ART HISTORY

PORTABLE EDITION | BOOK 6 | FOURTH EDITION

ART HISTORY

Eighteenth to Twenty-First Century Art

MARILYN STOKSTAD

Judith Harris Murphy Distinguished Professor of Art History Emerita
The University of Kansas

MICHAEL W. COTHREN

Scheuer Family Professor of Humanities
Department of Art, Swarthmore College

CONTRIBUTOR

Joy Sperling

Prentice Hall

Boston   Columbus   Indianapolis   New York   San Francisco   Upper Saddle River
Amsterdam   Cape Town   Dubai   London   Madrid   Milan   Munich   Paris   Montréal   Toronto
Delhi   Mexico City   São Paulo   Sydney   Hong Kong   Seoul   Singapore   Taipei   Tokyo

Editorial Director: Craig Campanella
Editor-in-Chief: Sarah Touborg
Senior Sponsoring Editor: Helen Ronan
Editorial Project Manager: David Nitti
Editorial Assistant: Carla Worner
Editor-in-Chief, Development: Rochelle Diogenes
Development Editors: Margaret Manos and Cynthia Ward
Media Director: Brian Hyland
Media Editor: Alison Lorber
Media Project Manager: Rich Barnes
Director of Marketing: Brandy Dawson
Senior Marketing Manager: Kate Mitchell
Marketing Assistant: Craig Deming
Senior Managing Editor: Ann Marie McCarthy
Assistant Managing Editor: Melissa Feimer
Production Project Managers: Barbara Cappuccio and Marlene Gassler
Senior Operations and Manufacturing Manager: Nick Sklitsis
Senior Operations Specialist: Brian Mackey
Manager of Design Development: John Christiana
Art Director and Interior Design: Kathy Mrozek
Cover Design: Kathy Mrozek
Site Supervisor, Pearson Imaging Center: Joe Conti
Pearson Imaging Center: Corin Skidds, Robert Uibelhoer, and Ron Walko
Cover Printer: Lehigh-Phoenix Color
Printer/Binder: Courier/Kendallville

This book was designed by
Laurence King Publishing Ltd, London
www.laurenceking.com

Commissioning Editor: Kara Hattersley-Smith
Senior Editors: Melissa Danny/Sophie Page
Production Manager: Simon Walsh
Page Design: Nick Newton/Randell Harris
Photo Researcher: Emma Brown
Copy Editors: Tessa Clark/Jenny Knight/Robert Shore/
Johanna Stephenson
Proofreader: Jennifer Speake
Indexer: Sue Farr

Cover photo: John Singleton Copley, *Thomas Mifflin and Sarah Morris (Mr. and Mrs. Mifflin)*. 1773. Oil on canvas, 61⅜ × 48″ (156.5 × 121.9 cm). Philadelphia Museum of Art. © 2007 Photo The Philadelphia Museum of Art/Art Resource/Scala, Florence.

Credits and acknowledgments borrowed from other sources and reproduced, with permission, in this textbook appear on the appropriate page within text or on the credit pages in the back of this book.

Library of Congress Cataloging-in-Publication Data
Stokstad, Marilyn
    Art History / Marilyn Stokstad, Michael W. Cothren; contributors,
Frederick M. Asher … [eg al.]. —4th ed.
    p. cm.
    Includes bibliographical references and index.
    ISBN-13: 978-0-205-74422-0 (hardcover : alk. paper)
    ISBN-10: 0205-74422-2 (hardcover : alk. paper)
    1. Art—History. I. Cothren, Michael Watt. II. Asher, Frederick M. III
Title.
N5300.S923 2011
709—dc22   2010001489

10 9 8 7 6 5 4 3 2 1

Prentice Hall
is an imprint of

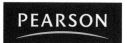

www.pearsonhighered.com

ISBN 10: 0-205-79096-8
ISBN 13: 978-0-205-79096-8

CONTENTS

Ordering Options

Art History is offered in a variety of formats to suit any course need, whether your survey is Western, global, comprehensive or concise, online or on the ground. Please contact your local representative for ordering details or visit www.pearsonhighered.com/art. In addition to this combined hardcover edition, *Art History* may be ordered in the following formats:

Volume I, Chapters 1–17 (ISBN: 978-0-205-74420-6)
Volume II, Chapters 17–32 (ISBN: 978-0-205-74421-3)

Art History **Portable Edition** has all of the same content as the comprehensive text in six slim volumes. Available in value-package combinations (Books 1, 2, 4, and 6) to suit **Western-focused survey** courses or available individually for period or region specific courses.
Book 1: Ancient Art, Chapters 1–6
Book 2: Medieval Art, Chapters 7, 8, 14–17
Book 3: A View of the World: Part One, Chapters 8–13
Book 4: Fourteenth to Seventeenth Century Art, Chapters 17–22
Book 5: A View of the World: Part Two, Chapters 23–28
Book 6: Eighteenth to Twenty-first Century Art, Chapters 29–32

Books À La Carte Give your students flexibility and savings with the new Books à la Carte edition of *Art History*. This edition features exactly the same content as the traditional textbook in a convenient three-hole-punched, loose-leaf version—allowing students to take only what they need to class. The Books à la Carte edition costs less than a used text—which helps students save about 35% over the cost of a new book.
Volume I, Books à la Carte Edition, 4/e
(ISBN: 978-0-205-79557-4)
Volume II, Books à la Carte Edition, 4/e
(ISBN: 978-0-205-79558-1)

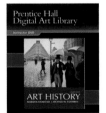 **CourseSmart Textbooks Online** is an exciting new choice for students looking to save money. As an alternative to purchasing the print textbook, students can subscribe to the same content online and save up to 50% off the suggested list price of the print text. For more information, or to subscribe to the CourseSmart eTextbook, visit www.coursesmart.com.

Combined Volume (ISBN: 978-0-205-80032-2)
Volume I (ISBN: 978-0-205-00189-7)
Volume II (ISBN: 978-0-205-00190-3)

Digital Resources

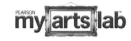 www.myartslab.com This dynamic website provides a wealth of resources geared to meet the diverse teaching and learning needs of today's instructors and students. Keyed specifically to the chapters of *Art History*, Fourth Edition, MyArtsLab's many tools will encourage students to experience and interact with works of art. Here are some of the key features:

- A complete **Pearson e-Text** of the book, enriched with multimedia, including: a unique human scale figure by all works of fine art, an audio version of the text read by the author, primary source documents, video demonstrations, and much more. Students can highlight, make notes and bookmark pages.
- 360 degree **Architectural Panoramas** for most of the major monuments in the book help students understand buildings from the inside and out.
- **Closer Look Tours** These interactive walkthroughs offer an in-depth look at key works of art, enabling the student to zoom in to see detail they could not otherwise see on the printed page or even in person. Enhanced with expert audio, they help students understand the meaning and message behind the work of art.
- A **Gradebook** that reports progress of students and the class as a whole.
- Instructors can also download the Instructor's Manual & Test Item File, PowerPoint questions for Classroom Response Systems, and obtain the PearsonMyTest assessment generation program.
- **MyArtsLab with e-Text** is available for no additional cost when packaged with any version of *Art History*, 4/e; it is also available standalone for less than the cost of a used text, and it is also available without e-Text for an even lower price.

The Prentice Hall Digital Art Library Instructors who adopt *Art History* are eligible to receive this unparalleled resource containing all of the images in *Art History* at the highest resolution (over 300 dpi) and pixellation possible for optimal projection and easy download. This resource features over 1,600 illustrations in jpeg and in PowerPoint, an instant download function for easy import into any presentation software, along with a unique zoom and "Save Detail" feature. (ISBN: 978-0-205-80037-7)

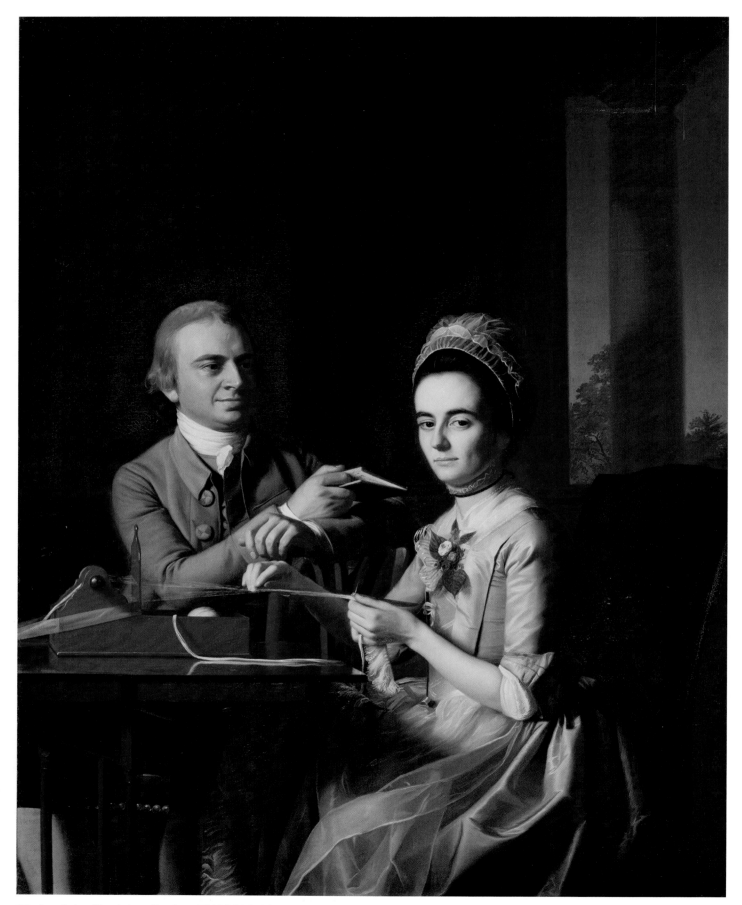

29-1 • John Singleton Copley **THOMAS MIFFLIN AND SARAH MORRIS (MR. AND MRS. MIFFLIN)**
1773. Oil on canvas, 61⅝ × 48″ (156.5 × 121.9 cm). Philadelphia Museum of Art.

EIGHTEENTH- AND EARLY NINETEENTH-CENTURY ART IN EUROPE AND NORTH AMERICA

The portrait by John Singleton Copley (1738–1815) of Thomas Mifflin and his wife, Sarah Morris (FIG. 29–1), was painted in 1773, the same year that American colonists protested against the British tax on tea by staging the Boston Tea Party—seizing British tea and tossing it into Boston harbor. The painting must have hung in the couple's Philadelphia home when Thomas Mifflin, a prominent merchant and politician, and other leading representatives of the colonies negotiated a strategy for the impending break with Britain at the First Continental Congress. Indeed, the painting reflects the couple's identity as American patriots, committed to the cause of independence.

Sarah, and not her famous husband, is the center of attention in this painting. She sits in the foreground dressed in a stylish silk dress decorated with expensive laces, a finely wrought lace cap atop her smoothly coiffed head. She is rich and elegant, but wears no jewelry except for a decorated choker. In fact, rather uncharacteristically for a woman of her social status, she is shown with her sleeves rolled up, working silk threads on the large wooden frame that sits on her polished table. Her work is domestic work, not the kind of activity normally chosen as the subject of a large and expensive portrait, but it was included here for important political reasons. She is weaving a type of decorative silk fringe that would have been imported from England in the past. By

including this frame, Copley demonstrates her commitment both to her home as a good and industrious wife, and also to the revolutionary cause as a woman without pretension who can manage well without British imported goods. Meeting the viewer's gaze with confidence and intelligence, she is clearly partner to her husband in the important work of resisting British colonial power.

John Singleton Copley was, by 1773, Boston's preeminent portrait painter and a wealthy man. (The Philadelphia Mifflins were in Boston the summer that Copley painted them.) His reputation stood on his remarkable ability to represent the upper strata of society in a clear, sharp, precise painting style that seemed to reveal not only every minute detail of his sitter's physical appearance and personality, but also the gorgeous satins, silks and laces of the women's dresses and the expensive polished furniture that were the signs of his patrons' wealth and status. Although his father-in-law was the Boston representative of the East India Company (whose tea was dumped into the harbor), Copley was nonetheless sympathetic to the revolutionary cause and, in fact, tried unsuccessfully to mediate the crisis in Boston. This portrait of Sarah and Thomas Mifflin was painted when Copley himself was ambivalent about the political future of the colonies, but his sitters reveal only their own sober commitment to the cause.

LEARN ABOUT IT

29.1 Discover how the ornate style of the Rococo era was a reflection of salon life among the aristocracy in eighteenth-century France.

29.2 Investigate Neoclassicism as a reflection of Enlightenment values with roots in the study of Classical antiquity in Rome.

29.3 Explore the many subjects of Romanticism, from the sublime in nature to the cruelty of the slave trade with a common interest in emotion and feeling.

29.4 Examine the Grand Manner in history painting and portraiture and the role of art academies.

29.5 Trace the complex political climate of the times through the work of Francisco Goya.

HEAR MORE: Listen to an audio file of your chapter **www.myartslab.com**

INDUSTRIAL, INTELLECTUAL, AND POLITICAL REVOLUTIONS

The American War of Independence was just one of many revolutions to shake the established order during the eighteenth and early nineteenth centuries. This was an age of radical change in society, thought, and politics, and while these transformations were felt especially in England, France and the United States, they had consequences throughout the West and, eventually, the world.

The transformations of this period were informed by a new way of thinking that had its roots in the scientific revolution of the previous century (see "Science and the Changing Worldview," page 756). In England, John Locke (1632–1704) argued that reasonable and rational thought should supplant superstition, and Isaac Newton (1643–1727) insisted upon empirical observation, rational evaluation, and logical consideration in mathematics and science. In 1702, Bernard de Fontenelle (1657–1757), a French popularizer of scientific innovation, wrote that he anticipated "a century which will become more enlightened day by day, so that all previous centuries will be lost in darkness by comparison." Over the course of the eighteenth century, this emphasis on thought "enlightened" by reason was applied to political and moral philosophy. Enlightenment thinking is marked by a conviction that humans are not superstitious beings ruled by God or the aristocracy, and that all men (some thinkers also included women) should have equal rights and opportunities for the pursuit of freedom, happiness, and fulfillment. Most Enlightenment philosophers believed that, when freed of past religious and political shackles, men and women could and would act rationally and morally. The role of the state was to protect and facilitate these rights, and when the state failed, the moral solution was to change it. Both the American Revolution of 1776 and the French Revolution of 1789 were justified on this basis.

The eighteenth century was also a period of economic and social transformation, set into motion by the Industrial Revolution. In 1700, Europe was still semi-feudal. Wealth and power belonged to the aristocracy, who owned the land and controlled the lives of poor tenant farmers. The Industrial Revolution replaced the land-based power of the aristocracy with the financial power of capitalists, who were able to use new sources of energy to mechanize manufacturing and greatly increase the quantity and profitability of saleable goods. Factory work lured the poor away from the countryside to the cities with the promise of wages and greater independence. The conditions that urban workers endured, however, were dreadful, both at their grueling factory jobs and in their overcrowded and unsanitary neighborhoods. These conditions would sow the seeds of dissent and revolution in several European countries in the mid nineteenth century. Industrialization also produced a large middle class that both bought and sold the new goods made in factories.

By the early nineteenth century, the aristocracy was weak and ineffectual in many nations, and virtually eliminated in France.

Upper-middle-class industrialists and merchants dominated European commerce, industry, and politics, and their beliefs and mores defined social norms. At the same time, the idealism of the Enlightenment had eroded, particularly in France in the wake of the Revolution, when the new republican form of government "by the people" brought chaos and bloodshed rather than order and stability. A new intellectual trend, known as Romanticism, started as a literary movement in the 1790s and served as a counterpoint to Enlightenment idealism. It critiqued the idea that the world was knowable and ruled by reason alone. The central premise of Romanticism was that an exploration of emotions, the imagination, and intuition—areas of the mind not addressed by Enlightenment philosophy—could lead to a more nuanced understanding of the world. Rather than one supplanting the other, Romanticism and Enlightenment thought co-existed as different parts of a complex whole.

THE ROCOCO STYLE

In the modern age, the shift from art produced at the behest of individual patrons—usually the monarchy, aristocracy, or Church—to art produced for sale to the industrial rich and even

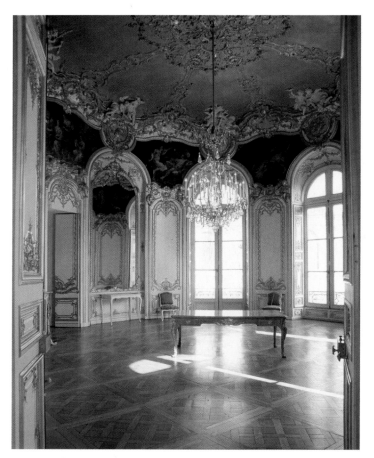

29-2 • Germain Boffrand SALON DE LA PRINCESSE, HÔTEL DE SOUBISE
Paris. Begun 1732. Library, Getty Research Institute, Los Angeles. Wim Swaan Photograph Collection (96, p. 21)

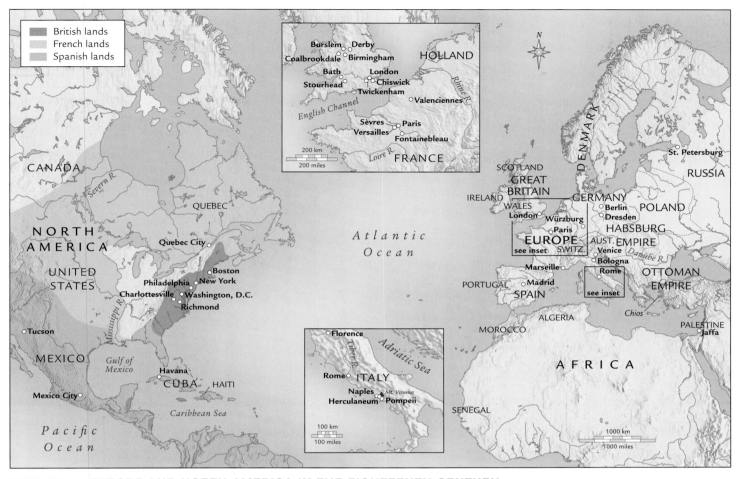

MAP 29–1 • EUROPE AND NORTH AMERICA IN THE EIGHTEENTH CENTURY

During the 18th century, three major artistic styles—Rococo, Neoclassicism, and Romanticism—flourished in Europe and North America.

the emerging middle classes had its roots in the Rococo when the court culture of Versailles changed to salon culture in Paris. The term *Rococo* combines the Italian word *barocco* (an irregularly shaped pearl, possibly the source of the word "baroque") and the French *rocaille* (a popular form of garden or interior ornamentation using shells and pebbles) to describe the refined and fanciful style that became fashionable in parts of Europe during the eighteenth century. The Rococo developed in France around 1715, when the duc d'Orléans, regent for the boy-king Louis XV (r. 1715–1774), moved his home and the French court from Versailles to Paris. The movement spread quickly across Europe **(MAP 29–1)**.

ROCOCO SALONS

The French court was happy to escape its confinement in the rural palace of Versailles and relocate to Paris. There courtiers built elegant town houses (in French, *hôtels*), whose social rooms may have been smaller than at Versailles, but were no less lavishly decorated. These became the center of social life for aristocrats who cultivated witty exchanges, elegant manners, and a luxurious life specifically dedicated to pleasure, leisure, and sensuality that frequently masked social insecurity and ambivalence. **Salons**, as

the rooms and the events held in them were known, were intimate, fashionable, and intellectual gatherings, often including splendid entertainments that mimicked in miniature the rituals of the Versailles court. The salons were hosted on a daily basis by accomplished, educated women of the upper class including Mesdames de Staël, de La Fayette, de Sévigné, and du Châtelet.

The Rococo style cannot be fully appreciated through single objects, but is evident everywhere in the salons, with their profusely decorated walls and ceilings bursting with exquisite three-dimensional embellishments in gold, silver, and brilliant white paint; their intimate, sensual paintings hung among the rich ornament; and their elaborate crystal chandeliers, mirrored walls, and delicate decorated furniture and tabletop sculptures. When these Parisian salons were lit by candles, they must have glittered with light reflected and refracted by the gorgeous surfaces. The rooms were no doubt also enlivened by the energy of aristocrats, fancifully dressed in a profusion of pastel blues, yellows, greens, and pinks to complement the light, bright details of the Rococo architecture, paintings, and sculptures around them.

The **SALON DE LA PRINCESSE** in the Hôtel de Soubise **(FIG. 29–2)**, designed by Germain Boffrand (1667–1754), was the

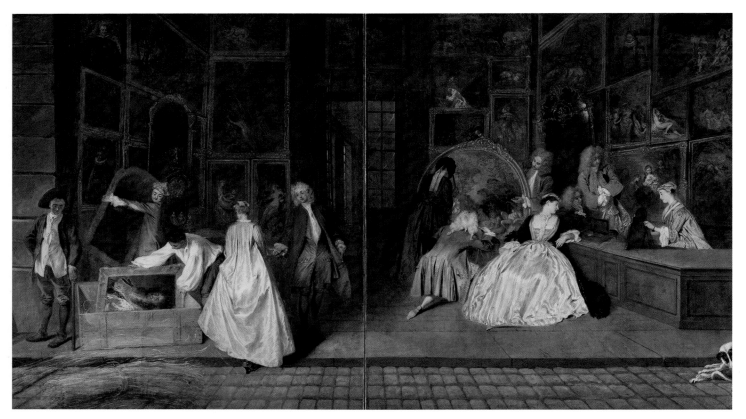

29-3 • Jean-Antoine Watteau THE SIGNBOARD OF GERSAINT
c. 1721. Oil on canvas, 5′4″ × 10′1″ (1.62 × 3.06 m). Stiftung Preussische Schlössen und Gärten Berlin-Brandenburg, Schloss Charlottenburg.

Watteau's signboard painting was designed for the Paris art gallery of Edmé-François Gersaint, a dealer who introduced to France the English idea of selling paintings by catalog. The systematic listing of works for sale gave the name of the artist and the title, the medium, and the dimensions of each work of art. The shop depicted on the signboard is not Gersaint's but an ideal gallery visited by elegant and cultivated patrons. The sign was so admired that Gersaint sold it only 15 days after it was installed. Later it was cut down the middle and each half was framed separately, which resulted in the loss of some canvas along the sides of each section. The painting was restored and its two halves reunited in the twentieth century.

EXPLORE MORE: Gain insight from a primary source on Jean-Antoine Watteau **www.myartslab.com**

setting for intimate gatherings of the Parisian aristocracy in the years prior to the French Revolution. Its delicacy and lightness are typical of French Rococo salon design of the 1730s, with architectural elements, rendered in sculpted stucco, including arabesques (characterized by flowing lines and swirling shapes), S-shapes, C-shapes, reverse C-shapes, volutes, and naturalistic plant forms. Intricate polished surfaces included carved wood panels called *boiseries* and inlaid wood designs on furniture and floors. The glitter of silver and gold against white and pastel shades and the visual confusion of mirror reflections all added to this Rococo interior.

ROCOCO PAINTING AND SCULPTURE

The paintings and sculpture that decorated Rococo salons and other elegant spaces contributed to their atmosphere of sensuality and luxury. Pictorial themes were often taken from Classical love stories, and sculpted ornaments were typically filled with *putti*, cupids, and clouds. The paintings of Jean-Antoine Watteau,

François Boucher, and John-Honoré Fragonard and the tabletop sculpture of Claude Michel, known as Clodion, were highly coveted in salon culture.

WATTEAU.   Jean-Antoine Watteau (1684–1721) was the originator and greatest proponent of the French Rococo style in painting. Born in the provincial town of Valenciennes, Watteau came to Paris around 1702, where he studied Rubens's paintings for Marie de' Medici (SEE FIG. 22–29), then displayed in the Luxembourg Palace, and the paintings and drawings of sixteenth-century Venetians such as Giorgione (SEE FIG. 20–21), which he saw in a Parisian private collection. Watteau perfected a graceful personal style informed by the fluent brushwork and rich colors of Rubens and the Venetians.

Watteau painted for the new urban aristocrats who frequently purchased paintings for their homes through art dealers in the city. His **SIGNBOARD OF GERSAINT (FIG. 29–3)** shows the interior of one of these shops. Painted for the art dealer Edmé-François Gersaint, the painting shows an art gallery filled with paintings from the Venetian and Netherlandish schools that Watteau admired. Indeed, the glowing satins and silks of the women's gowns pay homage to artists such as Gerard ter Borch (SEE FIG. 22–43). The visitors to the gallery are elegant ladies and gentlemen, at ease in these surroundings and apparently knowledgeable about painting, who create an atmosphere of aristocratic sophistication. At the left, a woman in shimmering pink satin steps across the threshold, ignoring her companion's outstretched hand, to watch the two porters packing. While one porter holds a mirror, the other carefully lowers into the wooden case a portrait of Louis XIV, which may be a reference to the name of Gersaint's shop, *Au Grand Monarque* ("At the Sign of the Great King"). It also suggests the passage of time, for Louis had died six years earlier.

Other elements in the work also suggest transience. On the left, the clock directly above the king's portrait, surmounted by an allegorical figure of Fame and sheltering a pair of lovers, is a **memento mori**, a reminder of mortality, suggesting that both love and fame are subject to the ravages of time. Well-established *vanitas* emblems are the easily destroyed straw (in the foreground) and the young woman gazing into the mirror (set next to a vanity case on the counter)—mirrors and images of young women looking at their reflections had been familiar symbols of the fragility of human life since the Baroque period. Notably, the two gentlemen at the end of the counter also appear to gaze at the mirror, and are thus also implicated in the *vanitas* theme. Watteau, who died from tuberculosis before he was 40, produced this painting during his last illness. Gersaint later wrote that he had completed the painting in eight days, working only in the mornings because of his failing health. When *The Signboard* was installed, it was greeted with almost universal admiration; Gersaint sold it within a month.

In his **PILGRIMAGE TO THE ISLAND OF CYTHERA (FIG. 29–4)**, painted four years earlier, Watteau portrayed an imaginary idyllic and sensual life of Rococo aristocrats but with the same melancholic undertone that hints at the fleeting quality of human happiness. The painting depicts a dream world in which beautifully dressed couples, accompanied by *putti*, conclude their day's romantic trysts on Cythera, the island sacred to Venus, the goddess of love, whose garlanded statue appears at the extreme right. The lovers, dressed in exquisite satins, silks, and velvets, gather in the verdant landscape. This kind of idyllic and wistfully melancholic vision charmed both early eighteenth-century Paris and most of Europe. Watteau painted *Pilgrimage to the Island of Cythera* in 1717

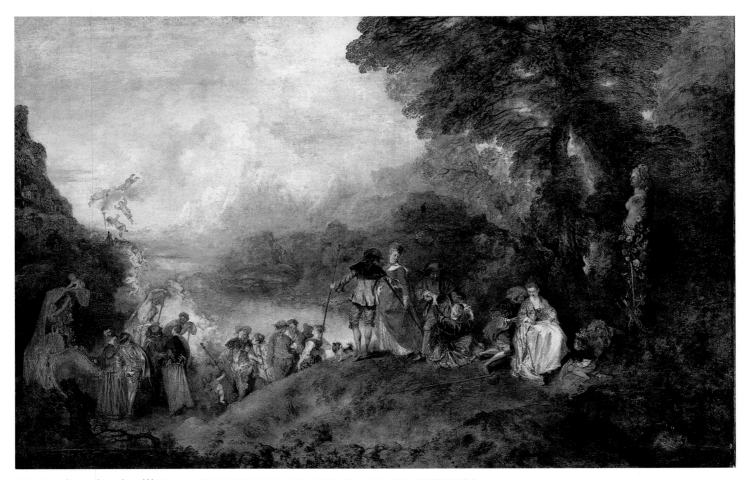

29-4 • Jean-Antoine Watteau PILGRIMAGE TO THE ISLAND OF CYTHERA
1717. Oil on canvas, 4'3" × 6'4½" (1.3 × 1.9 m). Musée du Louvre, Paris.

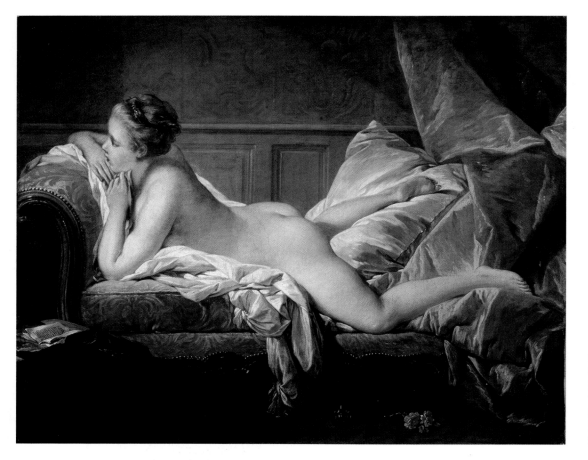

29–5 • François Boucher GIRL RECLINING: LOUISE O'MURPHY 1751. Oil on canvas, 28³/₄ × 23¹/₄″ (73 × 59 cm). Wallfaf-Richartz Museum, Cologne.

as his official examination canvas for admission to membership in the Royal Academy of Painting and Sculpture (see "Academies and Academy Exhibitions," page 924). Although there was no academic category to cover the painting, the academicians were so impressed by the canvas that they created a new category, the **fête galante**, or elegant outdoor entertainment, to describe this genre of painting.

BOUCHER.   The artist most closely associated with Parisian Rococo painting after Watteau's death is François Boucher (1703–1770). The son of a minor painter, Boucher in 1723 entered the workshop of an engraver where he was hired to reproduce Watteau's paintings for a collector, firmly establishing the future direction of his career.

After studying at the French Academy in Rome from 1727 to 1731, he settled in Paris and became an academician. Soon his life and career were intimately bound up with two women. The first was his artistically talented wife, Marie-Jeanne Buseau, who was a frequent model as well as a studio assistant to her husband. The other was Louis XV's mistress, Madame de Pompadour, who became his major patron and supporter. Pompadour was an amateur artist herself and took lessons in printmaking from Boucher. After he received his first royal commission in 1735, Boucher worked almost continuously on the decorations for the royal residences at Versailles and Fontainebleau. In 1755, he was

made chief inspector at the Gobelins tapestry manufactory, and provided designs for them as well as for the Sèvres porcelain and Beauvais tapestry manufactories. All these workshops produced both furnishings for the king and wares for sale on the open market by merchants such as Gersaint. Indeed, Boucher operated in a much more commercial market than artists in the previous century.

In 1765, Boucher became First Painter to the King. In this role he painted several portraits of Louis XV, scenes of daily life and mythological pictures, and a series of erotic works for private enjoyment often depicting the adventures of Venus. One such painting is **GIRL RECLINING: LOUISE O'MURPHY (FIG. 29–5)**. In this painting, the 18-year old Louise O'Murphy (whose identity is still debated by scholars), provocatively pink and completely nude, lies on her stomach on a couch. Her satiny pink and white clothing is strewn about beneath her, and pillows are scattered at her feet and on the floor; her hair is decorated with braids and a blue ribbon and a fallen pink rose lies on the floor. Louise's plump buttocks are displayed enticingly at the very center of the painting. There is little doubt about the subject of the painting; Boucher intended it to be overtly sensual. In contrast to Watteau's *fête galante*, in which nude gods, goddesses, and *putti* frolic around in unreal settings, the woman shown here is clearly human, contemporary, and lying in a very real Rococo room. Boucher's robust world of sensual pleasure recalls the style of Rubens (SEE FIG. 22–29), but Boucher has a lighter touch.

FRAGONARD. Another noteworthy master of French Rococo painting, Jean-Honoré Fragonard (1732–1806), studied with Boucher, who encouraged him to enter the competition for the Prix de Rome, the three- to five-year scholarship awarded to the top students in painting and sculpture graduating from the French Academy's art school. Fragonard won the prize in 1752 and spent the years 1756 to 1761 in Italy; however, it was not until 1765 that he was finally accepted as a member of the Royal Academy. He catered to the tastes of an aristocratic clientele, and, as a decorator of interiors, began to fill the vacuum left by Boucher's death in 1770.

Fragonard's **THE SWING** (FIG. 29–6) of 1767 was not part of an interior scheme. It was originally commissioned from painter Gabriel-François Doyen. Although the patron is unknown, Doyen's description reveals that the painting was clearly intended to be sensually explicit. He refused the commission, and gave it to

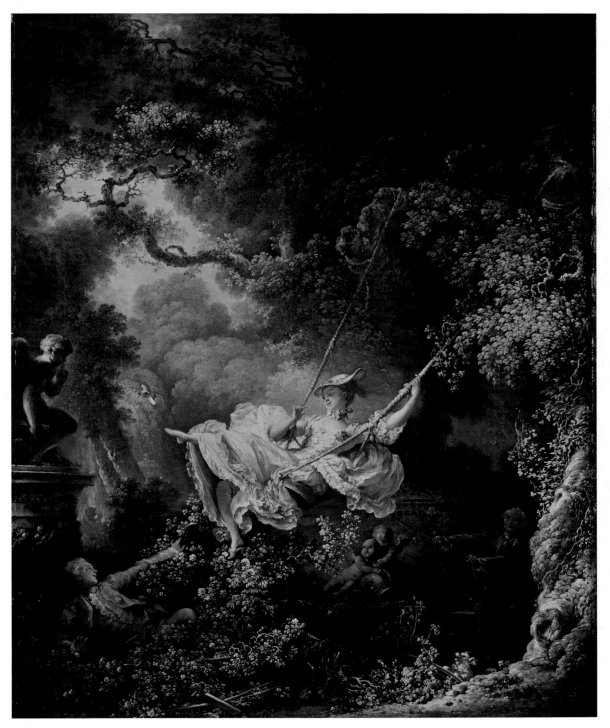

29-6 • Jean-Honoré Fragonard THE SWING
1766. Oil on canvas, 2′8⅝″ × 2′2″ (82.9 × 66 cm). The Wallace Collection, London.

Fragonard, who created a small jewel of a painting. The subject is a pretty young girl on a swing, being pushed by an elderly bishop obscured by the shadow of the bushes on the right. On the left, however, the girl's lover swoons, flushed with anticipation. As the swing approaches, he is rewarded with an unobstructed view of the girl's pretty legs. The young man reaches out to her with his hat as

if to make a mockingly useless attempt to cover the view, while she glances down and seductively tosses one shoe at him. The abandon of the lovers, the complicity of the sculpture of Cupid on the left, gesturing that he will not tell, the *putti* with a dolphin beneath the swing who seem to urge her on, and the poor bishop to the right, all work together to create an image that bursts with anticipation and desire, but also maintains a sense of humor.

CLODION. In the last quarter of the eighteenth century, the Rococo largely fell out of favor in France, its style and subject matter attacked for being frivolous at best and immoral at worst. One sculptor who clung onto the Rococo almost until the French Revolution, however, was Claude Michel, known as Clodion (1738–1814). Most of his work consisted of playful, erotic tabletop sculpture, mainly in unpainted terra cotta. Typical of his Rococo designs is the terra-cotta model he submitted to win a 1784 royal commission for a large monument to the invention of the hot-air balloon (FIG. 29–7). Hot-air balloons then were elaborately decorated with painted Rococo scenes, gold braid, and tassels. Clodion's balloon, decorated with bands of ornament, rises from a columnar launching pad in billowing clouds of smoke, assisted at the left by a puffing wind god with butterfly wings and heralded at the right by a trumpeting Victory. *Putti* stoke the fire basket, providing the hot air to make the balloon ascend, while others gather reeds for fuel and fly up toward them.

ROCOCO CHURCH DECORATION

The beginning of the Rococo signaled an end to the Church as a major patron of art in northern Europe. Although churches continued to be built and decorated, the dominance of the Church and hereditary aristocracy as patrons diminished significantly. The Rococo proved, however, to be a powerful vehicle for spiritual experience and there were several important churches built in the style, showing how one visual style can have many meanings in society. One of the most opulent Rococo churches still standing in German-speaking Europe is that of the church of the Vierzehnheiligen (the "Fourteen Auxiliary Saints" or "Holy Helpers") designed by Johann Balthasar Neumann (1687–1753) and constructed between 1743 and 1772. The plan (FIG. 29–8), which is based on six interpenetrating oval spaces of varying sizes around a vaulted ovoid center, recalls that of Borromini's Baroque church of San Carlo alle Quattro Fontane in Rome (SEE FIG. 22–7). But the effect here is airy lightness. In the nave (FIG. 29–9), the Rococo love of undulating surfaces with overlays of decoration creates a visionary world where flat wall surfaces scarcely exist. Instead, the viewer is surrounded by clusters of pilasters and engaged columns interspersed with two levels of arched openings to the side aisles, and large clerestory windows illuminating the gold and white of the interior. The foliage of the fanciful capitals is repeated in arabesques, wreaths, and the ornamented frames of irregular panels lining the vault. An ebullient sense of spiritual uplift is achieved by the complete integration of architecture and decoration.

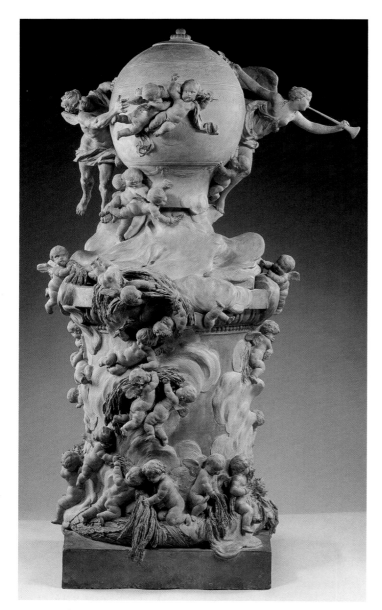

29-7 • Clodion THE INVENTION OF THE BALLOON
1784. Terra-cotta model for a monument, height 43½″ (110.5 cm). The Metropolitan Museum of Art, New York. Rogers Fund and Frederick R. Harris Gift, 1944 (44.21a b)

Clodion had a long career as a sculptor in the exuberant, Rococo manner seen in this work commemorating the 1783 invention of the hot-air balloon. During the austere revolutionary period of the First Republic (1792–1795), he became one of the few Rococo artists to adopt successfully the more acceptable Neoclassical manner. In 1806, he was commissioned by Napoleon to provide the relief sculpture for two Paris monuments, the Vendôme Column and the Carrousel Arch near the Louvre.

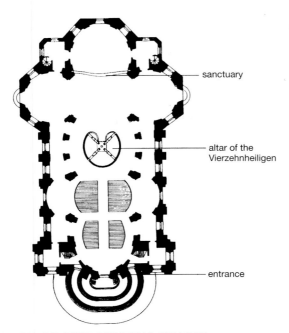

sanctuary

altar of the
Vierzehnheiligen

entrance

29-8 • PLAN OF THE CHURCH OF THE VIERZEHNHEILIGEN
c. 1743. Near Bamberg, Bavaria, Germany.

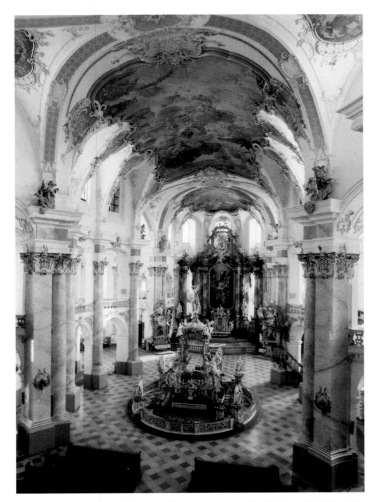

29-9 • Johann Balthasar Neumann INTERIOR, CHURCH OF THE VIERZEHNHEILIGEN
1743–1772. Near Bamberg, Bavaria, Germany.

ITALY: THE GRAND TOUR AND NEOCLASSICISM

From the late 1600s until well into the nineteenth century, the education of a wealthy young northern European or American gentleman—few women were considered worthy of such education—was completed on the **Grand Tour**, an extended visit to the major cultural sites of southern Europe. Accompanied by a tutor and an entourage of servants, the Grand Tourist began in Paris, moved on to southern France to visit a number of well-preserved Roman buildings and monuments there, then headed to Venice, Florence, Naples, and Rome. As the repository of the Classical and Renaissance pasts, Italy was the focus of the Grand Tour.

Italy, and Rome in particular, was also the primary destination for artists and scholars interested in the Classical past. In addition to the ancient architecture and sculpture to be found in collections throughout Rome, the nearby sites of Pompeii and Herculaneum offered sensational new material for study and speculation (see Chapter 6). These two prosperous Roman towns, buried by a sudden volcanic eruption in 79 CE, were discovered by archaeologists in the mid eighteenth century.

The artists and intellectuals who were inspired by the Classical past contributed to early Neoclassicism, which was both a way of viewing the world and a visual style. Neoclassicism (*neo* means "new") sought to present Classical ideals and subject matter in a style derived from Classical Greek and Roman sources. Neoclassical paintings reflect the frozen forms, tight compositions, and shallow space of ancient relief sculpture. Because the ancient world was considered the font from which British and European democracy, secular government, and civilized thought and action flowed, its art was viewed as the embodiment of timeless civic and moral lessons. Neoclassical paintings and sculptures were frequently painted for and displayed in public places in order to inspire patriotism, nationalism, and courage in defense of the state. Neoclassicism was frequently used in Britain, America, and especially France as a visual expression of the state or government.

GRAND TOUR PORTRAITS AND VIEWS

Artists in Italy benefitted not only from their access to authentic works of antiquity, but also from the steady stream of wealthy art collectors on the Grand Tour. Tourists visited the studios of important Italian artists in order to view and purchase works that could be brought home and displayed as evidence of their cultural travels.

CARRIERA. Wealthy European visitors to Italy frequently sat for portraits by Italian artists. Rosalba Carriera (1675–1757), the leading portraitist in Venice in the first half of the eighteenth century, worked mainly in pastel, a medium better suited than slow-drying oil to accommodate sitters whose time in the city was limited.

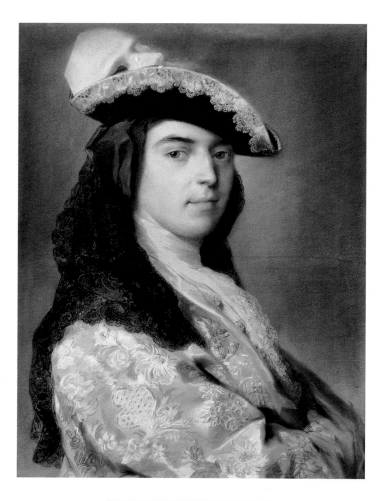

29-10 • Rosalba Carriera **CHARLES SACKVILLE, 2ND DUKE OF DORSET**
c. 1730. Pastel on paper, 25 × 19″ (63.5 × 48.3 cm). Private collection.

Pastel is a fast and versatile medium: Pastel crayons, made of pulverized pigment bound to a chalk base by weak gum water, can be used to sketch quickly and spontaneously, or they can be rubbed and blended on the surface of paper to produce a shiny and highly finished surface.

Carriera began her career designing lace patterns and painting miniature portraits on the ivory lids of snuffboxes before she graduated to pastel portraits. Her portraits were so widely admired that she was awarded honorary membership of Rome's Academy of Saint Luke in 1705, and was later admitted to the academies in Bologna and Florence. In 1720, she traveled to Paris, where she made a pastel portrait of the young Louis XV and was elected to the Royal Academy of Painting and Sculpture, despite the 1706 rule forbidding the further admission of women. Returning to Italy in 1721, she established herself in Venice as a portraitist of handsome young men such as the British aristocrat **CHARLES SACKVILLE, 2ND DUKE OF DORSET (FIG. 29–10)**.

CANALETTO. A painted city view was by far the most prized souvenir of a stay in Venice. Two kinds of views were produced in Venice: the **capriccio** ("caprice," plural *capricci*), an imaginary

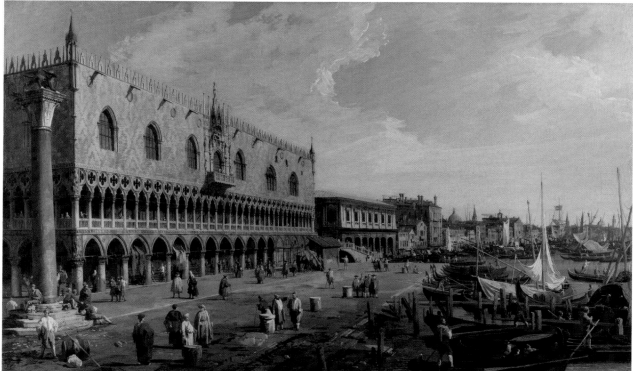

29-11 • Canaletto **THE DOGE'S PALACE AND THE RIVA DEGLI SCHIAVONI**
Late 1730s. Oil on canvas, 24⅛ × 39¼″ (61.3 × 99.8 cm). National Gallery, London. Wynn Ellis Bequest 1876 (NG 940)

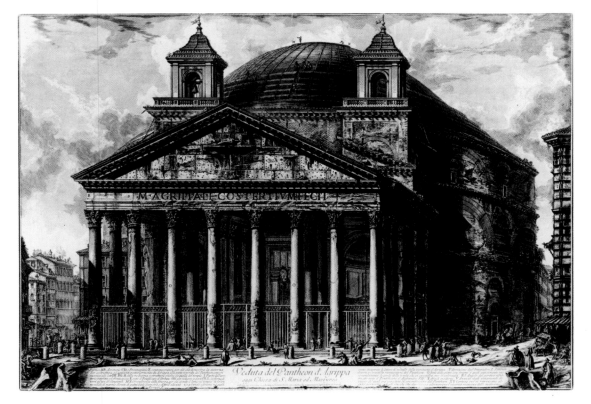

29–12 • Giovanni Battista Piranesi **VIEW OF THE PANTHEON, ROME**
From the Views of Rome series, first printed in 1756. Etching, 18⅜₆ × 27⅛″ (47.2 × 69.7 cm). Kupferstich-kabinett, Staatliche Museen, Berlin.

landscape or cityscape in which the artist mixed actual structures, such as famous ruins, with imaginary ones to create attractive compositions; and the **veduta** ("view;" plural *vedute*), a more naturalistic rendering of famous views and buildings, well-known tourist attractions, and local color in the form of tiny figures of the Venetian people and visiting tourists. *Vedute* often encompassed panoramic views of famous landmarks, such as **THE DOGE'S PALACE AND THE RIVA DEGLI SCHIAVONI (FIG. 29–11)** by the Venetian artist Giovanni Antonio Canal, called Canaletto (1697–1768). It was thought that Canaletto used the camera obscura (see page 967) to render his *vedute* with exact topographical accuracy, but his drawings show that he seems to have worked freehand. In fact, his views are rarely topographically accurate and more often than not are composite images: It is a mark of his skill that Canaletto makes us want to believe that his *vedute* are "real." He painted and sold so many to British visitors that his dealer sent him to London from 1746 to 1755 to paint views of the English capital city for his British clients, who included several important aristocrats as well as King George III.

PIRANESI.   The city of Rome was also captured in *vedute* for the pleasure of tourists and armchair travelers, most notably by Giovanni Battista Piranesi (1720–1778). Trained in Venice as an architect, he moved to Rome and studied etching, eventually establishing a publishing house and becoming one of the century's most successful printmakers. Piranesi produced a large series of *vedute* of ancient Roman monuments and ruins. His **VIEW OF THE PANTHEON (FIG. 29–12)** is informed by a careful study of ancient

Roman architecture. Piranesi succeeds in breathing life into his images by creating grand, monumental scenes.

NEOCLASSICISM IN ROME

The intellectuals and artists who came to study and work in Rome often formed communities with a shared interest in Neoclassical ideals. A British coterie, for example, included Angelica Kauffmann (SEE FIG. 29–26), Benjamin West (SEE FIG. 29–27), and Gavin Hamilton, all of whom contributed to early Neoclassicism. Communities of artists from France and Germany were also established. One of the most influential communities of the period formed at the Villa Albani on the outskirts of Rome, under the sponsorship of Cardinal Alessandro Albani (1692–1779).

Cardinal Albani built his villa in 1760–1761 specifically to house and display his vast collection of antique sculpture, sarcophagi, intaglios (objects in which the design is carved out of the surface), cameos, and vases, and it became one of the most important stops on the Grand Tour. The villa was more than a museum: It was also a place to buy art and artifacts. Albani sold items to artists and tourists alike, to help satisfy the growing craze for antiquities; unfortunately, many were faked or heavily restored by artisans in the cardinal's employ.

In 1758 Albani hired Johann Joachim Winckelmann (1717–1768), the leading theoretician of Neoclassicism, as his secretary and librarian. The Prussian-born Winckelmann became an expert on Classical art while working in Dresden, where the French Rococo style that he deplored was still fashionable. In 1755, he published a pamphlet, *Thoughts on the Imitation of Greek*

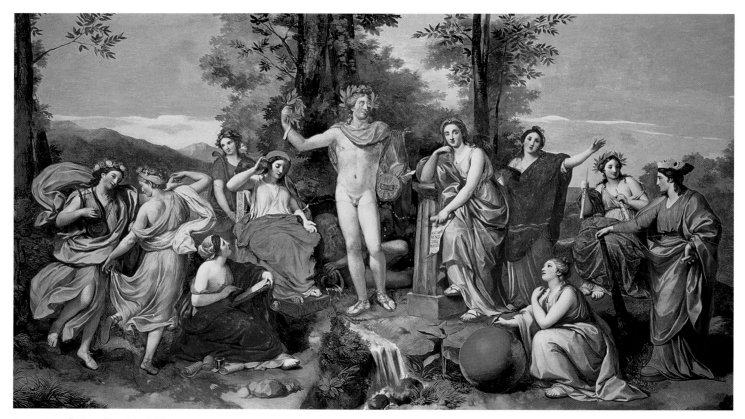

29–13 • Anton Raphael Mengs **PARNASSUS**
Ceiling fresco in the Villa Albani, Rome. 1761.

Works in Painting and Sculpture, in which he attacked the Rococo as decadent, arguing that modern artists could only claim their status as legitimate artists by imitating Greek art. Shortly afterward he went to work for Albani in Rome. In 1764, he published a second influential treatise, *The History of Ancient Art*, often considered one of the earliest art-historical studies. Here Winckelmann analyzed the history of art for the first time as a succession of period styles, an approach which later became the norm for art history books (including this one).

MENGS. Winckelmann's closest friend and colleague in Rome was a fellow German, Anton Raphael Mengs (1728–1779). In 1761 Cardinal Albani commissioned Mengs to create a painting for the ceiling of the great gallery in his new villa **(FIG. 29–13)**. To our eyes Mengs's **PARNASSUS** ceiling may seem stilted, but it is nevertheless significant as the first full expression of Neoclassicism in painting. The scene is taken from Classical mythology. Mount Parnassus in central Greece was where the ancients believed Apollo (god of poetry, music, and the arts) and the nine Muses (female personifications of artistic inspiration) resided. Mengs depicted Apollo standing at the center, almost nude and in the pose of the famous *Apollo Belvedere* in the Vatican collection; he holds a lyre and olive branch to represent artistic accomplishment. Around him are the Muses and their mother, Mnemosyne (Memory, leaning on a Doric column). Mengs arranged his figures in a roughly symmetrical, pyramidal

composition parallel to the picture plane, like the relief sculpture he had studied at Herculaneum. Winckelmann praised this work, claiming that it captured the "noble simplicity and calm grandeur" of ancient Greek sculpture. Shortly after completing this work Mengs left for Spain, where he served as court painter until 1777. Similarly, other artists from Rome moved around Europe, bringing Neoclassical ideas with them.

CANOVA. The theories of the Albani–Winckelmann circle were applied most vigorously by sculptors in Rome, who remained committed to Neoclassicism for almost 100 years. The leading Neoclassical sculptor of the late eighteenth and early nineteenth centuries was Antonio Canova (1757–1822). Born near Venice into a family of stonemasons, he settled in Rome in 1781, where he adopted the Neoclassical style under the guidance of the Scottish painter Gavin Hamilton and quickly became the most sought-after European sculptor of the period.

Canova specialized in two types of sculpture: grand public monuments for Europe's leaders, and erotic mythological subjects for the pleasure of private collectors. His **PAULINE BORGHESE AS VENUS (FIG. 29–14)** falls into the latter category, although it was commissioned by one of the most powerful rulers of Europe in the later eighteenth century, Emperor Napoleon of France (1769–1821). The subject is Napoleon's sister, Pauline, whom the emperor had arranged to marry Prince Camillo Borghese, a member of the

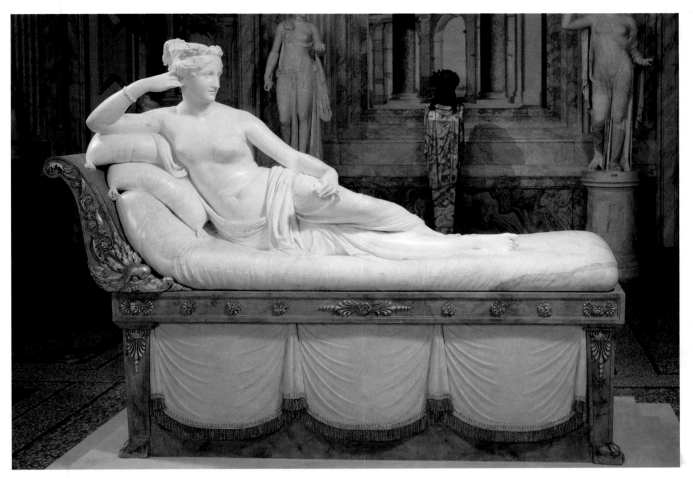

29-14 • Antonio Canova PAULINE BORGHESE AS VENUS
1808. Marble, length 6′7″ (218.4 cm). Galleria Borghese, Rome.

famous Roman Borghese family. Pauline wished to be portrayed as Venus. She is shown semi-nude, reclining on a divan with the golden apple given to Venus by Paris, prince of Troy, as a sign that she was the fairest of the three major goddesses. The cushions and drapery seem impossibly real. The glistening white marble evokes the sensuality of Hellenistic sculpture, and the grey, white, and gold marble base brings a materiality to the sculpture above. Pauline's husband was displeased with the sculpture, which seemed to confirm rumors about his wife's questionable behavior, and installed the sculpture in a private room in the Villa Borghese, where it remains today.

NEOCLASSICISM AND EARLY ROMANTICISM IN BRITAIN

British tourists and artists in Italy were the leading supporters of early Neoclassicism, partly because of the burgeoning taste for revival styles at home. Nonetheless, the British interest in Classical revival styles was inflected slightly differently from Roman Neoclassicism. While Roman Neoclassicism looked to the past in order to revive a sense of moral and civic virtue, many later eighteenth-century British artists harnessed the concept of civic

virtue to patriotism to create more Romantic works of art dedicated specifically to the British nation. It is in British art and literature that we find the beginnings of Romanticism.

Like Neoclassicism, Romanticism describes not only a style but also an attitude: It celebrates the individual and the subjective, while Neoclassicism celebrates the universal and the high-minded. Romanticism takes its name and many of its themes from the "romances"—novellas, stories, and poems written in Romance (Latin-derived) languages. The term "Romantic" suggests something fantastic or novelistic, perhaps set in a remote time or place, infused by a poetic, melancholic, or even terrifying spirit. One of the best examples of early Romanticism in literature is *The Sorrows of Young Werther* (1774) by Johann Wolfgang von Goethe (1749–1832), in which a sensitive, outcast young man fails at love and kills himself. This is a story about a troubled individual who loses his way; it does not recall ancient virtues or civic responsibility.

Neoclassicism and Romanticism existed side by side in the later eighteenth and early nineteenth centuries, the two ways of looking at the world each serving a purpose in society. Neoclassicism tended to be a more public art form, and Romanticism more individual and private. Sometimes Neoclassicism even functioned within Romanticism.

THE CLASSICAL REVIVAL IN ARCHITECTURE AND DESIGN

The vogue for the Classical spread throughout the arts in late eighteenth-century England. Ancient Greece and Rome provided impeccable pedigrees for British buildings, utensils, poetry, and even clothing fashions. Women donned white muslin gowns and men curled their hair forward in imitation of Classical statues. In the 1720s, a group of professional architects and wealthy amateurs in Britain, led by the Scot Colen Campbell (1676–1729), stood against what they viewed as the immoral extravagance of the Italian Baroque. They advocated a return to the austerity and simplicity of the Classically inspired architecture of Andrea Palladio, and his country houses in particular.

CHISWICK HOUSE.   Designed in 1724 by its owner, Richard Boyle, the third Earl of Burlington (1695–1753), **CHISWICK HOUSE** **(FIG. 29–15)** is a fine example of British Neo-Palladianism. Burlington visited several of Palladio's country houses in Italy and was particularly struck by the Villa Rotonda (SEE FIG. 20–40), which inspired his plan for Chiswick House. The building plan **(FIG. 29–16)** shares the bilateral symmetry of Palladio's villa, although its central core is octagonal rather than round and there are only two entrances. The main entrance, flanked now by matching

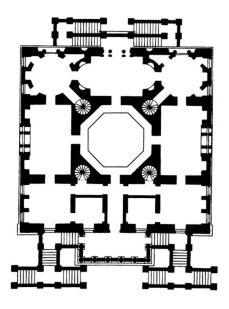

29-16 • PLAN OF CHISWICK HOUSE
1724.

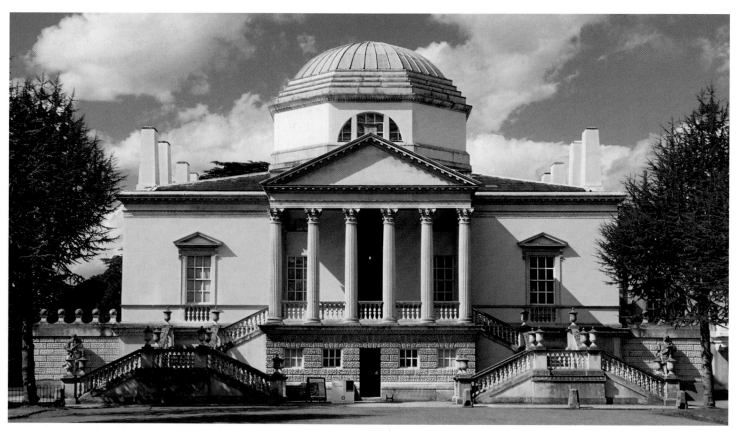

29-15 • Richard Boyle (Lord Burlington) CHISWICK HOUSE
West London, England. 1724–1729. Interior decoration (1726–1729) and new gardens (1730–1740) by William Kent.

SEE MORE: Click the Google Earth link for Chiswick House www.myartslab.com

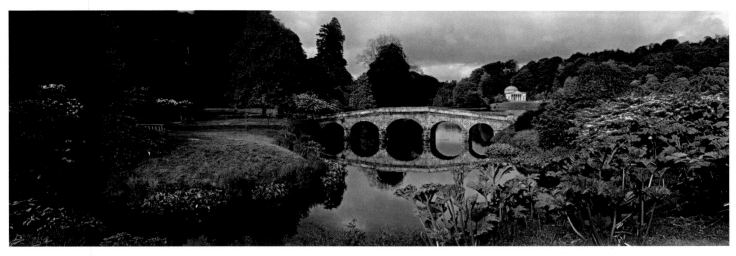

29-17 • Henry Flitcroft and Henry Hoare **THE PARK AT STOURHEAD**
Wiltshire, England. Laid out 1743, executed 1744–1765, with continuing additions.

staircases, is a Roman temple front, an imposing entrance for the earl. Chiswick's elevation is characteristically Palladian, with a main floor resting on a basement, and tall, rectangular windows with triangular pediments. The few, crisp details seem perfectly suited to the refined proportions of the whole. The result is a lucid evocation of Palladio's design.

When in Rome, Burlington persuaded the English expatriate William Kent (1685–1748) to return to London as his collaborator. Kent designed Chiswick's surprisingly ornate interior as well as its grounds, the latter in a style that became known throughout Europe as the English landscape garden. Kent's garden abandoned the regularity and rigid formality of Baroque gardens (see "Garden Design," page 760). It featured winding paths, a lake with a cascade, irregular plantings of shrubs, and other effects that imitated the appearance of a natural rural landscape—while it was, in fact, carefully designed and manicured.

STOURHEAD. Following Kent's lead at Chiswick, landscape architecture flourished in England in the hands of such designers as Lancelot ("Capability") Brown (1716–1783) and Henry Flitcroft (1697–1769). In the 1740s, the banker Henry Hoare began redesigning the grounds of his estate at Stourhead in Wiltshire **(FIG. 29–17)** with the assistance of Flitcroft, a protégé of Burlington. The resulting gardens at Stourhead carried Kent's ideas for the English garden much further. Stourhead is a perfect example of the English **picturesque** garden: Its conception and views intentionally mimic the compositional devices of "pictures" by French landscape painter Claude Lorrain (SEE FIG. 22–56), whose paintings were popular in England. The picturesque view illustrated here shows a garden designed with "counterfeit neglect": It is carefully designed to look natural and unkempt. The small lake is crossed by a rustic bridge, while in the background we see a "folly," a miniature version of the Pantheon in Rome. The park is punctuated by other Classically inspired temples, copies of antique statues, artificial grottoes, a rural

cottage, a Chinese bridge, a Gothic spire, and even a Turkish tent: The result is a delightful mixture of styles and cultures that successfully combines the Neoclassical and the Romantic. Inside the house, Hoare commissioned Mengs to paint *The Meeting of Antony and Cleopatra*, a work that similarly combines Classical history with a Romantic subject.

WEDGWOOD. The interiors of country houses like Chiswick and Stourhead were designed partly as settings for the art collections of British aristocrats, which included antiquities as well as a range of Neoclassical paintings, sculpture, and decorative wares (see "A Closer Look," page 919). The most successful producer of Neoclassical decorative art was Josiah Wedgwood (1730–1795). In 1769, near his native village of Burslem, he opened a pottery factory called Etruria after the ancient Etruscan civilization in central Italy known for its pottery. His production-line shop had several divisions, each with its own **kilns** (firing ovens) and workers trained in individual specialties. A talented chemist, in the mid 1770s Wedgwood perfected a fine-grained, unglazed, colored pottery which he called **jasperware**. His most popular jasperware featured white figures against a blue ground, as in **THE APOTHEOSIS OF HOMER** vase **(FIG. 29–18)**. The low-relief decoration was designed by the sculptor John Flaxman, Jr. (1755–1826), who worked for Wedgwood from 1775 to 1787. Flaxman based this scene on a book illustration portraying a particular Greek vase in the collection of William Hamilton (1730–1803), a leading collector of antiquities and one of Wedgwood's major patrons. Flaxman simplified the original design to accommodate both the popular and idealized notion of ancient Greek art and the demands of mass production.

The socially conscious Wedgwood, informed by Enlightenment thinking, established a village for his employees and showed concern for their well-being. He was active in the international effort to halt the African slave trade and abolish slavery. In an

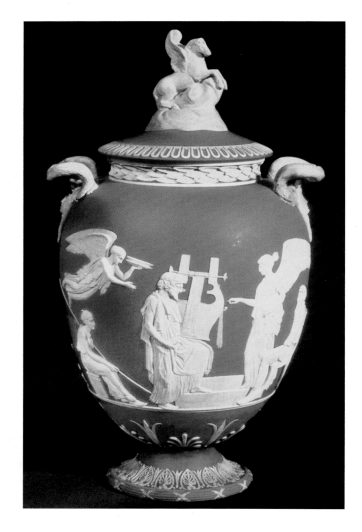

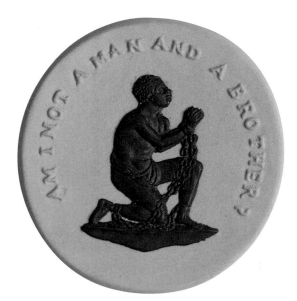

29–19 • William Hackwood for Josiah Wedgwood "AM I NOT A MAN AND A BROTHER?"
1787. Black-and-white jasperware, 1⅜ × 1⅜″ (3.5 × 3.5 cm).
Trustees of the Wedgwood Museum, Barlaston, Staffordshire, England

29–18 • Josiah Wedgwood THE APOTHEOSIS OF HOMER
Made at the Wedgwood Etruria factory, Staffordshire, England.
1790–1795. White jasperware body with a mid-blue dip and white
relief, height 18″ (45.7 cm). Relief of *The Apotheosis of Homer* adapted
from a plaque by John Flaxman, Jr., 1778. Trustees of the Wedgwood
Museum, Barlaston, Staffordshire, England

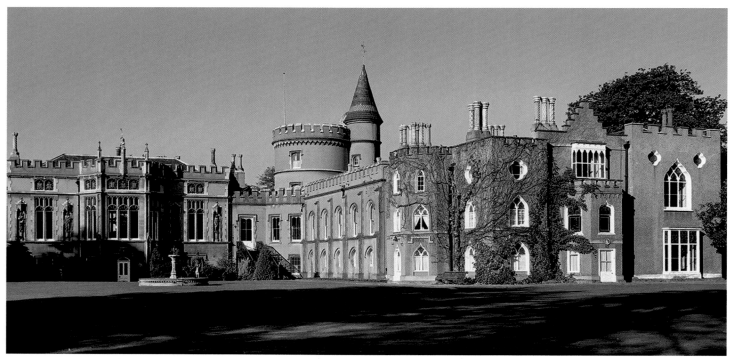

29–20 • Horace Walpole and others STRAWBERRY HILL
Twickenham, England. 1749–1776.

A CLOSER LOOK

Georgian Silver

Elizabeth Morley **GEORGE III TODDY LADLE, 1802**; Alice and George Burrows **GEORGE III SNUFFBOX, 1802**; Elizabeth Cooke **GEORGE III SALVER, 1767**; Ann and Peter Bateman **GEORGE III GOBLET, 1797**; Hester Bateman **GEORGE III DOUBLE BEAKER, 1790** National Museum of Women in the Arts, Washington, D.C. Silver Collection assembled by Nancy Valentine. Purchased with funds donated by Mr. and Mrs. Oliver Grace and family

All of the objects shown here bear the marks of silver shops run either wholly or partly by women, who played a significant role in the production of silver during the Georgian period—the years from 1714 to 1830, when Great Britain was ruled by four successive kings named George.

This goblet was used for drinking punch, a potent alcoholic beverage enjoyed by British high society. The gilded interior protected the silver from the acid in alcoholic drinks.

The filled goblets would have been served on a flat salver.

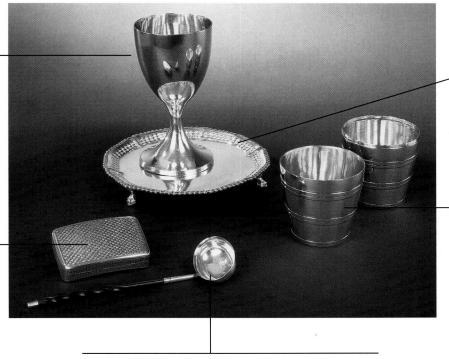

This box contained snuff, a pulverized tobacco inhaled by both men and women of the upper class. This snuffbox has curved sides for easy insertion into the pocket of a gentleman's tight-fitting trousers.

These "double beaker" cups are also for drinking punch. The smaller size made them convenient for use when traveling.

This ladle was used to pour punch from a bowl into a goblet. Its twisted whalebone handle floats, making it easy to retrieve from the bowl.

SEE MORE: View the Closer Look feature for Georgian Silver **www.myartslab.com**

attempt to publicize the abolitionist cause, he commissioned the sculptor William Hackwood (c. 1757–1839) to design an emblem for the British Committee to Abolish the Slave Trade, formed in 1787. Hackwood created a small medallion of black-and-white jasperware, with a cameo likeness of an African man kneeling in chains, and the legend **"AM I NOT A MAN AND A BROTHER?" (FIG. 29–19)**. Wedgwood sent copies of the medallion to Benjamin Franklin, the president of the Philadelphia Abolition Society, and to others in the abolitionist movement. The image was so compelling that the women's suffrage movement in the United States later used it to represent a woman in chains with the motto "Am I Not a Woman and a Sister?"

THE GOTHIC REVIVAL IN ARCHITECTURE AND DESIGN

The Gothic Revival style emerged alongside the Neoclassical in Britain in the mid eighteenth century and spread to several other nations after 1800. An early advocate of the Gothic Revival was the conservative politician and author Horace Walpole (1717– 1797). In 1764, Walpole published *The Castle of Otranto*, widely regarded as the first Gothic novel. This tale of mysterious and supernatural happenings, set in the Middle Ages, almost single-handedly launched a fashion for the Gothic. In 1749, Walpole began to remodel his country house, **STRAWBERRY HILL**, transforming it into the kind of Gothic castle that he described in his fiction (**FIG. 29–20**). Working with several friends and architects, over the next

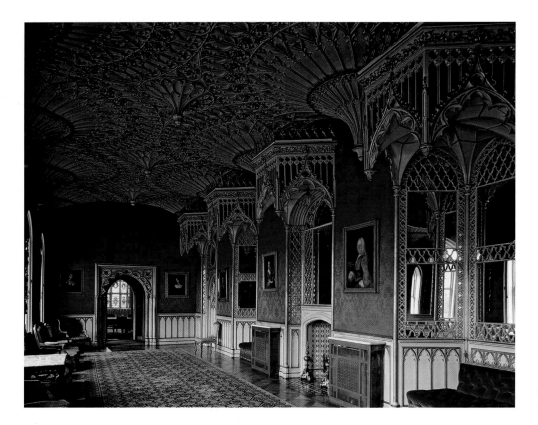

29-21 • Horace Walpole, John Chute, and Richard Bentley PICTURE GALLERY SHOWING FAN-VAULTED CEILING, STRAWBERRY HILL
After 1754.

30 years he added decorative **crenellations** (alternating higher and lower sections along the top of a wall), tracery windows, and turrets, to create an imaginary Gothic castle. The interior, too, was redesigned according to Walpole's interpretation of the British historical past. In the **PICTURE GALLERY** (**FIG. 29–21**), he drew on engravings of medieval architecture from antiquarian books in his library. The gallery ceiling is designed after that of the Chapel of Henry VII at Westminster, but transformed to suit Walpole's taste: For example, there is a very unmedieval strawberry design on the fan vaults.

TRENDS IN BRITISH PAINTING

In the mid nineteenth century, portraiture remained a popular genre in British painting among those with the means to purchase art. But a taste was also developing for other subjects, such as moralizing satire and caricature, ancient and modern history, scenes from British literature, and British landscape and people. Whatever their subject matter, many of the paintings and prints created in Britain reflected Romantic sensibilities and Enlightenment values, including an interest in social change, an embrace of natural beauty, and an enthusiasm for science and technology.

THE SATIRIC SPIRIT. The industrialization of Britain created a large and affluent middle class with the disposable income to purchase smaller and less formal paintings such as landscapes and genre scenes, as well as prints. Relatively inexpensive printed versions of paintings could also be sold to large numbers of people. William Hogarth (1697–1764) capitalized on this new market for

art and was largely responsible for reviving the British print industry in the eighteenth century.

Trained as a portrait painter, Hogarth believed art should contribute to the improvement of society. He worked within the flourishing culture of satire in Britain directed at a variety of political and social targets. He illustrated works by John Gay, a writer whose 1728 play *The Beggar's Opera* portrayed all classes as corrupt, but caricatured aristocrats in particular as feckless. In about 1730, Hogarth began illustrating moralizing tales of his own invention in sequences of four to six paintings, which he then produced in sets of mass-produced prints, enabling him to both maximize his profits and reach as many people as possible.

Between 1743 and 1745, Hogarth produced his *Marriage à la Mode* suite, inspired by Joseph Addison's 1712 essay in the *Spectator* promoting the concept of marriage based on love rather than on aristocratic machinations. In his series of paintings and later prints, Hogarth portrays the sordid story and sad end of an arranged marriage between the children of an impoverished aristocrat and a social-climbing member of the newly wealthy merchant class. In the opening scene of the series, **THE MARRIAGE CONTRACT** (**FIG. 29–22**), the cast of characters is assembled to legalize the union. At the right of the painting sits Lord Squanderfield, raising his gouty right foot on a footstool as he points to his lengthy family tree (with a few wilted branches), which goes all the way back to medieval knights, as if to say that the pile of money in front of him on the table is not payment enough for the marriage contract he is being asked to sign. Young Squanderfield, a fop and a simpleton, sits on the far left, admiring himself in the mirror and ignoring his

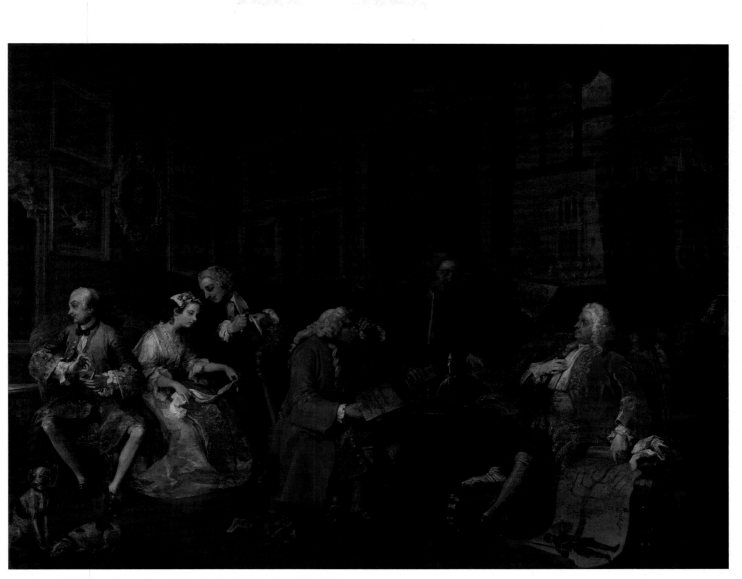

29-22 • William Hogarth THE MARRIAGE CONTRACT
From *Marriage à la Mode*, 1743–1745. Oil on canvas, 27½ × 35¾" (69.9 × 90.8 cm). National Gallery, London.

future wife as he takes a pinch of snuff. His neck is already showing signs of syphilis. The unhappy bride-to-be is extravagantly dressed but rather plain, and her wedding ring is threaded through a handkerchief to wipe away her tears. In the center, her father, the uncultured but wealthy merchant in the brash red coat, leans forward to study Lord Squanderfield's pedigree, an empty sack of money at his feet. The other men are lawyers, including the slippery Silvertongue, who is sharpening the quill that will seal the young couple's fate. The next five scenes of this sad tale describe the progressively disastrous results of such a union.

Hogarth hoped to create a distinctively British style of art, free of obscure mythological references and encouraging the self-improvement in viewers that would lead to social progress. His contempt for the decadent tastes of the aristocracy can be seen in the comic detail of the paintings hanging on Lord Squanderfield's walls. Hogarth wanted to entertain and amuse his audiences, but at the same time his acerbic wit lays open the tensions of class and wealth so prevalent in the Britain of his day. Hogarth's work

became so popular that in 1745 he was able to give up portraiture, which he considered a deplorable form of vanity.

PORTRAITURE. Sir Joshua Reynolds (1723–1792) was a generation younger than Hogarth, and represented the mainstream of British art at the end of the century. After studying Renaissance art in Italy, Reynolds settled in London in 1753, where he worked vigorously to educate artists and patrons to appreciate Classically inspired history painting. In 1768, he was appointed the first president of the Royal Academy (see "Academies and Academy Exhibitions," page 924). His *Fifteen Discourses to the Royal Academy* (1769–1790) set out his theories on art in great detail. He argued that artists should follow rules derived from studying the great masters of the past, especially those who worked in the Classical tradition; he claimed that the ideal image communicated universal truths, and that artists should avoid representations based solely on observation, as these paintings merely communicated base reality.

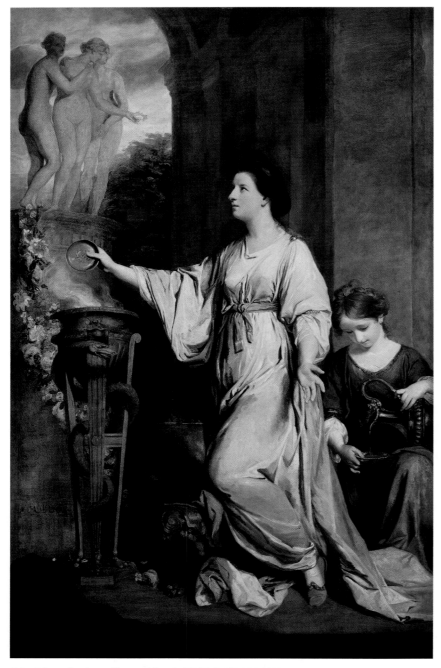

29-23 • Joshua Reynolds LADY SARAH BUNBURY SACRIFICING TO THE GRACES
1765. Oil on canvas, 7'10" × 5' (2.42 × 1.53 m). The Art Institute of Chicago. Mr. and Mrs. W. W. Kimball Collection, 1922.4468

Lady Sarah Bunbury was one of the great beauties of her era. A few years before this portrait was painted, she turned down a proposal of marriage from George III.

EXPLORE MORE: Gain insight from a primary source on Joshua Reynolds **www.myartslab.com**

Reynolds was able to combine his own taste for history painting with his patrons' desire for images of themselves by developing a type of historical or mythological portraiture that he called the **Grand Manner**. **LADY SARAH BUNBURY SACRIFICING TO THE GRACES** (FIG. 29–23) is just such a portrait. The large scale of the canvas suggests that it is a history painting, and its details evoke a Classical setting. Framed by a monumental Classical pier and arch, and dressed in a classicizing costume, Lady Sarah plays the part of a Roman priestess making a sacrifice to the Three Graces, personifications of female beauty. Portraits such as this were intended for the public rooms, halls, and stairways of aristocratic residences. Reynolds's Grand Manner portraits were widely celebrated, and his London studio was abuzz with sitters, patrons, and assistants. But Reynolds experimented with his paints, so many of his canvases have faded badly.

A counterpoint to Reynolds's style of portraiture is found in the art of Thomas Gainsborough (1727–1788). Gainsborough later set up a studio in Bath, a resort frequented by the rich and fashionable, and catered to his clients' tastes for the informal poses and natural landscapes introduced to England by Van Dyck in the 1620s. Gainsborough's earlier unfinished **ROBERT ANDREWS AND FRANCES CARTER (FIG. 29–24)**, painted soon after their wedding in 1748, shows the wealthy young rural landowner and his wife posed on the grounds of their estate, with the Sudbury River and the hills of Suffolk in the background. The youthful Frances Carter sits stiffly on a decorative seat, her fine dress arranged around her (the pheasant on her lap is unfinished), while her husband appears more relaxed, his gun in hand and his favorite dog at his side. The couple's good care of the land is revealed as well: The neat rows of corn stocks and stubble in the foreground show Robert Andrews's use of the seed drill and plant husbandry. Sheep and horses graze in separate fields. The significance of this painting lies in the natural pose of the couple, the depictions of their land and the pride they take in it, and the artist's emphasis on nature as the source of bounty and beauty. The painting prefigures the English landscapes of Constable half a century later.

THE ROMANCE OF SCIENCE. In the English Midlands, artist Joseph Wright of Derby (1734–1797) shows a similar admixture of Enlightenment aspirations, industrial innovation, and Romantic sensibility in his depiction of **AN EXPERIMENT ON A BIRD IN THE AIR-PUMP (FIG. 29–25)**. Wright set up his studio during the first wave of the Industrial Revolution, and many of his patrons were self-made wealthy industrial entrepreneurs. Wright belonged to the Lunar Society, a group of industrialists (including Wedgwood), merchants, traders, and progressive aristocrats who met monthly in or near Birmingham

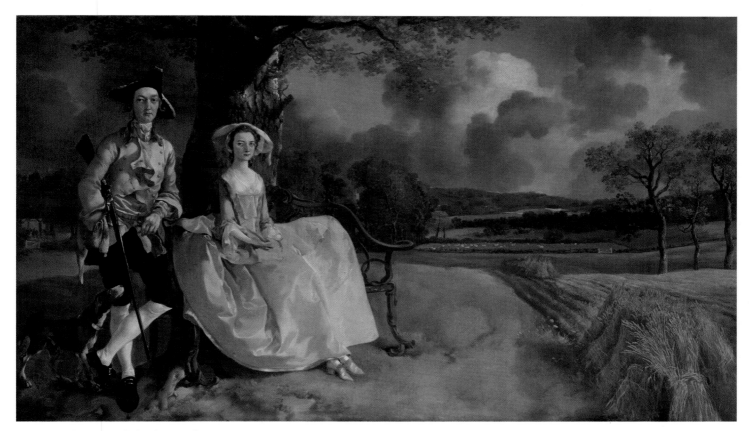

29-24 • Thomas Gainsborough **ROBERT ANDREWS AND FRANCES CARTER (MR. AND MRS. ANDREWS)**
c. 1748–1750. Oil on canvas, 27½ × 47″ (69.7 × 119.3 cm). National Gallery, London.

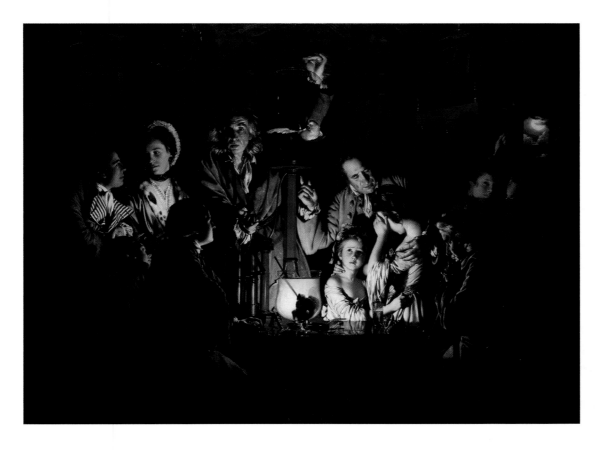

29-25 • Joseph Wright of Derby **AN EXPERIMENT ON A BIRD IN THE AIR-PUMP**
1768. Oil on canvas, 6 × 8′ (1.82 × 2.43 m). National Gallery, London.

Academies and Academy Exhibitions

During the seventeenth century, the French government founded a number of **academies** for the support and instruction of students in literature, painting and sculpture, music and dance, and architecture. In 1664, the Royal Academy of Painting and Sculpture in Paris began to mount occasional exhibitions of members' recent work. This exhibition came to be known as the Salon because it was held in the Salon Carré in the Palace of the Louvre. As of 1737, the Salon was held every other year, with a jury of members selecting the works to be shown.

History paintings (based on historical, mythological, or biblical narratives and generally conveying a high moral or intellectual idea) were accorded highest place in the Academy's hierarchy of genres, followed by historical portraiture, landscape painting, various other forms of portraiture, genre painting, and still life. The Salon shows were the only public art exhibitions of importance in Paris, so they were highly influential in establishing officially approved styles and in molding public taste; they also consolidated the Academy's control over the production of art.

In recognition of Rome's importance as a training ground for aspiring history painters, the Royal Academy of Painting and Sculpture opened a French Academy in Rome in 1666. A competitive "Prix de Rome," or Rome Prize, enabled the winners to study in Rome for three to five years. A similar prize was established by the French Royal Academy of Architecture in 1720. Many Western cultural capitals emulated the French academic model: Academies were established in Berlin in 1696, Dresden in 1705, London in 1768, Boston in 1780, Mexico City in 1785, and New York in 1802. Members of London's Royal Academy of Arts are depicted in Johann Zoffany's portrait of 1771–1772.

Although there were several women members of the European academies of art before the eighteenth century, their inclusion amounted to little more than an honorary recognition of their achievements. In France, Louis XIV proclaimed in his founding address to the Royal Academy that its purpose was to reward all worthy artists "without regard to the difference of sex," but this resolve was not put into practice. Only seven women gained the title of "Academician" between 1648 and 1706, after which the Royal Academy was closed to women. Nevertheless, four more women were admitted by 1770; however, the men, worried that women would become "too numerous," limited the total number of female members to four. Young women were neither admitted to the Academy School nor allowed to compete for Academy prizes, both of which were required for professional success. They fared even worse at London's Royal Academy. The Swiss painters Mary Moser and Angelica Kauffmann were both founding members in 1768, but no other women were elected until 1922, and then only as associates.

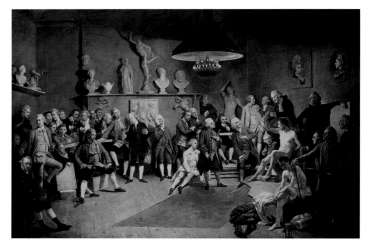

Johann Zoffany ACADEMICIANS OF THE ROYAL ACADEMY
1771–1772. Oil on canvas, 47½ × 59½″ (120.6 × 151.2 cm). The Royal Collection, Windsor Castle, England.

Zoffany's group portrait of members of the London Royal Academy reveals how mainstream artists were taught in the 1770s. The painting shows artists, all men, setting up a life-drawing class and engaging in lively conversation. The studio is decorated with the Academy's study collection of Classical statues and plaster copies. Propriety prohibited the presence of women in life-drawing studios, so Zoffany includes Royal Academicians Mary Moser and Angelica Kauffmann in portraits on the wall on the right.

to exchange ideas about science and technology. As part of the society's attempts to popularize science, Wright painted a series of "entertaining" scenes of scientific experiments.

The second half of the eighteenth century was an age of rapid technological change (see "Iron as a Building Material," page 926), and the development of the air-pump was among the many scientific innovations of the time. Although primarily used to study the properties of gas, it was also widely used in dramatic public demonstrations of scientific principles. In the experiment shown here, air was pumped out of the large glass vessel above the scientist's head until the bird inside collapsed from lack of oxygen. Before it died, air was reintroduced by a simple mechanism at the top. Wright depicts the moment before air is reintroduced, engaging the viewer with the excitement of the moment: Dramatically lit from below by a single light source on the table, the scientist peers out of the picture and gestures like a magician about to perform a trick. By delaying the reintroduction of air, the scientist has created considerable suspense. The three men on the left watch the experiment with great interest, while the young girls on the right have a more emotional response to

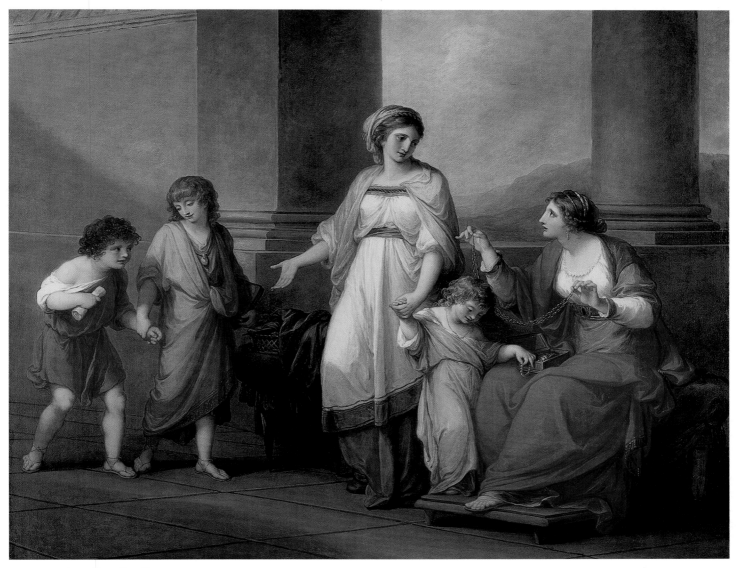

29-26 • Angelica Kauffmann CORNELIA POINTING TO HER CHILDREN AS HER TREASURES
c. 1785. Oil on canvas, 40 × 50″ (101.6 × 127 cm). Virginia Museum of Fine Arts, Richmond, Virginia. The Adolph D. and
Wilkins C. Williams Fund

the proceedings. One man is lost in thought, perhaps contemplating the meaning of life, as he stares at a skull suspended in fluid. The moon shines in through the window, a reference to the name of the Lunar Society. Science, the painting suggests, holds the potential for wonder, excitement, and discovery about matters of life and death.

HISTORY PAINTING.   By the time it was adapted to Neoclassicism, history painting had long been considered the highest form of art. The Swiss history painter Angelica Kauffmann (1741–1807), trained in Italy and one of the greatest exponents of early Neoclassicism, arrived in London in 1766 to great acclaim, inspiring British artists to paint Classical history paintings and British patrons to buy them. She was welcomed immediately into Joshua Reynolds's inner circle; in 1768 she was one of only two women artists named among the founding members of the Royal Academy (see "Academies and Academy Exhibitions," opposite).

Already accepting portrait commissions at age 15, Kauffmann painted Winckelmann's portrait in Rome, became an ardent practitioner of Neoclassicism, and was elected to the Academy of Saint Luke, also in Rome. Most eighteenth-century women artists specialized in the "lower" painting genres of portraiture or still life, but Kauffmann boldly embarked on an independent career as a history painter. In London, where she lived from 1766 to 1781, she produced numerous history paintings, many of them with subjects drawn from Classical antiquity. After her return to Italy, Kauffmann painted **CORNELIA POINTING TO HER CHILDREN AS HER TREASURES (FIG. 29–26)** for an English patron. The scene in the painting took place in the second century BCE, during the

In 1779, Abraham Darby III built a bridge over the Severn River at Coalbrookdale in Shropshire, England, a town typical of industrial England, with factories and workers' housing filling the valley. Built primarily for function, the bridge demonstrated a need for newer, better transportation routes for moving industrial goods. Its importance lies in the fact that it is probably the first large-scale example of the use of structural metal in bridge building, in which iron struts replace the heavy, hand-cut stone voussoirs of earlier bridges. Five pairs of cast-iron, semicircular arches form a strong, economical 100-foot span. In functional architecture such as this, the available technology, the properties of the material, and the requirements of engineering in large part determine form, often producing an unintended new aesthetic. Here, the use of metal made possible the light, open, skeletal structure sought by builders since the twelfth century. Cast iron was quickly adopted for the construction of such engineering wonders as the soaring train stations of the nineteenth century, leading ultimately to such marvels as the Eiffel Tower (FIG. 30–1).

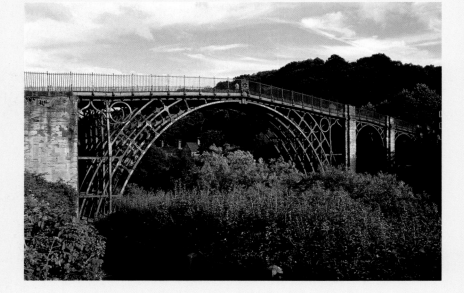

Abraham Darby III
SEVERN RIVER BRIDGE
Coalbrookdale, England. 1779.

republican era of Rome. A woman visitor shows Cornelia her jewels and then asks to see those of her hostess. In response, Cornelia shows her daughter and two sons, saying: "These are my most precious jewels." Cornelia exemplifies the "good mother," a popular theme among some later eighteenth-century patrons who preferred Classical subjects that taught metaphorical lessons of civic virtue. The value of her maternal dedication is emphasized by the fact that her sons, Tiberius and Gaius Gracchus, grew up to be political reformers. Kauffmann's composition is severe and Classical, but she softens the image with warm, subdued lighting and with the tranquil grace of her figures.

Kauffmann's devotion to Neoclassical history painting emerged during her friendship with American-born Benjamin West (1738–1820) in Rome. West studied in Philadelphia before he left for Rome in 1759, where he met Winckelmann and became a student of Mengs. In 1763, he moved permanently to London, where he specialized in Neoclassical history painting. In 1768, along with Kauffmann and Reynolds, he became a founding member of the Royal Academy.

Two years later, West shocked Reynolds and his other academic friends with his painting **THE DEATH OF GENERAL WOLFE** (FIG. 29–27), which seemed to break completely with Neoclassicism and academic history painting. West argued that history painting was not dependent on dressing figures in Classical costume; in fact, it could represent a contemporary subject as long as the grand themes and elevated message remained intact. Thus, West's painting, and the genre it spawned, came to be known as "modern history" painting. At first, George III and Joshua Reynolds were appalled, but modern history pieces had too strong an attraction for both British collectors and the British public. The king eventually commissioned one of the four replicas of the painting.

West's painting glorifies the British general James Wolfe, who died in 1759 in a British victory over the French for the control of Quebec during the Seven Years War (1756–1763). West depicted Wolfe in his red uniform expiring in the arms of his comrades under a cloud-swept sky. In fact, Wolfe actually died at the base of a tree, surrounded by two or three attendants, but the laws of artistic decorum demanded a much nobler scene. Thus, though West's

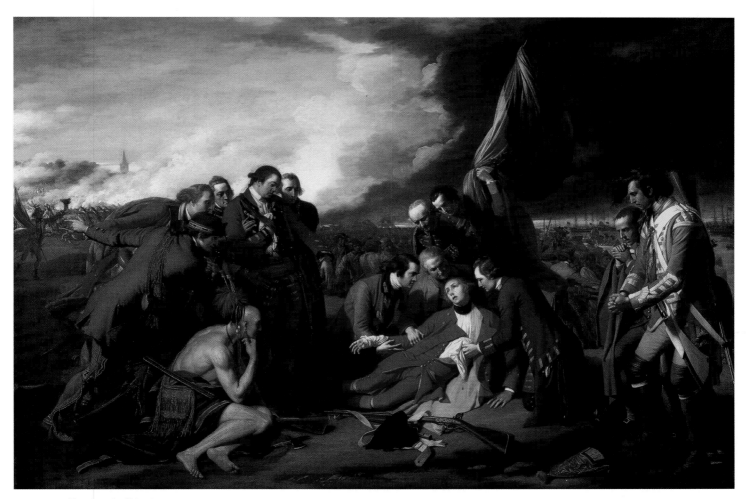

29-27 • Benjamin West THE DEATH OF GENERAL WOLFE
1770. Oil on canvas, 4'11½" × 7' (1.51 × 2.14 m). National Gallery of Canada, Ottawa. Transfer from the
Canadian War Memorials, 1921. Gift of the 2nd Duke of Westminster, Eaton Hall, Cheshire, 1918

The famous actor David Garrick was so moved by this painting that he enacted an impromptu interpretation of the dying
Wolfe in front of the work when it was exhibited at the Royal Academy.

painting seems naturalistic, it is not an objective document, nor was it intended to be. West employs the Grand Manner that Reynolds proposed in his *Discourses*, celebrating the valor of the fallen hero, the loyalty of the British soldiers, and the justice of their cause. To indicate the North American setting, West also included at the left a Native American warrior who contemplates the fallen Wolfe. This was another fiction, since the Native Americans in this battle fought on the side of the French, but his presence here establishes the North American site of the event. The dramatic illumination increases the emotional intensity of the scene, as do the poses of Wolfe's attendants, arranged to suggest a Lamentation over the dead Christ. Extending the analogy, the British flag above Wolfe replaces the Christian cross. Just as Christ died for humanity, Wolfe sacrificed himself for the good of the nation. The brilliant color, emotional intensity, and moralizing message made this image extremely popular with the British public. It was translated into a print and received the widest circulation of any image in Britain up to that time.

ROMANTIC PAINTING. The emotional drama of West's painting helped launch Romanticism in Britain. Among its early practitioners was John Henry Fuseli (1741–1825), who arrived in London from his native Switzerland in 1764. Trained in theology, philosophy, and the Neoclassical aesthetics of Winckelmann (whose writings he translated into English), Fuseli quickly became a member of London's intellectual elite. Joshua Reynolds encouraged Fuseli to become an artist, and in 1770 he left England to study in Rome, where he spent most of the next eight years. His encounter with the sometimes tortured and expressive aspects of both Roman sculpture and Michelangelo's painting led him not to Neoclassicism but to develop his own powerfully expressive style. In his work, Fuseli drew more heavily on the passion of some Roman art, and later that of Michelangelo, than on the ancient Greek art admired by Winckelmann.

Back in London, Fuseli established himself as a history painter, but he specialized in dramatic subjects drawn from Homer, Dante,

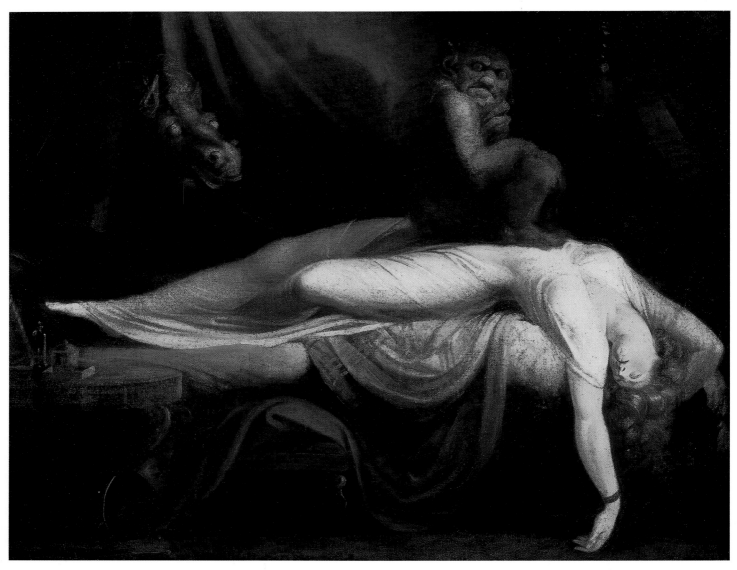

29-28 • John Henry Fuseli THE NIGHTMARE
1781. Oil on canvas, 39¾ × 49½" (101 × 127 cm). The Detroit Institute of Arts. Gift of Mr. and Mrs. Bert Smokler and Mr. and Mrs. Lawrence A. Fleischmann

Fuseli was not popular with the English critics. One writer said that his 1780 entry in the London Royal Academy exhibition "ought to be destroyed," and Horace Walpole called another painting in 1785 "shockingly mad, mad, mad, madder than ever." Even after achieving the highest official acknowledgment of his talents, Fuseli was called "the Wild Swiss" and "Painter to the Devil." But the public appreciated his work, and *The Nightmare*, exhibited at the Royal Academy in 1782, was repeated in at least three more versions and its imagery was disseminated through prints published by commercial engravers. One of these prints would later hang in the office of the Austrian psychoanalyst Sigmund Freud, who believed that dreams were manifestations of the dreamer's repressed desires.

Shakespeare, and Milton. His interest in the dark recesses of the human mind led him to paint supernatural and irrational subjects. In **THE NIGHTMARE (FIG. 29–28)**, he depicts a woman sprawled across a divan with her head thrown back. She is oppressed by a gruesome incubus (or *mara*, an evil spirit) crouching on her pelvis. According to legend, the incubus was believed to feed by stealing women and having sex with them; in her erotic dream the woman dreams that the incubus is about to feed upon her. In the background a horse with wild, phosphorescent eyes thrusts its head into the room through a curtain. The image communicates fear of

the unknown and unknowable, and sexuality without restraint. The painting was exhibited at the Royal Academy in 1782, and although not well received by Fuseli's peers, it clearly struck a chord with the public. He painted at least four versions of this subject and prints of it had a wide circulation.

Fuseli's friend William Blake (1757–1827), a highly original poet, painter, and printmaker, was also inspired by the dramatic aspect of Michelangelo's art. Trained as an engraver, he enrolled briefly at the Royal Academy, where he quickly rejected the teachings of Reynolds, believing that rules hinder rather than aid

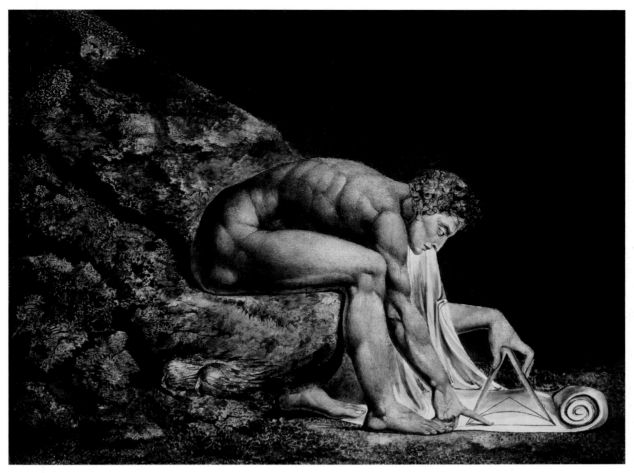

29-29 • William Blake NEWTON
1795–c. 1805. Color print finished in ink and watercolor, 18⅛ × 23⅝″ (46 × 60 cm). Tate, London.

creativity. He became a lifelong advocate of probing the unfettered imagination. For Blake, the imagination provided access to the higher realm of the spirit and reason was confined to the lower world of matter.

Blake was interested in probing the nature of good and evil, developing an idiosyncratic form of Christian belief, drawing on elements from the Bible, Greek mythology, and British legend. His "prophetic books," designed and printed in the mid 1790s, brought together painting and poetry to explore themes of spiritual crisis and redemption. Thematically related to the prophetic books are an independent series of 12 large color prints that he executed mostly in 1795, which may have some overarching theme; it is not obvious, however, what it is. These include the large print of **NEWTON (FIG. 29–29)**, the epitome of eighteenth-century rationalism, naked in a cave and obsessed with reducing the universe to a mathematical drawing with his compasses.

John Singleton Copley, whose portrait of the Mifflins is described above (SEE FIG. 29–1), moved from Boston to London after the Revolutionary War, never to return to his native country. In London, he established himself as a portraitist and painter of modern history in the vein of fellow American expatriate Benjamin West. Copley's most successful modern history painting was **WATSON AND THE SHARK (FIG. 29–30)**, commissioned by Brook Watson, a wealthy London merchant and Tory politician, in 1778. Copley's painting dramatizes an episode of 1749, in which the 14-year-old Watson was attacked by a shark while swimming in Havana Harbor, and lost part of his right leg before being rescued by his comrades. Copley's pyramidal composition is made up of figures in a boat and the hapless Watson in the water with a highly imaginary shark set against the backdrop of the harbor. Several of the figures were inspired by Classical sources, but the scene portrayed is anything but Classical. In the foreground, the ferocious shark rushes on the helpless, naked Watson, while at the prow of the rescue boat a man raises his harpoon to attack the shark. At the left, two of Watson's shipmates strain to reach him while others in the boat look on in alarm. An African man, standing at the apex of the painting, holds a rope that curls over Watson's extended right arm, connecting him to the boat.

Some scholars have read the African figure as a servant waiting to hand the rope to his white master, but his inclusion has also been interpreted in more overtly political terms. The shark attack on Watson in Havana Harbor occurred while he was working in the transatlantic shipping trade, one aspect of which involved the shipment of slaves from Africa to the West Indies. At the time when

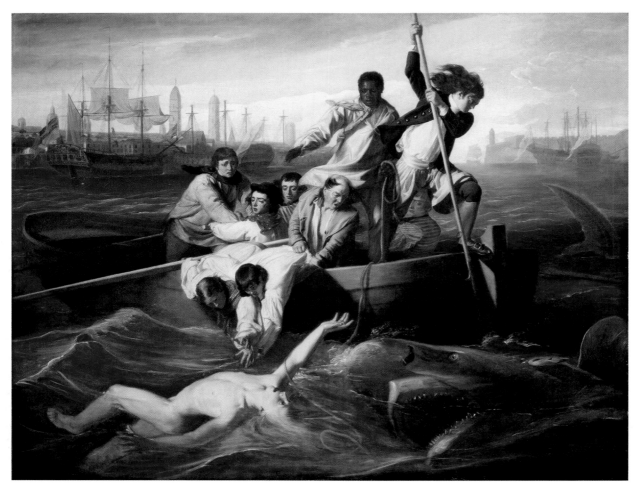

29–30 • John Singleton Copley WATSON AND THE SHARK
1778. Oil on canvas, 5'10¾" × 7'6½" (1.82 × 2.29 m). National Gallery of Art, Washington, D.C. Ferdinand Lammot Belin Fund

Watson commissioned this painting, debate was raging in the British Parliament over the interconnected issues of the Americans' recent Declaration of Independence and the slave trade. Several Tories, including Watson, opposed American independence, highlighting the hypocrisy of American calls for freedom from the British Crown while the colonists continued to deny freedom to African slaves. Indeed, during the Revolutionary War the British offered freedom to every runaway American slave who joined the British army or navy.

Copley's painting, its subject doubtless dictated by Watson, may therefore indicate Watson's sympathy for American slaves; or the figure may be included simply to indicate that the event took place in Havana. Copley was one of the first artists in the capital to exhibit his modern history paintings in public places around London, making money by charging admission fees and advertising his large paintings for sale. His sensational images and exhibitions took advantage of the spectacular displays of the *Phantasmagoria* (a sensational magic lantern display with smoke, mirrors, lights, and gauze "ghosts"), panoramas, dioramas, and the Eidophusikon (a miniature theater with special effects) of London in the early nineteenth century.

LATER EIGHTEENTH-CENTURY ART IN FRANCE

In late eighteenth-century France, the Rococo was replaced by Enlightenment ideas and by the gathering storm clouds of revolution. French art moved increasingly toward Neoclassicism. French architects held closer to Roman proportions and sensibility, while painters and sculptors increasingly embraced didactic Classicism and a plain Classical style.

ARCHITECTURE

French architects of the late eighteenth century generally considered Classicism not one of many alternative artistic styles but as the single, true style. Winckelmann's argument that "imitation of the ancients" was the key to good taste was taken to heart in France. The leading French Neoclassical architect was Jacques-Germain Soufflot (1713–1780), whose Church of Sainte-Geneviève **(FIG. 29–31)**, known today as the **PANTHÉON**, is the most typical Neoclassical building in Paris. In it, Soufflot attempted to integrate three traditions: the Roman architecture he had seen on two trips to Italy; French and English Baroque Classicism; and the Palladian style

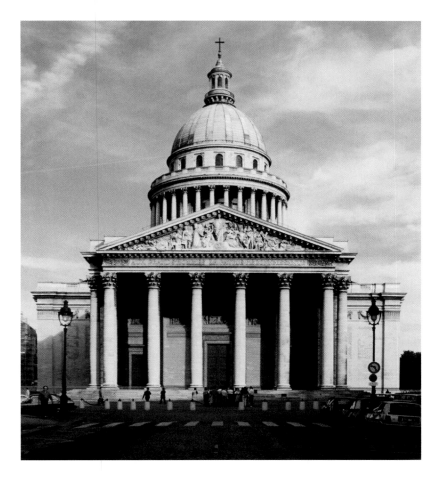

29-31 • Jacques-Germain Soufflot PANTHÉON (CHURCH OF SAINTE-GENEVIÈVE)
Paris. 1755–1792.

This building has an interesting history. Before it was completed, the Revolutionary government in control of Paris confiscated all religious properties to raise desperately needed public funds. Instead of selling Sainte-Geneviève, however, they voted in 1791 to make it the Temple of Fame for the burial of Heroes of Liberty. Under Napoleon I (r. 1799–1814), the building was resanctified as a Catholic church and was again used as such under King Louis-Philippe (r. 1830–1848) and Napoleon III (r. 1852–1870). Then it was permanently designated a nondenominational lay temple. In 1851, the building was used as a physics laboratory. Here the French physicist Jean-Bernard Foucault suspended his now-famous pendulum in the interior of the high crossing dome, and by measuring the path of the pendulum's swing proved his theory that the Earth rotated on its axis in a counterclockwise motion. In 1995, the ashes of Marie Curie, who had won the Nobel Prize in chemistry in 1911, were moved into this "memorial to the great men of France," making her the first woman to be enshrined there.

being revived at the time in England. The façade of the Panthéon, with its huge portico, is modeled on the proportions of ancient Roman temples. The dome, on the other hand, was inspired by seventeenth-century architecture, including Sir Christopher Wren's St. Paul's Cathedral in London (SEE FIG. 22–60), while the radical geometry of its central-plan Greek cross (FIG. 29–32)

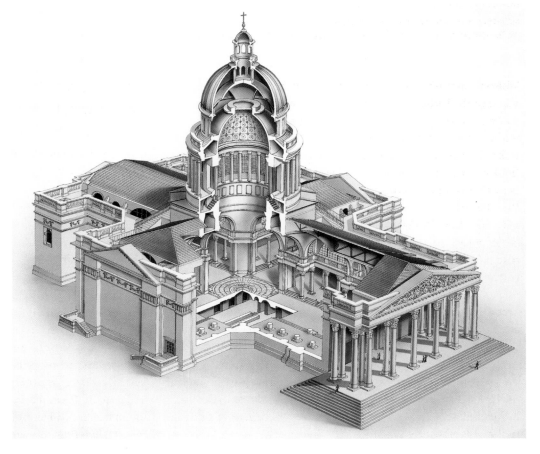

29-32 • PANTHÉON (CHURCH OF SAINTE-GENEVIÈVE), CUTAWAY ILLUSTRATION

SEE MORE: Click the Google Earth link for the Panthéon (Church of Sainte-Geneviève) www.myartslab.com

owes as much to Burlington's Neo-Palladian Chiswick House (SEE FIG. 29–16) as it does to Christian tradition. The Panthéon, however, is not simply the sum of its parts. Its rational, ordered plan is constructed with rectangles, squares, and circles, while its relatively plain surfaces communicate severity and powerful simplicity.

PAINTING AND SCULPTURE

While French painters such as Boucher, Fragonard, and their followers continued to work in the Rococo style in the later decades of the eighteenth century, a strong reaction against the Rococo had set in by the 1760s. A leading detractor of the Rococo was Denis Diderot (1713–1784), whose 32-volume compendium of knowledge and skill, the *Encyclopédie* (produced in collaboration with Jean le Rond d'Alembert, 1717–1783) served as an archive of Enlightenment thought in France. In 1759, Diderot began to write reviews of the official Salon for a periodic newsletter for wealthy subscribers, and he is generally considered to be the founder of modern art criticism. Diderot believed that it was art's proper function to "inspire virtue and purify manners," a function that the Rococo was not designed to fulfill.

CHARDIN. Diderot greatly admired Jean-Siméon Chardin (1699–1779), an artist who as early as the 1730s began to create moralizing pictures in the tradition of seventeenth-century Dutch

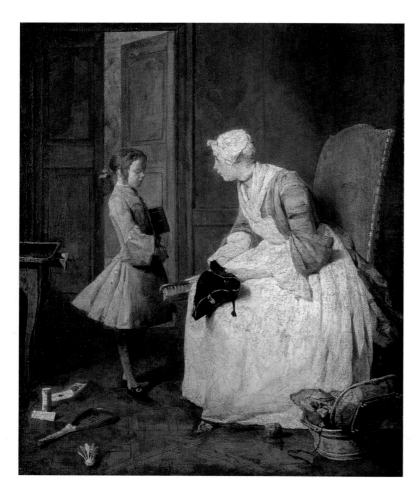

genre painting by focusing on carefully structured but touching scenes of everyday middle-class life. THE GOVERNESS (FIG. 29–33), for instance, shows a finely dressed boy with books under his arm, being addressed by his governess as she prepares to brush his tricorn (three-cornered) hat. Scattered on the floor are a racquet, a shuttlecock, and playing cards, the childish pleasures that the boy leaves behind as he prepares to go to his studies and, ultimately, to a life of responsible adulthood. The work suggests the benevolent exercise of authority and willing submission to it.

GREUZE. Diderot reserved his highest praise for Jean-Baptiste Greuze (1725–1805), and his own plays of the late 1750s served as a source of inspiration for Greuze's painting. Diderot expanded the traditional range of theatrical works in Paris from mostly tragedy and comedy to include the *drame bourgeois*, the middle-class drama, and "middle tragedy," later called the "melodrama," both moralizing plays that communicated moral and civic lessons through simple, clear stories of ordinary life. Greuze's domestic genre paintings, such as THE VILLAGE BRIDE (FIG. 29–34), were visual counterparts to Diderot's *drame bourgeois* and 'middle tragedy'. In this painting, Greuze presents the action on a shallow, stagelike space under a dramatic spotlight. An elderly father reaches out to his affectionate family as he hands the dowry for his daughter to his new son-in-law; a notary records the event. The young couple link arms but are not overly familiar with one another; the bride is held by her mother and sister. In contrast to Hogarth's marriage contract (SEE FIG. 29–22), Greuze's painting demonstrates that virtue and poverty can coexist. This kind of highly emotional, theatrical, and moralizing genre scene was widely praised in Greuze's time, offering a counterpoint to early Neoclassical history painting in France.

VIGÉE-LEBRUN. While Greuze painted scenes of the poor and middle class, Marie-Louise-Élisabeth Vigée-Lebrun (1755–1842) became famous as Queen Marie Antoinette's favorite portrait painter. Vigée-Lebrun was also notable for her election into the French Royal Academy of Painting and Sculpture, which then made only four places available to women. In 1787, she painted MARIE ANTOINETTE WITH HER

29-33 • Jean-Siméon Chardin THE GOVERNESS
1739. Oil on canvas, 18⅛ × 14¾″ (46 × 37.5 cm). National Gallery of Canada, Ottawa. Purchase, 1956

Chardin was one of the first French artists to treat the lives of women and children with sympathy and to portray the dignity of women's work in his images of young mothers, governesses, and kitchen maids. Shown at the Salon of 1739, *The Governess* was praised by contemporary critics, one of whom noted "the graciousness, sweetness, and restraint that the governess maintains in her discipline of the young man about his dirtiness, disorder, and neglect; his attention, shame, and remorse; all are expressed with great simplicity."

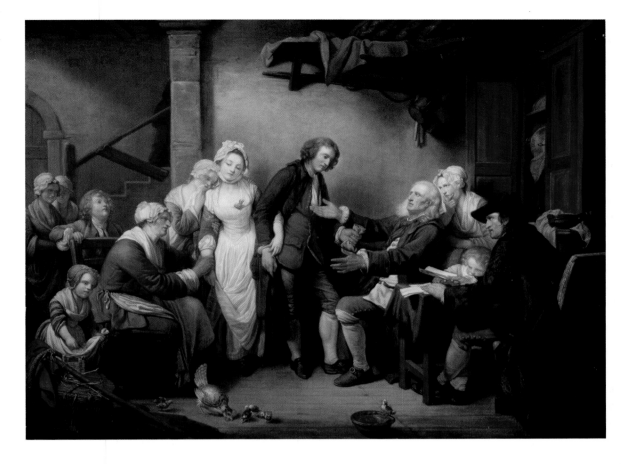

CHILDREN (FIG. 29–35). Drawing on the theme of the "good mother" seen earlier in Angelica Kauffmann's Neoclassical painting of Cornelia (SEE FIG. 29–26), Vigée-Lebrun portrays the queen as a kindly, stabilizing mother to try to counter public perceptions of her as selfish, extravagant, and immoral. The queen maintains her regal pose, as is appropriate, but her children are depicted more sympathetically: The princess leans affectionately against her mother's arm and the little dauphin, the heir to a throne he would never inherit, points to the empty cradle of a recently deceased sibling. The image alludes to the allegory of Abundance and is intended to assure peace and prosperity for France under the reign of her husband, Louis XVI, who came to the throne in 1774 but was executed, as was she, in 1792 during the Reign of Terror.

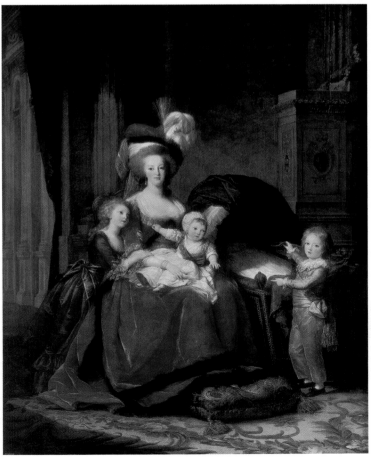

29–35 • Marie-Louise-Élisabeth Vigée-Lebrun
PORTRAIT OF MARIE ANTOINETTE WITH HER CHILDREN
1787. Oil on canvas, 9′1½″ × 7′5⅝″ (2.75 × 2.15 m). Musée National du Château de Versailles.

As the favorite painter to the queen, Vigée-Lebrun escaped from Paris with her daughter on the eve of the Revolution of 1789 and fled to Rome. After a very successful self-exile working in Italy, Austria, Russia, and England, the artist finally resettled in Paris in 1805 and again became popular with Parisian art patrons. Over her long career, she painted about 800 portraits in a vibrant style that changed very little over the decades.

DAVID. The most important French Neoclassical painter of the era was Jacques-Louis David (1748–1825), who dominated French art for over 20 years during the French Revolution and the subsequent reign of Napoleon. In 1774, he won the Prix de Rome and spent six years there, studying antique sculpture and learning the principles of Neoclassicism. After his return to Paris, he produced a series of severely plain Neoclassical paintings extolling the antique virtues of stoicism, masculinity, and patriotism.

Perhaps the most significant of these works was the **OATH OF THE HORATII** (FIG. **29–36**) of 1784–1785. A royal commission, the work reflects the taste and values of Louis XVI, who along with his minister of the arts, Count d'Angiviller, was sympathetic to the Enlightenment. Like Diderot, d'Angiviller and the king believed that art should improve public morals. One of d'Angiviller's first official acts was to ban indecent nudity from the Salon of 1775 and commission a series of didactic history paintings. David's

commission for the *Oath of the Horatii* in 1784 was part of that general program.

The subject of the painting was inspired by the drama *Horace*, written by the great French playwright Pierre Corneille (1606–1684), which was in turn based on ancient Roman historical texts; the patriotic oath-taking incident depicted by David here, however, is not taken directly from these sources and seems to have been the artist's own invention. The scene is set in the seventh century BCE, at a time when Rome and its rival, Alba, a neighboring city-state, agreed to settle a border dispute and avert a war by holding a battle to the death between the three sons of Horace (the Horatii), representing Rome, and the three Curatii, representing Alba. In David's painting, the Horatii stand with arms outstretched toward their father, who reaches to them with the swords on which they pledge to fight and die for Rome. The power running through the outstretched fingers of young men to their father almost makes him

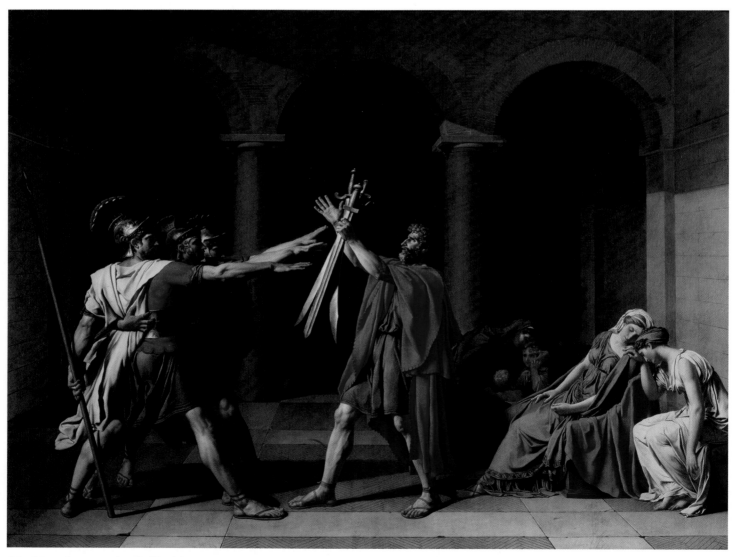

29-36 • Jacques-Louis David OATH OF THE HORATII
1784–1785. Oil on canvas, 10′8¼″ × 14′ (3.26 × 4.27 m). Musée du Louvre, Paris.

EXPLORE MORE: Gain insight from a primary source on Jacques-Louis David **www.myartslab.com**

step back. In contrast to the upright, muscular angularity of the men, the group of weeping women and frightened children are limp. They weep for the lives of both the Horatii and the Curatii. Sabina (in the center) is a sister of the Curatii, and also married to one of the Horatii; Camilla (at the far right) is sister to the Horatii and engaged to one of the Curatii. David's composition, which separates the men from the women and children spatially using framing background arches, dramatically contrasts the young men's stoic and willing self-sacrifice with the women's emotional collapse.

The emotional intensity of this history painting pushed French academy rules on decorum to the limit. Originally commissioned by the monarchy, it quickly and ironically became an emblem of the 1789 French Revolution. Its message of patriotism and sacrifice for the greater good effectively captured the mood of the leaders of the new French Republic established in 1792. As the revolutionaries abolished the monarchy and titles of nobility, took education out of the hands of the Church, and wrote a declaration of human rights, David joined the leftist Jacobin party and served very briefly as President of the National Convention in 1792 and as President of the Jacobin Club.

In 1793, David painted the death of the Jacobin leader, Jean-Paul Marat (**FIG. 29–37**). A radical journalist, Marat lived simply among the packing cases that he used as furniture, writing pamphlets urging the abolition of aristocratic privilege. Because he suffered from a painful skin ailment, he would often write while sitting in a medicinal bath. Charlotte Corday, a supporter of an opposition party, held Marat partly responsible for the 1792 riots in which hundreds of political prisoners judged sympathetic to the king were killed, and in retribution she stabbed Marat as he sat in his bath. David avoids the potential for sensationalism in the

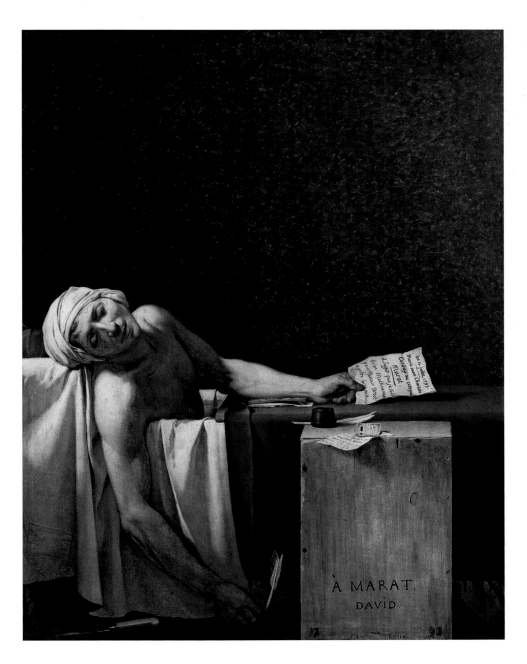

29-37 • Jacques-Louis David
DEATH OF MARAT
1793. Oil on canvas, 5′5″ × 4′2½″ (1.65 × 1.28 m). Musées Royaux des Beaux-Arts de Belgique, Brussels.

In 1793, David was elected a deputy to the National Convention and was named propaganda minister and director of public festivals. Because he supported Robespierre and the Reign of Terror, he was twice imprisoned after its demise in 1794, albeit under lenient conditions that allowed him to continue painting.

subject by portraying the tragic aftermath: the dead Marat slumped in his bathtub, his right hand still holding a quill pen, while his left hand grasps the letter that Corday used to gain access to his home. The simple wooden block beside the bath, which Marat used as a desk, is inscribed with Marat's name and the painter's dedication, and becomes his tombstone. David's painting is a tightly composed, powerfully stark image. The background is blank and undifferentiated, adding to the quiet mood of the piece in the way that the background of the *Oath of the Horatii* added to its drama. The color of Marat's pale body is echoed by the bloodstained sheets on which he lies; he is framed by the dark background and green blanket draped over the bath. David has transformed an ugly, brutal scene into one of somber eloquence. Marat's pose, which echoes Michelangelo's Sistine *Pietà* (SEE FIG. 20–9), implies that, like Christ, Marat was a martyr for the people.

The French Revolution eventually degenerated into mob rule in 1793–1794 as various political parties ruthlessly executed thousands of their opponents in what became known as the Reign of Terror. David, as a Jacobin, served a two-week term as president, during which time he signed several arrest warrants. When the Jacobins lost power in 1794, he was twice imprisoned, but he later emerged as a supporter of Napoleon and reestablished his career at the height of Napoleon's ascendancy to power.

GIRODET-TRIOSON. David was a charismatic and influential teacher who trained most of the major French painters of the 1790s and early 1800s. His teaching is evident, for example, in the **PORTRAIT OF JEAN-BAPTISTE BELLEY (FIG. 29–38)** by Anne–Louis Girodet-Trioson (1767–1824). The painting combines the restrained color and composition of early David with a relaxed new elegance. In addition, this portrait has a significant political aspect. The Senegal-born Belley (1747?–1805) was a former slave who was sent to Paris as a representative to the French Convention by the colony of Saint-Domingue (now Haiti). The Haitian Revolution of 1791, in which African slaves overturned the French colonial power, resulted in the first republic to be ruled by freed African slaves. In 1794, Belley led the successful legislative campaign to abolish slavery in the colonies and to grant full citizenship to people of African descent. In the portrait, Belley leans casually on the pedestal of a bust of the abbot Guillaume Raynal (1711–1796), the French philosopher whose 1770 book condemned slavery and paved the way for such legislation, making the portrait a tribute to both Belley and Raynal. Napoleon reestablished slavery in the Caribbean islands in 1801, but the revolt continued until 1804, when Haiti finally achieved full independence.

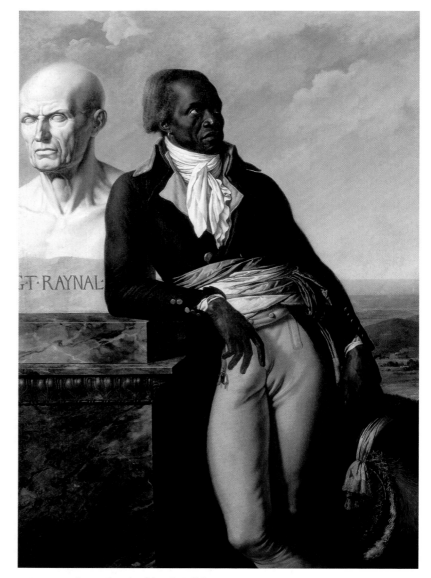

29-38 • Anne-Louis Girodet-Trioson **PORTRAIT OF JEAN-BAPTISTE BELLEY**
1797. Oil on canvas, 5'2½" × 3'8½" (1.59 × 1.13 m).
Musée National du Château de Versailles.

LABILLE-GUIARD. Also reflecting the revolutionary spirit of the age, the painter Adélaïde Labille-Guiard (1749–1803) championed the rights of women artists. Elected to the French Royal Academy of Painting and Sculpture in the same year as Vigée-Lebrun, Labille-Guiard asserted her worthiness for this honor in a **SELF-PORTRAIT WITH TWO PUPILS** that she submitted to the Salon of 1785 **(FIG. 29–39)**. The painting was a response to sexist rumors that her work, and that of Vigée-Lebrun, had actually been painted by men. In a witty role reversal, the only male in this monumental painting of the artist at her easel is her father, shown in a bust behind her canvas, as her muse, a role usually played by women. While the self-portrait flatters the painter, it also portrays Labille-Guiard as a force to be reckoned with, a woman who engages the gaze of the viewer uncompromisingly, and whose students are serious and intent on their study. In the year following the French Revolution, Labille-Guiard successfully petitioned the Royal Academy of Painting and Sculpture to end the restriction that limited its membership to four women. The reform was later reversed by the revolutionary government as it became more authoritarian.

HOUDON. The French Neoclassical sculptor Jean-Antoine Houdon (1741–1828), who studied in Italy between 1764 and 1768 after winning the Prix de Rome, imbued the Classical style with a new realism. His commitment to Neoclassicism began during his stay in Rome through his contact with the leading artists and theorists of the movement. He carved busts and full-length statues of a number of important figures of his era, including Diderot, Voltaire, Jean-Jacques Rousseau, Catherine the Great, Thomas Jefferson, Benjamin Franklin, Lafayette (a Revolutionary hero), and Napoleon. On the basis of his bust of Benjamin Franklin, Houdon was commissioned by the Virginia State Legislature to make a portrait of its native son **GEORGE WASHINGTON** to be installed in the Neoclassical Virginia state capitol building designed by Jefferson. In 1785, Houdon traveled to the United States to

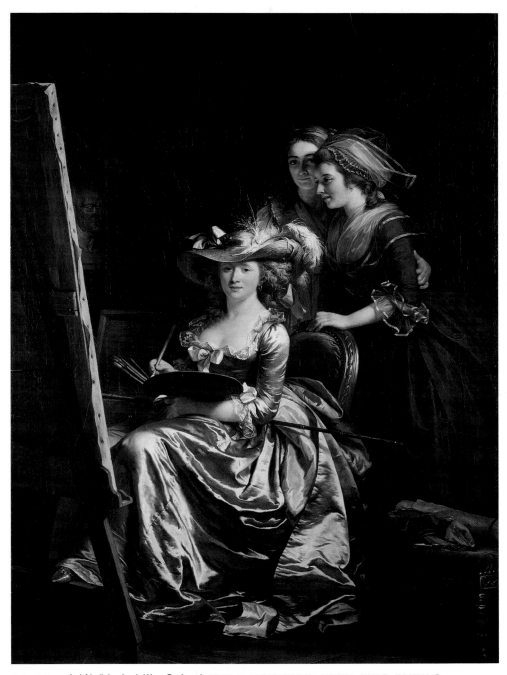

29–39 • Adélaïde Labille-Guiard **SELF-PORTRAIT WITH TWO PUPILS**
1785. Oil on canvas, 6'11" × 4'11½" (2.11 × 1.51 m). Metropolitan Museum of Art, New York.
Gift of Julia A. Berwind, 1953 (53.225.5)

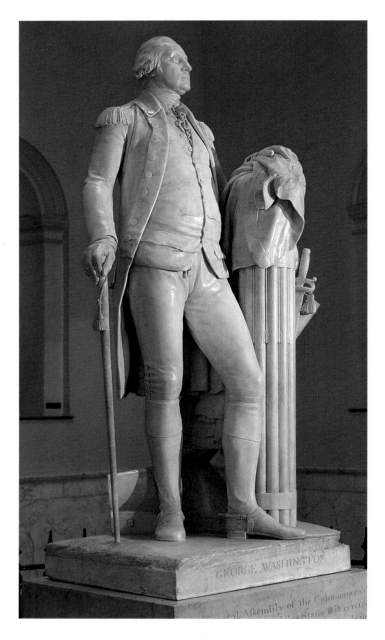

The plow blade behind Washington alludes to Cincinnatus, a
Roman soldier of the fifth century BCE who was appointed dictator and
dispatched to defeat the Aequi, who had besieged a Roman army.
After the victory, Cincinnatus resigned the dictatorship and returned to
his farm. Washington's contemporaries compared him with Cincinnatus
because, after leading the Americans to victory over the British, he
resigned his commission and went back to farming rather than seeking
political power. Just below Washington's waistcoat hangs the badge of
the Society of the Cincinnati, founded in 1783 by the officers of the
disbanding Continental Army who were returning to their peacetime
occupations. Washington lived in retirement at his Mount Vernon,
Virginia, plantation for five years before his 1789 election as the first
president of the United States.

ART IN SPAIN AND SPANISH AMERICA

In the first half of the eighteenth century, the Spanish art world was
marginalized by Philip V, who awarded most royal commissions
to foreign artists. Mengs's art for Charles III brought Neoclassicism
to Spain, but Neoclassicism was not embraced by Spanish artists
in the way that the Baroque had been in the previous century.
In the late eighteenth century, however, the Spanish court
appointed as court painter one of the greatest artists of the period,
Francisco Goya y Lucientes (1746–1828), whose work defies easy
categorization.

The Spanish commissioned art in their American colonies as
well. The art and architecture of these distant lands tended to
reflect both the continuing influence of the Spanish Baroque and
the artistic traditions of native peoples. Both the symbolism and
the artistic vocabulary of the two cultures were joined in the new
art of Mexico and the American Southwest.

PORTRAITURE AND PROTEST IN SPAIN: GOYA

Goya was introduced to the Spanish royal workshop in 1774, when
he produced tapestry cartoons under the direction of Mengs. He
painted for Charles III and served as court painter to Charles IV,
but he also belonged to an intellectual circle that embraced the
ideals of the French Revolution, and his work began to criticize
subtly the court in which he served.

King Charles IV, threatened by the possibility of similar social
upheaval in Spain, reinstituted the Inquisition soon after the
French Revolution, halted reform, and even prohibited the entry
of French books into Spain. Goya responded to this new situation
by creating a series of prints aimed at the ordinary people, with
whom he identified. *Los Caprichos* (*The Caprices*) is a folio of 80
etchings produced between 1796 and 1798. The overall theme of
the series is that reason ignored is a sleeping monster. In the print
entitled **THE SLEEP OF REASON PRODUCES MONSTERS (FIG.
29–41)**, the slumbering personification of Reason is haunted by a
menagerie of demonic-looking owls, bats, and a cat that are let
loose when Reason sleeps. Other *Caprichos* enumerate the follies

make a cast of Washington's features and a bust in plaster, returning
to Paris to execute the life-size marble figure **(FIG. 29–40)**. The
sculpture represents Washington in the Classical manner but with
contemporary clothes, much as Benjamin West had represented
General Wolfe (SEE FIG. 29–27). Houdon draws on the Classical
ideals of dignity, honor, and civic responsibility. Washington wears
the uniform of a general, the rank he held in the Revolutionary
War, but he also rests his left hand on a Roman *fasces*, a bundle of 13
rods (representing the 13 colonies) tied together with an axe face,
that served as a Roman symbol of authority. Attached to the *fasces*
are both a sword of war and a plowshare of peace. Significantly,
Houdon's Washington does not touch the sword.

Houdon's studio produced a steady supply of replicas of his
sculptures as part of a cult of great men promoted by Enlightenment
thinkers as models of virtue and patriotism.

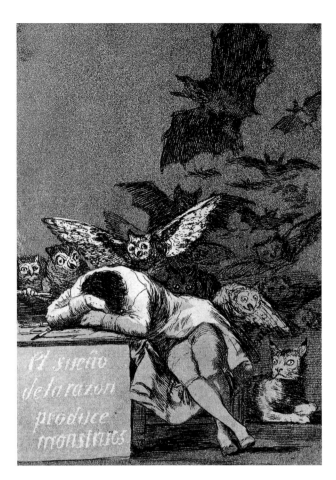

29–41 • Francisco Goya THE SLEEP OF REASON PRODUCES MONSTERS
No. 43 from *Los Caprichos* (*The Caprices*). 1796–1798; published 1799. Etching and aquatint, 8½ × 6″ (21.6 × 15.2 cm). Courtesy of the Hispanic Society of America, New York.

After printing about 300 sets of this series, Goya offered them for sale in 1799. He withdrew them two days later without explanation. Historians believe that he was probably warned by the Church that if he did not do so he might have to appear before the Inquisition because of the unflattering portrayal of the Church in some of the etchings. In 1803, Goya donated the plates to the Royal Printing Office.

of Spanish society that Goya and his circle considered equally monstrous. His implicit goal with this series was to incite action: He tried to market his etchings as Hogarth had done in England, but his work aroused controversy and was brought to the attention of his royal patrons. To deflect additional controversy, Goya presented the metal plates of the series to the king, suggesting that the images were not intentionally critical of the monarchy. He was torn between his position as a court painter who owed allegiance to the king and his passionate desire for a more open Spain.

His large portrait of the **FAMILY OF CHARLES IV** (FIG. 29–42) reveals some of Goya's ambivalence. He clearly wanted his patron to connect the portrait to an earlier Spanish royal portrait, *Las Meninas* by Velázquez (SEE FIG. 22–23), thereby raising his own status as well as that of the king. Like Velázquez, Goya includes

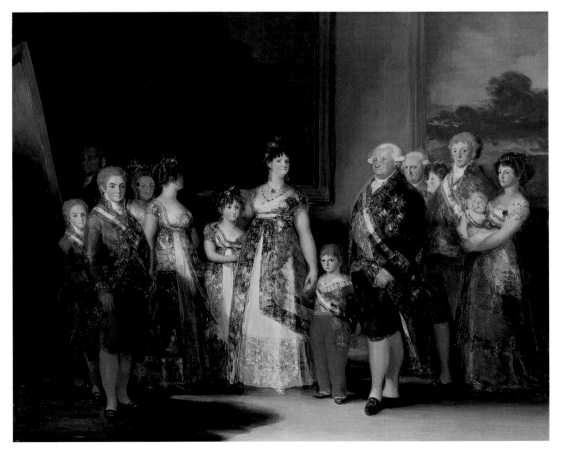

29–42 • Francisco Goya FAMILY OF CHARLES IV
1800. Oil on canvas, 9′12″ × 11′ (2.79 × 3.36 m). Museo del Prado, Madrid.

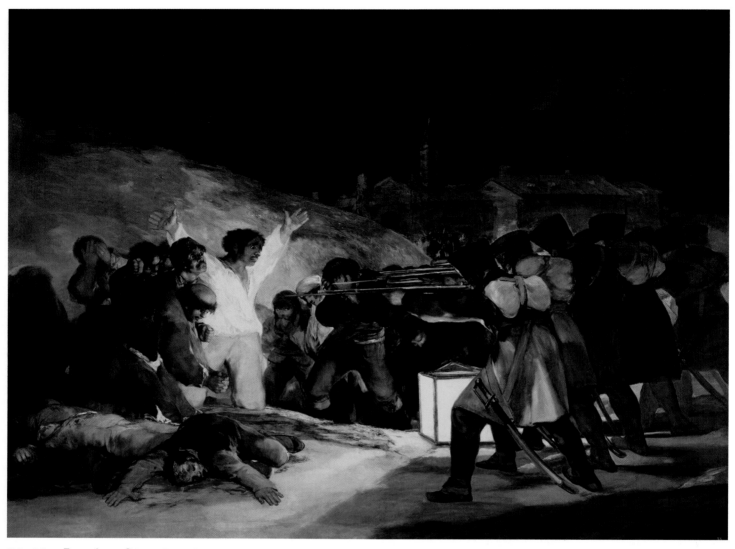

29-43 • Francisco Goya **THIRD OF MAY, 1808**
1814–1815. Oil on canvas, 8'9" × 13'4" (2.67 × 4.06 m). Museo del Prado, Madrid.

himself in the painting, to the left behind the easel. The king and queen appear at the center of this large family portrait, surrounded by their immediate family. The figures are formal and stiff. Much has been written about how Goya seems to show his patrons as faintly ridiculous here: Some of the subjects seem bored; the some-what dazed king, chest full of medals, stands before a relative who looks distractedly out of the painting (perhaps the face was added at the last minute); the double-chinned queen gazes obliquely out of the canvas (at that time she was having an open affair with the prime minister); their eldest daughter, to the left, stares into space; and another, older relative behind seems almost surprised to be there. One French art critic even described the painting as resembling "The corner baker and his family after they have won the lottery." Yet the royal family was apparently satisfied with Goya's depiction. At a time when the authority of the Spanish aristocracy was crumbling, this complex representation of conflicted emotions, aspirations, and responsibilities may have struck a chord with them.

In 1808, Napoleon conquered Spain and placed his brother, Joseph Bonaparte (1768–1844), on the Spanish throne. At first many Spanish citizens, Goya included, welcomed the French, who brought political reform, including a new, more liberal constitution. But on May 2, 1808, a rumor spread through Madrid that the French planned to kill the royal family. The people rose up against the French and a day of bloody street fighting ensued, followed by mass arrests. Hundreds were herded into a convent and then executed by a French firing squad before dawn on May 3. Goya's impassioned memorial to that slaughter **(FIG. 29–43)** portrays the victims as defenseless and frightened. The French are shown as a row of faceless executioners, the pose of the victim in white seems almost Christlike. This painting is not a cool, didactic representation of civic sacrifice like David's *Oath of the Horatii* (SEE FIG. 29–36), it is an image of blind terror and desperate fear. There is no moral here, only hopeless rage. Everything about this work is Romantic: the sensational current event, the loose brushwork, the poses based on reality, the off-balance composition, and the dramatic lighting. When asked why he painted such a brutal scene, Goya responded: "To warn men never to do it again." Thus, his painting moves from the relative restraint of the court to impassioned Romanticism.

Soon after, the Spanish monarchy was restored. Ferdinand VII (r. 1808; 1814–1833) once again reinstated the Inquisition and abolished the new constitution. In 1815, Goya was called before the Inquisition and charged with obscenity for an earlier painting of a female nude. He was acquitted and retired to his home outside Madrid, where he vented his anger at the world in a series of nightmarish "black paintings" rendered directly on the walls, and then spent the last four years of his life in France.

THE ART OF THE AMERICAS UNDER SPAIN

In the wake of the Spanish conquest of Central and South America, indigenous religions and their practice were suppressed. Temples were torn down and replaced with Roman Catholic churches, and Franciscan, Dominican, and Augustinian friars worked to convert the indigenous populations. Some missionaries were so appalled by the conquerors' brutal treatment of the native peoples that they petitioned the Spanish king to help improve conditions.

In the course of the Mesoamericans' forced conversion to Roman Catholicism, Christian symbolism became inextricably mixed with the symbolism of their own long-held religious beliefs. An example of this admixture can be seen in early colonial **atrial crosses**, carved by indigenous sculptors. Missionaries placed these crosses in church atriums, where converts gathered for education in Christianity. The sixteenth-century **ATRIAL CROSS** now in the Basilica of Guadalupe near Mexico City **(FIG. 29–44)** is richly carved in low relief, reflecting native sculptural traditions. The images show a complex interweaving of Christian and native religions. The Christian symbols were probably taken from the illustrated books and Bibles of the missionaries, and represent the Arms of Christ, or the "weapons" that Christ used to defeat the devil: the holy face, placed where his head would appear on a crucifix; the crown of thorns, draped around the cross bar; and the holy shroud, wrapped around the cross's arms. (The image of the holy face is believed to have been miraculously impressed on a cloth used by Veronica to wipe the face of the suffering Christ before his death.) Winged angel heads and pomegranates surround the inscription at the top as symbols of regeneration. While the cross represents Christ's redemption of humanity in Christianity, it is also symbolic of the tree of life in Mesoamerican religions. The blood that sprays out where the nails pierce the hands of Christ are a reference to his sacrifice; the representation of sacrificial blood may also refer to native religions.

Images of the Virgin Mary also took on a Mesoamerican inflection after she was believed to have appeared in Mexico. In one such case, in 1531, a Mexican named Juan Diego claimed that the Virgin Mary visited him and told him to build a church on a hill

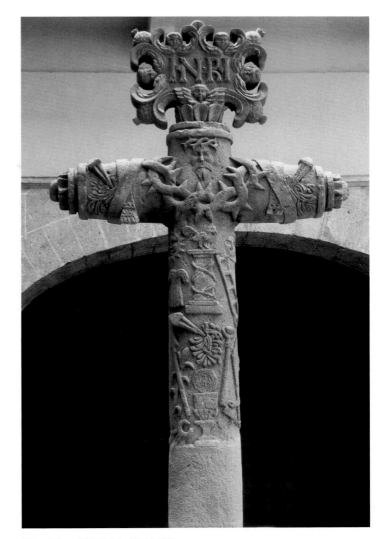

29-44 • ATRIAL CROSS
Before 1556. Stone, height 11′3″ (3.45 m). Chapel of the Indians, Basilica of Guadalupe, Mexico City.

where an Aztec goddess had once been worshiped. She also apparently caused flowers to bloom so that Juan Diego could show them to the archbishop as proof of his vision. When Juan Diego opened his bundle of flowers, the cloak he had used to wrap them is said to have borne the image of a Mexican Mary. A European version of this image, known as the Virgin of the Immaculate Conception, also became popular in Spain. The site of the vision was renamed Guadalupe after Our Lady of Guadalupe in Spain, and it became a venerated pilgrimage center. In 1754, the pope declared the Virgin of Guadalupe, as depicted here in a 1779 work by Sebastian Salcedo, the patron saint of the Americas **(FIG. 29–45)**.

Spanish colonial builders tried to replicate the architecture of their native country in the Americas. One of the finest examples of Spanish-influenced architecture is the **MISSION SAN XAVIER DEL BAC**, in the American Southwest near Tucson, Arizona **(FIG. 29–46)**. In 1700, the Jesuit priest Eusebio Kino (1644–1711) began laying the foundations for San Xavier del Bac using stone quarried

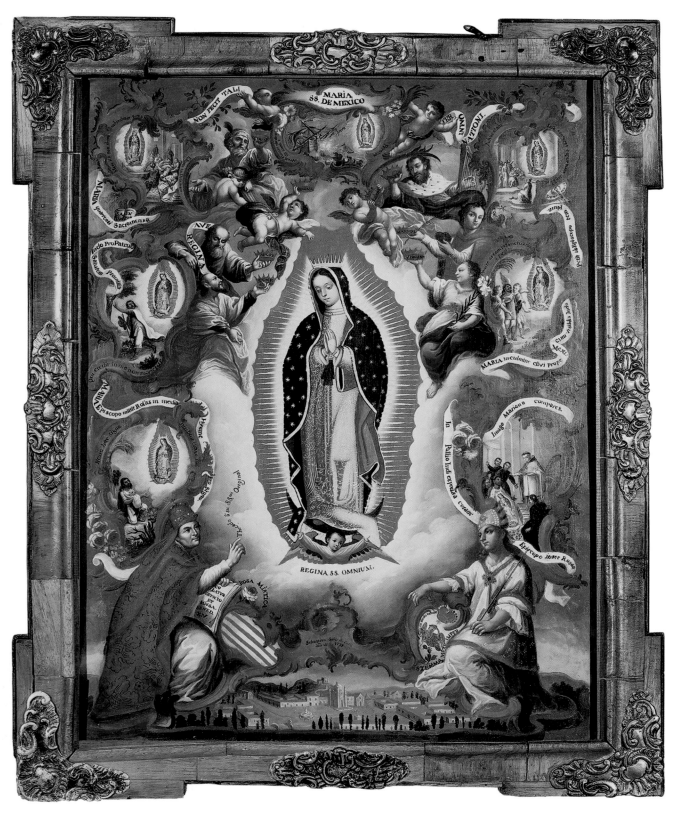

29–45 • Sebastian Salcedo VIRGIN OF GUADALUPE
1779. Oil on panel and copper, 25 × 19″ (63.5 × 48.3 cm). Denver Art Museum.

At the bottom right is the female personification of New Spain (Mexico) and at the left is Pope Benedict XIV (pontificate 1740–1758), who in 1754 declared the Virgin of Guadalupe to be the patroness of the Americas. Between the figures, the sanctuary of Guadalupe in Mexico can be seen in the distance. The four small scenes circling the Virgin represent the story of Juan Diego, and at the top three scenes depict Mary's miracles. The six figures above the Virgin represent Hebrew Bible prophets and patriarchs and New Testament apostles and saints.

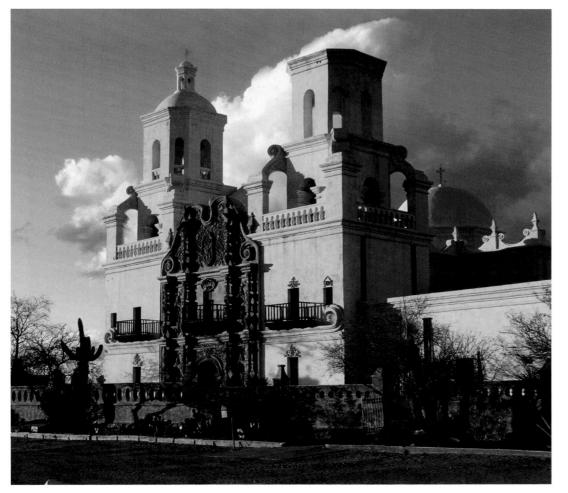

locally by people of the Pima nation. The Pima had already laid out the desert site with irrigation ditches, so, as Father Kino wrote in his reports, there would be running water in every room and workshop of the new mission. In 1768, before construction began, the site was turned over to the Franciscans as part of a larger change in Spanish policy toward the Jesuits. Father Kino's vision was eventually realized by the Spanish Franciscan Juan Bautista Velderrain, who arrived at the mission site in 1776.

This huge church, 99 feet long with a domed crossing and flanking bell towers, is unusual for the area because it was built of bricks and mortar rather than adobe, which is made from earth and straw. The basic structure was finished by the time of Velderrain's death in 1790, and the exterior decoration was completed by his successor in 1797. The façade of San Xavier is not a copy of Spanish architecture, although the focus of visual attention on the central entrance to the church and its Spanish Baroque decoration is clearly in the tradition of Pedro de Ribera in Madrid. Since the mission was dedicated to Francis Xavier, his statue once stood at the top of the portal decoration, and there are still four female saints, tentatively identified as Lucy, Cecilia, Barbara, and Catherine of Siena, in the niches. Hidden in the sculpted mass is one humorous element: a cat confronting a mouse, which inspired a local Pima saying: "When the cat catches the mouse, the end of the world will come" (cited in Chinn and McCarty, p. 12).

EARLY NINETEENTH-CENTURY ART: NEOCLASSICISM AND ROMANTICISM

Neoclassicism and Romanticism existed side by side well into the nineteenth century in European and American art. Neoclassicism survived in both architecture and sculpture beyond the middle of the century, as patrons and artists continued to use it to promote the virtues of democracy and republicanism. The longevity of Neoclassicism was also due in part to its embrace by art academies, where training rested on a study of antique sculpture and of the work of past artists, such as Raphael. The Neoclassical vision of art as embodying universal standards of taste and beauty complemented the academy's idea of itself as a repository of tradition in fast-changing times.

Romanticism, whose roots in eighteenth-century Britain have been discussed (pages 927–930), took a variety of forms in the early nineteenth century. The common thread connecting these continued to be an emphasis on emotional expressiveness and the unique experiences and tastes of the individual. Romantic paintings often explored dramatic subject matter taken from literature, current events, the natural world, or the artist's own imagination, with the goal of stimulating the viewer's sentiments and feelings. Romantic architecture experimented with the idea of matching a building's style to the personal needs, desires, and even fantasies of the patron.

NEOCLASSICISM AND ROMANTICISM IN FRANCE

Paris increasingly established itself as a major artistic center in the nineteenth century. The École des Beaux-Arts attracted students from all over Europe and the Americas, as did the **ateliers** (studios) of Parisian academic artists who offered private instruction. Artists competed fiercely for a spot in the Paris Salon, the annual exhibition that gradually opened to those who were not Academy members. Between 1800 and 1830, the academy system was the arbiter of artistic success in Paris. At the beginning of the nineteenth century there was a deep division between the *poussinistes* and *rubénistes* (see "Grading the Old Masters," page 764). The *poussinistes* argued that line, in the style of Poussin (SEE FIG. 22–54), created fundamental structure in a painting and should drive the work; the *rubénistes* argued that essential structure could be achieved more eloquently through a sophisticated use of rich, warm color, as demonstrated by Rubens (SEE FIG. 22–26). Similarly, the relative value of the *esquisse*, a preliminary sketch for a much larger work, was debated. Some argued that it was simply a tool for the larger, finished work, while others increasingly argued that the fast, impulsive expression of imagination captured in the *esquisse* made the finished painting seem dull and flat by comparison. This emphasis on expressiveness is seen in the blossoming of Romanticism in the period from 1815 to 1830.

THE GRAND MANNER PAINTINGS OF DAVID AND GROS. With the rise of Napoleon Bonaparte, Jacques-Louis David reestablished his dominant position in French painting. David saw in Napoleon the best hope for realizing France's Enlightenment-oriented political goals, and Napoleon saw in David a tested propagandist for revolutionary values. As Napoleon gained power and extended his rule across Europe, reforming law codes and abolishing aristocratic privilege, he commissioned David and his students to document his deeds.

David's glorification of Napoleon is already evident in his 1800 painting **NAPOLEON CROSSING THE SAINT-BERNARD** (or *Bonaparte Crossing the Alps*) (FIG. 29–47). Napoleon is represented in the Grand Manner, with David using artistic license to imagine how Napoleon might have appeared as he led his troops over the Alps into Italy. He is shown exhorting

his troops to follow as he charges uphill on his rearing horse. His horse's flying mane and wild eyes, and his own swirling cape convey energy, impulse, and power. He charges past the heavy guns and troops in the background. When Napoleon fell from power in 1814, David went into exile in Brussels, where he died in 1825.

Antoine-Jean Gros (1771–1835) began working in David's studio as a teenager and eventually vied with his master for commissions from Napoleon. Gros traveled with Napoleon in Italy in 1797 and later became an official chronicler of his military campaigns. His painting **NAPOLEON IN THE PLAGUE HOUSE AT JAFFA (FIG. 29–48)** is also a representation of an actual event in the Grand Manner. During Napoleon's campaign against the Ottoman Turks in 1799, bubonic plague broke out among his troops. Napoleon decided to try to quiet the fears of the still-healthy soldiers by visiting the sick and dying, who were housed in a

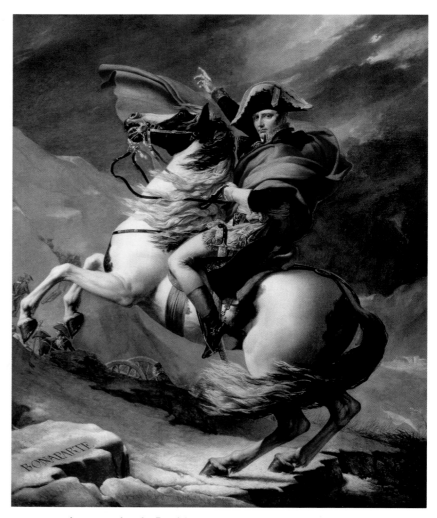

29–47 • Jacques-Louis David NAPOLEON CROSSING THE SAINT-BERNARD
1800–1801. Oil on canvas, 8'11″ × 7'7″ (2.7 × 2.3 m). Musée National du Château de la Malmaison, Rueil-Malmaison.

David flattered Napoleon by reminding the viewer of two other great generals from history who had led armies across the Alps—Charlemagne and Hannibal—by inscribing the names of all three in the rock in the lower left.

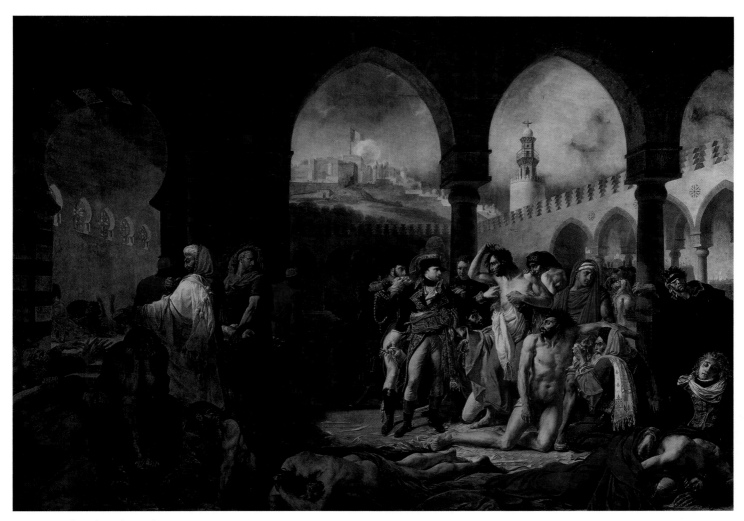

29–48 • Antoine-Jean Gros NAPOLEON IN THE PLAGUE HOUSE AT JAFFA
1804. Oil on canvas, 17′5″ × 23′7″ (5.32 × 7.2 m). Musée du Louvre, Paris.

converted mosque in the town of Jaffa (then part of the Ottoman Empire, and now in Israel). The format of Gros's painting—a shallow stage and a series of arcades behind the main protagonists—seems to have been inspired by David's *Oath of the Horatii*. But Gros's painting is quite different from David's: His color is more vibrant and his brushwork more spontaneous. The overall effect is Romantic, not simply because of the dramatic lighting and the wealth of details, both exotic and horrific, but also because the main action is meant to incite veneration of Napoleon the man more than republican virtue. At the center of the painting, surrounded by a small group of soldiers and a doctor, Napoleon reaches toward the sores of one of the victims in a pose that was meant to evoke Christ healing the sick with his touch. The huddled figures to the left remind us of the mouth of hell in Michelangelo's *Last Judgment* (SEE FIG. 20–34). At that time there was a rumor that shortly after Napoleon's visit to Jaffa, he ordered the remaining sick to be poisoned. Gros may have been aware of this rumor when he painted Napoleon as small and tentative compared to the Arab doctors and even the sick.

GÉRICAULT. Théodore Géricault (1791–1824) was a major early Romantic painter in Paris, although his career was cut short by his untimely death at age 32. After a brief stay in Rome in 1816–1817, where he discovered the art of Michelangelo, Géricault returned to Paris determined to paint a great modern history painting. He chose for his subject the scandalous and sensational shipwreck of the *Medusa* (see "*The Raft of the 'Medusa,'*" pages 946–947). In 1816, the *Medusa*, a ship carrying around 400 French colonists bound for Senegal, ran aground close to its destination. Its captain, an incompetent aristocrat commissioned by the newly restored monarchy of Louis XVIII, reserved all six lifeboats for himself, his officers, and several government representatives. The remaining 152 people were set adrift on a makeshift raft. When those on the raft were rescued 13 days later, only 15 had survived, some by living on human flesh. Since the captain had been a political appointee, the press used the horrific story to indict the monarchy for this and other atrocities in French-ruled Senegal. The moment in the story that Géricault chose to depict is one fraught with emotion, as the survivors on the raft experience both the fear that

The Raft of the "Medusa"

Théodore Géricault's monumental *The Raft of the "Medusa"* (FIG. A) fits the definition of a history painting in that it is a large (16 by 23 feet), multi-figured composition that represents an event in history. It may not qualify, however, on the basis of its function— to expose incompetence and a willful disregard for human life rather than to ennoble, educate, or remind viewers of their civic responsibility. The hero of this painting is also an unusual choice for a history painting; he is not an emperor or a king, or even an intellectual, but Jean Charles, a black man from French Senegal who showed endurance and emotional fortitude in the face of extreme peril.

The painting speaks powerfully through a composition that is arranged in a pyramid of bodies. The diagonal that begins in the lower left extends upwards to the waving figure of Jean Charles; the diagonal beginning with the dead man in the lower right extends through the mast and billowing sail, directs our attention to a huge wave. The painting captures the moment between hope of rescue and despair that the distant ship has not seen the survivors. The figures are emotionally suspended between hope of salvation and fear of imminent death. Significantly, the "hopeful" diagonal in Géricault's painting terminates in the vigorous figure of Jean Charles. By placing him at the top of the pyramid of survivors and giving him the power to save his comrades by signaling to the rescue ship, Géricault suggests metaphorically that freedom is often dependent on the most oppressed members of society.

Géricault prepared his painting carefully, using each of the prescribed steps for history painting in the French academic system. The work was the culmination of extensive study and experimentation. An early pen drawing (*The Sighting of the "Argus,"* FIG. B) depicts the survivors' hopeful response to the appearance of the rescue ship on the horizon at the extreme left. Their excitement is in contrast to the mournful scene of a man grieving over a dead youth on the right side of the raft. The drawing is quick, spontaneous and bursting with energy, like the *esquisse*. A later pen-and-wash drawing (FIG. C) reverses the composition, creates greater unity among the figures, and establishes the modeling of their bodies through light and shade. This is primarily a study of light and shade. Other

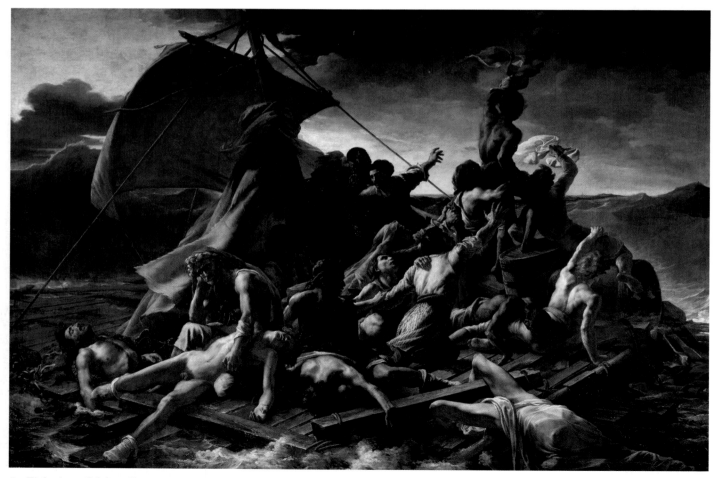

A. Théodore Géricault **THE RAFT OF THE "MEDUSA"**
1818–1819. Oil on canvas, 16'1" × 23'6" (4.9 × 7.16 m). Musée du Louvre, Paris.

studies would have focused on further analyses of the composition, arrangement of figures, and overall color scheme. The drawings look ahead to the final composition of the *The Raft of the "Medusa,"* but both still lack the figure of Jean Charles at the apex of the painting and the dead and dying figures at the extreme left and lower right, which fill out the composition's base.

Géricault also made separate studies of many of the figures, as well as of actual corpses, severed heads, and dissected limbs (FIG. D) supplied to him by friends who worked at a nearby hospital. For several months, according to Géricault's biographer, "his studio was a kind of morgue. He kept cadavers there until they were half-decomposed, and insisted on working in this charnel-house atmosphere…" However, he did not use cadavers for any specific figures in *The Raft of the "Medusa."* Rather, he traced the outline of his final composition onto its large canvas, and then painted each body directly from a living model, gradually building up his composition figure by figure. He drew from corpses and body parts in his studio to make sure that he understood the nature of death and its impact on the human form.

Indeed, Géricault did not describe the actual physical condition of the survivors on the raft: exhausted, emaciated, sunburned, and close to death. Instead, following the dictates of the Grand Manner, he gave his men athletic bodies and vigorous poses, evoking the work of Michelangelo and Rubens (Chapters 20 and 22). He did this to generalize and ennoble his subject, elevating it above the particulars of a specific shipwreck in the hope that it would speak to more fundamental human conflicts: humanity against nature, hope against despair, and life against death.

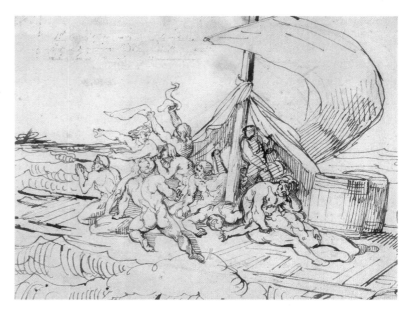

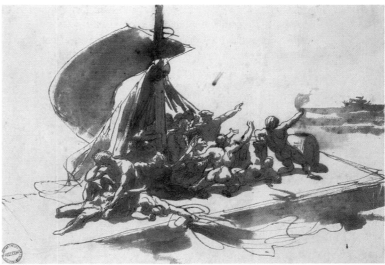

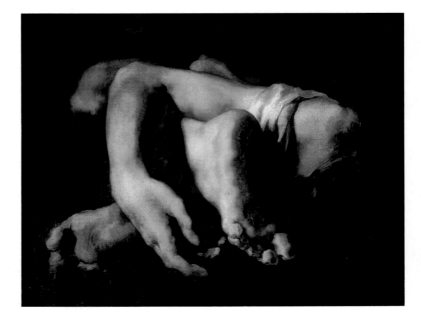

B. Théodore Géricault **THE SIGHTING OF THE "ARGUS"** (top)
1818. Pen and ink on paper, 13¾ × 16⅛″ (34.9 × 41 cm). Musée des Beaux-Arts, Lille.

C. Théodore Géricault **THE SIGHTING OF THE "ARGUS"** (middle)
1818. Pen and ink, sepia wash on paper, 8⅛ × 11¼″ (20.6 × 28.6 cm). Musée des Beaux-Arts, Rouen.

D. Théodore Géricault **STUDY OF HANDS AND FEET** (bottom)
1818–1819. Oil on canvas, 20½ × 25³⁄₁₈″ (52 × 64 cm). Musée Fabre, Montpellier.

the distant ship might pass them by and the hope that they will be rescued.

Géricault exhibited *The Raft of the "Medusa"* at the 1819 Salon, where it caused a great deal of controversy. Most contemporary French critics and royalists interpreted the painting as a political jibe at the king, on whose good grace many academicians depended, while independent liberals praised Géricault's attempt to expose corruption. This debate raises the larger question of the point at which a painting crosses the line between art and political advocacy. If David's and Gros's paintings of Napoleon still fall under the definition of contemporary history painting for supporting the state, does Géricault's painting fall outside it because it criticizes the state or because the intention of the painting was to shock and horrify rather than to edify and ennoble? Admittedly, Géricault's painting is sensationalist and topical, but it also conforms to academy rules in every other way (see *"The Raft of the 'Medusa,'"*

pages 946–947). The crown refused to buy the canvas, so Géricault exhibited it commercially on a two-year tour of Ireland and England; the London exhibition alone attracted more than 50,000 paying visitors.

DELACROIX. The French novelist Stendhal characterized the Romantic spirit when he wrote, "Romanticism in all the arts is what represents the men of today and not the men of those remote, heroic times which probably never existed anyway." Eugène Delacroix (1798–1863), the most important Romantic painter in Paris after Géricault's early death, depicted contemporary heroes and victims engaged in the violent struggles of the times. In 1830, he created his masterpiece, **LIBERTY LEADING THE PEOPLE: JULY 28, 1830 (FIG. 29–49)**, a painting that encapsulated the history of France after the fall of Napoleon. When Napoleon was defeated in 1815, the victorious neighboring nations reimposed a monarchy

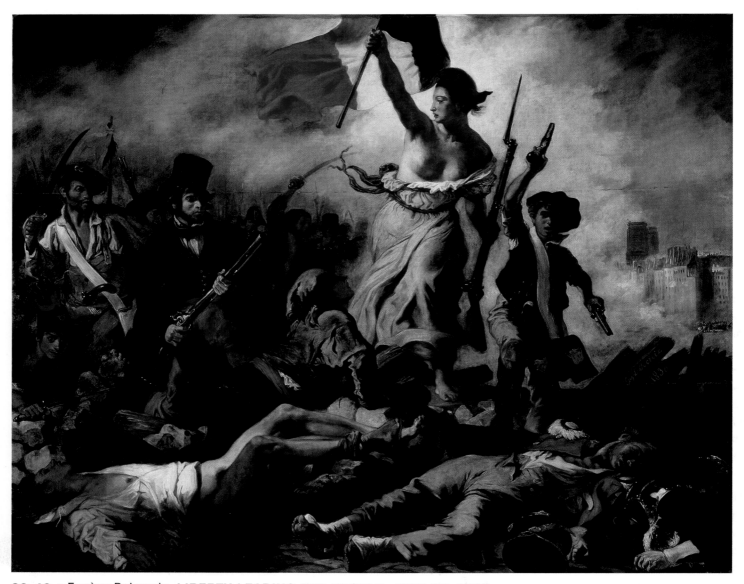

29-49 • Eugène Delacroix LIBERTY LEADING THE PEOPLE: JULY 28, 1830
1830. Oil on canvas, 8′6½″ × 10′8″ (260 × 325 cm). Musée du Louvre, Paris.

on France under Louis XVIII, brother of the last pre-revolutionary monarch. The king's power was limited by a constitution and a parliament, but the government became more conservative as years passed, undoing many revolutionary reforms. Louis's successor, Charles X, reinstated press censorship, returned education to the control of the Catholic Church, and limited voting rights. These actions triggered a large-scale uprising in the streets of Paris. Over the course of three days in July 1830, the Bourbon monarchical line was overthrown and Charles X was replaced by a more moderate king from the Orleanist line, who promised to abide by a new constitution. This period in French history is known as the "July Monarchy."

Delacroix memorialized the July 1830 revolution just a few months after it took place. His large modern history painting reports significant events, but it also departs from facts in ways appropriate to the intended message. His revolutionaries are a motley crew of students, craftworkers, day laborers, and even children and top-hatted intellectuals. They stumble forward through the smoke of battle, crossing a barricade of refuse and dead bodies. The towers of Notre-Dame are visible through the smoke and haze of the background. This much of the work is plausibly accurate. Their leader, however, is an energetic, allegorical figure of Liberty, personified by a gigantic, muscular, half-naked woman charging across the barricade with the revolutionary flag in one hand and a bayoneted rifle in the other. Delacroix has literally placed a Classical allegorical figure in the thick of battle, replete with a contemporary weapon and Phrygian cap (the ancient symbol for a freed slave and the cap used by the insurgents). He presents the event as an emotionally charged moment, full of passion, turmoil and danger. He chooses to show the moment just before the ultimate sacrifice, as the revolutionaries charge the barricades to near-certain death, making this a dramatic example of Romanticism.

29-50 • François Rude DEPARTURE OF THE VOLUNTEERS OF 1792 (THE MARSEILLAISE)
1833–1836. Limestone, height approx. 42′ (12.8 m). Arc de Triomphe, Place de l'Étoile, Paris.

RUDE. Artists working for the July Monarchy increasingly used the more dramatic subjects and styles of Romanticism to represent the 1830 revolution, just as Neoclassical principles had been used to represent the previous revolution. Early in the July Monarchy, the minister of the interior decided, as an act of national reconciliation, to complete the triumphal arch on the Champs-Élysées in Paris begun by Napoleon in 1806. François Rude (1784–1855) received the commission for a sculpture to decorate the main arcade with a scene that commemorated the volunteer army that had halted a Prussian invasion in 1792–1793. Beneath the urgent exhortations of the winged figure of Liberty, the volunteers surge forward, some nude, some in Classical armor **(FIG. 29–50)**. Despite these Classical details, the overall impact of this sculpture is Romantic. The crowded, excited group stirred patriotism in Paris, and the

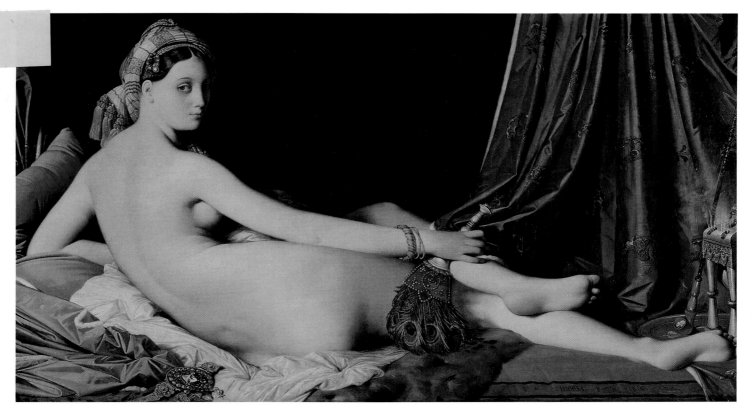

29-51 • Jean-Auguste-Dominique Ingres LARGE ODALISQUE
1814. Oil on canvas, approx. 35 × 64″ (88.9 × 162.5 m). Musée du Louvre, Paris.

During Napoleon's campaigns against the British in North Africa, the French discovered the exotic Near East. Upper-middle-class European men were particularly attracted to the institution of the harem, partly as a reaction against the egalitarian demands of women of their own class that had been unleashed by the French Revolution.

sculpture quickly became known simply as **THE MARSEILLAISE**, the name of the French national anthem written in 1792, the same year as the action depicted.

INGRES.   Jean-Auguste-Dominique Ingres (1780–1867) served as director of the French Academy in Rome between 1835 and 1841. As a teacher and theorist, Ingres became one of the most influential artists of his time. His paintings offer another variant on the Romantic and Neoclassical, combining the precise drawing, formal idealization, Classical composition, and graceful lyricism of Raphael (SEE FIG. 20–6) with an interest in creating sensual and erotically charged images.

Although Ingres fervently desired to be accepted as a history painter, it was his paintings of female nudes and his portraits of women that made him famous. He painted numerous versions of the **odalisque**, an exoticized version of a female slave or concubine in a sultan's harem. In his **LARGE ODALISQUE (FIG. 29–51)**, the cool gaze of the odalisque is leveled at her master, while she twists her naked body in a sinuous, snakelike reclining pose, revealing a calculated eroticism. The cool blues of the divan and the curtain at the right heighten the effect of her cool, white skin and blue eyes; she is Ingres's and his patrons' fantasy of a "white" slave. The exotic details of her headdress, fan, and the

jeweled object in the foreground add to her languid sensuality. Ingres's commitment to academic line and formal structure was grounded in his Neoclassical training, but his fluid, attenuated female nudes are much more in the Romantic tradition.

Although Ingres complained that making portraits was a "considerable waste of time," his skill in rendering a physical likeness in a scintillating way and in mimicking the material qualities of clothing, hairstyles, and jewelry in paint was unparalleled. He painted many life-size and highly polished portraits, but he also produced—usually in just a day—exquisite, small portrait drawings that are extraordinarily fresh and lively. The charming **PORTRAIT OF MADAME DÉSIRÉ RAOUL-ROCHETTE (FIG. 29–52)** is a flattering yet credible interpretation of the relaxed and elegant sitter. With her gloved right hand, Madame Raoul-Rochette has removed her left-hand glove, drawing attention to her social status (traditionally, fine kid gloves were worn by members of the European upper class, who did not work with their hands) and her marital status (a wedding band is on her left hand). Her shiny taffeta dress, with its fashionably high waist and puffed sleeves, is rendered with deft yet light strokes that suggest rather than describe the fabric. Greater emphasis is given to her refined face and elaborate coiffure, which Ingres has drawn precisely and modeled with subtle handling of light and shade.

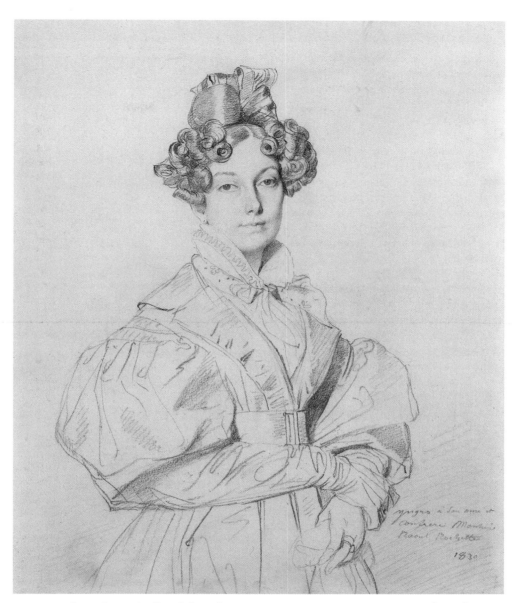

29–52 • Jean-Auguste-Dominique Ingres **PORTRAIT OF MADAME DÉSIRÉ RAOUL-ROCHETTE**

1830. Graphite on paper, 12⅝ × 9½″ (32.2 × 24.1 cm). Cleveland Museum of Art, Ohio.
Purchase from the J. H. Wade Fund (1927.437)

Madame Raoul-Rochette (1790–1878), née Antoinette-Claude Houdon, was the youngest daughter of the famous Neoclassical sculptor Jean-Antoine Houdon (SEE FIG. 29–40). In 1810, at age 20, she married Désiré Raoul-Rochette, a noted archaeologist, who later became the secretary of the Académie des Beaux-Arts (Academy of Fine Arts, founded in 1816 to replace the French Royal Academy of Painting and Sculpture) and a close friend of Ingres. Ingres's drawing of Madame Raoul-Rochette is inscribed to her husband, whose portrait Ingres also drew around the same time.

EXPLORE MORE: Gain insight from a primary source about Jean-Auguste-Dominique Ingres **www.myartslab.com**

DAUMIER. Honoré Daumier (1808–1879) came to Paris from Marseille in 1816. He studied drawing at the Académie Suisse, but he learned the technique of **lithography** (see page 952) as assistant to the lithographer Bélaird. He published his first lithograph in 1829, at age 21, in the weekly satirical magazine *La Silhouette*. In the wake of the 1830 revolution in Paris, Daumier began supplying pictures to *La Caricature*, an anti-monarchist, pro-republican magazine, and the equally partisan *Le Charivari*, the first daily newspaper illustrated with lithographs. In 1834, Daumier made a lithographic print of the atrocities on **RUE TRANSNONAIN (FIG. 29–53)**. A government guard was shot and killed on this street during a demonstration by workers, and in response the guards

Lithography, invented in the mid 1790s, is based on the natural antagonism between oil and water. The artist draws on a flat surface—traditionally, fine-grained stone (*lithos* is Greek for stone)—with a greasy, crayonlike instrument. The stone's surface is first wiped with water and then with an oil-based ink. The ink adheres to the greasy areas but not to the damp ones. After a series of such steps, a sheet of paper is laid face down on the inked stone, pressed together with a scraper, and then rolled through a flatbed press. This transfers ink from stone to paper, thus making lithography (like relief and intaglio) a direct method of creating a printed image. Unlike earlier processes, however, grease-based lithography enables the artist to capture the subtleties of drawing with crayon and a liquid mixture called *tusche*. Francisco Goya, Théodore Géricault, Eugène Delacroix, Honoré Daumier, and Henri de Toulouse-Lautrec used the medium to great effect.

Daumier is probably the greatest exponent of lithography in the nineteenth century. The technique was widely used in France for fine-art prints and to illustrate popular magazines and even newspapers. By the 1830s, the print trade in France had exploded. Artists could use lithography to produce their own prints without the cumbersome, expensive, and time-consuming intermediary of the engraver. Daumier's lithograph of *The Print Lovers* shows three men who have fixed their attention on the folio of prints in front of them, despite being surrounded by works of art packed tightly on the wall behind them. By the end of the nineteenth century, inexpensive prints were in every house and owned by people at every level of society.

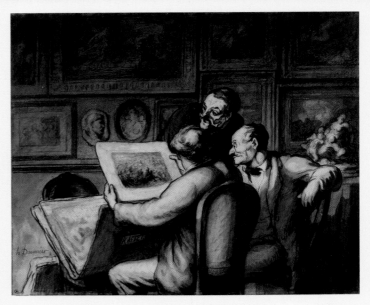

Honoré Daumier THE PRINT LOVERS
Watercolor, black pencil, black ink, gray wash, 10⅛ × 12⅛"
(25.8 × 30.7 cm). Musée du Louvre, Paris.

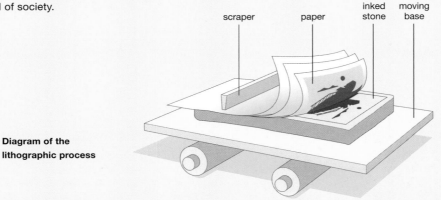

scraper   paper   inked   moving
                       stone   base

**Diagram of the
lithographic process**

SEE MORE: View a video about the process of lithography **www.myartslab.com**

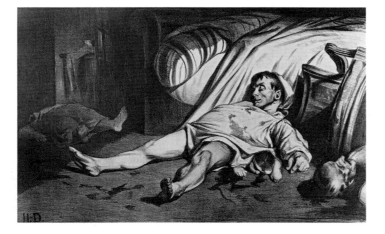

killed everyone in the building where they believed the marksman was hiding. The moment shown by Daumier is the bloody aftermath of the event, a family disturbed from their sleep and then murdered. The wife lies in the shadows to the left, her husband in the center of the room, and an elderly man to the right. It takes a few minutes for the viewer to realize that under the central figure's back there are also the bloody head and arms of a murdered child. Daumier was known for his biting caricatures and social commentary in print form, but this image is one of his most powerful.

**29-53 • Honoré Daumier RUE TRANSNONAIN,
LE 15 AVRIL 1834**
Lithograph, 11 × 17⅜" (28 × 44 cm). Bibliothèque Nationale, Paris.

ROMANTIC LANDSCAPE PAINTING

The Romantics saw nature as ever-changing, unpredictable, and uncontrollable, and they interpreted its many aspects as analogous to equally unpredictable and changeable human moods and emotions. They found nature awesome, fascinating, powerful, domestic, and delightful. The landscape became perhaps the most important visual vehicle for Romantic thought.

CONSTABLE. John Constable (1776–1837), the son of a successful miller, claimed that the quiet domestic landscape of his youth in southern England had made him a painter before he ever picked up a paintbrush. Although he was trained at the Royal Academy, he was equally influenced by the British topographic watercolor tradition of the late eighteenth century and by seventeenth-century Dutch landscape painting (SEE FIG. 22–46). After moving to London in 1816, he dedicated himself to painting monumental views of the agricultural landscape (known as "six-footers"), which he considered as important as history painting. Constable's commitment to contemporary English subjects was so strong that he opposed the establishment of the English National Gallery of Art in 1832 on the grounds that it might distract painters by enticing them to paint foreign or ancient themes in unnatural styles.

THE HAY WAIN (FIG. 29–54) of 1821 shows a quiet, slow-moving scene from Constable's England. It has the fresh color and sense of visual exactitude that persuades viewers to believe that it must have been painted directly from nature. Constable made numerous drawings and small-scale color studies for his open-air paintings, but the final works were carefully constructed images produced in the studio. The paintings are very large even for landscape themes of historic importance, never mind views derived from the local landscape. *The Hay Wain* represents England as Constable imagined it had been for centuries—comfortable, rural and idyllic. Even the carefully rendered and meteorologically correct details of the sky seem natural. The painting is, however, deeply nostalgic, harking back to an agrarian past that was fast disappearing in industrializing England.

TURNER. Joseph Mallord William Turner (1775–1851) is often paired with Constable. Both were landscape painters of roughly the same period, but Turner's career followed a different path. He

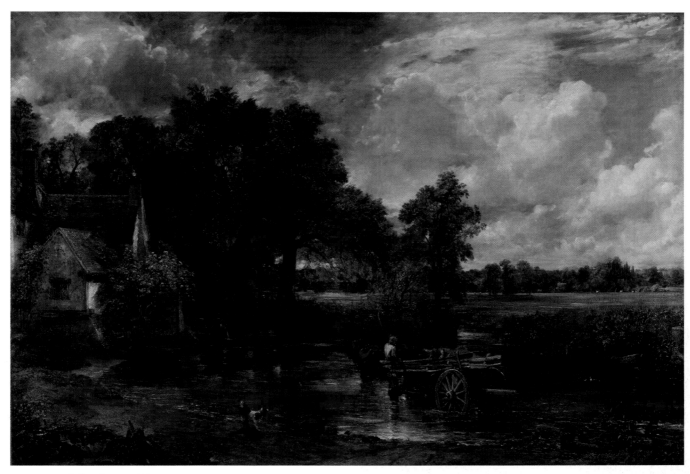

29–54 • John Constable THE HAY WAIN
1821. Oil on canvas, 51¼ × 73″ (130.2 × 185.4 cm). National Gallery, London. Gift of Henry Vaughan, 1886

EXPLORE MORE: Gain insight from a primary source by John Constable **www.myartslab.com**

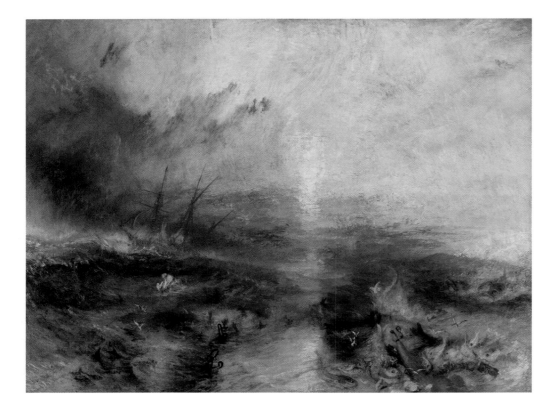

29–55 • Joseph Mallord William Turner **SLAVERS THROWING OVERBOARD THE DEAD AND DYING—TYPHOON COMING ON ("THE SLAVE SHIP")**
1840. Oil on canvas, 35¾ × 48¼" (90.8 × 122.6 cm). Museum of Fine Arts, Boston.

SEE MORE: View a video on Joseph Mallord William Turner **www.myartslab.com**

29–56 • Joseph Mallord William Turner **THE BURNING OF THE HOUSES OF LORDS AND COMMONS, 16TH OCTOBER 1834**
Oil on canvas, 36¼ × 48½" (92.1 × 123.2 cm). Philadelphia Museum of Art. The John Howard McFadden Collection, 1928

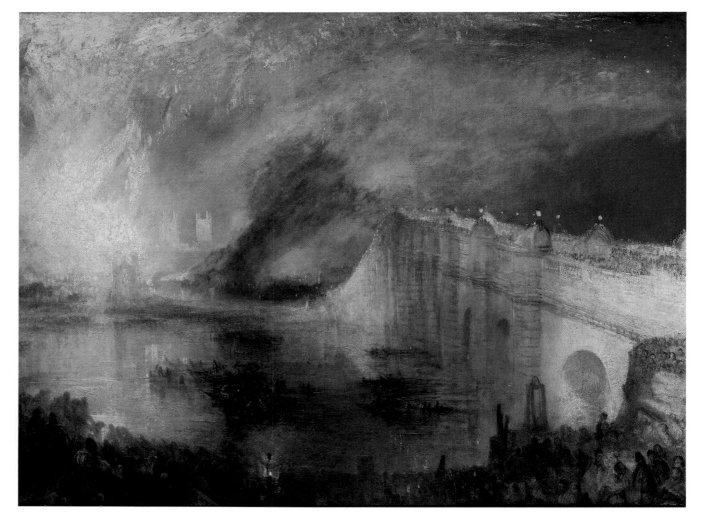

entered the Royal Academy in 1789, was elected a full academician at the unusually young age of 27, and later became a professor at the Royal Academy Schools. During the 1790s, Turner helped revolutionize the British watercolor tradition by rejecting careful underdrawing and topographic accuracy in favor of a freer application of paint and more generalized atmospheric effects. By the late 1790s, he was also exhibiting large-scale oil paintings of grand natural scenes and historical subjects. In his later work he sought to capture the **sublime**, a concept defined by philosopher Edmund Burke (1729–1797) as something that strikes awe and terror into the heart of the viewer. There is no real threat, however; the sublime is experienced vicariously and it is therefore thrilling and exciting.

Turner engages with contemporary social and political issues in his art on a sublime and cataclysmic scale. One of his later works, **SLAVERS THROWING OVERBOARD THE DEAD AND DYING —TYPHOON COMING ON ("THE SLAVE SHIP") (FIG. 29–55)**, depicts an event of genuine horror, based on an account in Thomas Clarkson's *The History of the Abolition of the Slave Trade* (1783), which was reprinted in 1840. Clarkson described the captain of a slave ship caught in the path of a typhoon. It was widely believed that insurance companies reimbursed for slaves lost at sea but not for those who died from sickness on board ship. In the foreground of Turner's painting, not readily recognizable and never quite legible, are the writhing bodies of slaves thrown overboard but still shackled together, fighting in vain for their lives. The fiery swirl of the sun, storm, and waves overwhelms these doomed souls.

Blazing color and light also dominate Turner's portrayal of **THE BURNING OF THE HOUSES OF LORDS AND COMMONS, 16TH OCTOBER 1834 (FIG. 29–56)**, which thrills with a sense of drama. We are not the only ones transfixed by the sight of a magnificent conflagration here: The foreground of the painting shows the south bank of the Thames packed with spectators. The fire was a national tragedy. London's ancient Houses of Parliament in Westminster Palace had witnessed some of the most important events in English history. The fire completely destroyed the House of Lords and left the House of Commons without a roof. Turner himself was witness to the scene and hurriedly made watercolor sketches; within a few months he had the large painting ready for exhibition. The brilliant light and color is the true theme of this painting, explaining why Turner was called "the painter of light."

COLE.   Thomas Cole (1801–1848) was one of the first great professional landscape painters in the United States. Cole emigrated from England at age 17 and by 1820 was working as an itinerant portrait painter. With the help of a patron, he traveled in Europe between 1829 and 1832; upon his return to the United States he settled in New York and became a successful landscape painter. He frequently worked from observation when making sketches for his paintings, but, like most landscape painters of his generation, he produced his large finished works in the studio during the winter months.

In the mid 1830s, Cole painted **THE OXBOW (FIG. 29–57)** for exhibition at the National Academy of Design in New York. He

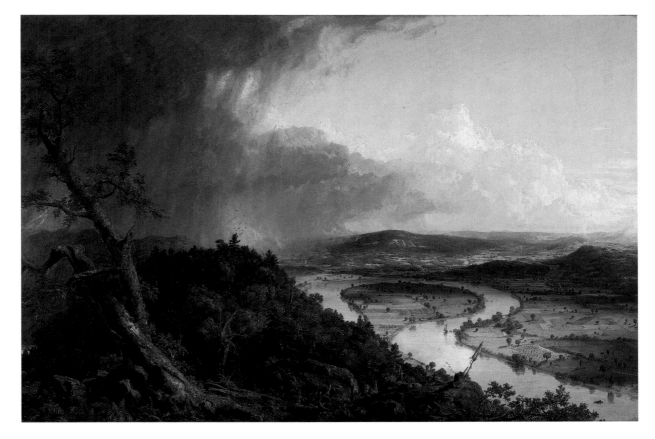

29-57 •
Thomas Cole
THE OXBOW
1836. Oil on canvas, 51½ × 76″ (1.31 × 1.94 m). Metropolitan Museum of Art, New York. Gift of Mrs. Russell Sage, 1908 (08.228)

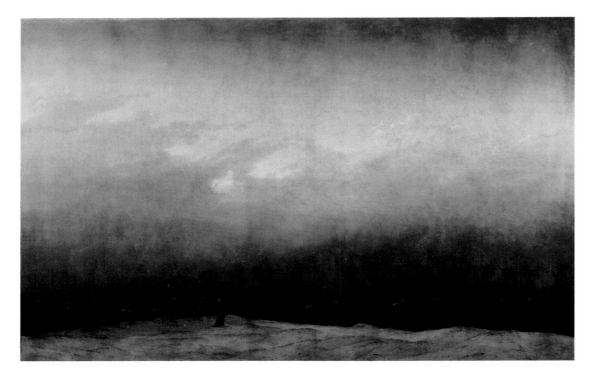

29-58 • Caspar David Friedrich **MONK BY THE SEA**
1809. Oil on canvas,
43 × 67¾″ (110 × 172 cm).
Nationalgalerie, Berlin.

considered this one of his "view" paintings because it represents a specific place and time. Although most of his other view paintings were small, this one was for exhibition at the National Academy, so it is monumentally large. Its scale allows for a sweeping view of a spectacular oxbow bend in the Connecticut River from the top of Mount Holyoke in western Massachusetts. Cole wrote that the American landscape lacked the historic monuments that made European landscape interesting; there were no castles on the Hudson River of the kind found on the Rhine, and there were no ancient monuments in America of the kind found in Rome. On the other hand, he argued, America's natural wonders, such as this oxbow, should be viewed as America's natural "antiquities." The painting's title tells us that Cole depicts an actual spot, but, like other landscape painters who wished to impart a larger message about the course of history in their work, he composed the scene to convey the landscape's grandeur and significance, exaggerating the steepness of the mountain and setting the scene below a dramatic sky. Along a great sweeping arc produced by the dark clouds and the edge of the mountain, he contrasts the two sides of the American landscape: its dense, stormy wilderness and its congenial, pastoral valleys with settlements. The fading storm seems to suggest that the land is bountiful and ready to yield its fruits to civilization.

FRIEDRICH.   In Germany, the Romantic landscape painter Caspar David Friedrich (1774–1840) considered landscape as a vehicle through which to achieve spiritual revelation. As a young man, he was influenced by the writings and teachings of Gotthard Kosegarten, a local Lutheran pastor and poet who taught that the divine was visible through a deep personal connection with nature. Kosegarten argued that just as God's book was the Bible, the landscape was God's "Book of Nature." Friedrich studied at the Copenhagen Academy before settling in Dresden, where the poet Johann Wolfgang von Goethe encouraged him to make landscape the principal subject of his art. He sketched from nature but painted in the studio, synthesizing his sketches with his memories of and feelings about nature. In **MONK BY THE SEA (FIG. 29–58)**, a long expanse of dark, moody beach is differentiated from the sky by no more than a vague horizon. The tiny figure of a monk contemplates the vastness and sublimity of the landscape from the edge of the water. The coastline is mysteriously quiet and fog has drawn a veil over most of the details of the landscape, creating a mood that is hushed and solemn.

Friedrich's landscape paintings were popular among members of the emerging nationalist movement in Germany after Napoleon's invasion in 1806. Interestingly, his work became less popular after Napoleon's defeat in 1815.

GOTHIC AND NEOCLASSICAL STYLES IN ARCHITECTURE

A mixture of Neoclassicism and Romanticism motivated architects in the early nineteenth century, many of whom worked in either mode, depending on the task at hand. Neoclassicism in architecture often imbued secular public buildings with a sense of grandeur and timelessness, while Romanticism evoked, for instance, the Gothic past with its associations of spirituality and community.

GOTHIC ARCHITECTURE.   The British claimed the Gothic as part of their patrimony and erected a plethora of Gothic Revival buildings in the nineteenth century, among them the **HOUSES OF**

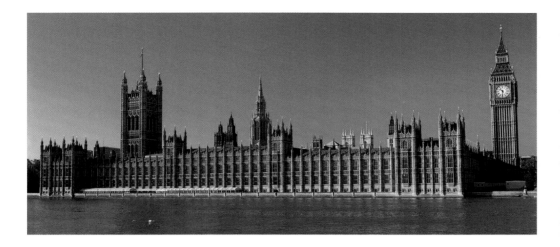

29–59 • Charles Barry and Augustus Welby Northmore Pugin **HOUSES OF PARLIAMENT, LONDON** 1836–1860. Royal Commission on the Historical Monuments of England, London.

Pugin published two influential books in 1836 and 1841, in which he argued that the Gothic style of Westminster Abbey was the embodiment of true English genius. In his view, the Greek and Roman Classical orders were stone replications of earlier wooden forms and therefore fell short of the true principles of stone construction.

PARLIAMENT (FIG. 29–59). After Westminster Palace had burned down in 1834, in the fire so memorably painted by Turner (SEE FIG. 29–56), the British government announced a competition for a new building to be designed in the English Perpendicular Gothic style, and to harmonize with the neighboring Westminster Abbey, the thirteenth-century church where English monarchs are crowned.

Charles Barry (1795–1860) and Augustus Welby Northmore Pugin (1812–1852) won the commission. Barry was responsible for the basic plan of the new building, whose symmetry suggests the balance of powers within the British parliamentary system; Pugin provided the intricate Gothic decoration laid over Barry's essentially Classical plan. The leading advocate of Gothic architecture in his era, Pugin published *Contrasts* in 1836, in which he compared the troubled modern era of materialism and mechanization unfavorably with the Middle Ages, which he represented as an idyllic epoch of deep spirituality and satisfying handcraft. For Pugin, Gothic was not a style but a principle, like Classicism. The Gothic, he insisted, embodied two "great rules" of architecture: "first, that there should be no features about a building which are not necessary for convenience, construction or propriety; second, that all ornament should consist of enrichment of the essential structure of the building."

In the nineteenth century, architects used the Gothic primarily for Roman Catholic and Anglican (Episcopalian in the United States) churches. The British-born American architect Richard Upjohn (1802–1878) designed many of the most important Gothic Revival churches in the United States, including **TRINITY CHURCH** in New York (**FIG. 29–60**). With its tall spire, long nave, and squared-off chancel, Trinity church quotes the early fourteenth-century British Gothic style particularly admired by Anglicans and Episcopalians. Every detail is rendered with historical accuracy, but the vaults are plaster, not masonry. The stained-glass windows above the altar were among the earliest of their kind in the United States.

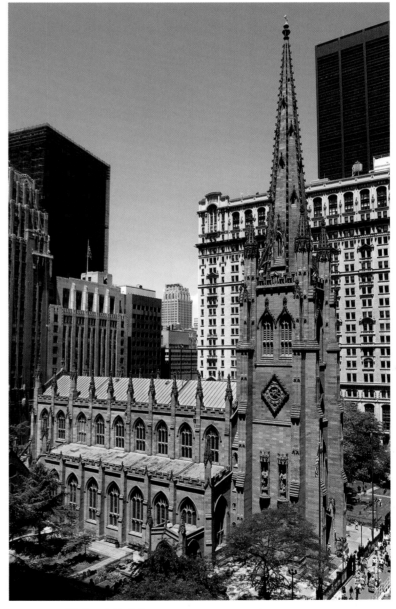

29–60 • Richard Upjohn **TRINITY CHURCH, NEW YORK CITY** 1839–1846.

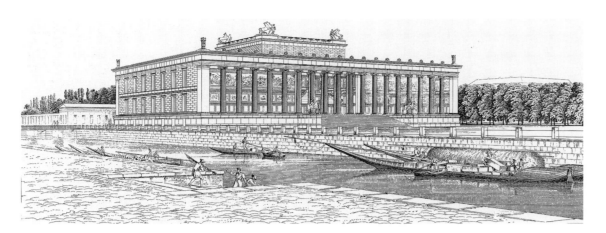

NEOCLASSICAL ARCHITECTURE. In several European capitals in the early nineteenth century, national museums were designed in the Neoclassical style, which positioned the new buildings as both temples of culture and displays of nationalism. Perhaps the most significant of these was the **ALTES MUSEUM** in Berlin, designed in 1822 by Karl Friedrich Schinkel (1781–1841) and built between 1824 and 1830 (**FIG. 29–61**). The Altes Museum (Old Museum) was commissioned to display the royal art collection, and was thus built directly across from the Baroque royal palace on an island on the Spree River in the heart of Berlin. The museum's imposing façade consists of a screen of 18 Ionic columns raised on a platform with a central staircase. Attentive to the problem of lighting artworks on both the ground and the upper floors, Schinkel created interior courtyards on either side of a central rotunda.

Tall windows on the museum's outer walls provide natural illumination, and partition walls perpendicular to the windows eliminate glare on the varnished surfaces of the paintings on display.

Large public works in the Neoclassical style were also constructed in the United States. The most significant and symbolic Neoclassical building in Washington, D.C. is the **U.S. CAPITOL**, initially designed in 1792 by William Thornton (1759–1828), an amateur architect. His monumental plan featured a large dome over a temple front flanked by two wings to accommodate the House of Representatives and the Senate. In 1803, President Thomas Jefferson (1743–1826), also an amateur architect, hired a British-trained professional, Benjamin Henry Latrobe (1764–1820), to oversee the actual construction of the Capitol. Latrobe modified Thornton's design by adding a grand staircase and Corinthian colonnade on the

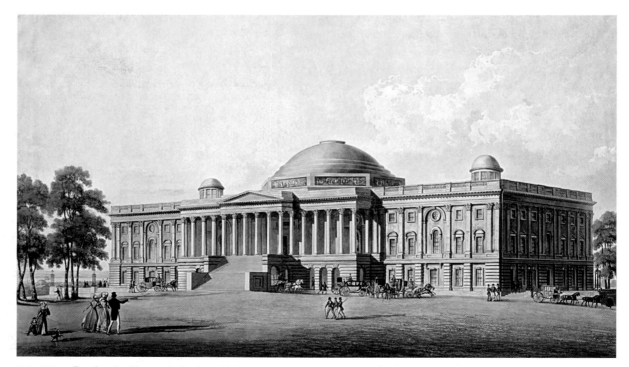

29–62 • Benjamin Henry Latrobe **U.S. CAPITOL, WASHINGTON, D.C.**
c. 1808. Engraving by T. Sutherland, 1825. New York Public Library. I. N. Phelps Stokes Collection, Myriam and Ira Wallach Division of Art, Prints, and Photographs

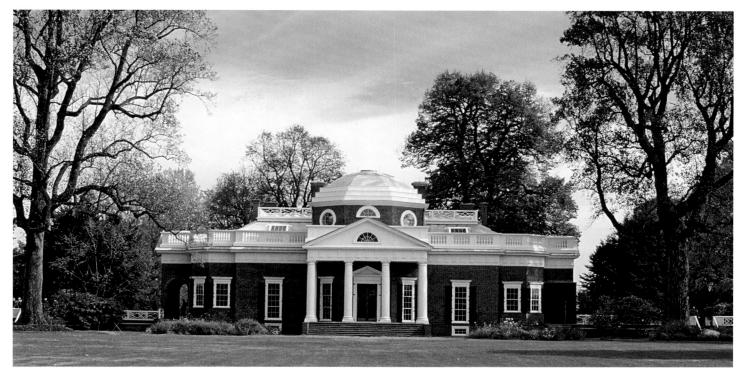

29-63 • Thomas Jefferson MONTICELLO
Charlottesville, Virginia. 1769–1782, 1796–1809.

SEE MORE: View multimedia features on Monticello **www.myartslab.com**

east front **(FIG. 29–62)**. After the British gutted the building in the war of 1812, Latrobe repaired the wings and designed a higher dome. Seeking new symbolic forms for the nation within the traditional Classical vocabulary, he also created a variation on the Corinthian order for the interior by substituting indigenous crops such as corn and tobacco for the Corinthian order's acanthus leaves. In 1817, he resigned his post. The reconstruction was completed under Charles Bulfinch (1763–1844), and another major renovation, resulting in a much larger dome, began in 1850.

Jefferson's designs for the mountaintop home he called **MONTICELLO** (Italian for "little mountain") near Charlottesville, Virginia, is an example of Neoclassical architecture in a private setting **(FIG. 29–63)**. Jefferson began the first phase of construction (1769–1782) when Virginia was still a British colony, and he based his design on the English Palladian style (see Chiswick House, FIG. 29–15). By 1796, however, he had become disenchanted with both the English and their architecture, and had come to admire French architecture while serving as the American minister in Paris. He then embarked upon a second building campaign at Monticello (1796–1809), enlarging the house and redesigning its brick and wood exterior so that its two stories appeared from the outside as one large story, in the manner then fashionable in Paris. The modern worlds of England, France, and America, as well as the ancient worlds of Greece and Rome, come together in this residence. In the second half of the nineteenth century, cultural borrowings would take on an even broader global scope.

THINK ABOUT IT

29.1 Summarize some of the key stylistic traits of French Rococo art and architecture, and explain how these traits relate to the social context of salon life. Then analyze one Rococo work from the chapter and explain how it is typical of the period style.

29.2 Write about how the Enlightenment interest in archaeology propelled the new movement of Neoclassicism in the eighteenth century.

29.3 Explain why artists as visually diverse as Delacroix and Friedrich can be classified under the category of Romanticism. Then evaluate the merits and pitfalls of "Romanticism" as a classifying term.

29.4 Discuss attitudes toward subject matter in the academies of Europe, particularly France and England. Explain what was included and excluded in the academic Grand Manner and why.

29.5 Write about the political climate during Francisco Goya's life, and then, through an analysis of his *Third of May, 1808* (FIG. 29–43), demonstrate how politics affected his art.

PRACTICE MORE: Compose answers to these questions, get flashcards for images and terms, and review chapter material with quizzes **www.myartslab.com**

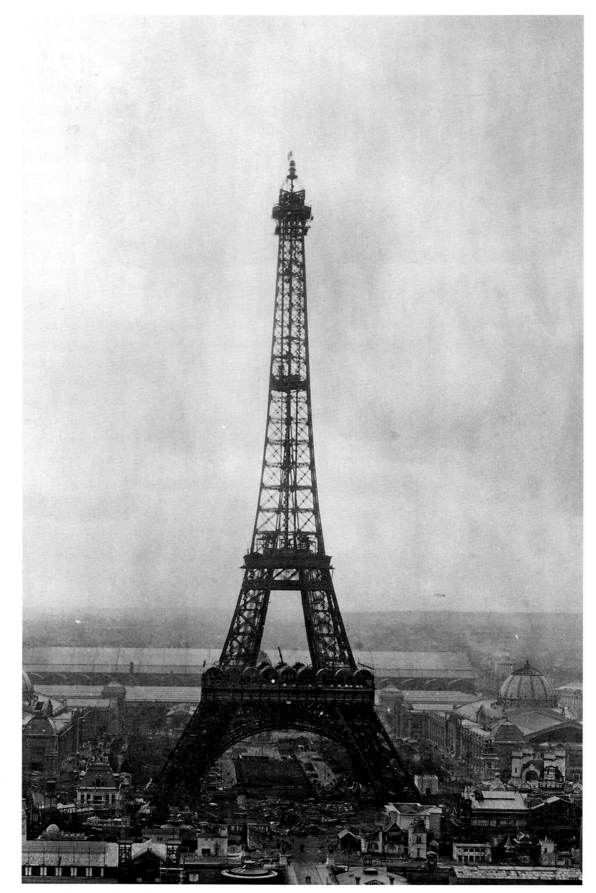

30-1 • Gustave Eiffel **EIFFEL TOWER** Paris. 1887–1889.

MID- TO LATE NINETEENTH-CENTURY ART IN EUROPE AND THE UNITED STATES

THE EIFFEL TOWER (FIG. 30–1) was designed and built by Gustave Eiffel (1832–1923) for the 1889 Universal Exposition in Paris. When completed, it stood 984 feet tall and was the tallest structure in the world, taller than the Egyptian pyramids or Gothic cathedrals. The Eiffel Tower served as the entrance to and was the main attraction of the Universal Exposition, one of more than 20 such international fairs staged throughout Europe and the United States in the second half of the nineteenth century. These events showcased and compared international industry, science, and the applied, decorative, and fine arts. An object of pride for the French nation, the Eiffel Tower was intended to demonstrate France's superior engineering, technological and industrial knowledge, and power. Although originally conceived as a temporary structure, it still stands today.

The initial response to the Eiffel Tower was mixed. In 1887, a group of 47 writers, musicians, and artists wrote to *Le Temps* protesting "the erection … of the useless and monstrous Eiffel Tower," which they described as "a black and gigantic factory chimney." Gustave Eiffel, however, said, "I believe the tower will have its own beauty," and that it "will show that we [the French] are not simply an amusing people, but also the country of engineers." Indeed, when completed, the Eiffel Tower quickly became an international symbol of advanced thought and modernity among artists, and was admired by the public as a wondrous spectacle. The great French theorist Roland Barthes described it in 1979 as the "universal symbol of Paris."

The tower was one of the city's most photographed structures in 1889, its immensity dwarfing the tiny buildings below. Copies of photographs taken by professional and commercial photographers were sold to thousands of tourists visiting the Universal Exposition. This photograph, from late March 1889, shows the tower still under construction but almost complete; the bottom two tiers with the fairgrounds below show evidence of rapid last-minute construction.

LEARN ABOUT IT

30.1 Evaluate the role played by academic art and architecture in the art world of the late nineteenth century.

30.2 Examine the early experiments that led to the emergence of photography as a new art form.

30.3 Analyze the ways in which the movement toward realism in art reflected the social and political concerns of the nineteenth century.

30.4 Investigate the origins of Impressionism and describe its form and content.

30.5 Compare and contrast the several manifestations of Post-Impressionism.

HEAR MORE: Listen to an audio file of your chapter **www.myartslab.com**

EUROPE AND THE UNITED STATES IN THE MID TO LATE NINETEENTH CENTURY

The technological, economic, and social transformations set in motion by the Industrial Revolution intensified in the nineteenth century. Increasing demands for coal and iron necessitated improvements in mining, metallurgy, and transportation. Likewise, the development of the locomotive and steamship facilitated the shipment of raw materials and merchandise, made passenger travel easier, and encouraged the growth of cities (SEE MAP 30–1). These changes also set in motion a vast population migration, as the rural poor moved to cities to find work in factories, mines, and mechanical manufacturing. Industrialists and entrepreneurs enjoyed new levels of wealth and prosperity in this system, but conditions for workers—many of them women and children—were often abysmal. Although new government regulations led to some improvements, socialist movements condemned the exploitation of workers by capitalist factory owners and advocated communal or state ownership of the means of production and distribution.

In 1848, workers' revolts broke out in several European capitals. In that year also, Karl Marx and Friedrich Engels published the *Communist Manifesto*, which predicted the violent overthrow of the bourgeoisie (middle class) by the proletariat (working class), the abolition of private property, and the creation of a classless society. At the same time, the Americans Lucretia Mott and Elizabeth Cady Stanton organized the country's first women's rights convention, in Seneca Falls, New York. They called for the equality of women and men before the law, property rights for married women, the acceptance of women into institutions of higher education, the admission of women to all trades and professions, equal pay for equal work, and women's suffrage.

The nineteenth century also witnessed the rise of imperialism. In order to create new markets for their products and to secure access to cheap raw materials and cheap labor, European nations established numerous new colonies by dividing up most of Africa and nearly a third of Asia. Colonial rule frequently suppressed indigenous cultures while exploiting the economic development of colonized areas.

Scientific discoveries led to the telegraph, telephone, and radio. By the end of the nineteenth century, electricity powered lighting, motors, trams, and railways in most European and American cities. Developments in chemistry created many new products, such as aspirin, disinfectants, photographic chemicals, and more effective explosives. The new material of steel, an alloy of iron and carbon, was lighter, harder, and more malleable than iron, and replaced it in heavy construction and transportation. In medicine and public health, Louis Pasteur's purification of beverages through heat (pasteurization) and the development of vaccines, sterilization, and antiseptics led to a dramatic decline in mortality rates all over the Western world.

Some scientific discoveries challenged traditional religious beliefs and affected social philosophy. Geologists concluded that the Earth was far older than the estimated 6,000 years sometimes claimed by biblical literalists. In 1859, Charles Darwin proposed that life evolved through natural selection. Religious conservatives attacked Darwin's account, which seemed to deny divine creation and even the existence of God. Some of his more extreme supporters, however, suggested that the "survival of the fittest" had advanced the human race, with certain types of people—particularly the Anglo-Saxon upper classes—achieving the pinnacle of social evolution. "Social Darwinism" provided a rationalization for the poor conditions of the working class and a justification for colonizing the "underdeveloped" parts of the world.

In the arts, industrialists, merchants, professionals, the middle classes, some governments, and national academies of art became new sources of patronage. Large annual exhibitions in European and American cultural centers took on increasing importance as a means for artists to show their work, win prizes, attract buyers, and gain commissions. Cheap illustrated newspapers and magazines published art criticism that influenced the reception and production of art, both making and breaking artistic careers, and commercial art dealers emerged as important brokers of art and taste.

The second half of the nineteenth century saw vast changes in how art was conceptualized and created. Some artists became committed political or social activists as industrialization and social unrest continued, while others retreated into their own imagination. Some responded to the ways in which photography transformed vision and perception, many setting themselves up as photographers, while other artists emulated the new medium's clarity in their own work. Still others investigated the difference between photography's detailed but superficial description of visual reality and a deeper, more human reality as a source of inspiration, and others explored the artistic potential of photography's sometimes visually unbalanced compositions, its tendency to compress the illusion of depth and assert its flatness, its lack of an even focus across the picture plane or sometimes the reverse, or even the inability of early photography to "see" red and green equally, causing blank areas of white and black in a photograph. Thus, by the late nineteenth century, while many artists were exploring the reliability of observed reality, others were venturing into the realm of abstraction.

FRENCH ACADEMIC ARCHITECTURE AND ART

The Académie des Beaux-Arts (founded in 1816 to replace the disbanded Royal Academy of Painting and Sculpture) and its official art school, the École des Beaux-Arts, continued to exert a powerful influence over the visual arts in France during the nineteenth century. Academic artists controlled the Salon juries, and major public commissions routinely went to academic architects, painters,

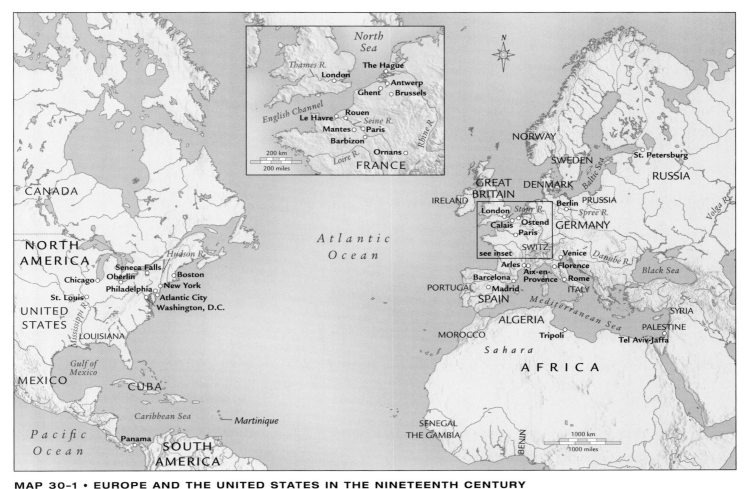

MAP 30–1 • EUROPE AND THE UNITED STATES IN THE NINETEENTH CENTURY

In the nineteenth century, Europe and the United States became increasingly industrialized and many European nations established colonial possessions around the world. Paris was firmly established as the center of the Western art world.

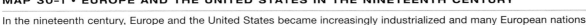

and sculptors. Artists and architects from Europe and the United States came to Paris to study the conventions of academic art.

Academic art and architecture frequently depended upon motifs drawn from historic models—a practice called **historicism**. Elaborating on earlier Neoclassical and Romantic revivals, historicist art and architecture encompassed the sweep of history. Historicists often combined allusions to several different historical periods in a single work. Some academic artists catered to the public taste for exotic sights with Orientalist paintings (see "Orientalism," page 966). These works also combined disparate elements, borrowing from Egyptian, Turkish and Indian cultures to create an imaginary Middle Eastern world.

ACADEMIC ARCHITECTURE

In 1848, after rioting over living conditions erupted in French cities, Napoleon III launched sweeping new reforms. The riots devastated Paris's central neighborhoods, and Georges-Eugène Haussmann (1809–1891) was engaged to redraw the street grid and rebuild the city. Haussmann's ideal was to impose a new rational plan of broad avenues, parks, and open public places upon the medieval heart of Paris. He demolished entire neighborhoods of narrow, winding, medieval streets, summarily evicting the poor from their slums, and replaced them with grand new buildings erected along wide, straight, tree-lined avenues that were suitable for horse-drawn carriages and strolling pedestrians.

The **OPÉRA (FIG. 30–2)**, a new city opera house designed by Charles Garnier (1825–1898) and now one of the major Parisian landmarks, was built at an intersection of Haussmann's grand avenues. Accessible from all directions, the Opéra was designed with transportation and vehicular traffic in mind, and with a modern cast-iron internal frame; yet in other respects it is a masterpiece of historicism based mostly on the Baroque style, revived here to recall an earlier period of greatness in France. The massive façade, featuring a row of paired columns over an arcade, was intended to recall the seventeenth-century wing of the Louvre, an association meant to suggest the continuity of the French nation and to flatter Emperor Napoleon III by comparing him favorably with King Louis XIV. The building's primary function—as a place of entertainment for Napoleon III, his entourage, and the French social elite—accounts for its luxurious

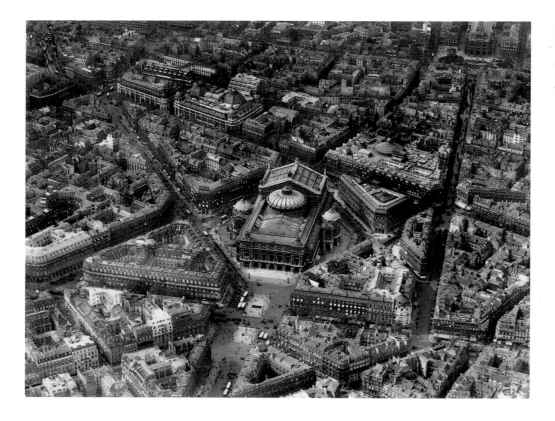

30-2 • Charles Garnier **OPÉRA**
Paris. 1861–1874.

SEE MORE: Click the Google
Earth link for the Opéra, Paris
www.myartslab.com

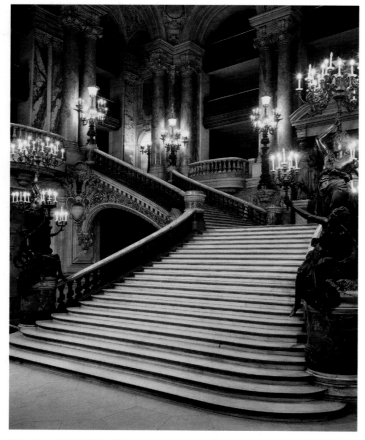

30-3 • GRAND STAIRCASE, OPÉRA

SEE MORE: View a panorama of the interior of the
Opéra **www.myartslab.com**

detail. The interior, described as a "temple of pleasure," was even more opulent, with neo-Baroque sculptural groupings, heavy gilded decoration, and a lavish mix of expensive, polychromed materials. The highlight of the interior may not have been the spectacle on stage so much as that on the grand, sweeping Baroque staircase **(FIG. 30–3)**, where members of the Paris elite displayed themselves. As Garnier said, the purpose of the Opéra was to fulfill human desires: to hear, to see, and to be seen.

ACADEMIC PAINTING AND SCULPTURE

The taste that dominated painting and sculpture in the Académie des Beaux-Arts by the mid nineteenth century was termed the *juste milieu*, or "middle way," taste. We can see the flavor of the *juste milieu* in **THE BIRTH OF VENUS** by Alexandre Cabanel (1823–1889), one of the leading academic artists of the time **(FIG. 30–4)**. After studying with an academic master, Cabanel won the Prix de Rome in 1845, and was awarded top honors at the Salon three times in the 1860s and 1870s. In his version of this mythological subject, a copy of which by Adolphe Jourdan is seen here, Venus is carried along by the waves, as flying *putti* herald her arrival with conch shells. Cabanel's mastery of anatomy, flesh tones, and the sea surface derives from his training and skillful technique. The image has a strong erotic charge, though, in the languid limbs, arched back, and hooded eyes of Venus. This combination of mythological pedigree and erotic appeal proved irresistible to Napoleon III, who bought *The Birth of Venus* for his private collection. For more on Jourdan's copy see "The Mass Dissemination of Art," page 974.

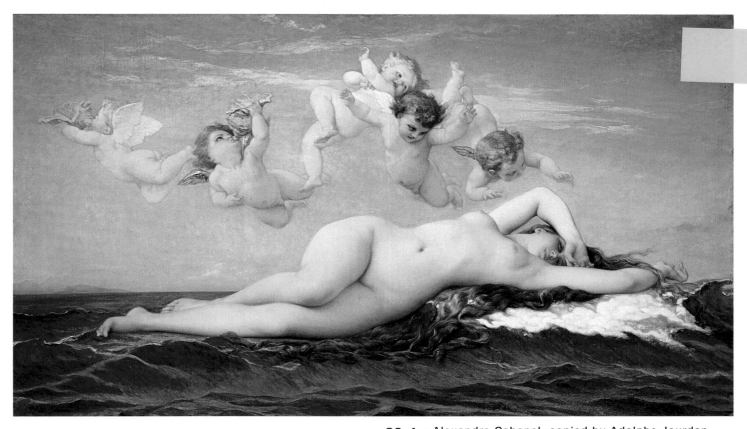

30-4 • Alexandre Cabanel, copied by Adolphe Jourdan
THE BIRTH OF VENUS
c. 1864. Oil on canvas, 33 × 53″ (85.2 × 135.8 cm). Dahesh Museum of Art, New York. 2002.37

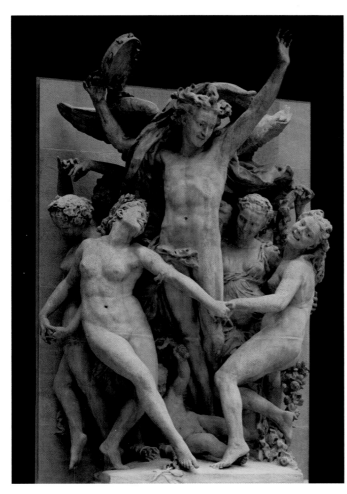

30-5 • Jean-Baptiste Carpeaux **THE DANCE**
1867–1868. Plaster, height approx. 15′ (4.6 m). Musée de l'Opéra, Paris.

Although academic and avant-garde artists are sometimes thought simply to have been in opposition, their relationship was more complex. Some academic artists experimented within academic conventions, while avant-garde artists held many academic conventions in high esteem and even sought academic approval. The academic artist Jean-Baptiste Carpeaux (1827–1875) illustrates the kind of experimentation that took place within the Académie des Beaux-Arts. Carpeaux, who had studied at the École des Beaux-Arts under the Romantic sculptor François Rude (SEE FIG. 29–50), was commissioned to carve a large sculptural group for the façade of the Opéra (SEE FIG. 30–2). In this work, **THE DANCE (FIG. 30–5)**, a winged male personifying Dance leaps up joyfully in the midst of a compact group of mostly nude female dancers, embodying the theme of uninhibited Dionysian revelry. Like Cabanel's *Birth of Venus*, the work imbues a mythological subject with erotic connotations.

Orientalism

The Snake Charmer by Jean-León Gérôme (1824–1904), painted around 1870, is an example of Orientalism in art. In it Gérôme portrays the nineteenth-century fantasy of the Middle East. The painting shows a young boy, entirely naked, handling a python, while an older man behind him plays a fipple flute, and a group of mercenaries watches. The setting is a large blue-tiled room decorated with calligraphic patterns. The scene is painted with an almost photographic clarity and attention to detail, leading us to think that it is an accurate representation of a specific event. Gérôme traveled to the Middle East several times, and was praised by critics of the 1855 Salon for his ethnographic accuracy. Yet the overall narrative of Gérôme's *Snake Charmer* is a complete fiction, mixing Egyptian, Turkish, and Indian cultures together in a fantastic pastiche.

Orientalism, the fascination with Middle Eastern cultures, dates in France to Napoleon's 1798 invasion of Egypt and his rampant looting of objects from the country for the Louvre Museum, which he opened in 1804. Between 1809 and 1822, the 24-volume *Description de l'Egypte*, recording the people, lands, and culture of Egypt, was published. In the 1840s and 1850s, photographic studios were established by British, French, and Italian photographers at major tourist sites in the Middle East in order to provide photographs for visitors and armchair tourists at home, thus fueling a popular interest in the region.

Orientalism is found in both academic and avant-garde art in the nineteenth century. The scholar Edward Said described Orientalism as the colonial gaze in which the colonizer gazes upon the colonized Orient (the Middle East rather than Asia) as something to possess, as a "primitive" or "exotic" playground for the "civilized" European visitor, in which "native" men are savage and despotic and "native" women are sultry and sexually available. The "orientalizing" impulse continued throughout the nineteenth century. Like that of Gérôme, the art of Ingres is replete with Orientalism (SEE FIG. 29–51).

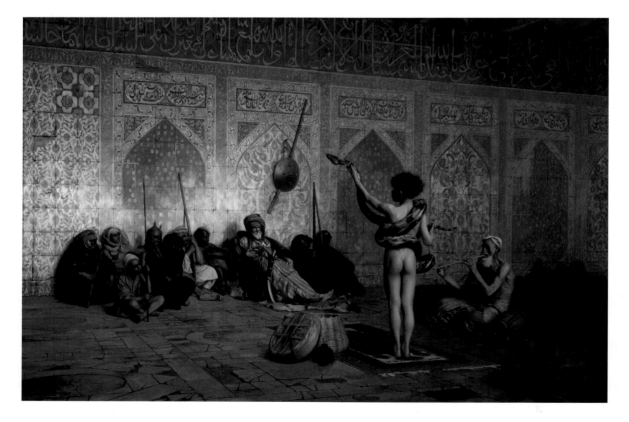

Jean-Léon Gérôme
THE SNAKE CHARMER
c. 1870. Oil on canvas, 33 × 48⅛″ (83.8 × 122.1 cm). Clark Art Institute, Williamstown, MA. Acquired by Sterling and Francine Clark, 1942. 1955.51

Unlike Cabanel's figures, Carpeaux's were not smooth and generalized in a Neoclassical manner and this drew criticism from some academicians. The arrangement of his sculptural group seemed too spontaneous, the facial expressions of the figures too vivid, their musculature too exact, their bone structure and proportions too much of this world, rather than of an ideal one. Carpeaux's work signaled a new direction in academic art, reflecting the values of the new generation of patrons from the industrial and merchant classes. These practical new collectors were less interested in art that idealized than in art that brought the ideal down to earth.

EARLY PHOTOGRAPHY IN EUROPE AND THE UNITED STATES

The nineteenth-century desire to record the faces of the new mercantile elite, their achievements and possessions, and even the imperial possessions of nations, found expression in photography. Since the late Renaissance, artists and others had sought a mechanical method for drawing from nature. One early device was the **camera obscura** (Latin, meaning "dark chamber," see page 970), which consists of a darkened room or box with a lens through which light passes, projecting onto the opposite wall (or box side) an upside-down image of the scene, which an artist can then trace. By the nineteenth century, a small, portable *camera obscura* or even lighter *camera lucida* had become standard equipment for artists. Photography developed as a way to fix—that is, to make permanent—the images produced by a *camera obscura* (later called a "camera") on light-sensitive material.

Photography had no single "inventor." Several individuals worked on the technique simultaneously, each contributing some part to a process that emerged over many years. Around 1830, a handful of experimenters understood ways to "record" the image, but the last step, "stopping" or "fixing" that image so that further exposure to light would not further darken the image, proved difficult to achieve.

In France, while experimenting with ways to duplicate his paintings, Louis-Jacques-Mandé Daguerre (1787–1851) discovered that a plate coated with light-sensitive chemicals and exposed to light for 20 to 30 minutes would reveal a "latent image" when then exposed to mercury vapors. By 1837, he had developed a method of fixing his image by bathing the plate in a solution of salt, and he vastly improved the process by using the chemical hyposulphate of soda (known as "hypo") as suggested by Sir John Frederick

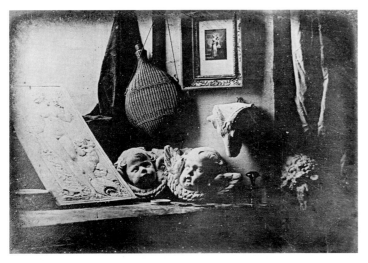

30-6 • Louis-Jacques-Mandé Daguerre THE ARTIST'S STUDIO
1837. Daguerreotype, 6½ × 8½" (16.5 × 21.6 cm). Société Française de Photographie, Paris.

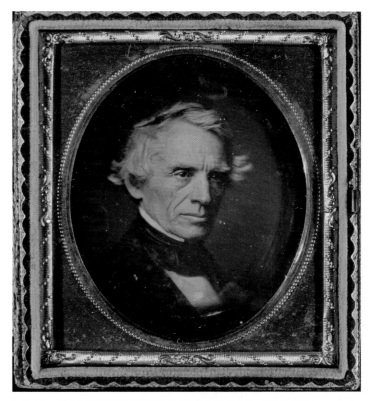

30-7 • DAGUERREOTYPE OF SAMUEL FINLEY BREESE MORSE
c. 1845. Sixth plate daguerreotype. The Daguerreotype Collection of the Library of Congress, Washington, D.C.

Herschel (1792–1871). The final image was negative, but when viewed upon a highly polished silver plate it appeared positive. The resulting picture could not be duplicated easily and was very fragile, but its quality was remarkably precise. In Daguerre's photograph of his studio tabletop **(FIG. 30–6)**, the details are exquisite (impossible to see in reproduction, even using today's technology) and the composition mimics the conventions of still-life painting. Daguerre, after he patented and announced his new technology, produced an early type of photograph called a **daguerreotype**, in August 1839.

Even before Daguerre announced his photographic technique in France, the American artist Samuel Morse (1791–1872) traveled to Paris to negotiate an exchange of information about his invention, the telegraph, for information about Daguerre's photography. Morse introduced the daguerreotype process to America within weeks of Daguerre's announcement, and by 1841 had reduced exposure times enough to take portrait photographs **(FIG. 30–7)**.

At the same time in England, Henry Fox Talbot (1800–1877), a wealthy amateur, made negative copies of engravings, lace, and plants by placing them on paper soaked in silver chloride and exposing them to light. He also found that the negative image on paper could be exposed again on top of another piece of paper to create a positive image, thus discovering the negative-positive process that became the basis of photographic printing. Talbot's negative could be used more than once, so he could produce a

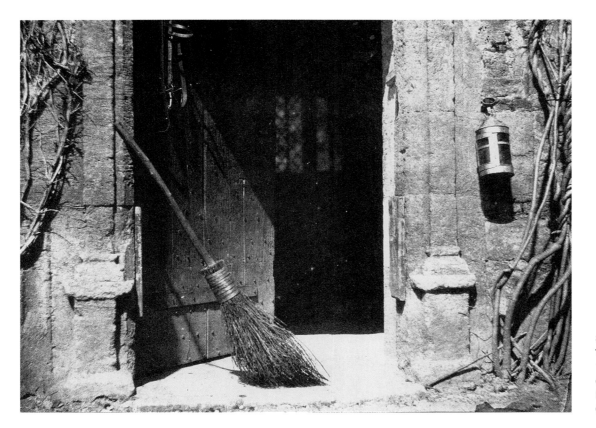

30-8 • Henry Fox Talbot
THE OPEN DOOR
1843. Salt-paper print from a
calotype negative. Science
Museum, London. Fox Talbot
Collection

number of positive images inexpensively. But the **calotype**, as he later called it, produced a soft, fuzzy image. When he heard of Daguerre's announcement, Talbot rushed to make his own announcement and patent his process. The term for these processes —photography, derived from the Greek for "drawing with light"—was coined by Herschel.

The emerging technology of photography was quickly put to use for making a visual record for contemporary audiences and future generations. Early on, however, photographers also experimented with the expressive possibilities of the new medium and worked to create striking compositions. Between 1844 and 1846, Talbot published a book in six parts entitled *The Pencil of Nature*, illustrated entirely with salt-paper prints made from calotype negatives. Most of the photographs were of idyllic rural scenery or carefully arranged still lifes; they were presented as works of art rather than documents of a precisely observed reality. Talbot realized that the imprecision of his process could not compete with the commercial potential of the daguerreotype, and so rather than trying to do so, he chose to view photography in visual and artistic terms. In **THE OPEN DOOR** (**FIG. 30–8)**, for example, shadows create a repeating pattern of diagonal lines that contrast with the vertical lines of the architecture. The photograph expresses nostalgia for a rural way of life that was fast disappearing in industrial England.

Other early photographers worked on assignment and chose the photographic process that best suited their final product. In 1851, the French government decided to commission photographs of the major architectural monuments of France, in part because so much of ancient France had been destroyed during the Revolution. Édouard-Denis Baldus (1813–1882) was one of several photographers assigned to make photographs for the Mission Héliographique through the Commission des Monuments Historiques. He relied on many techniques, including calotypes, wet-plate/collodion negatives, albumen prints, and heliogravure. Since the photographs had to be reproduced for publication, he was unable to use daguerreotypes. Ironically, despite intense competitive national pride over the French and English versions of photography, some of the best calotypes were made in France and some of the best daguerreotypes in England and the United States. This albumen print by Baldus, **HOUSE WITH STAIRCASE** (**FIG. 30–9)** is one of 11 photographs that he took for his famous folio *Vues de Paris en Photographie*.

American photographers used wet-plate glass negative and albumen paper print processes to document the momentous events of the Civil War (1861–1865). Timothy O'Sullivan (c. 1840– 1882) was a "camera operator" for Matthew Brady (1822–1896) at the beginning of the conflict, and, working with Alexander Gardner (1821–1882), he made war photographs that were distributed widely. **THE HOME OF THE REBEL SHARPSHOOTER** (**FIG. 30–10)** was taken after the Battle of Gettysburg in July 1863. The technical difficulties were considerable. Wet-plate technology required that the glass plate used to make the negative be coated with a sticky substance holding the light-sensitive chemicals; if the plate dried, the photograph could not be taken. Likewise, if dust contaminated the plate, the image would also be ruined. Long

THE BEGINNINGS OF THE AVANT-GARDE: REALISM AND BEYOND

In reaction to the rigidity of academic training, some French artists began to consider themselves members of an **avant-garde**, meaning "advance guard" or "vanguard." The term was coined by the French military during the Napoleonic era to designate the forward units of an advancing army that scouted territory that the main force would soon occupy. Avant-garde artists saw themselves as working in advance of an increasingly bourgeois society. The term was first mentioned in connection with art around 1825 in the political programs of French utopian socialists. Henri de Saint-Simon (1760–1825) suggested that in order to transform modern industrialized society into an ideal state, it would be necessary to gather together an avant-garde of intellectuals, scientists, and artists to lead France into the future.

In 1831, the architect Eugène Viollet-le-Duc applied the term to the artists of Paris in the aftermath of the revolution of 1830. Viollet-le-Duc vehemently opposed the French academic system of architectural training. His concept of the avant-garde called for a small elite of independent radical thinkers, artists, and architects to break away from the Académie des Beaux-Arts and the norms of society in order to forge new thoughts, ideas, and ways of looking at the world and art. He foresaw that this life would require the sacrifice of artists' reputations and sales of their work. Most avant-garde artists were neither as radical nor as extreme as Viollet-le-Duc, and, as we have seen, the relationship between the Académie des Beaux-Arts and the avant-garde was complex. Nonetheless, the idea was embraced by a number of artists who have come to characterize the period.

REALISM AND REVOLUTION

In the modern world of Paris at mid-century—a world plagued by violence, social unrest, overcrowding, and poverty—the grand, abstract themes of academic art seemed irrelevant to those thinkers who would come to represent the avant-garde. Rising food prices, high unemployment, political disenfranchisement, and government inaction led to a popular rebellion and the overthrow of the July Monarchy by a coalition of socialists, anarchists, and workers (see page 949), but conflicts among the reformers led to another uprising, in which more than 10,000 of the working poor were killed or injured in their struggle against the new government's forces. Against this social and political backdrop a new intellectual movement, known as Realism, originated in the novels of Émile Zola, Charles Dickens, Honoré de Balzac, and others who wrote about the lives of the urban lower classes. Realism in art was less of a style than a commitment to paint the modern world honestly, without turning away from the brutal truths of life for many ordinary people.

COURBET. Gustave Courbet (1819–1877) was one of the first artists to call himself "avant-garde" or "Realist." A big, blustery man, he was, in his own words, "not only a Socialist but a democrat and a Republican: in a word, a supporter of the whole Revolution." Born and raised near the Swiss border in the French town of Ornans, he moved to Paris in 1839. The street fighting in Paris in 1848 radicalized him and was a catalyst for two large canvases that have come to be regarded as the defining works of Realism. In 1849, he painted the first of these, **THE STONE BREAKERS** (FIG. 30–12).

At over 5 feet high and 8 feet wide, *The Stone Breakers* depicted a young boy and an old man crushing rock to produce

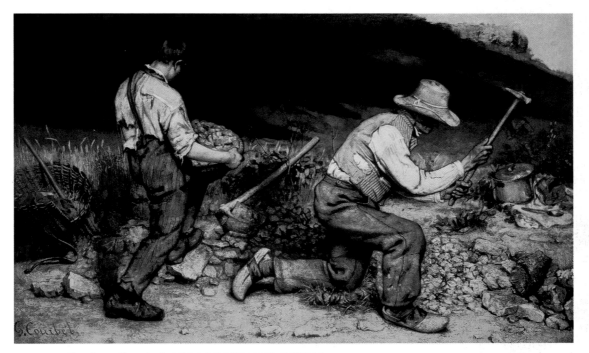

30-12 • Gustave Courbet THE STONE BREAKERS
1849. Oil on canvas, 5′3″ × 8′6″ (1.6 × 2.59 m). Formerly Gemäldegalerie, Dresden. Destroyed in World War II.

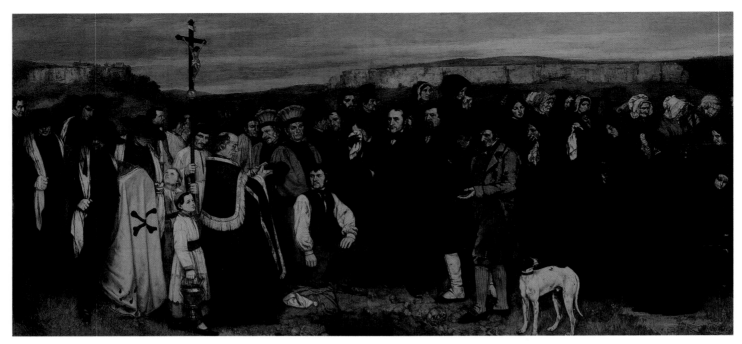

30–13 • Gustave Courbet A BURIAL AT ORNANS
1849. Oil on canvas, 10'3½" × 21'9" (3.1 × 6.6 m). Musée d'Orsay, Paris.

A Burial at Ornans was inspired by the 1848 funeral of Courbet's maternal grandfather, Jean-Antoine Oudot, a veteran of the Revolution of 1789. The painting is not meant as a record of that particular funeral, however, since Oudot is shown alive in profile at the extreme left of the canvas, his image adapted by Courbet from an earlier portrait. The two men to the right of the open grave, dressed not in contemporary but in late eighteenth-century clothing, are also revolutionaries of Oudot's generation. Their proximity to the grave suggests that one of their peers is being buried. Courbet's picture may be interpreted as linking the revolutions of 1789 and 1848, both of which sought to advance the cause of democracy in France.

the gravel used for roadbeds: the lowliest, most backbreaking form of work. Stonebreakers represent the disenfranchised peasants on whose backs modern life was being built. The younger figure strains to lift a large basket of rocks to the side of the road. Although he wears a tattered shirt and trousers, his boots are of modern make. The older man, almost broken by the work, pounds the rocks as he kneels. He wears the more traditional clothing of a peasant, including traditional wooden clogs. The boy represents a grim future, while the man signifies an increasingly obsolete rural past. Both are faceless laborers. Courbet described the inspiration for this painting:

> [N]ear Maisières [in the vicinity of Ornans], I stopped to consider two men breaking stones on the highway. It's rare to meet the most complete expression of poverty, so an idea for a picture came to me on the spot. I made an appointment with them at my studio for the next day … . On the one side is an old man, seventy … . On the other side is a young fellow … in his filthy tattered shirt … . Alas, in labor such as this, one's life begins that way, and it ends the same way.

Two things are clear from this description: Courbet intended to make a political statement, and he invited the men back to his studio so that he could study them more carefully, following academic methods.

By rendering labor on the scale of a history painting, Courbet intended to provoke. In academic art, monumental canvases on this scale were reserved for heroic subjects; by his work, Courbet suggests that even the lowest in society could be venerated as heroes. Instead of the usual highly finished academic style and inspiring message, his canvas reveals the brutality of modern life, his rough use of paint, dull, dark colors, awkward poses, and stilted composition making the scene feel realistic, gloomy, and degrading. In 1865, his friend, the anarchist philosopher Pierre-Joseph Proudhon (1809–1865), described *The Stone Breakers* as the first socialist picture ever painted, "an irony of our industrial civilization, which continually invents wonderful machines to perform all kinds of labor … yet is unable to liberate man from the most backbreaking toil." Courbet himself described the work as a depiction of "injustice."

Courbet began to paint **A BURIAL AT ORNANS (FIG. 30–13)** immediately after *The Stone Breakers*. Also exhibited at the 1850–1851 Salon, it is a vast painting, measuring roughly 10 by 21 feet, and depicts a burial on a life-size scale. A crush of people attend the graveside service. In the center, the gravedigger kneels over the gaping hole in the ground; to the left the clergy seem distracted and bored, perhaps reflecting the indifference of the institutional order of France after the 1848 revolution; to the right, the huddle of rural mourners, Courbet's heroes of modern life, weep in various states of grief, while in the highlighted foreground, closest to viewers, a bored altar boy and a distracted dog focus attention away from the central activity of the assembled crowd. Although painted on a scale befitting the funeral of a hero, Courbet's depiction has none of the idealization of traditional history painting; instead, it shows all the awkward, blundering numbness of a real funeral, with an emphasis on its brutal, physical reality. When shown at the Salon, the painting was attacked by critics who objected to the elevation of a provincial funeral to the scale of history painting, to Courbet's disrespect for the rules of academic composition, and even to the lack of any suggestion of the afterlife. Courbet had submitted his work to the Salon knowing that it would be denounced, however. He purposefully challenged the prescribed subjects, style, and finish of academic painting to establish his avant-garde position and to create controversy, which he embraced. When the 1854 Salon was cancelled and some of his works were refused for the International Exposition of 1855, Courbet had a temporary building constructed on rented land near the fair's Pavilion of Art and installed a show of his own works that he called the "Pavilion of Realism," clearly asserting his independence from the Salon as many other artists would also do later.

MILLET.   Similar claims of political radicalism were made about Jean-François Millet (1814–1875), although he denied them. Millet grew up on a farm but lived and worked in Paris between 1837 and 1848. He was awarded a state commission (with stipend) for his part in the 1848 revolution, allowing him to move to Barbizon, just south of Paris where he painted the hardships of the rural poor.

Among the best known of Millet's works is **THE GLEANERS** (**FIG. 30–14**), which shows three women gathering stray grain from the ground after harvest time. Despite its warm colors, the scene is one of extreme poverty. Gleaning was a form of relief offered to the rural poor by landowners, although it required hours of backbreaking work to collect enough wheat to make a single

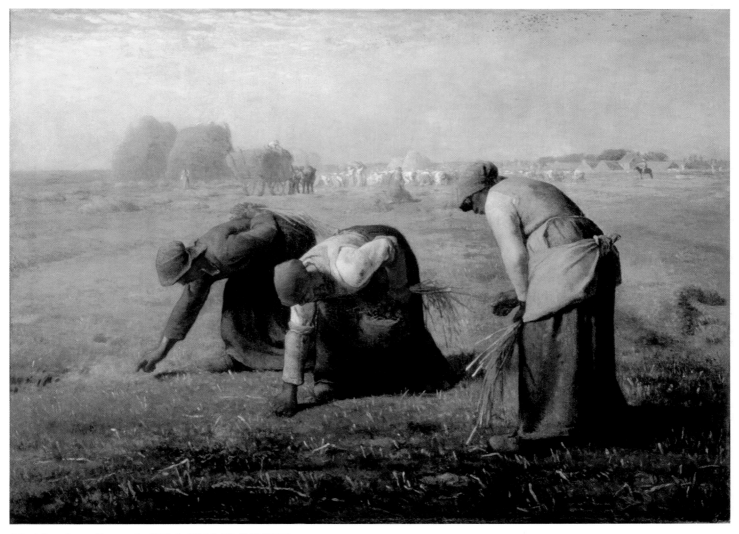

30–14 • Jean-François Millet THE GLEANERS
1857. Oil on canvas, 33 × 44″ (83.8 × 111.8 cm). Musée d'Orsay, Paris.

The Mass Dissemination of Art

Just as contemporary artists can distribute photographic reproductions of their work, in the eighteenth century, artists used engraving or etching to reproduce their work for distribution to a larger audience.

Works of art that won prizes or created controversy were often engraved for reproduction. Artists generally hired specialists to render their work in print form, and sold prints at bookstores or magazine stands. J. M. W. Turner used a team of engravers to capture the delicate tonal shadings of his works. An engraved copper plate could be printed upward of 100 times before the repeated pressing took its toll on image quality. In the later nineteenth century, artists increasingly used steel engraving, wood engraving, and lithography for printing. Those more durable surfaces could print up to 10,000 copies of an image without much loss of quality, though only a few artists experienced such demand.

One of the canniest self-marketers of the century was Alexandre Cabanel. After Napoleon III bought *The Birth of Venus*, the artist sold the reproduction rights to the art dealer Adolphe Goupil, who in turn hired other artists (in this case Adolphe Jourdan) to create at least two smaller-scale copies of the work (one of which is FIG. 30–4). After the original artist had approved the copies and signed them, the dealer used these as models for engravers who cut the steel plates. The dealer then sold the smaller versions of the work.

Another example of a work that was widely reproduced is Frederic Church's *Heart of the Andes* (1859), which was so popular in New York and London that it had to be protected by a rope; the painting was sold for $10,000, at that date the highest price ever paid for a painting by an American artist.

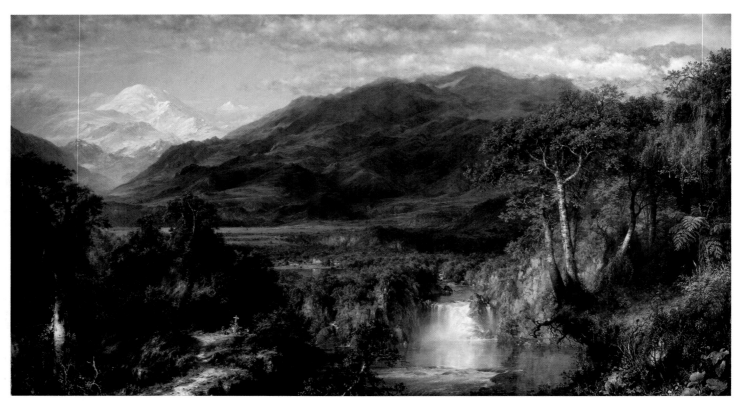

Frederic Church HEART OF THE ANDES
1859. Oil on canvas, 66⅛ × 119¼″ (168 × 302.9 cm). Metropolitan Museum of Art, New York. Bequest of Margaret E. Dows, 1909

loaf of bread. Two women are bent over to reach the tiny stalks of grain remaining on the ground. A third woman straightens to ease her back. When Millet exhibited the painting in 1857, critics noted its implicit social criticism and described the work as "Realist."

COROT.   Another, more romantic and less political approach to depicting rural life can be seen in the paintings of Jean-Baptiste-Camille Corot (1796–1875). Corot painted historical landscapes early in his career, but steadily moved toward more "naturalistic"

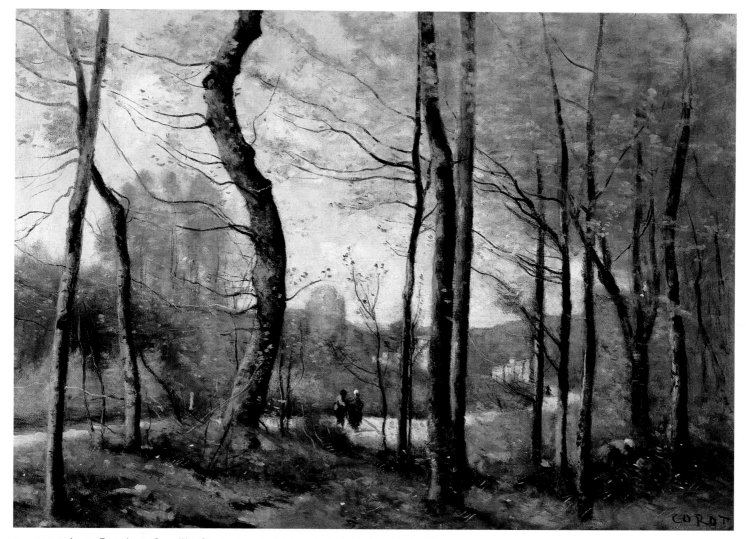

30–15 • Jean-Baptiste-Camille Corot FIRST LEAVES, NEAR MANTES
c. 1855. Oil on canvas, 13⅜ × 18⅛″ (34 × 46 cm). Carnegie Museum of Art, Pittsburgh, Pennsylvania.

and intimate scenes of rural France. **FIRST LEAVES, NEAR MANTES (FIG. 30–15)** depicts a scene infused with the soft mist of early spring in the woods. Corot's feathery brushwork representing the soft, new foliage contrasts with the stark, vertical tree trunks and branches, and, together with the fresh green of the new undergrowth, creates a perfectly balanced sense of a clear spring day. A man and woman pause to talk on the road winding from left to right through the painting, while a woman labors in the woods at the lower right. Corot invites us to imagine ourselves in the picture and feel the crisp, bright air. These images of peaceful country life held great appeal for Parisians who had experienced the chaos of the 1848 revolution and who lived in an increasingly crowded, noisy, and fast-paced metropolis.

BONHEUR.   Among the period's most popular painters of farm life was Rosa Bonheur (1822–1899), who was raised in Paris but was drawn to the countryside. Bonheur's success in what was then a male domain owed much to the socialist convictions of her parents, who belonged to a radical utopian sect, founded by the Comte de Saint-Simon (1760–1825), that believed not only in the equality of women but also in a future female Messiah. Bonheur's father, a drawing teacher, provided most of her artistic training.

Bonheur dedicated herself to realistic depictions of modern farm animals, which were becoming increasingly obsolete as technology and industrialization transformed farming. She studied her subjects intensely by reading zoology books and making detailed studies in stockyards and slaughterhouses. (To gain access to these all-male preserves, she received police permission to dress in men's clothing.) Her professional breakthrough came at the Salon of 1848, where she showed eight paintings and won a first-class medal. **THE HORSE FAIR (FIG. 30–16)**, painted in 1853, was based on a horse market near Salpêtrière, but was also partly inspired by the Parthenon marbles in London and by the art of Géricault. The scene portrays the display of splendid Percheron horses by their grooms, some walking obediently in their circle,

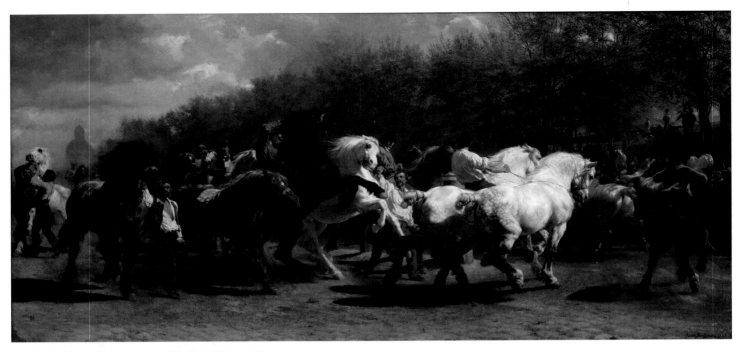

30–16 • Rosa Bonheur THE HORSE FAIR
1853–1855. Oil on canvas, 8′¼″ × 16′7½″. Metropolitan Museum of Art, New York.

EXPLORE MORE: Gain insight from a primary source on Rosa Bonheur **www.myartslab.com**

others rearing up, not yet quite broken. *The Horse Fair* has been interpreted by some scholars as a commentary on the lack of rights for women in the 1850s, but it was not read that way at the time. Although a monumental painting (at more than 8 by 16 feet) of farm animals, normally lower-ranking subjects, it was highly praised at the 1848 Salon. When the painting later toured throughout Britain and the United States, members of the public paid to see it. It was widely disseminated in print form on both sides of the Atlantic, and was purchased for the new Metropolitan Museum of Art in New York in 1889. Bonheur became so famous working within the Salon system that in 1865 she received France's highest award, membership in the Legion of Honor, becoming the first woman to be awarded its Grand Cross.

THE PAINTER OF MODERN LIFE: MANET

Along with the concept of the avant-garde, the second great concept that shaped art in France at this time was the idea of modernity. The experience of modernity—of constant change and renewal—is linked to the dynamic nature of city life. The themes of the modern city and of political engagement with modern life in an industrialized world are key to understanding the development of painting and literature in France in the second half of the nineteenth century.

Poet and essayist Charles Baudelaire argued that, in order to speak for their time and place, artists' work had to be infused with the idea of modernity. Modernity called for modern urban subjects and a new approach to seeing and representing the visual world—a break with the past in order to better comprehend and comment on the present. Especially after the invention of photography, art was expected to offer new ways of representing reality. One who rose to the challenge was the French painter Édouard Manet (1832–1883).

LE DÉJEUNER SUR L'HERBE. At mid-century, the Académie des Beaux-Arts increasingly opened Salon exhibitions to non-academic artists, resulting in a surge in the number of works submitted to, and inevitably rejected by, the Salon jury. In 1863, the jury turned down nearly 3,000 works, leading to a storm of protest. In response, Napoleon III tried to mediate the dispute by ordering an exhibition of the refused work called the *Salon des Refusés* ("Salon of the Rejected Ones"). Featured in it was Manet's painting **LE DÉJEUNER SUR L'HERBE (THE LUNCHEON ON THE GRASS) (FIG. 30–17).** A well-born Parisian who had studied in the early 1850s with the independent artist Thomas Couture (1815–1879), Manet had by the early 1860s developed a strong commitment to Realism, largely as a result of his friendship with the poet Baudelaire who called for a "Painter of Modern Life." Manet's *Le Déjeuner sur l'Herbe* invokes Baudelaire's spirit, and in doing so scandalized contemporary viewers all the way up to Napoleon III himself. Ironically, the resulting *succès de scandale* ("success from scandal") helped establish Manet's career as a radical artist.

The most scandalous aspect of the painting was the "immorality" of Manet's theme: a suburban picnic featuring two fully dressed bourgeois gentlemen (in fact, Manet's brother, wearing the hat of a student, and his brother-in-law), a naked woman to the front left, and another scantily dressed woman in the background. Manet's

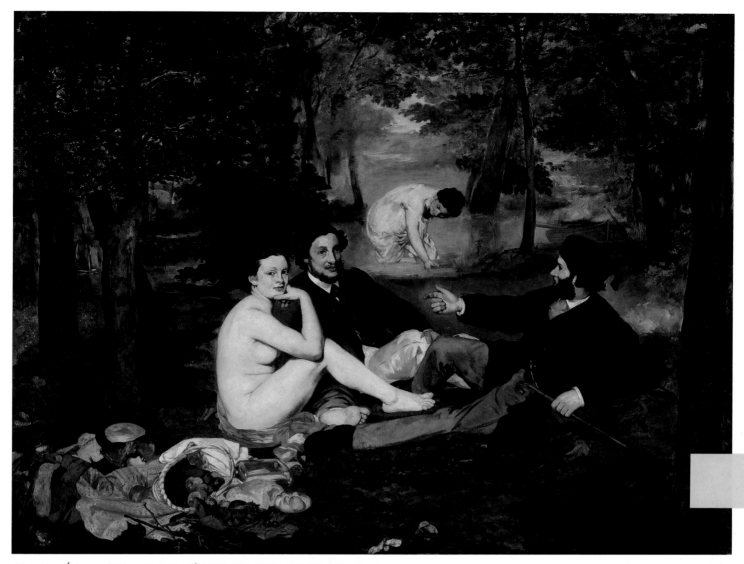

30–17 • Édouard Manet LE DÉJEUNER SUR L'HERBE (THE LUNCHEON ON THE GRASS)
1863. Oil on canvas, 7′ × 8′8″ (2.13 × 2.64 m). Musée d'Orsay, Paris.

audience assumed that these women were prostitutes, and the men their customers. Equally shocking were its references to important works of art of the past, which Académie des Beaux-Arts artists were expected to make, combined with its crude, unvarnished modernity. In contrast, one of the paintings that gathered most renown at the official Salon in that year was Alexandre Cabanel's *Birth of Venus* (SEE FIG. 30–4), which, because it presented nudity in a conventionally acceptable, Classical environment, was favorably reviewed and quickly entered the collection of Napoleon III.

Manet apparently conceived of *Le Déjeuner sur l'Herbe* as a modern version of a Venetian Renaissance painting in the Louvre, the *Pastoral Concert*, then believed to be by Giorgione but now attributed to both Titian and Giorgione or to Titian exclusively (SEE FIG. 20–22). Manet's composition also refers to a Marcantonio Raimondi engraving of Raphael's *The Judgment of Paris*—itself based on Classical reliefs of river gods and nymphs. Manet's modern interpretation of the scene, however, combined with his

modern style, was intentionally provocative. The stark lighting of his nude, the cool colors, the flat, cutout quality of his figures who seem as if they are set against a painted backdrop, all suggest the seamier side of city life. Presenting this under a flimsy guise of academic art underlined Manet's subversiveness.

OLYMPIA.   Shortly after completing *Le Déjeuner sur l'Herbe*, Manet painted **OLYMPIA (FIG. 30–18)**, its title alluding to a socially ambitious prostitute of the same name in a novel and play by Alexandre Dumas the Younger. Like *Le Déjeuner sur l'Herbe*, Manet's *Olympia* was based on a Venetian Renaissance source, Titian's "*Venus*" *of Urbino* (SEE FIG. 20–24), which Manet had earlier copied in Florence. At first, his painting appears to pay homage to Titian's in its subject matter (at that time believed to be a Venetian courtesan) and composition. However, Manet made his modern counterpart the very antithesis of Titian's. Titian's female is curvaceous and softly rounded, Manet's is angular and flattened;

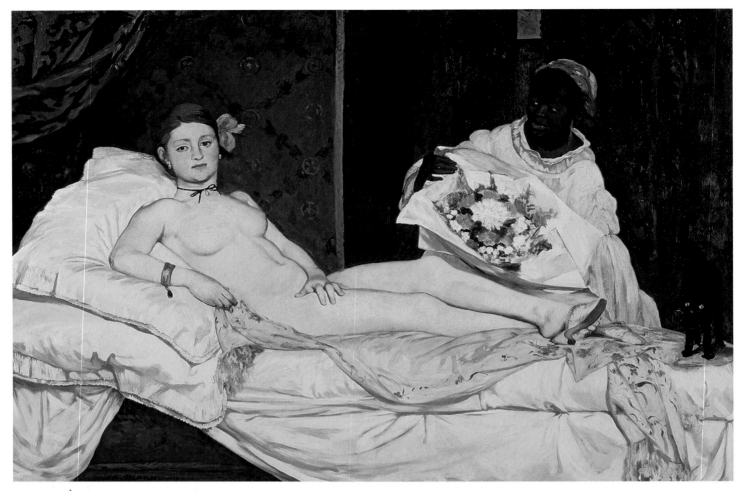

30–18 • Édouard Manet OLYMPIA
1863. Oil on canvas, 4′3″ × 6′2¼″ (1.31 × 1.91 m). Musée du Louvre, Paris.

Titian's colors are warm and rich, Manet's are cold and harsh, like a photograph; Titian's Venus looks coyly at the male spectator, Manet's Olympia appears coldly indifferent. Our relationship with Olympia is underscored by the reaction of her cat, which—unlike the sleeping dog in the Titian—arches its back at us. Finally, instead of looking up at us, Olympia gazes down at us, indicating that she is in the position of power and that we are subordinate, akin to the black servant at the foot of the bed who brings her a bouquet of flowers. In reversing the Titian, Manet overturns the entire tradition of the accommodating female nude. Not surprisingly, conservative critics vilified *Olympia* when it was exhibited at the Salon of 1865.

Manet generally submitted his work to every Salon, but when several were rejected in 1867, he did as Courbet had done in 1855: He asserted his independence by renting a hall nearby and staging his own show. This made Manet the unofficial leader of a group of progressive artists and writers who gathered at the Café Guerbois in the Montmartre district of Paris. Among the artists who frequented the café were Degas, Monet, Pissarro, and Renoir, all of whom would soon exhibit together as the Impressionists and follow Manet's lead in challenging academic conventions.

LATER WORKS. Manet worked closely with all of these artists and frequently painted themes similar to the Impressionists, even occasionally employing a lighter Impressionist palette of colors, but always retaining his previous dedication to the portrayal of modern urban life. In 1874, for instance, he painted **BOATING (FIG. 30–19)** in which two figures sit in a boat on a sunny summer day. The man, a *canotier* or lower-class boatman, is dressed in the standard uniform of white round-neck shirt and pants with a flat straw hat (boater). He has the helm of the boat. The young girl with him sits uneasily in the boat, neither comfortable in her position nor in her dress. The fact that she has no chaperone hints at impropriety. Despite the apparent Impressionist subject and colors, there is a gritty urban realism to Manet's painting that is in stark contrast to Morrisot's more idyllic and upper-class *Summer's Day* (SEE FIG. 30–30).

Manet's *A Bar at the Folies-Bergère* (see "A Closer Look," page 980) returns to the complex theme of gender and class relations in modern urban life. Here is a hard-working young girl serving drinks at a bar in the famous nightclub. She has an unfashionably ruddy face and hands scrubbed raw. In the glittering light created by the electric bulbs and mirrors of the café-concert frequented by Manet and his compatriots she seems stiff and distant. She

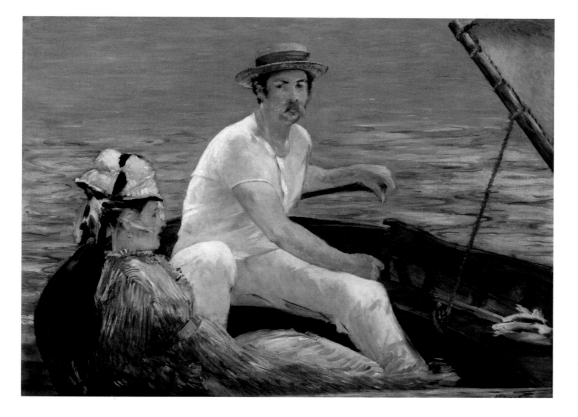

30–19 • Édouard Manet
BOATING
1874. Oil on canvas, 38¼ × 51¼"
(97.2 × 130.2 cm).
Metropolitan Museum of Art,
New York. H. O. Havemeyer
Collection, 1929

refuses to meet the gaze of her client. The barmaid is at once detached from the scene and part of it, one of the many items on display for purchase. This image is about sexualized looking and the barmaid's uneasy reflection in the mirror, which seems to acknowledge that both her class and gender expose her to visual and even sexual consumption.

RESPONSES TO REALISM BEYOND FRANCE

Artists of other nations embraced their own forms of realism in the period after 1850 as the social effects of urbanization and industrialization began to be felt in their countries. While these artists did not label themselves as Realists like their contemporaries in France, they did share their interest in presenting an unflinching look at grim reality and the difficult lives of the working poor.

REALISM IN RUSSIA: THE WANDERERS.   In Russia, a variant on French Realism developed in relation to a new concern for the peasantry. In 1861, the tsar abolished serfdom, emancipating Russia's peasants from the virtual slavery they had endured on the large estates of the aristocracy. Two years later, a group of painters inspired by the emancipation declared allegiance both to the peasant cause and to freedom from the St. Petersburg Academy of Art, which had controlled Russian art since 1754. Rejecting what they considered the escapist aesthetics of the Academy, the members of the group dedicated themselves to a socially useful realism. Committed to bringing art to the people in traveling exhibitions, they called themselves "The Wanderers." By the late 1870s, members of the group, like their counterparts in music and

literature, had also joined a nationalist movement to reassert what they considered to be an authentic Russian culture rooted in the traditions of the peasantry, rejecting the Western European customs that had long predominated among the Russian aristocracy.

Ilya Repin (1844–1930), who attended the St. Petersburg Academy and won a scholarship to study in Paris, joined the Wanderers in 1878 after his return to Russia. He painted a series of works illustrating the social injustices then prevailing in his homeland, including **BARGEHAULERS ON THE VOLGA (FIG. 30–20)**, which features a wretched group of peasants condemned to the brutal work of pulling ships up the Volga River. To heighten our sympathy for these workers, Repin placed a youth in the center of the group, a young man who will soon be as worn out as his companions unless something is done to rescue him. Thus the painting is a call to action.

REALISM IN THE UNITED STATES.   Realism was not a term used in the United States, but there were several kinds of realism in American art. Thomas Eakins (1844–1916), for instance, made a series of uncompromising paintings that were criticized for their controversial subject matter. Born in Philadelphia, Eakins trained at the Pennsylvania Academy of the Fine Arts, but since he regarded the training in anatomy as not rigorous enough—lacking realism, as he might have put it—he supplemented his training at the Jefferson Medical College nearby. He later studied at the École des Beaux-Arts in Paris and then spent six months in Spain, where he encountered the profound realism of Baroque artists Jusepe de Ribera and Diego Velázquez (SEE FIGS. 22–19, 22–21). After he returned

A Bar at the Folies-Bergère

by Édouard Manet, 1881–1882. Oil on canvas. 37¾ × 51¼″ (95.9 × 130 cm).
Courtauld Gallery, London. P.1934.SC.234

In the late nineteenth century, the café-concert was frequented by avant-garde artists such as Degas, Seurat, and Manet. The Folies-Bergère was one of the largest of these café-concerts in Paris, offering circuses, musicals, and vaudeville acts. Note the legs of a trapeze artist who is part of the spectacle to the upper left.

Reflected in the mirror are members of the elegant crowd who have come to the performances at the Folies-Bergère. The men are dressed in top hats and the women in rich costumes. Though their opera glasses they observe lazily the many glittering spectacles performed for their benefit as the electric light dances off the crystal chandelier behind the young girl's head.

The barmaid looks out of the painting at us as if we are her next customer, but she stands stiffly and formally, neither acknowledging nor smiling at us; her sleeves are rolled up and she seems weary from her work. On the other hand, she seems to lean forward to engage in conversation with the top-hatted client in her mirror reflection, suggesting either Manet's intention to create an ambiguous narrative or a curved mirror.

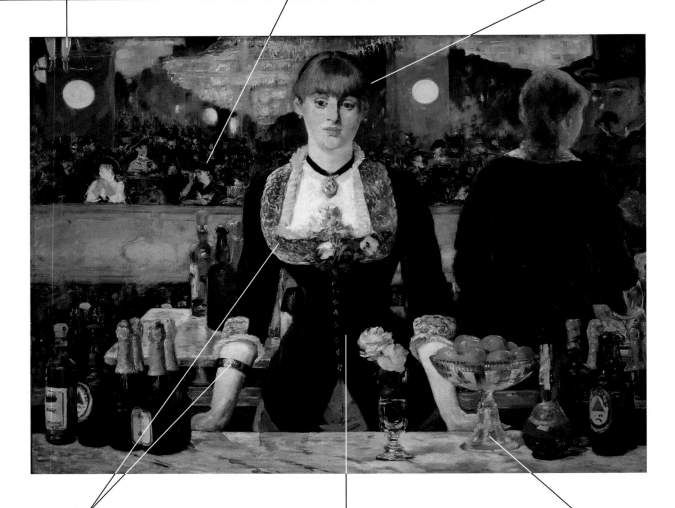

The bangles and lace at the barmaid's wrists and neck suggest a rise in the availability of consumption goods in the shops and department stores of the modern city, perhaps implying that the barmaid, who displays herself like the luscious oranges to the right, is also available for purchase.

Manet presents the Folies-Bergère as a place where the enjoyments of alcohol, the circus and vaudeville, and even sexual transactions take place. The weary girl stands at the bar, barely differentiated from her background, like one of so many glittering objects on display, to be consumed both visually and sexually.

On the marble bar-top Manet has spread a glorious still life of liquor bottles, tangerines, and flowers to entice the customer.

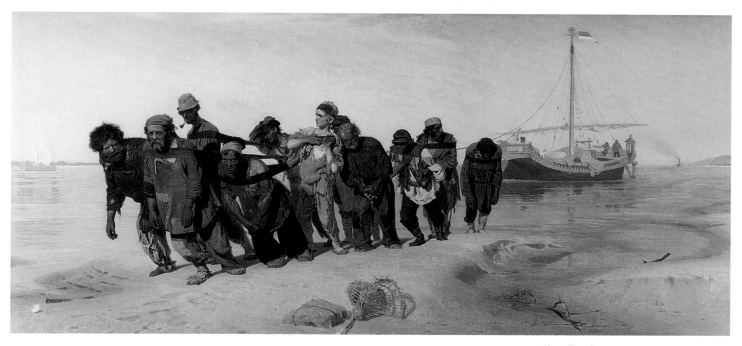

30-20 • Ilya Repin BARGEHAULERS ON THE VOLGA
1870–1873. Oil on canvas, 4'3¾" × 9'3" (1.3 × 2.81 m). State Russian Museum, St. Petersburg.

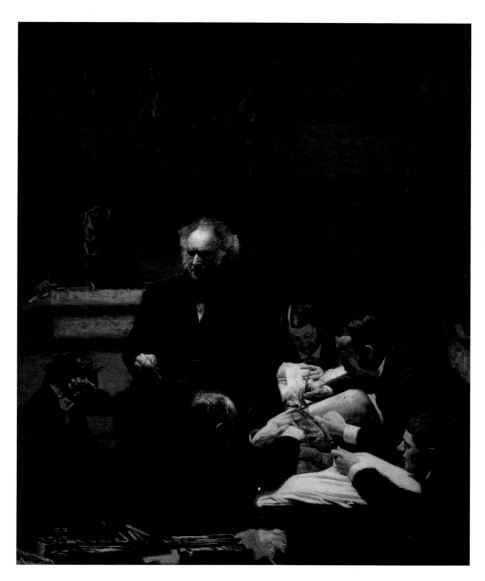

to Philadelphia in 1870, he specialized in frank portraits and scenes of everyday life whose lack of conventional charm generated little popular interest. But he was a charismatic teacher, and was soon appointed director of the Pennsylvania Academy.

THE GROSS CLINIC (FIG. 30–21) was one of Eakins's most controversial paintings. Although created specifically for the 1876 Philadelphia centennial show, it was rejected for the fine-art exhibition and relegated to the display area for scientific and medical inquiry. The painting shows Dr. Samuel David Gross performing an operation that he pioneered, as

30-21 • Thomas Eakins THE GROSS CLINIC
1875. Oil on canvas, 8' × 6'5" (2.44 × 1.98 m). Philadelphia Museum of Art, Pennsylvania.

Eakins, who taught anatomy and figure drawing at the Pennsylvania Academy of the Fine Arts, disapproved of the academic technique of drawing from plaster casts. In 1879, he said, "At best, they are only imitations, and an imitation of an imitation cannot have so much life as an imitation of nature itself." He added, "The Greeks did not study the antique … the draped figures in the Parthenon pediment were modeled from life, undoubtedly."

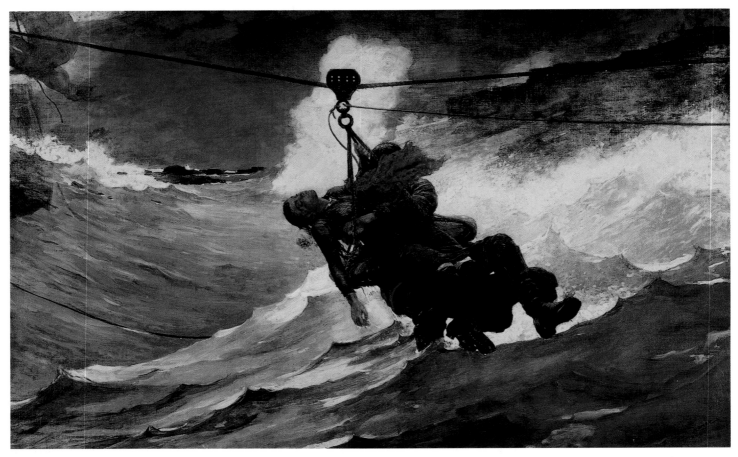

30-22 • Winslow Homer THE LIFE LINE
1884. Oil on canvas, 28¾ × 44⅝″ (73 × 113.3 cm). Philadelphia Museum of Art, Pennsylvania. The George W. Elkins Collection

In the early sketches for this work, the man's face was visible. The decision to cover it focuses more attention
not only on the victim, but also on the true hero, the mechanical apparatus known as the "breeches buoy."

he pauses to lecture to students taking notes in the background. The figures assisting the surgery are highlighted, but the rest of the operating theater is in deep shadow. Dr. Gross is dressed in street clothes, typical surgical attire before sterile procedure was introduced, and as he pauses he reveals his bloody hand. The stockinged feet of the patient, a young boy, are visible; his mother shields her eyes in horror. In the mid nineteenth century, surgeons were regarded with fear, especially teaching surgeons who frequently thought of the poor as objects on which to practice; for the poor, a visit to the hospital frequently meant death. Eakins captures the sinister aspect of Gross's fearsome skill. But the dramatic light that evokes both Rembrandt and the Spanish Baroque is significant because it illuminates the forehead of the doctor, thus acknowledging the intellect of this brilliant surgeon.

Winslow Homer (1836–1910) also painted with an unadorned realism later in his life. Born in Boston, he began his career as a 21-year-old freelance illustrator for popular periodicals such as *Harper's Weekly*, which sent him to cover the Civil War in 1862. In 1867, after a ten-month sojourn in France, he returned to make painted versions of the nostalgic rural scenes that had figured

in his illustrations for magazines. He developed a commitment to depicting the working poor after he spent 1881–1882 in a tiny English fishing village on the rugged North Sea coast. Moved by the hard lives and strength of character of the people there, he turned from idyllic subjects to themes of heroic struggle against natural adversity. In England, he was particularly impressed by the "breeches buoy," a mechanical apparatus used for rescue at sea. During the summer of 1883, he made sketches of one imported by the lifesaving crew in Atlantic City, New Jersey. The following year he painted **THE LIFE LINE** (FIG. 30–22), which depicts a coastguard saving a shipwrecked woman with the use of a breeches buoy—a testament not simply to valor but also to ingenuity.

The sculptor Edmonia Lewis (1845–c. 1911) was born in New York State to a Chippewa mother and an African-American father; she was orphaned at the age of 4, and raised by her mother's family. As a teenager, with the help of abolitionists, she attended Oberlin College, the first college in the United States to grant degrees to women, and then moved to Boston. Her highly successful busts and medallions of abolitionist leaders and Civil War heroes financed her move to Rome in 1867.

Galvanized by the struggle for equality of newly freed slaves, Lewis created **FOREVER FREE** (**FIG. 30–23**) as a memorial to the Emancipation Proclamation. Although it retains Neoclassical forms, this sculpture addresses a modern issue—the end of slavery in America. The standing African-American man raises his hand with the broken shackles still attached; next to him a woman kneels and prays in thanks. This sculpture not only celebrates emancipation, but also subtly reflects white attitudes towards women and people of color. Lewis creates her female as less racialized and more submissive than her male counterpart so that

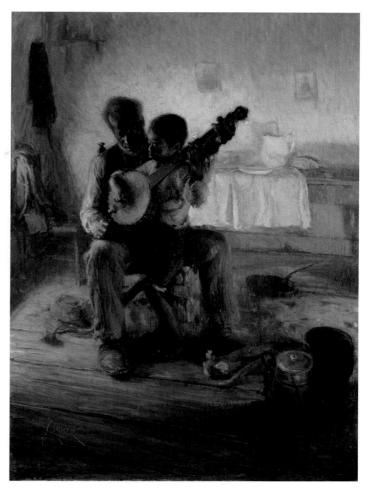

30-24 • Henry Ossawa Tanner THE BANJO LESSON
1893. Oil on canvas, 49 × 35½″ (124.4 × 90 cm). Hampton University Museum, Virginia.

the figure would better reflect the concept of ideal womanhood and be more appealing to white audiences.

Henry Ossawa Tanner (1859–1937) was the most successful African-American painter of the late nineteenth and early twentieth centuries. The son of a bishop in the African Methodist Episcopal Church, Tanner grew up in Philadelphia, sporadically studied art with Thomas Eakins at the Pennsylvania Academy of the Fine Arts between 1879 and 1885, and then worked as a photographer and drawing teacher in Atlanta. In 1891, he moved to Paris to further his academic training. In the early 1890s, Tanner began making paintings with African-American themes, as he put it, to paint the "serious and pathetic side of life." Tanner's **THE BANJO LESSON** (**FIG. 30–24**) shows an elderly man teaching a young boy seated on his lap to play the banjo. Both are serious and intent. Their poverty fades as they concentrate together. Mutuality, respect, patience, and attention connect the man and child. Although the banjo player was a common derogatory caricature of African-Americans, Tanner takes up the theme and transforms it into a subject of dignity and pride. He turned to biblical painting after a trip to Palestine in 1897.

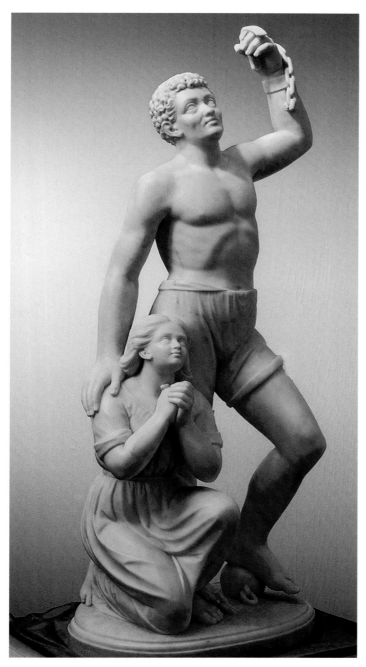

30-23 • Edmonia Lewis FOREVER FREE
1867. Marble, 41¼ × 22 × 17″ (104.8 × 55 × 43.2 cm). Howard University Art Gallery, Washington, D.C.

IMPRESSIONISM

The generation of French painters maturing around 1870 also painted modern urban subjects, but from a perspective very different from that of Manet and the Realists. These artists painted the upper middle class at leisure in the countryside and in the city, and although several members of this group painted rural scenes, their point of view tended to be that of a city person.

In April 1874, a group of artists, including Paul Cézanne, Edgar Degas, Claude Monet, Berthe Morisot, Camille Pissarro, and Pierre-Auguste Renoir, exhibited together in Paris under the title of the Société Anonyme des Artistes Peintres, Sculpteurs, Graveurs, etc. (Anonymous Corporation of Artist-Painters, Sculptors, Engravers, etc.). Pissarro organized the group along the lines advocated by anarchists such as Proudhon, who urged citizens to band together into self-supporting grass-roots organizations, rather than relying on state-sanctioned institutions. Pissarro envisioned the Société as a mutual aid group for artists who opposed the state-funded Salons. While the Impressionists are the best remembered of its members today, at the time the group included artists working in several styles. All 30 participants agreed not to submit anything that year to the Salon, which had in the past often rejected their work. This exhibition was a declaration of independence from the Académie and a bid to gain the public's attention directly.

While their exhibition received some positive reviews, one critic, Louis Leroy, writing in the satirical journal *Charivari*, seized upon the title of Monet's painting *Impression: Sunrise* (SEE FIG. 30–26), and dubbed the entire exhibition "impressionist." Leroy sought to ridicule the fast, open brushstrokes and unfinished look of some of the paintings, but Monet and his colleagues liked the name and kept it as it aptly described their aim to render the fleeting moment in paint. Seven more Impressionist exhibitions were held between 1876 and 1886, with the membership of the group varying slightly on each occasion; only Pissarro participated in all eight shows. The relative success of these exhibitions prompted other artists to organize their own alternatives to the Salon, and by 1900 the independent exhibition and gallery system had all but replaced the Salon system in Paris. This in turn brought to an end the Académie des Beaux-Arts' control over the display of art and thus centrally determined artistic "standards" effectively ended.

THE LANDSCAPE

Claude Monet (1840–1926) was a leading exponent of Impressionism. Born in Paris but raised in the port city of Le Havre, he trained briefly with an academic teacher but soon established his own studio. His friend Charles-François Daubigny urged him to "be faithful to his impression" and suggested that he create a floating studio on a boat and paint *en plein air* (outdoors). Monet's early works depict a side of modernity that the Realists did not show. Like other Impressionists, he was more interested in creating a modern painting style than in producing biting social commentary, although his thematic focus was also modern life. The Impressionists celebrated the semi-rural pleasures of outings to the suburbs

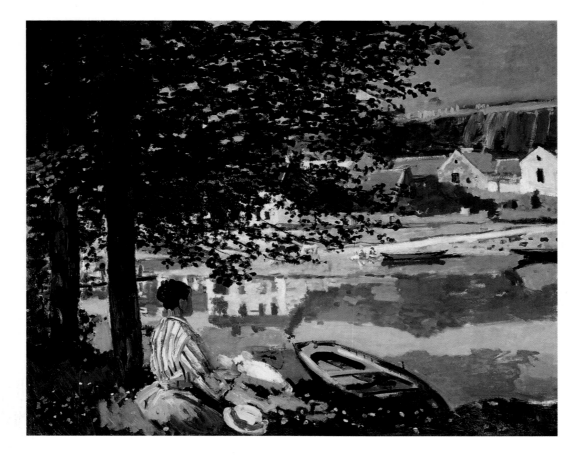

**30-25 • Claude Monet
ON THE BANK OF THE SEINE, BENNECOURT**
1868. Oil on canvas, 32 × 39⅔″ (81.5 × 100.7 cm). Art Institute of Chicago. Potter Palmer Collection, 1922.427

EXPLORE MORE: Gain insight from a primary source on Claude Monet **www.myartslab.com**

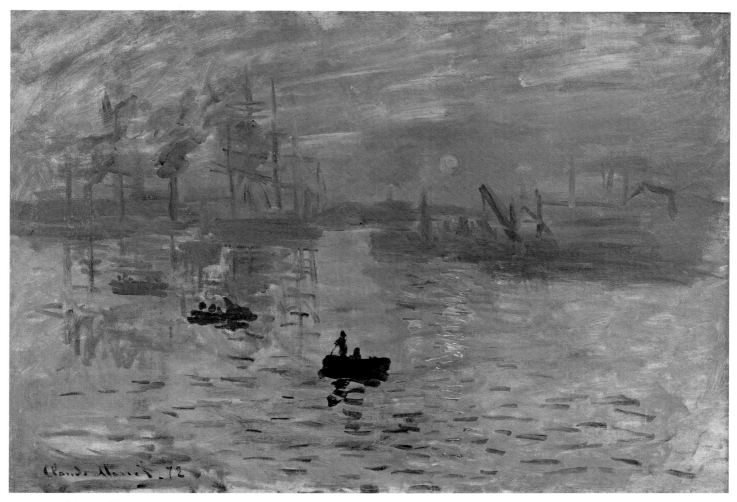

30-26 • Claude Monet IMPRESSION: SUNRISE
1872. Oil on canvas, 19 × 24⅜″ (48 × 63 cm). Musée Marmottan, Paris.

afforded by the Paris train system. Few early works depict locations far from Paris; most feature the Parisian middle and upper middle classes out walking, boating, and visiting the fashionable new parks in the city or at places just outside of town.

Many of Monet's early works include shimmering expanses of water, such as **ON THE BANK OF THE SEINE, BENNECOURT (FIG. 30–25)**, a scene of a young woman in summer, sitting under trees on a riverbank, a small row boat on the river in front of her. At first we think this is a country scene; on closer inspection, however, we see a landing and several buildings on the far bank, and other boats on the water. It is quite a crowded scene, but the intense brightness of Monet's colors makes the first impression one of pure sunlight. (One critic even complained that the painting made his eyes hurt.) To achieve this effect, Monet dispensed entirely with underpainting as taught by the Académie des Beaux-Arts, instead applying flat expanses of pure color directly onto the canvas, unmixed and straight from the tube. The invention of the collapsible metal paint tube in 1841 led to the manufacture of ready-to-use oil colors that painters could conveniently pack and take with them. No longer confined to grinding colors in a studio,

artists like Monet could now paint anywhere. Eschewing the tedium of the academic program for painting, Monet sought to capture the play of light quickly, before it changed. This was a new, modern landscape. As he said: "The Romantics have had their day."

In the summer of 1870, the Franco-Prussian War broke out and Monet fled to London, where he spent time with Pissarro and his future art dealer, Paul Durand-Ruel. The disastrous loss of the major industrial regions of Alsace and Lorraine to Prussia at the end of the war had an equally disastrous impact on the French economy. In Paris, for two months between March and May 1871, the working classes rose up and established the Commune, a working-class city government, the suppression of which led to an estimated 20,000 dead and 7,500 imprisoned. The horror rocked Paris and made people fearful. Courbet was imprisoned for a short time and, in artists' circles, the fear of being branded as an enemy of the state sent a chill through everyone. After 1871, overt political commentary in French art diminished, and the challenge of the avant-garde was expressed increasingly as a rebellion in style.

In 1873, just after returning to Paris, Monet painted **IMPRESSION: SUNRISE (FIG. 30–26)**, a view of the sun rising in

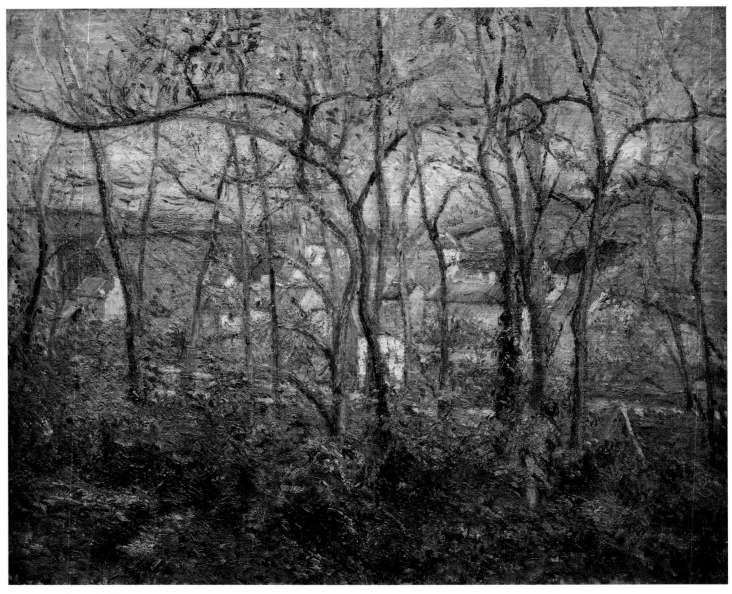

30-27 • Camille Pissarro WOODED LANDSCAPE AT L'HERMITAGE, PONTOISE
1878. Oil on canvas, 18⅝₁₆ × 22⅛₁₆″ (46.5 × 56 cm). Nelson-Atkins Museum of Art, Kansas City, Missouri. Gift of Dr. and Mrs. Nicholas S. Pickard

the morning fog over the harbor at Le Havre. The painting is rendered almost entirely as color alone. The foreground is eliminated and the horizon line disappears among steamships and docks in the background; forms and atmosphere are shimmering shapes in color. We find our bearings in this painting slowly, but once we do, we "feel" the scene with our eyes. Monet registers the intensity and shifting forms of a first sketch and renders it as the final work of art. The criticism leveled against his paintings was that they were not "finished." The American painter Lilla Cabot Perry, who befriended Monet in his later years, recalled him telling her:

> When you go out to paint, try to forget what objects you have before you—a tree, a house, a field, or whatever. Merely think, Here is a little square of blue, here an oblong of pink,

here a streak of yellow, and paint it just as it looks to you, the exact color and shape, until it gives your own naive impression of the scene before you.

Monet's friend and fellow artist Camille Pissarro (1830–1903) offered a new image of the landscape in a style similar to Monet's. He painted scenes where the urban meets the rural; some of his paintings portray the rural landscape alone, but many show urban visitors to the countryside or small towns or factories embedded in the land as the city encroaches upon them. Born in the Dutch West Indies to French parents and raised near Paris, Pissarro studied art in Paris during the 1850s and early 1860s. In 1870, while he and Monet lived in London, Pissarro embraced the ideas that would later become known as Impressionism. The two artists worked together in England, trying to capture what Pissarro described as "plein air light and fugitive effects." The impact on both painters was a lightening of color intensity and hue, and a loosening of brushstroke.

Following his return to France, Pissarro settled in Pontoise, a small, hilly village northwest of Paris where he worked for most of the 1870s in an Impressionist style, using high-keyed color and short brushstrokes to capture fleeting qualities of light and atmosphere. In the late 1870s, his painting became more visually complex and the colors darkened again. His **WOODED LANDSCAPE AT L'HERMITAGE, PONTOISE (FIG. 30–27)**, for instance, has a foreground composition of trees that screens the view of a rural path and village behind, flattening space and even partly masking the figure at the lower right. Pissarro applies his paint thickly here, with a multitude of short, multi-directional brushstrokes.

THE FIGURE

In contrast, the Impressionist painter Pierre-Auguste Renoir (1841–1919) focused most of his attention on figure painting, producing mostly images of the upper middle class at leisure. When he met Monet at the École des Beaux-Arts in 1862, he was in fact working as a figure painter. Monet encouraged him to lighten his palette and to paint outdoors, and by the mid 1870s Renoir was combining a spontaneous handling of natural light with animated figural compositions. In his **MOULIN DE LA GALETTE (FIG. 30–28)**, for example, Renoir depicts crowds dancing in dappled sunlight that falls through the trees. The Moulin de la Galette (the "Pancake Mill"), in the Montmartre section of Paris, was an old-fashioned Sunday afternoon dance hall, which opened its outdoor courtyard during good weather. In this painting, Renoir has glamorized the working-class clientele of the dance hall by placing his artist friends and their models in their midst. These attractive people are shown in attitudes of relaxed congeniality, smiling, dancing, and chatting. He underscores the innocence of their flirtations by including children in the painting in the lower left, while emphasizing the ease of their relations through the relaxed informality of the scene. The overall mood is knit together by sunlight falling through the

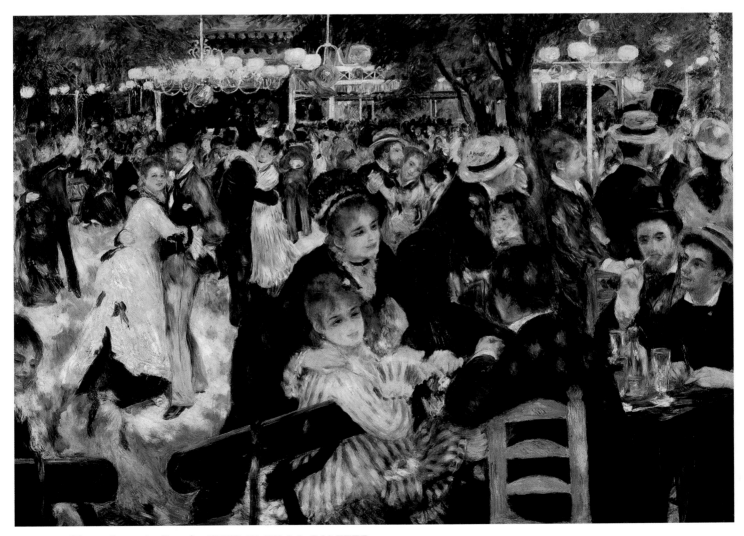

30-28 • Pierre-Auguste Renoir **MOULIN DE LA GALETTE**
1876. Oil on canvas, 4′3½″ × 5′9″ (1.31 × 1.75 m). Musée d'Orsay, Paris.

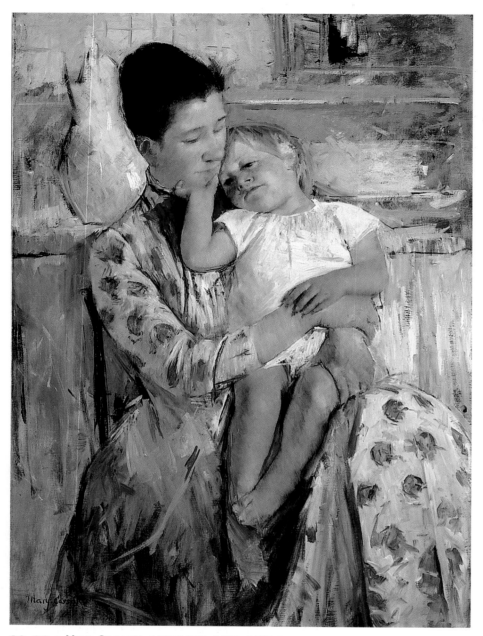

30–29 • Mary Cassatt MOTHER AND CHILD
c. 1890. Oil on canvas, 35½ × 25⅜" (90.2 × 64.5 cm). Wichita Art Museum, Kansas.

academic training, eventually settling in France. The realism of the figure paintings she exhibited at the Salons of the early and mid 1870s attracted the attention of Degas, who invited her to participate in the fourth Impressionist exhibition in 1879. Although she, like Degas, remained a studio painter and printmaker, her distaste for what she called the "tyranny" of the Salon jury system made her one of the group's staunchest supporters.

Cassatt focused her artistic career on the world she knew best: the domestic and social life of upper-middle-class women. Around 1890 she painted **MOTHER AND CHILD (FIG. 30–29)**, one of many representations of the theme in her career. The painting shows the intimate contact between a mother and child after a bath and just before the child falls asleep. The drowsy face and flushed cheeks of the child and the weight of its limbs have a natural quality to them, even though the space occupied by the figures seems flattened. The solidly modeled forms of the hands and faces contrast with the strong, broad, and unfinished quality of the brushstrokes of the lower part of the mother's dress and the background. Cassatt elevates this small vignette of modern life into a homage to motherhood. Though she lived as an expatriate, Cassatt retained her connections in the United States, and when her friends and relatives came to visit she encouraged them to buy art by the Impressionists, thus creating a market for their work in the United States even before one developed in France.

The French artist Berthe Morisot (1841–1895) also defied societal conventions to become a professional painter, and her work also took as its main subject the female figure. Morisot and her sister, Edma, copied paintings in the Louvre and studied with several teachers, including Corot, in the late 1850s and early 1860s. The sisters exhibited their art in the five Salons between 1864 and 1868, the year they met Manet. In 1869, Edma married and gave up painting to devote herself to domestic duties, but Berthe continued painting, even after her 1874 marriage to Manet's brother, Eugène, and the birth of their daughter in 1879. Morisot sent nine paintings to the first exhibition of the Impressionists in 1874 and showed her work in all but one of their subsequent shows.

As a respectable bourgeois lady, Berthe Morisot was not free to prowl the city looking for modern subjects, and, like Cassatt's,

trees and Renoir's soft brushwork weaving blues and purples through the crowd and around the canvas. This idyllic image of a carefree time and place encapsulates Renoir's idea of the essence of art: "For me a picture should be a pleasant thing, joyful and pretty—yes pretty! There are quite enough unpleasant things in life without the need for us to manufacture more."

The American expatriate Mary Cassatt (1844–1926; SEE FIG. 30–32) also exhibited her work with the Impressionists and, like Renoir, became highly skilled in compositions that focused on the figure. Born near Pittsburgh to a well-to-do family, she studied at the Pennsylvania Academy of the Fine Arts in Philadelphia between 1861 and 1865, and then moved to Paris for further

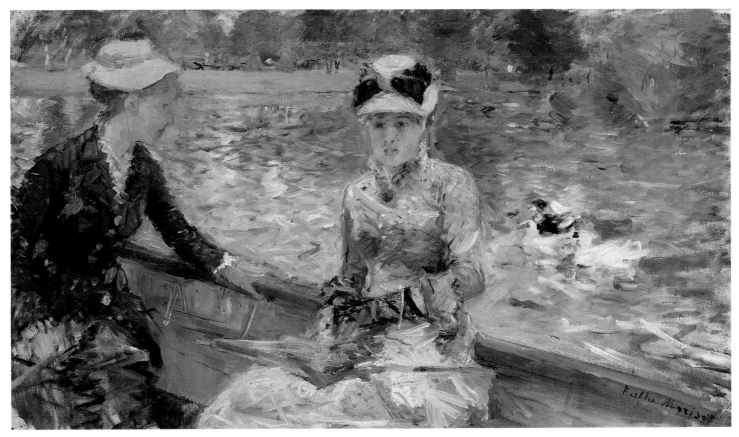

30-30 • Berthe Morisot SUMMER'S DAY
1879. Oil on canvas, 17¹³⁄₁₆ × 29⁵⁄₁₆″ (45.7 × 75.2 cm). National Gallery, London. Lane Bequest, 1917

her painting was confined to depictions of women's lives, a subject she knew well. In the 1870s, she painted in an increasingly fluid and painterly style, flattening her picture plane and making her brushwork more visible. In her oil painting **SUMMER'S DAY (FIG. 30–30)**, Morisot shows two elegant young ladies on a pleasant outing on the lake of the fashionable Bois du Boulogne. Unlike the figures in Manet's *Boating* (SEE FIG. 30–19), Morisot's women are properly accompanied by each other, and their ferry is steered by an unseen boatman who is at their behest. First exhibited in the fifth Impressionist exhibition in 1880, *Summer's Day* explores the formal side of Impressionism: Its brushstrokes and colors are skillfully handled. While Morisot was unable to comment on modern city life in ways her brother-in-law might, she nevertheless painted intensely modern pictures.

MODERN LIFE

Subjects of urban work and leisure also attracted Edgar Degas (1834–1917), although his vision is closer to Realism in its social commentary. Instead of painting out of doors, Degas composed his pictures in the studio from working drawings and photographs. He received rigorous academic training at the École des Beaux-Arts in the mid 1850s and subsequently spent three years in Italy studying the Old Masters. Assured compositional structure and intensity of line were hallmarks of his art throughout his career.

The son of a Parisian banker, Degas's painting themes and style were closer to Manet's than to the Impressionists'. In the 1870s, he began painting the modern life of the city: the racetrack, the music hall, and the opera, often focusing on those working to provide the entertainment rather than on their audience. He became the painter of the Paris ballet in the 1870s and 1880s at a time when it was in decline. Degas did not draw or paint actual dancers in rehearsal; rather, he hired dancers, often very young "ballet rats," to come to his studio to pose for him. His ballet paintings and pastels contain acerbic social commentary. **THE REHEARSAL ON STAGE (FIG. 30–31)**, for example, is a contrived scene, not an actual event. Many dancers' poses are uncharacteristic of the actual ballet but are included to show how the life of a dancer is tiresome, involving tedious hours of work. In this pastel, several young dancers look bored or exhausted, and to the far right sit two gentleman visitors who, the artist may be suggesting, pay to see the girls practice. The composition is set in a raked space, as if viewed from a box close to the stage. The abrupt foreshortening is emphasized by the dark scrolls of the double basses that jut up from the lower left. The angular viewpoint may derive from Japanese prints, which Degas collected, while the cropping of figures on the left suggests photography, which he also practiced. The Realist novelist Edmond de Goncourt (1822–1896), a friend of Degas, described him as capturing "the soul of modern life."

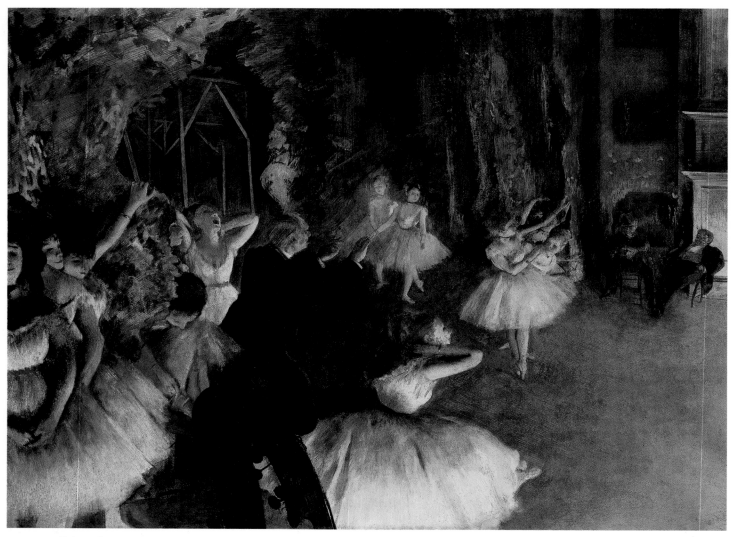

30-31 • Edgar Degas THE REHEARSAL ON STAGE
c. 1874. Pastel over brush-and-ink drawing on thin, cream-colored wove paper, laid on bristol board, mounted on canvas, 21⅜ × 28¾" (54.3 × 73 cm). Metropolitan Museum of Art, New York. Bequest of Mrs. H. O. Havemeyer Collection, Gift of Horace Havemeyer, 1929 (29.160.26)

In the right background of Degas's picture sit two well-dressed, middle-aged men, who enjoy their intimacy with the dancers at informal rehearsal. Because ballerinas generally came from lower-class families and exhibited their scantily clad bodies in public—something prohibited for "respectable" bourgeois women—they were widely assumed to be sexually available, and they often attracted the attentions of wealthy men willing to support them in exchange for sexual favors. Thus several of Degas's ballet pictures also include one or more of the dancers' mothers, who would accompany their daughters to rehearsals and performances in order to safeguard their virtue.

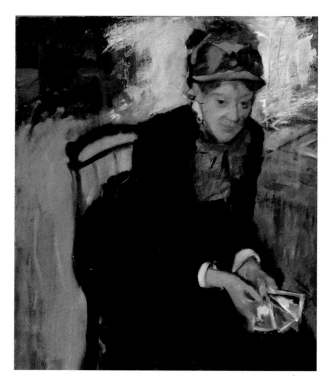

30-32 • Edgar Degas PORTRAIT OF MARY CASSATT
1880–1884. Oil on canvas, 28⅛ × 23⅛" (71.4 × 58.7 cm). National Portrait Gallery, Smithsonian Institution, Washington, D.C.

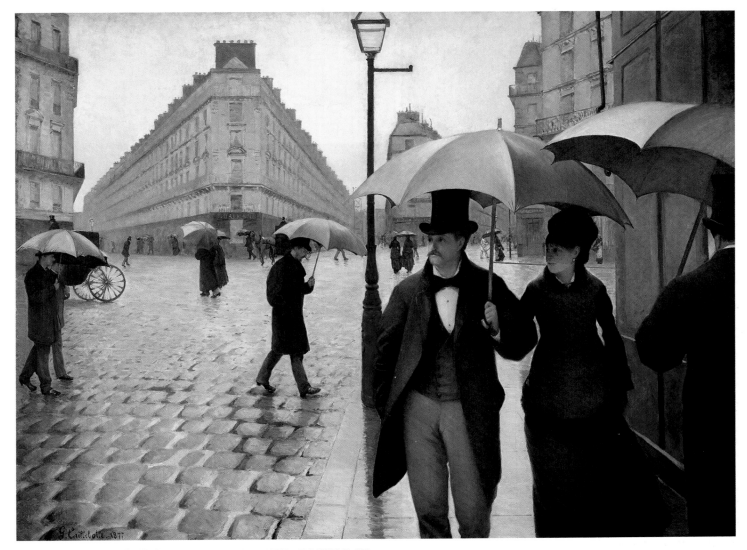

30-33 • Gustave Caillebotte PARIS STREET, RAINY DAY
1877. Oil on canvas, 83½ × 108¾″ (212.2 × 276.2 cm). Art Institute of Chicago. Part of the Charles H. and
Mary F. S. Worcester Fund

Degas's **PORTRAIT OF MARY CASSATT (FIG. 30–32)** is very different from his ballet pictures. It shows Cassatt as an uncharacteristically strong, intense, and intelligent woman for her time. She leans forward in her chair as if to engage the viewer in conversation in the midst of playing cards. Cassatt carved out a career for herself painting in a radical style and earned the respect of artists like Degas at a time when such professionalism in women was frowned upon. In this portrait Degas shows Cassatt's sharp intellect, something he rarely revealed in other paintings of women.

Gustave Caillebotte (1848–1894), another friend of Degas, was involved in organizing several Impressionist exhibitions; he also purchased the work of his friends, amassing a large collection of paintings. He studied with an academic teacher privately and qualified for the École des Beaux-Arts, but never attended. Caillebotte was fascinated by the streets of Paris, especially Haussmann's modernized street plan, and his subjects and compositions characteristically represent modern life. His **PARIS STREET, RAINY DAY (FIG. 30–33)** has an unconventional, almost telescopic composition that tilts the perspective. The street itself seems to be the subject of this painting; the people are huddled under umbrellas or pushed to the sides of the composition. The figure to the far right is even cropped in half, as in a photograph, and the couple strolling toward us are squeezed between him and the lamppost.

LATE NINETEENTH-CENTURY ART AND THE BEGINNINGS OF MODERNISM

The Realists and Impressionists continued to contribute to avant-garde art until the late nineteenth century, but by the mid 1880s they had relinquished their dominance to a younger generation of artists. The period after Impressionism seems less unified and less directed, involving artists from several different nations taking art in many new visual directions. This generation of artists increasingly defined avant-garde art in terms of visual experimentation, working to develop the precise manner of painting appropriate to their message. Some reinterpreted art as an expression of an interior world of the imagination, while others reconstructed the world around them in paint using new visual languages.

These artists included French Post-Impressionists, who explored inner ways of expressing the outer world, sometimes escaping from the city to the countryside or even to far-flung places; late nineteenth-century French sculptors, who studied the passionate physicality of the human form; British artists, inspired by medieval history in both painting and design; Symbolist artists, who retreated into fantastical and sometimes horrifying worlds of the imagination; Art Nouveau artists, who rejected the rational order of the industrial world to create images and designs ruled by the writhing, moving asymmetrical shapes of growing plants; and even landscape designers, who recast the urban cityscape into a rambling natural landscape.

At the end of the century and late in his life, Paul Cézanne (see pages 1007–1009) altered this course by returning to an intense visual study of the world around him, scrutinizing it like a specimen on a dissecting table and urging younger artists to consider new ways of creating meaning in painting. In 1906, the year Cézanne died, a retrospective exhibition of his life's work in Paris revealed his methods to the next generation of artists, the creators of Modernism.

POST-IMPRESSIONISM

The English critic Roger Fry coined the term "Post-Impressionism" in 1910 to describe a diverse group of painters whose work he had collected for an exhibition. He acknowledged that these artists did not share a unified style or approach to art, but they all used Impressionism as a springboard for their individual expressions of modernity in art.

SEURAT. Georges Seurat (1859–1891) was born in Paris and trained at the École des Beaux-Arts. He was dedicated to the clarity of structure that he found in Classical relief sculpture, and to

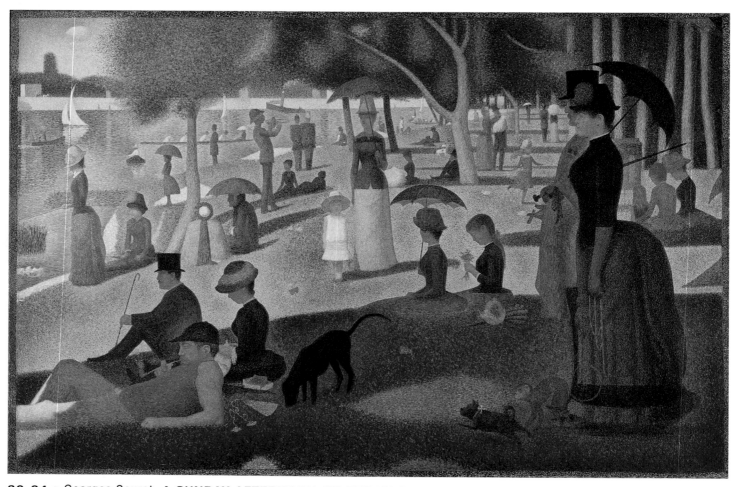

30-34 • Georges Seurat A SUNDAY AFTERNOON ON THE ISLAND OF LA GRANDE JATTE
1884–1886. Oil on canvas, 6′9½″ × 10′1¼″ (207 × 308 cm). Art Institute of Chicago. Helen Birch Bartlett Memorial Collection

the seemingly systematic but actually quite emotive use of color suggested by optics and color theory. He was particularly interested in the "law of the simultaneous contrast of colors" formulated by Michel-Eugène Chevreul in the 1820s. Chevreul observed that adjacent objects not only cast reflections of their own color onto their neighbors, but also create in them the effect of their **complementary color**. Thus, when a blue object is set next to a yellow one, the eye will detect in the blue object a trace of purple, the complement of yellow, and in the yellow object a trace of orange, the complement of blue.

Seurat explored how color hues and tones adjacent to one another create this visual effect of a third color. He studied carefully which hues could be combined, and in what proportions, to produce the effect of a particular color. His goal was to find ways to create retinal vibrations that enlivened the painted surface. He painted in distinctive short, multi-directional strokes of almost pure color, in what came to be known by the various names of "Divisionism" (the term preferred by Seurat), "Pointillism," and "Neo-Impressionism." In theory, these juxtaposed small strokes of color would merge in the viewer's eye to produce the impression of other colors. When perceived from a certain distance they would appear more luminous and intense than the same colors seen separately, while on close observation Seurat's strokes and colors would remain distinct and separate, creating an almost abstract arrangement of color and shape.

Seurat's monumental painting **A SUNDAY AFTERNOON ON THE ISLAND OF LA GRANDE JATTE (FIG. 30–34)** was first exhibited at the eighth and final Impressionist exhibition in 1886. He presented this large canvas as a "demonstration" piece to prove his worth as an artist and to advertise his smaller works. The painting contained 11 colors, with the purest hue of each that he could find. He laid these out in a single row on his palette, while creating a second, upper row of the same colors mixed with white and a third lower row mixed with black. He painted the entire canvas using this range of colors. When viewed from a distance of about 9 feet, the painting reads as figures in a park rendered in many colors and tones; but when viewed from a distance of 3 feet, the individual marks of color become more distinct and the forms begin to dissolve into abstraction.

The painting represents a sunny Sunday afternoon, the newly designated official day off for French working families to spend time together. The park, on the island of the Grande Jatte, just west of Paris, was accessible by train. There was a social hierarchy in Parisian parks in the late nineteenth century; the Bois du Boulogne (SEE FIG. 30–30) was an upper-middle-class park in an area of grand avenues, whereas the Grande Jatte faced a lower-class industrial area across the river. The figures represent a range of lower-middle-class "types" that would have been easily recognizable to the nineteenth-century viewer, such as the strolling man and his companion to the right, usually identified as a *boulevardier* (or citified dandy) and a *cocotte* (a single woman of the demi-monde), or the *canotier* (working-class oarsman) to the left.

VAN GOGH. Among the artists to experiment with Divisionism, Impressionism and modernity was the Dutch painter Vincent van Gogh (1853–1890), who transformed his artistic sources into a highly expressive personal style. The oldest son of a Protestant minister, Van Gogh worked as an art dealer, a teacher, and an evangelist before deciding in 1880 to become an artist. After brief periods of study in Brussels, The Hague, and Antwerp, in 1886 he moved to Paris, where he discovered the Parisian avant-garde. Van Gogh adapted Seurat's Divisionism, for instance, by applying brilliantly colored paint in multi-directional strokes of **impasto** (thick applications of paint) to give his pictures a turbulent emotional energy and a palpable surface texture.

Van Gogh was a socialist who believed that modern life, with its constant social change and focus on progress and success, alienated people from one other and from themselves (see "Modern Artists and World Cultures: Japonisme," pages 994–995). His own paintings are efforts to communicate his emotional state and establish a connection between artist and viewer, thereby overcoming the emotional barrenness that he felt modern society created. In a prolific output over only ten years, he produced paintings that would contribute significantly to the later emergence of Expressionism, in which the artist's emotional intensity overrides fidelity to the actual appearance of things. Van Gogh described his working method in a letter to his brother:

I should like to paint the portrait of an artist friend who dreams great dreams, who works as the nightingale sings, because it is his nature. This man will be fair-haired. I should like to put my appreciation, the love I have for him, into the picture. So I will paint him as he is, as faithfully as I can— to begin with. But that is not the end of the picture. To finish it, I shall be an obstinate colorist. I shall exaggerate the fairness of the hair, arrive at tones of orange, chrome, pale yellow. Behind the head—instead of painting the ordinary wall of the shabby apartment, I shall paint infinity, I shall do a simple background of the richest, most intense blue that I can contrive, and by this simple combination, the shining fair head against this rich blue background, I shall obtain a mysterious effect, like a star in the deep blue sky.

One of the most famous examples of this approach is **THE STARRY NIGHT (FIG. 30–35)**, painted from careful observation and the artist's imagination. Above the quiet town, the sky pulsates with celestial rhythms and blazes with exploding stars. Contemplating life and death in a letter, Van Gogh wrote: "Just as we take the train to get to Tarascon or Rouen, we take death to reach a star." This idea is rendered visible in this painting by the cypress tree, a traditional symbol of both death and eternal life, which rises dramatically to link the terrestrial and celestial realms. The brightest star in the sky is actually a planet, Venus, which is associated with love. It is possible that the picture's extraordinary energy also expresses Van Gogh's euphoric hope of gaining in death the love that had eluded him in life. The painting is a riot of

Modern Artists and World Cultures: Japonisme

In 1887, Vincent van Gogh painted *Japonaiserie: Flowering Plum Tree*. He was deeply affected by recently imported examples of Japanese art and prints, which he appreciated for their "exotic" visual effects. Japan was opened to Western trade and diplomacy in 1853, after a lengthy isolation, and in 1855 trade agreements permitted the regular exchange of goods with Japan. Among the first Japanese art objects to come to Paris was a sketchbook entitled *Manga* by Hokusai (1760–1849), which was eagerly passed around by Parisian artists. Several of them began to collect Japanese objects; the 1867 Paris International Exposition mounted the first show of Japanese prints in Europe; and immediately thereafter, Japanese lacquers, fans, bronzes, hanging scrolls, kimonos, ceramics, illustrated books, and **ukiyo-e** (prints of the "floating world," the realm of geishas and popular entertainment) began to appear for sale in specialty shops, art galleries, and even some department stores in Paris. The French obsession with Japan reached such a level by 1872 that the art critic Philippe Burty named the phenomenon **Japonisme**.

Vincent van Gogh admired the design and handcrafted quality of Japanese prints, which he both owned and copied. His *Japonaiserie: Flowering Plum Tree* is largely copied from Hiroshige's woodblock print *Plum Orchard, Kameido*. Van Gogh makes use of the same flattened tree with its asymmetrical branches, thin, shooting twigs, and tiny blossoms in his foreground; the same smaller trees in the middle ground; and the same railing in the background, behind which can be seen several figures and a small hut. Van Gogh has also appropriated Hiroshige's color scheme and flattened picture plane, as well as his banners of text. But he also made significant changes in his adaptation. He flattened the scene more extremely than Hiroshige had done. His grass is a uniform blanket of green, the flat gray trees with hard black outlines are flat and undifferentiated, and it is not clear whether the yellow blossoms are in front of or behind the thickly painted red sky. Indeed, Hiroshige's print suggests greater spatial depth than Van Gogh's imitation. Van Gogh also frames his painting with a bold, rather crudely painted orange frame with pseudo-Japanese characters scrawled around it, as if to accentuate the "primitiveness" of the image and its source. Van Gogh knew little about Japanese culture and less about the Japanese painting or printmaking tradition. He uses the Hiroshige print as a prompt in order to conjure up what he saw as a simpler, more "primitive" culture than his own, at a time when other artists, such as Paul Gauguin traveled the world in search of "primitive" cultures to inspire their art.

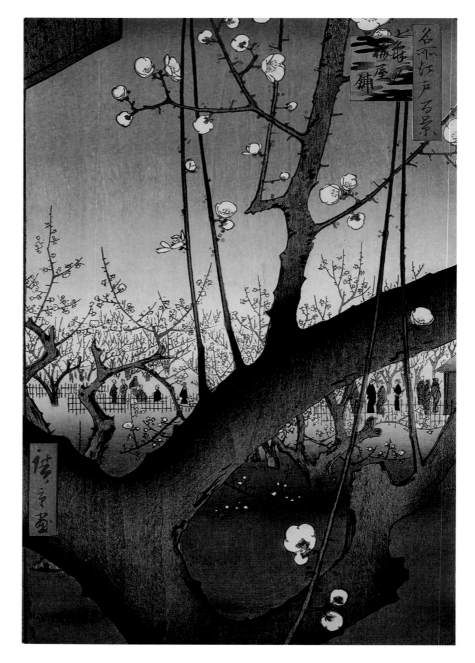

Hiroshige PLUM ORCHARD, KAMEIDO

1857. From *One Hundred Famous Views of Edo*. Woodblock print, 13¼ × 8⅝″ (33.6 × 47 cm). Brooklyn Museum, New York.

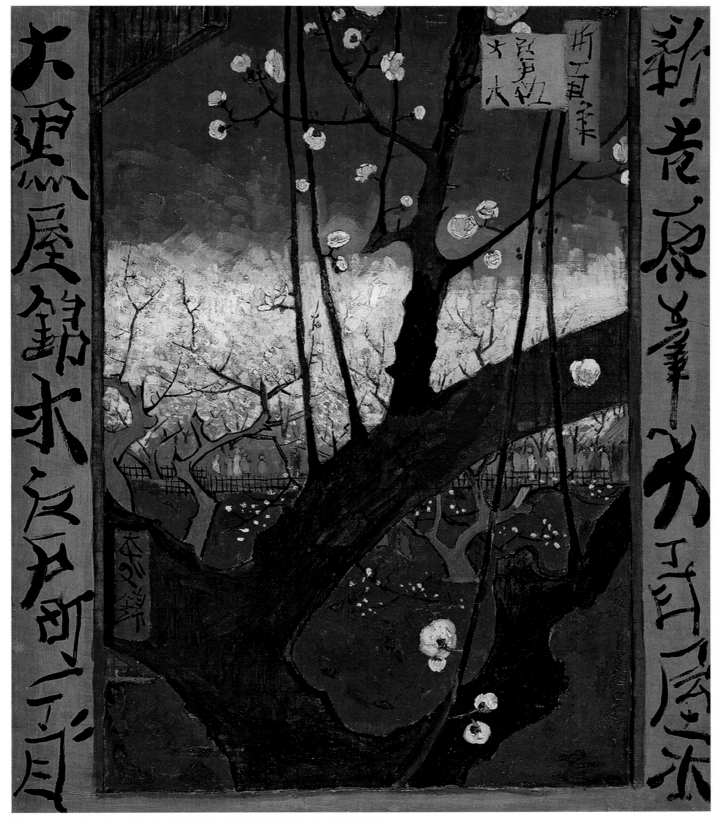

Vincent van Gogh JAPONAISERIE: FLOWERING PLUM TREE
1887. Oil on canvas, 21½ × 18″ (54.6 × 45.7 cm). Vincent van Gogh Museum, Amsterdam.

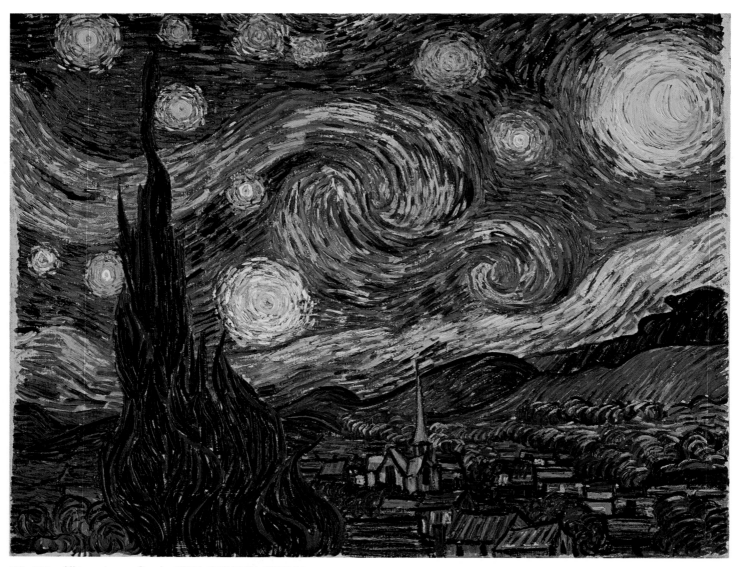

30-35 • Vincent van Gogh THE STARRY NIGHT
1889. Oil on canvas, 28¾ × 36¼" (73 × 93 cm). Museum of Modern Art, New York.
Acquired through the Lillie P. Bliss Bequest (472.1941)

brushwork, as rail-like strokes of intense color writhe across its surface. Van Gogh's brushwork is immediate, expressive, and intense. During the last year and a half of his life, he experienced repeated psychological crises that lasted for days or weeks. While they were raging, he wanted to hurt himself, heard loud noises in his head, and could not paint. The stress and burden of these attacks led him to the asylum where he painted *The Starry Night*, and eventually to suicide in July 1890.

GAUGUIN. In painting from imagination as much as from nature in *The Starry Night*, Van Gogh may have been following the advice of his friend Paul Gauguin (1848–1903), who once counseled another artist: "Don't paint from nature too much. Art is an abstraction. Derive this abstraction from nature while dreaming before it, and think more of the creation that will result." Gauguin's

art abstracts from nature like Van Gogh's, and it laid foundations for even more abstracted art in the twentieth century. Born in Paris to a Peruvian mother and a radical French journalist father, Gauguin lived in Peru until age 7. During the 1870s and early 1880s, he enjoyed a comfortable bourgeois life as a stockbroker, painting in his spare time under the tutelage of Pissarro. Between 1880 and 1886, he exhibited in the final four Impressionist exhibitions. In 1883, he lost his job during a stock market crash; three years later he abandoned his wife and five children to pursue a full-time painting career. Gauguin knew firsthand the business culture of his time and came to despise it, writing disparagingly to a friend of "the European struggle for money." Believing that escape to a more "primitive" place would bring with it the simpler pleasures of life, Gauguin lived for extended periods in the French province of Brittany between 1886 and

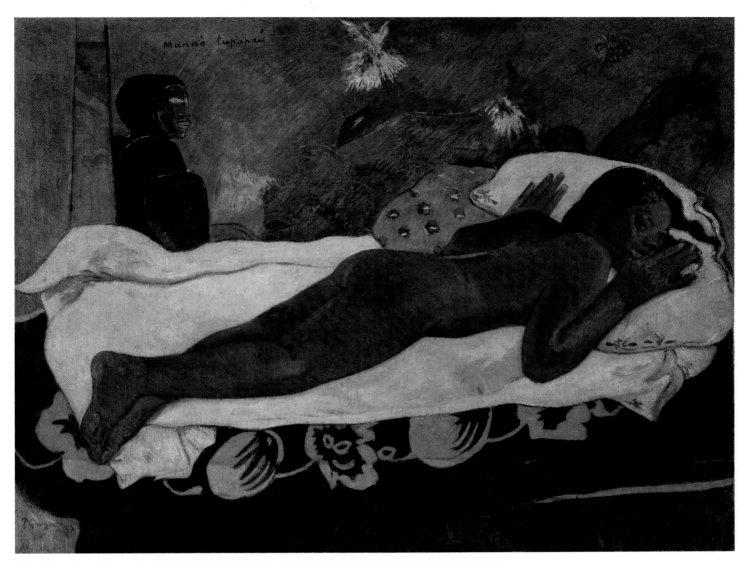

30–36 • Paul Gauguin MANAO TUPAPAU (SPIRIT OF THE DEAD WATCHING)
1892. Oil on burlap mounted on canvas, 28⅝ × 36⅝″ (73 × 92 cm). Collection Albright-Knox Art Gallery, Buffalo, NY.
A. Conger Goodyear Collection, 1965.

EXPLORE MORE: Gain insight from a primary source on Paul Gauguin **www.myartslab.com**

1891, traveled to Panama and Martinique in 1887, spent two months in Arles with Van Gogh in 1888, and then in 1891 sailed for Tahiti, a French colony in the South Pacific. After a final sojourn in France in 1893–1895, Gauguin returned to the Pacific, where he died in 1903.

Gauguin's art was inspired by sources as varied as medieval stained glass, folk art, and Japanese prints; he sought to paint in a "primitive" way employing the so-called "decorative" qualities of folk art such as brilliantly colored flat shapes, an anti-naturalist use of color, and thick, black outlines to feign "primitiveness." Gauguin called his style "synthetism," because he believed it synthesized observation and the artist's feelings about a subject in an abstracted application of line, shape, space, and color.

MANAO TUPAPAU (THE SPIRIT OF THE DEAD KEEP WATCH) **(FIG. 30–36)** portrays a thickly outlined, androgynous nude figure lying prone on a bed, close to sleep. In the background the spirit

of the dead watches over the figure. Gauguin implicitly suggests that this painting represents a scene from Tahitian religion, but there is no evidence that this is the case. The painting is not intended to be naturalistic or realistic, evoking a mood rather than representing a specific scene. Like many of Gauguin's works, this painting shows the late nineteenth-century desire to "get away" from the oppressive life of the city, and to get back to so-called "primitive" versions of culture.

LATE NINETEENTH-CENTURY ART IN BRITAIN

In the 1840s, Britain also encountered social and political upheaval. The depression of the "hungry forties," the Irish Potato Famine, and the Chartist Riots threatened social stability in England. Artists in Britain at mid century painted scenes of religious, medieval, or moral exemplars using a tight realistic style that was quite different from French Realism.

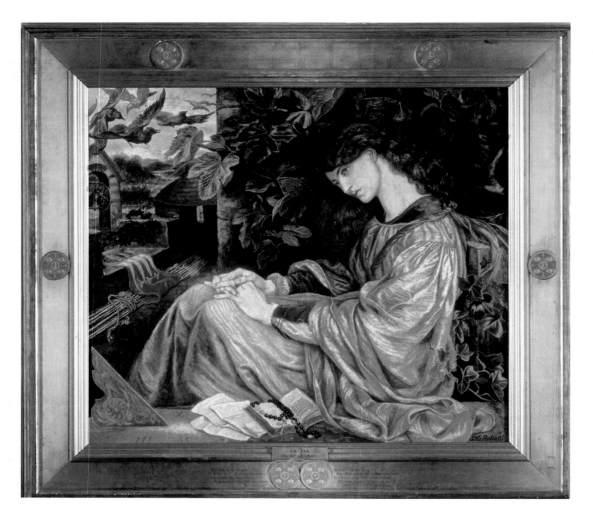

30-37 • Dante Gabriel Rossetti **LA PIA DE' TOLOMEI**
1868–1869. Oil on canvas, 41½ × 47½" (105.4 × 119.4 cm). Spencer Museum of Art, The University of Kansas, Lawrence.

ROSSETTI AND THE PRE-RAPHAELITES. In 1848, seven young London artists formed the Pre-Raphaelite Brotherhood in response to what they considered the misguided practices of contemporary British art. Instead of the "Raphaelesque" conventions taught at the Royal Academy, the Pre-Raphaelites looked back to the Middle Ages and early Renaissance (before Raphael) for a beauty and spirituality that they found lacking in their own time. The Pre-Raphaelites invoked what they imagined was the more moralistic and "real" art of this earlier time.

Dante Gabriel Rossetti (1828–1882) was a leading member and spokesperson of the Pre-Raphaelite Brotherhood, although his art grew increasingly visionary in later years. His painting **LA PIA DE' TOLOMEI** (FIG. 30–37) illustrates a scene from Dante's

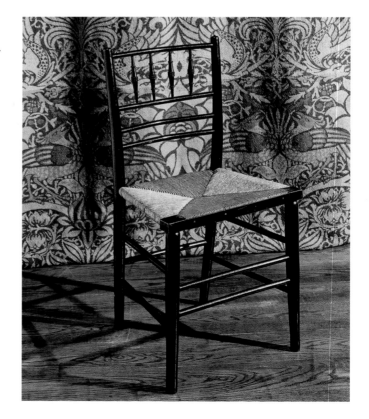

30-38 • FOREGROUND: Philip Webb **SINGLE CHAIR FROM THE SUSSEX RANGE**
In production from c. 1865. Ebonized wood with rush seat, 33 × 16½ × 14" (83.8 × 42 × 35.6 cm).

BACKGROUND: William Morris **"PEACOCK AND DRAGON" CURTAIN**
1878. Handloomed jacquard-woven woolen twill, 12'10½" × 11'5⅝" (3.96 × 3.53 m). Chair and curtain manufactured by Morris & Company. The William Morris Gallery, London Borough of Waltham Forest.

Art on Trial in 1877

This is a partial transcript of Whistler's testimony at the libel trial that he initiated against the art critic John Ruskin. Whistler's responses often provoked laughter, and the judge at one point threatened to clear the courtroom.

Q: What is your definition of a Nocturne?

A: I have, perhaps, meant rather to indicate an artistic interest alone in the work, divesting the picture from any outside sort of interest which might have been otherwise attached to it. It is an arrangement of line, form, and color first … The *Nocturne in Black and Gold* [SEE FIG. 30–39] is a night piece, and represents the fireworks at Cremorne.

Q: Not a view of Cremorne?

A: If it were called a view of Cremorne, it would certainly bring about nothing but disappointment on the part of beholders. It is an artistic arrangement. It was marked 200 guineas …

Q: I suppose you are willing to admit that your pictures exhibit some eccentricities; you have been told that over and over again?

A: Yes, very often.

Q: You send them to the gallery to invite the admiration of the public?

A: That would be such a vast absurdity on my part that I don't think I could.

Q: Did it take you much time to paint the *Nocturne in Black and Gold*? How soon did you knock it off?

A: I knocked it off in possibly a couple of days; one day to do the work, and another to finish it.

Q: And that was the labor for which you asked 200 guineas?

A: No, it was for the knowledge gained through a lifetime.

The judge ruled in Whistler's favor; Ruskin had indeed libeled him. But he awarded Whistler damages of only one farthing. Since in those days the person who brought the suit had to pay all the court costs, the case ended up bankrupting the artist.

Purgatory in which La Pia (the Pious One), wrongly accused of infidelity and locked up by her husband, is dying. The rosary and prayer book at her side refer to her piety, while the sundial and ravens suggest the passage of time and her impending death. La Pia's continuing love for her husband is represented by his letters, which lie under her prayer book. The luxuriant fig leaves that surround her are traditionally associated with shame, and they seem to suck her into themselves. They have no source in Dante, but are relevant to Rossetti: Jane Burden, his model for this and many other paintings as well as his lover, was the wife of his friend William Morris. La Pia twists at her wedding ring in the painting. It is hard to believe that this painting about La Pia's imprisonment for adultery is not also about Rossetti and Jane Burden.

MORRIS AND THE ARTS AND CRAFTS MOVEMENT. Other British artists drew inspiration from the medieval past as a panacea for modern life in London. William Morris (1834–1896) worked briefly as a painter under the influence of the Pre-Raphaelites before turning his attention to interior design and decoration. Morris's interest in crafts developed in the context of a widespread reaction against the shoddy design of industrially produced goods. Unable to find satisfactory furnishings for his new home after his marriage in 1859, Morris designed and constructed them himself, with the help of friends, later founding a decorating firm to produce a full range of medieval-inspired objects. Although many of the furnishings offered by Morris & Company were expensive, one-of-a-kind items, others, such as the rush-seated chair illustrated here **(FIG. 30–38)**, were inexpensive and simple,

intended as a handcrafted alternative to machine-made furniture. Concerned with creating a "total" environment, Morris and his colleagues designed not only furniture but also stained glass, tiles, wallpaper, and fabrics, such as the "Peacock and Dragon" curtain seen in the background of FIGURE 30–38.

Morris inspired what became known as the Arts and Crafts Movement. He rebelled against the idea that art was a highly specialized product made for a small elite, and he hoped to usher in a new era of art for the people. He said in lectures: "I do not want art for a few, any more than education for a few, or freedom for a few." A socialist, Morris opposed mass production and the deadening impact of factory life on the industrial worker. He argued that when laborers made handcrafted objects, they had the satisfaction of being involved in the entire process of creation and thus produced honest and beautiful things. He was inspired by the romance of the medieval craft tradition, ignoring its harsh realities.

WHISTLER. The American expatriate James Abbott McNeill Whistler (1834–1903) also focused his attention on the rooms and walls where art was hung, but he did so more to satisfy elitist tastes for beauty for its own sake. He also became embroiled in several artistic controversies that laid the groundwork for the art of the next century. After flunking out of West Point in the early 1850s, Whistler studied art in Paris, where he was briefly influenced by Courbet's Realism; the two artists painted several seascapes together. He settled in London in 1859, after which his art began to take on a more "decorative" quality that he called "aesthetic"

30–39 • James Abbott McNeill Whistler NOCTURNE IN BLACK AND GOLD, THE FALLING ROCKET
1875. Oil on panel, 23¾ × 18⅜″ (60.2 × 46.7 cm). Detroit Institute of Arts, Detroit, Michigan. 46.309

EXPLORE MORE: Gain insight from a primary source about James Abbott McNeill Whistler's *Nocturne in Black and Gold, The Falling Rocket*
www.myartslab.com

and which increasingly diverged from observed reality. He believed that the arrangement of a room (or a painting) could be aesthetically pleasing in itself, without reference to the outside world. He was among the first artists to hang art in a single horizontal row on a wall, rather than "stacked" in Salon style. He even occasionally designed exhibition rooms for his art, with the aim of creating a total harmony of objects and space.

Whistler's ideas about art were revolutionary. He was among the first artists to conceive of his paintings as abstractions from rather than representations of observed reality, and he was among the first to collect Japanese art, fascinated by its "decorative" (see page 997) line, color, and shape, although he understood little about its meaning or intent. By the middle of the 1860s, Whistler began to

entitle his works "Symphonies" and "Arrangements," suggesting that their themes resided in their compositions rather than their subject matter. He painted several landscapes with the musical title "Nocturne," and when he exhibited some of these in 1877, he drew the scorn of England's leading art critic, John Ruskin (1819–1900), a supporter of the Pre-Raphaelites and their moralistic intentions. Decrying Whistler's work as carelessly lacking in finish and purpose, Ruskin's review asked how an artist could "demand 200 guineas for flinging a pot of paint in the public's face."

The most controversial painting in Whistler's 1877 exhibition was **NOCTURNE IN BLACK AND GOLD, THE FALLING ROCKET (FIG. 30–39)**, and Ruskin's objections to it precipitated one of the most notorious court dramas in art history. Painted in restricted tonalities, at first glance the work appears completely abstract. In fact, the painting is a night scene depicting a fireworks show over a lake at Cremorne Gardens in London, with viewers vaguely discernible along the lake's edge in the foreground. The term "Nocturne" was taken from the titles of piano compositions by the Romantic composer Frederic Chopin: Whistler wanted to evoke an association between the abstract qualities of art and music. After reading Ruskin's review, Whistler sued the critic for libel (see "Art on Trial in 1877," page 999). He deliberately turned the courtroom into a public forum in which both to defend and advertise his art. On the witness stand, he defended his view that art has no higher purpose than creating visual delight, claiming that paintings need not have a subject matter. While Whistler never made a completely abstract painting, his theories were integral to the development of abstract art in the next century.

SYMBOLISM

The move toward abstraction can also be seen in Symbolism, an international movement in art and literature that comprised a loose affiliation of artists making works addressing the irrational fears, desires, and impulses of the human mind. A fascination with the dark recesses of the mind emerged over the last decades of the nineteenth century, encompassing photographic and scientific examinations of the nature of insanity, as well as a popular interest in the spirit world of mediums. Some Symbolist artists sought escape from modern life in irrational worlds of unrestrained emotion as described by authors such as Edgar Allan Poe (1809–1849), whose terrifying stories of the supernatural were popular across Europe. It is not coincidental that Sigmund Freud (1856–1939), who compared artistic creation to the process of dreaming, wrote his pioneering *The Interpretation of Dreams* (1900) during this period.

The Symbolists rejected the values of rationalism and material progress that dominated modern Western culture, choosing instead to explore the nonmaterial realms of emotion, imagination, and spirituality. Ultimately the Symbolists sought a deeper and more mysterious reality than the one encountered in everyday life, which they conveyed through strange and ambiguous subject matter and stylized forms that suggest hidden and elusive meanings. They transformed appearances in order to give pictorial form to psychic experience, and they often compared their works to dreams.

Symbolism in painting closely paralleled a similar movement among poets and writers who also abjured materialism and who retreated into fantasy worlds conjured from their imaginations. For example, Joris-Karl Huysmans's novel *À Rebours* (*Against the Grain*), published in 1884, has a single character, an aristocrat named Des Esseintes, who locked himself away from the world because "Imagination could easily be substituted for the vulgar realities of things." Claiming that nature was irrelevant, Des Esseintes mused: "Nature has had her day" and "wearied aesthetes" should take refuge in artworks "steeped in ancient dreams or antique corruptions, far removed from the manner of our present day."

MOREAU. A visionlike atmosphere pervades the later work of Gustave Moreau (1826–1898), an older academic artist whom the Symbolists regarded as a precursor. The Symbolists particularly admired Moreau's renditions of the biblical Salome, the young Judaean princess who, at the instigation of her mother, Herodias, performed an erotic dance before her stepfather, Herod, and demanded as reward the head of John the Baptist (Mark 6:21–28). In **THE APPARITION** (FIG. 30–40), exhibited at the Salon of 1876, the seductive Salome confronts a vision of the saint's severed head,

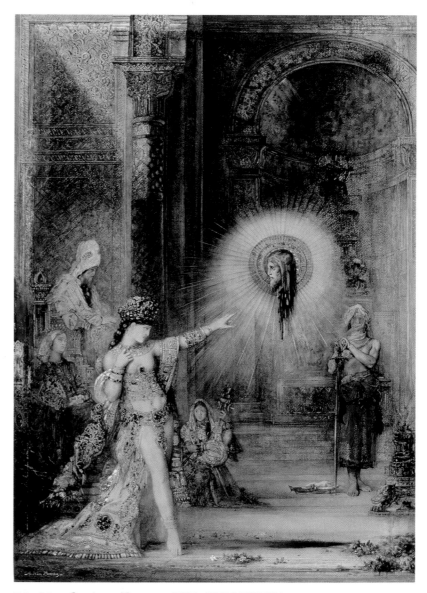

30-40 • Gustave Moreau THE APPARITION
1874–1876. Watercolor on paper, 41⅝₆ × 28⅜₆" (106 × 72.2 cm). Musée du Louvre, Paris.

which hovers open-eyed in midair, dripping blood yet also radiating holy light. Moreau depicted this sensual and macabre scene and its exotic setting in linear detail, with touches of jewel-like color to create an atmosphere of voluptuous decadence that amplifies Salome's role as *femme fatale* who uses her sensuality to destroy her male victim.

The Symbolists, like many smaller groups of artists in the late nineteenth century, staged independent art exhibitions; they were not interested in the approbation of the general public. Unlike the Impressionists, for instance, who hired halls, printed programs, and charged a small admission fee for their exhibitions, the Symbolists mounted more modest shows. During the 1889 Universal Exposition, they hung some works in a café a few blocks away from the grounds, with the result that the exhibition went almost unnoticed by the press.

MUNCH. Symbolism originated in France but had a profound impact on the avant-garde in other countries, where it frequently took on Expressionist tendencies. In Norway, Edvard Munch (1863–1944) produced a body of work that shows the terrifying workings of an anguished mind. **THE SCREAM (FIG. 30–41)** is the stuff of nightmares and horror movies; its harsh swirling colors and lines throw us wildly around the painting, but bring us right back to where we started, trapped between going forward into an unknown horror and going back into a known one. Munch described how the painting began: "One evening I was walking along a path; the city was on one side,

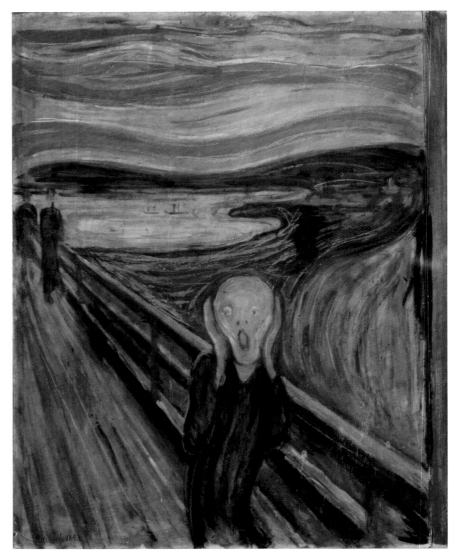

30–41 • Edvard Munch THE SCREAM
1893. Tempera and casein on cardboard, 36 × 29″ (91.3 × 73.7 cm).
Nasjonalgalleriet, Oslo.

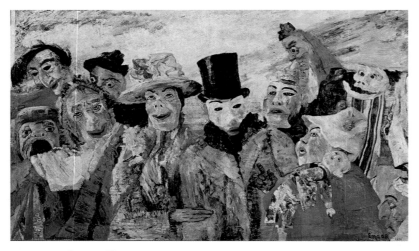

30–42 • James Ensor THE INTRIGUE
1890. Oil on canvas, 35½ × 59″ (90.3 × 150 cm). Koninklijk Museum voor Schone Kunsten, Antwerp.

and the fjord below. I was tired and ill … . I sensed a shriek passing through nature … . I painted this picture, painted the clouds as actual blood." A silent scream echoes throughout the painting.

ENSOR. The Belgian painter and printmaker James Ensor (1860–1949) brought together Symbolist and Expressionist tendencies in equally terrifying paintings. He studied for four years at the Brussels Academy, but spent the rest of his life in the nearby coastal resort town of Ostend. **THE INTRIGUE (FIG. 30–42)** shows a tightly packed group of people bustling and jostling towards us. Their faces are covered with blank, sometimes eyeless masks modeled on the grotesque papier-mâché masks that his family sold for the pre-Lenten carnival, a major holiday in Ostend. These disturbing faces create a mindless

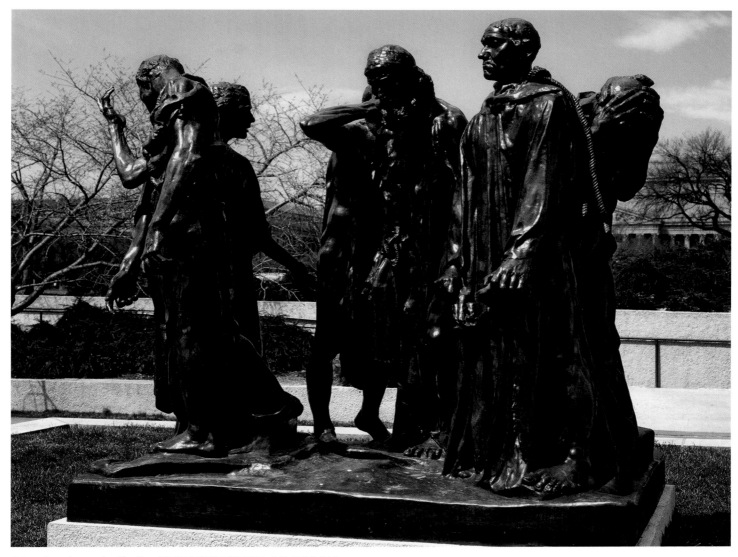

30–43 • Auguste Rodin THE BURGHERS OF CALAIS
1884–1889. Bronze, 6'10½" × 7'11" × 6'6" (2.1 × 2.4 × 2 m). Hirshhorn Museum and Sculpture Garden,
Smithsonian Institution, Washington, D.C. Gift of Joseph H. Hirshhorn, 1966

crowd that seems to move menacingly upon us. Ensor's acidic
colors and deliberately crude handling increase the sense of
danger. The threat posed by this picture, however, is located firmly
in the mind.

LATE NINETEENTH-CENTURY FRENCH SCULPTURE

A defiance of conventional expectations and an interest in emotional
expressiveness also characterize the work of late nineteenth-century
Europe's most successful and influential sculptor, Auguste Rodin
(1840–1917), and his contemporary Camille Claudel (1864–1943).
Born in Paris and trained as a decorative craftworker, Rodin failed
on three occasions to gain entrance to the École des Beaux-Arts
and consequently spent the first 20 years of his career as an assistant
to other sculptors and decorators. After a trip to Italy in 1875,
where he saw the sculpture of Donatello and Michelangelo, Rodin
developed a style of vigorously modeled figures in unconventional,

even awkward poses, which was simultaneously scorned by
academic critics and admired by the general public.

Rodin's status as a major sculptor was confirmed in 1884,
when he won a competition to create **THE BURGHERS OF CALAIS**
(FIG. 30–43), commissioned to commemorate an event from the
Hundred Years War. In 1347, Edward III of England offered to
spare the besieged city of Calais if six leading citizens (or
burghers)—dressed only in sackcloth with rope halters and
carrying the keys to the city—surrendered themselves to him for
execution. Rodin shows the six volunteers preparing to give
themselves over to what they assume will be their deaths. Rodin
defies academic conventions: Instead of elevating the hostages as
heroes, he brings them down off their pedestal and places them at
eye level. Instead of noble resignation, they show anguish and
despair. Entirely unidealized, these awkward figures are restless,
agitated, and distressed. Their exaggerated expressions, lengthened

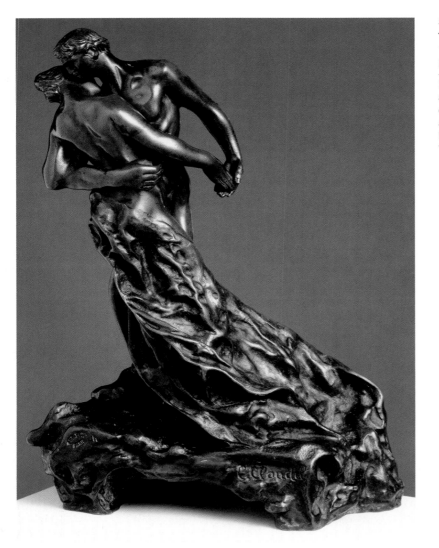

30-44 • Camille Claudel
THE WALTZ
1892–1905. Bronze, height 9⅞" (25 cm).
Neue Pinakothek, Munich.

French composer Claude Debussy,
a close friend of Claudel, displayed a cast
of this sculpture on his piano. Debussy
acknowledged the influence of art and
literature on his musical innovations.

arms, enlarged hands and feet, and heavy cloaks accentuate their burden; they seem unable to take another step. The discomfort and raw emotional power of this sculpture were not what the commissioners at Calais expected. Nevertheless, Rodin's ability to stylize human physicality for expressive purposes transformed late nineteenth-century sculpture and paved the way for subsequent sculptural abstractions.

Camille Claudel (1864–1943) was an assistant in Rodin's studio while he worked on *The Burghers of Calais*. Claudel studied sculpture from 1879 to 1883, before becoming Rodin's student. She also became his mistress; their often-stormy relationship lasted 15 years. Most often remembered for her dramatic life story, Claudel enjoyed independent professional success but suffered a breakdown that sent her to a mental hospital for the last 30 years of her life.

One of Claudel's most celebrated works is **THE WALTZ (FIG. 30–44)**, of which she produced several versions in various sizes between 1892 and 1905. The sculpture depicts a dancing couple, both nude, although the woman's lower body is covered with long, flowing drapery. In Claudel's original conception, the figures were entirely nude; she was forced to add the drapery after an inspector from the Ministry of Fine Arts declared their sensuality unacceptable, and recommended that her state commission for a marble version of the work be revoked. The subject of the waltz alone was controversial at this time because of the close contact demanded of dancers. Claudel added enough drapery to persuade the inspector to reinstate the commission, but she never finished it. She did, however, modify *The Waltz*, casting it in bronze as a tabletop sculpture. In this version, the spiral flow of the cloth creates the illusion of rapturous movement as the dancers twirl together, nearly losing their balance.

ART NOUVEAU

The swirling mass of drapery in Claudel's *The Waltz* has a stylistic affinity with Art Nouveau (French for "new art"), a movement launched in the early 1890s that permeated all aspects of European art, architecture, and design for more than a decade. Like the contemporary Symbolists, the practitioners of Art Nouveau largely rejected the values of modern industrial society and sought new aesthetic forms that combined a pre-industrial sense of beauty with fresh asymmetrical designs. They drew particular inspiration

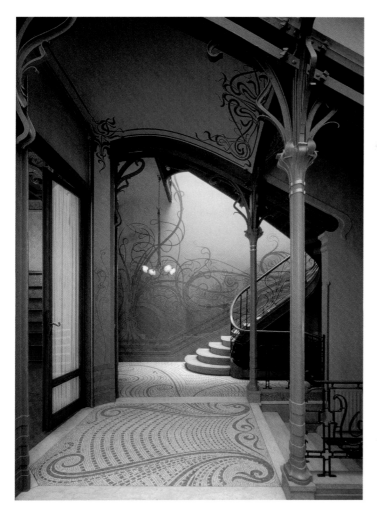

30–45 • Victor Horta **STAIRWAY, TASSEL HOUSE**
Brussels. 1892–1893.

from nature, especially from organisms such as vines, snakes, flowers, and winged insects, whose delicate and sinuous forms were adapted to their graceful and attenuated linear designs. Following a commitment to organic principles, practitioners of Art Nouveau also sought to harmonize all aspects of design into a beautiful whole, as found in nature itself.

HORTA. The artist most responsible for developing the Art Nouveau style in architecture was the Belgian Victor Horta (1861–1947). Trained at the academies in Ghent and Brussels, Horta worked in the office of a Neoclassical architect in Brussels for six years before opening his own practice in 1890. In 1892, he received his first important commission, a private residence in Brussels for a Professor Tassel. The result, especially the house's entry hall and staircase **(FIG. 30–45)**, was strikingly original. The ironwork, wall decoration, and floor tiles were all designed in an intricate series of long, graceful curves. Although Horta's sources are still debated, he was apparently impressed by the stylized linear designs of the English Arts and Crafts Movement of the 1880s. His concern for integrating the various arts into a more unified whole,

like his reliance on a refined decorative line, derived in part from English reformers such as William Morris.

GAUDÍ. The application of graceful linear arabesques to all aspects of design, evident in the entry hall of the Tassel House, began a vogue that spread across Europe. In Spain, where the style was called *Modernismo*, the major practitioner was the Catalan architect Antonio Gaudí i Cornet (1852–1926). Gaudí integrated natural forms into the design of buildings and parks that are still revolutionary in their dynamic freedom of line.

In 1904, the wealthy industrialist Josep Batlló commissioned Gaudí to design a private residence to surpass the lavish houses of other prominent families in Barcelona. Gaudí retained the underlying structure of the building that existed in the space for Batlló's new home, but completely transformed the façade and interior spaces. The façade **(FIG. 30–46)** is a dreamlike fantasy of undulating sandstone sculptures and multicolored glass and tile

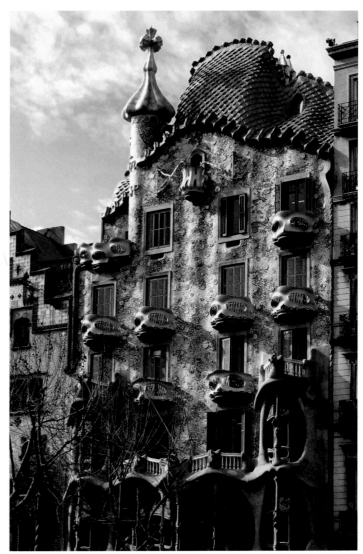

30–46 • Antonio Gaudí **CASA BATLLÒ**
43 Passeig de Gracia, Barcelona. 1900–1907.

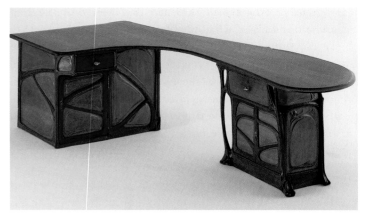

30-47 • Hector Guimard DESK
c. 1899 (remodeled after 1909). Olive wood with ash panels, 28¾ ×
47¾" (73 × 121 cm). Museum of Modern Art, New York.
Gift of Madame Hector Guimard

district of Paris that housed the most bohemian of the avant-garde
artists. In the late 1880s, Toulouse-Lautrec dedicated himself to
depicting the nightlife of Montmartre, and the cafés, theaters,
dance halls, and brothels that he himself frequented.

Toulouse-Lautrec made roughly 30 posters between 1891 and
1901 for several of the more famous nightspots, advertising their
most popular dancers. One of his most famous features the
notoriously limber café dancer **JANE AVRIL** performing the
infamous can-can **(FIG. 30–48)**. Toulouse-Lautrec places Avril on a
stage that zooms into the background, with the hand and face of a
double-bass player, part of the instrument, and pages of music
framing the lower right of the poster. The bold foreshortening and
prominent placement of the bass recall the compositions of Degas
(SEE FIG. 30–31), but the overall feeling of the image is quite
different. Toulouse-Lautrec's image emphasizes Avril's sexuality in
order to draw in the crowds, while Degas's pastels reveal visual

surfaces that mix the Islamic, Gothic, and Baroque visual
traditions of Barcelona in imaginative ways. The gaping
lower-story windows are the source of the building's
nickname, the "house of yawns," while the use of what
look like giant human tibia for upright supports led to its
other nickname, the "house of bones." The roof resembles
a recumbent dragon with overlapping tiles as scales. A
fanciful turret rises at its edge, recalling the sword of St.
George—patron of Catalonia—plunged into the back of
his legendary foe. Gaudí's highly personal alternative to
academic historicism and modern industrialization in
urban buildings such as this reflects his affinity with Iberian
traditions as well as his concern to provide imaginative
organic surroundings to enrich the lives of city dwellers.

GUIMARD. In France, Art Nouveau was also sometimes
known as the *Style Guimard* after its leading French
practitioner, Hector Guimard (1867–1942). Guimard
worked in an eclectic manner during the early 1890s, but
in 1895 he met and was influenced by Horta. He went on
to design the famous Art Nouveau-style entrances for the
Paris Métro (subway) and devoted considerable effort to
interior design and furnishings, such as this **DESK** that he
made for himself **(FIG. 30–47)**: Instead of a static and
stable object, Guimard handcrafted an asymmetrical,
organic entity that seems to undulate and grow.

TOULOUSE-LAUTREC. Henri de Toulouse-Lautrec (1864–
1901) was born into an aristocratic family in the south of
France. He had a genetic disorder and suffered several
childhood accidents that halted his growth and left him
physically disabled. He moved to Paris in 1882, where he
had private academic training and then discovered the
work of Degas, which changed his artistic perspective. He
also discovered Montmartre, the low-class entertainment

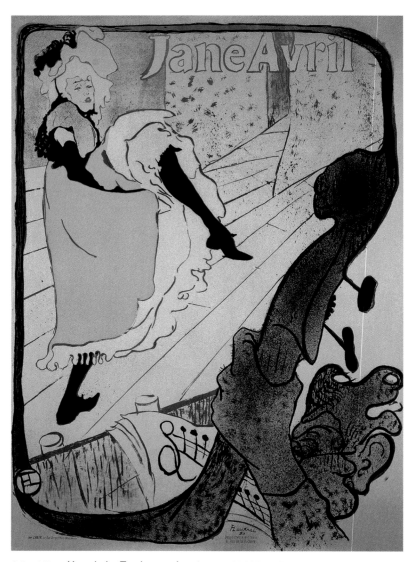

30-48 • Henri de Toulouse-Lautrec JANE AVRIL
1893. Lithograph, 50½ × 37" (129 × 94 cm).
San Diego Museum of Art.
Gift of the Baldwin M. Baldwin Foundation (1987.32)

beauty in the roughest raw material. Toulouse-Lautrec outlines his forms, flattens his space, and suppresses modeling to accommodate the cheap colored lithographic printing technique he used, which afforded only three or four colors. His curving lines and the hand-drawn lettering are also distinctively Art Nouveau.

CÉZANNE AND THE BEGINNINGS OF MODERNISM

No artist had a greater impact on the next generation of Modern painters than Paul Cézanne (1839–1906). The son of a prosperous banker in the southern French city of Aix-en-Provence, Cézanne studied art first in Aix and then in Paris, where he participated in the circle of Realist artists around Manet. His early pictures, somber in color and coarsely painted, often depicted Romantic themes of drama and violence, and were consistently rejected by the Salon.

In the early 1870s, Cézanne changed his style under the influence of Pissarro. He adopted a bright palette and broken brushwork, and began painting landscapes. Like the Impressionists,

with whom he exhibited in 1874 and 1877, Cézanne dedicated himself to the study of what he called the "sensations" of nature. Unlike the Impressionists, however, he did not seek to capture transitory effects of light and atmosphere; instead, he created highly structured paintings of an ordered nature through a methodical application of color that merged drawing and modeling into a single process. His professed aim was to "make of Impressionism something solid and durable, like the art of the museums."

Cézanne's dedicated pursuit of this goal is evident in his repeated paintings of **MONT SAINTE-VICTOIRE**, a mountain close to his home in Aix, which he depicted in hundreds of drawings and about 30 oil paintings between the 1880s and his death in 1906. The view here **(FIG. 30–49)** presents the mountain rising above the Arc Valley, which is dotted with buildings and trees, and crossed at the far right by a railroad viaduct. Framing the scene to the left is an evergreen tree, which echoes the contours of the mountains, creating visual harmony between the two principal elements of the

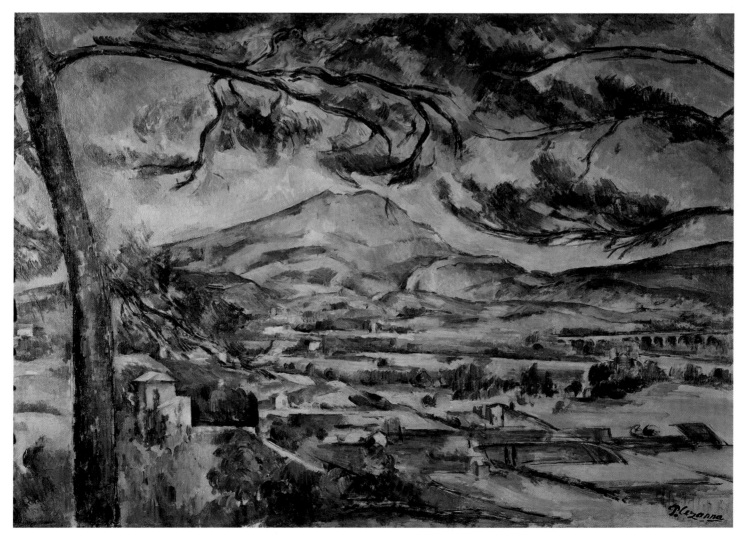

30–49 • Paul Cézanne **MONT SAINTE-VICTOIRE**
c. 1885–1887. Oil on canvas, 25½ × 32″ (64.8 × 92.3 cm). Courtauld Institute of Art Gallery, London. P.1934.SC.55

SEE MORE: View a video about Paul Cézanne's *Mont Sainte-Victoire* **www.myartslab.com**

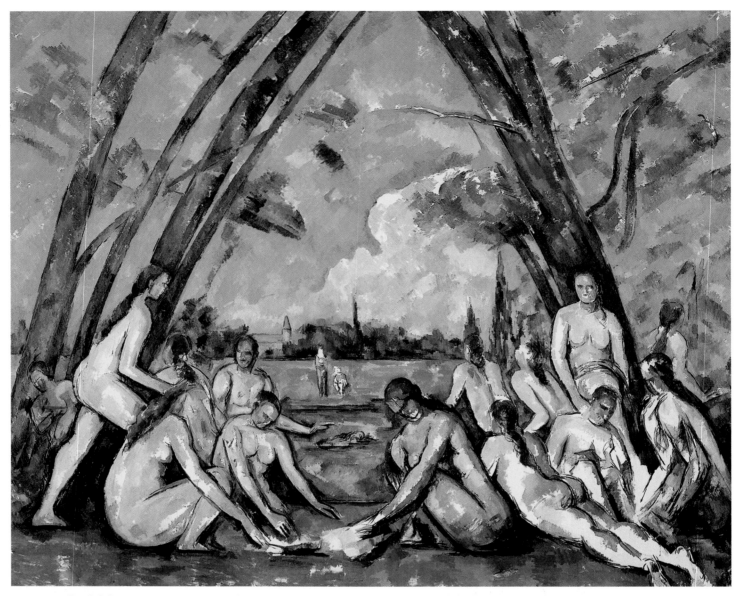

30–50 • Paul Cézanne **THE LARGE BATHERS**
1906. Oil on canvas, 6′10″ × 8′2″ (2.08 × 2.49 m). Philadelphia Museum of Art. The W. P. Wilstach Collection

composition. The even light, still atmosphere, and absence of human activity create the sensation of hermetic stillness.

Cézanne's handling of paint is deliberate and controlled. His brushstrokes, which vary from short, parallel hatchings to light lines to broader swaths of flat color, weave together the elements of the painting into a unified but flattened visual space. The surface design vies with the pictorial effect of receding space, generating tension between the illusion of three dimensions within the picture and the physical reality of its two-dimensional surface. Recession into depth is suggested by the tree in the foreground—a *repoussoir* (French for "something that pushes back") that helps draw the eye into the valley—and by the transition from the saturated hues in the foreground to the lighter values in the background, creating an effect of atmospheric perspective. But recession into depth is challenged by other more intense colors in

both the foreground and background, and by the tree branches in the sky, which follow the contours of the mountain, subtly suggesting that the two are on the same plane. Photographs of this scene show that Cézanne created a composition in accordance with a harmony that he felt the scene demanded, rather than from the details of the scene itself. His commitment to the painting as a work of art, which he called "something other than reality"—not a representation of nature but "a construction after nature"—was crucial for modern art of the next century.

Cézanne enjoyed little professional success until the last years of his life, at which time his paintings became more complex internally and less tied to observed reality. **THE LARGE BATHERS** (**FIG. 30–50**) was probably begun in the last year of his life and left unfinished. This canvas, the largest he ever painted, returns in several ways to the academic conventions of the history painting: it is a multi-figured painting of nude figures in a landscape setting that suggests a mythological theme. The bodies cluster in two pyramidal groups at the left and right sides of the painting, beneath a canopy of trees that opens in the middle onto a triangular expanse of water, landscape, and sky. The figures assume statuesque poses (the crouching figure at the left quotes the Hellenistic *Crouching Venus* that Cézanne copied in the Louvre) and seem to exist in a timeless realm. Using a restricted palette of blues, greens, ochers, and roses, laid down over a white ground, Cézanne suffuses the picture with a cool light that emphasizes the scene's remoteness from everyday life. Despite its unfinished state, *The Large Bathers* brings nineteenth-century painting full circle by reviving the Arcadian landscape, a much earlier category of academic painting, while opening a new window on the radical rethinking of the fundamental practice and purpose of art.

THE ORIGINS OF MODERN ARCHITECTURE

The history of late nineteenth-century architecture reflects a dilemma faced by the late nineteenth-century industrial city, caught between the classicizing tradition of the Beaux-Arts academic style and the materials, construction methods, and new aesthetic of industry. The École des Beaux-Arts, although weakened in painting by the end of the century, came into its own as the training ground for European and American architects after

1880, while industrialization in places like Chicago simultaneously demanded new ways of thinking about tall and large buildings.

TECHNOLOGY AND STRUCTURE

The pace of life sped up considerably over the course of the nineteenth century. Industrialization allowed people to manufacture more, consume more, travel more, and do more, in greater numbers than before. Industrialization caused urbanization, which in turn demanded more industrialization. A belief in the perfectibility of society spawned more than 20 international fairs celebrating innovations in industry and technology. One of the first of these took place in London in 1851. The Great Exhibition of the Industry of All Nations was mounted by the British to display their industrial might, assert their right to empire, and quell lingering public unrest after the 1848 revolutions elsewhere in Europe. The centerpiece of the Great Exhibition, the Crystal Palace, introduced new modern building techniques and aesthetics.

THE CRYSTAL PALACE.   The revolutionary construction of **THE CRYSTAL PALACE (FIG. 30–51)**, created by Joseph Paxton (1803–1865), featured a structural skeleton of cast iron that held iron-framed glass panes measuring 49 by 30 inches, the largest size that could be mass-produced at the time. Prefabricated wooden ribs and bars supported the panes. The triple-tiered edifice was the largest space ever enclosed up to that time—1,851 feet long, covering more than 18 acres, and providing almost a million

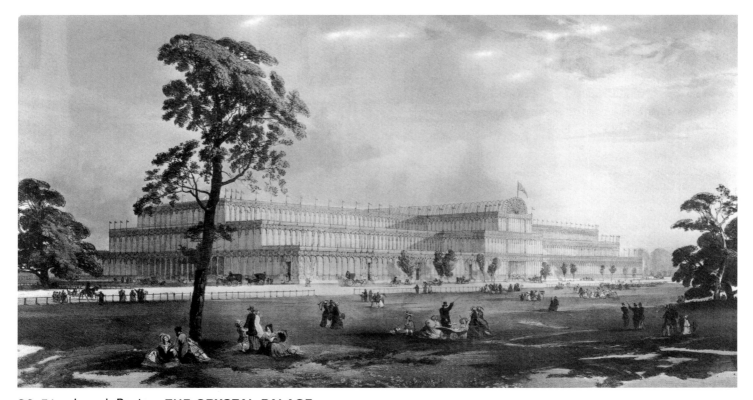

30-51 • Joseph Paxton THE CRYSTAL PALACE
London. 1850–1851. Iron, glass, and wood. (Print of the Great Exhibition of 1851; printed and published by Dickinson Brothers, London, 1854.)

square feet of exhibition space. The central vaulted transept— based on the design for new cast-iron railway stations—rose 108 feet to accommodate a row of the elm trees dear to Prince Albert, the husband of Queen Victoria. By the end of the exhibition, 6 million people had visited it, most agreeing that the Crystal Palace was a technological marvel. Even so, most architects and critics, still wedded to Neoclassicism and Romanticism, considered it a work of engineering rather than legitimate architecture because the novelty of its iron and glass frame overshadowed its Gothic Revival style.

BIBLIOTHÈQUE NATIONALE. Henri Labrouste (1801–1875) trained as an architect at the École des Beaux-Arts, where he also taught. Labrouste had a radical desire to fuse the École's historicizing approach to architecture with the technical innovations of industrial engineering. Although reluctant to push his ideas at the École, he pursued his goals in his architecture. The **BIBLIOTHÈQUE NATIONALE (FIG. 30–52)** is an example of this fusion. The ceiling is a series of domes with glass-covered oculi that light the reading room. The domes rest on thin iron arches and columns that open the space visually. The domes are faced

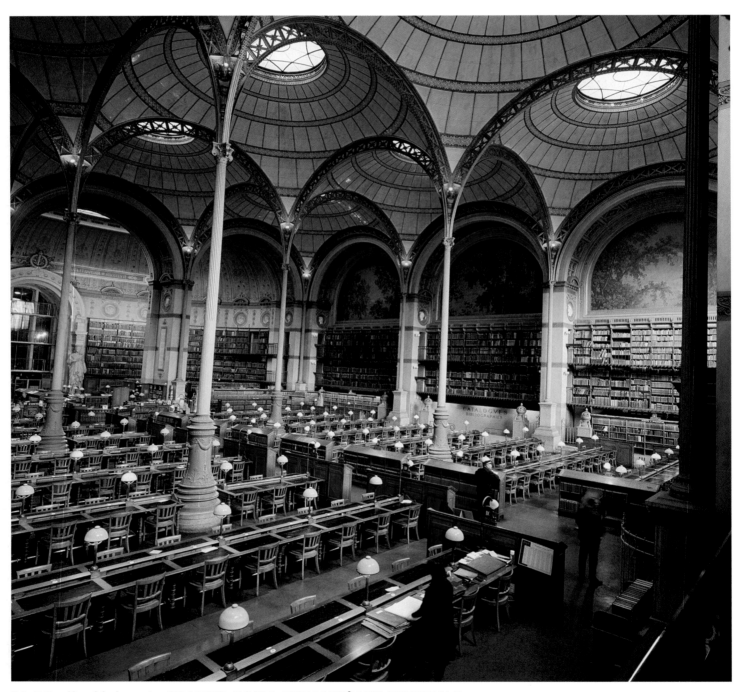

30-52 • Henri Labrouste **READING ROOM, BIBLIOTHÈQUE NATIONALE**
Paris. 1862–1868.

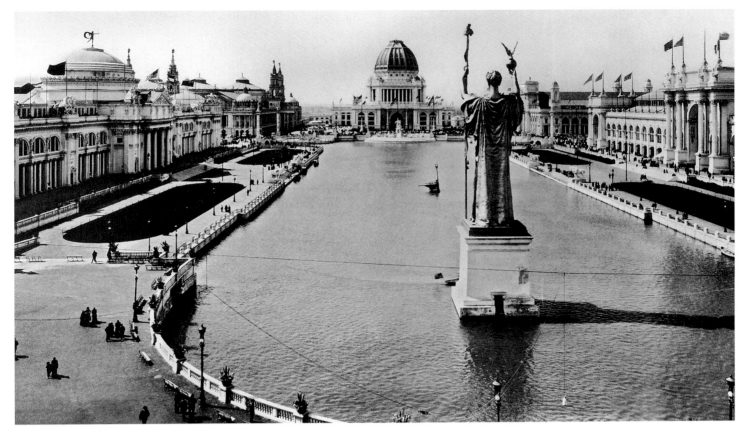

30-53 • COURT OF HONOR, WORLD'S COLUMBIAN EXPOSITION
Chicago. 1893. View from the east.

with bright white ceramic tiles, strong metal bookshelves are arranged around the walls, and a metal trelliswork and triumphal arch complete with caryatids define the spaces. The mixture of historical allusions and the vast open space made possible by industrial materials is thoroughly modern.

THE CHICAGO SCHOOL OF ARCHITECTURE

In the United States, a new architecture evolved to accommodate the needs of the modern city. In America up until this time, as in Europe, major architectural projects were expected to embody the Beaux-Arts tradition and its historicist associations. But the modern city required new building types for industry, transportation, commerce, storage, and residences. These new building types needed to accommodate more people and more activities in urban areas where land prices were skyrocketing. Chicago was a case in point. As the transportation hub for grain, livestock, and other produce transplanted from the rural Midwest to the cities of the east and west coasts, Chicago became a populous, wealthy city by the 1890s; its stock exchange was one of the most active in the nation. As new department stores, commercial facilities, and office buildings were designed, primarily with practical needs in mind, Chicago also became the cradle for an entirely new way of thinking about urban design and construction in which function gave birth to architectural form.

WORLD'S COLUMBIAN EXHIBITION. Richard Morris Hunt (1827–1895) was the first American to study architecture at the École des Beaux-Arts in Paris. Extraordinarily skilled in Beaux-Arts historicism and determined to raise the standards of American architecture, he built in every accepted style, including Gothic, French Classicist, and Italian Renaissance. After the Civil War, Hunt built many lavish mansions, emulating aristocratic European models for a growing class of wealthy eastern industrialists and financiers.

Late in his career, Hunt supervised the design of the 1893 World's Columbian Exposition in Chicago, commemorating the 400th anniversary of Christopher Columbus's arrival in the Americas. Rather than focus on the engineering wonders of previous fairs (although the first ferris wheel was built for the fair), the Chicago planning board decided to build "permanent buildings—a dream city." (In fact, the exposition buildings were temporary, and constructed from staff, a mixture of plaster and fibrous materials, rather than masonry.) To create a sense of unity among the buildings, a single style for the fair was settled upon: a Classical style, alluding to ancient Greece and republican Rome to reflect America's pride in its own democratic institutions as well as its emergence as a world power. A photograph of Hunt's design for the Administration Building at the end of the **COURT OF HONOR (FIG. 30–53)** shows the Beaux-Arts style of the so-called "White City."

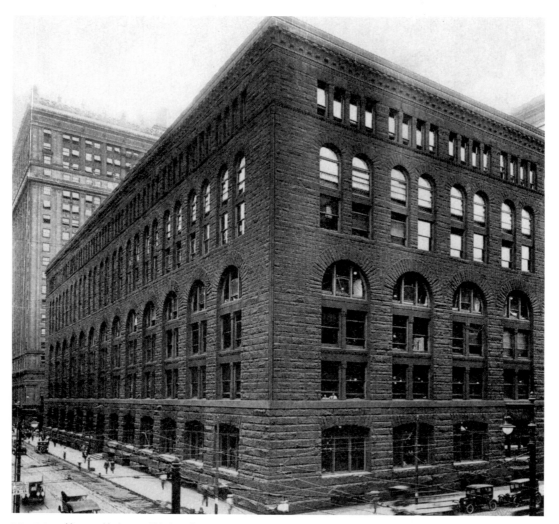

30-54 • Henry Hobson Richardson **MARSHALL FIELD WHOLESALE STORE**
Chicago. 1885–1887. Demolished c. 1935.

The World's Columbian Exposition was intended to be a model of the ideal American city—clean, spacious, carefully planned, and Classically styled—in contrast to the soot and over-crowding of most unplanned American cities. Frederick Law Olmsted, the designer of New York City's Central Park (see "The City Park," page 1014), was responsible for the landscape design of the exposition. He converted the marshy lakefront into a series of lagoons, canals, ponds, and islands, some laid out formally, as in the White City, and others informally, as in the "Midway," containing the busy conglomerate of pavilions of "less civilized" nations. Between these two parts stood a ferris wheel, which provided a spectacular view of the fair and the city. After the fair, most of its buildings were demolished, but Olmsted's landscaping has remained.

RICHARDSON. The second American architect to study at the École des Beaux-Arts was Henry Hobson Richardson (1838–1886). Born in Louisiana and educated at Harvard, Richardson returned from Paris in 1865 to settle in New York. He designed architecture in a variety of revival styles and became famous for a robust, rusticated style known as Richardsonian Romanesque. In 1885, he designed the **MARSHALL FIELD WHOLE-SALE STORE** in Chicago (FIG. 30–54). The design drew on the heavy, blocklike shapes and imposing scale of Italian Renaissance palazzos such as the Medici-Riccardi palace in Florence (SEE FIG. 19–5), and occupied most of a city block. The rough stone facing, the arched windows, and the decorated cornice all evoke historical architectural antecedents. Even so, Richardson's eclecticism resulted in a readily identifiable personal style.

Plain and sturdy, Richardson's building was a revelation to the young architects of Chicago then engaged in rebuilding the city after the disastrous fire of 1871. About the same time, new technology for producing steel, a strong, cheap alloy of iron, created new structural opportunities for architects. William Le Baron Jenney (1832–1907) built the first steel-skeleton building in Chicago; his lead was quickly followed by younger architects, known as the Chicago School. The rapidly rising cost of urban land made tall buildings desirable; structural steel and the electric elevator, first manufactured in 1889, made them possible.

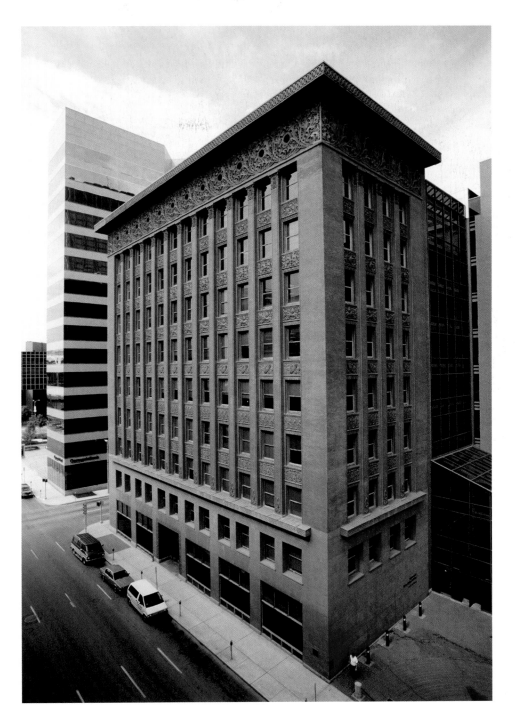

30–55 • Louis Sullivan
WAINWRIGHT BUILDING
St. Louis, Missouri. 1890–1891.

SEE MORE: Click the
Google Earth link for the
Wainwright Building
www.myartslab.com

SULLIVAN.   Equipped with new structural materials and improved passenger elevators, driven by new economic considerations, and inspired by Richardson's departure from Beaux-Arts historicism, the Chicago School architects produced a new kind of building—the skyscraper—and a new style of architecture. An example of their work, and evidence of its rapid spread throughout the Midwest, is Louis Sullivan's **WAINWRIGHT BUILDING** in St. Louis, Missouri (**FIG. 30–55**). The Boston-born Sullivan (1856–1924) studied for a year at the Massachusetts Institute of Technology (MIT), home of the United States' first formal architecture program, and for an equally brief period at the École des

Beaux-Arts in Paris, where he developed a distaste for historicism. He settled in Chicago in 1875, partly because of the building boom there that had followed the fire of 1871, and in 1883 he entered into a partnership with the Danish-born engineer Dankmar Adler (1844–1900).

Sullivan's first major skyscraper, the Wainwright Building, has a U-shaped plan that provides an interior light-well for the illumination of inside offices. The ground floor, designed to house shops, has wide plate-glass windows for the display of merchandise. The second story, or mezzanine, also features large windows for the illumination of the shop offices. Above the mezzanine rise seven

Parks originated during the second millennium BCE in China as enclosed hunting reserves for kings and the nobility. In Europe, from the Middle Ages to the eighteenth century, they remained private recreation grounds for the privileged. The first urban park intended for the public was in Munich, Germany. Laid out by Friedrich Ludwig von Sckell in 1789–1795 in the picturesque style of an English landscape garden (SEE FIG. 29–17), the park contained irregular lakes, gently sloping hills, broad meadows, and paths meandering through wooded areas.

The crowding and pollution of cities during the Industrial Revolution prompted the creation of large public parks whose green open spaces would help purify the air and provide city dwellers of all classes with a place for healthy recreation. Numerous municipal parks were built in Britain during the 1830s and 1840s and in Paris during the 1850s and 1860s, when Georges-Eugène Haussmann redesigned the former royal hunting forests of the Bois de Boulogne and the Bois de Vincennes in the English style favored by the emperor.

In American cities before 1857, the only public outdoor spaces were small squares found between certain intersections, or larger gardens, such as the Boston Public Garden, neither of which filled the growing need for varied recreational facilities in the city. For a time, landscaped suburban cemeteries in the picturesque style were popular sites for strolling, picnicking, and even horse racing—an incongruous set of uses that strikingly demonstrated the need for more urban parks.

The rapid growth of Manhattan in the nineteenth century spurred civic leaders to set aside parkland while open space still existed. The city purchased an 843-acre tract in the center of the island and in 1857 announced a competition for its design as Central Park. The competition required that designs include a parade ground, playgrounds, a site for an exhibition or concert hall, sites for a fountain and for a viewing tower, a flower garden, a pond for ice skating, and four east–west cross-streets so that the park would not interfere with the city's vehicular traffic.

The latter condition was pivotal to the winning design, drawn up by architect Calvert Vaux (1824–1895) and park superintendent Frederick Law Olmsted (1822–1903), which sank the crosstown roads in trenches hidden below the surface of the park and designed separate routes for carriages, horseback riders, and pedestrians.

Believing that the "park of any great city [should be] an antithesis to its bustling, paved, rectangular, walled-in streets," Olmsted and Vaux designed picturesque landscaping in the English tradition, with the irregularities of topography and planting used as positive design elements. Except for a few formal elements, such as the tree-lined mall that leads to the Classically designed Bethesda Terrace and Fountain, the park is remarkably informal and naturalistic. Where the land was low, Olmstead and Vaux further depressed it, installing drainage tiles and carving out ponds and meadows. They planted clumps of trees to contrast with open spaces, and exposed natural outcroppings of schist to provide dramatic, rocky scenery. They arranged walking trails, bridlepaths, and carriage drives through the park with a series of changing vistas. Views from the apartment houses of the wealthy on the streets surrounding the park were designed to be especially appealing. An existing reservoir divided the park into two sections. Olmsted and Vaux developed the southern half more completely and located most of the sporting facilities and amenities there, while leaving the northern half more like a nature reserve. Largely complete by the end of the Civil War, Central Park was widely considered a triumph, launching a movement to build similar parks in cities across the United States.

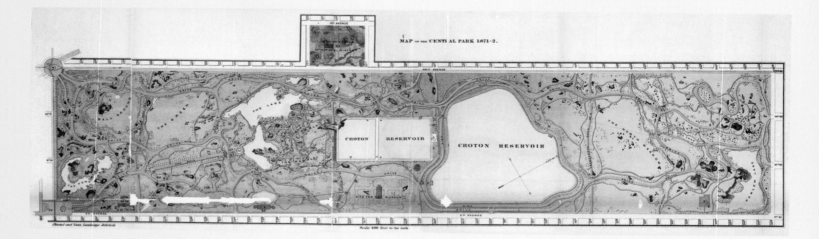

Frederick Law Olmsted and Calvert Vaux **MAP OF CENTRAL PARK, NEW YORK CITY**
Revised and extended park layout as shown in a map of 1873.

SEE MORE: View a simulation of the city park **www.myartslab.com**

identical floors of offices, lit by rectangular windows. An attic story houses the building's mechanical plant and utilities. The building is crowned by a richly decorated foliate frieze in terra-cotta relief, punctuated by bull's-eye windows and capped by a thick cornice slab.

The Wainwright Building's outward appearance clearly articulates three different levels of function: shops at the bottom, offices in the middle, and utility storage at the top. It illustrates Sullivan's philosophy of architecture summed up in his statement, "Form ever follows function." This idea was adopted as a credo by Modernist architects, who used it to justify removal of all surface decoration from buildings. Sullivan designed the Wainwright Building for function, but he also created an interesting and expressive building. The thick corner piers, for example, are not structurally necessary—since an internal steel-frame skeleton supports the building—but they emphasize its vertical thrust. The thinner piers between the office windows, which rise uninterrupted from the third story to the attic, echo and reinforce its spring and verticality. As Sullivan put it, a tall office building "must be every inch a proud and soaring thing, rising in sheer exultation."

In the Wainwright Building that exultation culminates in the rich vegetative ornament that swirls around the crown of the building, serving a decorative function like that of the foliated capital of a Classical column. The tripartite structure of the building itself suggests the Classical column with its base, shaft, and capital, reflecting the lingering influence of Classical design principles. Only in the twentieth century would Modern architects reject tradition entirely to create an architectural aesthetic that was decoration-free.

30.1 Discuss the interests and goals of French academic painters and sculptors and explain how their work differed from other art of the same time and place, such as that of the Realists and Impressionists.

30.2 Explain how the photographic process works and write about the roles played by Louis-Jacques-Mandé Daguerre and Henry Fox Talbot in the emergence of this medium.

30.3 Discuss Gustave Courbet's Realism in works such as *The Stonebreakers* (FIG. 30–12) and *A Burial at Ornans* (FIG. 30–13) in relation to the social and political issues of mid-century France.

30.4 Discuss the novel form and content of Impressionist paintings, and explain how both differ from those of traditional European painting. Make sure to reference works discussed in the chapter.

30.5 Distinguish among the various responses to Impressionism that constitute the concept of Post-Impressionism. Compare and contrast two Post-Impressionist paintings by different artists discussed in the chapter and explain how each offers an alternative to Impressionism.

PRACTICE MORE: Compose answers to these questions, get flashcards for images and terms, and review chapter material with quizzes **www.myartslab.com**

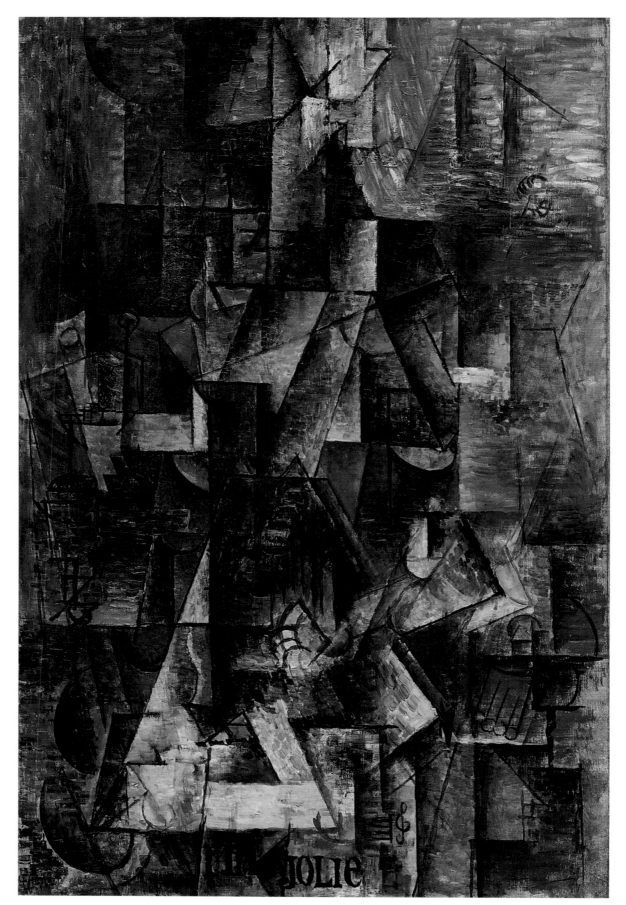

31-1 • Pablo Picasso MA JOLIE 1911–1912. Oil on canvas, 39⅜ × 25¾" (100 × 65.4 cm).
Museum of Modern Art, New York. Acquired through the Lillie P. Bliss Bequest (176.1945)

MODERN ART IN EUROPE AND
THE AMERICAS, 1900–1950

Pablo Picasso was a towering presence at the center of the early twentieth-century Parisian art world, transforming the form, meaning, and conceptual framework of Modern art. In his great Cubist work **MA JOLIE** (FIG. 31–1) of 1911–1912, Picasso challenges his viewers to think about the very nature of communication through painting. Remnants of the subjects Picasso worked from are evident throughout, but any attempt to reconstruct the subject—a woman with a stringed instrument— poses difficulties for the viewer. *Ma Jolie* ("My Pretty One") is in some sense a portrait, though hardly a traditional one. Picasso makes us work to see and to understand the figure. We can discover several things about Ma Jolie from the painting; we can see parts of her head, her shoulders, and the curve of her body, a hand or a foot. But in Paris in 1911, "Ma Jolie" was also the title of a popular song, so the inclusion of writing and a musical staff in the painting may also suggest other meanings. Our first impulse might be to wonder what exactly is pictured on the canvas. To that question, Picasso provided the sarcastic answer "It's My Pretty One!"

On the other hand, it might be argued that the human subject provided only the raw material for a formal, abstract arrangement. A subtle tension between order and disorder is maintained throughout this painting. For example, the shifting effect of the surface, a delicately patterned texture of grays and browns, is given regularity through the use of short, horizontal brushstrokes. Similarly, with the linear elements, strict horizontals and verticals dominate, although many irregular curves and angles are also evident. The combination of horizontal brushwork and right angles firmly establishes a grid that effectively counteracts the surface flux. Moreover, the repetition of certain diagonals and the relative lack of details in the upper left and upper right create a pyramidal shape. Thus, what at first may seem a chaotic composition of lines and muted colors turns out to be a well-organized unit. The aesthetic satisfaction of such a work depends on the way chaos seems to resolve itself into order.

LEARN ABOUT IT

31.1 Assess the impact of Cubism on abstract art in the early twentieth century.

31.2 Examine the different ways that artists in the Modern period responded directly or indirectly to the violence of war.

31.3 Investigate how Dada and Surrealism changed the form, content, and concept of art.

31.4 Analyze the relationship between function, form, and technology in early twentieth-century architecture.

31.5 Determine the political and economic impact of the Great Depression on interwar European and American art.

31.6 Assess how and why Abstract Expressionism transformed painting after 1940.

HEAR MORE: Listen to an audio file of your chapter **www.myartslab.com**

31 CHAPTER

EUROPE AND AMERICA
IN THE EARLY TWENTIETH CENTURY

At the beginning of the twentieth century, the fragile idea that "civilization" would inexorably continue to progress began to fissure and finally crack in an orgy of violence during World War I. Beginning in August 1914, the war initially pitted the Allies (Britain, France, and Russia) against the Central Powers (Germany and the Austro-Hungarian Empire) and the Ottoman Empire. The United States eventually entered the war on the side of Britain and France in 1917, the American contribution helping guarantee victory for the Allies the following year.

World War I transformed almost every aspect of politics, economics, and society in the Western world (MAP 31–1). The war was fought with twentieth-century technology but nineteenth-century strategies. Trench warfare and the Maxim gun caused the deaths of millions of soldiers and the horrible maiming of as many again. Europe lost an entire generation of young men; whole societies were shattered. The war also caused Europe to question the nineteenth-century imperial social and political order that had precipitated this carnage and foreshadowed a change in the character of warfare itself. Future wars would be over ideology rather than—as in the nineteenth century—territory.

In the first half of the twentieth century, three very different political ideologies struggled for world supremacy: communism (as in the U.S.S.R. and China), fascism (as in Italy and Germany), and liberal-democratic capitalism (as in America, Britain, and Western Europe). The October 1917 Russian Revolution led to the Russian Civil War, which in turn led to the triumph of the Bolshevik ("Majority") Communist Party, led by Vladimir Lenin, and to the founding of the U.S.S.R. in 1922. After Lenin's death and an internal power struggle, Joseph Stalin emerged as leader of the U.S.S.R.. Under Stalin, the U.S.S.R. annexed several neighboring states, suffered through the Great Purge of the 1930s, and lost tens of millions during the war against Nazi Germany.

Fascism first took firm root in Italy when Benito Mussolini came to power in October 1922. In Germany, meanwhile, the postwar democratic Weimar Republic was destroyed by a combination of rampant hyperinflation and the enmity between communists, socialists, centrists, Christian Democrats, and fascists. By the time of the 1932 parliamentary election, Germany's political and economic deterioration had paved the way for a Nazi Party victory and the promotion of its leader, Adolf Hitler, to chancellor. Fascism was not limited to Germany and Italy—it was widespread throughout Central and Eastern Europe and on the Iberian peninsula, where General Francisco Franco emerged victorious from the Spanish Civil War.

The economic impact of World War I was global. Although the United States emerged from it as the leading economic power in the world, the hyperinflation of Germany in the 1920s, the repudiation of German war debt under the Versailles Treaty, and the Stock Market Crash of 1929 in the United States plunged the Western world into a Great Depression that exacerbated political hostility between the major European countries, served as an incubator for fascism and communism in Europe, and tore apart the social and political fabric of Britain and America. In America, President Franklin D. Roosevelt created the New Deal programs in 1933 to stimulate the economy with government spending, and France and Britain took their first steps toward the modern welfare state. But ultimately the Great Depression was only ended by the military build-up of World War II. The latter lasted from 1939 to 1945, and the human carnage it caused both in battle and to civilians, particularly in German concentration camps, raised some difficult questions about the very nature of our humanity.

Changes in scientific knowledge were no less dramatic at this time. The foundations of Newtonian physics were shaken by Albert Einstein's publication of his Special Theory of Relativity and collapsed with the development of quantum theory by Niels Bohr, Werner Heisenberg, and Max Planck. These theories also unlocked the Pandora's box of nuclear energy, first opened when the British split the atom in 1919, and unleashed on the world when America dropped nuclear bombs on Japan in 1945.

The twentieth century also witnessed amazing new innovations in technology and manufacturing: the first powered flight (1903); the mass manufacture of automobiles (1909); the first public radio broadcast (1920); the electrification of most of Western Europe and North America (1920s); and the development of television (1926) and the jet engine (1937), to mention only a few. Technology led both to better medicines for prolonging life and to more efficient warfare, which shortened it. Information about the outside world became even more accessible with the advent of radio, television, and film. Where the visual culture of the nineteenth century was based on paper, that of the early twentieth century was based on photographs and films.

Just as quantum physics fundamentally altered our understanding of the physical world, developments in psychology fundamentally altered our conception of how the mind works and consequently how humans view themselves. In 1900, Austrian psychiatrist Sigmund Freud published *The Interpretation of Dreams*, which posited that our behavior is often motivated by powerful forces that are below our level of awareness. The human unconscious, as he described it, has strong urges for love and power that we simply cannot act upon if society is to remain peaceful and whole. Our psychic lives are not wholly, or even usually, guided by reason alone, but often by these urges that we may be unaware of. Thus we are always attempting to strike a balance between our rational and irrational sides, often erring on one side or the other. Also in 1900, Russian scientist Ivan Pavlov began feeding dogs just after ringing a bell. Soon the dogs salivated not at the sight of food but at the sound of the bell. The discovery that these "conditioned reflexes" also exist in humans showed that if we manage the external stimuli we can control people's appetites. Political leaders of all stripes soon took advantage of this fact.

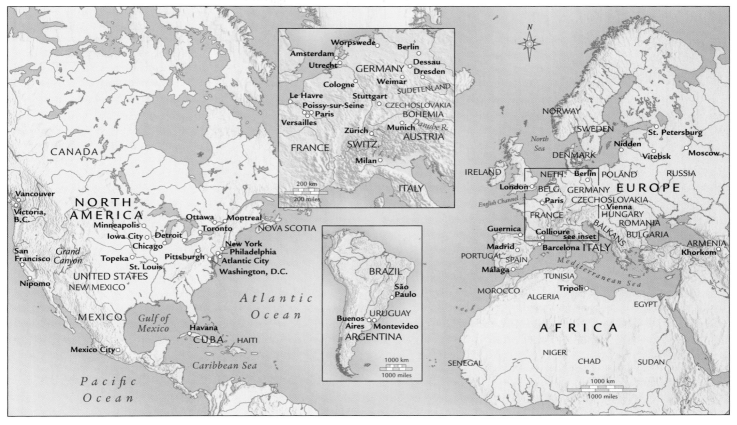

MAP 31-1 • EUROPE, THE AMERICAS, AND NORTH AFRICA, 1900–1950

The first half of the twentieth century was a time of exciting new technologies and increased access of ordinary people to consumer items, but it was also a time of cataclysmic social, economic, and political change, and a time when millions died in prison camps and wars. These changes, some for the better and some for the worse, shaped the art of the early twentieth century.

EARLY MODERN ART IN EUROPE

Modern artists invented myriad new ways of seeing our world. Few read academic physics or psychology texts, but they lived in a world that was being transformed by such fields, along with so many other technological advances. Modern art was frequently subversive and intellectually demanding, and it was often visually, socially, and politically radical. In the modern period it seemed as if every group of artists developed a manifesto or statement of intent along with their art, leading this to be described later as the age of "isms."

Yet most Modern art was still bound to the idea that a work of art, regardless of how it challenged vision and thought, was still a precious object—a painting or a sculpture or a designed object. Only a few artistic movements of this time, notably Dada and some elements of Surrealism, both of them prompted by the horrors of World War I, challenged this idea; their artistic preoccupations provided the foundation for much art after 1950.

THE FAUVES: WILD BEASTS OF COLOR

The Salon system still operated in France, but the ranks of artists dissatisfied with its conservative precepts were swelling. In 1903, a group of malcontents including André Derain (1880–1954), Henri Matisse (1869–1954), Georges Rouault (1871–1958), and Albert Marquet (1875–1947) organized the first Salon d'Automne (Autumn Salon) exhibition, so named to suggest its opposition to the official Salon show that took place every spring. The Autumn Salon, which continued until after World War I, promised juries more open to avant-garde art. The first major Modern movement of the twentieth century made its debut in this Salon's disorderly halls. Paintings by Derain, Matisse, and Maurice de Vlaminck (1876–1958) displayed in the exhibition in 1905 were filled with explosive colors and blunt brushwork. Responding to these characteristics in his review of the show, the critic Louis Vauxcelles described the young painters as *fauves* ("wild beasts"), the French term by which they soon became known. These artists took the French tradition of color and strong brushwork to new heights of intensity and expressive power, and entirely rethought the picture's surface.

Among the first major Fauve works were paintings that Derain and Matisse made in 1905 in Collioure, a Mediterranean port. Derain's **MOUNTAINS AT COLLIOURE (FIG. 31–2)** is painted in short, broad strokes of pure color. By placing the complementary colors of blue and orange together, as in the mountain range, or red and

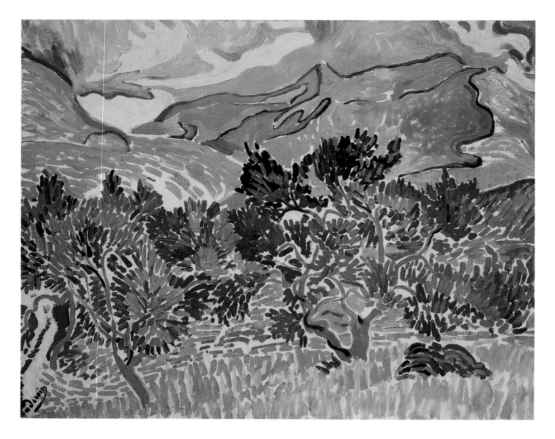

31-2 • André Derain
MOUNTAINS AT COLLIOURE
1905. Oil on canvas, 32 × 39½″
(81.5 × 100 cm). National Gallery
of Art, Washington, D.C. John Hay
Whitney Collection

green together, as in the trees, the artist intensifies the hue of each. The scene is painted in a range of seminaturalistic colors—the trees are sort-of green, their trunks are sort-of brown, and the grass is a kind-of green. It is visibly a landscape, but it is also a self-conscious exercise in painting. The colors are so bright that they seem to advance or push forward out of the picture plane (instead of creating an illusion of space behind it): As a consequence, we are very aware that what we are looking at is a flat canvas decorated with paint. This tension, along with explosive color, generates a visual energy that positively pulses from the painting. Derain described his colors as "sticks of dynamite," and his stark juxtapositions of complementary hues as "deliberate disharmonies."

Equally interested in such deliberate disharmonies was Matisse, whose **THE WOMAN WITH THE HAT** (FIG. 31–3) proved particularly controversial at the 1905 Autumn Salon because of its thick swatches of crude, arbitrary, nonnaturalistic color and its broad and blunt brushwork—the sitter, an otherwise conventional subject for a portrait, has a thick green stripe across her brow and down her nose. The uproar did not stop siblings Gertrude and Leo Stein, among the most important American patrons of avant-garde art at this time, from purchasing the work in 1905.

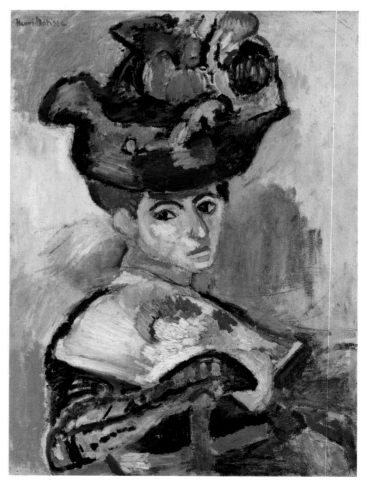

31-3 • Henri Matisse **THE WOMAN WITH THE HAT**
1905. Oil on canvas, 31¾ × 23½″ (80.6 × 59.7 cm). San Francisco Museum of Modern Art. Bequest of Elise S. Haas

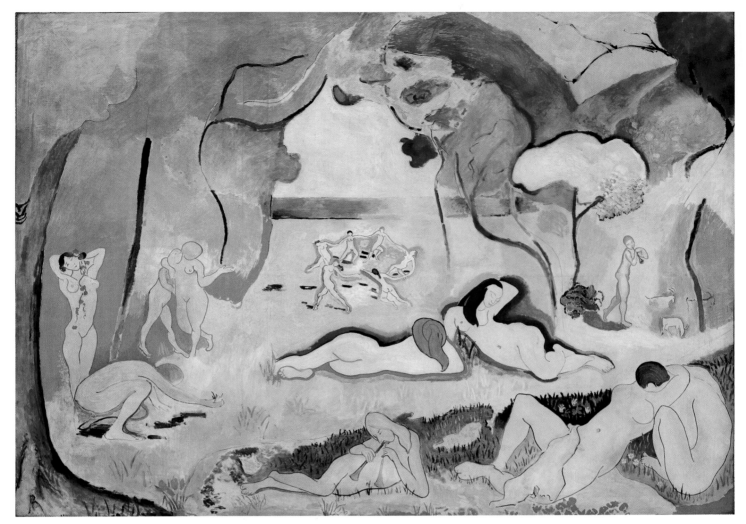

31-4 • Henri Matisse LE BONHEUR DE VIVRE (THE JOY OF LIFE)
1905–1906. Oil on canvas, 5′8½″ × 7′9¾″ (1.74 × 2.38 m). The Barnes Foundation, Merion, Pennsylvania. BF 719

The same year, Matisse also started **LE BONHEUR DE VIVRE (THE JOY OF LIFE)** (**FIG. 31–4**), a large pastoral landscape depicting a golden age—a reclining nude in the foreground plays pan pipes, another piper herds goats in the right mid-ground, lovers laze in the foreground while others frolic in dance in the background. Like Cézanne's *Large Bathers* of the same time (SEE FIG. 30–50), *The Joy of Life* is academic in scale and theme, but it is avant-garde in other respects—in the way the figures appear "flattened" and in the distortion of the spatial relations between them. Matisse emphasizes expressive color and draws on the tradition of folk art in his use of unmodeled forms and strong outlines. As he explained in 1908: "What I am after, above all, is expression." In the past, an artist might express feeling through the figure poses or facial expressions that the characters in the painting had. But now, he wrote, "The whole arrangement of my picture is expressive. The place occupied by figures or objects, the empty spaces around them, the proportions, everything plays a part." As for the colors he used: "The chief aim of color should be to serve expression as well as possible."

PICASSO, PRIMITIVISM, AND THE COMING OF CUBISM

Of all Modern art "isms" created before World War I, Cubism probably had the most influence on later artists. The joint invention of Pablo Picasso (1881–1973) and Georges Braque (1882–1963), Cubism proved a fruitful launching pad for both artists, allowing each to comment on modern life and to investigate how we perceive the world.

PICASSO'S EARLY ART.   Of all the "Modern" artists working in Paris, the undisputed capital of the art world prior to 1950, Picasso probably had the most significant impact on avant-garde art with this radical rethinking of how and what art communicates. Born in Málaga, Spain, Picasso was an artistic child prodigy. During his teenage years at the National Academy in Madrid, he made highly polished works that portended a bright future, had he stayed on a conservative artistic path. But his restless temperament led him to Barcelona in 1899, where he involved himself in avant-garde circles. In 1900, he traveled to Paris and moved there permanently in 1904. During this period he painted

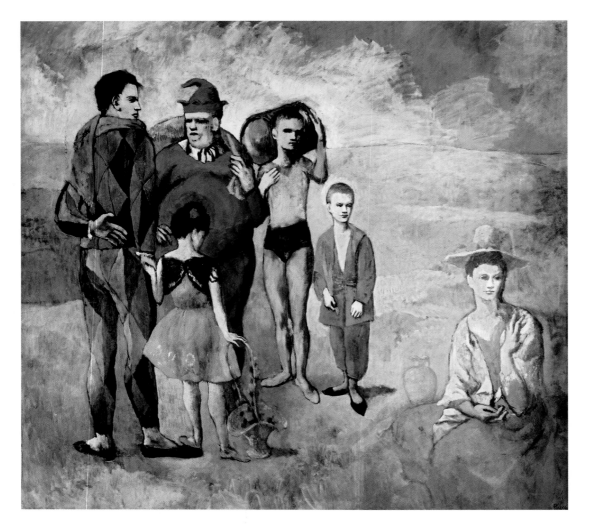

31–5 • Pablo Picasso
FAMILY OF SALTIMBANQUES
1905. Oil on canvas, 6′11¾″ × 7′6⅜″ (2.1 × 2.3 m). National Gallery of Art, Washington, D.C.
Chester Dale Collection

the outcasts of both cities in weary poses using a coldly expressive blue palette (his Blue Period). These paintings seem to have been motivated by Picasso's political sensitivity to those he considered victims of modern capitalist society, which eventually led him to join the Communist Party.

In 1904–1905, Picasso joined a larger group of Paris-based avant-garde artists and became fascinated with the subject of *saltimbanques* (traveling acrobats). He rarely painted them performing, however, focusing instead on the hardships of their existence on the margins of society. In **FAMILY OF SALTIMBANQUES** **(FIG. 31–5)**, a painting from his Rose Period (so called because of the introduction of that color into his palette), five *saltimbanques* stand in weary silence to the left, while a sixth, a woman, sits in curious isolation on the right. All of the *saltimbanques* seem psychologically withdrawn, as uncommunicative as the empty landscape they occupy. Picasso began to sell these works to a number of important collectors around 1905.

Around 1906, Picasso became one of the first artists in Paris to study and actively use images from African art in his paintings. This encounter with "primitive" art and art beyond the Western tradition would prove decisive in his career. In 1906, the Louvre installed a newly acquired collection of sixth- and fifth-century

BCE sculpture from the Iberian peninsula (present-day Spain and Portugal), but it was an exhibition of African masks that he saw around the same time that really changed the way Picasso thought about art. The exact date of this encounter is not known, but it might have occurred at the Musée d'Éthnographie du Trocadéro (now the Musée du Quai Branly) which was opened to the public in 1882, or at the Musée Permanent des Colonies (now the Musée National des Arts d'Afrique et d'Océanie), or in any number of stores in the city that sold "primitive" objects, mostly brought back from French colonies in Africa. Picasso greatly admired the expressive power and formal strangeness of the African masks that he saw. Since African art was relatively inexpensive, he also bought several pieces and kept them in his studio.

The term **primitivism**, as applied to the widespread tendency among Modern artists to scour the art of other cultures beyond the Western tradition for inspiration, is not benignly descriptive, since it implicitly makes a statement about perceptions of relative cultural superiority and inferiority. The inherent assumption is that Western culture is superior, more civilized, more developed, and more complex than other cultures, which are less civilized, less developed, and simpler than our own. It could be argued that, just as colonizing nations exploited "primitive" ones in the nineteenth century for their raw materials and labor to increase their own wealth and power, so Western artists exploited the visual cultures of "primitive" nations merely to amplify ideas about themselves. Many early Modern artists thus represented other cultures and their art without understanding, or really caring to understand, how the cultures actually functioned or how their art was used—this was the case with Picasso.

Picasso was certainly influenced by African art when he created **LES DEMOISELLES D'AVIGNON (THE YOUNG LADIES OF AVIGNON) (FIG. 31–6)**, one of the most radical and complex paintings of the twentieth century. The artist deliberately sends mixed messages in this work, beginning with the title: Avignon was the seat of a papal court in the fourteenth century, so it may mean that these figures are young ladies of the court; on the other hand, Avignon was also a red-light district in Barcelona, which would suggest that they are prostitutes—the most common interpretation of the scene. The work's boldness does not end with its controversial subject matter. Picasso may have undertaken such a large (nearly 8 feet square) painting in competition with both Matisse (who exhibited *The Joy of Life* in the 1906 Salon) and Cézanne (whose *Large Bathers* was shown the same year). Like Matisse and Cézanne,

Picasso revives and renegotiates the ideas of large-scale academic history painting, making use of the traditional subject of nude women shown in an interior space. There are other echoes of the Western tradition in the handling of the figures: The two in the center display themselves to the viewer like *Venus Anadyomene* (Venus Rising from the Sea), while that to the left stands in a rigid pose like an Archaic Greek figure (SEE FIG. 5–16) and the one seated on the right might suggest the pose of Manet's *Le Déjeuner sur l'Herbe* (SEE FIG. 30–17). Other visual references are Iberian and African. An Iberian influence is evident specifically in the faces of the three leftmost figures, with their flattened features and wide, almond-shaped eyes. The faces of the two right-hand figures, painted in a radically different style, were inspired by African art.

We see the African references not only in the masklike faces, but also in the handling of their forms in space. The women in the painting are flattened and fractured into sharp angular shapes. The space they inhabit is equally fractured and convulsive. The central pair of *demoiselles* raise their arms in a traditional gesture of accessibility but contradict it with their hard, piercing gazes and firm mouths. Even the fruit displayed in the foreground, perhaps a symbol of female sexuality, seems dangerous. The women, Picasso

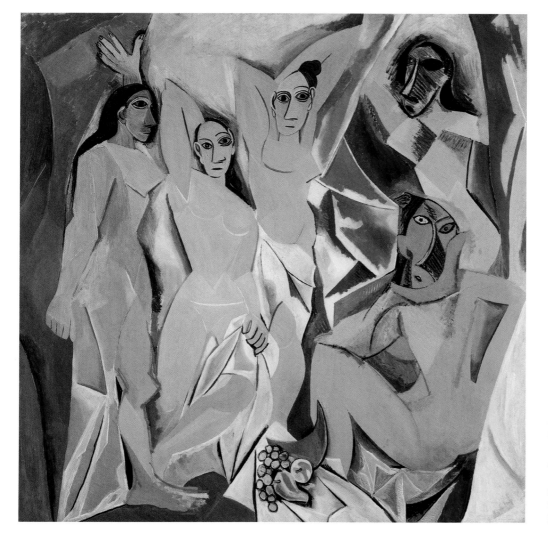

31-6 • Pablo Picasso LES DEMOISELLES D'AVIGNON (THE YOUNG LADIES OF AVIGNON)
1907. Oil on canvas, 8′ × 7′8″ (2.43 × 2.33 m). Museum of Modern Art, New York. Acquired through the Lillie P. Bliss Bequest (333.1939)

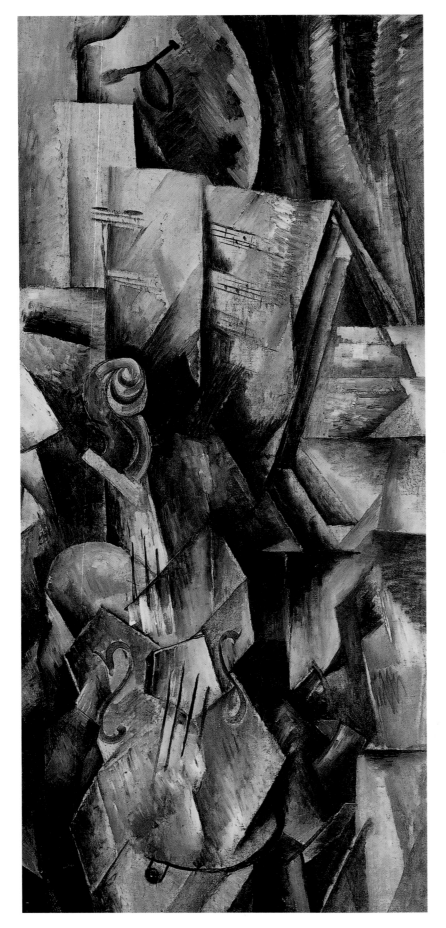

suggests, are not the gentle and passive creatures that men would like them to be. With this viewpoint he contradicts much of the tradition of erotic imagery since the Renaissance. Likewise, his treatment of space shatters the orderly perspective first proposed in Renaissance painting.

Most of Picasso's friends were shocked by his new work. Matisse, for example, accused Picasso of making a joke of Modern art and threatened to break off their friendship. But one artist, Georges Braque, responded positively—he saw in *Les Demoiselles d'Avignon* a potential for new visual experiments. Picasso used broken and distorted forms expressionistically to convey his view of women, which some feminists have described as misogynist. But what secured Picasso's place in the Parisian avant-garde was the revolution in form that *Les Demoiselles d'Avignon* inaugurated. Braque responded eagerly to Picasso's formal innovations and set out, alongside Picasso, to develop them. This painting inaugurated two phases of Cubism: Analytic and Synthetic.

ANALYTIC CUBISM. In 1907–1908, Picasso and Braque began a close working relationship that lasted until the latter went to war in 1914. According to Braque: "We were like two mountain climbers roped together."

Braque, a year younger than Picasso, was born near Le Havre, France, where he trained as a decorator. In 1900, he moved to Paris and began painting brightly colored landscapes in the Fauvist manner, but it was the 1906 Cézanne retrospective that established his future course. Picasso's *Demoiselles* sharpened his interest in altered form and compressed space and emboldened Braque to experiment in ways that built on Cézanne's late art.

Braque's 1908–1909 VIOLIN AND PALETTE (FIG. 31–7) shows the kind of relatively small-scale still-life paintings that the two artists experimented with initially. In it, the move toward the gradual abstraction of recognizable subject matter and space is evident. The still-life items are not arranged in illusionistic depth but are pushed close to the picture plane in a shallow space. Braque knits the various elements—a violin, an artist's palette, and some sheet music—together into a single shifting surface of forms and colors. In some areas of the painting, these formal elements have lost not only their

31-7 • Georges Braque VIOLIN AND PALETTE
1909–1910. Oil on canvas, 36⅛ × 16⅞″ (91.8 × 42.9 cm). Solomon R. Guggenheim Museum, New York. 54.1412

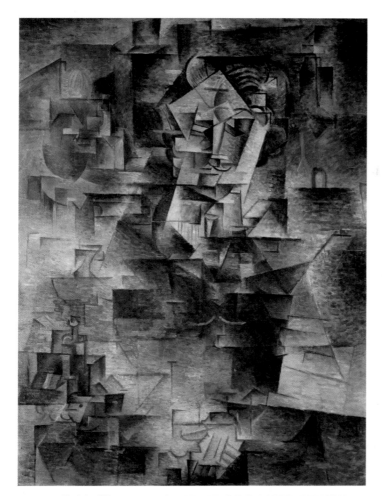

31-8 • Pablo Picasso PORTRAIT OF DANIEL-HENRY KAHNWEILER
1910. Oil on canvas, 39½ × 28⅝″ (100.6 × 72.8 cm). Art Institute of Chicago.

different approach to the breaking up of forms. Picasso and Braque did not simply fracture objects visually, they picked them apart and rearranged their component parts. Thus, Analytic Cubism resembles the actual process of perception. When we look at an object, we are likely to examine it from various points of view and reassemble our glances into a whole object in our brain. Picasso and Braque shattered their subjects into jagged forms analogous to momentary, partial glances, but they reassembled the pieces to communicate meaning rather than to represent observed reality.

SYNTHETIC CUBISM.   Works such as *Ma Jolie* brought Picasso and Braque to the brink of complete abstraction, but in the spring of 1912 they pulled back and began to create works that suggested more visually discernible subjects. Neither artist wanted to break the link to reality; Picasso said that there was no such thing as completely abstract art, because "You have to start somewhere." This second major phase of Cubism is known as Synthetic Cubism because of the way the artists created complex compositions by combining and transforming individual elements, as in a chemical synthesis. Picasso's **GLASS AND BOTTLE OF SUZE (FIG. 31–9)**, like many of the works he and Braque created from 1912 to 1914, is a

natural spatial relations but their coherent shapes as well. Where representational motifs remain—the violin, for example—Braque fragmented them to facilitate their integration into the compositional whole.

Picasso's 1910 Cubist **PORTRAIT OF DANIEL-HENRY KAHNWEILER (FIG. 31–8)** shows the artist's first and most important art dealer in Paris, who saved many artists from destitution by buying their early works: He was an early champion of Picasso's art, being one of the first to recognize the significance of *Les Demoiselles*. His impressive stable of artists included—in addition to Picasso—Braque, André Derain, Ferdinand Léger, and Juan Gris. Being German, Kahnweiler was forced to flee France for Switzerland during World War I, and being Jewish, he was forced into hiding in Paris during World War II.

Braque's and Picasso's paintings of 1909 and 1910 initiated what is known as Analytic Cubism because of the way the artists broke objects into parts as if to analyze them. The works of 1911 and early 1912, such as Picasso's *Ma Jolie* (SEE FIG. 32–1), are also grouped under the Analytic label, although they reflect a

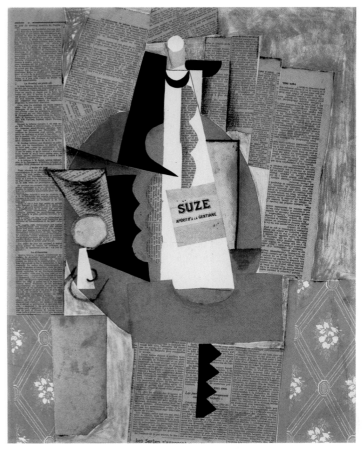

31-9 • Pablo Picasso GLASS AND BOTTLE OF SUZE
1912. Pasted paper, gouache, and charcoal, 25¾ × 19¼″ (65.4 × 50.2 cm). Washington University Gallery of Art, St. Louis, Missouri.

collage (from the French *coller*, meaning "to glue"), a work composed of separate elements pasted together. At the center, newsprint and construction paper are assembled to suggest a tray or round table supporting a glass and a bottle of liquor with an actual label. Around this arrangement Picasso pasted larger pieces of newspaper and wallpaper. The composition is Cubist; its angular shapes overlap in a shallow space. The elements together evoke not only a place—a bar—but also an activity: the viewer alone with a newspaper, enjoying a quiet drink. However, the newspaper clippings deal with the First Balkan War of 1912–1913, which contributed to the outbreak of World War I. Picasso may have wanted to underline the modernity of his art with this reference to the political chaos then building in the Balkans.

Picasso employed collage three-dimensionally to produce Synthetic Cubist sculpture, such as **MANDOLIN AND CLARINET** **(FIG. 31–10)**. Composed of wood scraps, the sculpture suggests the Cubist subject of two musical instruments, here shown at right angles to each other. Sculpture had traditionally been either carved, modeled, or cast, but Picasso's sculptural collage was new. In works such as this, Picasso introduced the sculptural technique of **assemblage**, giving sculptors the option not only of carving or modeling but also of constructing their works out of found objects and unconventional materials. Another of Picasso's innovations was his introduction of space into the interior of the sculpture. The parts of the sculpture do not fit perfectly together, leaving gaps and holes. Moreover, the white central piece describes a semicircle that juts outward toward the viewer. The sculpture creates volume by using both forms and spaces rather than mass alone. Thus Picasso challenged the traditional conception of sculpture as a condensed solid form.

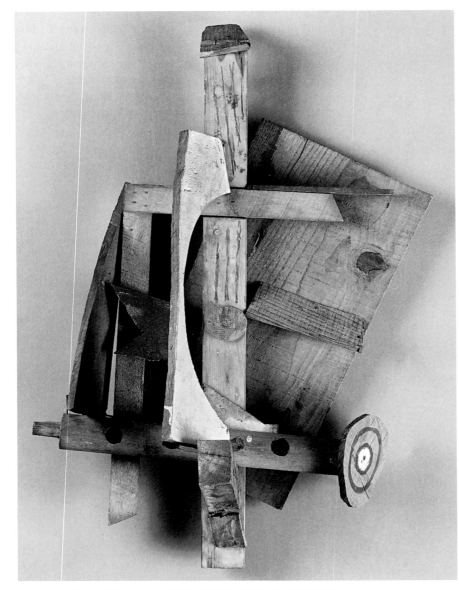

31–10 • Pablo Picasso MANDOLIN AND CLARINET
1913. Construction of painted wood with pencil marks, 25⅝ × 14⅛ × 9″ (58 × 36 × 23 cm). Musée Picasso, Paris.

THE BRIDGE AND PRIMITIVISM

Simultaneously with all this activity in Paris, a group of radical German artists came together in Dresden as Die Brücke (The Bridge), taking their name from a passage in Friedrich Nietzsche's *Thus Spake Zarathustra* (1883) which described contemporary humanity's potential as a "bridge" to a more perfect humanity in the future. Formed in 1905, The Bridge included architecture students Fritz Bleyl (1880–1966), Erich Heckel (1883–1970), Ernst Ludwig Kirchner (1880–1938), and Karl Schmidt-Rottluff (1884–1976). Other German and northern European artists later joined the group, which continued in existence until 1913. These artists hoped The Bridge would be a gathering place for "all revolutionary and surging elements" who opposed Germany's "pale, overbred, and decadent" society.

Drawing on northern visual prototypes, such as Van Gogh or Munch, and adopting traditional northern media such as woodcuts, these artists created intense, brutal, expressionistic images of alienation in response to Germany's fast, intensive, and brutal urbanization. Not surprisingly, their favorite motifs were the natural world and the nude body—nudism was also a growing cultural trend in Germany in those years, as city dwellers forsook the city to reconnect with nature. Karl Schmidt-Rottluff's **THREE NUDES—DUNE PICTURE FROM NIDDEN** **(FIG. 31–11)** portrays three bulky but flattened female nudes. By integrating these nude women into their surroundings, Schmidt-Rottluff makes them seem "natural" and the landscape "feminine," in contrast to more masculine

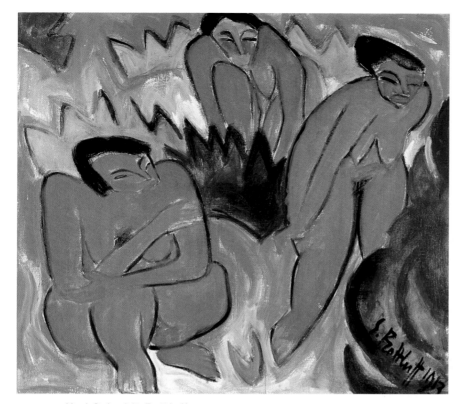

31-11 • Karl Schmidt-Rottluff THREE NUDES—DUNE PICTURE FROM NIDDEN
1913. Oil on canvas, 38⅝ × 41¾″ (98 × 106 cm). Staatliche Museen zu Berlin, Preussischer Kulturbesitz, Nationalgalerie.

to him from European carnivals (SEE FIG. 30–42). By collapsing these traditions together, Nolde transforms sources drawn from art beyond the Western tradition into a European nightmare full of horror and implicit violence. The gaping mouths and hollow eyes of the hideously colored and roughly drawn masks seem to mock the viewer, appearing to advance from the picture plane. Nolde also uses the juxtaposition of complementaries to intensify his colors and the violent emotions they are intended to communicate. On the eve of World War I, Nolde accompanied a German scientific expedition to New Guinea, explaining that what attracted him to the arts of Oceania was their "primitivism," their "absolute originality, the intense and often grotesque expression of power and life in very simple forms—that may be why we like these works of native art." Nolde stopped frequenting The Bridge's studio in 1907 but remained friendly with the group's members.

During the summers, members of The Bridge returned to nature, visiting remote areas of northern Germany, but in 1911 they moved to Berlin—perhaps preferring to imagine rather than actually live the simple life. Their images of cities,

"rational" culture. In this painting, the three "primitive" women actually seem to become part of nature. Their bright red flesh is separated from the background only by their dark outlines. They are like huge "earth mothers," a likely intentional association since the *Woman from Willendorf* (SEE FIG. 1–7) had been discovered in Austria and presented to the world with great fanfare only five years earlier, in 1908. The immediate juxtaposition of the complementary colors red and green serves to intensify both colors and creates an example of bold, intense northern Expressionism.

Although not part of the original Bridge group, Emil Nolde (1867–1956) joined in 1906 and quickly became its most committed member. Nolde originally trained in industrial design, studying academic painting privately in Paris for a few months in 1900, but he never painted as he was taught. Rather, Nolde regularly visited ethnographic museums to study the tribal arts of Africa and Oceania. He was impressed by the radical and forceful visual presence of the figural arts that he saw there. One result of his research was **MASKS (FIG. 31–12)** of 1911, in which he seems to refer both to the masks he studied in Paris, and to those familiar

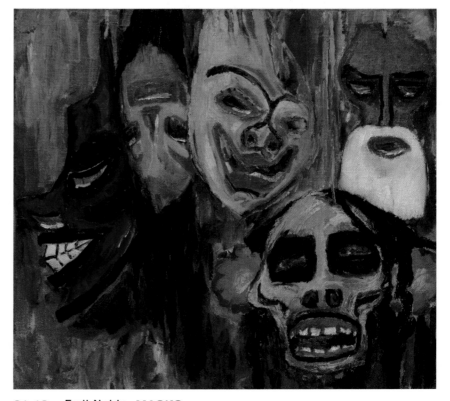

31-12 • Emil Nolde MASKS
1911. Oil on canvas, 28¾ × 30½″ (73.03 × 77.47 cm). Nelson-Atkins Museum, Kansas City, Missouri. Gift of the Friends of Art, 5490

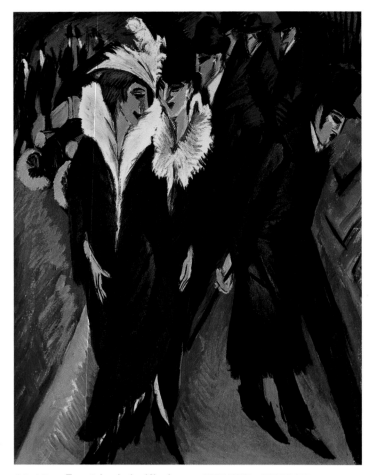

31–13 • Ernst Ludwig Kirchner STREET, BERLIN
1913. Oil on canvas, 47½ × 35⅞″ (120.6 × 91 cm). Museum of Modern Art, New York. Purchase (274.39)

especially Berlin, are powerfully critical of urban existence. In Ernst Ludwig Kirchner's **STREET, BERLIN (FIG. 31–13)**, two prostitutes—their profession advertised by their large feathered hats and fur-trimmed coats—strut past well-dressed bourgeois men whom they view as potential clients. They seem to have deliberately embarrassed the man to their left, smirking as he hurriedly refocuses his attention on the shop window to the right. The women and men appear as artificial and dehumanized figures, with masklike faces and stiff gestures. Their bodies crowd together, but they are psychologically distant from one another. The harsh biting colors, tilted perspective, and piercingly sharp brushstrokes make this a disturbing Expressionistic image of urban degeneracy and alienation.

INDEPENDENT EXPRESSIONISTS

Beyond the members of The Bridge, many other artists in Germany and Austria worked in an Expressionist mode before World War I. One, Käthe Kollwitz (1867–1945), was committed to working-class causes and pursued social change primarily through printmaking because of this cheap and easily disseminable medium's potential to reach a wide audience. Between 1902 and 1908, she produced a series of seven etchings showing the

sixteenth-century German Peasants' War. **THE OUTBREAK (FIG. 31–14)**, a lesson in the power of group action, portrays the ugly fury of the peasants as they charge forward armed only with farm tools, bent on revenge against their oppressors for years of abuse. The faces of the two figures at the front of the charge are particularly grotesque while the leader, Black Anna—whom Kollwitz modeled on herself—signals the attack with a gesture that is inhumanly fierce. Her arms silhouetted against the sky, and the crowded mass of workers with their farm tools, form a passionate picture of political revolt.

Like Kollwitz, Paula Modersohn-Becker (1876–1907) studied at the Berlin School of Art for Women. In 1898, she moved to Worpswede, an artists' retreat in rural northern Germany. Dissatisfied with the Worpswede artists' naturalistic approach to rural life, after 1900 she made four trips to Paris to view recent developments in Post-Impressionist painting. Although obviously informed by the "primitivizing" tendencies of other artists such as Gauguin (SEE FIG. 30–36) toward women at the time, her physically small and yet monumental **SELF-PORTRAIT WITH AN AMBER NECKLACE (FIG. 31–15)** subverts those same tendencies. Modersohn-Becker appears as a kind of earth mother, surrounded by plants and with flowers in her hair and hands, but she also has a powerful, human presence. Modersohn-Becker looks out of the canvas at us, calmly returning our gaze and establishing her humanity. While painted in the manner of other Modernists, this tender self-portrait reveals an artist of strong independent ideas and a woman of sharp intelligence.

In contrast to Modersohn-Becker's gentle self-portrait, **SELF-PORTRAIT NUDE (FIG. 31–16)** of 1911 by the Austrian artist Egon Schiele (1890–1918) conveys physical and psychological torment. Schiele's father died insane from untreated syphilis when the artist

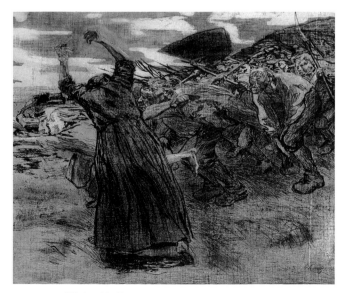

31–14 • Käthe Kollwitz THE OUTBREAK
From the *Peasants' War* series. 1903. Etching, 20 × 23⅓″ (50.7 × 59.2 cm). Kupferstichkabinett, Staatliche Museen zu Berlin, Preussischer Kulturbesitz. Kunstmuseum, Switzerland (1748)

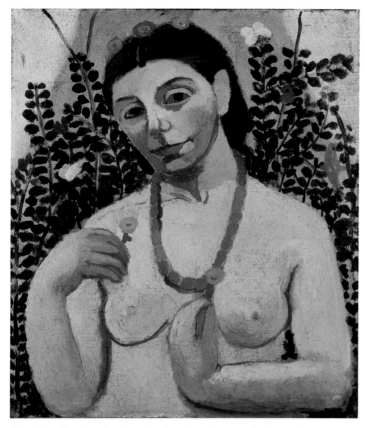

31–15 • Paula Modersohn-Becker **SELF-PORTRAIT WITH AN AMBER NECKLACE**
1906. Oil on canvas, 24 × 19¾″ (61 × 50 cm).
Öffentliche Kunstsammlung Basel.

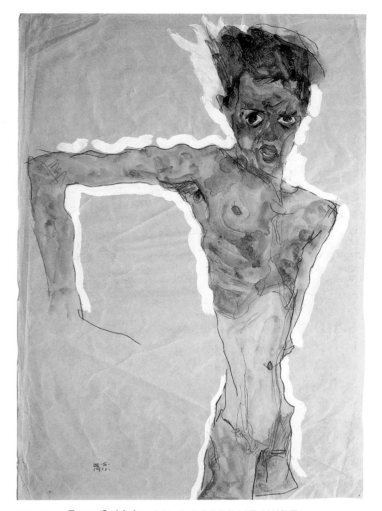

31–16 • Egon Schiele **SELF-PORTRAIT NUDE**
1911. Gouache and pencil on paper, 20¼ × 13¾″ (51.4 × 35 cm).
Metropolitan Museum of Art, New York. Bequest of Scofield Thayer, 1982
(1984.433.298)

was just 14, and as a result Schiele had a tendency to conflate suffering and sexuality throughout his life. In many drawings and watercolors, Schiele portrays women in demeaning, sexually explicit poses that emphasize their animal nature, and in his self-portraits the artist turns the same harsh gaze upon himself, revealing deep ambivalence toward sexuality and the body in his art and his life. In *Self-Portrait Nude*, he stares out of the picture with anguish, his emaciated body stretched and displayed in a halo of harsh light. Mutilated and impotent, he has neither right hand nor genitals. The missing body parts have been interpreted in Freudian fashion as the artist's symbolic self-punishment for indulgence in masturbation, then commonly believed to lead to insanity.

SPIRITUALISM OF THE BLUE RIDER

Formed in Munich by the Russian artist Vassily Kandinsky (1866–1944) and the German artist Franz Marc (1880–1916), Der Blaue Reiter ("The Blue Rider") was named for a popular image of a blue knight, the St. George on the city emblem of Moscow. Just as St. George had been a spiritual leader in society, so The Blue Rider aspired to offer spiritual leadership in the arts. Its first exhibition was held in December 1911 and included the work of 14 artists working in a wide range of styles, from realism to radical abstraction.

By 1911, Marc was mostly painting animals rather than humans. He had a spiritual affinity to animals, which he felt were more "primitive" and thus purer than humans, enjoying a more spiritual relationship with nature. He rendered them in big, bold forms painted in almost-primary colors. In **THE LARGE BLUE HORSES (FIG. 31–17)**, the animals merge into a homogenous unit. Their sweeping contours reflect the harmony of their collective existence and echo the curved lines of the hills behind them, suggesting that they are also in harmony with their surroundings. The blue of the horses alludes to St. George and to the spirituality of the natural world.

Born into a wealthy family in Moscow, Kandinsky initially trained as a lawyer, but after visiting exhibitions of Modern art in Germany and taking private art lessons, he gave up the legal profession, moved to Munich, and established himself as an artist. His early works make frequent reference to Russian folk culture, which he admired for its "primitivism."

Kandinsky may have been a synesthete—i.e. someone who "hears" colors and "sees" sound. Whether he was or not, his art is

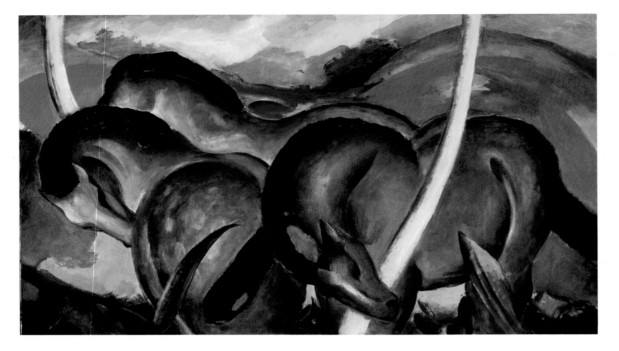

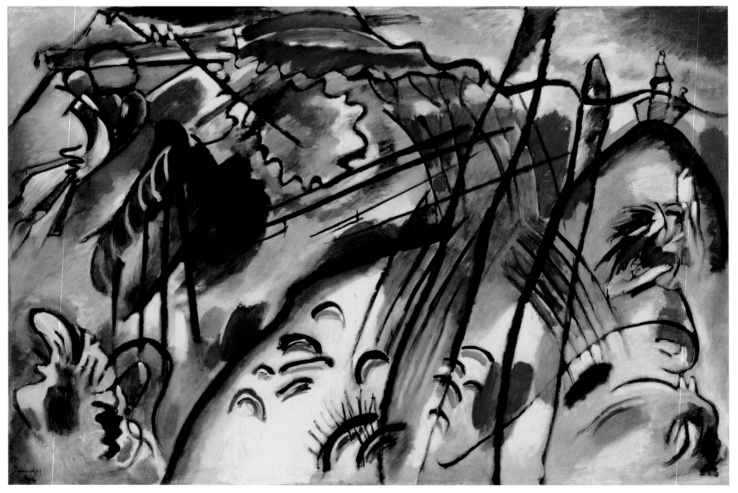

31-18 • Vassily Kandinsky IMPROVISATION 28 (SECOND VERSION)
1912. Oil on canvas, 43⅞ × 63⅞" (111.4 × 162.2 cm). Guggenheim Museum, New York. Gift, Solomon R. Guggenheim. 37.239

EXPLORE MORE: Gain insight from a primary source by Vassily Kandinsky **www.myartslab.com**

clearly that of an artist for whom sound and color were inextricably linked. His early study of the work of Whistler (SEE FIG. 30–39) convinced him that the arts of painting and music were related: Just as a composer organizes sound, so a painter organizes color and form. Kandinsky was particularly interested in the music of the Austrian composer Arnold Schoenberg, who around 1910 introduced a momentous change in musical history. All Western music since antiquity was previously based on the arrangement of notes into scales, or modes (such as today's common major and minor), and composers chose the scale they worked in for expressive reasons. Particularly since the Baroque period, each note in any given scale had a role to play, and these roles operated in a clear hierarchy that served to reinforce what became known as the "tonal center," a kind of home base or place of repose in the musical composition. Schoenberg eliminated the tonal center and treated all tones equally, denying the listener any place of repose and instead prolonging the tension (and thus, he felt, the expression) of his music indefinitely. Kandinsky contacted the composer and was delighted to find out that he also painted in an Expressionist style. Kandinsky believed that if music could exist without a tonal center, could art exist without subject matter?

Kandinsky was thus one of the first artists to investigate the theoretical possibility of purely abstract painting. He gave his works musical titles, such as "Composition" and "Improvisation," and aspired to make paintings that responded to his inner state rather than an external stimulus and which would be entirely autonomous, making no reference to the visible world. In 1912, he painted a series of works, including **IMPROVISATION 28 (FIG. 31–18)**, that he claimed was the first truly abstract art. In these, Kandinsky's colors leap and dance, with different colors expressing different emotions. For Kandinsky, painting was a utopian spiritual force. He believed that art's traditional focus on accurate rendering of the physical world was a basically materialistic quest. Art should not depend so much on mere physical reality. He hoped that his paintings would lead humanity toward a deeper awareness of spirituality and the inner world. Rather than searching for correspondence between the painting and the world where none is intended, the artist asks us to look at the painting as if we were hearing a symphony, responding instinctively and spontaneously to this or that passage, and then to the total experience. Kandinsky further explained the musical analogy in his book *Concerning the Spiritual in Art*: "Color directly influences the soul. Color is the keyboard, the eyes are the hammers, the soul is the piano with many strings. The artist is the hand that plays, touching one key or another purposively, to cause vibrations in the soul."

Despite Kandinsky's noble aspirations, however, works such as *Improvisation 28* are not entirely abstract. They often retain a vestige of the landscape—Kandinsky found references to nature the hardest to transcend—as well as suggestions of horses, boats, and oars. But these half-recognized forms increasingly act in his works as a kind of punctuation mark to increase or decrease our speed, or raise or lower our emotions, as our eyes fly around his canvases.

EXTENSIONS OF CUBISM

As Cubism emerged from the studios of Braque and Picasso, it was clear to the art world that they had altered the artistic discourse irrevocably. Cubism's way of viewing the world resonated with artists all over Europe, in Russia, and even in the United States. These artists interpreted Cubism in their own ways, significantly broadening and extending its visual message beyond the ideas and objects of Picasso and Braque.

FRANCE. Robert Delaunay (1885–1941) and his wife, the Ukrainian-born Sonia Delaunay-Terk (b. Sonia Stern, 1885–1979), took the relatively monochromatic and relatively static forms of Cubism in a new direction. Delaunay's early work was inflected with Fauvist color; he also had a deep interest in communicating spirituality through color and participated in Blue Rider exhibitions. In 1910, he began to fuse this intense interest in color with Cubist forms to create paintings celebrating the modern city and modern technology. In **HOMAGE TO BLÉRIOT (FIG. 31–19)**, Delaunay pays tribute to Louis Blériot, the French pilot who in 1909 became the first person to fly across the English Channel, by

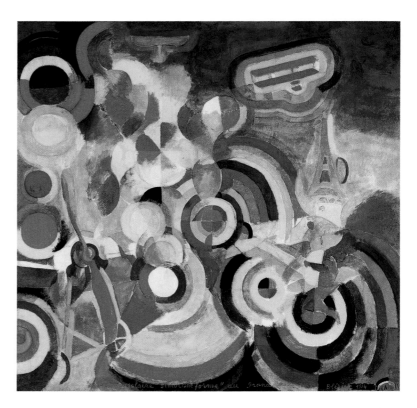

31–19 • Robert Delaunay HOMAGE TO BLÉRIOT
1914. Tempera on canvas, 8'2½" × 8'3" (2.5 × 2.51 m).
Öffentliche Kunstsammlung Basel, Kunstmuseum, Basel, Switzerland. Emanuel Hoffman Foundation

portraying his airplane flying over the Eiffel Tower, the Parisian symbol of modernity. The brightly colored circular forms that fill the rest of the canvas suggest the movement of the airplane's propeller, a blazing sun in the sky, and the great rose window of the Cathedral of Notre-Dame, representing Delaunay's ideas of "progressive" science and spirituality. This painting's fractured colors suggest both the power of the Christian God's light and the fast-moving parts of modern machinery.

The critic Guillaume Apollinaire labeled the art of both Robert and Sonia Delaunay "Orphism" after Orpheus, the legendary Greek poet whose lute playing charmed wild beasts, thus implying that their art had similar power. They preferred the term "simultaneity," a concept based on Michel-Eugène Chevreul's law of the simultaneous contrast of colors that proposed collapsing spatial distance and temporal sequence into the simultaneous "here and now" to create a harmonic unity out of the disharmonious world. They envisioned a simultaneity that combined the modern world of airplanes, telephones, and automobiles with spirituality.

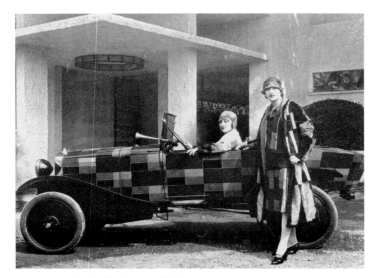

31–20 • Sonia Delaunay-Terk CLOTHES AND CUSTOMIZED CITROËN B-12 (EXPO 1925 MANNEQUINS AVEC AUTO)
From *Maison de la Mode*, 1925.

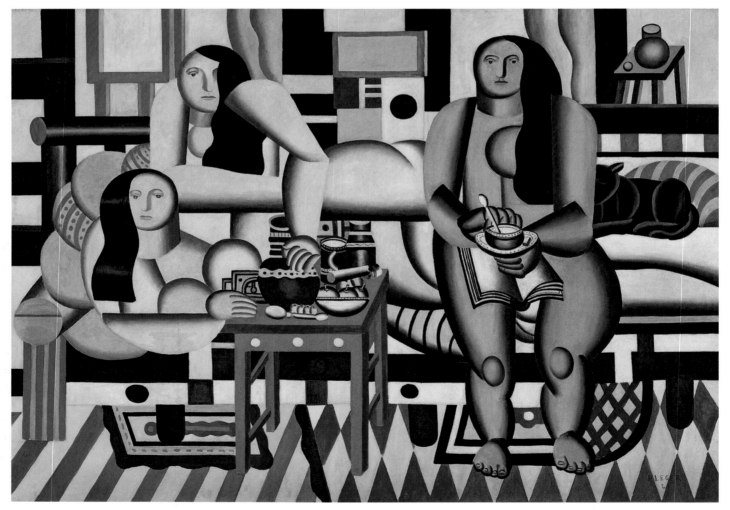

31–21 • Fernand Léger THREE WOMEN
1921. Oil on canvas, 6′½″ × 8′3″ (1.84 × 2.52 m). Museum of Modern Art, New York. Mrs. Simon Guggenheim Fund

Sonia Delaunay (née Terk) produced Orphist paintings with Robert, but she was also an important fabric and clothing designer. She created new clothing patterns similar to Cubist paintings that she called Simultaneous Dresses and exhibited a line of inexpensive ready-to-wear garments with bold geometric designs at the important 1925 International Exposition of Modern Decorative and Industrial Arts. She decorated a Citroën sports car to match one of her ensembles for the exhibition (FIG. 31–20), choosing the sports car as an expression of the new automobile age, because like her clothing this car was produced inexpensively for a mass market and because the small three-seater was designed specifically to appeal to the newly independent woman of the time, Delaunay's clientele base. Sadly, there are only black-and-white photographs of these designs.

Technology also fascinated Fernand Léger (1881–1955), who painted a more static but brilliantly colored version of Cubism based on machine forms. THREE WOMEN (FIG. 31–21) is a Purist, machine-age version of the French academic subject of the reclining nude. Purism was developed in Paris by Le Corbusier (b. Charles-Édouard Jeanneret, 1887–1965) and Amédée Ozenfant in a 1925 book, *The Foundation of Modern Art*, that argued for a return to clear, ordered forms and ideas to express the efficient clarity of the machine age. In Léger's painting, the women's forms are constructed from large machinelike planes arranged in an asymmetrical geometric grid that both embodies a cool Classicism and suggests an arrangement of plumbing parts. The women are dehumanized; they have identical, bland, round faces; they seem to be assembled from standard, interchangeable parts; and the brightly colored background suggests fantastic plumbing. The exuberant colors and patterns that surround the women suggest an orderly industrial society in which everything has its place.

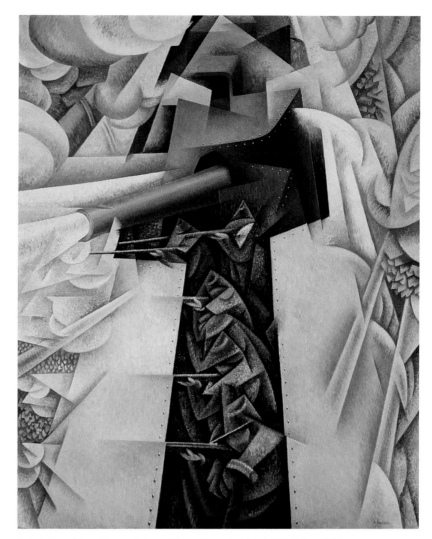

31-22 • Gino Severini ARMORED TRAIN IN ACTION
1915. Oil on canvas, 45⅝ × 34⅞″ (115.8 × 88.5 cm). Museum of Modern Art, New York. Gift of Richard S. Zeisler. 287.86

ITALY. In Italy, technology and speed were combined with Cubism to create Futurism. In 1908, Italy was a state in crisis: There were huge disparities of wealth between the north and south; four-fifths of the country was illiterate; poverty and near-starvation were rampant; and as many as 50,000 people had recently died in one of the nation's worst earthquakes. On February 20, 1909, the Milanese poet and editor Filippo Tommaso Marinetti (1876–1944) published his "Foundation and Manifesto of Futurism" on the front page of the Parisian newspaper *Le Figaro*, in which he attacked everything old, dull, and "feminine," and proposed to shake Italy free of its past by embracing an exhilarating, "masculine," "futuristic," and even dangerous world based on the thrill, the speed, energy, and power of modern urban life.

In April 1911, a group of Milanese artists followed Marinetti's manifesto with the "Technical Manifesto of Futurist Painting," in which they demanded that "all subjects previously used must be swept aside in order to express our whirling life of steel, of pride, of fever, and of speed." Some of these artists traveled to Paris for a Futurist exhibition in 1912, after which they harnessed the visual forms of Cubism to their love of machines, speed, and war.

Gino Severini (1883–1966) signed the "Technical Manifesto" while living in Paris, where he served as an intermediary between the Italian-based Futurists and the French avant-garde. Perhaps more than other Futurists, Severini embraced the concept of war as a social cleansing agent. In 1915, he painted **ARMORED TRAIN IN ACTION** (FIG. 31–22), which was probably based on a photograph of a Belgian armored car on a train going over a bridge. Severini uses the jagged forms and splintered overlapping surfaces of Cubism to describe a tumultuous scene of smoke, violence, and cannon blasts issuing from the speeding train as seen from a dizzying and disorienting viewpoint.

In 1912, Umberto Boccioni (1882–1916) argued for a Futurist "sculpture of environment," in which form should explode in a

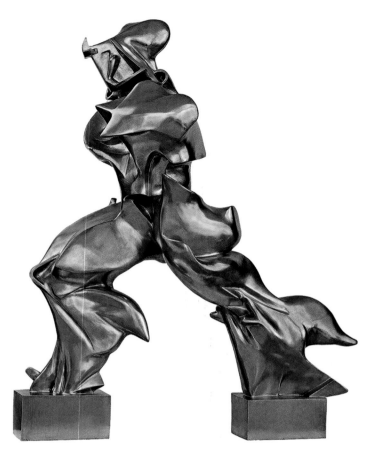

31-23 • Umberto Boccioni UNIQUE FORMS OF CONTINUITY IN SPACE
1913. Bronze, 43⅞ × 34⅞ × 15¾" (111 × 89 × 40 cm). Museum of Modern Art, New York. Acquired through the Lillie P. Bliss Bequest (231.1948)

EXPLORE MORE: Gain insight from a primary source by Filippo Tommaso Marinetti **www.myartslab.com**

violent burst of motion from the closed and solid mass of traditional sculpture into the surrounding space. In **UNIQUE FORMS OF CONTINUITY IN SPACE (FIG. 31–23)**, Boccioni portrays a figure striding powerfully through space, like the ancient *Nike (Victory of Samothrace)* (SEE FIG. 5–56), with muscular forms like wings flying out energetically behind it. Many of Boccioni's sculptures made use of unconventional materials; this sculpture was actually made of plaster. It was cast in bronze after the artist's death. In keeping with his Futurist ideals, Boccioni celebrated Italy's entry into World War I by enlisting and was killed in combat.

RUSSIA. By 1900, Russian artists and art collectors in the cosmopolitan cities of St. Petersburg and later Moscow had begun to embrace avant-garde art and to travel to Paris regularly. Russian artists also drew on Futuristic ideas about the possibility of technology and the aesthetic of speed to modernize Russia. In 1912, Russian Futurist artists, also known as Cubo-Futurists, claiming to have emerged independently of Italian Futurism, began to move toward abstraction in art.

Natalia Goncharova's (1881–1962) **ELECTRIC LIGHT** of 1913 **(FIG. 31–24)** shows a brightly artificial new electric light fracturing and dissolving its surrounding forms. Goncharova also combined Russian folk art with abstraction in costumes and sets for several of Sergei Diaghilev's Ballet Russes stagings, including *Le Coq d'or* (1914), *Night on Bald Mountain* (1923) and the 1926 revival of Stravinsky's *Firebird*.

After 1915, Kazimir Malevich (1878–1935) emerged as the leader of the Moscow avant-garde. According to his later reminiscences, "in the year 1913, in my desperate attempt to free art from the burden of the object, I took refuge in the square form and exhibited a picture which consisted of nothing more than a black square on a white field." *The Black Square* was one of the backdrops for Mikhail Matiushin's Russian futurist opera, *Victory Over the Sun.* Malevich exhibited 39 works of art, consisting of flat, abstract shapes collaged together which he termed Suprematism, at the "Last Futurist Exhibition of Paintings: 0.10," held in St. Petersburg in the winter of 1915–1916. One work, **SUPREMATIST PAINTING (EIGHT RED RECTANGLES) (FIG. 31–25)**, consists of eight red rectangles arranged diagonally on a white painted ground. Malevich described Suprematism as "the supremacy of pure feeling in creative art."

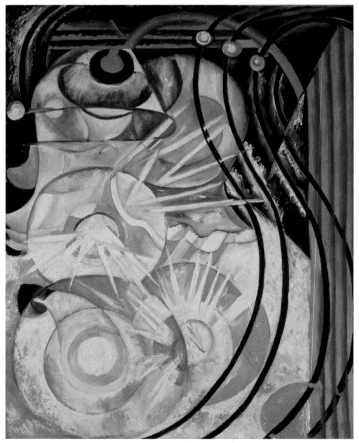

31-24 • Natalia Goncharova ELECTRIC LIGHT
1913. Oil on canvas, 41½ × 32" (105.5 × 81.3 cm). Musée National d'Art Moderne, Centre National d'Art et de Culture Georges Pompidou.

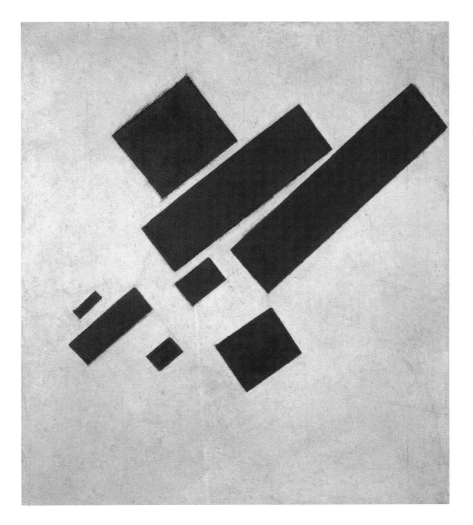

31-25 • Kazimir Malevich
**SUPREMATIST PAINTING
(EIGHT RED RECTANGLES)**
1915. Oil on canvas, 22½ × 18⅞"
(57 × 48 cm). Stedelijk Museum,
Amsterdam.

EXPLORE MORE: Gain insight
from a primary source by
Kazimir Malevich
www.myartslab.com

At the same time Vladimir Tatlin (1885–1953) began to construct entirely abstract sculptures that he entitled **CORNER COUNTER-RELIEFS (FIG. 31–26).** He created these sculptures from various nonprecious, nonart materials such as metal, glass, wood, plaster, and wire. Although his move away from sculpture conceived of as mass and traditional materials may have been inspired by a visit to Picasso's studio, Tatlin's art created an entirely new formal and conceptual language for sculpture by actively using open and negative space, eliminating sculpture's reliance on mass and monumentality, and producing fragile and physically unstable objects that not only had no bases but actually hung in the corners of rooms—the space formerly reserved for religious icons. In effect, Tatlin intended these "Counter-Reliefs" to be modern abstract replacements of the icons of the old Russian faith.

TOWARD ABSTRACTION IN SCULPTURE

It is clear that sculpture underwent a revolution as profound as that of painting in the years prior to World War I. Not all change involved new materials: The Romanian artist Constantin Brancusi (1876–1957) settled in Paris in 1904 and became immediately captivated by the "primitive" art on display in the city. He admired the semi-abstracted forms of much art beyond the Western tradition, believing that the artists who made such art succeeded in capturing the "essence" of their subject. In Brancusi's search for a sculptural essence he, like Picasso, rejected superficial realism. Brancusi wrote, "What is real is not the external form but the

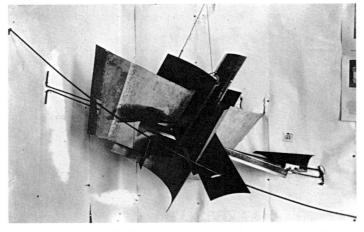

31-26 • Vladimir Tatlin CORNER COUNTER-RELIEF
1915. Mixed media, 31½ × 59 × 29½" (80 × 150 × 75 cm). Present whereabouts unknown.

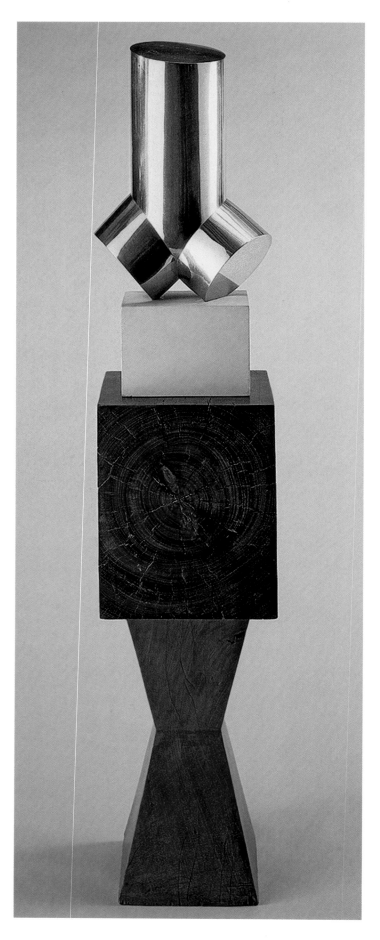

31-27 • Constantin Brancusi TORSO OF A YOUNG MAN
1924. Bronze on stone and wood bases; combined figure and bases
40⅜ × 20 × 18¼″ (102.4 × 50.5 × 46.1 cm). Hirshhorn Museum and
Sculpture Garden, Smithsonian Institution, Washington, D.C.

essence of things. Starting from this truth it is impossible for anyone to express anything essentially real by imitating its exterior surface." In his 1924 **TORSO OF A YOUNG MAN (FIG. 31–27),** Brancusi distills and abstracts the young man's torso and upper legs into three essential but beautifully carved and polished marble forms.

The egg symbolized the potential for birth, growth, and development for Brancusi. It was a perfect but organic ovoid that contained life in its essence. In **THE NEWBORN (FIG. 31–28),** he conflates its shape with the disembodied head of a human infant to suggest the essence of humanity at the moment of birth.

DADA: QUESTIONING ART ITSELF

When the Great War broke out in August 1914, most European leaders thought it would be over by Christmas. Both sides reassured their populations that the efficiency of their armies and bravery of their soldiers would ensure a speedy resolution and that the political status quo would resume. These hopes proved illusory. World War I was the most brutal and costly in human history to date. On the Western Front in 1916 alone, Germany lost 850,000 soldiers, France 700,000, and Great Britain 400,000. The conflict settled into a vicious stalemate on all fronts as each side deployed new killing technologies such as improved machine guns, flame throwers, fighter aircraft, and poison gas. On the home front, governments exerted control over industry and labor to manage the war effort, and ordinary people were forced to endure food rationing, propaganda attacks, and shameless war profiteering.

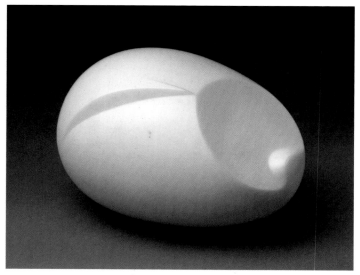

31-28 • Constantin Brancusi THE NEWBORN
1915. Marble, 5¾ × 8¼ × 5⅞″ (14.6 × 21 × 14.8 cm). Philadelphia
Museum of Art. Louise and Walter Arensberg Collection. 195.134.10

Horror at the enormity of the carnage and loss arose on many fronts. One of the first artistic movements to address the slaughter and the moral questions it posed was Dada. If Modern art until that time questioned the traditions of art, Dada went further to question the concept of art itself. Witnessing how thoughtlessly life was discarded in the trenches, Dada mocked the senselessness of rational thought and even the foundations of modern society. It embraced a "mocking iconoclasm," even in its name, which has no real or fixed meaning. *Dada* is baby talk in German; in French it means "hobbyhorse"; in Romanian and Russian, "yes, yes"; in the Kru African dialect, "the tail of a sacred cow." Dada artists annihilated the conventional understanding of art as something precious, replacing it with a strange and irrational art about ideas and actions rather than about objects.

Dada was a transnational movement with several quite distinct local manifestations that arose almost simultaneously in the cities of Zürich, New York, Paris, and Berlin, as Paris temporarily relinquished its place at the center of the art world in 1914.

HUGO BALL AND THE CABARET VOLTAIRE. Dada's opening moment was probably the first performance of poet Hugo Ball's poem "Karawane" at the Cabaret Voltaire. Ball (1886–1927) and his companion, Emmy Hennings (d. 1949), a nightclub singer, moved from Germany to neutral Switzerland when World War I broke out and opened the Cabaret Voltaire in Zürich on February 5, 1916. Their cabaret was based loosely on the bohemian artists' cafés of prewar Berlin and Munich, and its mad irrational world became a meeting place for exiled avant-garde writers and artists of various nationalities who shared Ball's and Hennings's disgust for the war.

At the Cabaret Voltaire, Ball recited one of his sound poems, **"KARAWANE" (FIG. 31–29)**, while wearing a strange costume, with his legs and body encased in blue cardboard tubes and a white-and-blue "witch doctor's hat," as he called it, on his head. He also wore a huge, gold-painted cardboard cape that flapped when he moved his arms and lobsterlike cardboard hands or claws. He solemnly recited his poem, the text of which can be seen in the photograph and which comprised a list of nonsensical sounds. Ball's poetry renounced "the language devastated and made impossible by journalism," and mocked traditional poetry and the rationality of adulthood by creating a new, randomly based and wholly incomprehensible private language that seemed to mimic baby talk.

MARCEL DUCHAMP. Although not formally a member of the movement, Marcel Duchamp (1887–1968) created some of Dada's most complex and challenging works. He also took Dada to New York when he moved there to escape the war in Europe. In Paris in 1912, Duchamp experimented with Cubism by painting *Nude Descending a Staircase*, one of the most controversial works to be included later in the Armory Show (see page 1042). By the time Duchamp arrived in the United States, he had discarded painting, which he claimed had become for him a mindless activity, and he devised the Dada concept that he termed the **readymade**, in

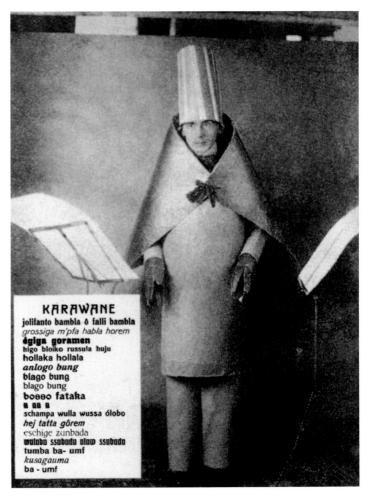

31–29 • HUGO BALL RECITING THE SOUND POEM "KARAWANE"
Photographed at the Cabaret Voltaire, Zürich, 1916.

which he transformed ordinary, often manufactured objects into works of art.

On arrival in New York in 1915, Duchamp was warmly welcomed by the American art world. He was invited to become a founding member of the American Society of Independent Artists, and was appointed chair of the hanging committee for its first annual "Forum" exhibition in 1917. The show was advertised as unjuried: Any work of art submitted (for the fee of $6) would be hung. Yet, in Dada fashion, Duchamp spent almost two years devising a work of art that would be so shocking and offensive that it would have to be rejected, thus commenting on the contemporary process of art making and its exhibition. The piece that he created was a common porcelain urinal that he purchased from a plumber, which he turned on one side so that it was no longer functional and signed it "R. Mutt" in a play on the name of the urinal's manufacturer, J. L. Mott Iron Works. He submitted it anonymously to the exhibition and it was indeed rejected.

FOUNTAIN (FIG. 31–30) of 1917 was, and still is, one of the most controversial works of art of the modern age. In it Duchamp asks: What is the essence of a work of art? How much can be

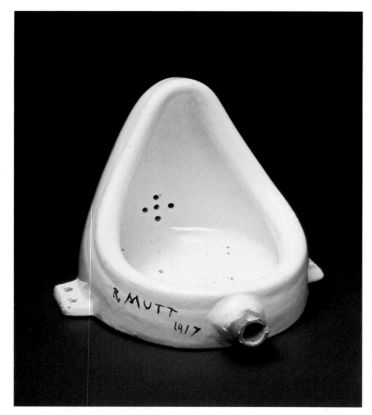

31-30 • Marcel Duchamp FOUNTAIN
1917. Porcelain plumbing fixture and enamel paint, height 24⅝"
(62.5 cm). Photograph by Alfred Stieglitz. Philadelphia Museum of Art,
Pennsylvania. Louise and Walter Arensberg Collection (1998-74-1)

SEE MORE: View a video on Marcel Duchamp
www.myartslab.com

stripped away before the essence of art disappears? Since Whistler's
famous court case (see "Art on Trial in 1877," page 999), most
avant-garde artists would have responded that a work of art need
be neither descriptive nor well-crafted but, before 1917, none
would have argued, as Duchamp does in this piece, that "art" might
be primarily conceptual. For centuries, artists regularly employed
studio assistants to craft parts, if not all, of the art objects that they
designed. In some ways Duchamp translated that practice into
modern terms by arguing that art objects might not only be
crafted (in part) by others, but that the objects of art could actually
be manufactured for the artist in the mass-produced world.
In a clever twist of logic, Duchamp simultaneously makes a
commentary on consumption, modernity, and the irrationality of
the modern age by arguing that the "readymade" work of art, as a
manufactured object, simply bypasses the craft tradition. Duchamp
translated this idea into physical form in *Fountain*.

Fountain is one of the most transgressive works of art in Western
history. It is still funny, mad, and obscene; it refers openly to
bathroom functions, to humanity's most degraded functions and
vulnerable states, and it challenges every assumption made about the
nature of art. When *Fountain* was rejected, as Duchamp anticipated it
would be, the artist resigned from the Society in mock horror, and

published an unsigned editorial in a Dada journal detailing what he
described as the scandal of the R. Mutt case. He wrote: "The only
works of art America has given are her plumbing and bridges,"
adding, "Whether Mr. Mutt with his own hands made the fountain
or not has no importance. He CHOSE it. He took an ordinary article of life, placed it so that its useful significance disappeared under the
new title and point of view—created a new thought for that object."

After Duchamp returned to Paris, he challenged the French
art world with a piece that he entitled **L.H.O.O.Q. (FIG. 31–31)**, and
that he described as a "modified readymade." In 1911, Leonardo's
famous *Mona Lisa* (SEE FIG. 20–5) was stolen from the Louvre and
it took two years to recover it. While missing, however, the
painting became even more famous than when it had actually been
on public display, being widely and badly reproduced on postcards,
posters, and in advertising. Duchamp chose to comment on the
nature of fame and on the degraded image of the *Mona Lisa* in
L.H.O.O.Q. In 1919, he purchased a cheap postcard reproduction
of the *Mona Lisa* and drew a mustache and beard on her famously

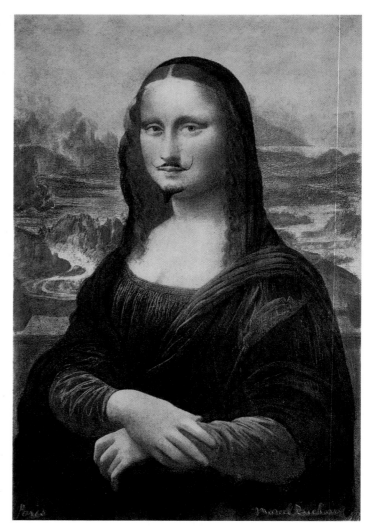

31-31 • Marcel Duchamp L.H.O.O.Q.
1919. Pencil on reproduction of Leonardo da Vinci's *Mona Lisa*.
7¾ × 4¾" (19.7 × 12.1 cm). Philadelphia Museum of Art, Pennsylvania.
Louise and Walter Arensberg Collection

enigmatic face. In doing so he turned a sacred cultural artifact into an object of crude ridicule. The letters that he scrawled across the bottom of the card, "L.H.O.O.Q.," when read aloud sound phonetically similar to the French slang phrase *elle a chaud au cul*, politely translated as "she's hot for it," thus adding a crude sexual innuendo to the already cheapened image. Like *Fountain*, this work challenges preconceived notions about morality or virtue being a basis for art and introduces disgust as a viable artistic subject. Indeed, as one of Dada's founders said: "Dada was born of disgust."

Duchamp made only a few readymades. In fact, he created very little art at all after about 1922, when he devoted himself mostly to chess. When asked about his occupation, he described himself as a "retired artist," but his ideas have been among the most influential on art produced since 1960.

BERLIN DADA. Early in 1917, Hugo Ball and the Romanian-born poet Tristan Tzara (1896–1963) organized the Galerie Dada. Tzara also edited the magazine *Dada*, which quickly attracted the attention of like-minded artists and writers in several European capitals and in the United States. The movement spread farther when expatriate members of Hugo Ball's circle in Switzerland returned to their homelands after the war. Richard Huelsenbeck (1892–1974), for instance, took Dada to Germany, where he helped found the Club Dada in Berlin in April 1918.

Dada pursued a slightly different agenda and took on different forms in each of its major centers. A distinctive feature of Berlin Dada was its agitprop agenda. It also produced an unusually large amount of visual art—especially collage and **photomontage** (photographic collage)—compared to the more literary forms of Dada elsewhere.

Kurt Schwitters (1887–1948), for instance, who met Huelsenbeck and other Dadaists in 1919, used discarded rail tickets, postage stamps, ration coupons, beer labels, and other street detritus to create visual poetry. Schwitters termed his two- and three-dimensional works of art, made out of the wasted ephemera of the industrial world, *Merzbilder*. *Merz* was Schwitters's term for the refuse he collected; *Bild* is German for "picture." In his "Merz Pictures," Schwitters's collaged together fragments of newspaper and other printed material with drawn or painted images. He wrote that garbage demanded equal rights with painting. In **MERZBILD 5B** (FIG. 31–32), Schwitters has collaged printed fragments from the street with newspaper scraps to comment on the postwar disorder of defeated Germany. One fragment describes the brutal overthrow of the short-lived socialist republic in Bremen.

Hannah Höch (1889–1978) produced even more pointed political photomontages. Between 1916 and 1926, she worked for Verlag, Berlin's largest publishing house, designing decorative

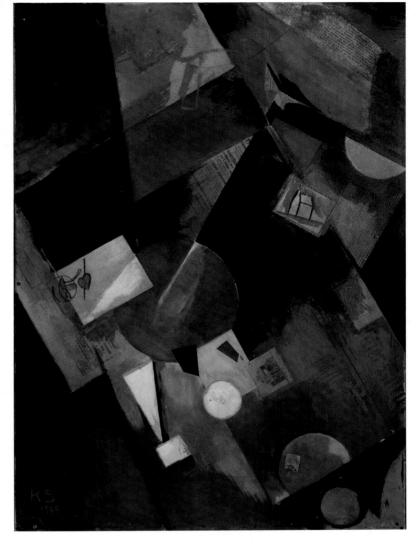

31–32 • Kurt Schwitters MERZBILD 5B (PICTURE-RED-HEART-CHURCH)
April 26, 1919. Collage, tempera, and crayon on cardboard, 32⅞ × 23¾" (83.4 × 60.3 cm). Guggenheim Museum, New York. 52.1325

patterns and writing articles on crafts for a women's magazine. Höch considered herself part of the women's movement in the 1920s. She disapproved of contemporary mass-media representations of women and had to fight for her place as the sole woman among the Berlin Dada group, one of whom described her contribution disparagingly as merely conjuring up beer and sandwiches. In **CUT WITH THE DADA KITCHEN KNIFE THROUGH THE LAST WEIMAR BEER-BELLY CULTURAL EPOCH IN GERMANY (FIG. 31–33)**, Höch collages images and words from the popular press, political posters, and photographs to create a complex and angry critique of the Weimar Republic in 1919. She shows women physically cutting apart the beer-bloated German establishment in this photomontage and includes portraits of androgynous Dada characters, such as herself and several other Berlin Dada artists, along with Marx and Lenin. It is tempting to wonder which side she really thinks her fellow Dadaists stand on.

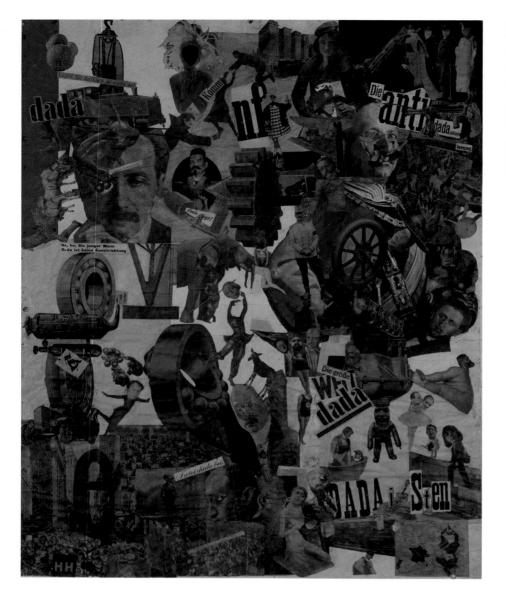

31–33 • Hannah Höch CUT WITH THE DADA KITCHEN KNIFE THROUGH THE LAST WEIMAR BEER-BELLY CULTURAL EPOCH IN GERMANY
1919. Collage, 44⅞ × 35⅜″ (114 × 90 cm). Nationalgalerie, Staatliche Museen zu Berlin, Berlin.

EXPLORE MORE: Gain insight from a primary source on Hannah Höch
www.myartslab.com

MODERNIST TENDENCIES IN AMERICA

When avant-garde Modern art was first widely exhibited in the United States, it received a cool welcome. While some American artists did work in abstract or Modern ways, most preferred to work in a more naturalistic manner, at least until around 1915.

THE ASHCAN SCHOOL

In the first decade of the twentieth century, a vigorous realist movement coalesced in New York City around the charismatic painter and teacher Robert Henri (1865–1929), who rejected the idyllic Impressionist imagery of the previous generation in America. Henri told his students: "Paint what you see. Paint what is real to you." In 1908, he organized an exhibition of artists called The Eight, four of whom trained and worked as newspaper illustrators and whose exhibition introduced scenes of gritty urban life in New York City to American art. Five of The Eight, who painted the street life of the immigrant poor specifically, were dubbed the Ashcan School.

Henri greatly admired Manet's paintings of modern life and the art of the Spanish Baroque. He traveled to Spain where, in 1906, he painted **LA REINA MORA** (FIG. 31–34). "La Reina Mora" (the Moorish Queen) was the stage name of Milagros Morena, a well-known Andalusian dancer. In the painting Moreno stands proudly in a red-flowered costume with a fringed skirt, a luxurious silver-white shawl, and pink satin dancing shoes, wearing several rings on her fingers, a golden bracelet around one wrist, and two decorative necklaces around her neck. Her jet-black hair is dressed with ribbons or flowers. Morena's face is covered with a whitish makeup that is in contrast to the darker skin of her neck and arms, making her strong black eyebrows, deep dark eyes, rouged cheeks, and red lips stand out dramatically.

STIEGLITZ AND THE "291" GALLERY

The chief proponent of European Modern art in the United States was the photographer Alfred Stieglitz (1864–1946), who in the years before World War I organized several small exhibitions

In his own photographs, Stieglitz tried to compose poetic images of romanticized urban scenes. In **THE FLATIRON BUILDING** (**FIG. 31–35**), the tree trunk to the right is echoed by branches in the grove farther back, and in the wedge-shaped Flatiron Building to the rear. An arc of chairs and a low wall behind seem to encircle the trees. The entire scene is suffused with a misty wintery atmosphere, which the artist created by manipulating his viewpoint, exposure, and possibly both the negative and positive images.

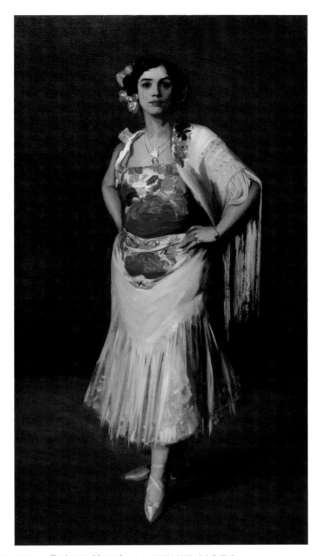

31-34 • Robert Henri **LA REINE MORA**
1906. Oil on canvas, 78 × 42¹⁄₁₆″ (198 × 107 cm). Museum purchase from the Jere Abbott Acquisitions Fund, Colby Museum of Art.

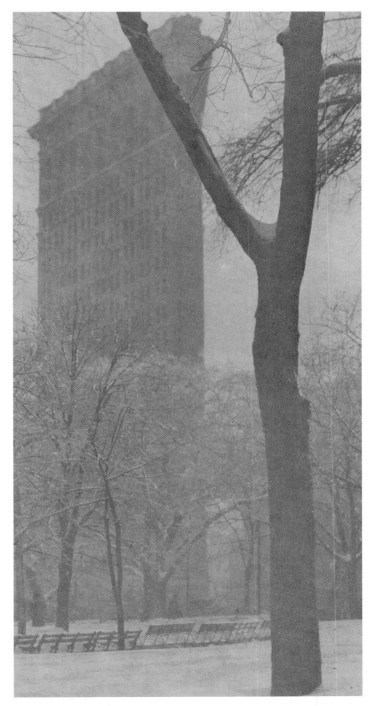

31-35 • Alfred Stieglitz **THE FLATIRON BUILDING**
1903. Photogravure, 6¹¹⁄₁₆ × 3⁵⁄₁₆″ (17 × 8.4 cm) mounted. Metropolitan Museum of Art, New York. Gift of J. B. Neumann, 1958 (58.577.37)

featuring the art of major Modernists at a tiny gallery at 291 Fifth Avenue, known simply as 291. Stieglitz, like Kahnweiler in Paris, supported many of the early American Modernist painters and photographers in New York. As a photographer himself, he sought to establish the legitimacy of photography as a fine art with these exhibitions.

Born in New Jersey to a wealthy German immigrant family, Stieglitz studied photography in the 1880s at the Technische Hochschule in Berlin, quickly recognizing photography's artistic potential. In 1890, he began to photograph New York City street scenes. He promoted his views through an organization called the Photo-Secession, founded in 1902, and two years later opened the 291 gallery. By 1910, this gallery had become a focal point for both photographers and artists, with Stieglitz giving shows (sometimes their first) to artists such as Arthur Dove, John Marin, and Georgia O'Keeffe, and bringing to America the art of European artists such as Kandinsky, Braque, Cézanne, and Rodin.

Ironically, Stieglitz softens and romanticizes the Flatiron Building, one of New York's earliest skyscrapers and a symbol of the city's modernity. The magazine *Camera Work*, a high-quality photographic publication that Stieglitz edited, and which published this photograph in photogravure form in 1903, also featured numerous photogravures of American and European Modernist art as well as some important American Modern art criticism.

THE ARMORY SHOW AND HOME-GROWN MODERNISM

In 1913, Modernist art arrived in New York en masse with an enormous exhibition held in the drill hall of the 69th Street Armory. Walt Kuhn (1877–1949) and Arthur B. Davies (1862–1928), a member of The Eight, were the principal organizers of the "Armory Show," which featured more than 1,600 works, a quarter of them by European artists. Most of the art, even Modernist art, was well received and sold well, but the art of a few European Modernists, including Matisse and Duchamp in particular, caused a public outcry. Some of the latter were described as being "cousins to the anarchists," and when selected works from the exhibition traveled on to Chicago, a few faculty and some students of the School of the Art Institute even hanged Matisse in effigy, while civic leaders called for a morals commission to investigate the show. Yet the exhibition consolidated American Modernist art and inspired its artists, who subsequently found more enthusiastic collectors and exhibition venues.

One of the most significant early American Modernists was Arthur Dove (1880–1946). Dove studied the work of the Fauves in Europe in 1907–1909, and he even exhibited at the Autumn Salon. After returning home, he began making abstract nature studies about the same time as Kandinsky, although each was unaware of the other. Dove's **NATURE SYMBOLIZED NO. 2 (FIG. 31–36)** is one of a remarkable series of small works that reveals his beliefs about the spiritual power of nature. But while Kandinsky's art focuses on an inner vision of nature, Dove rendered his deeply felt experience within the landscape in abstract terms, saying that he had "no [artistic] background except perhaps the woods, running streams, hunting, fishing, camping, the sky." Dove supported himself by farming in rural Connecticut, but he exhibited his art in New York and was both well received by and connected to the New York art community.

Another pioneer of American Modernism who exhibited at the Armory Show was Marsden Hartley (1877–1943), who was also a regular exhibitor at the 291 gallery. Between 1912 and 1915, Hartley lived mostly abroad, first in Paris, where he discovered Cubism, then in Berlin, where he began to paint colorful Expressionistic art. Around 1914, however, Hartley developed a powerfully original and intense style of his own in *Portrait of a German Officer* (see "A Closer Look," page 1044), a tightly arranged composition of boldly colored shapes and patterns, interspersed with numbers, letters, and fragments of German military imagery that refer symbolically to Hartley's fallen lover.

Georgia O'Keeffe (1887–1986) was born in rural Wisconsin, studied and taught art sporadically between 1905 and 1915, and was "discovered" by Stieglitz when a New York friend showed

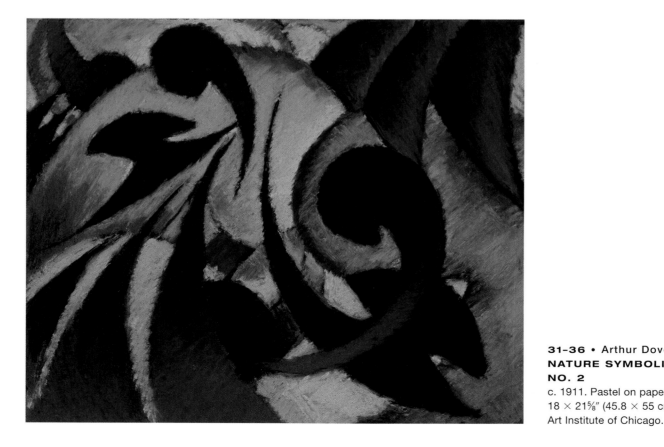

31-36 • Arthur Dove
NATURE SYMBOLIZED
NO. 2
c. 1911. Pastel on paper,
18 × 21⅝" (45.8 × 55 cm).
Art Institute of Chicago.

him some of her charcoal drawings. Stieglitz's reported response was: "At last, a woman on paper!" In 1916, Stieglitz included O'Keeffe's work in a group show at 291 and gave her a solo exhibition the following year. O'Keeffe's flower paintings were described by critics as essentially feminine and vaginal. Stieglitz did little to dissuade this reading of O'Keeffe's art and, in fact, did quite a bit to promote it. O'Keeffe objected strenuously to this critical caricature, claiming that she was an artist, not just a woman artist.

O'Keeffe moved to New York in 1918 and married Stieglitz in 1924. In 1925, she began to paint New York skyscrapers, which were acclaimed at the time as embodiments of American inventiveness and energy. But paintings such as **CITY NIGHT (FIG. 31–37)** are not unambiguous celebrations of lofty buildings. O'Keeffe frequently portrayed her architectural subjects from a low vantage point so that they appear to loom ominously over the

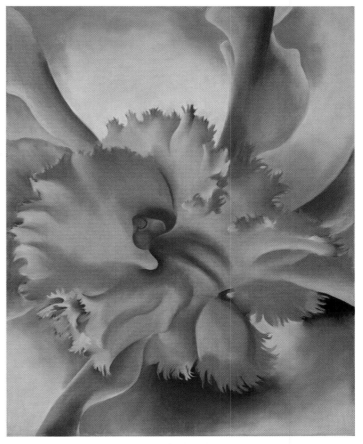

31-38 • Georgia O'Keeffe AN ORCHID
1941. Pastel on board, 21¾ × 27⅝″ (55.2 × 70.2 cm). Museum of Modern Art, New York. Bequest of Georgia O'Keeffe (556.1990)

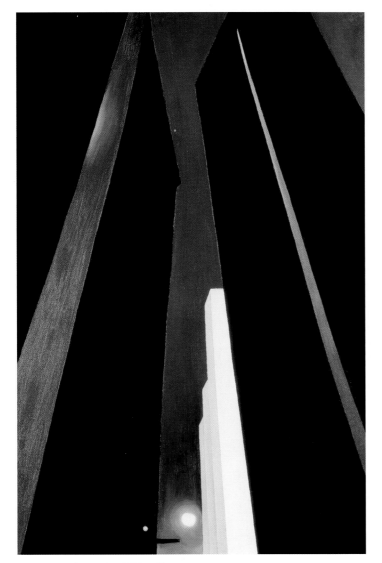

31-37 • Georgia O'Keeffe CITY NIGHT
1926. Oil on canvas, 48 × 30″ (123 × 76.9 cm). Minneapolis Institute of Arts.

viewer; in *City Night*, for instance, the dark tonalities, stark forms, and exaggerated perspective produce a sense of menace that also appears in the art of other American Modernists.

In 1925, O'Keeffe also began to exhibit a series of close-up paintings of flowers that remain among her best-known subjects. In **AN ORCHID (FIG. 31–38)**, O'Keeffe brings the heart of the heavy sensual flower to the very front of the picture plane, revealing its inner organs and soft, delicate surfaces. Whether intentionally sexual or not, these works drip with sensuality. In 1929, O'Keeffe began spending her summers in New Mexico and moved there permanently in the 1940s.

EARLY MODERN ARCHITECTURE

New industrial materials and engineering innovations enabled twentieth-century architects to create tall buildings of unprecedented height that vastly increased the usable space in structures built on scarce and valuable city lots. At the same time that Modern artists in Europe rejected the decorative in painting and sculpture, American architects increasingly embraced the plain geometric shapes and undecorated surfaces of skyscraper architecture.

Portrait of a German Officer

by Marsden Hartley, 1914. Oil on canvas, 68¼ × 41⅜″ (1.78 × 1.05 m). Metropolitan Museum of Art, New York. The Alfred Stieglitz Collection, 1949 (49.70.42)

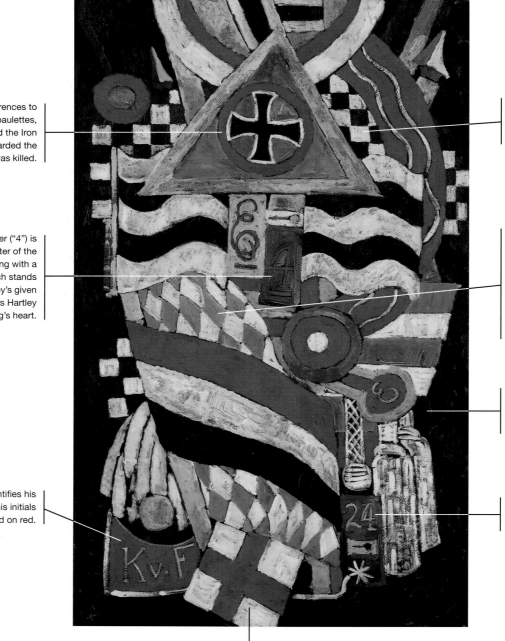

Symbolic references to Freyburg include epaulettes, lance tips, and the Iron Cross he was awarded the day before he was killed.

His regiment number ("4") is shown at the center of the abstracted chest along with a red cursive "E," which stands for "Edmund" (Hartley's given name). This places Hartley over Freyburg's heart.

Hartley identifies his subject with his initials ("Kv.F") in gold on red.

The black-and-white checkerboard patterns evoke Freyburg's love of chess.

The blue-and-white diamond pattern comes from the Bavarian flag; the red, white, and black bands constitute the flag of the German Empire, adopted in 1871; and the black-and-white stripes are those of the historic flag of Prussia.

The funereal black background heightens the intensity of the foreground colors.

The young man's age ("24") is noted in gold on blue.

While living in Berlin in 1914, Hartley fell in love with a young Prussian lieutenant, Karl von Freyburg, whom Hartley described as "in every way a perfect being—physically, spiritually, and mentally." Freyburg's death in World War I devastated Hartley, who memorialized his fallen lover in this symbolic portrait.

SEE MORE: View the Closer Look feature for *Portrait of a German Officer* **www.myartslab.com**

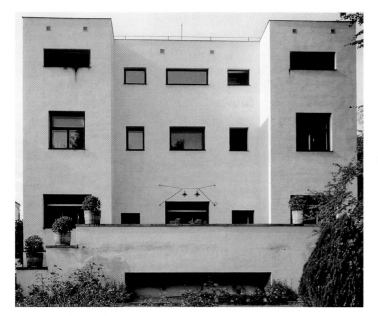

31–39 • Adolf Loos STEINER HOUSE
Vienna. 1910.

EUROPEAN MODERNISM

In Europe, a stripped-down and severely geometric style of Modern architecture developed, partly in reaction to the natural organic lines of Art Nouveau. In Vienna, Adolf Loos (1870–1933), one of the pioneers of European architectural Modernism, insisted in his 1913 essay "Ornament and Crime" that "The evolution of a culture is synonymous with the removal of ornament from utilitarian objects." For Loos, ornament was a sign of cultural degeneracy. Thus his **STEINER HOUSE** (FIG. 31–39) is a stucco-covered, reinforced concrete construction without decorative embellishment. Loos argued that the exterior's only function was to provide protection from the elements; the placement of the plain rectangular windows, for instance, was ostensibly determined by interior needs.

The most important French Modern architect was Le Corbusier, who established several important precepts that influenced architects for the next half-century. His **VILLA SAVOYE** (FIG. 31–40), a private home outside Paris, is an icon of the International Style (see "The International Style," page 1057) that also reflects his Purist ideals in its rectilinear design and lack of ornamentation. It is also one of the best expressions of Le Corbusier's **domino construction** system, first elaborated in 1914, in which slabs of ferroconcrete (concrete reinforced with steel bars) rest on six free-standing steel posts, placed at the positions of the six dots on a domino playing piece. Over the next decade Le Corbusier further explored the possibilities of the domino system and in 1926 published "The Five Points of a New Architecture," in which he proposed raising houses above the ground on **pilotis** (free-standing posts); using flat roofs as terraces; using movable partition walls slotted between supports on the interior and **curtain walls** (nonloadbearing exterior walls) to allow greater design flexibility; and using ribbon windows (windows that run the length of the wall). All of these became features of Modern architecture. Le Corbusier described the Villa Savoye as "a machine for living in," meaning that it was designed as rationally as a car or a machine. He also developed designs for mass-produced standardized housing as many architects did after World War I to help rebuild Europe's destroyed infrastructure.

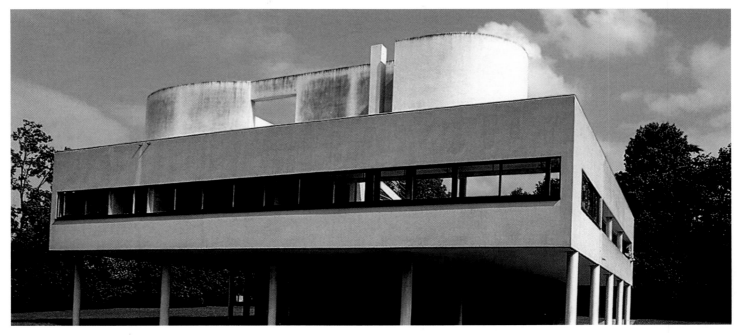

31–40 • Le Corbusier VILLA SAVOYE
Poissy-sur-Seine, France. 1929–1930.

EXPLORE MORE: Click the Google Earth link for Villa Savoye **www.myartslab.com**

AMERICAN MODERN ARCHITECTURE

CONNECTION TO THE LAND. Frank Lloyd Wright (1867–1959) was not only America's most important Modernist architect, he was also one of the most influential architects in the world in the early twentieth century. After briefly studying engineering at the University of Wisconsin, Wright apprenticed to a Chicago architect, then spent five years with the firm of Dankmar Adler and Louis Sullivan (SEE FIG. 30–55), eventually becoming their chief drafter. In 1893, Wright established his own office, specializing in domestic architecture. Around 1900, he and several other architects in the Oak Park suburb of Chicago began to design low, horizontal houses with flat roofs and heavy overhangs that echoed the flat plains of the prairie in the Midwest. This group of architects was known as the Prairie School.

The **FREDERICK C. ROBIE HOUSE (FIG. 31–41)** is one of Wright's early masterpieces in the **Prairie Style**. It was designed around a central chimney (to radiate heat throughout the house in the bitter Chicago winter), and features a low, flat overhanging roof (to shade against the summer sun) with open porches for sleeping outside in the cool of summer nights. The roof is dramatically cantilevered on both sides of the chimney. The windows are arranged in low bands around the house; many are stained glass, creating a colored screen between the interior of the house and the outside world while also inviting the viewer to look through the windows into the garden beyond.

The horizontal emphasis continues inside. The main living level is one long space divided into living and dining areas by a free-standing fireplace. There are no dividing walls. Wright visited the Japanese exhibit at the 1893 Chicago World's Fair and was deeply influenced by the aesthetics of Japanese architecture, particularly its use of space and screenlike windows (see "*Shoin* Design," page 819). Wright's homes frequently featured built-in closets and bookcases, and he hid heating and lighting fixtures when possible. He also designed and arranged the furniture for his interiors **(FIG. 32–42)**. Here, the chairs are machine-cut in modern geometric designs, while their high backs huddle around the table to create the intimate effect of a room within a room. Wright integrated lights and flower holders into the posts closest to the table's corners so that there would no need for lights or flowers on the table.

Wright had an uneasy relationship with European Modernist architecture. Although he routinely used new building materials such as concrete, glass, and steel, he also tried to create a more natural sensibility by connecting his buildings to their sites using brick, wood, or local stone. He was uninterested in the machine aesthetic of Le Corbusier.

FALLINGWATER (FIG. 31–43) in rural Pennsylvania is perhaps the best-known expression of Wright's conviction that buildings should not simply sit *on* the landscape but exist *in* it. Fallingwater was commissioned by Edgar Kaufmann, a Pittsburgh department

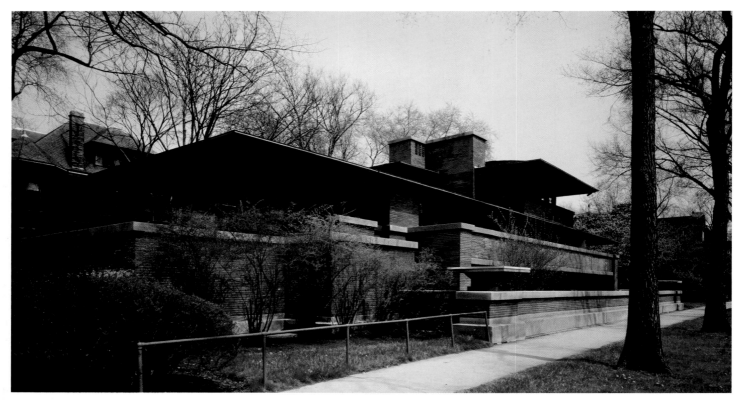

31-41 • Frank Lloyd Wright FREDERICK C. ROBIE HOUSE
Chicago. 1906–1909.

EXPLORE MORE: Click the Google Earth link for the Robie House **www.myartslab.com**

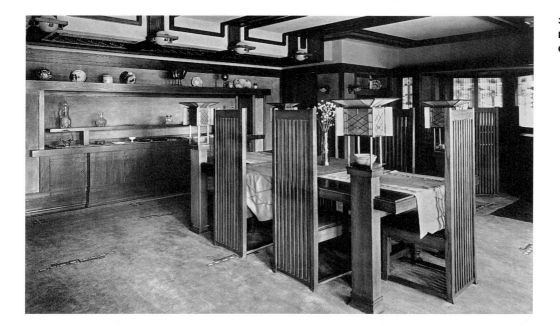

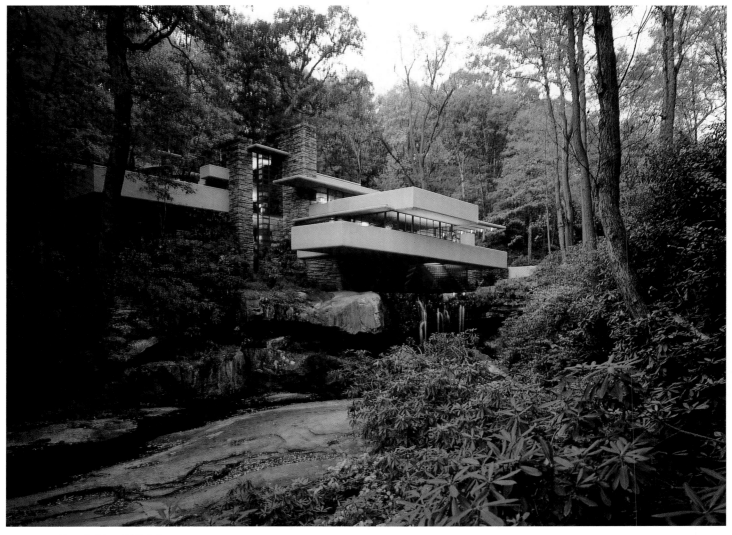

31–43 • Frank Lloyd Wright EDGAR KAUFMANN HOUSE, FALLINGWATER
Mill Run, Pennsylvania. 1937.

SEE MORE: View an animated video of Fallingwater **www.myartslab.com**

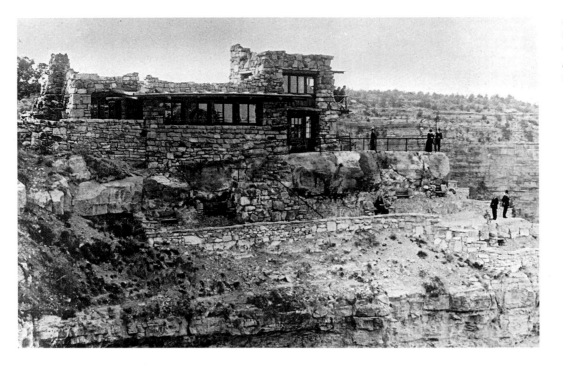

31–44 • Mary Colter
LOOKOUT STUDIO
Grand Canyon National Park,
Arizona. 1914. Grand Canyon National
Park Museum Collection

store owner, to replace a family summer cottage on the site of a waterfall and a pool where his children played. To Kaufmann's surprise, Wright decided to build the new house right into the cliff and over the pool, allowing the waterfall to flow around and under the house. A large boulder where the family had sunbathed in the summers was used for the central hearthstone of the fireplace. In a dramatic move that engineers questioned (with reason, as subsequent history has shown), Wright used cantilevers to extend a series of broad concrete terraces out from the cliff to parallel the huge slabs of rock below. The terraces are all poured concrete, but Wright painted them a soft earth tone; he made use of local wood and stone wherever possible. Wright preferred to design rural or suburban structures and disliked the inner city. When asked what could be done to improve city architecture, Wright responded: "Tear it down."

Mary Colter (1869–1958) also expressed a strong connection to the land in her architecture. Born in Pittsburgh and educated at the California School of Design in San Francisco, she spent much of her career as an architect and decorator for the Fred Harvey Company, which operated luxury hotels throughout the Southwest. Colter was an avid student of Native American art, especially the architecture of the Hopi and Pueblo peoples, and her buildings quoted liberally from those traditions. She designed several visitor facilities at Grand Canyon National Park, of which **LOOKOUT STUDIO** (FIG. 31–44) is one of the most dramatic. The building perches on the edge of the chasm; its foundation is the natural rock of the canyon, and its walls are built from stones quarried nearby. The roofline is deliberately irregular to echo the surrounding canyon wall. Inside, Colter used exposed logs for many of the structural supports and ceiling, in homage to Hopi architecture. The only concession to modernity is a liberal use of

glass windows and a cement floor. Colter's work on hotels and railroad stations throughout the region helped to establish the distinctive Southwest style.

THE AMERICAN SKYSCRAPER. After 1900, New York City assumed a lead over Chicago in the development of the skyscraper, whose soaring height was made possible by the use of the steel-frame skeleton for structural support (see "The Skyscraper," page 1050). New York clients rejected the more utilitarian Chicago style of Louis Sullivan and others, preferring the historicizing approach then still popular on the east coast. The **WOOLWORTH BUILDING** (FIG. 31–45), designed by the Minnesota-based firm of Cass Gilbert (1859–1934), was the world's tallest building at 792 feet and 55 floors when first completed. Its Gothic-style external details, inspired by the soaring towers of late medieval churches, gave the building a strong visual personality. Because of its Gothic style, Gilbert called it his "Cathedral of Commerce."

ART BETWEEN THE WARS IN EUROPE

World War I had a devastating effect on Europe's artists and architects. Many artists responded to the destruction and loss of a generation of young men by criticizing the European tradition, while others sought to rebuild. Either way, much of the art created between 1919 and 1939 addressed the needs and concerns of society directly.

UTILITARIAN ART FORMS IN RUSSIA

In the 1917 Russian Revolution, the radical socialist Bolsheviks overthrew the tsar, withdrew Russia from the world war, and turned inward to fight a civil war that lasted until 1920 and led to the establishment of the U.S.S.R. (Union of Soviet Socialist Republics). Most Russian avant-garde artists enthusiastically supported the Bolsheviks and were initially supported by them.

CONSTRUCTIVISM. The case of Aleksandr Rodchenko (1891–1956) is fairly representative. An early associate of Malevich (SEE FIG. 31–25), Rodchenko used drafting tools to make abstract drawings. He exhibited as a Suprematist in 1921 when he showed three large, flat, monochromatic panels painted red, yellow, and blue, which he titled *Last Painting* (now lost). After this, he renounced painting as a basically selfish activity and condemned self-expression as weak and socially irresponsible.

Also in 1921, Rodchenko helped to establish the Constructivists, a post-revolutionary group of artists dedicated to working collectively for the good of the state who described themselves as workers who literally "constructed" art for the people. Rodchenko was convinced that self-expression in art did not contribute enough to society, so after 1921 he worked as a photographer producing posters, books, textiles, and theater sets to promote communism.

In 1925, Rodchenko designed a model workers' club for the Soviet Pavilion at the Paris International Exposition of Modern Decorative and Industrial Arts (FIG. 31–46). Rodchenko designed the club for ease of use and simplicity of construction; the furniture was made of wood because Soviet industry was best equipped for mass production in wood. The high, straight backs of the chairs were meant to promote a physical and moral posture of uprightness among the workers.

Another artist active in early Soviet Russia was El Lissitzky (1890–1941), who, after the Revolution, was invited to teach architecture and graphic arts at the Vitebsk School of Fine Arts where Malevich also taught. By 1919, Lissitzky was both teaching and using a Constructivist vocabulary for propaganda posters and

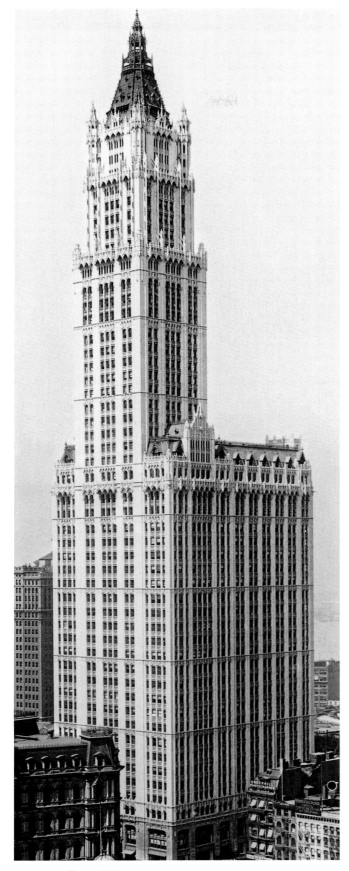

31–45 • Cass Gilbert WOOLWORTH BUILDING
New York. 1911–1913. Collection of the New York Historical Society, New York

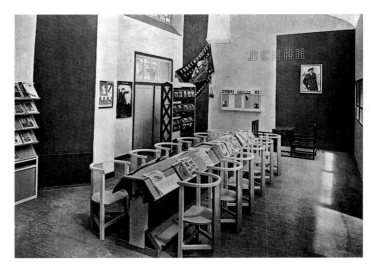

31–46 • Aleksandr Rodchenko WORKERS' CLUB
Exhibited at the International Exposition of Modern Decorative and Industrial Arts, Paris. 1925. Rodchenko-Stepanova Archive, Moscow

The development of the skyscraper design and aesthetic depended on several things: The use of metal beams and girders for the structural-support skeleton; the separation of the building-support structure from the enclosing wall layer (the cladding); the use of fireproof materials and measures; the use of elevators; and the overall integration of plumbing, central heating, artificial lighting, and ventilation systems. The first generation of skyscrapers, built between about 1880 and 1900, were concentrated in the Midwest, chiefly in Chicago and St. Louis (SEE FIG. 30–55). Second-generation skyscrapers, mostly with over 20 stories, date from after 1895 and are found more frequently in New York. The first tall buildings were free-standing towers, sometimes with a base, such as the Woolworth Building of 1911–1913 (SEE FIG. 31–45). New York City's Building Zone Resolution of 1916 introduced mandatory setbacks—decreases in girth as the building rose—to ensure light and ventilation to adjacent sites. Built in 1931, the 1,250-foot setback form of the Empire State Building, diagrammed here, has a streamlined design. The Art Deco exterior cladding (see inset below) conceals the structural elements and mechanisms such as elevators that make its great height possible. The Empire State Building was the tallest building in the world when it was built and its distinctive profile ensures that it remains one of the most recognizable even today.

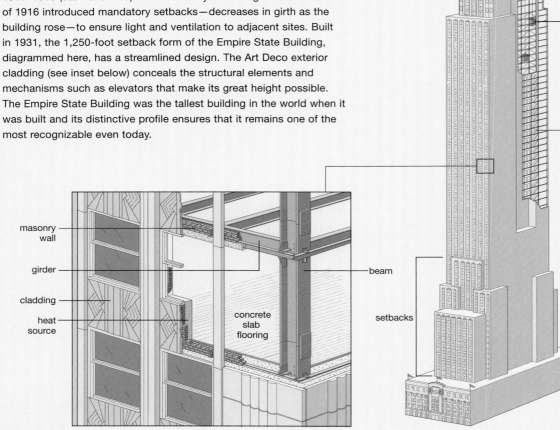

elevator
shafts
(layer two)

stairwells
(layer one)

masonry
wall

girder

cladding

heat
source

concrete
slab
flooring

beam

setbacks

skyscraper

SEE MORE: View a simulation of skyscraper construction **www.myartslab.com**

for work that he called the Proun (pronounced "pro-oon"), thought to be an acronym for the Russian *proekt utverzhdenya novogo* ("project for the affirmation of the new"). Although most Prouns were paintings or prints, a few were installed in specific sites (**FIG. 31–47**) to create a total environment. Lissitzky rejected painting as too personal and imprecise, preferring to "construct" Prouns for the collective using the less personal instruments of mechanical drawing. Like many other Soviet artists of the late 1920s, Lissitzky also turned to more socially engaged projects such

as architectural design, typography, photography, and photomontage for publication.

SOCIALIST REALISM.   In the mid 1920s, Soviet artists increasingly rejected abstraction in favor of a more universally accessible, and thus more politically useful, Socialist Realism that was ultimately established as official Soviet art. Many of Russia's pioneering Modernists and Constructivists, including Rodchenko, made the change willingly because they were already committed to the

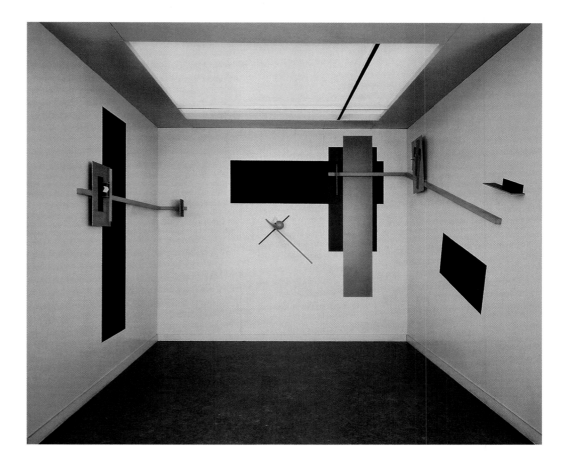

31-47 • El Lissitzky PROUN SPACE
Created for the Great Berlin Art Exhibition. 1923, reconstruction 1965. Stedelijk Van Abbemuseum, Eindhoven, The Netherlands.

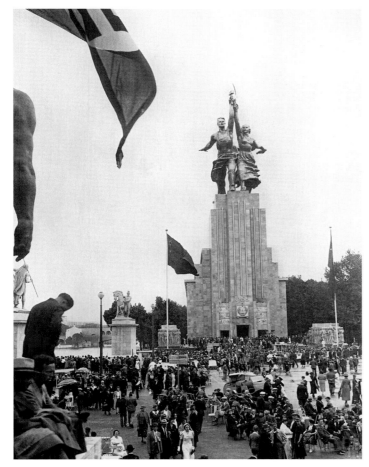

national cause, but others, who refused to change, were fired from public positions and lost public support.

The move to Socialist Realism was led by the Association of Artists of Revolutionary Russia (AKhRR), founded in 1922 to depict Russian workers, peasants, revolutionary activists, and the Red Army. AKhRR sought to document the history of the U.S.S.R. by promoting its leaders and goals. Artists were commissioned to create public paintings and sculptures as well as posters for mass distribution; their subjects were heroic or inspirational people and themes, and their style was an easily readable realism.

Vera Mukhina (1889–1953) was a member of AKhRR and is best known for her 78-foot-tall stainless-steel sculpture of a **WORKER AND COLLECTIVE FARM WOMAN (FIG. 31–48)** made for the Soviet Pavilion at the Paris Universal Exposition of 1937. The sculpture shows a powerfully built male factory worker and an equally powerful female farm laborer with their hammer and sickle held high in the air, reflecting the same tools as appeared on the Soviet flag. The figures are portrayed as equals, partners in their common cause, striding purposefully into the future with determined faces set and their windblown clothing billowing behind them.

31-48 • Vera Mukhina WORKER AND COLLECTIVE FARM WOMAN
Sculpture for the Soviet Pavilion, Paris Universal Exposition. 1937. Stainless steel, height approx. 78′ (23.8 m).

RATIONALISM IN THE NETHERLANDS

In the Netherlands after World War I, abstraction took a different turn than in the U.S.S.R. The Dutch artist Piet Mondrian (1872–1944) encountered Cubism on a trip to Paris in 1912 where he began to abstract animals, trees, and landscapes, searching for their "essential" form. After his return to the Netherlands, he met Theo van Doesburg (1883–1931) who, in 1917, started a magazine named *De Stijl* (*The Style*) that became a focal point for Dutch artists, architects, and designers after the war. In the magazine, Van Doesburg argued that there are two kinds of beauty: sensual or subjective beauty, and a higher, rational, and universal beauty and that De Stijl (note the term translates as "*The* Style" rather than "*A* Style") artists should aspire to create the latter kind of beauty. Mondrian adhered to De Stijl's rational, universal beauty by eliminating everything sensual or subjective from his paintings, but he also followed M. H. J. Schoenmaekers's ideas about Theosophy, as expressed in his 1915 book *New Image of the World*. Schoenmaekers argued that an inner visual construction of nature consisted of a balance between opposing forces, such as heat and cold, male and female, order and disorder, and that artists might represent this inner construction in abstract paintings by using only horizontal and vertical lines and primary colors.

Mondrian's later paintings seem to be visual embodiments of both Schoenmaekers's theory and De Stijl's artistic ideas. In **COMPOSITION WITH YELLOW, RED, AND BLUE** (FIG. **31–49**), for example, Mondrian uses three primary colors (red, yellow, and blue), three neutrals (white, gray, and black), and a grid of horizontal and vertical lines in his search for the essence of higher beauty and the balance of forces. Mondrian's opposing lines and colors balance a harmony of opposites that he called a "dynamic equilibrium" and which he achieved by carefully plotting an arrangement of colors, shapes, and visual weights grouped asymmetrically around the edges of a canvas, with the center acting as a blank white fulcrum. Mondrian hoped that De Stijl would have applications in the real world and would help to create an entirely new visual environment for living, designed according to the rules of a "universal beauty" that, when perfectly balanced, would both balance and purify the world. Mondrian said that he hoped to be the world's last artist, because, while art brought humanity to everyday life, when "universal beauty" infused all aspects of life, there would no longer be a need for art.

The architect and designer Gerrit Rietveld (1888–1964) applied Mondrian's principles of dynamic equilibrium and De Stijl's theories to architecture to create one of the most important examples of the International Style (see "The International Style,"

31-49 • Piet Mondrian
COMPOSITION WITH YELLOW, RED, AND BLUE, 1927
1927. Oil on canvas, 14⅞ × 13¾″ (37.8 × 34.9 cm). The Menil Collection, Houston.
© 2010 Mondrian/Holtzman Trust c/o HCR International, Virginia 20186 USA

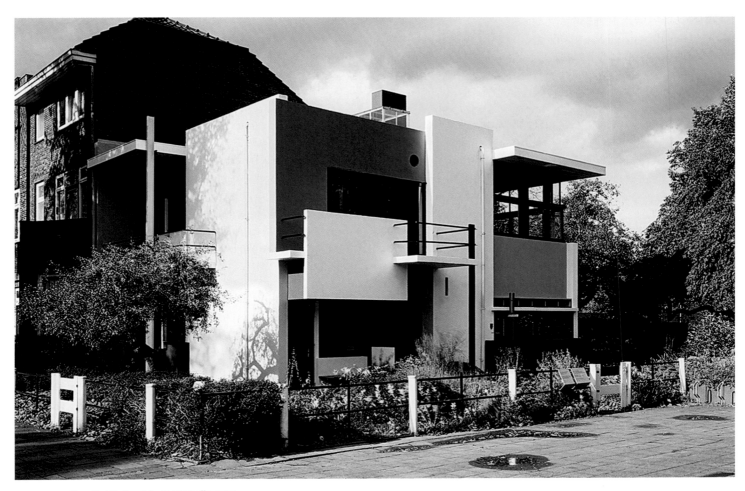

31-50 • Gerrit Rietveld **SCHRÖDER HOUSE**
Utrecht, the Netherlands. 1925.

EXPLORE MORE: Click the Google Earth link for the Schröder House
www.myartslab.com

page 1057). The radically asymmetrical exterior of the **SCHRÖDER HOUSE** in Utrecht (**FIG. 31–50**) is composed of interlocking gray and white planes of varying sizes, combined with horizontal and vertical accents in primary colors and black. The **"RED-BLUE" CHAIR** (**FIG. 31–51**) echoes the arrangement in the interior, where sliding partitions allow modifications in the spaces used for sleeping, working, and entertaining. The patron of the house, Truus Schröder-Schröder, wanted a home that suggested an elegant austerity, with basic necessities sleekly integrated into a balanced and restrained whole.

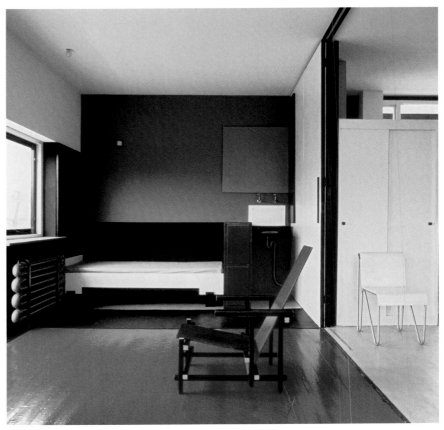

31-51 • Gerrit Rietveld **INTERIOR, SCHRÖDER HOUSE, WITH "RED-BLUE" CHAIR**
1925.

BAUHAUS ART IN GERMANY

In Germany, the creators of the Bauhaus ("House of Building"), which had been founded by Walter Gropius (1883–1969) in Weimar in 1919, found the strict geometric shapes and lines of Purism and De Stijl too rigid and argued that a true German architecture and design should emerge organically. At the Bauhaus, Gropius brought together German architects, designers, and craft workers whose collective creative energy could be harnessed to create an integrated system of design and production based on German traditions and styles. Gropius believed that he could revive the spirit of collaboration of the medieval building guilds (*Bauhütten*) that had erected Germany's cathedrals.

Although Gropius's "Bauhaus Manifesto" of 1919 declared that "the ultimate goal of all artistic activity is the building," the Bauhaus offered no formal training in architecture until 1927. Gropius's students were allowed to begin architectural training only after they completed a mandatory foundation course and received full training in design and crafts in the Bauhaus workshops. These included pottery, metalwork, textiles, stained glass, furniture, wood carving, and wall paintings. In 1922, Gropius also added a new emphasis on industrial design and the next year hired the Hungarian-born László Moholy-Nagy (1895–1946) to reorient the workshops toward more functional design suitable for mass production.

In 1925, when the Bauhaus moved to Dessau, Gropius designed its new building. Although the structure openly acknowledges its reinforced concrete, steel, and glass materials, there is also a balanced asymmetry to its three large cubic areas that was intended

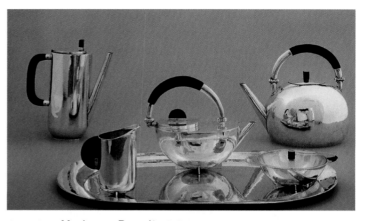

31–53 • Marianne Brandt COFFEE AND TEA SERVICE
1924. Silver and ebony, with Plexiglas cover for sugar bowl. Bauhaus Archiv, Berlin.

to convey the dynamism of modern life **(FIG. 31–52)**. A glass-panel wall wraps around two sides of the workshop wing of the building to provide natural light for the workshops inside, while a parapet below demonstrates how modern engineering methods could create light, airy spaces. Both Moholy-Nagy and Gropius left the Bauhaus in 1928. The school eventually moved to Berlin in 1932, but lasted only one more year before the new German chancellor, Adolf Hitler, forced its closure (see "Suppression of the Avant-Garde in Nazi Germany," page 1055). Hitler opposed Modern art on two grounds: First, it was cosmopolitan and not nationalistic enough; second, he believed it to be overly influenced by Jews. The first was a matter of opinion; the second was patently untrue.

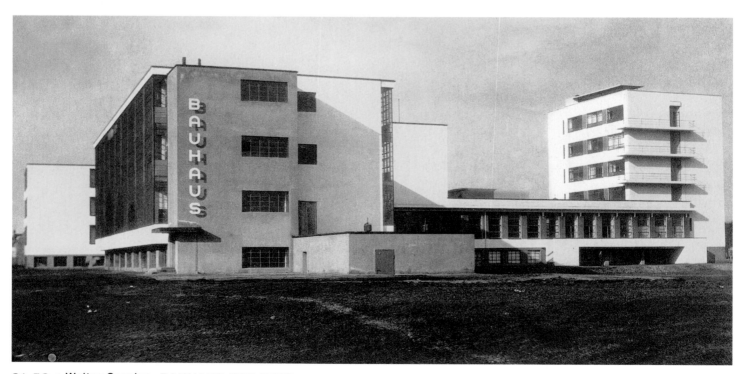

31–52 • Walter Gropius BAUHAUS BUILDING
Dessau, Germany. 1925–1926. View from northwest.

Suppression of the Avant-Garde in Nazi Germany

In the 1930s, the avant-garde was increasingly disparaged by Hitler and the rising Nazi Party. This led to a concerted effort to suppress it. One of the principal targets was the Bauhaus. Through much of the 1920s, classes there were taught by important artists such as Paul Klee, Vassily Kandinsky, Josef Albers, and Ludwig Mies van der Rohe. But they struggled against an increasingly hostile and reactionary political climate. As early as 1924, conservatives accused the Bauhaus of being not only educationally unsound but also politically subversive. To avoid having the school shut down by the opposition, Gropius moved it to Dessau in 1925, at the invitation of Dessau's liberal mayor, but he left office soon after the relocation and his successors faced increasing political pressure to close the school as it was a prime center of Modernist practice. The Bauhaus was forced to move again in 1932, this time to Berlin.

After Adolf Hitler came to power in 1933, the Nazi Party mounted an even more aggressive campaign against Modern art. In his youth Hitler had been a mediocre landscape painter, and he developed an intense hatred of the avant-garde. During the first year of his regime, the Bauhaus was forced to close permanently. A number of the artists, designers, and architects who had been on its faculty—including Albers, Gropius, and Mies—fled to the United States.

The Nazis also attacked German Expressionist artists, whose often-intense depictions of German politics and the economic crisis after the war criticized the state and whose frequent caricatures of German facial features and body types undermined Nazi attempts to redraw Germans as idealized Aryans. Expressionist and avant-garde art was removed from museums and confiscated, and artists were forbidden to buy paint or canvas and were subjected to public intimidation.

In 1937, the Nazi leadership organized an exhibition of what they termed "Degenerate Art" in an attempt to ridicule the banned Modern art and erase its makers. The Nazis described the avant-garde and Modernism as sick and degenerate, presenting the confiscated paintings and sculptures as specimens of pathology and scrawling slogans and derisive commentaries on the walls of the exhibition (see illustration). Ironically, the exhibition of 650 paintings, sculptures, prints, and books confiscated from German museums and artists was viewed by as many as 2 million people in four months in Munich, and by another 1 million on its three-year tour of German cities.

Large numbers of confiscated works that were supposed to be destroyed were looted by Nazi officials and sold in Switzerland in exchange for foreign currency. The ownership of much of the surviving art is still in question. Many artists fled to neighboring countries or the United States, but some, such as Ernst Ludwig Kirchner, whose *Street, Berlin* (SEE FIG. 31–13) was included in the "Degenerate Art" exhibit, were driven to suicide by their loss. Even the work of artists sympathetic to the Nazi position was not safe. Emil Nolde (SEE FIG. 31–12), who joined the Nazi Party in 1932, also had his art confiscated.

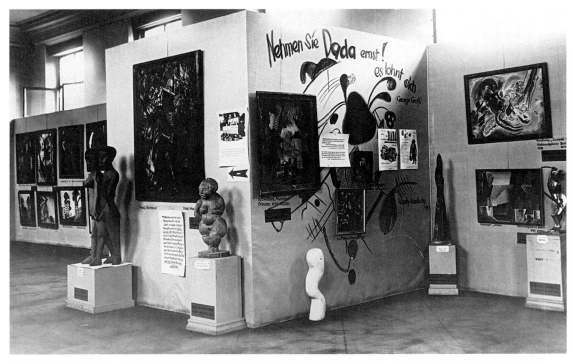

THE DADA WALL IN ROOM 3 OF THE "DEGENERATE ART" ("ENTARTETE KUNST") EXHIBITION
Munich. 1937.

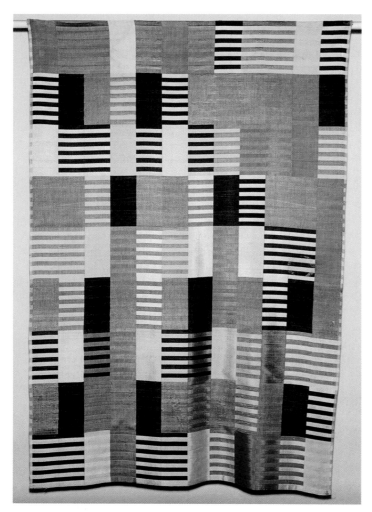

31-54 • Anni Albers WALL HANGING
1926. Silk, two-ply weave, 5′11⅝₆″ × 3′11⅝″ (1.83 × 1.22 m).
Busch-Reisinger Museum, Harvard University, Cambridge,
Massachusetts. Association Fund

Marianne Brandt's (1893–1983) elegant tea and coffee service (**FIG. 31–53**), handcrafted in silver, is an example of the collaboration between design and industry at the Bauhaus. This set was a prototype for mass production in cheaper metals such as nickel silver. After the Bauhaus moved to Dessau, Brandt also designed lighting fixtures and table lamps for mass production, earning much-needed revenue for the school. After Moholy-Nagy and Gropius's departure, Brandt took over the metal workshop for a year before she too left, in 1929. As a woman in the otherwise all-male metal workshop, Brandt made an exceptional contribution to the Bauhaus.

Although it was claimed that women were admitted to the Bauhaus on an equal basis with men, Gropius opposed their education as architects and channeled them into what he considered the more gender-appropriate workshops of pottery and textiles. Berlin-born Anni Albers (b. Annelise Fleischmann, 1899–1994) arrived at the school in 1922 and married the Bauhaus graduate and professor Josef Albers (1888–1976) in 1925. Obliged

to enter the textiles workshop rather than the painting studio, Anni Albers made "pictorial" weavings and wall hangings (**FIG. 31–54**) that were so innovative they actually replaced paintings on the walls of several modern buildings. Her decentralized, rectilinear designs make reference to the aesthetics of De Stijl, but differ in their open acknowledgment of the natural process of weaving. Albers's goal was "to let threads be articulate … and find a form for themselves to no other end than their own orchestration."

SURREALISM AND THE MIND

At the same time in France in the early 1930s, a group of artists and writers took a very different approach to Modernism in a revolt against logic and reason. The Surrealists embraced the irrational, disorderly, aberrant, and even violent social interventions. Surrealism emerged initially as an offshoot of Dada from the mind of the poet André Breton (1896–1966). Breton trained in medicine and psychiatry and served in a neurological hospital during World War I where he used Freudian analysis on shell-shocked soldiers. By 1924, Breton, still drawn to the vagaries of the human mind, published the "Manifesto of Surrealism" in which he interpreted Freud's theory that the human mind is a battleground where the irrational forces of the unconscious mind wage a constant war against the rational, orderly, and oppressive forces of the conscious mind. Breton wanted to explore humanity's most base, irrational, and forbidden sexual desires, fantasies, and violent instincts by freeing the conscious mind from reason. As Breton wrote in 1934, "we still live under the rule of logic." Thus, he and other Surrealists developed strategies to liberate the unconscious using dream analysis, free association, automatic writing, word games, and hypnotic trances. Surrealists studied acts of "criminal madness" and the "female mind" in particular, believing the latter to be weaker and more irrational than the male mind. Breton believed that the only way to improve the war-sick society of the 1920s was to discover the more intense "surreality" that lay beyond rational constraint.

AUTOMATISM. Surrealist artists employed a variety of techniques, including **automatism**, to release the mind from conscious control and to produce surprising new juxtapositions of imagery and forms. Max Ernst (1891–1976), a self-taught German artist who collaborated in Dada in Cologne and later joined Breton's circle in Paris, was particularly inventive in his use of automatism. In 1925, Ernst developed the automatist technique of **frottage**, in which he rubbed a pencil or crayon over a piece of paper placed on a textured surface. The resulting image stimulated Ernst's imagination. As he gazed at it, he began to see fantastic creatures, plants, and landscapes that he articulated more clearly with additional drawing. Ernst adapted frottage to painting, calling this new technique **grattage**. He created images by scraping layers of paint over a canvas laid over a textured surface, and then "revealing" the imagery he saw in the paint with additional painting. **THE HORDE** (**FIG. 31–55**) shows a nightmarish scene of

After World War I, increased exchanges between Modern architects led to the development of a common formal language, transcending national boundaries, which came to be known as the International Style. The term gained wide currency as a result of a 1932 exhibition at the Museum of Modern Art in New York, "The International Style: Architecture Since 1922," organized by the architectural historian Henry-Russell Hitchcock and the architect and curator Philip Johnson. Hitchcock and Johnson identified three fundamental principles of the style.

The first was "the conception of architecture as volume rather than mass." The use of a structural skeleton of steel and ferroconcrete made it possible to eliminate loadbearing walls on both the exterior and interior. The building could then be wrapped in a skin of glass, metal, or masonry, creating the effect of enclosed space (volume) rather than dense material (mass). Interiors featured open, free-flowing plans providing maximum flexibility in the use of space.

The second was "regularity rather than symmetry as the chief means of ordering design." Regular distribution of structural supports and the use of standard building parts promoted rectangular regularity rather than the balanced axial symmetry of Classical architecture. The avoidance of Classical balance also encouraged an asymmetrical disposition of the building's components, such as doors and windows.

The third was the rejection of "arbitrary applied decoration." The new architecture depended on the intrinsic elegance of its materials and the formal arrangement of its elements to produce harmonious aesthetic effects. In sum, the most extreme International Style building would be an unadorned glass box.

According to Hitchcock and Johnson, the International Style originated in the Netherlands (in De Stijl), France (in Purism), and Germany (at the Bauhaus). After the exhibition and publication of the catalog listing the characteristics of the International Style in 1932, it spread to the United States.

The first concentrated manifestation of the International Style was in 1927 at the Deutscher Werkbund's Weissenhofsiedlung exhibition in Stuttgart, Germany, directed by Ludwig Mies van der Rohe (1886–1969), an architect who, like Gropius, was associated with the Bauhaus in Germany. The purpose of this semipermanent show was to present a range of model homes that used new technologies and made no reference to historical styles. The buildings in the exhibition featured flat roofs, plain walls, off-center openings, and rectilinear designs by Mies, Gropius, Le Corbusier, and others.

The conceptual clarity of the International Style allowed it to remain vital until the 1970s, especially in the United States, where many of its original European architects, such as Mies and Gropius, who had escaped Hitler and the rise of Nazism in Germany in the 1930s, practiced.

---

wooden-looking monsters who advance against some unseen opponent. Like much of Ernst's other work of the period, this frightening image seems to evoke the horrors of World War I that Ernst had experienced firsthand in the German army.

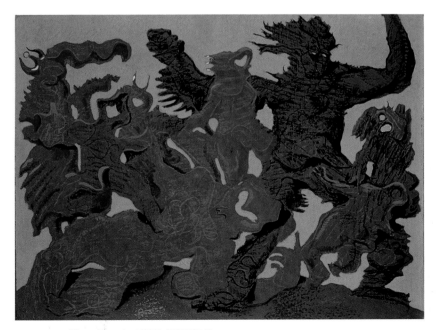

31-55 • Max Ernst THE HORDE
1927. Oil on canvas, 44⅞ × 57½″ (114 × 146.1 cm). Stedelijk Museum, Amsterdam.

UNEXPECTED JUXTAPOSITIONS. The paintings of Salvador Dalí (1904–1989) include more recognizable figures and forms but they also reveal the visual wonders of a subconscious mind run wild. Dalí trained at the San Fernando Academy of Fine Arts in Madrid, where he mastered the traditional methods of illusionistic representation, and traveled to Paris in 1928, where he met the Surrealists. Dalí's contribution to Surrealist theory was the "paranoid-critical method," in which he cultivated the paranoid's ability to misread, mangle, and misconstrue ordinary appearances, thus liberating himself from the shackles of conventional thought. Dalí then painted what he had imagined.

Dalí's paintings generally deal with a few key themes: sexuality, violence, and putrefaction. In the **BIRTH OF LIQUID DESIRES (FIG. 31–56)**, we see a large yellow **biomorphic** form (an organic shape resembling a living organism) that looks like a monster's face, a painter's palette, or a woman's body as the backdrop for four figures. A woman in white embraces a hermaphroditic figure who stands with one foot in a bowl that is being filled with liquid by a third figure, partially hidden, while a fourth figure enters a cavernous hole to the left. On a thick black cloud above the scene the question is posed: "Consign: to waste the total slate?" Dalí claimed that he arrived at his

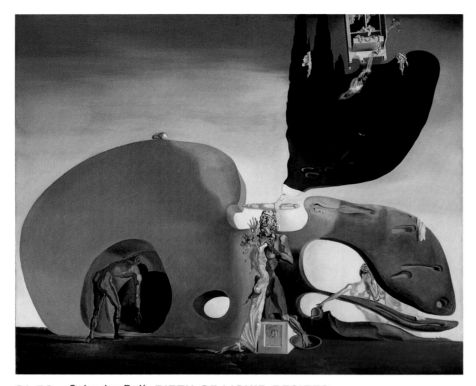

31-56 • Salvador Dalí BIRTH OF LIQUID DESIRES
1931–1932. Oil and collage on canvas, 37⅞ × 44¼″ (96.1 × 112.3 cm). Guggenheim Museum, New York. Peggy Guggenheim Collection. 76.2553 PG 100

surreality. One of the most disturbingly exquisite and mockingly humorous examples is **OBJECT (LUNCHEON IN FUR) (FIG. 31–57)**, by the Swiss artist Meret Oppenheim (1913–1985). Oppenheim was one of the few women invited to participate in the Surrealist movement. Surrealists generally treated women as their muses or as objects of study, but not their equals: Picasso even claimed to have "given" Oppenheim the idea for this sculpture. *Object* consists of an actual cup, saucer, and spoon covered with the fur of a Chinese gazelle (chosen for its resemblance in texture to pubic hair). It transposes two objects (a tea setting and gazelle fur) from their ordinary reality, recontextualizes them in an irrational new surreality, and transforms them into an uncanny object that is simultaneously desirous and deeply disturbing.

BIOMORPHIC ABSTRACTION. The Catalan artist Joan Miró (1893–1983) exhibited regularly with the Surrealists but never formally joined the movement. Miró's biomorphic abstraction is also intended to free the mind from rationality, but in a more benign manner. His **COMPOSITION (FIG. 31–58)** of 1933 is populated by curving biomorphic primal or mythic shapes and forms that are arranged by chance, and seem to emerge from the artist's mind uncensored, like doodles, to dance gleefully around the canvas. The Surrealists used the free association of doodling to relax the conscious mind and allow images to bubble up from the unconscious. Miró reportedly doodled on his canvases before working up in paint the shapes and forms revealed there. His forms do seem to take shape before our eyes, but their identity is always in flux. Miró was also fascinated by children's art, which he thought of as spontaneous

imagery by writing down his nightmares and merely painting what his paranoid-critical mind had conjured up. Dalí's images are thus, as Breton advocated, "the true process of thought, free from the exercise of reason and from any aesthetic or moral purpose." They defy rational interpretation although they trigger fear, anxiety, and even regression in our empathetic minds.

Dalí's strangely compelling art also draws on the Surrealist interest in unexpected juxtapositions of disparate realities. Surrealists argued that by juxtaposing several disparate ordinary objects in strange new contexts artists could create an uncanny

31-57 • Meret Oppenheim
OBJECT (LUNCHEON IN FUR)
1936. Fur-covered cup, diameter 4⅜″ (10.9 cm); fur-covered saucer, diameter 9⅜″ (23.7 cm); fur-covered spoon, length 8″ (20.2 cm); overall height, 2⅞″ (7.3 cm). Museum of Modern Art, New York.

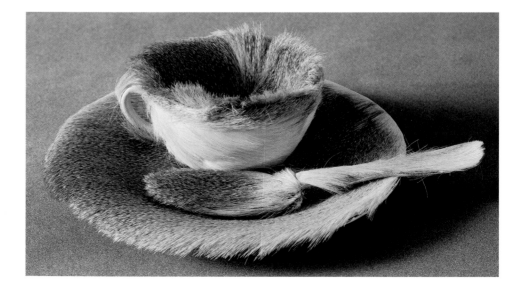

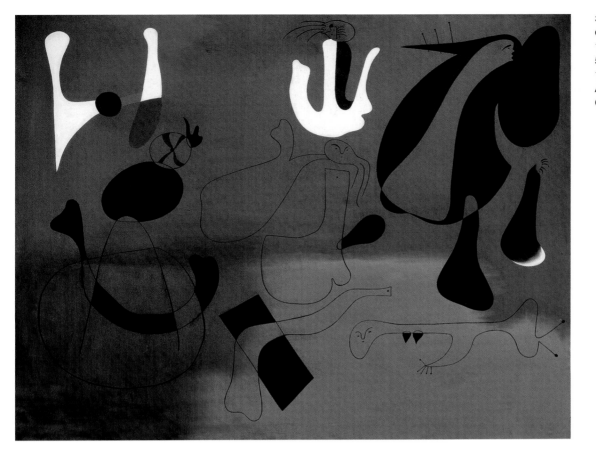

31–58 • Joan Miró
COMPOSITION
1933. Oil on canvas,
51¼ × 63½″ (130.2 ×
161.3 cm). Wadsworth
Athenaeum, Hartford,
Connecticut.

and expressive and, although he was a well-trained artist himself, he said that he wished he could learn to paint with the freedom of a child.

If Miró's paintings suggest movement, the American artist Alexander Calder (1898–1976) actually made biomorphic forms move. Calder trained as an engineer and took some art classes before traveling to Paris in 1926. Although not an official member of the movement, his sculpture was particularly admired by the Surrealists, with whom he exhibited on occasion. Calder came from a family of monumental sculptors, so it is not surprising that he reacted against his heritage by exploring the use of light new industrial materials in his sculpture. Like other sculptors of his generation, he explored negative space, removed sculpture from its pedestal, and hung it from the ceiling. The movement in Calder's art is not driven by motors; his sculptures are brushed into movement by air currents that make his unstable balanced forms bob and dip independently and seemingly randomly. Calder's metal sculptures, which are attached to wire arms and hung from the ceiling, are termed **mobiles**. **LOBSTER TRAP AND FISH TAIL (FIG. 31–59)** is composed of delicately balanced flat biomorphic forms and wire. At first it seems to be abstract, but the title works on our imagination to help us find the lobster trap and fish tail as they bob and spin

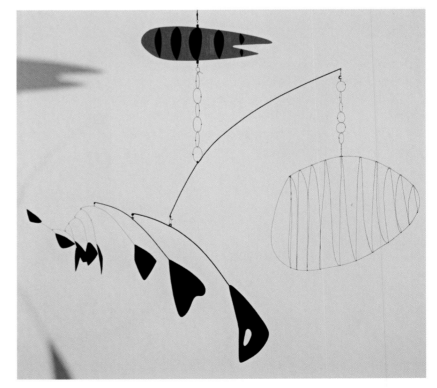

31–59 • Alexander Calder LOBSTER TRAP AND FISH TAIL
1939. Painted steel wire and sheet aluminum, approx. 8′6″ × 9′6″ (2.6 × 2.9 m). Museum of Modern Art, New York.
Commissioned by the Advisory Committee for the Stairwell of the Museum (590.139.a–d)

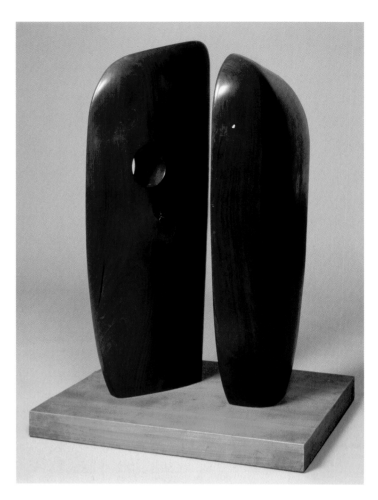

31-60 • Barbara Hepworth FORMS IN ECHELON
1938. Wood, 42½ × 23⅔ × 28″ (108 × 60 × 71 cm). Tate Gallery, London. Presented by the artist 1964 © Bowness, Hepworth Estate

EXPLORE MORE: Gain insight from a primary source by Barbara Hepworth **www.myartslab.com**

to create the terrifyingly funny possibility that the lobster or the fish will get caught in the trap.

UNIT ONE IN ENGLAND

In 1933, the English artists Barbara Hepworth (1903–1975), Henry Moore (1898–1986), and Paul Nash (1889–1946), along with the poet and critic Herbert Read (1893–1968), founded Unit One. Although short-lived, this group promoted the use of hand-crafted, Surrealist-influenced biomorphic forms in sculpture, brought new energy to British art in the 1930s, and exerted a lasting impact on British sculpture.

Hepworth studied at the Leeds School of Art and made exquisitely crafted sculptures punctuated with holes so that air and light could pass through them. **FORMS IN ECHELON (FIG. 31–60)** consists of two biomorphic shapes carved in highly polished wood. The artist merely described these sculptures as organic. She hoped that viewers would let their eyes play around them, letting their imaginations generate associations and meanings.

Moore also carved sculptural abstractions punctured by holes, although his sculptures were more obviously based on the human form. He also studied sculpture at the Leeds School of Art and then

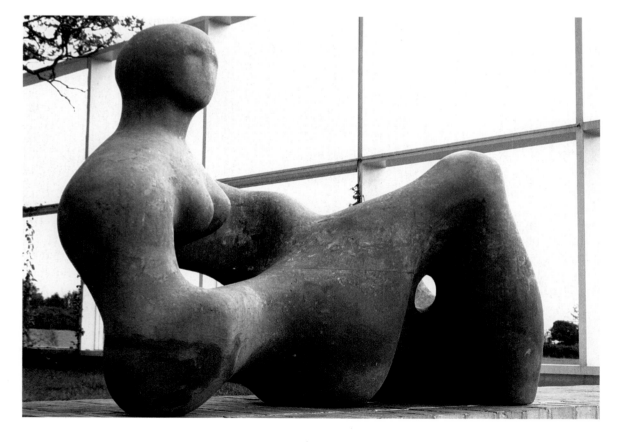

31-61 • Henry Moore RECUMBENT FIGURE
1938. Hornton stone, 35 × 52 × 29″ (88.9 × 132.7 × 73.7 cm).

at the Royal College of Art in London. The African, Oceanic, and Pre-Columbian sculpture that he saw at the British Museum had a more powerful impact on his developing aesthetic than his training at the college. He felt that the work of artists beyond the Western tradition showed a greater respect for the inherent qualities of materials such as stone or wood than that of Western artists.

The reclining female nude is the dominant theme of Moore's art. The massive simplified body in **RECUMBENT FIGURE (FIG. 31–61)** refers to the *chacmool*, a reclining human form in Toltec and Maya art (SEE FIG. 12–13). Moore's carving also demonstrates a sensitivity to the inherent qualities of his stone, which he sought out in remote quarries, always insisting that each of his sculptures was labeled with the specific kind of stone he had used. While certain aspects of the human body are clearly defined in this piece, such as the head, breasts, supporting elbow, and raised knee, other parts seem to flow together into an undulating mass suggestive of a hilly landscape. The cavity at the center inverts our expectations about the solid and void. In 1937, Moore wrote: "A hole can itself have as much shape-meaning as a solid mass."

MODERN ART IN THE AMERICAS BETWEEN THE WARS

In American art between the wars, the need for a national visual identity emerged, but the United States is a large, diverse nation that has so many "identities" that, despite attempts to consolidate the fiction of a single, essentially Anglo-Saxon national identity, the work of African-American artists, immigrant artists, women artists, and others became more visible at this time.

THE HARLEM RENAISSANCE

In the 1930s, hundreds of thousands of African Americans migrated from the rural, mostly agricultural American South to the urban, industrialized North to escape racial oppression and find greater social and economic opportunities. This Great Migration prompted the formation of the nationwide New Negro movement and the Harlem Renaissance in New York, which called for greater social and political activism among African Americans.

Harlem's wealthy middle-class African-American community produced some of the nation's most talented artists of the 1920s and 1930s, such as the jazz musician Duke Ellington, the novelist Jean Toomer, and the poet Langston Hughes. The movement's intellectual leader was Alain Locke (1886–1954), a critic and philosophy professor who argued that black artists should seek their artistic roots in the traditional arts of Africa rather than in mainstream American or European art.

James Van Der Zee (1886–1983) was a studio photographer who made carefully crafted portraits of the Harlem upper middle classes. He opened his studio in 1916 and worked both as a news reporter and a society photographer. **COUPLE WEARING RACCOON COATS WITH A CADILLAC (FIG. 31–62)** shows a wealthy man and woman posing with their new car in 1932, at the height of the

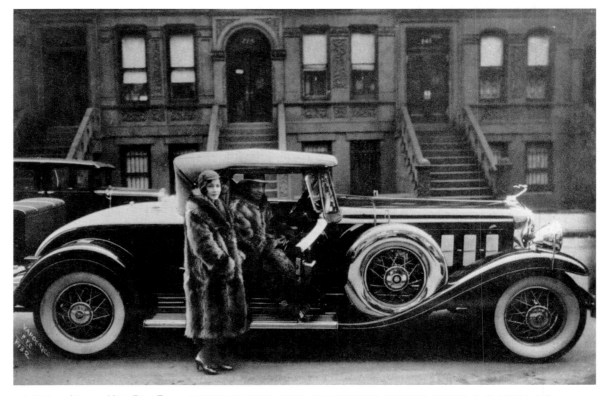

31-62 • James Van Der Zee COUPLE WEARING RACCOON COATS WITH A CADILLAC, TAKEN ON WEST 127TH STREET, HARLEM, NEW YORK
1932. Gelatin-silver print.

Guernica

In January 1937, as the Spanish Civil War between the Republicans and the Nationalists began to escalate, the Spanish artist Pablo Picasso, who was then living in Paris, was commissioned to make a large painting for the Spanish Pavilion of the 1938 Paris Exposition. He was unsure what he might create for the exposition, a direct descendant of the nineteenth-century World's Fairs that resulted in the Crystal Palace and the Eiffel Tower. The 1938 Spanish Pavilion was the first Spanish national pavilion at any World's Fair.

On April 26, 1937, Nationalist-supporting German bombers attacked the town of Guernica in the Basque region of Spain, killing and wounding 1,600 civilians. The cold-blooded and calculating nature of the attack on Guernica was inhuman. For more than three hours, 25 bombers dropped 100,000 pounds of explosives on the town, while more than 20 fighter planes strafed anyone caught in the streets trying to flee destroyed or burning buildings. Fires burned in Guernica for three days. By the end, one-third of the town's population was killed or wounded and 75 percent of its buildings had been destroyed. The attack seemed to serve no military purpose, other than to allow Franco's Nationalist forces to terrorize civilian populations, but the true horror was revealed when it was discovered that the German commander planned the massacre merely as a "training mission" for the German air force.

Horrified, Picasso now had his subject for the Fair. On May 1, 1 million protesters marched in Paris and the next day Picasso made his first preliminary sketches for his visual response to this Spanish Civil War atrocity. Picasso was trained in the academic tradition and he planned his GUERNICA as an immense history painting detailing the historic, and ignoble, events of the attack. He made several preliminary sketches (esquisses) to develop the composition, colors, and so on, moving on to canvas only after ten days of intensive planning. He worked at the painting itself, changing figures, altering colors, and developing his themes, for another month.

Guernica is a complex painting layered with meaning. Picasso rarely used specific or obvious symbolism in his art, preferring to let individual viewers interpret specific details differently. What is beyond question is that Guernica is a scene of brutality, chaos, terror, and suffering. Painted in black, white, and dark blue, the image resonates with anguish. It freezes figures in mid-movement in stark black and white as if caught by the flashbulb of a reporter's camera. There is a bull in the upper left, a wounded horse in the center, and several broken human forms along with a giant light bulb like an eye at the top, a lamp below it, and smoke and fire visible beyond the destroyed room in which the action takes place. The details of the painting have been interpreted in many ways: The bull and horse have been described as standing for Nationalist and Republican forces respectively, as well as the reverse. The light bulb, javelin, dagger, lamp, and bird have also been ascribed specific meanings. But Picasso refused to be pinned down; he said that Guernica is about massacred people and animals—beyond that, the meaning is fluid.

Guernica was installed in the Spanish Pavilion with other works of art supporting the Republican cause, including Alexander Calder's Fontaine de Mercure, seen in the foreground of this photograph, and works by Joan Miró, filmmaker Luis Buñuel, and others. Picasso did not want Guernica to be shown in Spain while the Nationalist leader, General Franco, ruled, so it was hung in the Museum of Modern Art in New York for years, before finally being installed in the Reina Sofía in Madrid in 1981, six years after Franco's death. A tapestry of Guernica has hung in the United Nations Building in New York since 1985.

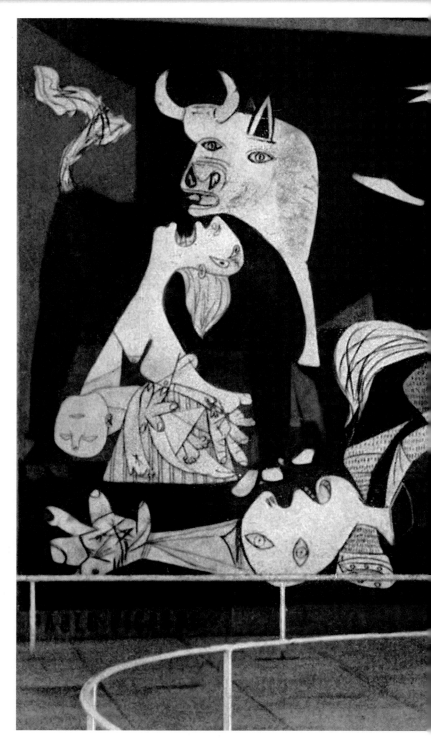

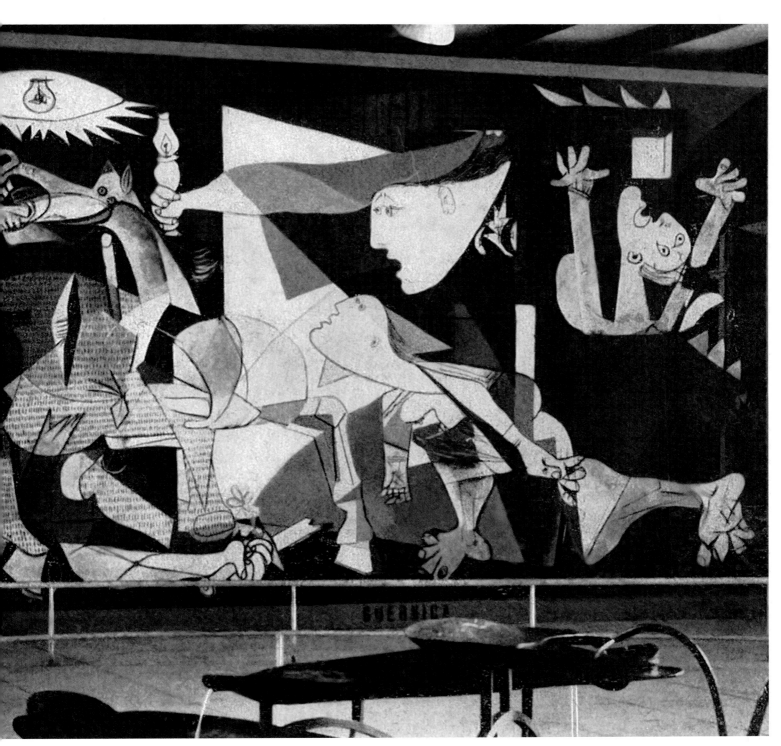

Pablo Picasso GUERNICA
1937. Oil on canvas, 11'6" × 25'8" (3.5 × 7.8 m). Museo Nacional Centro de Arte Reina Sofía, Madrid. On permanent loan from the Museo del Prado, Madrid. Shown installed in the Spanish Pavilion of the Paris Exposition, 1937.

In the foreground: Alexander Calder's *Fontaine de Mercure* (Mercury Fountain). 1937. Mercury, sheet metal, wire rod, pitch, and paint, 44 × 115 × 77" (122 × 292 × 196 cm). Fundacio Joan Miró, Barcelona.

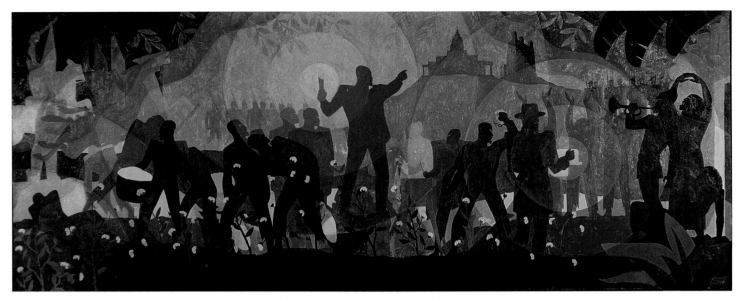

31-63 • Aaron Douglas ASPECTS OF NEGRO LIFE: FROM SLAVERY THROUGH RECONSTRUCTION
1934. Oil on canvas, 5′ × 11′7″ (1.5 × 3.5 m). Schomburg Center for Research in Black Culture, New York Public Library.

Great Depression. The photograph reveals the glamor of Harlem, then the center of African-American cultural life.

The painter Aaron Douglas (1898–1979), from Topeka, Kansas, moved to New York City in 1925. He developed a collaged silhouette style that owes much to African art, and that became a fundamental characteristic of later African-American art (SEE FIG. 32–70). His **ASPECTS OF NEGRO LIFE: FROM SLAVERY THROUGH RECONSTRUCTION (FIG. 31–63)** was painted for the Harlem branch of the New York Public Library under the sponsorship of the Depression-era Public Works of Art Project. To the right in the painting, Douglas shows slaves celebrating the Emancipation Proclamation of 1863. Concentric circles of light seem to emanate from the Proclamation itself. At the center of the composition, a figure in orator pose gestures dramatically and points to the United States Capitol in the background, as if urging all African Americans, some of whom are shown still picking cotton, to exercise their right to vote. To the left, Union soldiers leave the South after Reconstruction, while Ku Klux Klan members, hooded and on horseback, ride in as if to remind viewers that the fight for civil rights has only just been joined.

The career of sculptor Augusta Savage (1892–1962) reflects the myriad difficulties faced by African Americans in the art world. Savage studied at Cooper Union in New York but her first application to study in Europe in 1923 was turned down because of her race. In a letter of protest to the institution's administration, she wrote: "Democracy is a strange thing. My brother was good enough to be accepted in one of the regiments that saw service in France during the war, but it seems his sister is not good enough to

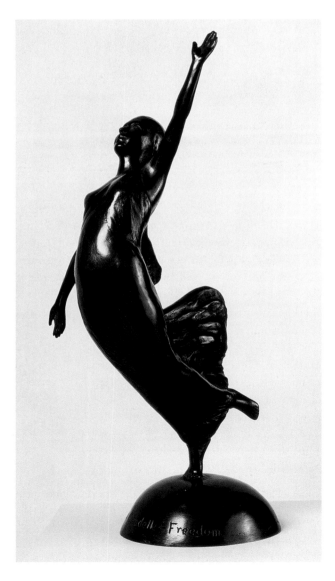

31-64 • Augusta Savage LA CITADELLE: FREEDOM
1930. Bronze, 14½ × 7 × 6″ (35.6 × 17.8 × 15.2 cm).
Howard University Art Collection, Washington, D.C.

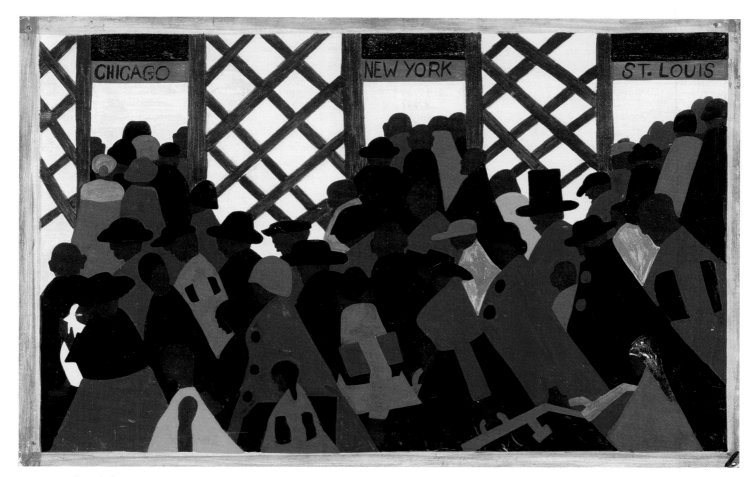

31-65 • Jacob Lawrence **THE MIGRATION SERIES, PANEL NO.1: DURING WORLD WAR I THERE WAS A GREAT MIGRATION NORTH BY SOUTHERN AFRICAN AMERICANS** 1940–1941. Tempera on masonite, 12 × 18″ (30.5 × 45.7 cm). The Phillips Collection, Washington, D.C.

be a guest of the country for which he fought." Finally, in 1930, Savage was able to study in Paris. On her return to the United States, she made sculptural portraits of several African-American leaders, including Marcus Garvey and W. E. B. DuBois. She was inspired by the story of the Haitian Revolution in 1791 following the Slave Revolt (SEE FIG. 29–38). In **LA CITADELLE: FREEDOM (FIG. 31–64)**, Savage portrays a female figure raising her hand to the sky like the figure of freedom as she balances on the toes of one foot and flies through the air. La Citadelle was the castle residence of one of Haiti's first leaders of African heritage and which, for Savage, represented the possibility and promise of freedom and equality.

Savage established a small private art school in Harlem for which she received Federal funds under the Works Progress Administration (see "Federal Patronage for American Art During the Depression," page 1066) to transform it into the Harlem Community Art Center. Hundreds of these centers were eventually established all over the country, but Savage's became an unofficial salon for Harlem artists, poets, composers, dancers, and historians.

One of the best-known artists to emerge from the Harlem Community Art Center was Jacob Lawrence (1917–2000).

Lawrence devoted much of his early work to the depiction of African-American history, which he recounted in several series of narrative paintings on small panels, each accompanied by a text. The themes of these series include the history of Harlem and the lives of Haitian revolutionary leader Toussaint L'Ouverture and American abolitionist John Brown. In 1940–1941, Lawrence created his most expansive series, entitled **THE MIGRATION OF THE NEGRO**, in which 60 panels chronicle the Great Migration, a journey that brought Lawrence's own parents from South Carolina to Atlantic City, New Jersey. The first panel **(FIG. 31–65)** shows African-American migrants streaming through the doors of a Southern train station on their way to Chicago, New York, or St. Louis. Lawrence's boldly abstracted silhouette style, with its flat bright shapes and colors, is superficially similar to Cubism, but in fact draws consciously and more directly on the African visual sources that inspired Picasso. Lawrence later also illustrated books by Harlem Renaissance authors.

RURAL AMERICA

In the 1930s, other artists, known collectively as the Regionalists, began to paint Midwestern themes. In 1931, at the height of the

Federal Patronage for American Art During the Depression

In the early 1930s, during the Great Depression, President Franklin D. Roosevelt's New Deal established a series of programs to provide relief for the unemployed and to revive the nation's economy. These programs included several initiatives to supply work to American artists. The Public Works of Art Project (PWAP), set up in late 1933 to employ needy artists, lasted only five months but it supported 4,000 artists, who produced more than 15,000 works. The Section of Painting and Sculpture in the Treasury Department was established in October 1934 and lasted until 1943; it commissioned murals and sculpture for public buildings, although technically it was not a relief program because artists were paid only when they won a commission. The Federal Art Project (FAP) of the Works Progress Administration (WPA), which ran from 1935 to 1943, succeeded the PWAP. The WPA was the most important work-relief agency of the Depression era and had employed more than 6 million workers by 1943. Its programs supporting the arts included the Federal Theater Project, the Federal Writers' Project, and the FAP. About 10,000 artists participated in the FAP, producing a staggering 108,000 paintings, 18,000 sculptures, 2,500 murals, and thousands of prints, photographs, and posters. All of this art became public property. The murals and sculptures, commissioned for public buildings such as train stations, schools, hospitals, and post offices, reached a particularly wide audience. Many can still be seen today, but most of the easel paintings were sold as "plumber's canvas" and destroyed.

To build public support for Federal assistance in rural America, the Resettlement Agency (RA) and Farm Security Administration (FSA) hired photographers to document the effects of the Depression across the country. These photographs were available, copyright-free, to any newspaper, magazine, or publisher. They are still available, copyright-free, today. San Francisco-based Dorothea Lange (1895–1965), an RA/FSA photographer between 1935 and 1939, documented the plight of migrant farm laborers who fled the Dust Bowl conditions of the Great Plains and then flooded California looking for work.

MIGRANT MOTHER, NIPOMO, CALIFORNIA shows Florence Thompson, a 32-year-old mother of seven children, as representative of the poverty suffered by thousands of migrant workers in California. Lange's photograph is carefully constructed to tug at the heartstrings. It is taken very close to the subject so that we sympathize with the mother's worn expression and resolve. The composition reminds us of the images of the sorrowful Madonna as she contemplates the loss of her son (SEE FIG. 20–9). What Lange chose to eliminate from this photograph, but is recorded in other photographs of the same scene, are the makeshift tent in which the family is camped, the dirty dishes on a battered trunk, trash strewn around the campsite, and, most significant, Thompson's teenage daughter. Lange wanted this photograph to evoke the purity and moral worth of her subject, for whom she sought Federal aid; she could not allude to the fact that Thompson was a teenage mother, or even that she was Cherokee. *Migrant Mother* (then unidentified by name) became the "poster child" of the Great Depression, and her powerfully sad distant gaze still resonates with audiences today, demonstrating the propaganda power of the visual image.

During the Depression, the FAP paid a generous average salary of about $20 a week (a salesclerk at Woolworth's earned only about $11) for painters and sculptors to devote themselves full time to art. New York City's painters, in particular, developed a group identity, meeting in the bars and coffeehouses of Greenwich Village to discuss art. The FAP thus provided the financial grounds on which New York artists built a sense of community—a community that produced the Abstract Expressionists, and allowed New York to supersede Paris as the center of activity for Western art.

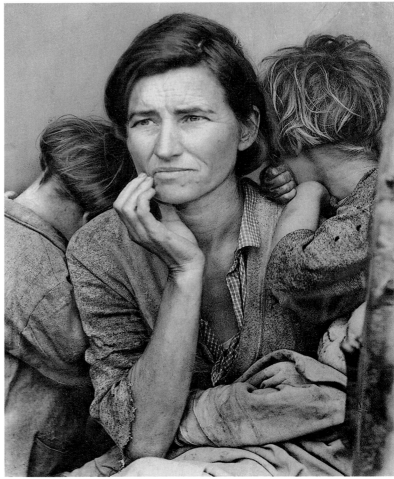

Dorothea Lange **MIGRANT MOTHER, NIPOMO, CALIFORNIA**
February 1936. Gelatin-silver print. Library of Congress, Washington, D.C.

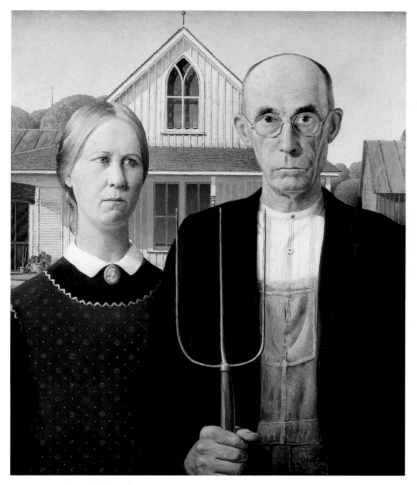

31-66 • Grant Wood AMERICAN GOTHIC
1930. Oil on beaverboard, 29⅞ × 24⅞″ (74.3 × 62.4 cm).
Art Institute of Chicago.

Depression, Grant Wood (1891–1942), who later taught at the University of Iowa, created **AMERICAN GOTHIC (FIG. 31–66)**, which was purchased by the Art Institute of Chicago and established Wood's national fame. *American Gothic* shows an elderly father with his unmarried daughter standing in front of their Gothic Revival framed house. The couple is dressed in old-fashioned clothes for the time. Wood's sister Nan and his dentist posed for the figures and the house was modeled on an actual house in Eldon, Iowa. The daughter in the scene wears a home-made ricrac-edged apron and Wood's mother's cameo. The father clutches an old-fashioned three-tined pitchfork and the house behind them is a modest small-town home. The daughter's long sad face echoes her father's; she is unmarried and likely to stay that way. In 1931, husbands were hard to come by in the Midwest because many of the young men had fled from the farms to the city of Chicago for jobs. The painting is tightly and carefully painted in homage to the Flemish Renaissance painters that Wood admired. This image stood for everything good and everything bad about the heartland in the 1930s.

CANADA

In the nineteenth century, Canadian artists, like their counterparts in the United States, began to assert their independence from European art by painting Canada's great untamed wilderness. A number of Canadians, however, still studied in Paris at the end of the century, using academic realism to paint figurative subjects, while others painted the Canadian landscape through the lens of Impressionism. In 1907, the Canadian Art Club was founded in Toronto, Ontario.

LANDSCAPE AND IDENTITY. In the early 1910s, a younger group of Toronto artists, many of whom worked for the same commercial art firm, began to sketch together, adopting the rugged landscape of the Canadian north as an expression of Canadian national identity.

A key figure in this movement was Tom Thomson (1877–1917), who, as of 1912, spent the warm months of each year in Algonquin Provincial Park, a large forest reserve 180 miles north of Toronto. He made numerous small, swiftly painted, oil-on-board sketches as the basis for the full-size paintings that he executed in his studio during the winter. A sketch made in the spring of 1916 led to **THE JACK PINE (FIG. 31–67)**. This tightly organized composition features a stylized pine tree rising from a rocky foreground and silhouetted against a luminous background of lake and sky, horizontally divided by

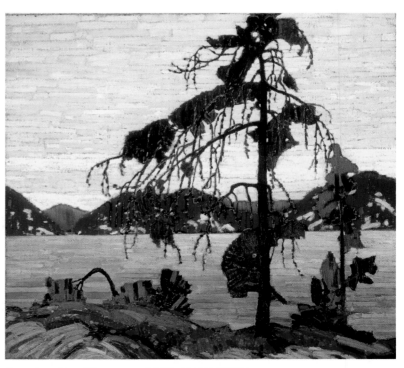

31-67 • Tom Thomson THE JACK PINE
1916–1917. Oil on canvas, 49⅞ × 54½″ (127.9 × 139.8 cm). National Gallery of Canada, Ottawa, Ontario. Purchase, 1918

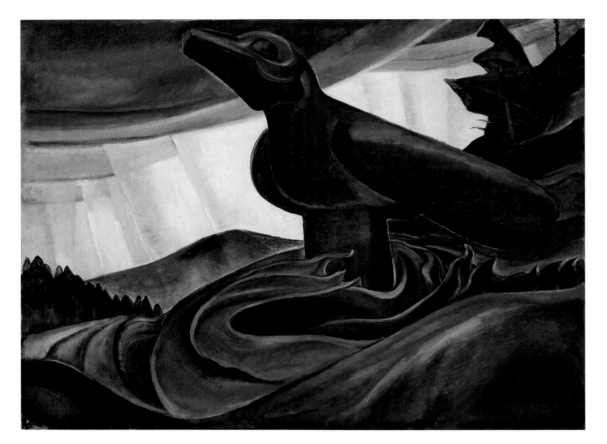

cold blue hills. The painting's arresting beauty and reverential mood suggest a divine presence in the lonely northern landscape and have made it an icon of Canadian national art. In 1917, Thomson tragically drowned.

NATIVE AMERICAN INFLUENCE. Born in Victoria, British Columbia, the West Coast artist Emily Carr (1871–1945) studied art in San Francisco, England, and Paris. On a 1907 trip to Alaska she encountered the monumental carved poles of Northwest Coast Native peoples and resolved to document these "real art treasures of a passing race." Over the next 23 years, Carr visited more than 30 such sites across British Columbia, making drawings and watercolors as a basis for oil paintings. After a commercially unsuccessful exhibition of her Native subjects, Carr returned to Victoria in 1913, opened a boardinghouse, and painted very little for the next 15 years. In 1927, however, she was invited to participate in an exhibition of West Coast art at the National Gallery of Canada. On her trip east for the show's opening Carr met members of the Group of Seven, which had been established in 1920 by some of Tom Thomson's former colleagues, who rekindled her interest in painting.

With the Group of Seven, Carr developed a dramatic and powerfully sculptural style full of dark, brooding energy. **BIG RAVEN (FIG. 31–68)**, based on a 1912 watercolor, shows an abandoned village in the Queen Charlotte Islands where Carr found a carved raven on a pole, the surviving member of a pair that

originally marked a mortuary house. In her autobiography Carr described the raven as "old and rotting," but in the painting she shows it as strong and majestic, thrusting dynamically above the swirling vegetation, a symbol of enduring spiritual power and national pride.

MEXICO

The Mexican Revolution of 1910 overthrew the 35-year dictatorship of General Porfirio Díaz and was followed by ten years of political instability. In 1920, however, the reformist president Álvaro Obregón came to power and finally restored political order. As in the U.S.S.R., the leaders of the new government engaged artists in the service of the people and state. Obregón's government commissioned several Mexican artists to decorate public buildings with murals celebrating the history, life, and work of the Mexican people. These murals were to be executed in a naturalistic style because, in the opinion of the new government, abstract art was incompatible with and incomprehensible to the public at large.

Diego Rivera (1886–1957) was prominent in the Mexican mural movement. He enrolled in Mexico City's Academia de San Carlos at age 11. From 1911 to 1919, he lived in Paris where he met Picasso and David Siqueiros (1896–1974), another Mexican muralist. Both Rivera and Siqueiros were dedicated to creating a revolutionary mural art in public buildings and in the service of the people. In 1920–1921, Rivera traveled to Italy to study Renaissance

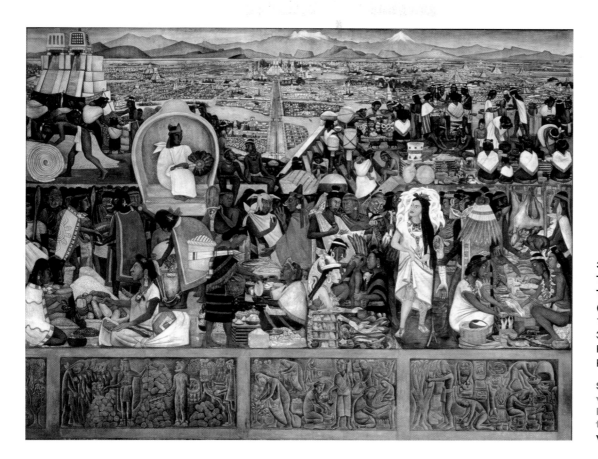

31-69 • Diego Rivera
THE GREAT CITY OF TENOCHTITLAN (DETAIL)
1945. Mural, 16′1¾″ × 31′10¼″ (4.92 × 9.71 m). Patio corridor, National Palace, Mexico City.

SEE MORE: View a video about Diego Rivera's fresco technique
www.myartslab.com

frescoes; he also visited ancient Mexican indigenous sites to study mural paintings. **THE GREAT CITY OF TENOCHTITLAN (FIG. 31–69)** is one of the murals that Rivera painted for the National Palace in Mexico City, a cycle depicting the history of Mexico using stylized forms and brilliant local colors. Rivera also painted murals in the United States. In 1929, he married Frida Kahlo.

The art of Frida Kahlo (1907–1954) is an admixture of autobiography and traditional Mexican folk painting. **THE TWO FRIDAS (FIG. 31–70)** shows a double image of the artist that expresses an identity split between European and Mexican heritages (her father was German and her mother part indigenous Mexican). The European Frida wears a Victorian dress while the Mexican Frida wears a traditional Mexican costume. The Mexican Frida holds a small sculpture of an

31-70 • Frida Kahlo **THE TWO FRIDAS**
1939. Oil on canvas. 5′8½″ × 5′8½″ (1.74 × 1.74 m). Museo de Arte Moderno, Instituto Nacional de Bellas Artes, Mexico City.

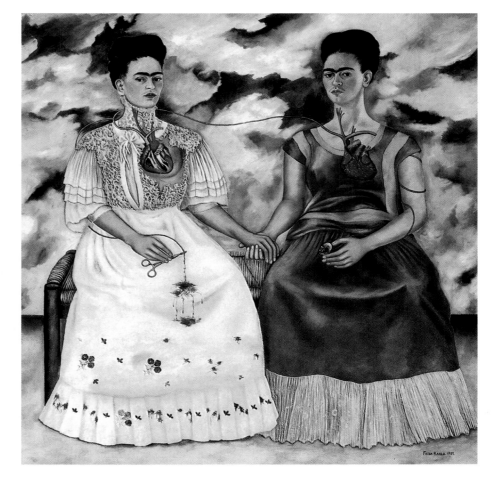

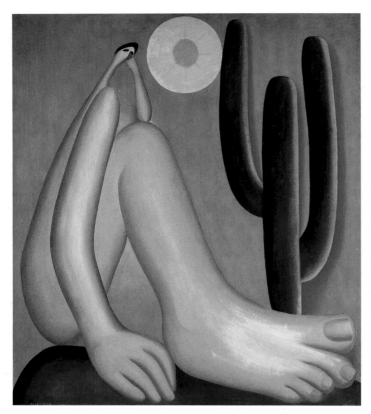

31-71 • Tarsila do Amaral ABAPORÚ (THE ONE WHO EATS)
1928. Oil on canvas, 34 × 29″ (86.4 × 73.7 cm). Museo de Arte Latinoamericano, Buenos Aires. Courtesy of Guilherme Augusto do Amaral/Malba-Coleccion Constantini, Buenos Aires

used to declare their artistic independence from Europe. Modern Art Week brought avant-garde poets, dancers, and musicians as well as visual artists to São Paulo and took on a distinctly confrontational character. Poets derided their elders in poetry, dancers enacted modern versions of traditional dances, and composer Hector Villa-Lobos (1887–1959) appeared on stage in a bathrobe and slippers to play new music based on Afro-Brazilian rhythms.

In 1928, the São Paulo poet Oswald de Andrade, one of Modern Art Week's organizers, wrote the *Anthropophagic Manifesto* proposing a tongue-in-cheek if radical solution to Brazil's seeming dependence on European culture. He suggested that Brazilians should imitate the ancient Brazilians' response to Portuguese explorers arriving on their shore: Eat them. He mockingly described this relationship as anthropophagic or cannibalistic and proposed that Brazilians should gobble up European culture, digest it, let it strengthen their Brazilianness, and then get rid of it.

The painter who most closely embodies this irreverent attitude is Tarsila do Amaral (1887–1974), a daughter of the coffee-planting aristocracy who studied in Europe with Fernand Léger (SEE FIG. 31–21), among others. Her painting **ABAPORÚ (THE ONE WHO EATS)** (FIG. 31–71) shows an appreciation of the art of Léger

ancient god, while the European Frida holds a forceps: A blood vessel connects the god to the forceps through the hearts of the two Fridas. Kahlo suffered a broken pelvis in an accident at 17, and endured a lifetime of surgical interventions—this work alludes to her constant pain, as well as to the Aztec custom of human sacrifice by heart removal. The significance of Kahlo's art, apart from its memorable self-expression, lies in its investigation of larger issues of Mexican identity. This painting addresses issues of mixed heritage in Mexico, sexuality, and gender identity within the context of Kahlo's own life.

BRAZIL

Other Latin American art was dominated by the academic tradition in the nineteenth century; several nations had thriving academies, large art communities, and significant numbers of artists traveling to Paris to study. By 1914, artists in many Latin American countries had begun to paint national themes in their own versions of Impressionism. After the war, artists who studied abroad also brought home ideas drawn from Modern art and the European avant-garde which they translated into a specifically Latin American vision. For instance in 1922, as Brazil marked the centenary of its independence from Portugal, the avant-garde in São Paulo celebrated with Modern Art Week, an event Brazilian artists

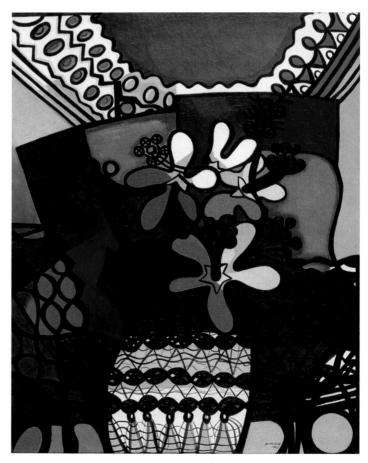

31-72 • Amelia Peláez MARPACÍFICO (HIBISCUS)
1943. Oil on canvas, 45½ × 35″ (115.6 × 88.9 cm). Art Museum of the Americas, Washington, D.C. Gift of IBM

and Brancusi (SEE FIGS. 31–27, 31–28), which Tarsila collected. But she has cleverly inserted several "tropical" clichés into her own work in the abstracted forms of a cactus and a lemon-slice sun. The subject is Andrade's irreverent cannibal who sits in an almost caricatural Brazilian landscape, as if to say: If Brazilians are caricatured abroad as cannibals, then let us act like cannibals. As Andrade wrote in one of his manifestos: "Carnival in Rio is the religious outpouring of our race. Richard Wagner yields to the samba. Barbaric but ours. We have a dual heritage: The jungle and the school."

CUBA

Cuba's 1920s avant-garde was one of the most interdisciplinary, consisting of anthropologists, poets, composers, and even a few scientists, who gathered in Havana and called themselves "The Minority." They issued a manifesto in 1927 repudiating government corruption, "Yankee imperialism," and dictatorship on any continent. "Minority" artists, they urged, should pursue a new, popular, Modern art rooted in Cuban soil.

Amelia Peláez (1896–1968) left Cuba for Paris shortly after this manifesto was issued. When she returned home, she joined the anthropologist Lydia Cabrera to study Cuban popular and folk arts. Her paintings focus on the woman's realm—the domestic interior—and national identity, as in **MARPACÍFICO (HIBISCUS) (FIG. 31–72)**. The overall language of this work is Cubist, as seen in the flattened overlapping forms and compressed pictorial space, but it shows a mirror, a tabletop, and local hibiscus flowers embroidered in paint with heavy black outlines and pure color that would be instantly recognizable in Cuba as representing the flat fan-shaped stained-glass windows that decorate many Cuban homes.

POSTWAR ART IN EUROPE AND THE AMERICAS

FIGURAL RESPONSES AND *ART INFORMEL* IN EUROPE

The horrors of World War II surpassed even those of World War I. The human loss was almost too profound and grotesque to comprehend. Between loss of life in action, those killed in work camps and death camps (concentration camps), those lost to starvation, and those lost in the bombing of civilian targets, more than 30 million people died and a further estimated 40 million people were displaced. The unimaginable horror of the concentration camps and the awful impact of the dropping of nuclear bombs shook humanity to its core. Winston Churchill described the extent of the catastrophe: "What is Europe now? A rubble heap, a charnel house, a breeding ground of pestilence and hate."

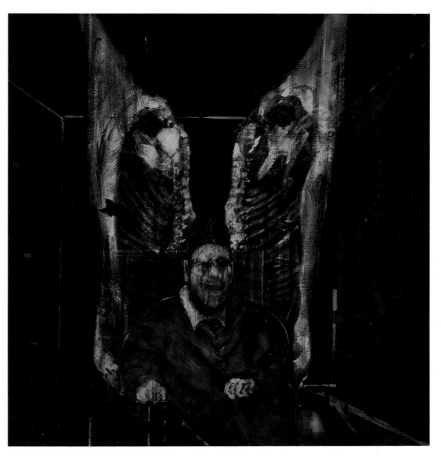

31-73 • Francis Bacon HEAD SURROUNDED BY SIDES OF BEEF
1954. Oil on canvas, 50¾ × 48″ (129 × 122 cm). Art Institute of Chicago.
Harriott A. Fox Fund

Most European artists in the immediate postwar period used their art to try to come to terms with what they had experienced, many debating about how best to do this: Some artists worked figuratively while others painted abstractions.

In England, Francis Bacon (1909–1992) used his canvases to capture the horrors that haunted him. Bacon was self-taught and produced very few pictures until the 1940s. He served as an air-raid warden during World War II and saw the bloody impact of the bombing of civilians in London firsthand. In **HEAD SURROUNDED BY SIDES OF BEEF (FIG. 31–73)**, Bacon shows the imperious Pope Innocent X reduced to an anguished and insubstantial man howling in a black void as two bloody sides of beef enclose him in a claustrophobic box that contains his frightful screams and amplifies his terror. The painting was directly inspired by Diego Velázquez's portrait of Pope Innocent X (1650) and by Rembrandt paintings of dripping meat. Bacon wrote of his art: "I hope to make the best human cry in painting … to remake the violence of reality itself."

One of the most distinctive postwar European art movements was *Art Informel* ("formless art"), which was also called *tachisme* (*tache* is French for "spot" or "stain"). *Art Informel* was promoted by the French critic Michel Tapié (1909–1987) who suggested that art should express an authentic concept of postwar humanity through simple, honest marks.

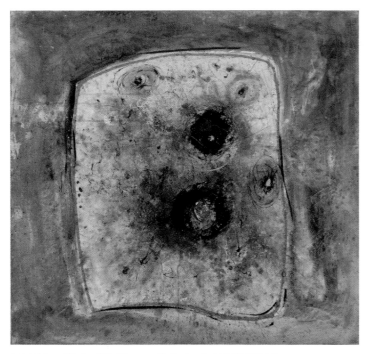

31-74 • Wols (Wolfgang Schulze) PAINTING
1944–1945. Oil on canvas, 31⅞ × 32″ (81 × 81.1 cm). Museum of Modern Art, New York. Gift of D. and J. de Menil Fund (29.1956)

knew both Picasso and the Surrealists, and was forced to return to Cuba when the Nazis invaded France. He found himself on the same ship as the Surrealist leader André Breton; Lam disembarked at Havana while Breton traveled on to New York. Lam explored his African-Cuban heritage in the company of anthropologist Lydia Cabrera and novelist Alejo Carpentier. His work from the late 1940s is deeply informed by African-Cuban art, the polytheistic spirituality imagery of *santería*, and his anti-colonial stance in Cuba. The jagged, semi-abstracted forms of **ZAMBEZIA, ZAMBEZIA (FIG. 31–75)** might recall European Modernism, but are actually derived from *santería* religious ritual. The central figure is a composite *santería* deity. "Zambezia" was the early colonial name for Zimbabwe in southeastern Africa, which at the time that this painting was created was still a British colonial possession known as Rhodesia. Much earlier, Zambezia was also a source for slaves who were brought to Cuba. Lam said of his art: "I wanted with all my heart to paint the drama of my country … . In this way I could act as a Trojan horse spewing forth hallucinating figures with the power to surprise, to disturb the dreams of the exploiters."

In Buenos Aires, two groups of artists formed immediately after the war: Arte Concreto-Invención and Madí. At the time

The informal leader of *Art Informel* was Wolfgang Schulze, called Wols (1913–1951), who lived through the dislocation and devastation experienced by millions in Europe in the 1930s and 1940s. Born in Germany, Wols was resolutely anti-Nazi and left his homeland when Hitler came to power. He settled in Paris where he became a photographer working for *Vogue* and *Harper's Bazaar*. When the Germans occupied France, he fled to Spain but was arrested, had his passport confiscated, and was deported to spend the rest of the war as a stateless person in a refugee camp in southern France. When the war ended, Wols moved back to Paris and began painting again, producing passionate pictures by applying paint with whatever came to hand, scraping his heavy surfaces with a knife and allowing the paint to drip and run. **PAINTING (FIG. 31–74)** represents a disease-ridden and violent world in which the semi-abstracted forms resemble either cells or dark muddy bacterial growths. Wols was temporarily supported by the French philosopher and novelist Jean-Paul Sartre, but died of food poisoning in 1951.

LATIN AMERICAN EXPERIMENTS

In Cuba, Wifredo Lam (1902–1980) created abstract and Surrealist paintings about the violence and anguish of his country's struggle against colonialism. Lam was of mixed Chinese, Spanish, and African heritage and brought issues of identity and self-discovery to his art. He studied at the National Academy in Havana, moved to Paris, where he

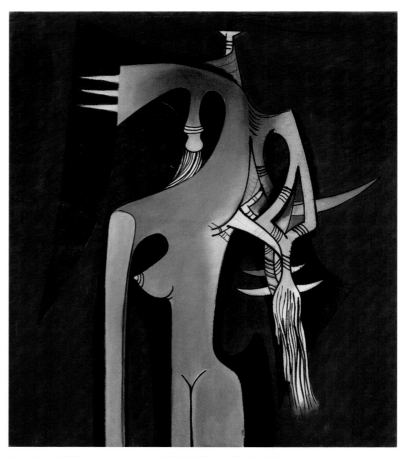

31-75 • Wifredo Lam ZAMBEZIA, ZAMBEZIA
1950. Oil on canvas, 49⅜ × 43⅝″ (125 × 110 cm). Solomon R. Guggenheim Museum, New York. Gift, Mr. Joseph Cantor, 1974.2095

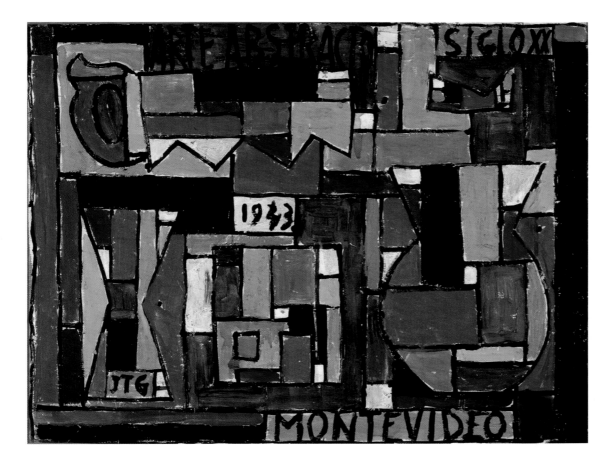

31–76 • Joaquín Torres-Garcia **ABSTRACT ART IN FIVE TONES AND COMPLEMENTARIES** 1943. Oil on board mounted on panel, 20½ × 26⅝″ (52.1 × 67 cm). Albright Knox Art Gallery, Buffalo, N.Y. Gift of Mr. and Mrs. Armand J. Castellani, 1979

Argentina was ruled by Juan Perón who admired Italy's fascist leader, Benito Mussolini (1883–1945), and who disliked Modern art profoundly. Thus, many of Argentina's artistic avant-garde were strongly antifascist. The best-known Latin American artist of the time was the Uruguayan Joaquín Torres-García (1874–1949), who established the "School of the South" in Montevideo, Uruguay's capital. Torres-García had spent 43 years in Europe before returning home after the war. His art was deeply rooted in the indigenous art of the Inca (SEE FIG. 26–8). He regarded ancient Uruguayan culture as a fertile soil in which to grow a new national and cultural visual identity. He used the stone patterns of Inca architecture in paintings that underscored for him the universal validity of abstract art. In **ABSTRACT ART IN FIVE TONES AND COMPLEMENTARIES (FIG. 31–76)**, Torres-García combines ideas of abstraction and Modernism with Inca imagery in a style that he named Constructive Universalism.

ABSTRACT EXPRESSIONISM

THE CENTER SHIFTS: POSTWAR ART IN NEW YORK

The United States recovered from World War II more quickly than Europe. Its territory was spared the ravages of war and the trauma it felt was limited to those Americans who saw action in Europe or the Pacific, to European refugees to the United States, and to Japanese-American citizens who had been interned. While the European art world took decades to recover and Paris lost its artistic vibrancy, New York, as the art historian Serge Guilbault wrote, "Stole the Idea of Modern Art."

Many leading European artists and writers escaped to the United States during World War II. By 1941, André Breton, Salvador Dalí, Fernand Léger, Piet Mondrian, and Max Ernst were all living in New York, where they altered the character and artistic concerns of the New York art scene. American artists were most deeply affected by the work of the European Surrealist artists in New York. Ultimately, however, Abstract Expressionist artists developed their own uniquely American artistic identities by drawing from, but radically reimagining, European and American Modernism.

The term "Abstract Expressionism" describes the art of a fairly wide range of artists in New York in the 1940s and early 1950s. It was not a formally organized movement but rather a loosely affiliated group of artists who worked in the city and were bound by a common purpose: to express their profound social alienation after World War II and to make new art that was both moral and universal.

The influential **formalist** (concerning form over content) critic Clement Greenberg urged the Abstract Expressionists to consider their paintings "autonomous" and completely self-referential objects. The best paintings, he argued, made no reference to the outside world, but had their own internal narrative and order. Abstract Expressionism was also deeply informed by the theories of the Swiss psychoanalyst Carl Jung (1875–1961), who described a collective unconscious shared by all humans. The Abstract Expressionists aspired to create heroic and sublime worlds in paint inhabited by universal symbolic forms. As the 1940s progressed, the symbolic content of their paintings became increasingly personal and abstract. Some Abstract Expressionists were interested in "primitive," mythic imagery and archaic, archetypal, and primal symbolism that connected all people through the collective unconscious; several used biomorphic forms or an individual symbolic language in their paintings; all made passionate and expressive statements on large canvases. The Abstract Expressionists also felt destined to make a major mark on art history; they were convinced that they had the power to transform the world with their art. Thus, Abstract Expressionists were brought together by four major endeavors: first, an interest in the tradition of painting, but a desire to rebel against it and to recalibrate the ideas of European Modernism; second, a desire to treat the act of painting on canvas as a self-contained expressive exercise; third, a mining of visual archetypes that Jung argued were embedded in the collective unconscious to communicate universal ideas in paint; and, fourth, the ambition to paint sublime art on a heroic scale. The critic Harold Rosenberg described two major categories of Abstract Expressionism: "Action painting" and "Color Field painting." The Abstract Expressionists disliked these terms arguing, with good reason, that they were too simplistic, but as general typologies go, the terms are useful.

THE FORMATIVE PHASE

Arshile Gorky (1904–1948) was older than the other Abstract Expressionists, but his ideas and images resonated deeply with them. Gorky (not his given name) was born in Armenia and fled with surviving family members to the United States in 1920 during the Ottoman Turkish genocide of the Armenian people. His mother did not survive long after her escape, leaving Gorky mostly alone. Gorky's painting is filled with the trauma of his loss: He threads idyllic images of his childhood home and garden through Surrealist and Jungian ideas about the collective unconscious to create visual memorials to the people and places he has lost.

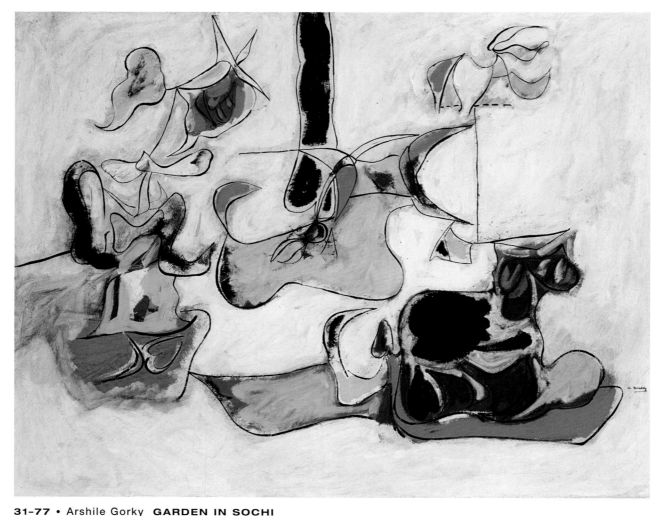

31–77 • Arshile Gorky **GARDEN IN SOCHI**
c. 1943. Oil on canvas, 31 × 39" (78.7 × 99.1 cm). Museum of Modern Art, New York.
Acquired through the Lillie P. Bliss Bequest (492.1969)

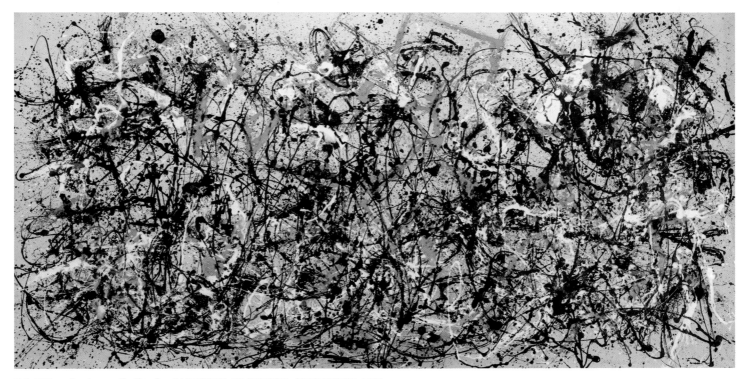

31-78 • Jackson Pollock AUTUMN RHYTHM (NUMBER 30)
1950. Oil on canvas, 8'9" × 17'3" (2.66 × 5.25 m). Metropolitan Museum of Art, New York.
George A. Hearn Fund, 1957 (57.92)

EXPLORE MORE: Gain insight from a primary source about Jackson Pollock
www.myartslab.com

Gorky's vision of his past world came together in a series of paintings of the early 1940s called **GARDEN IN SOCHI** (**FIG. 31–77**) in which Gorky's memories of his father's garden in Khorkom, Armenia are transformed into a mythical dreamscape. According to the artist, this garden was known locally as the Garden of Wish Fulfillment because it contained a rock upon which village women, his mother included, would rub their bared breasts and make a wish, and a "Holy Tree" to which people tied strips of clothing. In this painting, the mythical garden floats on a dense white ground. Various forms, shapes, and colors coalesce into a bare-breasted woman to the left, the Holy Tree to the center, strips of clothing, and "the beautiful Armenian slippers" that Gorky and his father wore in Khorkom. The painting simultaneously suggests vital life forces and an ancient connection to the earth. It also reveals Gorky's vision of a world that has been extinguished and exists only in his memory.

JACKSON POLLOCK AND ACTION PAINTING

Jackson Pollock (1912–1956) is perhaps the best-known artist associated with Abstract Expressionism. Pollock was born in Wyoming and moved to New York in 1930. By all accounts, Pollock was self-destructive from an early age. He developed a drinking problem by age 16, was reading Jung by 22, and was institutionalized for psychiatric problems and alcohol abuse at age 26. Friends described two Pollocks—one shy and sober, and the

other obnoxious and drunk. He entered Jungian psychotherapy in 1939 but was already acquainted with Jung's theory that visual images had the ability to tap into the primordial consciousness of viewers. Pollock was free of alcohol for most of the 1940s, the period when he was supported emotionally by Lee Krasner and when he created his most celebrated art.

Pollock began his career working figuratively but around 1940 moved toward abstraction. In 1943, he had his first solo exhibition at Peggy Guggenheim's gallery and was propelled into stardom by the critic Clement Greenberg, who, by 1947, described Pollock as "the most powerful painter in North America."

In the late 1940s, Pollock pushed beyond the Surrealist strategy of automatic painting by taking his canvas off the stretcher, placing it on the floor, and throwing, dripping, and dribbling paint onto it to create a sublime abstract calligraphy as it fell. In 1950, *Time* magazine described Pollock as "Jack the Dripper." In 1952, Rosenberg coined the term "Action painting," in an essay, "The American Action Painters." Rosenberg described the development and purpose of Action painting as follows: "At a certain moment the canvas began to appear to one American painter after another as an arena in which to act—rather than a space in which to reproduce, redesign, analyze, or 'express' an object, actual or imagined."

In 1950, Pollock's painted **AUTUMN RHYTHM (NUMBER 30)** (**FIG. 31–78**) while the filmmaker Hans Namuth filmed him (**FIG. 31–79**). In the fall of 1946, Pollock had begun to work in a

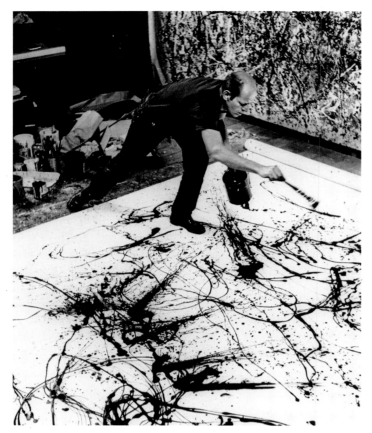

31-79 • Hans Namuth PHOTOGRAPH OF JACKSON POLLOCK PAINTING
The Springs, New York. 1950.

renovated barn, where he placed his canvases on the floor so that he could reach into them from all four sides. The German expatriate artist Hans Hofmann (1880–1966) had poured and dripped paint before Pollock, but Pollock's unrestrained gestures transformed the idea of painting and the way that artists viewed the canvas. Pollock painted by moving around and within the canvas, dripping and scoring commercial-grade enamel paint (rather than specialist artist's paint) onto it using sticks and trowels. Pollock's urgent arcs and whorls of paint have been described as chaotic, but he saw them as labyrinths that led the viewer along complex paths and into an organic calligraphic web of natural and biomorphic forms. Pollock's all-over composition lacks hierarchical arrangement; it has multiple moving focal points and it denies perspectival space. Yet, as the paint travels around the canvas in arcs and ellipses, it never escapes the edges of the canvas. There is also a top and a bottom: Turn the image upside down and it appears "wrong." Like a coiled spring, the painting seems full of anxious energy that is ready to explode at any moment.

Autumn Rhythm is heroic in scale: It is almost 9 feet tall by 17 feet wide and it engulfs the viewer's entire field of vision. According to Lee Krasner, Pollock was a "jazz addict" who spent many hours listening to the explosively improvised bebop of Charlie Parker and Dizzy Gillespie. Pollock was also interested in Native American art, which he associated with his western roots and which enjoyed widespread coverage in popular and art magazines in the 1930s. Pollock was particularly struck by the images and processes of Navajo sand painters who demonstrated their work at the Natural History Museum in New York. And, of course, he drew on Jung's theories of the collective unconscious. But Pollock was not merely

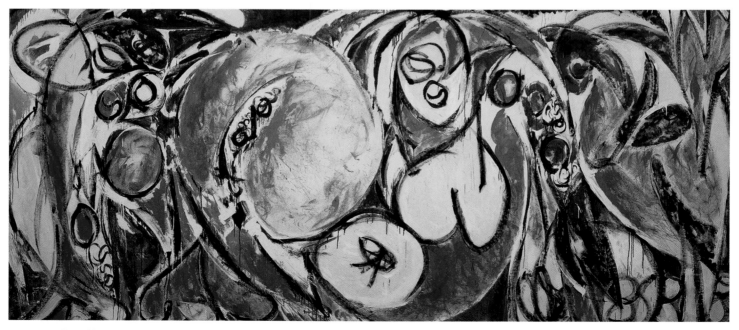

31-80 • Lee Krasner THE SEASONS
1957. Oil on canvas, 7'8¾" × 16'11¾" (2.36 × 5.18 m). Whitney Museum of American Art, New York. Purchased with funds from Frances and Sydney Lewis (by exchange), the Mrs. Percy Uris Purchase Fund, and the Painting and Sculpture Committee (87.7)

the sum of his parts. His paintings communicate on a grand, modern, but primal level. In a radio interview, he said that he was creating for "the age of the airplane, the atom bomb, and the radio."

OTHER ACTION PAINTERS. Lee Krasner (1908–1984) studied in New York with Hans Hofmann and produced fully nonrepresentational paintings with all-over compositions several years before Pollock. She moved in with Pollock in 1942 and virtually stopped painting in order to take care of him. They moved to Long Island in 1945, where she set up a small studio in a guest bedroom and produced small, tight, gestural paintings. After Pollock's death in an automobile crash in 1956, Krasner took over his studio and produced a series of large, dazzling gestural paintings that marked her re-emergence into the mainstream art world. Works such as **THE SEASONS** (FIG. 31–80) feature bold, sweeping curves that

express not only a new sense of liberation but also her powerful identification with the forces of nature in bursting, rounded forms and springlike colors. Krasner said that "Painting, for me, when it really 'happens' is as miraculous as any natural phenomenon."

In contrast, Willem de Kooning (1904–1997) wrote that "Art never seems to make me peaceful or pure." An immigrant from the Netherlands, de Kooning was friendly with several Modern artists including Elaine Marie Fried, whom he married. His view of the world was never simple or certain. He remarked: "I work out of doubt." De Kooning's painting was always highly structured and controlled. He made careful under-drawings, and painted and scraped several layers of paint in the process of creating a single canvas. His gestural strokes appear spontaneous but they are, in fact, the result of hours of experiment and failure. De Kooning painted strokes, scraped them off, and repeated the process until the exact

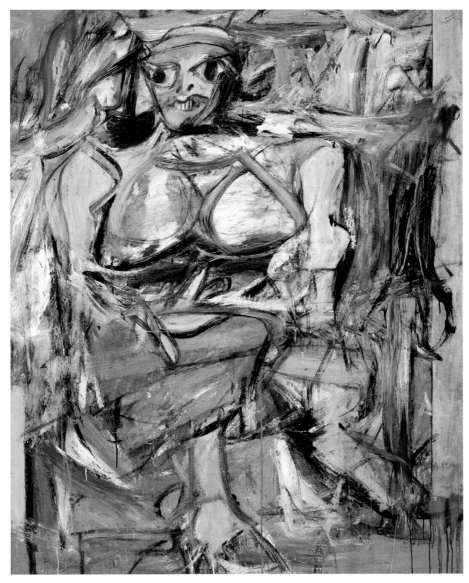

31-81 • Willem de Kooning WOMAN I
1950–1952. Oil on canvas, 75⅞ × 58″ (192.7 × 147.3 cm). Museum of Modern Art, New York.

mark he wanted emerged. In 1953, de Kooning shocked the art world by moving away from pure abstraction with a series of figurative paintings of women. **WOMAN I** (FIG. 31–81) took the artist two years to complete and de Kooning's wife Elaine estimated that he scraped and repainted it about 200 times. It portrays a figure who seems at once grotesque and rapacious, and the image is both hostile and sexist. It is powerfully sexual, full of implied violence, and intensely passionate. De Kooning described his "Woman" paintings as images of great fertility goddesses like the *Woman from Willendorf* (SEE FIG. 1–7), or as a composite of stereotypes taken from the media and film.

Abstract Expressionism spread quickly to Canada. In his native Montreal, the French Canadian painter Jean-Paul Riopelle (1923–2002) worked with Les Automatistes (The Automatists), a group of artists using the Surrealist technique of automatism to create abstract paintings. In 1947, Riopelle moved to Paris and, in the early 1950s, began to squeeze paint directly onto the canvas and spread it with a palette knife to create an all-over painting of bright swatches of color that are suggestive of broken shards of stained glass traversed by a network of spidery lines, as in **KNIGHT WATCH** (FIG. 31–82).

Helen Frankenthaler (b. 1928) visited Pollock's studio in 1951 and went on to create a more lyrical version of Action painting that had a significant impact on later artists. Like Pollock, she worked on the floor, but she poured paint onto the unprimed canvas in thin washes so that it soaked into the fabric rather than sitting on its surface. Frankenthaler

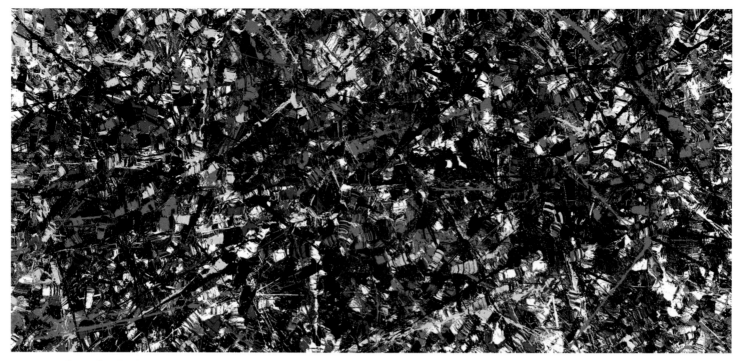

31–82 • Jean-Paul Riopelle KNIGHT WATCH
1953. Oil on canvas, 38 × 76⅝″ (96.6 × 194.8 cm). National Gallery of Canada, Ottawa, Ontario.

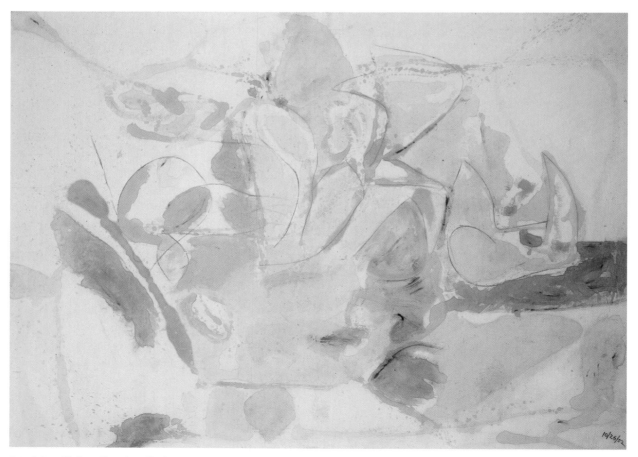

31–83 • Helen Frankenthaler MOUNTAINS AND SEA
1952. Oil and charcoal on canvas, 7′2¾″ × 9′8¼″ (2.2 × 2.95 m). Collection of the artist on extended loan to the National Gallery of Art, Washington, D.C.

described her process as starting with an aesthetic question or image and evolving as the process of painting took over as a self-expressive act. She described her working method: "I will sometimes start a picture feeling, What will happen if I work with three blues … ? And very often midway through the picture I have to change the basis of the experience. Or I add and add to the canvas.… When I say gesture, my gesture, I mean what my mark is. I think there is something now that I am still working out in paint; it is a struggle for me to both discard and retain what is gestural and personal." In **MOUNTAINS AND SEA (FIG. 31–83)**, Frankenthaler poured several colors onto the canvas and outlined selected forms in charcoal. The result reminded her of the coast of Nova Scotia where she frequently went to sketch.

COLOR FIELD PAINTING

New York School artists used abstract means to express various kinds of emotional states, not all of them as urgent or improvisatory as those of the Action painters. The Color Field painters moved in a different direction, painting large, flat areas of color to evoke more transcendent, contemplative moods in paint.

Mark Rothko (1903–1970) had very little formal art training but by 1940 was already producing paintings that were deeply influenced by the European Surrealists and by Jung's archetypal imagery. By the mid-1940s, Rothko began to paint very large canvases with rectangular shapes arranged in a vertical format in which he allowed his colors to bleed into one another. These canvases, such as **LAVENDER AND MULBERRY (FIG. 31–84)**, are

31-84 • Mark Rothko LAVENDER AND MULBERRY
1959. Oil on paper mounted on fiberboard, 37¾ × 24¾″ (95.9 × 62.8 cm). Hirshhorn Museum and Sculpture Garden, Smithsonian Institution, Washington, D.C.
Gift of Joseph H. Hirshhorn 1966

31–85 • Barnett Newman VIR HEROICUS SUBLIMIS
1950–1951. Oil on canvas, 95⅜ × 213¼″ (242 × 541.7 cm). Museum of Modern Art, New York. Gift of Mr. and Mrs. Ben Heller

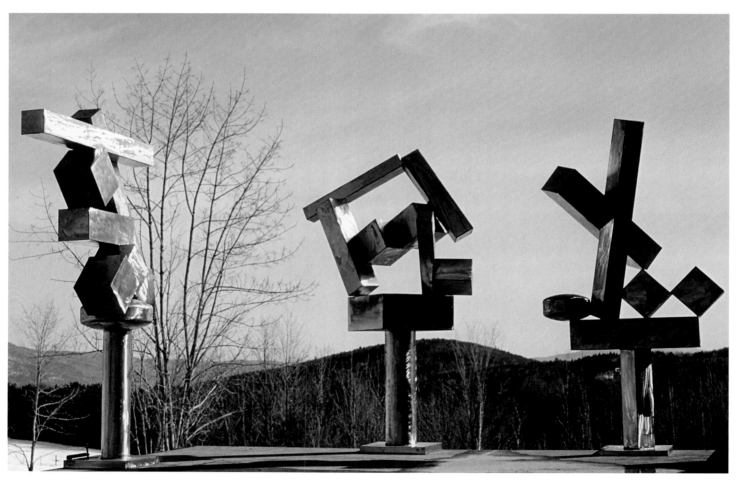

31–86 • David Smith CUBI
David Smith. *Cubi XVIII* (left), 1964. Stainless steel, 9′8″ (2.94 m). Museum of Fine Arts, Boston. *Cubi XVII* (center), 1963. Stainless steel, 9′2″ (2.79 m). Dallas Museum of Fine Arts, Dallas. *Cubi XIX* (right), 1964. Stainless steel, 9′5⅜″ (2.88 m). Tate Gallery, London. Shown installed at Bolton Landing, New York in 1965.

neither simply arrangements of flat geometric shapes on a canvas nor atmospheric landscapes. Rothko thought of his shapes as fundamental "ideas" expressed in rectangular form, unmediated by a recognizable subject, which sit in front of a painted field (hence the name "Color Field painting"). He preferred to show his paintings together in series or rows and lit indirectly to evoke moods of transcendental meditation.

Barnett Newman (1905–1970) also addressed modern humanity's existential condition in his very large canvases painted in one, often brilliant, color and torn or split by thin jagged lines in another color that he called "zips." Newman said that his art was about "[t]he self, terrible and constant." **VIR HEROICUS SUBLIMIS** (**FIG. 31–85**) shows how Newman's total concentration on a single color focuses his meaning. Newman's red painting does not describe any form; it presents an absolute state of redness in a vast canvas that is unbroken except for the dangerous zips of other colors that threaten to unbalance it. *Vir Heroicus Sublimis* (Latin for "Man, Heroic and Sublime") is heroic and sublime like the hero threatened by a fatal flaw. Many of Newman's paintings have religious overtones. Newman wrote: "The present painter is concerned not with his own feelings or with the mystery of his own personality but with the penetration into the world mystery. His imagination is therefore attempting to dig into metaphysical secrets. To that extent his art is concerned with the sublime."

SCULPTURE OF THE NEW YORK SCHOOL

Sculpture tended to resist the kind of instantaneous gestural processes developed by artists such as Pollock, although some sculptors managed to communicate both abstractly and Expressionistically in three dimensions. David Smith (1906–1965) learned to weld and rivet while working at an automobile plant in Indiana. He trained as a painter, but became a sculptor after seeing reproductions of welded metal sculptures by artists such as Picasso. Smith avoided the precious materials of traditional sculpture and created works out of standard industrial materials. After World War II, Smith began to weld horizontally formatted, open-form sculptures that were like drawings in space. The forms of the vertical **CUBI** series (**FIG. 31–86**) were actually determined by standardized, precut sizes of stainless-steel sheets. In photographs they sometimes look coldly industrial, but when observed outdoors as Smith intended, their highly burnished surfaces show the gestural marks of the sculptor's tools upon them, and reflect and refract the sun in different ways depending on the time of day, weather conditions, and distance from which they are viewed. Vaguely anthropomorphic like giant totemic figures, the sculptures are surprisingly organic when seen at close range.

THINK ABOUT IT

31.1 Discuss the impact that Cubism had on other avant-garde art styles in the early part of the twentieth century. Analyze its pattern of influence in at least two works from the chapter that demonstrate a substantial debt to Cubism.

31.2 Explain how World Wars I and II had an impact on the visual arts in Europe and North America in both direct and indirect ways. Give examples of both with reference to works from the chapter.

31.3 Explain how both Dada and Surrealism changed the form, content, and concept of art. Focus your answer around an analysis of one artwork discussed in the chapter from each of these two movements.

31.4 Write about Walter Gropius and the Bauhaus's attitude towards questions of form and function and discuss how Gropius and other early twentieth-century architects embodied those attitudes in their buildings. Contrast these buildings and attitudes with those studied in previous chapters.

31.5 Summarize the events of the Great Depression and discuss its impact on European and American art.

31.6 Discuss the goals and interests of the painters associated with Abstract Expressionism, and determine the role that Surrealism and other early twentieth-century avant-garde art movements had in the formation of this new movement in the 1940s.

PRACTICE MORE: Compose answers to these questions, get flashcards for images and terms, and review chapter material with quizzes **www.myartslab.com**

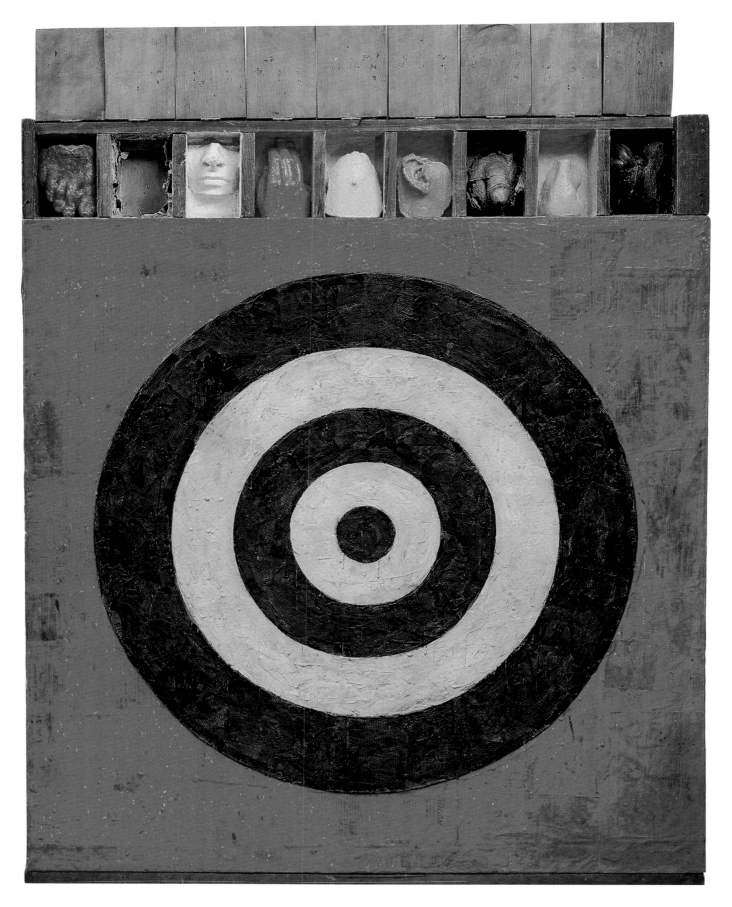

32–1 • Jasper Johns TARGET WITH PLASTER CASTS 1955. Encaustic and collage on canvas with objects, 51 × 44″ (129.5 × 111.8 cm). Collection Mr. and Mrs. Leo Castelli.

THE INTERNATIONAL SCENE SINCE 1950

In the early 1950s, a generation of younger artists in New York challenged the artistic assumptions of the previous generation of Abstract Expressionist artists. They believed that art should be firmly anchored in real life. Two artists in particular, Jasper Johns and Robert Rauschenberg, questioned the goals of the New York School as defined by Clement Greenberg's version of formalism: that art should be autonomous and internally coherent (deeply meaningful, with the act of painting as its subject, abstract, and with an all-over composition); that it should avoid the taint of popular culture and be viewed in the "white cube" of the gallery space; and that the artist should be vigilantly self-critical. In **TARGET WITH PLASTER CASTS** (FIG. 32–1), Johns not only stretches formalism to its limits, but he actually mocks it.

This work is neither a painting nor a sculpture but both; the cast body parts are arranged across the top of the work, parodying the nonhierarchical manner of Abstract Expressionism, but the target below is emphatically hierarchical. The flatness of the painted target suggests an all-over composition, but the target itself always has a central focus; the target and casts, moreover, make reference to popular culture and the world around Johns. The target also raises thorny questions about the nature of representation: Is this a painting of a target or is it an actual target? The meaning of this work is fluid and unfixed—it contains recognizable faces and a recognizable object (a target) but the purpose of their inclusion is unclear. Unlike that of the Abstract Expressionists, Johns's art is emotionally cool and highly cerebral. Like many artists after 1950, Johns reintroduces readily recognizable, real-world but strategically recontextualized, images and objects in order to question the form, appearance, content, and meaning of art. Thus, like much art after 1950, Johns's art is as intellectual as it is visual.

Johns and Rauschenberg were critical figures in the New York art world and beyond. They expanded the intellectual bases of Abstract Expressionism, cooled its passion and intensity, and made art that connected to and was inspired by the vastly expanded visual culture of postwar America. They also prefigured the next generation's interest in introducing popular culture into art, its investigation of the conceptual possibilities of art, its expanded understanding of the use of nonart materials in art, and its exploration of the performative possibilities of art.

LEARN ABOUT IT

32.1 Assess the ways in which artists since 1950 have introduced popular culture into their art.

32.2 Account for the "dematerialization" of the object since 1950 and account for its return after 1980.

32.3 Compare and contrast the impact of the three "waves" of feminism on art after 1950.

32.4 Examine how and why artists since 1950 have engaged with social, political, cultural, or religious issues.

32.5 Evaluate how globalism has created new opportunities, strategies, and subjects for artists today.

HEAR MORE: Listen to an audio file of your chapter **www.myartslab.com**

THE WORLD SINCE THE 1950S

The United States and the U.S.S.R. emerged from World War II as the world's most powerful nations. The Soviet occupation and sponsorship of communist governments in several Central and Eastern European states, and the emergence of the People's Republic of China in 1949 compelled the United States to attempt to contain the further expansion of Soviet power and communism into American spheres of influence, particularly in Western Europe, Japan, and Latin America. This precipitated a "Cold War" and what Winston Churchill described as the descending of an "Iron Curtain" across Europe (MAP 32–1). The United States initially provided both financial and political support to states sympathetic to American interests, but then resorted to military force, most notably in Korea (1950–1953) and then Vietnam (1954–1975). Europe lost most of its imperial holdings by the early 1960s, often after protracted guerilla wars of the kind that the French experienced in Vietnam and Algeria. The British granted India independence in 1946 and by 1971 had withdrawn from "East of Suez."

During the Cold War, the United States and the U.S.S.R. amassed large nuclear arsenals, eventually adopting a strategy of mutually assured destruction, which was supposed to deter nuclear war by threatening to destroy the civilian population on both sides. The Cold War effectively ended with the fall of the Berlin Wall in October 1989. When the Soviet Union dissolved in 1992, the United States emerged as the world's unchallenged superpower.

The United Nations, sponsored by American power, was established in 1945 to provide collective security and legitimacy to the Anglo-American design for a new postwar world order. It eventually emerged as a forum for the sovereign recognition of governments for the many newly independent states in Asia and Africa after the war. Despite the UN mandate to intervene in conflicts between states, however, its efforts to maintain global peace have proven inadequate in the face of ethnic and religious conflicts that have erupted around the world in regions such as the Indian subcontinent, central and eastern Africa, the Balkans, and the Middle East. The terrorist attacks on the World Trade Center and the Pentagon on September 11, 2001, exacerbated many of the preexisting racial, ethnic, and religious conflicts, and led to both civil wars and wars between states, most notably in the recent and controversial American-led wars in Afghanistan and Iraq.

THE ART WORLD SINCE THE 1950S

Artists have faced a number of major questions since 1950: What is art? Does it always have to be an object, is it an idea, or is it some combination of the two? In the period since 1950, artists have reconceptualized and reimagined art, producing radically new forms, content, ideas, and agendas. They have addressed increasingly divisive and complex social and political questions for which there is no right or wrong answer; artists have raised questions about gender, race, ethnicity, sexual orientation, religion, class, death, colonialism, terrorism, violence against the less powerful, and resistance to power. This art has not sought to edify us by showing

moral exemplars (as in Neoclassicism); rather it has challenged us to question our own morality, behavior, and complacency. Much of this art is difficult to look at and to understand; we are frequently assaulted and accused by it. It is rarely pretty. But today's art holds a mirror to contemporary life, revealing things that we might not see or hear in any other context, and it forces us to confront ourselves in that mirror. We may not like recent art initially, but once we learn something about it, we have to admit that, at its best, it has the power, like all great art, to affect us deeply.

THE EXPANDING ART WORLD

The generation of artists who began to make art in the 1950s increasingly addressed the real world, acknowledging its fragmentation, its relativism, and its messy relation to popular culture. Assemblage and collage artists broke apart the physical forms and the meanings of art along with the distinction between painting and sculpture, and high and low art. Pop artists investigated how advertising impacted vision and explored a newly visible domestic world. Photographers showed us aspects of the world around us that we had not seen, or had chosen not to see, before.

ASSEMBLAGE

In the 1950s, the visual artists Jasper Johns (b. 1930) and Robert Rauschenberg (1925–2008), and the composer John Cage (1912–1992) consciously introduced the world around them (rather than representations of it) into their art and music. Cage, who taught for a time at Black Mountain College near Asheville, North Carolina, explored the idea of creating music that brought the ambient noises of the world around him directly into his music. In 1952, Cage "composed" *4′33″* (4 minutes 33 seconds), which was first performed in Woodstock, New York. In this piece, the pianist came on stage, performed several different "movements" for four minutes and 33 seconds, and then closed the keyboard to signal the end of the work. The sound-piece consisted of actual sounds made by audience members as they rustled, shuffled, whispered, and coughed for 4′33″. Thus, this composition differs each time it is performed, gathering a new set of sounds and meanings in every new location and with every new audience. The form of *4′33″* is circumscribed by Cage's directions, but its content, the chance juxtaposition of seemingly random sounds, occurs spontaneously at each performance. The piece was engineered by the composer to create a work with open and multiple interpretations and to obscure the personality of the composer. Similarly, Johns and Rauschenberg in their assemblages brought or "assembled" disparate found objects and images in seemingly random constructions to create visual works of art with equally open-ended and multiple meanings that revealed little of the artist's personality.

Rauschenberg grew up in Texas and moved to New York to paint in 1947. He attended Black Mountain College where he studied with Cage and de Kooning (SEE FIG. 31–81). Rauschenberg

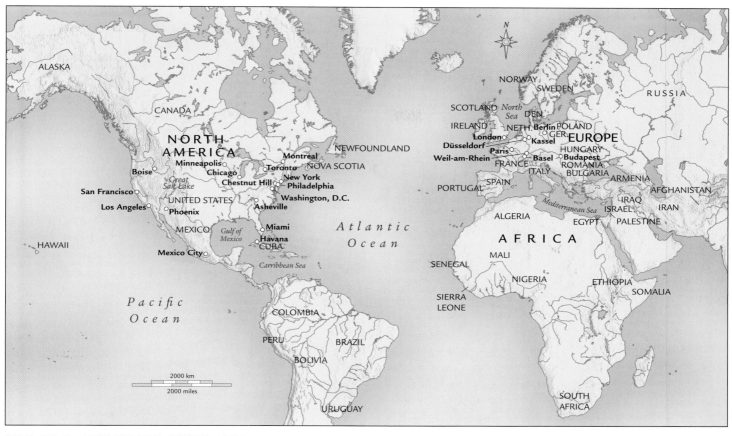

MAP 32–1 • THE WORLD SINCE 1950

International sites in the contemporary art world in the Americas, Europe, and Africa.

explored ways to "work in the gap between art and life." In 1951, he exhibited a series of brightly lit blank white paintings in which the shadows cast by viewers on the canvases became the content of the work; there are obvious visual parallels to Cage's *4′33″* of the following year.

Between 1955 and 1960, Rauschenberg made a series of objects that he entitled **combines** (combinations of painting and sculpture using nontraditional art materials). In one of these, **CANYON (FIG. 32–2)**, Rauschenberg brings together a roughly painted canvas with a stuffed eagle emerging from a box, a dirty pillow tied with cord suspended from a piece of wood, and a flattened steel drum. On the canvas itself Rauschenberg glued family photographs, images cut from newspapers and magazines, and fragments of political posters. *Canyon* is so dense with cultural references that it is impossible to find a single, unified meaning in the piece. In fact, Rauschenberg believed that viewers should find their own meaning in his art as if searching for metaphors for the experience of modern urban life. He said: "I only consider myself successful when I do something that resembles the lack of order [that] I sense."

Johns, Cage, and Rauschenberg collaborated on several theatrical events that extended the idea of the assemblage into temporal space in the late 1950s and early 1960s. Cage composed music while Johns and Rauschenberg designed sets and sometimes

actually performed. They worked with the Merce Cunningham Dance Company, which specialized in creating dance based on everyday actions such as waiting for a bus or reading a newspaper. Prior to these events, none of the participants informed the others what they were planning to do, so the performances became legendary in their unpredictability.

HAPPENINGS AND PERFORMANCE ART

In the 1950s and 1960s, several artists argued that the artistic process was as important as the finished object; these artists began to replace the traditional materials of art with the actions, movements, and gestures of their own bodies. These events were termed **Happenings** by Allan Kaprow but the more common term is **Performance art**. Performance art owes a debt to Pollock (SEE FIG. 31–79), whose physical enactment of the act of painting was transformed into a work of art in its own right, and to Cage, Johns, and Rauschenberg, who relied on spontaneous and unpredictable actions to provide a new set of variables for each of their events.

Performance art tears down the space that has traditionally existed between the viewer and the art object; the artwork literally comes to life and actively invades the space of the viewer, both physically and intellectually. Thus, Performance art is often radical, and assaultive. It also exists in the moment and, although often photographed or filmed, is ephemeral.

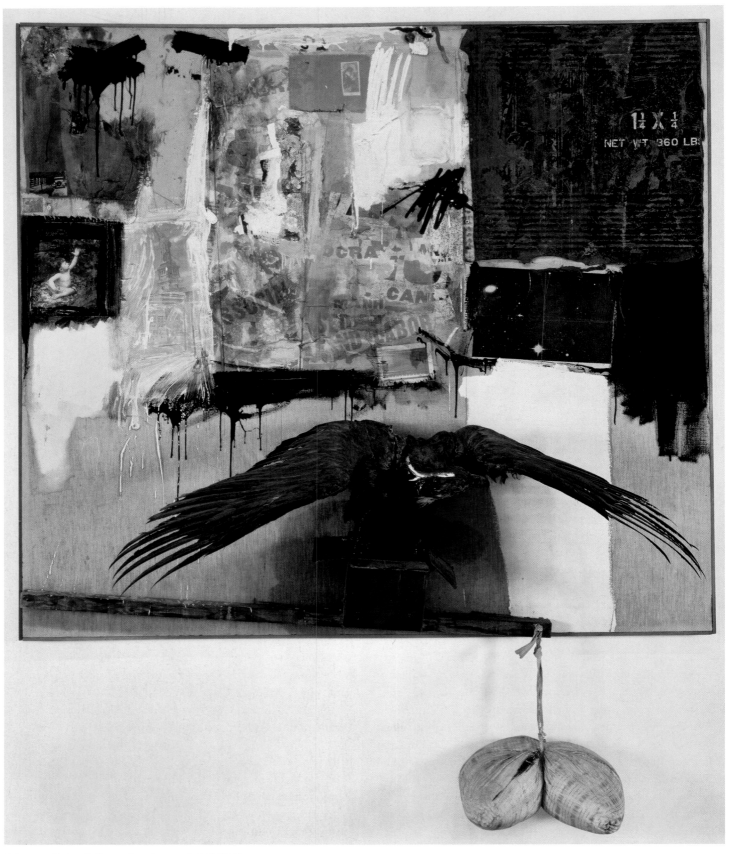

32-2 • Robert Rauschenberg CANYON
1959. Oil, pencil, paper, metal, photograph, fabric, wood on canvas, plus buttons, mirror, stuffed eagle, pillow tied with cord, and paint tube, 6′1″ × 5′6″ × 2′¾″ (1.85 × 1.68 × 0.63 m). Sonnabend Collection.

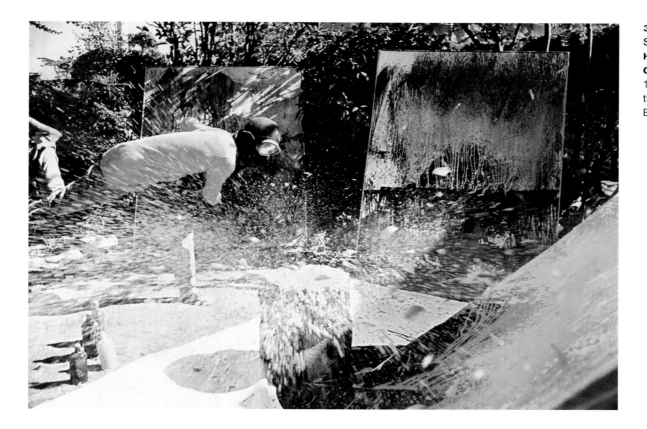

THE GUTAI GROUP. Some of the earliest postwar performances took place in Japan. In 1954, several Japanese artists formed the Gutai (meaning "embodiment") group to "pursue the possibilities of pure and creative activity with great energy." In Gutai performances, it was the act of creating itself that was the art-work. Gutai organized outdoor **installations**, theatrical events, and dramatic performances. At the second Gutai Exhibition in 1956, Shozo Shimamoto (b. 1928) performed **HURLING COLORS** (**FIG. 32–3**) by smashing bottles of paint against a canvas on the floor, thus pushing Pollock's gestural painting technique one step farther by suggesting that the work of art lay solely in the performance of a painting rather than in the object produced. In fact, Gutai artists regularly destroyed the physical products they created at the end of each performance.

KAPROW. In 1958, Allan Kaprow (1927–2006), also a student of John Cage, began to create environments and in 1959 Happenings. His 1961 piece **YARD** (**FIG. 32–4**) was staged in the walled garden space behind the Martha Jackson Gallery in Manhattan. Kaprow filled the space with used tires, tar paper, and barrels, and asked viewers to walk though it, to experience the smell and physicality of the rubber and the tar firsthand, recontextualized (removed from one context and placed in a new one to create new meaning) in the art gallery space. Kaprow later described how gallery audiences—more formally dressed then than they would be today, especially the women, who wore dresses and heels—experienced aspects of the urban environment in unfamil-iar and unanticipated ways as they tumbled in and over the tires.

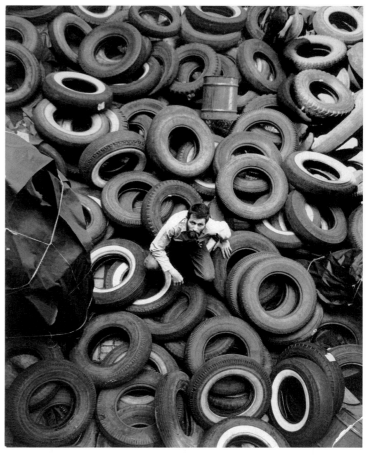

32-4 • Allan Kaprow **YARD**
1961. View of tires in court of Martha Jackson Gallery, New York, 1961.

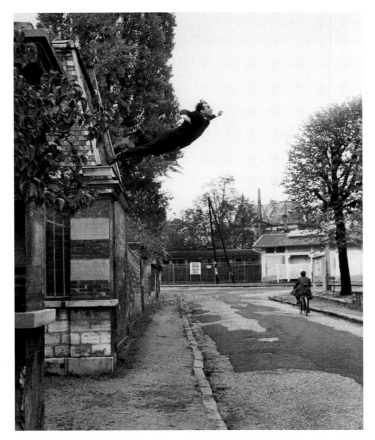

32-5 • Yves Klein LEAP INTO THE VOID
1960. Photograph of a performance by Yves Klein at Rue Gentil-Bernard, Fontenay-aux-Roses, October 1960, by Harry Shunk.

KLEIN. In Europe, Performance art occurred as part of the activities of the New Realism movement, a term coined by art critic Pierre Restany. Restany argued that the age of painting ended with the New York School and *Art Informel* and that thereafter art would take its form from the real world. He wrote: "The passionate adventure of the real, perceived in itself …. The New Realists consider the world a painting: a large, fundamental work of which they appropriate fragments."

The French artist Yves Klein (1928–1962) first staged his *Anthropometries of the Blue Period* in 1960. He invited members of the Paris art world to watch him direct three female models covered in blue paint as they pressed their naked bodies against large sheets of paper to the musical accompaniment of a 20-piece orchestra playing a single note. The performance was a commentary on the perceived pretentiousness of Pollock's action painting, of which Klein wrote: "I dislike artists who empty themselves into their paintings. They spit out every rotten complexity as if relieving themselves." Like Cage, Johns, and Rauschenberg, Klein orchestrated his performance but often removed himself from the act of crafting the final object. He used the nude female body as the subject of his painting by pressing the model's bodily imprint in paint directly onto the paper. Klein presents art making as a physical, gestural act and the final work of art as the imprint of either the artist or his model.

Klein is perhaps best known for the 1960 **LEAP INTO THE VOID** (FIG. 32–5), a manipulated photograph showing the artist leaping from a wall into the street, arms outstretched with apparently nothing but the pavement below him. The photograph was originally published to prove Klein's mock claim that he could

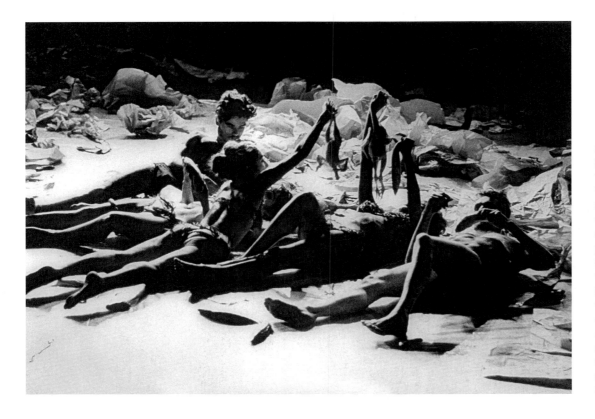

32-6 • Carolee Schneemann MEAT JOY
1964. Judson Church, New York City. Group performance: raw fish, chickens, sausages, wet paint, plastic, rope, and shredded scrap paper. First performed as part of the First Festival of Free Expression at the American Center in Paris. MOMA. 16mm film transferred to video (color, soundtrack collaged by CS), 6 min.
Acquired through the generosity of Katherine Farley and Jerry I. Speyer, Anna Marie and Robert F. Shapiro, and Marie-Josée and Henry R. Kravis

undertake lunar travel unaided, and was published again in a pamphlet denouncing NASA's bid to land a man on the moon as arrogant and foolish. Klein argued that his works were visible only as imprints, in this case his imprint on the pavement.

SCHNEEMANN. Many early Performance artists were women, whose bodies have been the object of the gaze in art for centuries. Performance art enabled women artists to control how their bodies were viewed and to look back and even challenge their audience. One of the most important early Performance artists was Carolee Schneemann (b. 1939), whose **MEAT JOY** (FIG. 32–6) was a radical feminist performance. *Meat Joy* was performed first with Jean-Jacques Lebel and the Kinetic Group Theater at the Festival de la Libre Expression in Paris, and a second time in New York, where it was filmed and photographed. In the performance eight men and women first undressed one another, then danced, rolled on the floor ecstatically, and played with a mixture of raw fish, raw sausages, partially plucked raw and bloody chickens, wet paint, and scraps of paper. The purpose was to make both performers and audience smell, taste, and feel viscerally the body and its fluids. The piece was variously described as an erotic rite and a celebration of flesh and blood. It countered the expectation that a work of art was something to be examined in the cool unemotional space of an art gallery with the viewer in control, replacing the traditional artwork with a performance that made the audience squirm as control was wrenched away from it by the performers.

PHOTOGRAPHY

Photography served as an important tool for documenting Performance art in the 1950s, but it was also an important medium in its own right. Although the 1955 "Family of Man" exhibition of photographs at the Museum of Modern Art, New York, curated by Edward Steichen, presented a world at peace and in harmony, and illustrated magazines such as *Life* projected an image of modern life as comfortable, suburban, white, and domestic, other photographers chose to convey an alternate view of society.

FRANK. Robert Frank (b. 1924), a Swiss photographer who emigrated to the United States in the 1940s, took gritty social portraits, trying to capture some of the disorder and disharmony that Johns and Rauschenberg presented in their art. In 1948, frustrated by the pressure and banality of news and fashion assignments, Frank abandoned his freelance work with magazines such as *Life* and *Vogue* and traveled to Peru and Bolivia. Four years later, he took a series of photographs documenting the lives of Welsh coalminers, before being awarded a one-year Guggenheim Fellowship in 1955 to travel around America photographing the "social landscape." Frank took more than 28,000 photographs that year, from which he chose 83 to publish in book form. But the images were so raw, grim, and full of biting social commentary that at first he was unable to find a publisher in the United States and so was forced to publish the book in France under the title *Les Américains* (1958). *The Americans* was finally published in the United States the following year with an introduction by Jack Kerouac, one of the leaders of the new Beat generation of authors who were critical of mainstream American values. In **TROLLEY, NEW ORLEANS** (FIG. 32–7), white passengers sit in the front of the bus, while African Americans sit in the back, as required by law at the time. The composition of the image, in which the rectangular symmetry of the windows frames and isolates the figures on the

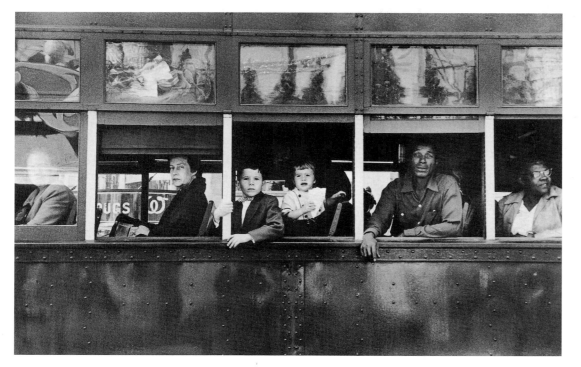

32-7 • Robert Frank
TROLLEY, NEW ORLEANS
1955–1956. Gelatin-silver print, 9 × 13″ (23 × 33 cm). Art Institute of Chicago.

trolley, underscores visually both the racial segregation and urban alienation inherent in the scene.

KEÏTA. In Africa in the late 1950s, Seydou Keïta (1921–2001) took photographs of the proud people of the newly independent nation of Mali. Keïta established a reputation as a portrait photographer and worked as a Mali government photographer. His photographs were among the first by an African to portray his own nation and people as affluent and urban rather than objectified as ethnographic subjects, as seen in magazines such as *National Geographic*. In the image shown here **(FIG. 32–8)**, the sitters occupy a visually luxurious space. The heavy, strong patterns of the wife's clothing contrast with the stark white of that of her husband and child. Keïta's elegant photograph presents individuals whose power and pride are communicated through their commanding poses and relaxed gestures. The sitters look out of the photograph at the viewer, returning our gaze, demanding that we see them as real people and as equals, whose sense of identity is as multivalent and as complex as our own. While Keïta made his photographs for domestic consumption, many were subsequently exhibited in Europe and the United States.

POP ART

In the late 1950s, several artists began to focus their attention on the explosion in visual culture, fueled by the growing presence of mass media and the rising disposable income of the postwar young. Pop art originated in Britain, but reached its zenith in the United States in the early 1960s. During this period individual and mass identity was increasingly determined by how people looked and dressed, and by what they consumed. Home ownership, cars, and the visible display of objects in the home were modeled on what appeared on television, in film, and in print advertising. Pop artists critiqued the fiction and superficiality of the perfect home and perfect person projected in this new popular culture.

HAMILTON. In the 1950s, an interdisciplinary collection of artists, architects, photographers, and writers came together as the Independent Group in London in order to discuss the place of art in a consumer society, periodically exhibiting at the Institute of Contemporary Arts. The government argued that Britain's postwar recovery was predicated on sustained consumption. Richard Hamilton (b. 1922) argued that modern mass visual culture was fast replacing traditional art for the public; movies, television, and advertising, not art, now defined beauty. Society's idols were no longer politicians or military heroes but inter-national movie stars; social status was increasingly measured by the number of one's possessions.

Thus Hamilton made collages of images drawn from advertising to create a vision of a disharmonious world of excessive consumption. In his 1955 work **JUST WHAT IS IT THAT MAKES TODAY'S HOMES SO DIFFERENT, SO APPEALING?** **(FIG. 32–9)**, Hamilton critiques advertising strategies by imitating them. The title parodies an advertising slogan, while the collage itself shows two figures named Adam and Eve in a domestic setting. Like the biblical Adam and Eve, these figures are almost naked, but this time the "temptations" to which they have succumbed are those of consumer culture. Adam has become a bodybuilder and Eve is a pin-up girl. In an attempt to recreate their lost Garden of Eden, this Adam and Eve have filled their home with all the best new products: a television, a tape recorder, a vacuum cleaner, modern furniture. On the wall in place of "high art" is a poster advertising a romance novel; beside this is a printed portrait of John Ruskin, the critic who accused the painter Whistler of destroying art (see "Art on Trial in 1877," page 999). Adam holds a huge Tootsie Pop, which the English critic Lawrence Alloway referenced when he described this work as "Pop art," thus naming the art movement. Like Rauschenberg's and Johns's assemblages in the United States,

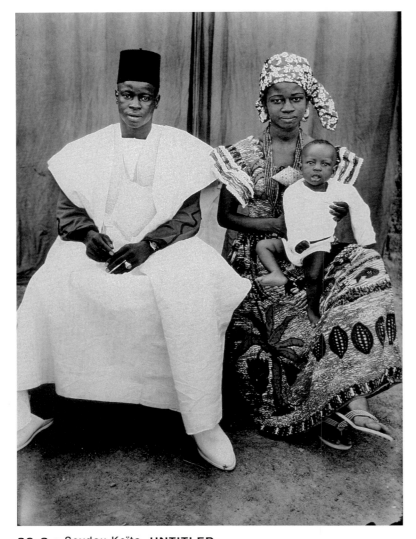

32-8 • Seydou Keïta UNTITLED
1952–1955. Gelatin-silver print, 24 × 20″ (61 × 50.8 cm).
Edition of ten.

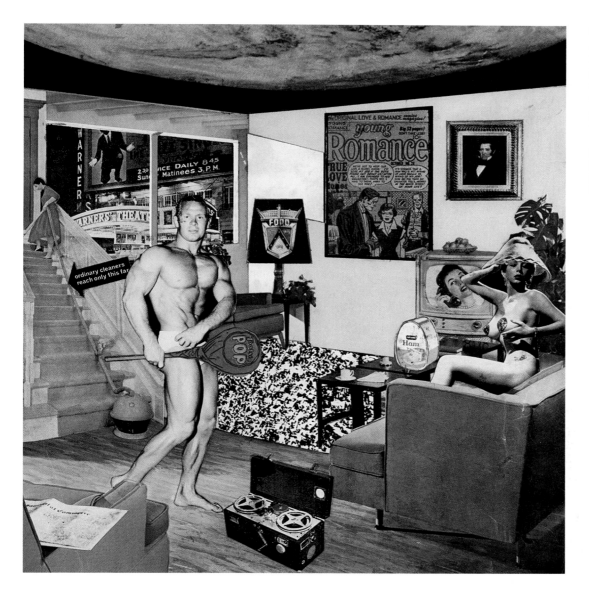

32-9 • Richard Hamilton
JUST WHAT IS IT THAT MAKES TODAY'S HOMES SO DIFFERENT, SO APPEALING?
1955. Collage, 10¼ × 9¾″ (26 × 24.7 cm). Kunsthalle Tübingen, Germany.

SEE MORE: View a podcast about Richard Hamilton's work
www.myartslab.com

Hamilton's collage comments on the visual overload of the 1950s and on culture's inability to differentiate between important and trivial images or between the advertising world and the real one. In 1968, Hamilton designed the cover for the Beatles's *White Album*, which significantly is devoid of any images at all.

WARHOL.　By 1960, several American artists, like the earlier British Pop artists, began to incorporate images from the burgeoning mass culture into their art. By comparison with their British peers, however, they developed a slicker Pop art style using common advertising mass-production techniques to give their art a flat, commercial feel, a stance that was also intended to show opposition to the presence of the hand of the artist in Abstract Expressionism. American Pop art both imitated and critiqued 1960s popular culture, often including images of newly independent women and their ambivalent relationship to domesticity. The emotional tone of Pop art was more ironic, camp, and cynically detached than the irreverent assemblage of Johns and Rauschenberg. Pop art flowered in the United States after 1962; it was dominated by the artistic giant and heir to Duchamp's ideas about the nature of art and the role of artists in art making, Andy Warhol (1928–1987).

Warhol created an immense body of work between 1960 and his death in 1987, including prints, paintings, sculptures, and films. He published *Interview* magazine, and even managed The Velvet Underground, a radical and hugely influential rock band. Warhol knew advertising culture well—he trained as a commercial artist. By 1962, he was using advertising from America's mass culture in his art, taking as his subjects popular consumer items such as Brillo boxes, Campbell's Soup cans, and Coca-Cola bottles, and reproducing them using the cheap industrial print method of **silkscreen** (in which a fine mesh silk screen is used as a printing stencil). Warhol argued that past art demanded thought and understanding, whereas advertising and celebrity culture demanded only immediate attention, very quickly becoming uninteresting and boring. In keeping with this position, he suggested that art should be like movie stars, interesting for 15 minutes.

In 1962, Marilyn Monroe died suddenly, an apparent suicide. Warhol's **MARILYN DIPTYCH** (FIG. 32–10) is one of a series of silkscreens that Warhol made immediately after the actress's death. He memorializes the screen image of Monroe, using a famous publicity photograph transferred directly onto silkscreen, thus rendering it flat and bland so that Monroe's signature features—her bleach-blond hair, her ruby lips, and her sultry blue-shadowed eyes—stand out as a caricature of the actress. The face portrayed is not that of Norma Jeane (Monroe's real name) but of Monroe the celluloid sex symbol as made over by the movie industry. Warhol made multiple prints from this screen, aided by a host of assistants working with assembly-line efficiency. (In 1965, Warhol even—ironically—named his studio "The Factory," further mocking the commercial aspect of his art by suggesting he was only in it for the profit.)

The Marilyn portrait, however, has deeper undertones. It is a diptych (see page 564) and thus evokes religious connotations, perhaps suggesting that Monroe was a martyred saint or goddess in the pantheon of departed movie stars. In another print, Warhol even surrounded her with a gold background of the kind found in Orthodox religious icons. Additionally, while the Monroes on the colored left side of the diptych are flat and undifferentiated, those on the right side, in black and white, fade in ghostly fashion as they are printed without the screen being reinked until all that is left of the original portrait is the shadow of an image of a person.

Warhol was one of the first artists to exploit the fact that while the mass media, television in particular, seem to bring us closer to the world, they also allow us to observe the world as voyeurs rather than as participants. We become desensitized to death and disaster by the constant repetition of images on television, and are able literally to switch off at any time. Warhol's art, especially in the *Marilyn Diptych*, is like television—the presentation is superficial and bland, uses seemingly mindless repetition, and inures us to the full impact of the tragic moment of death. Warhol, known for his quotable phrases, once said: "I am a deeply superficial person." Likewise the superficiality of his art is deeply intellectual.

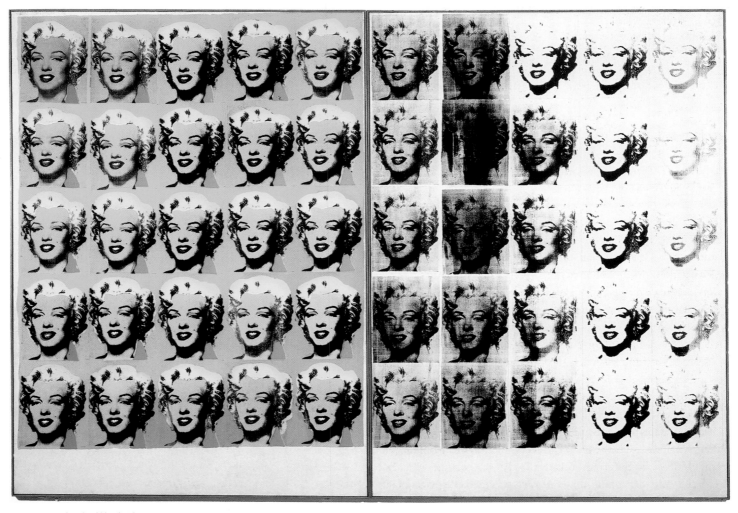

32-10 • Andy Warhol MARILYN DIPTYCH
1962. Oil, acrylic, and silkscreen on enamel on canvas, two panels, each 6′10″ × 4′9″ (2.05 × 1.44 m). Tate Gallery, London.

SEE MORE: View a video about the silkscreen process **www.myartslab.com**

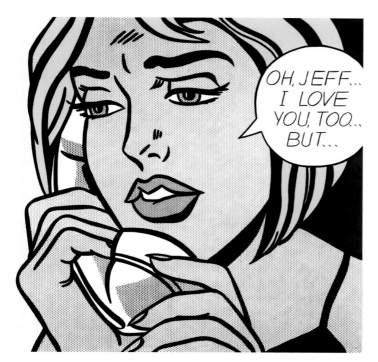

32–11 • Roy Lichtenstein OH, JEFF … I LOVE YOU, TOO … BUT …
1964. Oil and magna on canvas, 48 × 48″ (122 × 122 cm). Private collection.

EXPLORE MORE: Gain insight from a primary source by Roy Lichtenstein **www.myartslab.com**

LICHTENSTEIN. Roy Lichtenstein (1923–1997), who also investigated the various ways that popular imagery resonated with high art, used comic-book imagery in his art to critique mass-market imagery. In 1961, while teaching at Rutgers University with Allan Kaprow (SEE FIG. 32–4), Lichtenstein began to make paintings based on panels from war and romance comic books. In these, the source images are tightened and clarified to focus on significant emotions or actions that simultaneously represent and parody the flat, superficial ways in which a comic book communicates with its readers. Lichtenstein painted these images with heavy black outlines and flat primary colors, imitating the **Benday dots** used in the commercial printing of cartoons. **OH, JEFF … I LOVE YOU, TOO … BUT …** **(FIG. 32–11)** compresses an entire generic romance story into a single frame. In so doing, Lichtenstein suggests something of the superficiality of the media-saturated culture of the early 1960s.

OLDENBURG. Like Warhol and Lichtenstein, Claes Oldenburg (b. 1929) made ironic critiques of the new consumer culture, but in the case of the Swedish-born Oldenburg he turned his subjects into sculptural monuments. Oldenburg's humor is evident in his large-scale public projects, such as **LIPSTICK (ASCENDING) ON CATERPILLAR TRACKS (FIG. 32–12)**, made for his *alma mater*, Yale University. Oldenburg was invited to create this work by a group of graduate students from the School of Architecture who specified that they wanted a monument to the "Second American

Revolution" of the late 1960s, a period marked by student demonstrations against the Vietnam War. Oldenburg mounted a giant lipstick tube on top of steel tracks taken from a Caterpillar tractor. Visually the sculpture suggests both the warlike aggression of a mobile missile launcher and the eroticism of a lipstick, perhaps in a play on the popular slogan of the time, "make love, not war." The lipstick was to have included a suggestive balloonlike vinyl tip that could be pumped up with air and then left to deflate slowly, but the pump was never installed and the drooping tip, vulnerable to vandalism, was quickly replaced with a metal one. The lipstick monument was installed provocatively on a plaza in front of both the Yale War Memorial and the president's office. Not surprisingly, Oldenburg was asked to remove it. In 1974, however, he reworked the sculpture in the more permanent materials of fiberglass, aluminum, and steel and donated it to Yale, where it was placed in the courtyard of Morse College.

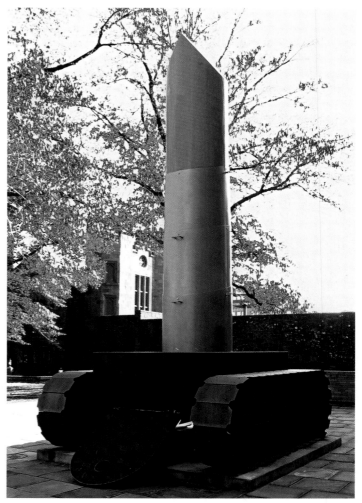

32–12 • Claes Oldenburg LIPSTICK (ASCENDING) ON CATERPILLAR TRACKS
1969, reworked 1974. Painted steel body, aluminum tube, and fiberglass tip, 21′ × 19′5½″ × 10′11″ (6.70 × 5.94 × 3.33 m). Yale University Art Gallery, New Haven, Connecticut.
Gift of Colossal Keepsake Corporation

THE DEMATERIALIZATION OF THE ART OBJECT

In the same decade that Pop artists critiqued the very visual world of popular culture, other artists questioned the role, purpose, and relevance of the art object in contemporary culture. Their restlessness parallels the social upheaval that marked the era of the mid-1960s and early 1970s. During this period, the youth of Europe and America questioned the authority and rights of the state with civil rights movements, massive rallies against the draft and the Vietnam War, environmentalist and feminist movements, and the Paris revolts of 1968. Women artists made their presence felt in large numbers, and many more artists made art to be viewed outside the gallery system. The decade ended with a move toward making noncommodifiable art and "dematerializing" the art object.

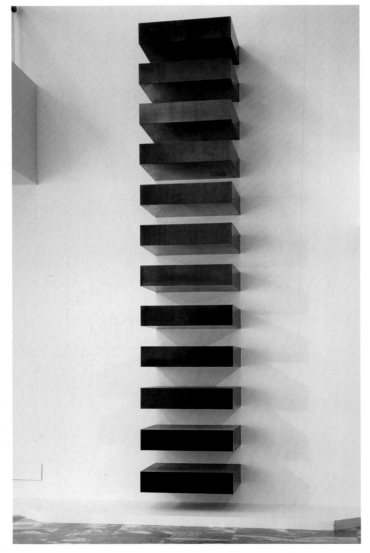

32-13 • Don Judd UNTITLED
1967. Lacquer on galvanized iron, 12 units, each 9 × 40 × 31″ (22.8 × 101.6 × 78.7 cm), installed vertically with 9″ (22.8 cm) intervals. Museum of Modern Art, New York. Helen Acheson Bequest (by exchange) and gift of Joseph Helman

MINIMALISM

Minimalism, which dominated the New York art discourse in the late 1960s, argued for the dematerialization of the art object. In the mid-1960s, a group of articulate young sculptors, including Donald Judd (1928–1994), Robert Morris (b. 1931), and Carl Andre (b. 1935), proposed what was variously called ABC Art, Primary Structures, or Minimalism. They produced slab- or box-like sculptures, frequently fabricated for them out of industrial materials such as Plexiglas, fluorescent lighting, steel, and mirrors, and so rejected the gesture and emotion invested in the hand-crafted object, as well as the traditional materials of sculpture. Judd and Morris described their theories eloquently in the journal *Artforum*. They asked viewers to try to comprehend their art objects as united wholes without a focal point, allowing the energy of the work and the viewers' interest to be dissipated throughout the object in a kind of entropy.

JUDD. In 1965, Donald Judd published the article "Specific Objects" in *Artforum*, where he argued that Minimalism should consist of real or "specific" objects. These were mathematically constructed shapes arranged without hierarchy, which could be read as complete objects at a single glance, were impersonal, and occupied the space of real things, having neither a base below nor a glass case around them. **UNTITLED** of 1967 **(FIG. 32–13)** consists of 12 identical rectangular units fabricated from galvanized iron and hung in a vertical row on the gallery wall. The arrangement is deliberately impersonal, avoiding allusion to any imagined subject. The objects are aggressively themselves. Judd provides the viewer with a set of clear, self-contained visual facts, setting the conceptual clarity and physical perfection of his art against the messy complexity of the real world.

MORRIS. Robert Morris explored the banal and uninteresting in his early art. By the early 1970s, he was making simple, unitary objects. **UNTITLED (MIRROR CUBE) (FIG. 32–14)** is a group of wooden cubes covered on all sides with mirror glass. They literally reflect and deflect any attempt to discover interest *in* the box. There is no point of focus—the boxes are constructed from industrial materials and hold no meaning within their form; instead they reflect the world around them. In fact, the artfulness of this piece lies almost entirely in the artistic concept behind it— the purposes and goals of the artist. The manifestos of Minimalism worked hand-in-hand with actual Minimalist objects to communicate the ideas of Minimal art, which the viewer had to work hard to learn how to read, understand, and appreciate.

Minimalism had its critics. The formalist critic Michael Fried, for instance, wrote that Minimal objects suffered from "objecthood" and held no more interest than any other nonart objects. He also criticized Minimalism for its "theatricality"—in his view, Minimalism, like Pop art, demanded immediate attention but could not hold a viewer's visual attention for very long and so became very boring very quickly.

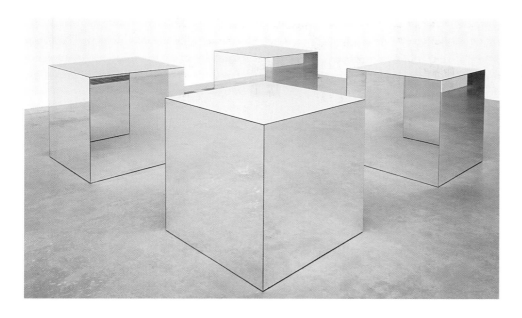

CONCEPTUAL AND PERFORMANCE ART

The logical extension of the Minimalist move away from the handcrafted art object was Conceptual art. Unlike Duchamp and Dada artists earlier in the century, who argued that the idea *is* the work of art, Conceptual artists argue that the "idea" and "form" of art are separable. Thus, for Conceptual artists there are times when a physical object is an appropriate vehicle for a work of art, other times when a performance is more appropriate, and still other times when a conceptual manifestation, sometimes in the form of written or spoken instructions, is most appropriate. Conceptual art literally "dematerialized" the art object by suggesting that the catalyst for a work of art is a concept and the means by which the concept is communicated can vary. The conceptual work of art usually leaves behind some visual trace, in the form of a set of instructions, writing on a chalkboard, a performance, photographs, or a piece of film, and in some cases even objects. Conceptual art is theoretically driven and is noncommodifiable because it leaves no precious object behind for purchase, although collectors and many museums now collect the "trace" objects left behind.

Beuys. Some of the most radical Conceptual art came out of Europe. Joseph Beuys (1921–1986) was perhaps the most significant early Conceptual artist. He served as a fighter pilot in the German Luftwaffe during World War II, when he claimed to have been shot down over the Crimea and saved by Tartars who wrapped him in animal fat and felt. There is no evidence that this actually occurred, although something traumatic clearly did happen to Beuys during the war. As an artist, Beuys developed a mysterious shamanistic persona, and created a repertoire of significant materials and objects that he used symbolically and performatively in his art in an attempt to explain the inexplicable to audiences. Beuys's symbolism was deeply personal and difficult for others to grasp. His art was about the desire to communicate and the complexities of that process.

In Beuys's **HOW TO EXPLAIN PICTURES TO A DEAD HARE (FIG. 32–15)**, the artist initially sat on a chair in a gallery surrounded by his own drawings, his head coated in honey and covered by a mask of gold leaf, and cradling a dead hare to which

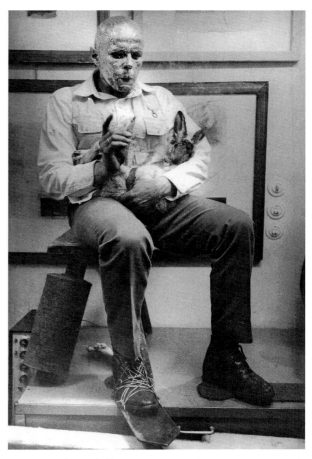

32-15 • Joseph Beuys **HOW TO EXPLAIN PICTURES TO A DEAD HARE**
1965. Photograph of performance.

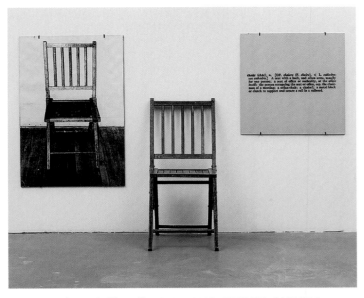

32-16 • Joseph Kosuth ONE AND THREE CHAIRS
1965. Wood folding chair, photograph of chair, and photographic enlargement of dictionary definition of chair; chair, 32⅜ × 14⅞ × 20⅞″ (82.2 × 37.8 × 53 cm); photo panel, 36 × 24⅛″ (91.4 × 61.3 cm); text panel 24⅛ × 24½″ (61.3 × 62.2 cm). Museum of Modern Art, New York. Larry Aldrich Foundation Fund (383.1970 a–c)

had as much chance of communicating fully with the dead hare as with another person. Thus he rendered visible the problems inherent in the normal means of communication. Beuys said: "Even a dead animal preserves more powers of intuition than some human beings."

KOSUTH.   Joseph Kosuth (b. 1945) abandoned painting in 1965 to examine the intersection between language and vision, the abstract idea and concrete imagery. His early work was indebted to Duchamp, semiotic theory, and the linguistic philosophy of Ludwig Wittgenstein (1889–1951). Kosuth is not interested in art that deals with beauty; his work is about the imperfect possibilities of communication, either visual or verbal. **ONE AND THREE CHAIRS (FIG. 32–16)** is a visual rendition of semiotic theory. In this piece there is an actual chair, a photograph of a chair, and a dictionary definition of "chair." The chair is an object, the photograph an imperfect visual representation of the idea of the same chair, and the dictionary definition is the literal abstraction of a chair. The title, *One and Three Chairs*, tells us that we can read this piece as one chair represented three different ways or as three different chairs. Either way, this work of art demonstrates the impossibility of precise representation and communication of an idea, leaving us with the question: Which is the "real" chair?

he muttered incomprehensibly. His left foot rested on felt, suggesting spiritual warmth, while his right foot rested on steel, symbolizing cold hard reason. He carried the dead hare around the gallery for several hours, quietly explaining his pictures to it, reasoning that he

NAUMAN.   In 1966–1967, the California-based artist Bruce Nauman (b. 1941) made a series of 11 color photographs based on wordplay and visual puns in which he cleverly complicated the

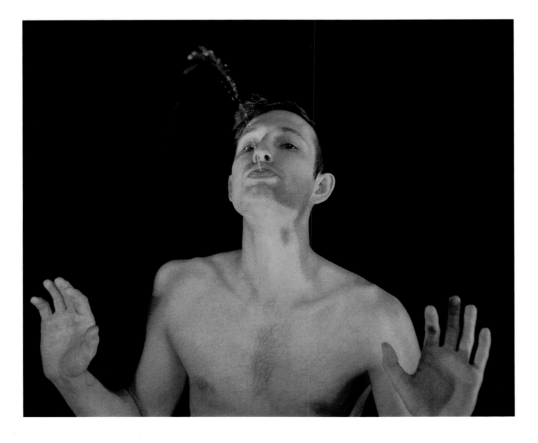

32-17 • Bruce Nauman SELF-PORTRAIT AS A FOUNTAIN
1966–1967. Color photograph, 19¾ × 23¾″ (50.1 × 60.3 cm). Courtesy Leo Castelli Gallery, New York.

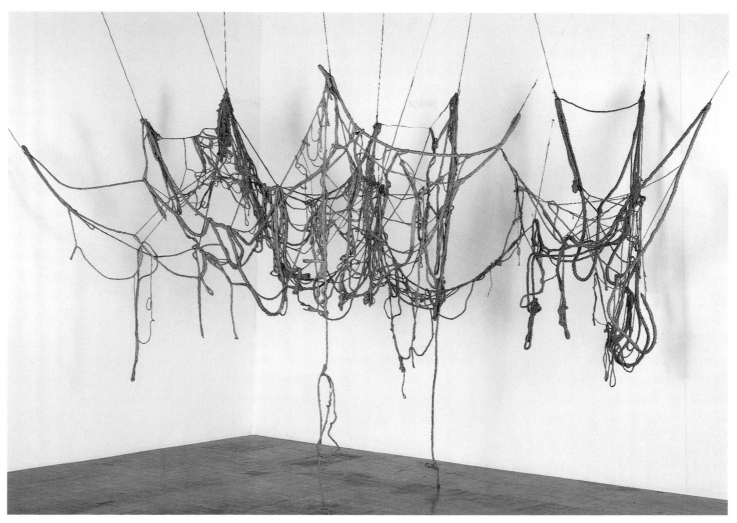

32–18 • Eva Hesse ROPE PIECE
1969–1970. Latex over rope, string, and wire; two strands, dimensions variable. Whitney Museum of American Art, New York.
Purchase, with funds from Eli and Edythe L. Broad, the Mrs. Percy Uris Purchase Fund, and the Painting and Sculpture Committee (88.17 a–b)

EXPLORE MORE: Gain insight from a primary source by Eva Hesse **www.myartslab.com**

problem of communication. In **SELF-PORTRAIT AS A FOUNTAIN (FIG. 32–17)**, for example, the bare-chested artist tips his head back and spurts water into the air, thereby showing us that he is a fountain, or perhaps the *Fountain*, the title of Duchamp's infamous urinal (SEE FIG. 31–30). Nauman, like Kosuth, leaves us with the question: Which is the "real" fountain? Is it our abstracted idea of a fountain alluded to in the title (conceptual), Nauman's claim to be a fountain (visual), or his sly reference to Duchamp's *Fountain* (literal)?

PROCESS ART

By the early 1970s, it was evident that Minimalism and Conceptualism had boxed art into an impossible absolutist corner—their reductivist approaches seemed too detached from a society that was being torn apart by social and political conflict. Some artists refused to eliminate personal meaning from their work, and in opposition to Minimalism they explored the physicality, personality, and even sensuality of the process of making art.

HESSE. Eva Hesse (1936–1970), for instance, infused her elegantly crafted art with personal history and meaning. She was born in Hamburg and narrowly escaped the Nazi Holocaust, moving to New York with her family in 1939. After graduating from the Yale School of Art in 1959, she painted dark Expressionistic self-portraits, but in 1964 began to make abstract sculpture that adapted the vocabulary of Minimalism to her own, more self-expressive purpose. She wrote: "For me art and life are inseparable. If I can name the content [of my art] … it's the total absurdity of life." **ROPE PIECE (FIG. 32–18)** is about instability; it takes on different forms and shapes each time it is installed. The work consists of several skeins of rope dipped in latex, knotted and tangled, and then hung from wires attached to the gallery ceiling. It is fragile and evocative, sensuous and delicate. Hesse embraced the instability, irrationality, and emotive power of art, reflecting her own life and emotions in the work. Her last pieces, made before her premature death from cancer, are heartbreaking.

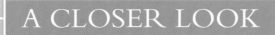
Plenty's Boast

by Martin Puryear, 1994–1995. Red cedar and pine.
68 × 83 × 118″ (172.7 × 210.8 × 299.7 cm). Nelson-Atkins Museum of Art, Kansas City, Missouri. Purchase of the Renee C. Crowell Trust (F95–16 A–C)

Puryear spent a year with the Peace Corps in Sierra Leone. He worked with African carpenters, learning their woodworking methods and skills. Note the gentle and beautifully irregular hand-finishing at the mouth of the sculpture and in the binding of its tail.

Puryear, who studied furnituremaking with James Krenov, is dedicated to maintaining the highest craft standards. Notice the radiating grain on the inside of the horn, the spiraling grain on its tail, and the exquisite quality of the joints.

The clarity, abstract nature, and monumental scale (it is 5½ feet tall) of the sculpture seem to refer to Minimalism, but evidence of the human hand in the crafting of the piece, as in the wobble in the line of the bell, suggests something closer to Process art.

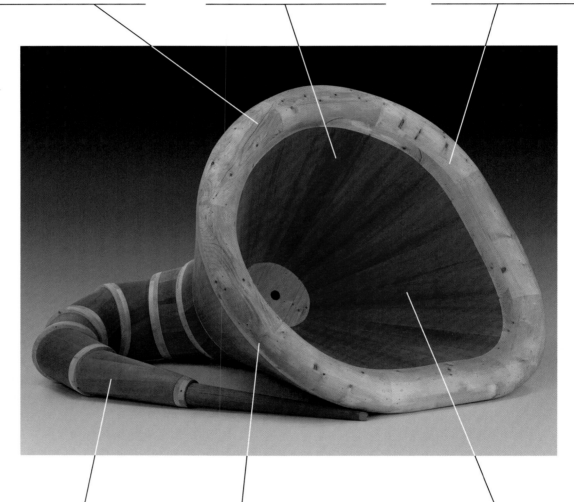

The twisting tail suggests the empty shell of a strange animal or plant. Although it is lying passively at the moment, it looks as if it could flex quickly (note the jointing) to deliver a deadly sting.

The bell shape evokes many forms, such as a musical horn, an old-fashioned gramophone horn, a flower's bell, or a cornucopia (horn of plenty).

Puryear wants viewers to see ghosts of resemblances in his allusive sculpture. Perhaps most obviously *Plenty's Boast* suggests a cornucopia, filled with the fruits of harvest and symbolizing abundance. But the cone is empty, implying an "empty boast"—a phrase suggested by the title.

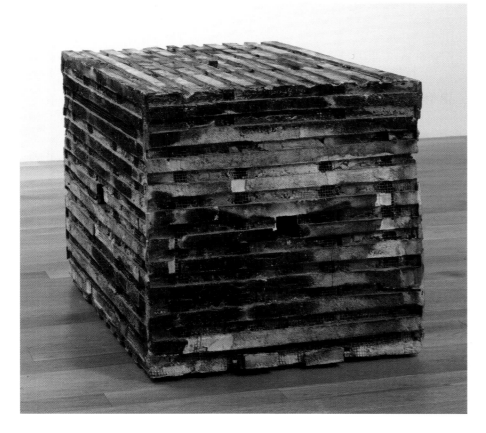

32-19 • Jackie Winsor BURNT PIECE
1977–1978. Cement, burnt wood, and wire mesh, 33⅞ × 34 × 34″ (86.1 × 86.4 × 86.4 cm). Gift of Agnes Gund. © 2009 Jackie Winsor 90.1991

WINSOR. Jackie Winsor's (b. 1941) elegant and moving **BURNT PIECE** (**FIG. 32–19**), constructed from wire mesh, cement, and burnt wood, which Winsor worked intensively, also subverts the boxlike shapes of Minimalist sculpture. The detail is really only visible on the inside; this is a closed, private, and secretive piece. The woodwork also refers to Winsor's childhood in Newfoundland, where her father was employed in the house-building trade.

FEMINISM AND ART

The idea of feminist art developed alongside the women's liberation movement of the 1960s. Both challenged one of the major unspoken conventions of art history: that great art could only be made by men. Since the 1960s, there have been three waves of feminist art and art history. A major aim of the first feminist artists and art historians was increased recognition for the accomplishment of women artists, both past and present. As feminists examined the history of art, they found that women had contributed to most of the movements of Western art but were almost never mentioned in histories of art. Feminists also attacked the traditional Western hierarchy that placed "the arts" (painting, sculpture, architecture) at a level of achievement higher than "the crafts" (ceramics, textiles, jewelry-making). Since most craft media have been historically dominated by women, favoring art over craft tends to relegate women's achievements to second-class status. Thus early feminist art tended to embrace craft media.

The first wave of feminist art and art history in the 1960s and early 1970s called for an increased recognition and acknowledgment of the accomplishments of women artists, past and present. Art historians salvaged the histories of as many women artists as possible, instating them in the "canon," and making the argument that they were as good as the male artists in it. Meanwhile feminist artists represented the physicality and sexuality of the female body as defined by women rather than as it appeared in male fantasies. This early feminist art was essentialist; it focused on women's bodies and defined gender in biological terms.

The second wave of feminist art defined gender in more relativist terms. In 1971, Linda Nochlin wrote a groundbreaking essay entitled "Why Have There Been No Great Women Artists," in which she argued that many women artists in history cannot be described as "great" if the only standard of judgment for "great" art is a masculine canon. Nochlin argued that art institutions had systematically denied women access to art education and opportunities available to men throughout history, thereby making competition on male terms impossible. Thus, the terms of the canon must be challenged and the art system changed so that women can compete on their own terms. Second-wave feminist artists deconstructed the canon by which art was currently judged and called for a re-evaluation of the place of so-called feminine arts, such as ceramics, textiles, jewelry-making, and miniature painting. They also challenged how women are looked at (gazed upon) by men in life and in art (Laura Mulvey and John Berger wrote on the "gaze" in 1973 and 1972, respectively).

Third-wave feminist art emerged in the 1990s. This latest generation of artists has addressed a plethora of other issues that discriminate against or denigrate women, including such hybrid ones as gender and class, gender and race, violence against women, postcolonialism, transgenderism, transnationalism, and eco-feminism. Third-wave feminist art explores the many strategies that women employ to navigate life.

CHICAGO AND SCHAPIRO. Born Judy Cohen, Judy Chicago (b. 1939) adopted the name of the city of her birth in order to free herself from "all names imposed upon her through male social dominance." In the late 1960s, she began making abstracted images

The Dinner Party

Judy Chicago's THE DINNER PARTY is a large, complex, mixed-media installation dedicated to hundreds of women and women artists rescued from anonymity by early feminist artists and historians. It took five years of collaborative effort to make, and it drew on the assistance of hundreds of female and several male volunteers working as ceramists, needleworkers, and china painters. *The Dinner Party* is composed of a large, triangular table, each side stretching 48 feet; Chicago conceived of the equilateral triangle as a symbol of both the feminine and the equalized world sought by feminism. The table rests on a triangular platform of 2,300 triangular porcelain tiles comprising the "Heritage Floor" that bears the names of 999 notable women from myth, legend, and history. Along each side of the table are 13 place settings representing famous women—13 being the number of men at the Last Supper as well as the number of

witches in a coven. The 39 women thus honored by individual place settings include the mythical, such as the goddess Ishtar and the Amazon, and historical personages such as the Egyptian queen Hatshepsut, the Roman scholar Hypatia, the medieval French queen Eleanor of Aquitaine, the author Christine de Pizan (see page 531), the Italian Renaissance noblewoman Isabella d'Este (see page 658), the Italian Baroque painter Artemisia Gentileschi (SEE FIG. 22–14), the eighteenth-century English feminist writer Mary Wollstonecraft, the nineteenth-century American abolitionist Sojourner Truth, and the twentieth-century American painter Georgia O'Keeffe (shown here).

Each larger-than-life place setting includes a 14-inch-wide painted porcelain plate, ceramic flatware, a ceramic chalice with a gold interior, and an embroidered napkin, sitting upon an elaborately ornamented runner. The runners are

decorated using stitching and weaving techniques and motifs appropriate to the time and place in which each woman lived. Most of the plates feature abstract designs based on female genitalia because, as Chicago said, "that is all [these women] had in common…. They were from different periods, classes, ethnicities, geographies, experiences, but what kept them within the same confined historical space" was their biological sex. The empty plates represent the fact that they "had been swallowed up and obscured by history instead of being recognized and honored."

The prominent place accorded to china painting and needlework in *The Dinner Party* both celebrates traditional women's crafts and argues for their place in the pantheon of "high art," while at the same time informing the viewer about some of the unrecognized contributions that women have made to history.

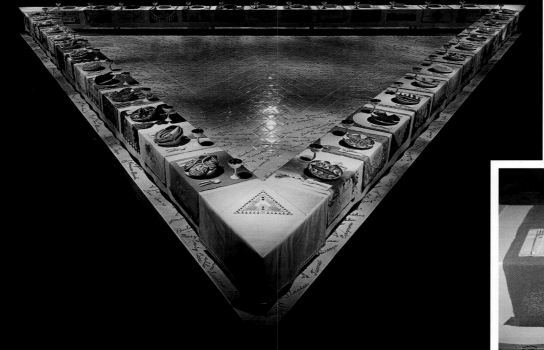

Judy Chicago THE DINNER PARTY
1974–1979. Overall installation view. White tile floor inscribed in gold with 999 women's names; triangular table with painted porcelain, sculpted porcelain plates, and needlework, each side 48 × 42 × 3′ (14.6 × 12.8 × 1 m). Brooklyn Museum of Art, New York.
Gift of the Elizabeth A. Sackler Foundation (2002.10)

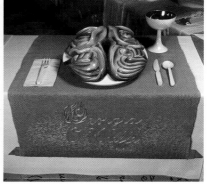

Georgia O'Keeffe
Place setting, detail of *The Dinner Party*.

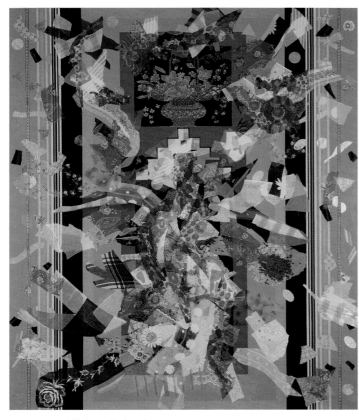

32-20 • Miriam Schapiro PERSONAL APPEARANCE #3
1973. Acrylic and fabric on canvas, 60 × 50″ (152.4 × 127 cm).
Private collection.

of female genitalia to challenge the male-dominated art world and to validate the female body and experience. In 1970, she established a feminist studio art course at Fresno State College (now California State University, Fresno) and the next year moved to Los Angeles to join the painter Miriam Schapiro (b. 1923) in establishing a Feminist Art Program at the new California Institute of the Arts (CalArts). At this time she also began to make *The Dinner Party*, one of the largest and best-known feminist artworks of the decade (see "*The Dinner Party*," opposite).

In 1971–1972, Chicago, Schapiro, and 21 of their female students created *Womanhouse*, a collaborative art environment located in a run-down Hollywood mansion which the artists renovated and filled with feminist installations. In collaboration with Sherry Brody, Schapiro also created *Dollhouse*, a mixed-media construction of several miniature rooms adorned with richly patterned fabrics. She subsequently began to incorporate pieces of fabric into her acrylic paintings, developing a type of work she called **femmage** (from "female" and "collage"). Schapiro's femmages, such as **PERSONAL APPEARANCE #3** (FIG. 32–20), celebrate traditional women's crafts. Schapiro later returned to New York to lead the Pattern and Decoration movement, a group of both female and male artists who merged the aesthetics of abstraction with ornamental motifs derived from women's craft, folk art, and art beyond the Western tradition in a nonhierarchical manner.

MENDIETA. Ana Mendieta (1948–1985) was born in Cuba but was sent to Iowa in 1961 as part of "Operation Peter Pan," which relocated 14,000 unaccompanied Cuban children after the 1959 revolution brought Fidel Castro and communism to power in Cuba. Mendieta never fully recovered from the trauma of her removal: A sense of personal dislocation haunted her and a desire to leave her bodily imprint on the earth drove her art. Mendieta used ritualistic actions in performances that connected her to the earth. She was inspired by both *santería*, the African-Cuban religion (SEE FIG. 31–75), and the work of Beuys (SEE FIG. 32–15). Mendieta produced more than 200 body works called "Silhouettes" in which she explored ways to "plant" herself in the earth. She recorded these performances in photographs and on film. The **TREE OF LIFE** series **(FIG. 32–21)** was created in Iowa, where she studied and lived. This photograph shows Mendieta with arms upraised like an earth goddess, pressed against a tree and covered in mud, as if to invite the tree to absorb her and connect her to her "maternal source." Like many of Mendieta's other works, this piece celebrates the notion that women have a deeper identification with nature than do men.

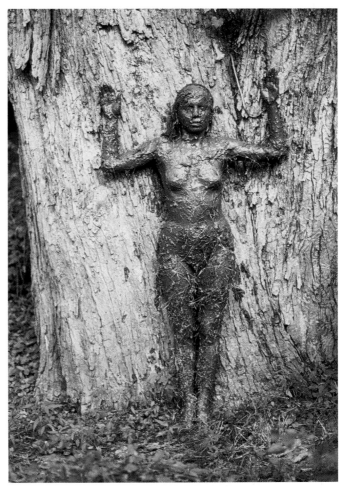

32-21 • Ana Mendieta UNTITLED, FROM THE TREE OF LIFE SERIES
1977. Color photograph, 20 × 13¼″ (50.8 × 33.7 cm). Courtesy of Galerie Lelong, New York and the estate of Ana Mendieta.

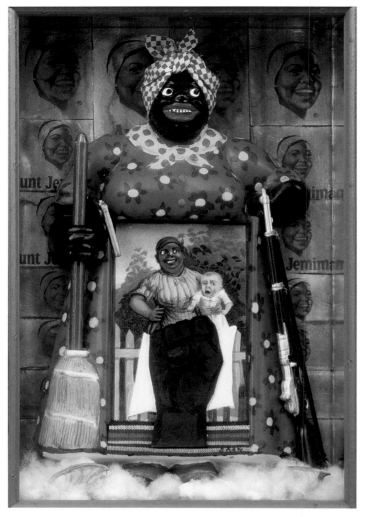

32-22 • Betye Saar THE LIBERATION OF AUNT JEMIMA
1972. Mixed media, 11¾ × 11⅞ × 2¾" (29.8 × 30.3 × 7 cm),
Berkeley Art Museum, University of California. Purchased with the aid of
funds from the National Endowment for the Arts (selected by The Committee for
the Acquisition of Afro-American Art)

SAAR. African-American sculptor Betye Saar (b. 1926) makes
works of art about race in America that are both militantly feminist
and racially activist. For **THE LIBERATION OF AUNT JEMIMA (FIG.
32–22)**, Saar created a collage out of appropriated two- and three-
dimensional images of the derogatory stereotype of a cheerfully
servile "mammy," here transformed into a militant black feminist.
The larger "mammy" figure is actually a notepad holder, to which
Saar has attached another picture of a "mammy" holding a crying
white child; in front of that is a large clenched black fist, the
symbol of Black Power. In place of a pencil the main "mammy"
holds a broom and a rifle. The rifle and fist contrast sharply with
the repeated images of a smiling Aunt Jemima in the background.
Saar's **appropriation** (taking material from one source and using
it, unaltered, in another) of contrasting images from popular
culture subverts and critiques the servile black female stereotype
by both liberating her and threatening the viewer.

EARTHWORKS AND SITE-SPECIFIC SCULPTURE

In the early 1970s, as Process artists reintroduced the handcrafted
into art, another group of artists began working with the earth as a
medium to be manipulated, crafted, and changed. Earth artists
used the land as their canvas. They made art outdoors, frequently
manipulating raw materials found at the site to create **earthworks**
that are usually **site-specific** (designed for a specific location). Some
of these artists created vast sculptures that altered the landscape
permanently, while others made ambitious works that only
temporarily changed a place. Some Earth art is located in remote
locations and is directly accessible to only a few people, while other
examples have been made available to many. Earth art, like
Performance and Conceptual art, is often intended to be noncommodifiable but it is frequently recorded in photographs and on film,
with the result that these images become collectable objects. Earth
art should not be confused with Environmental art: The former
uses the land (or city) as a place on which to make art, whereas the
latter seeks to draw attention to an imperiled natural environment.

SMITHSON. Robert Smithson (1938–1973) created **SPIRAL
JETTY (FIG. 32–23)**, one of the most significant earthworks, in
1970. This is a 1,500-foot spiraling earthen jetty that extends into
the Great Salt Lake in Utah. To Smithson, the Great Salt Lake
represented both a primordial ocean that cultivated life and a dead
sea that killed it. Smithson liked the way that skeletons of
abandoned oil rigs along the lake's shore looked like dinosaur
bones; his jetty was supposed to remind viewers of the remains of
ancient civilizations. Smithson also incorporated one of the few
living organisms found in the otherwise dead lake into his work: an
alga that turns a reddish color under certain conditions. Smithson's
Spiral Jetty is one vehicle wide: To create the jetty, earth was hauled
out into the lake in a huge land-moving truck.

Smithson used the spiral because it is an essential shape in
nature and has been used in human art for millennia. The spiral
curls and uncurls, endlessly suggesting growth and decay, creation
and destruction. Smithson ordered that no maintenance be done
on *Spiral Jetty*; he wanted the sculpture to be governed by the
natural elements over time. The work was intended to illustrate the
"ongoing dialectic" in nature between constructive and destructive
forces. The jetty is now covered with crystallized salt; it remains
visible today and can be seen on Google Earth.

CHRISTO AND JEANNE-CLAUDE. The most visible site-specific
artists in America were Christo Javacheff (b. 1935) and Jeanne-
Claude de Guillebon (1935–2009). Christo and Jeanne-Claude, as
they were known, embarked on vast projects (both rural and
urban) that sometimes took many years of planning to realize. In
1958, Christo emigrated from Bulgaria to Paris, where he met
Jeanne-Claude; they moved to New York together in 1964. Their
work was political and interventionist, frequently commenting
on capitalism and consumer culture by wrapping or packaging
buildings or large swatches of land in fabric: They "wrapped" the

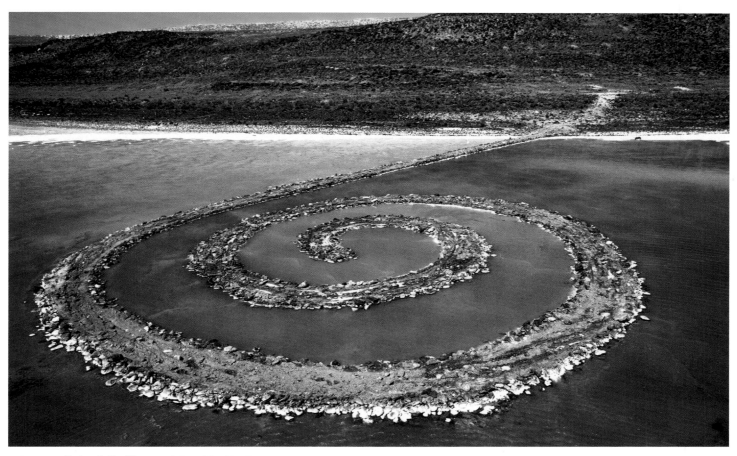

32–23 • Robert Smithson SPIRAL JETTY
1970. Mud, precipitated salt crystals, rocks, and water, length 1,500 × width 15′ (457 × 4.5 m). Great Salt Lake, Utah.
Collection: DIA Center for the Arts, New York

EXPLORE MORE: Click the Google Earth link for Spiral Jetty www.myartslab.com

Reichstag in Berlin and 1 million square feet of Australian coastline, for instance. In each case the process of planning and battling bureaucracies was part of the art, frequently taking years to complete. By contrast, the wrapping itself usually took only a few weeks and the completed project was in place for even less time. Christo and Jeanne-Claude funded each new project from the sale of books, Christo's original artworks like drawings, collages, and other ephemera relating to the preceding projects. In February 2005, Christo and Jeanne-Claude installed **THE GATES, CENTRAL PARK, NEW YORK, 1979-2005** (FIG. 32–24). This project took 26 years to realize, during which time the artists battled their way through various New York bureaucracies, meeting many obstacles and making changes to the work along the way. They finally installed 7,503 saffron-colored nylon panels on "gates" along 23 miles of pathway in Central Park. The brightly colored flapping panels enlivened the frigid February landscape and were an enormous public success. The installation lasted for only 16 days.

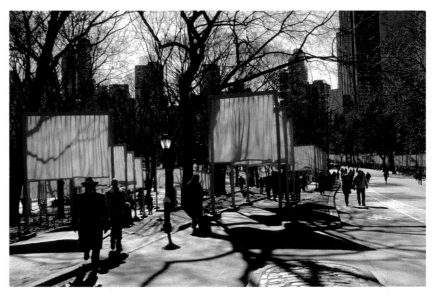

32–24 • Christo and Jeanne-Claude THE GATES, CENTRAL PARK, NEW YORK CITY, 1979-2005
1979–2005.

SEE MORE: View an interactive map of Christo's and Jeanne-Claude's *The Gates* www.myartslab.com

ARCHITECTURE: MID-CENTURY MODERNISM TO POSTMODERNISM

In architecture, the Modernist International Style endured until the 1970s. The International Style, with its plainly visible structure and rejection of historicism, dominated new urban construction in much of the world after World War II, which meant that the utopian and revolutionary aspects of Modernist architecture settled into a form that largely came to stand for corporate power and wealth. Several major European International Style architects, such as Walter Gropius (SEE FIG. 31–52), migrated to the United States and assumed important positions in architecture schools where they trained several generations of like-minded architects.

MID-CENTURY MODERNIST ARCHITECTURE

The most extreme examples of postwar International Style buildings were created by Ludwig Mies van der Rohe (1886–1969) (see "The International Style," page 1057), a former Bauhaus teacher and refugee from Nazi Germany. Mies designed the rectilinear glass towers that came to personify postwar capitalism. In the **SEAGRAM BUILDING** in New York City **(FIG. 32–25)**, designed with Philip Johnson, the building's crisp, clean

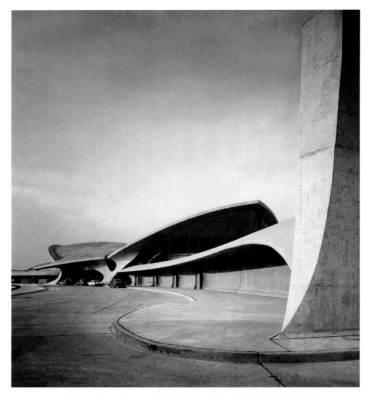

32-26 • Eero Saarinen **TRANS WORLD AIRLINES (TWA) TERMINAL, JOHN F. KENNEDY AIRPORT**
New York. 1956–1962.

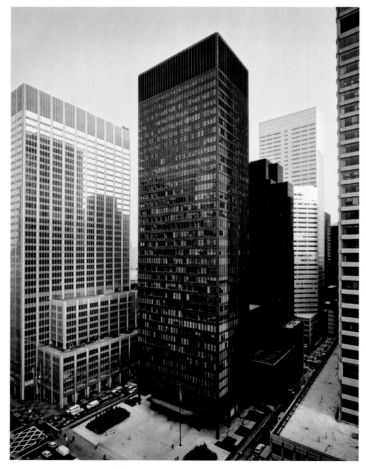

32-25 • Ludwig Mies van der Rohe and Philip Johnson
SEAGRAM BUILDING
New York. 1954–1958.

lines epitomize the standardization and impersonality that became synonymous with the modern corporation. Such buildings, with their efficient construction methods and use of materials, allowed the architect to pack an immense amount of office space into a building on a very small lot, which meant that they were also economical to construct. Although criticized for building relatively unadorned glass boxes, Mies advocated: "Less is more." He did, however, use nonfunctional, decorative bronze beams on the outside of the Seagram Building to echo the functional beams inside and give the façade a sleek, rich, and dignified appearance.

Although the pared-down, rectilinear forms of the International Style dominated the urban skyline, other architects departed from its impersonal principles so that, even in commercial architecture, expressive designs using new structural techniques and more materials also appeared. For instance, the **TRANS WORLD AIRLINES (TWA) TERMINAL (FIG. 32–26)** at John F. Kennedy Airport in New York City, by the Finnish-born American architect Eero Saarinen (1910–1961), breaks out of the box dramatically. Saarinen wanted to evoke the thrill and glamor of air travel, so he gave the TWA Terminal's roof two broad winglike canopies of reinforced concrete that suggest a huge bird about to take flight; the interior meanwhile consists of large, open, dramatically flowing spaces. Saarinen designed all of the building's interior details—from ticket counters to telephone booths—to complement his gull-winged shell.

Frank Lloyd Wright (SEE FIGS. 31–41, 31–42, 31–43) transformed museum architecture when he designed the **GUGGENHEIM**

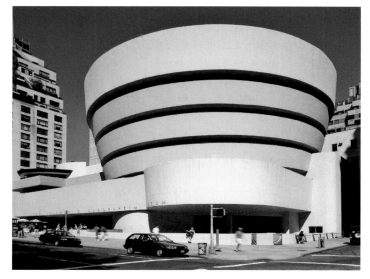

32-27 • Frank Lloyd Wright **SOLOMON R. GUGGENHEIM MUSEUM**
New York. 1943–1959.

EXPLORE MORE: Click the Google Earth link for the Guggenheim Museum **www.myartslab.com**

MUSEUM (FIG. 32–27) in New York as a sculptural work of art in its own right. The Guggenheim was designed to house Solomon Guggenheim's personal collection of Modern art and, like the TWA Terminal, was based on an organic shape, in this case a spiral. The museum's galleries spiral downward from a glass ceiling, wrapping themselves around a spectacular five-story atrium—Wright's plan was that visitors would begin by taking the elevator to the top floor and then walk down the sloping and increasingly widening ramp, enjoying Guggenheim's personal collection of paintings along the way. The interior today still has the intended intimacy of a "living room," despite having been altered by the museum's first directors. Wright wanted the building to contrast with skyscrapers like the Seagram Building and to become a Manhattan landmark—indeed, it is still one of the twentieth century's most distinctive museum spaces, and a favored site for installation and Performance art.

POSTMODERN ARCHITECTURE

In the 1970s, architects began to move away from the sleek glass-and-steel boxes of the International Style and to reintroduce quotations from past styles into their designs. Architectural historians trace the origins of this new style—Postmodernism—to the work of Jane Jacobs (1916–2006), who wrote *The Death and Life of Great American Cities* (1961), and the Philadelphian Robert Venturi (b. 1925), who rejected the abstract purity of the International Style by incorporating elements drawn from vernacular (meaning popular, common, or ordinary) sources into his designs.

Venturi parodied Mies van der Rohe's aphorism, "Less is more," with his own saying, "Less is a bore." He argued that Mies and other Modernist architects had ignored human needs in their quest for uniformity and sterility, and that Postmodernism should address the complex, contradictory, and heterogeneous mixture of "high" and "low" architecture that comprised the modern city. He said that new architecture should embrace eclecticism, so he reintroduced references to past architectural styles into his designs, and began to apply decoration to his buildings.

While writing his treatise on Postmodernism, *Complexity and Contradiction in Architecture* (1966), Venturi designed a house for his mother **(FIG. 32–28)** that illustrated many of his new ideas. The shape of the façade returns to the traditional Western "house" volumes and shapes that Modernists rejected because of their historical associations. Its vocabulary of triangles, squares, and circles is arranged in a complex asymmetry that subverts the symmetrical rigidity of Modernist design, while the curved molding over the door is simply decorative. The most disruptive element of the façade is the deep cleavage over the door, which opens to reveal a mysterious upper wall (which turns out to be a penthouse) and chimney top. The interior is also complex and contradictory. The irregular floor plan **(FIG. 32–29)**, including an odd stairway leading up to the second floor, is further complicated by irregular ceiling levels that are partially covered by a barrel vault. The overall structure makes reference to several previous buildings, including Michelangelo's Porta Pia in Rome and a nearby house designed by Venturi's mentor, Louis Kahn (1901–1974).

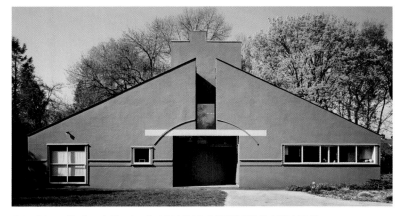

32-28 • Robert Venturi **VANNA VENTURI HOUSE**
Chestnut Hill, Pennsylvania. 1961–1964.

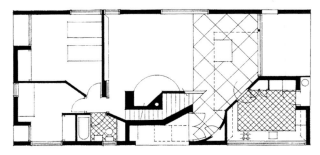

32-29 • **GROUND-FLOOR PLAN OF THE VANNA VENTURI HOUSE**

In the 1970s, Postmodern ideas were also applied to commercial architecture. One of the first examples was the **AT&T CORPORATE HEADQUARTERS** (now the Sony Building) in New York City **(FIG. 32–30)** by Philip Johnson (1906–2005). This elegant, granite-clad skyscraper has 36 oversized stories, making it as tall as the average 60-story building. It mimics its International Style neighbors with its smooth uncluttered skin, while its Classical window groupings set between vertical piers also echo nearby skyscrapers from much earlier in the century. But the overall profile of the building bears a whimsical resemblance to the shape of a Chippendale highboy, an eighteenth-century chest of drawers with a long-legged base—Johnson seems to have intended a pun on the terms "highboy" and "high-rise." The round notch at the top of the building as well as the rounded entryway at its base suggest the coin slot and coin return of an old pay telephone in a clever reference to Johnson's patron, the AT&T telephone company.

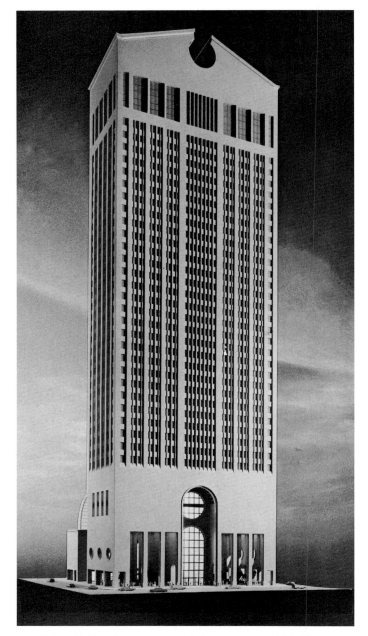

32-30 • Philip Johnson and John Burgee MODEL, AT&T CORPORATE HEADQUARTERS
New York. 1978–1983.

EXPLORE MORE: Click the Google Earth link for the AT&T Building (now the Sony Building)
www.myartslab.com

POSTMODERNISM

Scholars disagree about the exact date when the theories of Postmodernism filtered through the Western art world, but most agree that it took place in the early 1980s. By then, the Modern ideas of art as absolute, ideal, pure, or perfect, and of the artist as a serious, single-minded individual who held her/himself above and apart from society, were beginning to seem both arrogant and foolhardy to younger artists.

Rather than a style, Postmodernism is perhaps better thought of as a strategy for making art. Its manifestations are many and varied. Postmodern artists reject the seriousness of Modernism, creating visually interesting, messy, sometimes contrary, and often political images that mock the rules of Modern art. They "appropriate" or take images wholesale from both "high art" and "popular" sources, repositioning and recontextualizing them, making them partially their own, twisting and changing their meanings. Postmodern artists create new images and new meanings out of the old, welcoming oddity and eccentricity, and seriously questioning the idea of "originality."

Just as Modern art heralded an industrial, technological society, the advent of Postmodern art heralded a post-industrial, advanced capitalist society based on communication and information, and demanding a flexible population that embraces difference and change. Postmodern art reflects the **pluralism** (social and cultural diversity) of our globalized society, in which the only real constant is change and the only thing we have in common is difference. Postmodern art also embraces the vast visual culture of the 1980s, the age of personal computers, video cameras, cable television, and an emerging Internet culture; it harnesses images from this infinitely mutable world in which it is difficult to know what is real and what is not. As Andy Warhol observed presciently some time before, "I don't know where the artificial stops and the real starts."

PAINTING

Neo-Expressionism was one of the first international expressions of Postmodernism. It was launched by two highly visible exhibitions in London ("A New Spirit") and Berlin ("Zeitgeist") in the early 1980s. These exhibitions included large-scale figural Expressionist paintings that recovered the luxury of the painted surface. Neo-Expressionism was almost exclusively dominated by men: "A New Spirit" featured the art of 38 male artists and "Zeitgeist" featured the art of one female and 43 male artists.

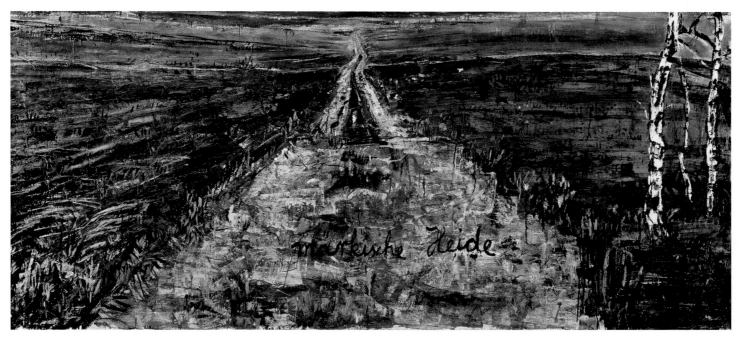

32-31 • Anselm Kiefer HEATH OF THE BRANDENBURG MARCH
1974. Oil, acrylic, and shellac on burlap, 3'10½" × 8'4"
(1.18 × 2.54 m). Stedelijk Van Abbemuseum, Eindhoven,
The Netherlands.

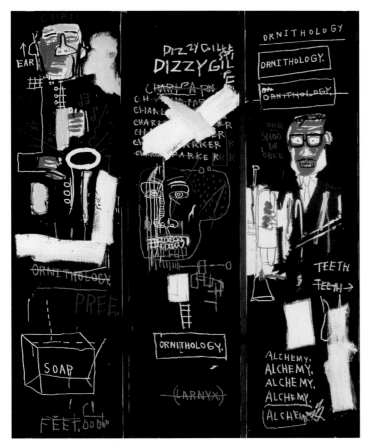

32-32 • Jean-Michel Basquiat HORN PLAYERS
1983. Acrylic and oil paintstick on canvas, three panels, overall 8' ×
6'5" (2.44 × 1.91 m). Broad Art Foundation, Santa Monica, California.

KIEFER. The German Neo-Expressionist Anselm Kiefer (b. 1945) was born in the final weeks of World War II. His work both pays homage to and critiques the art of the German Expressionists of the 1930s whose art was banned by the Nazis (see "Suppression of the Avant-Garde in Nazi Germany," page 1055). In the burned and barren landscape of his **HEATH OF THE BRANDENBURG MARCH (FIG. 32–31)**, Kiefer tries to come to grips with his country's Nazi past, building on the ideas of his teacher Beuys. Instead of simply documenting Nazism in this painting, Kiefer portrays both the devastating physical impact of the war on the Brandenburg Heath (near Berlin) and invokes Nazi history by scrawling the first words of the Nazi marching song "Märkische Heide, märkische Sand" across the road in the front of the painting, thus both quoting from the past and critiquing it.

BASQUIAT. In the United States, the tragically short-lived Jean-Michel Basquiat (1960–1988) made Neo-Expressionist paintings that grew out of graffiti art. The Brooklyn-born Basquiat was raised in middle-class comfort but rebelled by quitting high school and leaving home to become a street artist. For three years he covered the walls of lower Manhattan with short and witty philosophical texts signed with the tag "SAMO©." In 1980, Basquiat participated in the highly publicized "Times Square Show" which showcased the raw and aggressive styles of subway and graffiti artists. Basquiat said he wanted to make "paintings that look as if they were made by a child," but in reality his work is a sophisticated mix of appropriated imagery from Modern art combined with blunt references to race and the street.

HORN PLAYERS (FIG. 32–32) portrays legendary jazz musicians Charlie Parker (upper left) and Dizzy Gillespie (center right). Basquiat's urgent paint application and hurried lettering are strongly emotional and Expressionist, conveying a dedication to

The Guerrilla Girls

In 1984, the Museum of Modern Art mounted "An International Survey of Painting and Sculpture," an exhibition that supposedly displayed the most important art of the time, yet of the 169 (mostly white) artists included in the exhibition, only 13 were women. By way of a rejoinder to this and several other such exhibitions, the following year the radical feminist group the Guerrilla Girls was founded in New York to function, they said, as "the conscience of the art world." Its members wear gorilla masks to hide their identity and to prevent personal reprisals; they call themselves "girls" as a play on the demeaning term "girl" as applied to women. Each Guerrilla Girl takes as a pseudonym the name of a famous dead woman artist. They have declared that the new "f" word is feminism.

Their mandate is to reveal gender and racial inequities in the art world, to demonstrate against discrimination, and to fight for the rights of women and artists of color. The Guerrilla Girls use the strategies of guerrilla warfare—they act covertly and strike anonymously at the heart of their enemy. They compile statistics on discrimination in the art world, produce sharp, witty, sophisticated posters that draw on the best advertising theory, and paste these posters at night on walls in the art districts of New York close to offending galleries and museums. The posters are highly visible, damning, and very funny, and they have made a difference.

One of their most famous posters features a poster version of a reclining nude by Ingres and the words "Do women have to be naked to get into the Met. Museum?" As the poster explains, 85 percent of the nudes on display in the Metropolitan Museum at the time (1989) were women, while less than 5 percent of art in the museum was by women. Sadly, the Guerrilla Girls repeated their survey in 2005 and found that there were even fewer women artists (3 percent), but, as they said, at least there were more naked men!

THE ADVANTAGES OF BEING A WOMAN ARTIST delivers a clever, ironic, and sadly accurate list of the "benefits" of being a woman artist. Today's Guerrilla Girls have broadened their reach to address larger issues of race and political discrimination in the world. They have made significant differences in the art world, if not yet at the Met.

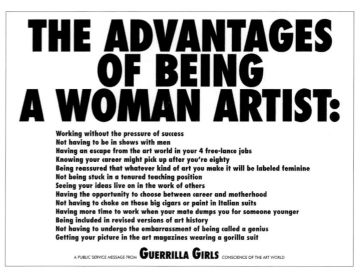

Guerrilla Girls **THE ADVANTAGES OF BEING A WOMAN ARTIST**
1988. Offset print, 17 × 22" (43.2 × 55.9 cm). Collection of the artists.

---

jazz and a passionate determination to foreground African-American subjects in an unsentimental way. Basquiat said: "Black people are never portrayed realistically, not even portrayed, in Modern art, and I'm glad to do that." He died from a heroin overdose at age 27.

RICHTER. Postmodern painting took many forms in addition to Neo-Expressionism. One of the most sophisticated Postmodern artists is the German artist Gerhard Richter (b. 1932), who rejected the idea of a single style in art, arguing that each painting's content should determine its form. In 1988, he made a series of paintings, including **MAN SHOT DOWN (1) ERSCHOSSENER (1) FROM OCTOBER 18, 1977** (FIG. 32–33). This series features life-size painted copies of grainy black-and-white newspaper photographs of the bodies of three members of the terrorist group the Red Army Faction

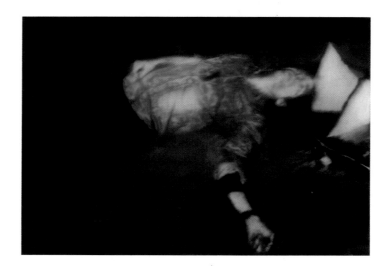

32-33 • Gerhard Richter MAN SHOT DOWN (1) ERSCHOSSENER (1) FROM OCTOBER 18, 1977
1988. Oil on canvas, 39½ × 55¼" (100 × 140 cm). Museum of Modern Art, New York. The Sidney and Harriet Janis Collection, gift of Philip Johnson, and acquired through the Lillie P. Bliss Bequest (all by exchange); Enid A. Haupt Fund; Nina and Gordon Bunshaft Bequest Fund; and gift of Emily Rauh Pulitzer. (169.1995.g.)

(commonly known as the Baader-Meinhof Gang), who were found dead in their prison cells in 1977, probably by suicide. They had been imprisoned for the kidnap and murder of Hans Martin Schleyer, president of the powerful German Federation of Industries. In his painting Richter simultaneously critiques the single-minded pursuit of a political ideologue willing to die for an idea, the role of the mass media in creating meaning in images (knowledge of the historical context of the events portrayed changes their meaning), and the value of the (in this case almost invisible) hand of the artist.

POSTMODERNISM AND GENDER

In 1982, the critic Craig Owens argued that Postmodernism represented a crisis in normal cultural authority because of the way it questioned the relative homogeneity of Modernism. Moreover, since photography, which had never been fully integrated into the canon, was perhaps the perfect medium for appropriating images, Owens argued that it might also be the ideal Postmodern medium. In addition, since feminism challenged the "patriarchy" (the masculine control of power in society) and Owens described Modernism as patriarchal, authoritative, single-minded, and driven by the quest for originality and artistic mastery, he also argued that feminists might be in a position to make the best Postmodern art. Since Postmodernism, feminism, and photography all forced viewers to confront difference, since all challenged the authority of the canon, and since none particularly valued originality or individual artistic mastery, Owens argued that feminists and photographers represented Postmodernism more completely than did the mostly male Neo-Expressionist painters. In keeping with this, in the 1980s many women artists used Postmodern strategies to create feminist art (see "The Guerrilla Girls," opposite).

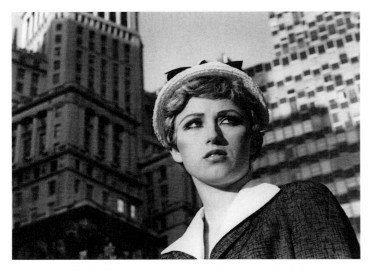

32-34 • Cindy Sherman **UNTITLED FILM STILL #21**
1978. Black-and-white photograph, 8 × 10″ (20.3 × 25.4 cm).
Courtesy of the artist and Metro Pictures, New York.

EXPLORE MORE: Gain insight from a primary source related to Cindy Sherman **www.myartslab.com**

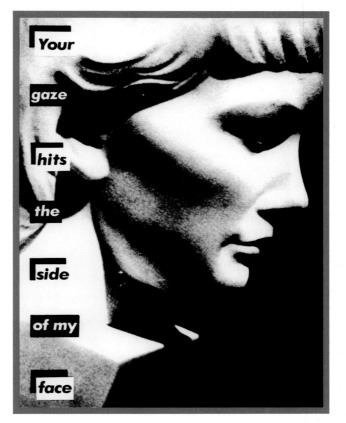

32-35 • Barbara Kruger **UNTITLED (YOUR GAZE HITS THE SIDE OF MY FACE)**
1981. Photograph, red painted frame, 55 × 41″ (140 × 104 cm). Mary Boone Gallery, New York.

SHERMAN. The "Untitled Film Stills" series by Cindy Sherman (b. 1954) exemplifies Postmodern strategies of looking. These photographs eerily resemble authentic still photographs from early 1960s films; they are even printed in black-and-white on 8 × 10″ paper in film-still format. But all are in fact contemporary photographs of Sherman herself in which she poses, appropriately made-up, in settings that seem to quote from the well-known plots of old movies. In **UNTITLED FILM STILL #21** (FIG. 32–34), for instance, she appears as a small-town girl who has moved to the big city to find work. Other photographs from the series show her variously as a Southern belle, a hardworking housewife, and a teenager waiting by the phone for a call. Critics have discussed these images in terms of second-wave feminism, as questioning the culturally constructed roles played by women in society, and as a critique of the male gaze. In these photographs, Sherman is both the photographer and the photographed. By assuming both roles, she complicates the relationship between the person looking and the person being looked at, and she subverts the way in which photographs of women communicate stereotypes.

KRUGER. Barbara Kruger (b. 1945) makes an even stronger point about how women are looked at in **UNTITLED (YOUR GAZE HITS THE SIDE OF MY FACE)** (FIG. 32–35). Kruger started her career as a designer for *Mademoiselle* magazine before beginning to make

32-36 • Faith Ringgold
TAR BEACH (PART I FROM THE WOMAN ON A BRIDGE SERIES)
1988. Acrylic on canvas, bordered with printed, painted, quilted, and pieced cloth, 74⅝ × 68½″ (190.5 × 174 cm).
Guggenheim Museum, New York.
Gift, Mr. and Mrs. Gus and Judith Lieber, 1988 (88.362)

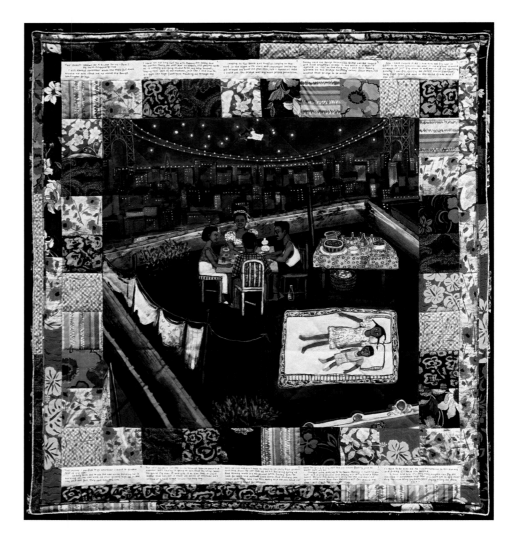

photo-based art. Her signature style is the black-and-white photographic image with red (three-color printing) used in cheap advertising. Kruger appropriates the imagery of advertising, its layout style, and its characteristic use of slogans, doing so both to suggest and to subvert the advertising image. In this photograph, she personalizes the relationship between the viewer and the viewed, addressing the former directly using the personal pronoun "you." In any figurative image, there is a person who looks (the spectator) and a person in the image who is looked at (the subject). The person who looks is active, while the person being looked at is passive. Usually it is the person who looks who holds the power of the "gaze" and implicitly subjugates the person being looked at.

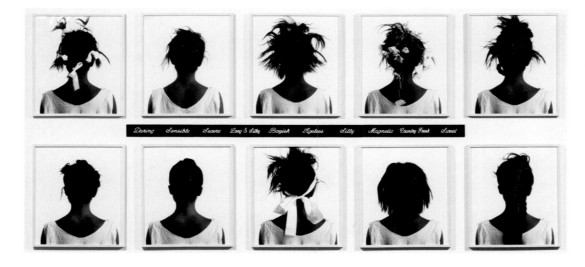

32-37 • Lorna Simpson
STEREO STYLES
1988. Ten black-and-white Polaroid prints and ten engraved plastic plaques, 5′4″ × 9′8″ (1.63 × 2.95 m) overall.
Private collection.

If the person being looked at returns, rejects, or deflects the gaze, however, the traditional power relationship is upset. That is what happens in Kruger's image, where the looker ("you") is blocked by the woman being looked at, who says that "your gaze" is deflecting by "the side of my face." Kruger's art is subversive and interventionist; she has printed her works on posters, on T-shirts, and even on pencils and pens.

POSTMODERNISM, RACE, AND ETHNICITY

Other artists have likewise used Postmodern strategies to draw attention to racial and ethnic difference, to advocate change, and to explore how race and gender combine to doubly silence artists.

RINGGOLD.   Faith Ringgold (b. 1930) draws on the tradition of African-American quiltmaking combined with the heritage of African textiles to make significant statements about race in America. In the early 1970s, Ringgold began to introduce traditional women's crafts into her art, painting on soft fabrics rather than on stretched canvases and framing her paintings with decorative quilted borders. Ringgold's mother, Willi Posey, a fashion designer and dressmaker, made the quilted borders until her death in 1981, after which Ringgold began to do the quilting herself. In 1977, Ringgold started writing her autobiography (*We Flew Over the Bridge: The Memoirs of Faith Ringgold*, 1995) but, unable to find a publisher, decided to sew her stories into quilts instead—what she termed "story quilting."

Animated by a feminist sensibility, Ringgold's story quilts are narrated by women and usually address women's issues. In **TAR BEACH** (FIG. 32–36), the narrator is 8-year-old Cassie Louise Lightfoot—although the story is actually based on Ringgold's own memories of growing up in Harlem. "Tar Beach" is the roof of the apartment building in which Ringgold's family lived and where they slept on hot summer nights. Ringgold describes it as a

magical place. Cassie and her brother lie on a blanket while their parents and neighbors play cards. She dreams that she can fly and that she can possess everything over which she passes. Another version of Cassie is shown flying over the George Washington Bridge, claiming it for herself; over a new union-constructed building, claiming it for her father who, as an African-American construction worker, was not allowed to join the union; and over an ice-cream factory, claiming "ice cream every night for dessert" for her mother. Cassie's fantasy reminds the viewer of the real social and economic prejudices that African Americans have faced in America's past and present.

SIMPSON.   In **STEREO STYLES** (FIG. 32–37), Lorna Simpson (b. 1960) arranges ten Polaroid photographs of African-American women photographed from behind in a double row. Each wears a different hairstyle. Adjectives describe the hairstyles variously and ironically as "Daring," "Sensible," "Severe," "Long and Silky," "Boyish," "Ageless," "Silly," "Magnetic," "Country Fresh," and "Sweet." Simpson frequently photographs African-American women with their faces turned away to suggest that they are seen only in terms of their bodies or, in this case, of their African-American hair styles. Her images ask us to consider how African-American women are stereotyped and the role that hair plays as an indicator of race, gender, and class in society.

BACA.   Judith F. Baca (b. 1946) pays tribute to her Mexican-American heritage in *The Great Wall of Los Angeles*, which looks back to the Mexican mural movement (SEE FIG. 31–69) to recount the history of California as seen through Mexican-, African-, and Japanese-American eyes. This detail, **THE DIVISION OF THE BARRIOS** (FIG. 32–38), depicts the residents of a Mexican-American neighborhood protesting futilely against the division of their neighborhood by a new freeway. Other scenes include the

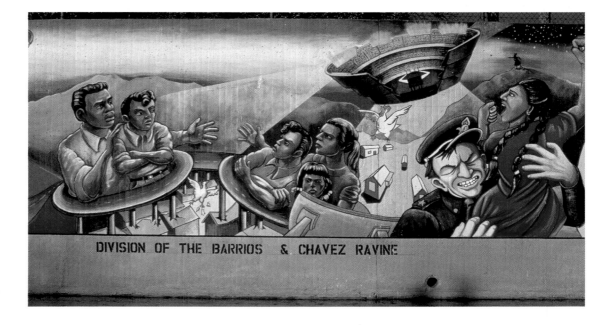

32-38 • Judith F. Baca THE DIVISION OF THE BARRIOS. DETAIL FROM THE GREAT WALL OF LOS ANGELES
1976–1983. Height 13′ (4 m), overall length approx. 2,500′ (762 m). Tujunga Wash Flood Control Channel, Van Nuys, California.

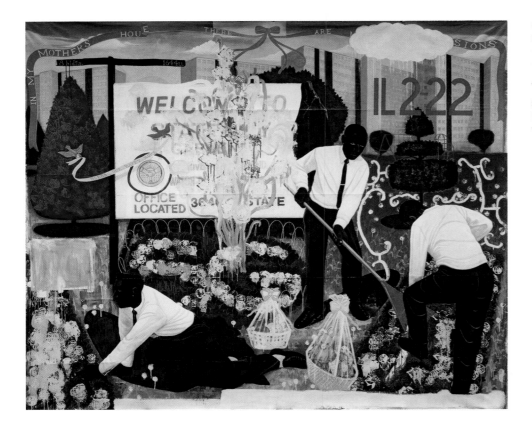

32–39 • Kerry James Marshall
MANY MANSIONS
1994. Acrylic on paper mounted on canvas,
114¼ × 135⅛″ (290 × 343 cm).
Art Institute of Chicago.

SEE MORE: View a video about
Kerry James Marshall
www.myartslab.com

deportation of Mexican-American citizens during the Great Depression and the internment of Japanese-American citizens during World War II. Baca's *The Great Wall of Los Angeles* was a collaborative effort involving many professional artists and hundreds of young people.

MARSHALL. **MANY MANSIONS** (FIG. 32–39) by African-American painter Kerry James Marshall (b. 1955) is a wry, ironic commentary on race, class, and poverty in American society. The work refers to Stateway Gardens, Chicago, one of the largest and most notoriously ill-maintained housing projects in America. The scandalously inadequate conditions were the subject of much debate prior to its long-overdue demolition in 2007. Marshall shows an unrealistically idyllic attempt by three African-American men, who are impossibly well dressed for gardening, to create an equally impossibly tidy garden that includes manicured topiary in the background and flowerbeds in the foreground. The painting includes a number of biting details, including the statement "In my mother's house there are many mansions," which both changes the gender of the biblical quotation (John 14:2) and comments on the disrepair of the projects by calling them, ironically, "mansions." Two cute cartoon bluebirds with a baby-blue ribbon fly into the scene like the birds that bring the fairy godmother's gifts to Cinderella in rags in the Disney film, while two Easter baskets neatly wrapped in plastic sit in the garden. The artist even takes a swipe at the fact that the condition of the projects was studied and cataloged and then ignored by the authorities by labeling his own picture "IL2-22" ("Illustration 2-22") in the upper right.

LUNA. James Luna (b. 1950) asks us to confront Native American stereotypes in his **THE ARTIFACT PIECE** (FIG. 32–40), first staged in a hall dedicated to a traditional ethnographic exhibition at the Museum of Man in San Diego in 1987. Luna lay, almost naked, in a glass display case filled with sand embedded with artifacts from his life, such as his favorite music and books, personal legal papers, and so on. Museum-style labels pointed to marks and scars on his body that he had acquired while drinking or fighting or in accidents. In this way, Luna literally turned his living body and his life into an ethnographic object for people to stare at, evaluate, and judge. By physically objectifying himself, he challenges our prejudices, stereotypes, and assumptions about Native Americans in general and about him specifically.

SCULPTURE

Finally, in the 1980s several sculptors became embroiled in controversies over the nature and purpose of sculpture. Some sculptures challenged sculptural orthodoxy by introducing images and objects appropriated from popular and mass culture into their art, while others raised questions about the rights of an artist to make art either deliberately confrontational or offensive. Debates also raged over the artist's rights and responsibilities when making government-funded site-specific sculptures in the public domain.

KOONS. Jeff Koons (b. 1955), the brilliant self-publicist and critic (or celebrant) of the superficial, consumption-crazy suburban society of the 1980s, with a sly reference to Duchamp (SEE FIG. 31–30), has deified household objects such as vacuum cleaners, inflatable bunny

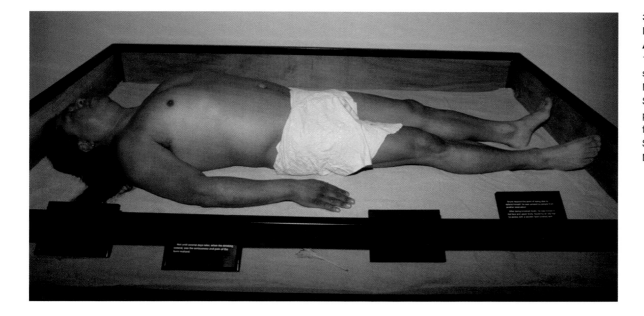

32-40 • James Luna **THE ARTIFACT PIECE** 1987–1990. First staged in 1987 at the Museum of Man, San Diego. Luna also performed the piece for "The Decade Show," 1990, in New York.

rabbits, topiary puppy dogs, porcelain pornography, and in this case a very scary embrace between the Pink Panther and a cheesy centerfold pin-up **(FIG. 32–41)**. At more than 3 feet tall, this sculpture is almost life-size, and the fact that it is made from porcelain, a material more commonly used for knick-knacks than a major sculpture, means that its surface is slick and glossy. The porcelain, the flat pastel colors that evoke Warhol's Marilyn Monroe portraits (SEE FIG. 32–10), and the cloying presence of the Pink Panther combine to produce a work that is both annoyingly bland and annoyingly attractive. Koons invites and even welcomes critical disapproval, embracing kitschy lower-middle–class consumer culture without seeming to critique it. Koons's work is openly materialistic and shallow, positively wallowing in popular culture.

SERRA.   Richard Serra (b. 1939) studied sculpture at Berkeley, Santa Barbara, and Yale. His early sculpture involved, among other things, draping vulcanized rubber in different arrangements and throwing molten lead against gallery walls. In the early 1970s, he began making sculptures from very large steel plates. In 1981, he won a commission from the General Services Administration (GSA) to create a sculpture, **TILTED ARC** (FIG. 32–42), for the plaza in front of the Javitz Federal Building in New York. Before commissioning it, the GSA saw plans of the proposed work and so knew both what it would look like and the effect it would have on the plaza. Once installed, the sculpture, a long curved Cor-Ten steel structure 120 feet long, 12 feet tall, and 2½ inches thick, bisected the plaza, completely changing it as a public space and making it impossible to hold concerts or performances there and difficult to use casually. Over time *Tilted Arc* rusted and was soon covered in graffiti and pigeon droppings. Public outrage against it was so intense that it was removed to a Brooklyn parking lot in 1986, creating a further furor, this time among artists and critics. Serra argued that moving the site-specific piece destroyed it and

filed a lawsuit on the grounds of censorship, but the Federal district court found no legal merit in his case.

Tilted Arc raised several important questions about the rights and responsibilities of artists as well as the obligations of those who fund such art. Serra intentionally changed (and for some spoiled)

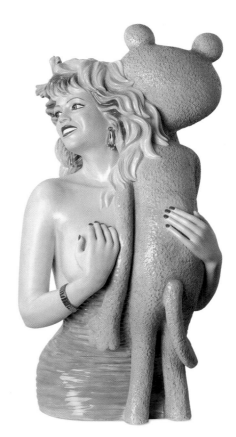

32-41 • Jeff Koons PINK PANTHER
1988. Porcelain, 41 × 20½″ × 19″ (104.1 × 52.1 × 48.3 cm).
Museum of Contemporary Art, Chicago.

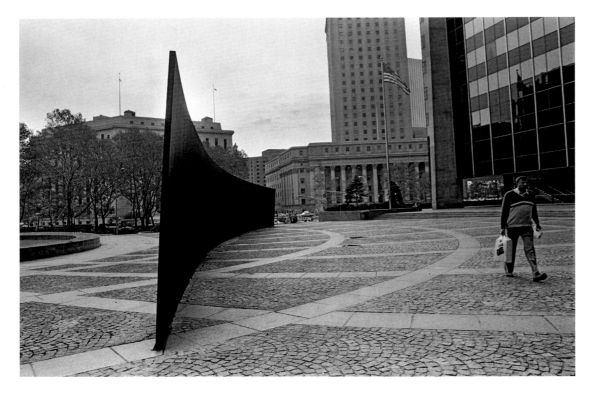

32-42 • Richard Serra
TILTED ARC
1981–1989. Jacob K. Javitz Federal Plaza, New York. Steel. Destroyed.

SEE MORE: View a video about Richard Serra's *Tilted Arc*
www.myartslab.com

Javitz Plaza. Moreover, in court he did not attempt to defend the aesthetics of his work. Rather, he argued that, once commissioned, he had a right to make the piece as planned. The case precipitated changes in the commissioning of public sculpture: Today neighborhood groups and local officials meet with artists in advance of public commissions. But important questions remain unresolved: Do these public safeguards produce better public sculpture? Or do they merely guarantee that it will be bland, inoffensive, and decorative?

LIN. Maya Lin (b. 1959) was an architecture student at Yale University in 1981 when she was awarded the commission for the **VIETNAM VETERANS MEMORIAL (FIG. 32–43)** in Constitution Gardens, Washington, D.C., A jury of architects, landscape architects, and sculptors selected her design for a simple and dramatic memorial cut into the ground in a V-shape. Two highly polished black granite slabs reach out from the deepest point of the memorial at the center. Each of these arms is 247 feet long, and they meet at a 130-degree angle where the slabs are 10 feet tall. The names of American soldiers killed or declared missing in action during the Vietnam War are listed chronologically as they died or were lost, beginning at the shallowest point to the left. The tallest part of the sculpture represents the year of the highest casualties. The black polished granite reflects the faces of visitors; as they read the names of the dead and missing, they see their own faces superimposed on them. The memorial, commissioned by Vietnam Veterans for Vietnam Veterans, serves both to commemorate the dead and missing and to provide a place where survivors can confront their own loss. This sculpture is one of the best-known works of public art in the United States and has transformed the way the nation mourns its war dead. Visiting it is a powerful and profound experience.

Yet, when it was first commissioned, the *Vietnam Veterans Memorial* was the subject of intense debate. It was described as a "black gash in the Mall," its black color contrasting with the white marble of the surrounding memorials. Lin was accused of creating a monument of shame, one critic going so far as to claim that black was the universal color of "shame, sorrow, and degradation in all races, all societies." Opposition to the sculpture was so intense in some quarters that a second, naturalistic sculpture showing three soldiers was commissioned and placed 120 feet from the wall in 1983; in 1993, another figurative sculpture of three nurses was added 300 feet to the south.

ART, ACTIVISM, AND CONTROVERSY: THE NINETIES

The passage from the 1980s to the 1990s was marked by what is commonly referred to as the "Culture Wars" (see "Controversies Over Public Funding for the Arts," page 1120), a confrontation between artists and public officials in America over freedom of speech and public funding for the arts, particularly with regard to the right to make art that might be considered offensive or obscene by others. At the same time many artists who had previously worked on the periphery of society and established art institutions began to claim center stage by making aggressive images about identity and unequal treatment on the grounds of gender, sexual orientation, race, or class. Many of these artists

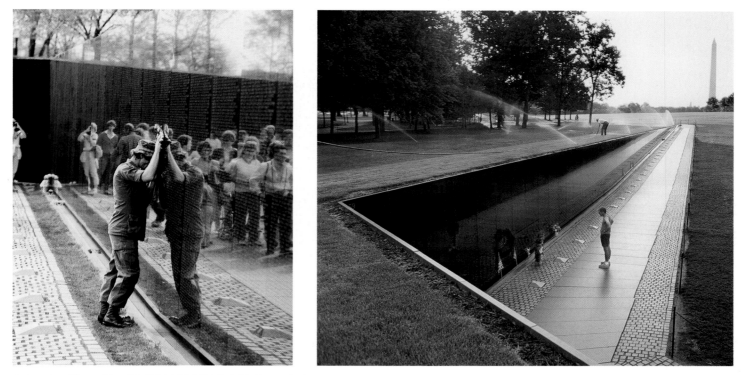

32-43 • Maya Lin VIETNAM VETERANS MEMORIAL
Washington, D.C. 1981–1983.

EXPLORE MORE: Click the Google Earth link for the Vietnam Veterans Memorial
www.myartslab.com

worked with passion and urgency as they or their friends and lovers died from AIDS. The 1990s was also the beginning of the digital age, when a new interest in the mutability of photography and film opened imaginative new vistas for artists.

THE CULTURE WARS

In the early 1990s, several previously marginalized younger artists achieved fame by producing narrative images deliberately intended to disrupt, provoke, and offend viewers. In the United States, Andres Serrano defamed an image of the Christian crucifix while Robert Mapplethorpe confronted audiences with openly gay sexuality. In the United Kingdom, Damien Hirst defiled the mortal remains of domestic animals while Chris Ofili created a racially and culturally hybrid Christian Madonna. The resulting social and political backlash triggered the Culture Wars.

SERRANO.   In 1987, Andres Serrano (b. 1950) created *Piss Christ* (see page 1120). Like other artists of the time, Serrano's art explores social taboos in deliberately confrontational and offensive ways. His art dances between the luxuriously beautiful and the abject: His photographs of the homeless, Klansmen, suicides, and murder victims have proven so difficult for some viewers that they have even been vandalized. *Piss Christ* is an almost 2-foot-high, brilliantly colored Cibachrome print of a Christian crucifix which the artist framed in a Plexiglas box filled with his own urine.

Serrano, who was raised a strict Catholic, has argued that this image is about confronting the physicality of the death of the body of Christ, sometimes too easily forgotten, and that it critiques the commercialization of Christ's image in the media, which is why it is also so provocative and offensive to others.

HIRST.   In London in the 1980s, a group of Young British Artists (YBAs) banded together to exhibit their work, led informally by Damien Hirst (b. 1965). In 1995, the Walker Art Center in Minneapolis mounted an exhibition entitled "Brilliant" featuring 22 British artists, many of whom used nontraditional materials and images in their art, had working-class backgrounds or sympathies, or had an adversarial relationship with mainstream society. Two years later, the London Royal Academy featured many of the same artists in "Sensation," an exhibition of art from the Charles Saatchi Collection, which consolidated the reputation of many YBAs. When the show traveled to the Brooklyn Museum in 1999, however, it was considered so offensive that the mayor of New York threatened to close the museum if it was not removed.

Damien Hirst is one of the most outrageous of the original YBAs and his most outrageous work of art, *For the Love of God* (2007), is a diamond-encrusted human skull with an asking price of $100m. His work is about the physical reality of death and the impossibility of imagining your own death; he frequently uses dead animals in his work. Hirst's art, although it is increasingly considered

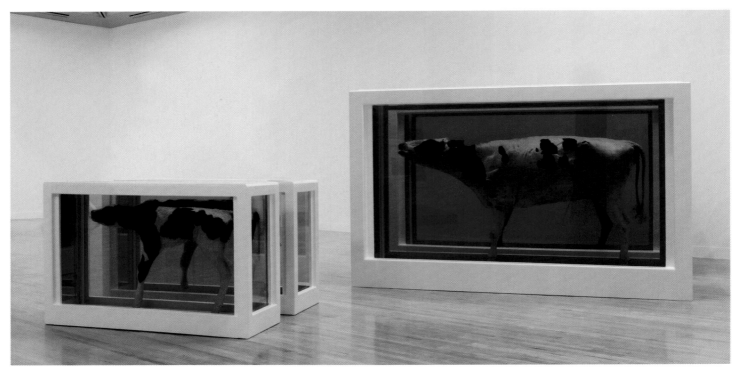

32–44 • Damien Hirst MOTHER AND CHILD DIVIDED
1993. Steel, GRP, composites, glass, silicone, cow, calf, and formaldehyde solution, two tanks at 74⅞ × 126⅞ × 43″
(190 × 322 × 109 cm), two tanks at 40⅛ × 66½ × 24⅝″ (102.5 × 169 × 62.5 cm). Tate Gallery, London.

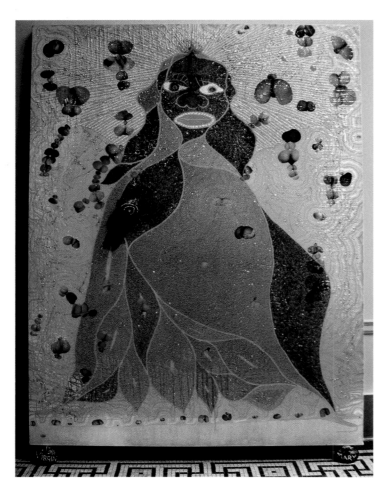

serious and even thoughtful and profound, has also, unsurprisingly, attracted considerable criticism. In **MOTHER AND CHILD DIVIDED (FIG. 32–44)**, the bodies of a cow and her calf are bisected vertically and longitudinally and displayed floating in museum vitrines (glass display cases) filled with formaldehyde. This sculpture resembles the kind of display that you might see in a natural history museum—but with some significant differences. The vitrines are arranged so that the viewer is able not only to walk around them but also between them and thus between the two halves of each cow. On the outside, these animals seem to retain an amazingly lifelike look (even their eyelashes and individual hairs are visible) as they float in the formaldehyde, but once we see the cleavages in their bones, muscles, organs, and flesh on the inside, the actuality of their death overwhelms us. When you also consider that British cattle were being slaughtered daily in an attempt to stop the spread of the terrifying BSE (Mad Cow Disease) in the 1990s, *Mother and Child Divided* creates a feeling of being caught between life and death, between mother and child, and between scientific presentation and, as in Serrano's work, a set of barely suppressed and disturbingly powerful emotions.

32–45 • Chris Ofili THE HOLY VIRGIN MARY
1996. Paper collage, oil paint, glitter, polyester resin, map pins, and elephant dung on linen, 7′11″ × 5′11⅝6″ (2.44 × 1.83 m). Saatchi Gallery, London.

OFILI. The art of the Nigerian-British artist Chris Ofili (b. 1968) provided the focal point for criticism of the 1999 "Sensation" exhibition at the Brooklyn Museum. Ofili exhibited **THE HOLY VIRGIN MARY (FIG. 32–45)**, a glittering painting of a stylized African Madonna which includes parts made from elephant dung and small found photographs of women's buttocks. Ofili, who spent a year in Zimbabwe studying the use of materials in art, explained that in many African nations there is a tradition of using found or salvaged objects and materials in both popular and high art. Ofili's painting is a contemporary bicultural reinvention of the Western Madonna tradition. It employs elephant dung to reinforce this black Madonna's connection to the art and religion of Zimbabwe and to represent her fertility. Then-mayor of New York Rudolph Giuliani and his allies, however, considered the picture so shocking and sacrilegious that they wanted it removed immediately or the exhibition closed.

ACTIVIST ART

The Culture Wars were fueled by a significant increase in Activist art in the 1990s. AIDS decimated the younger art scene in New York's East Village and triggered a global health crisis by mid-decade. Increasingly, anger over the agony of those dying from, and losing friends and lovers to, AIDS, combined with government inaction, spilled over into art. Thus the 1990s opened with angry art about the body, AIDS, and identity, as well as with art clamoring for acknowledgment of the discrimination faced by people of different races, ethnicities, classes, and sexual orientations. The Culture Wars were, in many ways, about artists searching for a place in the world when so many were fading from it.

GONZALEZ-TORRES. In the mid-1980s, the spread of the human immunodeficiency virus (HIV), the underlying cause of AIDS, had begun to reap its deadly harvest within the gay community.

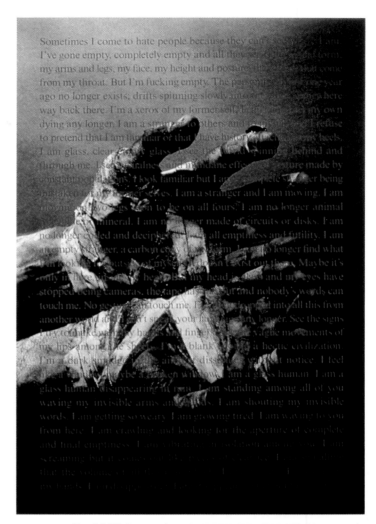

32–47 • David Wojnarowicz UNTITLED (HANDS)
1992. Silver print with silkscreened text, 38 × 26″ (96.5 × 66.0 cm).
Courtesy of the estate of David Wojnarowicz and PPOW Gallery, New York

Felix Gonzalez-Torres (1957–1996) created **UNTITLED (LOVERBOY) (FIG. 32–46)** in 1990 as his lover was dying from AIDS. The piece is deceptively simple: The artist placed a stack of pale blue paper on the gallery floor and invited visitors to take a sheet as they walked by. As each day of the exhibition passed, the stack of paper gradually diminished. The pale blue sheets slowly peeling away were a touching allegory of the slowly disappearing body and mind of Gonzalez-Torres's lover. The artist said: "I wanted to make something that would disappear completely." There is a poignant directness to this work. Gonzalez-Torres himself died of AIDS in 1996.

WOJNAROWICZ. David Wojnarowicz (1955–1992) railed against death before he too died from AIDS in 1992. In 1987, Wojnarowicz's lover Peter Hujar died from AIDS and the artist himself was diagnosed as HIV-positive. In response, he began to make forcefully aggressive art about the fear and confusion of watching a loved one die while facing one's own death. In **UNTITLED (HANDS) (FIG. 32–47)**, Wojnarowicz photographed, in black and white, two bandaged hands outstretched as if in a begging gesture.

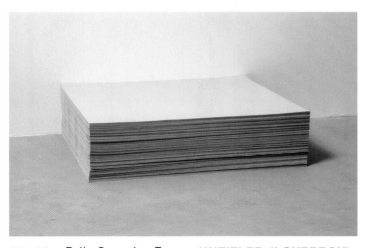

32–46 • Felix Gonzalez-Torres UNTITLED (LOVERBOY)
1990. Blue paper, endless copies, 7½ (at ideal height) × 29 × 23″
(19.1 × 73.7 × 58.4 cm). Installation view of inaugural solo exhibition, "Felix Gonzalez-Torres," at Andrea Rosen Gallery, New York, 1990.
ARG# GF1990-3

Superimposed is a text in angry red type taken from Wojnarowicz's book *Memories That Smell Like Gasoline*, in which he describes how he is hollowing out from the inside and becoming invisible as he dies. Parts of Wojnarowicz's book were reprinted in the catalog of an exhibition, "Witnesses Against Our Vanishing," which featured art by and about artists with AIDS and which became a flash point in the Culture Wars.

SMITH. In sculpture of the early 1990s, the physicality of the human body reasserted itself as a site for the discourse on AIDS. The sculptor Kiki Smith (b. 1954), who lost a sister to AIDS, explores the body, bodily functions, and the loss of physical control that the dying experience in works such as the 1990 **UNTITLED** (FIG. 32–48). This disturbing sculpture shows two life-size naked figures hanging passively, but not quite lifelessly, side by side a few inches above the ground. The figures, a woman and a man, are made from flesh-colored painted beeswax. The woman has milk dripping from her breasts and the man has semen dripping down his leg as if both have lost control of bodily functions that were once a source of vitality and pleasure. The figures evoke a profound sense of loss. Smith has written that our society abhors the reality of bodily functions, so we strive to conceal and control them, making our loss of control as death nears humiliating and frightening. This sculpture asks us to consider bodily control—both our own sense of control and the control that others exert on our body as we die—and suggests that relinquishing it may be as liberating as it is devastating.

WODICZKO. Some artists took their art beyond the gallery, not only advocating social change but working to make a tangible difference in society. In the late 1980s, Krzysztof Wodiczko (b. 1943) created **THE HOMELESS PROJECT VEHICLE** (FIG. 32–49), designed in collaboration with the homeless in New York as "an instrument for survival for urban nomads." Wodiczko wanted to draw attention to the problem of homelessness in New York, one of the richest cities in the richest country in the world. But he did not want simply to illustrate homelessness or evoke pity. Rather, he wanted to dramatize homelessness by making it visible while at the same time actually helping the homeless. *The Homeless Project Vehicle* is a modified and "upgraded" version of the shopping cart that so many homeless people use to carry around their worldly possessions. Wodiczko designed the cart with a waterproof and

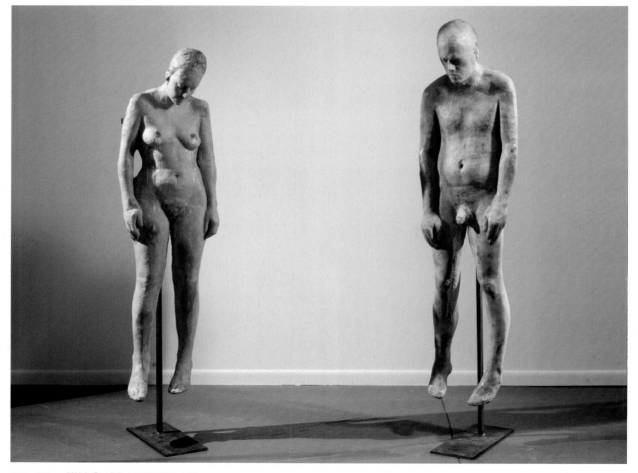

32-48 • Kiki Smith UNTITLED
1990. Beeswax with microcrystalline wax figures on metal stands, female figure installed height 6'1½" (1.87 m), male figure 6'4¹⁵⁄₁₆" (1.95 m). Whitney Museum of American Art, New York.

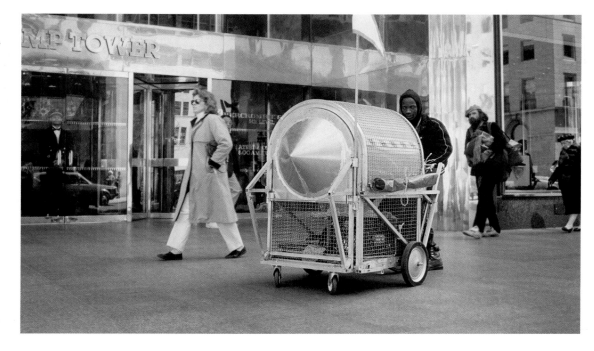

32-49 • Krzysztof Wodiczko **THE HOMELESS PROJECT VEHICLE** 1988–1989.

relatively safe sleeping pod, a series of baskets underneath in which to store belongings, and a brightly colored flag to indicate approach. The homeless who were lucky enough to get a vehicle were pleased with the way it worked, but the New York city authorities felt that the carts made the homeless too visible and they disappeared quickly.

WHITEREAD. The British sculptor Rachel Whiteread (b. 1963) made her reputation as a YBA by casting the inverse of everyday objects such as a bathtub or worn mattress to reveal the ghostliness of their absence. In 1993, however, she also drew attention to the invisibility of the urban poor with her largest and most controversial work, **HOUSE (FIG. 32–50)**. For this project, Whiteread cast the inner space of an entire three-story terraced house in concrete. The house was one of a row in London's East End slated for demolition by developers, who effectively erased the last vestiges of a community that had pulled together so heroically during the Blitz in World War II. *House* is about how memories are contained in places and times,

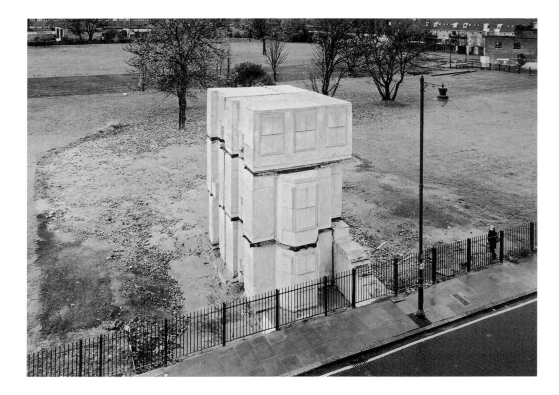

32-50 • Rachel Whiteread **HOUSE**
1993. Sprayed concrete. Corner of Grove and Roman roads, London. Destroyed 1994. Commissioned by Artangel Trust and Beck's, London. Received the Turner Prize, Tate Britain, London

Controversies Over Public Funding for the Arts

Should public money help pay for art that some taxpayers believe to be offensive and indecent? This question started a political battle in 1989–1990 after controversial works of art by Robert Mapplethorpe (1946–1989) and Andres Serrano (b. 1950) went on public display in exhibitions funded in part by the National Endowment for the Arts (NEA), an agency of the Federal government. The ensuing debate pitted artists and museum administrators against political and religious figures. This battle over artists' rights and responsibilities is now referred to as the "Culture Wars."

Serrano's PISS CHRIST was at the center of the debate. Serrano did not use public money directly to create this work, but the Southeastern Center for Contemporary Art (SECCA), which exhibited *Piss Christ* in a group exhibition, was a recipient of NEA funds. The Reverend Donald Wildmon, leader of the American Family Association, described *Piss Christ* as "hate-filled, bigoted, anti-Christian, and obscene," and told his many followers to flood Congress and the NEA with letters protesting the misuse of public funds. This resulted in several high-profile conservative Republican politicians joining his attack.

At the same time, the traveling exhibition "The Perfect Moment," a retrospective of the work of photographer Mapplethorpe, who had recently died from AIDS, was canceled by the Corcoran Gallery of Art in Washington, D.C., for fear that the show's content might cause offense. "The Perfect Moment" had been organized by the Institute of Contemporary Art (ICA) in Philadelphia, was NEA-funded, and included several homoerotic and sadomasochistic images. When it was shown in Cincinnati, the museum director was arrested. Additionally, four artists known as the "NEA Four" (Karen Finley, John Fleck, Holly Hughes, and Tim Miller), who made lesbian, gay, or radical feminist art, had their grants rescinded amid a flurry of debate. Congress slashed NEA funding by $45,000: the amount of Serrano's $15,000 SECCA grant, plus the ICA's $30,000 grant for the Mapplethorpe show. The NEA Four sued and won back their grants, but a so-called "obscenity clause" was added to NEA regulations requiring jurors to consider the "general standards of decency and respect for the diverse beliefs and values of the American public" when making awards.

During the next five years, the NEA was largely restructured by the Republican-controlled House of Representatives, some of whose members wanted to eliminate the agency altogether. In 1996, Congress reduced the NEA's budget by 40 percent.

Controversies over public funding continued, however. In 1999, the Brooklyn Museum of Art exhibited "Sensation: Young British Artists from the Saatchi Collection," causing another major controversy over public funding and offensive art. The Brooklyn Museum kept the show open in direct defiance of a threat from Mayor Rudolph Giuliani to eliminate city funding and evict the museum from its city-owned building if it persisted in showing art that he considered "sick" and "disgusting." Giuliani and Catholic leaders took particular offense at Chris Ofili's *The Holy Virgin Mary* (SEE FIG. 32–45). When the Brooklyn Museum of Art still refused to cancel the show, Giuliani withheld the city's monthly maintenance payment to the museum of $497,554 and filed a suit in the state court to revoke its lease. In response, the museum filed for an injunction against Giuliani's actions on the grounds that they violated the First Amendment and the United States District Court for the Eastern District of New York eventually barred Giuliani from punishing or retaliating against the museum in any way for mounting the exhibition. Giuliani had argued that Ofili's art fostered religious intolerance, but the court ruled that the government has "no legitimate interest in protecting any or all religions from views distasteful to them," adding that taxpayers "subsidize all manner of views with which they do not agree" and even those "they abhor."

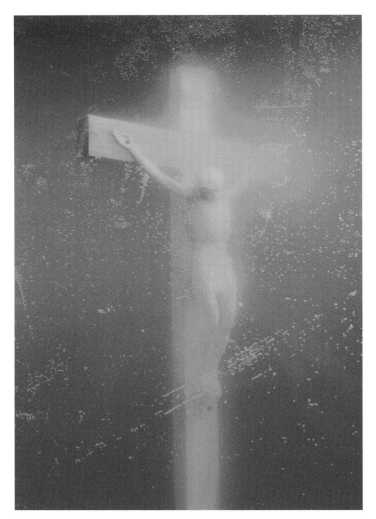

Andres Serrano PISS CHRIST
1989. Cibachrome print mounted on Plexiglas, 23½ × 16″ (59.7 × 40.6 cm).

and how easily they can be destroyed. As the other houses around it were demolished, Whiteread sprayed concrete on the inner walls of her house to make a cast of the space within it. Then she dismantled the house. The white concrete left behind outlined a ghostly trace of the space within the house that had once been someone's home. The publicity surrounding Whiteread's *House* brought to the fore several critical issues in British society, including homelessness, the costs and benefits of urban renewal, and the place of the working class in society. Whiteread's piece demonstrates how a work of visual art can articulate controversial issues in ways that are impossible using other means of communication. Whiteread intended *House* to make a political statement about "the state of housing in England; the ludicrous policy of knocking down homes like this and building badly designed tower blocks which themselves have to be knocked down after 20 years."

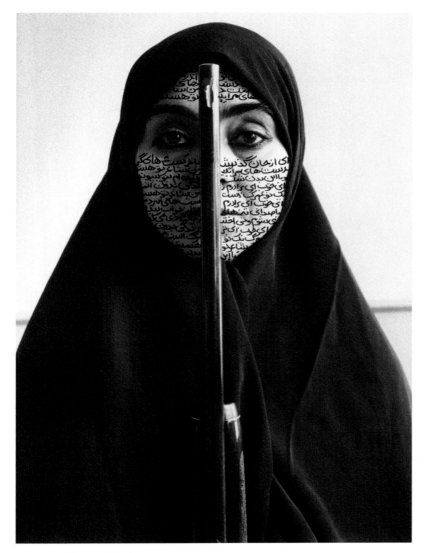

32–51 • Shirin Neshat REBELLIOUS SILENCE
1994. Black-and-white RC print and ink (photo taken by C. Preston), 11 × 14″ (27.9 × 35.6 cm). Barbara Gladstone Gallery, New York.

EXPLORE MORE: Gain insight from a primary source by Shirin Neshat **www.myartslab.com**

POSTCOLONIAL DISCOURSE

With increased migration and the expansion of global communications and economies, questions of personal, political, cultural, and national identity also emerged in the 1990s. Postcolonial artists began to explore issues of contested identity and the identity struggle of postcolonial peoples, and to investigate the dissonance produced by transnational (mis)communication between colonizers and the postcolonized. Many of these artists, such as Shirin Neshat and Rasheed Araeen, speak with unfamiliar but forthright and significant new artistic voices.

NESHAT. In **REBELLIOUS SILENCE (FIG. 32–51)** from her 1994 "Women of Allah" series of photographs, Shirin Neshat (b. 1957) explores how Iranian women are stereotyped by the West. Her photographs and videos assert that Islamic women's identities are more varied and complex than is frequently perceived. Each of Neshat's "Women of Allah" photographs portrays both a part of an Iranian woman's body, such as her hands or her feet, overwritten with Farsi text and with a weapon. In *Rebellious Silence*, the woman wears the traditional chador but her face is visible, written over with calligraphy and with a rifle barrel bisecting it vertically. The calligraphy and rifle barrel seem to protect her from the viewer, but they also create a sense of incomprehensibility or foreignness that prompts us to try to categorize her. Likewise, although the woman wears a chador, she looks directly and defiantly out of the photograph at us, meeting our gaze and returning it. She challenges us to acknowledge her as an individual, in this case a strong and beautiful woman; but the image simultaneously and paradoxically prompts us to see her as a stereotypical Iranian woman in a chador more than as an individual. Neshat's photograph asks us to confront our prejudices while also raising questions about women's power and feminism in contemporary Iran.

ARAEEN. Rasheed Araeen (b. 1935) is from Pakistan and lives in London. He founded the journal *Black Phoenix* in 1978, which in 1989 became *Third Text*, a leading journal on postcolonial art, culture, and ethnicity. In 1985–1986, Araeen made **GREEN PAINTING IV (FIG. 32–52)**, a work comprised of nine equal-sized panels. The five central panels contain photographs of the head of a young bull prepared for ritual sacrifice with garlands around its neck and framed by Urdu text. The other four panels are painted a flat green—the primary color in the Pakistani flag, an important color in Islam, and a color that Araeen associates with youthful rawness and flexibility, like a green twig. Yet the central panels also appear to form a crucifix. Araeen has said that his pictures are not just superimpositions of Western and Pakistani cultures, but are images that speak about "cutting and

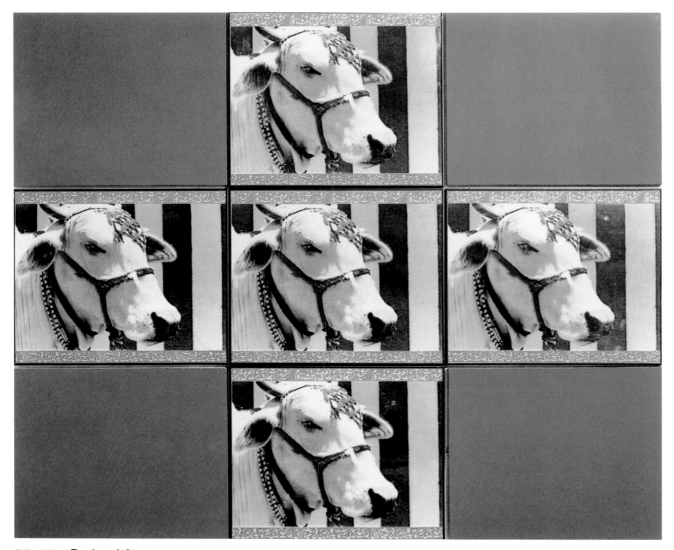

32-52 • Rasheed Araeen GREEN PAINTING IV
1985–1986. Five color photographs with Urdu text and acrylic on four plywood panels, 5′9″ × 6′10″ (1.75 × 2.08 m). Collection of the artist.

rupturing," that investigate postcolonial dissonance and miscommunication. He argues that when someone British or American sees the cross in his art, for instance, they almost invariably read Pakistani culture through a Christian lens, thereby distorting, misinterpreting, and stereotyping the "other." Araeen's art demands a more nuanced understanding of cultures on their own terms and according to their own visual languages.

SEARLE. Berni Searle (b. 1964) explores her South African identity in the wake of Apartheid in her art. In the **COLOR ME** series **(FIG. 32–53)**, she photographs her head and torso covered in powdered pigment that changes her skin color from red to yellow to brown to white. Searle asks us to see that race and identity are not as simple as skin pigmentation, and that superficial or skin-deep characteristics do not define a person. The fragility and impermanence of the pigmentation also underscore the instability of stereotypes and the complexity of real identity.

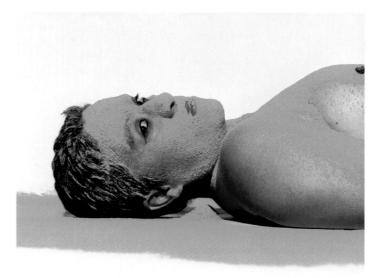

32-53 • Berni Searle
UNTITLED FROM COLOR ME SERIES
1998. Michael Stevenson Gallery, Cape Town.

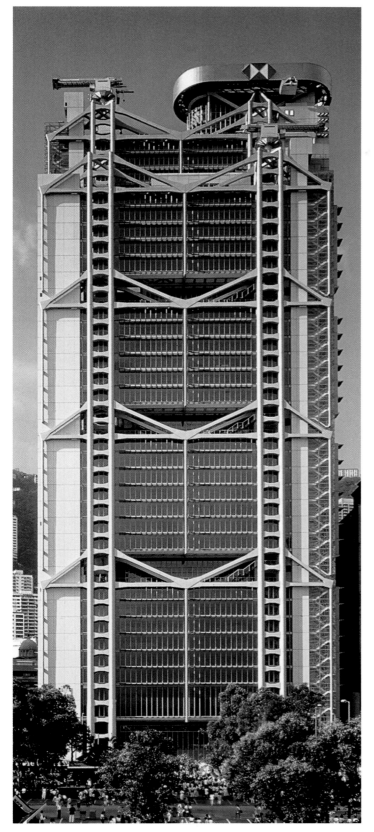

32-54 • Norman Foster HONG KONG & SHANGHAI BANK
Hong Kong. 1986.

SEE MORE: View a simulation about the Hong Kong & Shanghai Bank **www.myartslab.com**

HIGH TECH AND DECONSTRUCTIVIST ARCHITECTURE

Architecture and architectural practice was transformed in the 1980s and 1990s by computer-aided design (CAD) programs with 3-D graphics. These programs enabled architects to design structures virtually, to calculate engineering stresses faster and more precisely, to experiment with new ways to use advanced building technologies and materials, and to imagine new ways of composing a building's mass.

HIGH TECH ARCHITECTURE. High Tech architects broke out of the restrictive shape of the Modernist "glass box" (SEE FIG. 32–25) to experiment with dramatically designed engineering marvels. These buildings are characterized by a spectacular use of new technologies, materials, equipment, and components, and frequently by their visible display of service systems such as heating and power.

The **HONG KONG & SHANGHAI BANK (FIG. 32–54)** by the British architect Norman Foster (b. 1935) is among the most spectacular examples of High Tech architecture. Foster was invited to spare no expense in designing this futuristic 47-story skyscraper. The loadbearing steel skeleton, composed of giant masts and girders, is on the exterior. The individual stories hang from it, making possible the uninterrupted rows of windows that fill the building with natural light. In addition, the banking hall in the lower part of the building has a ten-story atrium space that is flooded with daylight refracted into it by motorized "sunscoops" at the top of the structure that are programmed to track the sun's rays and channel them into the building. The sole concession Foster makes to tradition in this design is his placement of two bronze lions flanking the public entrance. These were taken from the bank's previous headquarters; touching the lions before entering the bank is believed to bring good luck.

DECONSTRUCTIVIST ARCHITECTURE. Deconstructivist architecture, a more theory-based architecture than High Tech, emerged in the early 1990s. Deconstructivist architects deliberately disturb traditional architectural assumptions about harmony, unity, and stability to create "decentered," skewed, and distorted designs. Several Deconstructivist architects admire the aesthetic of Russian Suprematists and Constructivists (SEE FIGS. 31–26, 31–46), which they frequently combine with the principles of Deconstruction as developed by the French philosopher Jacques Derrida (1930–2004). Derridean Deconstruction asserts that no written text possesses a single, intrinsic meaning. For Derrida, meaning is always "intertextual," thus a product of one text's relationship to other texts: It is always "decentered," "dispersed," or "diffused" through an infinite web of "signs," which themselves have unstable meanings. Deconstructivist architecture is likewise intertextual, in that it plays with meaning by mixing diverse architectural features, forms, and contexts, and is decentered in its diffusion as well as in its perceived instability of both meaning and form.

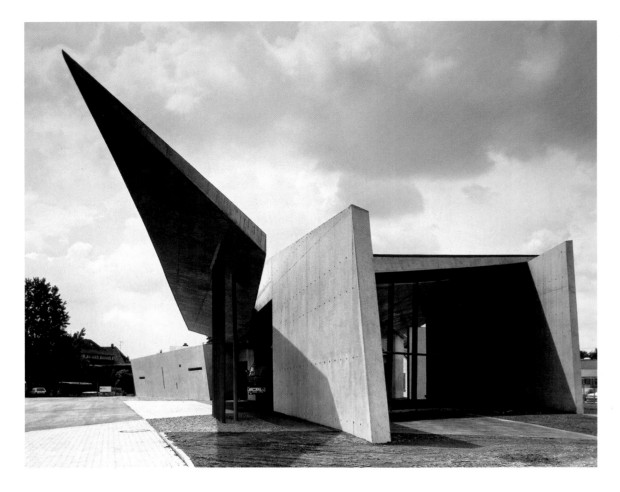

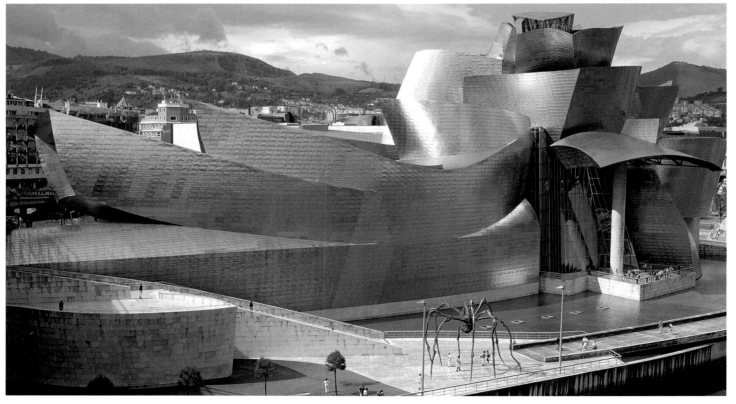

32–56 • Frank O. Gehry **GUGGENHEIM MUSEUM**
Bilbao, Spain. 1993–1997.

A good example of Deconstructivist architecture is the **VITRA FIRE STATION** in Weil-am-Rhein, Germany **(FIG. 32–55)** by the Baghdad-born architect Zaha Hadid (b. 1950), who studied in London and established her practice there in 1979. Formally influenced by the paintings of Kasimir Malevich (SEE FIG. 31–25), the Vitra Fire Station features reinforced concrete walls that lean into one another, meet at unexpected angles, and jut out dramatically into space, denying a sense of visual unity but creating a feeling of immediacy, speed, and dynamism appropriate to the building's function.

The Toronto-born, California-based Frank O. Gehry (b. 1929) also creates unstable and Deconstructivist building masses and curved winglike shapes that extend far beyond the building's mass. One of his most spectacular designs is the **GUGGENHEIM MUSEUM** in Bilbao, Spain **(FIG. 32–56)**. In the 1990s, art-museum designs became more and more spectacular as the museum increasingly came to define the visual landscape of cities. Gehry developed this asymmetrical design using a CATIA CAD program that enabled him to create a powerfully organic, sculptural structure. The complex steel skeleton is covered by a thin skin of silvery titanium that shimmers gold or silver depending on the time of day and the weather conditions. From the north the building resembles a living organism, while from other angles it looks like a giant ship, referencing the industry on which Bilbao has traditionally depended and thereby identifying the museum with the city. Despite the sculptural beauty of the museum, however, the interior is a notoriously difficult space in which to display art.

VIDEO AND FILM

In the last decades of the twentieth century, the rapid development and increasingly widespread availability of hand-held video cameras created a new medium for artists. Video artists rejected traditional forms and meanings to make art that was deliberately nonprecious, often using the video image to address the place and prevalence of television in our culture. Today Video art is even more prevalent because of the explosion in digital and visual imagery. In fact, most contemporary Video art is digitally produced, while innovations in projecting video and DVD images on large screens (or on any surface) have transformed how and where Video art is projected and to a certain extent its subject.

PAIK. One of the pioneers of Video art was the Korean-born Nam June Paik (1931–2006), who made experimental music in the late 1950s and early 1960s under the influence of John Cage. He began working with modified television sets in 1963, and began making Video art in 1965, the same year that Sony released the first portable video camera. Paik predicted that just "as collage technique replaced oil paint, the cathode ray [television] tube will replace the canvas." Later, he worked with live, recorded, and computer-generated images displayed on video monitors of varying sizes, which he often combined into works of art such as **ELECTRONIC SUPERHIGHWAY: CONTINENTAL U.S. (FIG. 32–57)**, a site-specific sculpture created for the Holly Solomon Gallery in New York. This featured a neon outline map of the United States set against a wall of dozens of computer-controlled video monitors

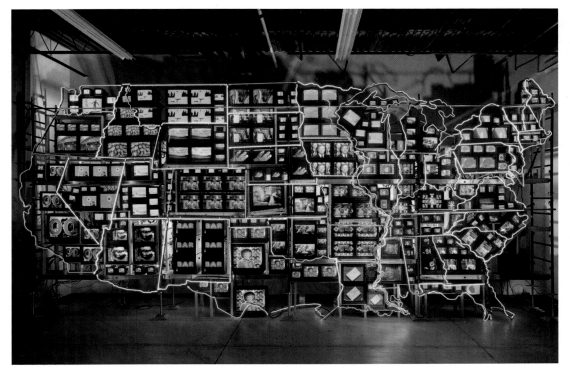

32-57 • Nam June Paik ELECTRONIC SUPERHIGHWAY: CONTINENTAL U.S.
1995. Forty-seven-channel closed-circuit video installation with 313 monitors, neon, steel structure, color, and sound, approx. 15 × 32 × 4′ (4.57 × 9.75 × 1.2 m). Courtesy Holly Solomon Gallery, New York.

displaying rapidly changing soundtracked images that reflected each state's culture and history. The work addresses both the prevalence and power of the mixed messages transmitted by television in our society. The monitor for New York State projected a closed-circuit live video feed of gallery visitors, who were thus transformed from passive spectators into active participants in the piece as the monitor constructed their media identity in front of them as they watched.

Viola. In 1996, the California video artist Bill Viola (b. 1951) created **THE CROSSING** (FIG. 32–58) which consists of a double projection of two brilliantly colored videos on opposite sides of a 16-foot screen. On one side, Viola projects a video loop of a silhouette of a man who slowly emerges from the background to fill the entire screen. As he does this, a drop of water starts to fall, growing in size as the man moves forward slowly until at last a deluge washes him away. The soundtrack meanwhile goes from a small dripping noise to a torrential roar. On the reverse screen, a similar scenario unfolds, except that this time the man appears in the background with tiny flames licking at his feet that grow into a wild conflagration that finally engulfs him. This side also has a soundtrack of the sound of the fire growing in intensity. But Viola's piece is about the way that vision informs perception, and there is in fact only one soundtrack—we simply perceive it differently according to whatever image we are watching. This video is profoundly sensory but also meditative; its elemental symbolism is informed by Viola's spirituality and intense study of world religions.

GLOBALISM: INTO THE NEW MILLENNIUM

In the last decade, the growth in international art exhibitions and art fairs has created new opportunities for artists, dealers, and collectors to meet and network in ways that, until quite recently, would have been considered impossible, or unproductive. Until recently the only truly international fora for new art were the Venice Biennale (established in 1903 and held every two years) and Documenta, in Kassel, West Germany (established in 1955 and held roughly every five years). Today there are at least 30 international biennial exhibitions around the world, as well as many more vast international art fairs: Art Basel in Switzerland, Art Basel Miami in Miami Beach, the Frieze Art Fair in London, the Armory Show in New York, and the Fiore Internationale d'Art Contemporain (FIAC) in Paris, to mention just a few. Finally, the Internet has allowed visual access to art globally. We can find information on practically any exhibited art, and much that is not exhibited, on

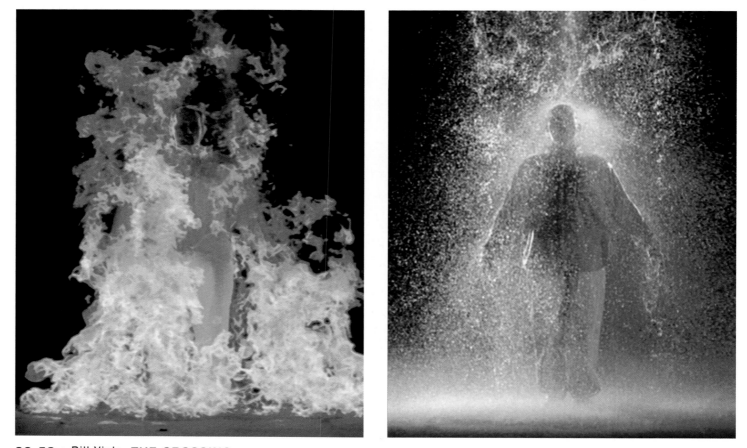

32-58 • Bill Viola THE CROSSING
1996. Video/sound installation with two channels of color video projection onto screens 16′ (4.88 m) high. Private collection.

our laptops. This new globalism has forced artists to question not just how their own identities but also how those of others are formed, and to realize that neither identity nor art is as simple or as univalent as it might have seemed as recently as in the 1990s.

Art in the new millennium seems to be heading in several directions simultaneously, constantly shifting and recalibrating new perspectives and concerns as part of an increasingly complicated global discourse. The art of our own times may be the most difficult to classify and analyze, but it has increasingly focused on global issues, raising questions about national identities, ethnic or racial identities, colonial and postcolonial identities, human rights, global economic, political, and natural environments, the widening divide between the rich and poor nations of the world, and technological change in every aspect of our lives. Today's artists are actively engaged in society at all levels and their art frequently reflects their ambition to be agents of change in troubling and unstable times.

ART AND TECHNOLOGY

STUDIO CRAFTS. Dale Chihuly (b. 1941) has been producing major public sculptures in glass for 30 years, but his creations are as fresh today as they were in 1975. Chihuly's sculptures are both technologically innovative and experimental. **THE SUN (FIG. 32–59)**, a multi-part blown-glass sculpture using the latest glass-making techniques, shows Chihuly's profound interest in natural forms and global energies. The sun bursts forth in a multitude of twisting, wriggling, spiraling forms as if the unremittingly intense light of Phoenix has taken physical shape and come to life. Brilliantly liquid, visually thrilling, and accessible, Chihuly's sculptures suggest a deeper connection with nature, inviting contemplation, meditation, and an awareness of global environmentalism.

DIGITAL PHOTOGRAPHY SINCE 2000. Photography has always been a malleable and mutable medium. Even in the nineteenth century photographs were manipulated to create fictional imagery out of what appeared to be a factual visual record. It is often difficult and time-consuming to manipulate a chemical-mechanical process, however, and it was only with the development of digital technology that manipulation became a fast, easy, and standard way to create photographic images.

The Canadian artist Jeff Wall (b. 1946) uses multiple digital photographs and elaborate stage sets to create large complex photographic narratives that he considers analogous to the history paintings of the nineteenth century, and which he exhibits as gloriously colored transparencies mounted in light boxes—the format frequently used in modern advertising in public places.

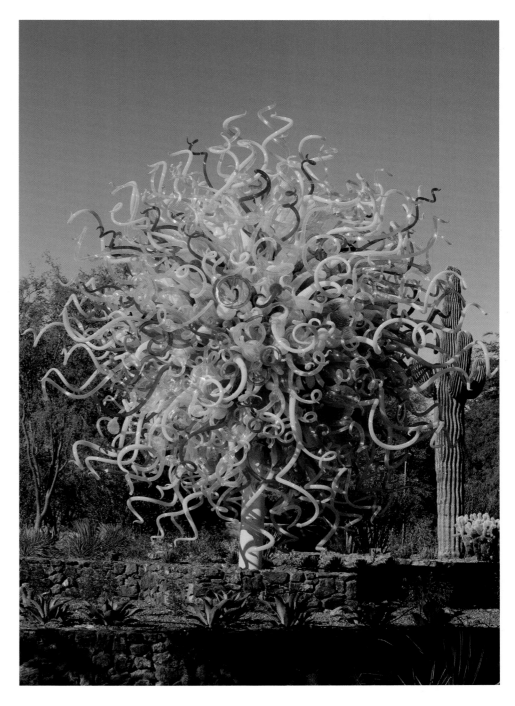

32-59 • Dale Chihuly THE SUN
2008. Desert Botanical Garden, Phoenix, Arizona. Installed November 22, 2008– May 31, 2009.

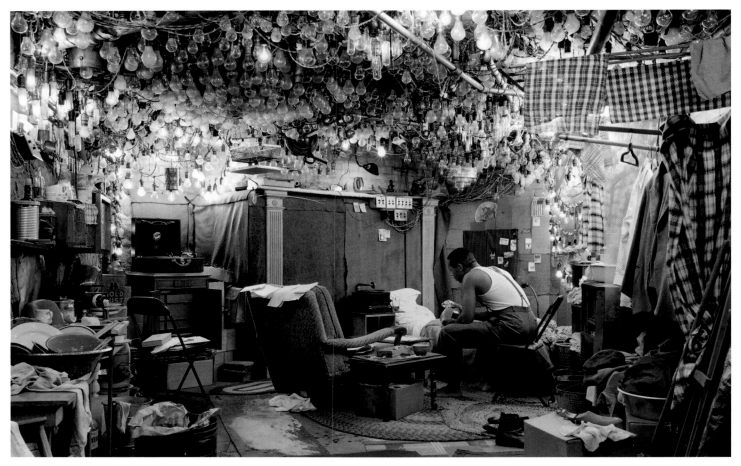

32-60 • Jeff Wall AFTER "INVISIBLE MAN" BY RALPH ELLISON, THE PREFACE
1999–2001. Transparency in lightbox, 68½ × 98⅝″ (174 × 250.5 cm).

EXPLORE MORE: Gain insight from a primary source related to Jeff Wall **www.myartslab.com**

Wall creates his photographs like a movie director, carefully designing the sets and posing his actors. He takes multiple photographs that he then combines digitally to create one final transparency. **AFTER "INVISIBLE MAN" BY RALPH ELLISON, THE PREFACE (FIG. 32–60)** is an elaborate composition for which Wall spent 18 months designing and constructing the sets and three weeks actually taking photographs. The image illustrates a passage from Ralph Ellison's 1951 novel about an African-American man's search for fulfillment that ends in disillusionment and retreat. Wall shows us the cellar room, "warm and full of light," to which Ellison's character retreats and which is heated and lit by 1,369 light bulbs powered by electricity stolen from the power company. For Ellison, these lights seem to illuminate the sad truth of the character's existence.

INSTALLATION ART. Tony Oursler's 2009 exhibition at Metro Pictures raises issues about how the average American constructs his or her identity in the digital age. The installation (art installed in a specific space for which it was made) included several oversized sculptural versions of the things that we cannot seem to live without today: an enormous cell phone entitled **MULTIPLEXED**

(FIG. 32–61), a giant five-dollar bill, a "forest of smoldering cigarettes," an arrangement of oversized self-help books, and a Genie bottle containing a video of the artist himself. Oursler's exhibition is a clever updating of Pop art's critique of consumer society, making sly references to Warhol, Oldenburg, and even Lichtenstein (SEE FIGS. 32–10, 32–11, 32–12). Objects come to life by means of superimposed animated video projections that make the cigarettes seem to burn, "Abe" Lincoln to pull faces, Oursler himself to try to escape his bottle, and the cell phone (in this illustration) to spew forth, as the press release states, "disjointed snippets of conversations." Oursler asks us to consider how the world of technology, constantly bombarding us with images, creates an intense visual overload and frames our concept of identity.

ART AND IDENTITIES

The artists featured in this final section investigate their individual and group identities—a growing and ever-more complex concern in the new millennium—in a wide range of ways, breaking down traditional distinctions between medium and message in the process, and dissolving boundaries to create art that is as interesting, exciting, difficult, and confusing as the world itself is today.

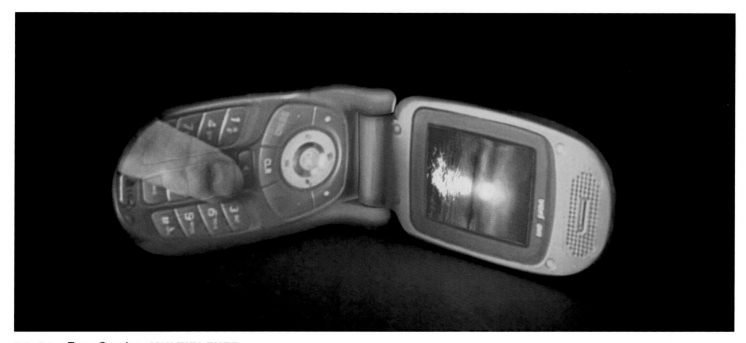

32-61 • Tony Oursler MULTIPLEXED
2008. Fiberglass, 37 × 33 × 17″ (94 × 83.8 × 43.2 cm).
MetroPicture (MP 574)

BARNEY. Between 1994 and 2002, Matthew Barney (b. 1967) created a now legendary series of films entitled *The Cremaster Cycle* in which he developed an arcane sexual mythology. The cycle is premised on the concept of gender mutability, questioning gender assignation and roles throughout. The cremaster muscle for which the series is named controls the ascent and descent of the testes, usually in response to changes in temperature but also in response to fear or sexual arousal, and it also determines sexual differentiation in the human embryo. Barney uses a diagrammatic representation of the cremaster muscle as his visual emblem throughout the series.

Each film has its own complex narrative and catalog of multilayered symbols. *Cremaster 3* (2002) describes the construction of the Chrysler Building in New York and features Richard Serra (SEE FIG. 32–42) as the architect. A segment of the film is set in the Guggenheim Museum's rotunda (SEE FIG. 32–27). Barney, playing Serra's apprentice and dressed in a peach-colored kilt and gagged, must accomplish a series of tasks to assert his supremacy over Serra. As in a video game, Barney scales the walls of the Guggenheim rotunda to complete a task on each level before gaining enlightenment. Along the way he is challenged by a line of Rockettes dressed as Masonic lambs, by warring punk-rock bands, by a leopard woman (played by Aimee Mullins), and finally by Serra. The settings and costumes are lavish, and the epic plot is baroquely interconnected. In **MAHABYN (FIG. 32–62)**, Barney and the leopard woman transform into Masons—they are shown here in modified Masonic costume.

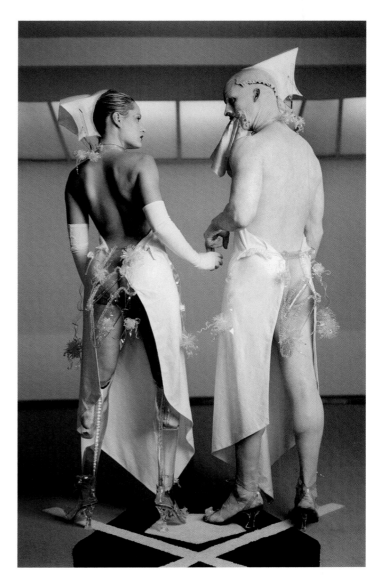

32-62 • Matthew Barney CREMASTER 3: MAHABYN
2002. 46½ × 54 × 1½″ (118 × 137 × 3.8 cm). Guggenheim Museum, New York.

The entire filmic cycle addresses the crisis of identity experienced by white, middle-class heterosexual male artists in America in an era seemingly dominated by identity politics.

BEECROFT. Vanessa Beecroft also set her **VB35** (FIG. 32–63) in the Guggenheim Museum's rotunda and also uses performance to examine gender roles, although she explores perceptions of the female body and femininity. Unlike Barney, she does not appear in her work. Many of Beecroft's performances refer obliquely to her own battle with anorexia. The artist numbers her performances—*vb35* is her 35th piece—and in it she questions both the nature of today's distorted concept of feminine beauty and voyeuristic looking. For the performance, Beecroft hired 15 professional fashion models, each of whom was fashionably thin, tall, and white. The models were directed to stand in a loose group, facing forward. Ten wore high heels and designer bikinis, while five wore nothing but high heels. They stood staring blankly ahead while the audience was permitted to observe them from the foyer or the ramp of the museum, thus acquiescing in the gaze that objectified them. The event was "invitation only" so the atmosphere was charged with

exclusivity, but Beecroft complicated this piece by heightening the tension in two ways: First, the group of professional models whose business it is to be looked at commanded the museum; and second, the audience was instructed to behave in very precise ways—they were not allowed to speak to the models, make eye contact with them, or invade their physical or emotional space in any way. This strategy cleverly inverted the normal relationship between looker and looked-at. A sexual charge filled the air, but ironically the models claimed control. Viewers found that they were intimidated and discomforted: They felt as though they had been caught in the act of looking illicitly. As one critic put it: "we found ourselves confronted by the cool authority of the art's nakedness, and we had no role to play … so we drifted and loitered."

GU. Wenda Gu (b. 1955) dedicates his art to bringing people together. Trained in traditional ink painting at China's National Academy of Fine Arts, he emigrated to the United States in 1987 and began an ongoing global project entitled the "United Nations Series" in 1992. Each "monument" in this series is made from human hair collected from barbershops and hair salons worldwide

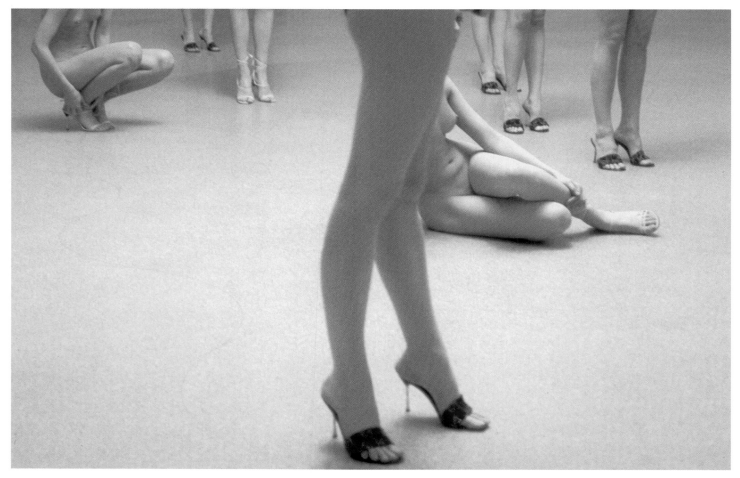

32-63 • Vanessa Beecroft VB35
1998. Performance.

EXPLORE MORE: Gain insight from a primary source by Vanessa Beecroft www.myartslab.com

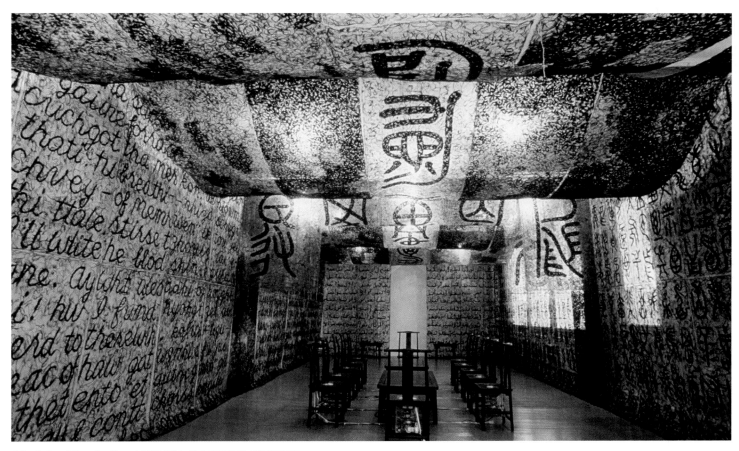

32-64 • Wenda Gu **UNITED NATIONS SERIES: TEMPLE OF HEAVEN**
1998. Installation with screens of human hair, wooden chairs and tables, and video. Commissioned by the Asia Society. Collection of the artist.

and which Gu presses into bricks or weaves into carpets and curtains covered with ideograms of his own invention. **UNITED NATIONS SERIES: TEMPLE OF HEAVEN (FIG. 32–64)** contains hair from many different nations and blended scripts based on Chinese, English, Hindi, and Arabic characters that "evoke the limitations of human knowledge." Gu also creates "national" monuments—examples have been installed in Poland, Israel, and Taiwan, among other places—made from hair collected in, and addressing issues specific to, that particular country. The "transnational" monuments from the "United Nations Series," on the other hand, address more global themes, using hair blended from several different countries to suggest a "brave new racial identity" for the new millennium.

OSPINA. In his series **COLOMBIA LAND (FIG. 32–65)**, the Colombian artist Nadín Ospina (b. 1960) uses Lego figures, blown up in photographs and sculptures to gargantuan size, to caricature stereotypical images of Colombia as a nation of drug lords and violence. *Colombia Land* is a funny but also sinister parody of a Legoland theme park. In this piece, Ospina mimics a typical *National Geographic* cover by placing a Lego bandit with an automatic weapon, bands of ammunition slung across his chest, and

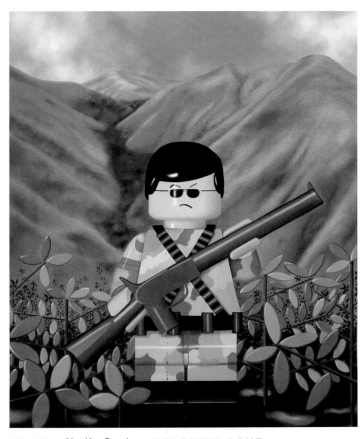

32-65 • Nadín Ospina **COLOMBIA LAND**
2004. Centro Cultural de la Universidad de Salamanca, Bogotá.

dark glasses hiding his eyes, amid a crop of drugs. Such a figure would be threatening were he not transformed into a child's toy. Ospina describes Colombia as "an art and culture hijacked by violence," and his art explores the cultural colonization of Colombia by Western European and American popular culture as well as Colombia's own complicated self-perceptions.

HAMMONS. A socially minded artist strongly committed to working in the public realm, David Hammons (b. 1943) is an outspoken critic of the gallery system in America, lamenting the lack of challenging content and representation of African Americans in exhibitions. He has described the art world as being "like Novocain. It used to wake you up but now it puts you to sleep." Hammons argues that only art that intervenes in and transacts with society is uncontaminated by commerce and still jolts people awake. In **UNTITLED (FIG. 32–66)**, the artist creates a witty but biting satire on the still ambiguous place of African Americans in American society. Hammons originally created this flag in 1990 for the Studio Museum, Harlem, in response to a controversy concerning the flying of the Confederate flag on public buildings in some states. It has since been installed in several other museums, including the Museum of Modern Art in New York in 2000. The colors in Hammons's flag are those of the Pan-African or Universal Negro Improvement Association and African Communities League flag, which was created in 1920 by African Americans to symbolize the "Rights of Negro Peoples of the World." The red stands for the blood that unites all people of African descent and that was spilled in the quest for liberation; the black stands for the symbolic nation of black people; and the green stands for the verdant lands of Africa. The piece makes a poignant and pointed comment about race in America.

SHONIBARE. Yinka Shonibare (b. 1962) is a British-Nigerian artist based in London. His art examines how identity is informed, perceived, and constructed through the twists and turns of colonial history, as well as class, race, and self-perception. **HOW TO BLOW UP TWO HEADS AT ONCE (LADIES) (FIG. 32–67)** is a life-size sculpture of two headless women whose skin color, and thus on a superficial level whose race, is indeterminate. Although the figures have women's bodies, they seem to have masculine hands. They face off against one another in a dueling pose with nineteenth-century flintlock pistols drawn and pointed at each other's absent heads. They wear what appear to be nineteenth-century costumes, but their brightly colored dresses are made of a Dutch wax fabric that is usually associated with West African nations. The complexities of the history and use of the fabric, and the way that Shonibare uses it, give us some idea of the multiple and eliding meanings in this sculpture. This brilliantly colored and patterned fabric, worn by millions of Africans today, originally came from Indonesia, was imported and copied by Dutch colonists in Africa, was manufactured in bulk in cotton mills in Manchester, England, and was then exported to West Africa, where it was copied, modified, transformed, and now possessed by West African cultures. Ironically, Shonibare buys the fabric for his sculptures at London's

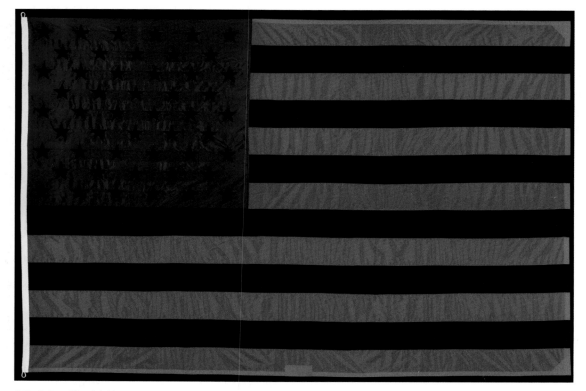

32–66 • David Hammons UNTITLED
2004. Studio Museum, Harlem. Nylon, 6 × 10′ (1.82 × 3 m). Gift of the artist (04.2.19)

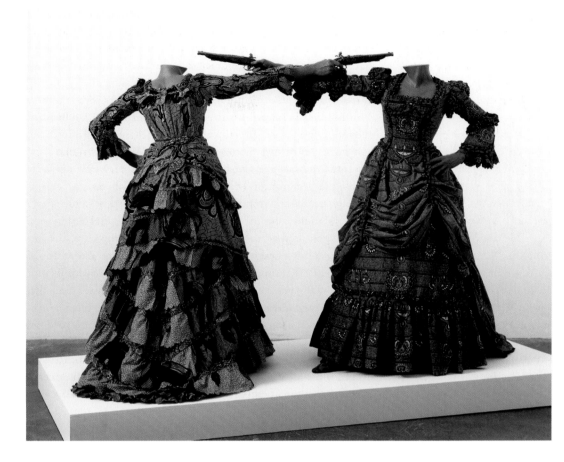

32-67 • Yinka Shonibare, MBE

HOW TO BLOW UP TWO HEADS AT ONCE (LADIES)
2006. Two fiberglass mannequins, two prop guns, Dutch, wax printed cotton textile, shoes, leather riding boots, plinth, 93½ × 63 × 48″ (237 × 160 × 122 cm). Museum purchase with funds provided by Wellesley College Friends of Art, 2007.124.1-2

Brixton market. Shonibare challenges our perceptions about issues of race, postcolonialism, property, ownership, violence, and class. His work, although witty and ironic, is also acerbic as it shows us the tangled web of forces that construct identity.

SIERRA.   Santiago Sierra (b. 1966), a Spanish artist who lives in Mexico City, addresses race, ethnicity, and the capitalist exploitation of the poor in his interventionist artworks. At the 49th Venice Biennale in 2001, Sierra created a very visible commentary on the luxurious indulgence and elitist atmosphere of the exhibition and on the relative invisibility of both poverty and race there. For this piece, Sierra paid 133 non-European men to dye their naturally black hair blond and to make themselves visible around Venice for the duration of the exhibition **(FIG. 32–68)**. The shocking white hair on dark-skinned men made them very visible and placed a group of individuals who normally melt into the background of society front and center, persistently reminding viewers of both their presence and their relative poverty—the only reason their hair was blond was because they needed the money.

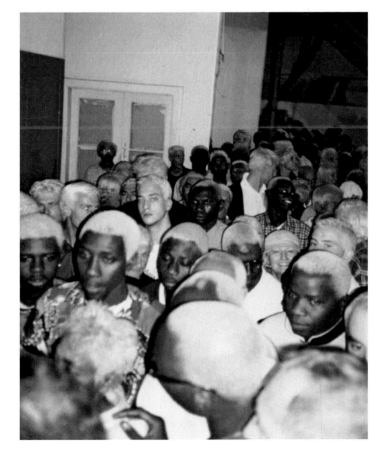

32-68 • Santiago Sierra 133 PEOPLE PAID TO HAVE THEIR HAIR DYED BLOND
2001. 49th Venice Biennale

Sierra paid 133 non-European men to dye their hair blond. In the exhibition, he presented video footage of the dyeing process.

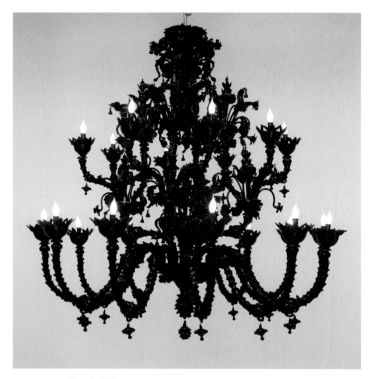

32-69 • Fred Wilson CHANDELIER MORI
2003. United States Pavilion, 50th Venice Biennale.

WILSON. In the 1990s, artists increasingly began to critique the constructed narratives of the traditional museum exhibition. The museum was acknowledged as a place in which curators, who make decisions about what to show and how to arrange works in an exhibition, create history rather than revealing it and, in the process, frequently reveal their own prejudices. Fred Wilson (b. 1954) is best known for *Mining the Museum* (1992), a brilliant interventionist piece in which he inverted and subverted the Baltimore Historical Society's collection. Wilson "mined" the museum's storage area and found that, while the objects on show were mostly about white history, there were numerous objects relating to African-American history in the vaults. He "inserted" many of these into the main museum display, including some horrific objects used to restrain African-American slaves, thereby upsetting and reshaping the story told in the original exhibition.

In 2003, Wilson represented the United States at the Venice Biennale with *Speak of Me As I Am*, a multi-part installation that focused on the history of Africans in Venice. This included several black sculptures made with Murano glass, a kind of glass made in Venice for centuries, set in a black-and-white tiled room with "graffiti" on the walls consisting of excerpts from African-American slave narratives and a video installation of Shakespeare's *Othello* being screened backwards. The title of the work, *Speak of*

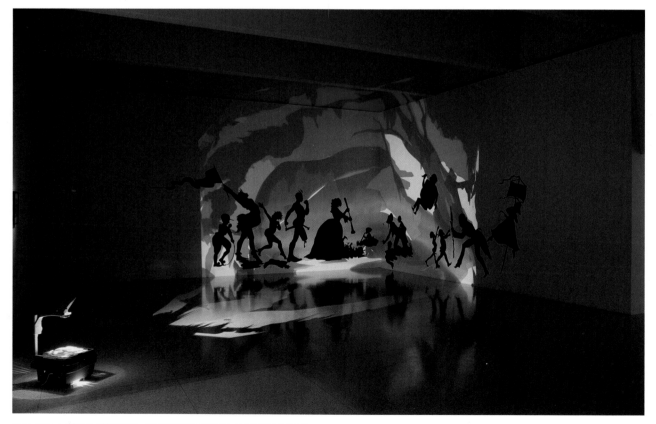

32-70 • Kara Walker DARKYTOWN REBELLION
2001. Cut paper and projection on wall, 14 × 37′ (4.3 × 11.3 m) overall. Musée d'Art Moderne Grand-Duc Jean, Luxembourg.

SEE MORE: View a video about Kara Walker **www.myartslab.com**

Me As I Am, is taken from words spoken by Othello, the "Moor," in Shakespeare's play. **CHANDELIER MORI** (FIG. 32–69), the chandelier from Wilson's installation, is also made from Murano glass but, unlike the brilliantly glittering Venetian glass chandeliers seen around the city, this one emphasizes blackness. The title suggests the *memento mori* or *vanitas* painting that reminds viewers that death comes to all of us, drawing attention to the fact that the commerce of Venice was built on the back of African labor and at the cost of African lives.

WALKER. It is fitting to end this book with some of the most challenging and provocative art made in America today. The art of Kara Walker (b. 1969) hits raw nerves, shocks, and horrifies. Walker makes her work by cutting large-scale silhouettes of figures out of black construction paper, waxing them to the walls of galleries, and illuminating them with projected light. In **DARKYTOWN REBELLION** (FIG. 32–70), a scene showing a slave revolt and massacre, the walls of the gallery are covered by black-silhouetted figures that tell an unfolding tale of horror. The room swirls with beautifully colored white, black, pink, green, blue, and yellow projected lights and shadows dancing on the walls. As we walk around the space looking at the figures, we step in front of the projector and our own shadows are cast on the walls, placing us uncomfortably close to or actually in the narrative. Walker's stories and caricatural figures are drawn variously from slave narratives, minstrel shows, advertising memorabilia, and even from Harlequin romance novels, blending fiction and fact to evoke a history of oppression and terrible violence—she does not balk at portraying unpleasant or painful bodily functions either, such as excretion, vomiting, and childbirth. Walker's characters are black and white stereotypes. She contrasts the tight, cramped features of her white characters with the stereotypical black features of her African Americans. She even refers to some of her characters as "nigger wenches" or "pickaninnies."

Walker plays on white fears of miscegenation and insecurities about racial purity. She pushes so far over the border of the acceptable that visiting one of her installations can be a terrifying and disruptive experience. Her figures disturb us intensely because of what they make us do. As silhouettes, they are all black, which means that we cannot identify their race by skin color. In order to read the narrative, however, we need to differentiate the characters and so have to look for other visual markers of race, making us draw upon an entire history of ugly stereotypes in the process. We are forced to examine the figures for thin or big lips, flat or curly hair, elegant or raggedy clothes. In this way Walker catches us in the act of being racist, making clear that she is speaking to us personally, not to some theoretical racist, and that racism is neither theoretical nor a thing of the past. As Walker has said: "It's interesting that as soon as you start telling the story of racism you start reliving it." She might also have said that when you experience her cycloramas, you become part of them.

Walker shows us that identity is not nearly as clear-cut as we would like to think. We are all complicated beings, constantly negotiating and renegotiating our place in the world, changing and reinventing ourselves. Kara Walker's art is not pleasant, but it changes us by altering our perception of the world. It makes us confront a world that we do not want to believe exists, and shows us that the work of visual artists—past, present, and future—can reveal things about the time and place in which it was created and about the world we inhabit in ways that are beyond the reach of any other form of communication.

THINK ABOUT IT

32.1 Discuss the emergence of Pop art in the 1950s and 1960s in the work of artists such as Richard Hamilton and Andy Warhol. Explain how and why Pop reacted to Abstract Expressionism.

32.2 Write about the importance of the dematerialized object in the art of postwar United States. Then discuss how representational art regained importance in later years, particularly after 1980, and explain the new forms that representation took.

32.3 Distinguish the three waves of feminism and assess their impact on the visual arts.

32.4 Analyze how contemporary American artists have used their art to address social and political issues surrounding race. Select and discuss the work of at least two artists from the chapter such as David Hammons, Kerry James Marshall, Kara Walker, or Fred Wilson.

32.5 Explain how globalism has impacted the visual arts and discuss how artists use contemporary strategies to speak to issues in their local cultures. Analyze one such artwork from the chapter.

PRACTICE MORE: Compose answers to these questions, get flashcards for images and terms, and review chapter material with quizzes www.myartslab.com

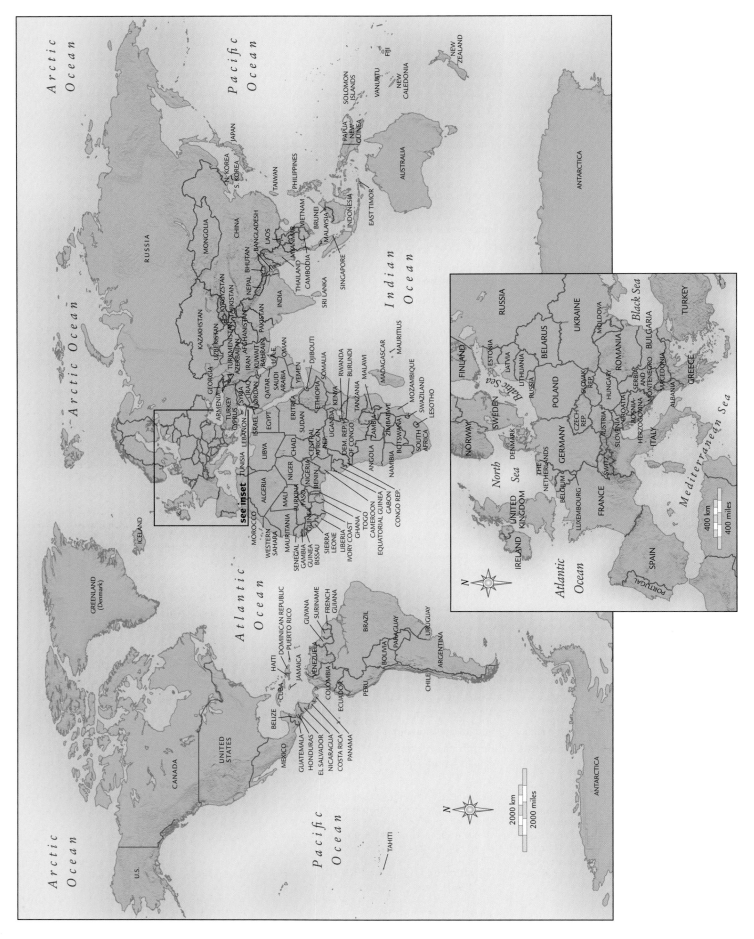

Arctic Ocean

Pacific Ocean

Arctic Ocean

NEW ZEALAND

FIJI

VANUATU

NEW CALEDONIA

SOLOMON ISLANDS

PAPUA NEW GUINEA

JAPAN

N. KOREA
S. KOREA

TAIWAN

PHILIPPINES

VIETNAM

BRUNEI

MALAYSIA

INDONESIA

EAST TIMOR

AUSTRALIA

ANTARCTICA

RUSSIA

MONGOLIA

CHINA

LAOS

MYANMAR

THAILAND
CAMBODIA

KAZAKHSTAN

UZBEKISTAN
TURKMENISTAN
KYRGYZSTAN
TAJIKISTAN

NEPAL BHUTAN

BANGLADESH

INDIA

SRI LANKA

SINGAPORE

Indian Ocean

GEORGIA
ARMENIA
TURKEY
AZERBAIJAN
SYRIA
CYPRUS
LEBANON
ISRAEL
JORDAN
IRAQ
IRAN
AFGHANISTAN
PAKISTAN
KUWAIT
BAHRAIN
QATAR
U.A.E.
OMAN
SAUDI ARABIA
YEMEN
DJIBOUTI
SOMALIA

ERITREA
ETHIOPIA
KENYA
UGANDA
RWANDA
BURUNDI
TANZANIA
MALAWI
MADAGASCAR
MAURITIUS
MOZAMBIQUE
SWAZILAND
LESOTHO
ZIMBABWE
ZAMBIA
BOTSWANA
SOUTH AFRICA
NAMIBIA
ANGOLA
DEM. REP. OF CONGO

EGYPT
SUDAN
CHAD
CENTRAL AFRICAN REP.
CONGO REP.
GABON
EQUATORIAL GUINEA
CAMEROON
TOGO
IVORY COAST
GHANA
BENIN
NIGERIA
NIGER
LIBYA
TUNISIA

see inset

MOROCCO
WESTERN SAHARA
ALGERIA
MALI
MAURITANIA
BURKINA FASO
GUINEA
SENEGAL
GAMBIA
GUINEA BISSAU
SIERRA LEONE
LIBERIA

ICELAND

GREENLAND (Denmark)

Atlantic Ocean

BRAZIL

GUYANA
SURINAME
FRENCH GUIANA

VENEZUELA
COLOMBIA
ECUADOR
PERU
BOLIVIA
PARAGUAY
URUGUAY
ARGENTINA
CHILE

DOMINICAN REPUBLIC
PUERTO RICO
HAITI
JAMAICA
CUBA
BELIZE
MEXICO
GUATEMALA
HONDURAS
EL SALVADOR
NICARAGUA
COSTA RICA
PANAMA

UNITED STATES

CANADA

U.S.

Arctic Ocean

Pacific Ocean

N

2000 km
2000 miles

TAHITI

ANTARCTICA

Inset

RUSSIA

FINLAND

ESTONIA
LATVIA
LITHUANIA
RUSSIA

Baltic Sea

BELARUS

UKRAINE

MOLDOVA

ROMANIA

Black Sea

BULGARIA

TURKEY

POLAND

CZECH REP.
SLOVAK REP.
HUNGARY
AUSTRIA
SLOVENIA
CROATIA
BOSNIA-HERZOGOVINA
SERBIA AND MONTENEGRO
MACEDONIA
ALBANIA
GREECE

GERMANY

SWITZ.

ITALY

Mediterranean Sea

NORWAY

SWEDEN

DENMARK

North Sea

THE NETHERLANDS
BELGIUM
LUXEMBOURG
FRANCE

UNITED KINGDOM

IRELAND

Atlantic Ocean

SPAIN

PORTUGAL

N

400 km
400 miles

abacus (p. 108)   The flat slab at the top of a **capital**, directly under the **entablature**.

abbey church (p. 239)   An abbey is a religious community headed by an abbot or abbess. An abbey church often has an especially large choir to provide space for the monks or nuns.

absolute dating (p. 12)   A method of assigning a precise historical date to periods and objects, based on known and recorded events in the region, as well as technically extracted physical evidence (such as carbon-14 disintegration). See also **radiometric dating, relative dating**.

abstract, abstraction (p. 8)   Any art that does not represent observed aspects of nature or transforms visible forms into a stylized image. Also: the **formal** qualities of this process.

academy (p. 924)   A place of study, the word coming from the Greek name of a garden near Athens where Plato and, later, Platonic philosophers held discussions. Academies of fine arts, such as the Academy of Drawing or the Royal Academy of Painting, were created to foster the arts by teaching, by discussion, by exhibitions, and occasionally by financial aid.

acanthus (p. 110)   A Mediterranean plant whose leaves are reproduced in architectural ornament used on **moldings, friezes**, and **Corinthian capitals**.

acropolis (p. 129)   The citadel of an ancient Greek city, located at its highest point and housing temples, a treasury, and sometimes a royal palace. The most famous is the Acropolis in Athens.

acroterion (acroteria) (p. 110)   An ornament at the corner or peak of a roof.

adobe (p. 393)   Sun-baked blocks made of clay mixed with straw. Also: the buildings made with this material.

aedicula (p. 609)   A decorative architectural frame, usually found around a niche, door, or window. An aedicula is made up of a **pediment** and **entablature** supported by **columns** or **pilasters**.

agora (p. 138)   An open space in a Greek town used as a central gathering place or market. See also **forum**.

aisle (p. 228)   Passage or open corridor of a church, hall, or other building that parallels the main space, usually on both sides, and is delineated by a row, or **arcade**, of **columns** or **piers**. Called side aisles when they flank the **nave** of a church.

album (p. 795)   A book consisting of a series of painting or prints (album leaves) mounted into book form.

allegory (p. 625)   In a work of art, an image (or images) that symbolizes an idea, concept, or principle, often moral or religious.

alloy (p. 23)   A mixture of metals; different metals melted together.

amalaka (p. 301)   In Hindu architecture, the circular or square-shaped element on top of a spire (**shikhara**), often crowned with a **finial**, symbolizing the cosmos.

ambulatory (p. 228)   The passage (walkway) around the **apse** in a **basilican** church or around the central space in a **central-plan building**.

amphora (p. 101)   An ancient Greek jar for storing oil or wine, with an egg-shaped body and two curved handles.

aniconic (p. 262)   A symbolic representation without images of human figures, very often found in Islamic art.

animal interlace or style (p. 427)   Decoration made of interwoven animals or serpents, often found in Celtic and early medieval Northern European art.

ankh (p. 51)   A looped cross signifying life, used by ancient Egyptians.

appropriation (p. 1102)   Term used to describe the practice of some postmodern artists of adopting images in their entirety from other works of art or from visual culture for use in their own art. The act of recontextualizing the appropriated image allows the artist to critique both it and the time and place in which it was created.

apse, apsidal (p. 192)   A large semicircular or polygonal (and usually **vaulted**) niche protruding from the end wall of a building. In the Christian church, it contains the altar. Apsidal is an adjective describing the condition of having such a space.

arabesque (p. 263)   A type of linear surface decoration based on foliage and **calligraphic** forms, usually characterized by flowing lines and swirling shapes.

arcade (p. 172)   A series of **arches**, carried by **columns** or **piers** and supporting a common wall or **lintel**. In a **blind arcade**, the arches and supports are **engaged** (attached to the wall) and have a decorative function.

arch (p. 271)   In architecture, a curved structural element that spans an open space. Built from wedge-shaped stone blocks called **voussoirs**, which, when placed together and held at the top by a trapezoidal **keystone**, form an effective space-spanning and weight-bearing unit. Requires **buttresses** at each side to contain the outward **thrust** caused by the weight of the structure. **Corbel arch** (p. 16): an arch or **vault** formed by **courses** of stones, each of which projects beyond the lower course until the space is enclosed; usually finished with a **capstone**. **Horseshoe arch** (p. 268): an arch of more than a half-circle; typical of western Islamic architecture. **Round arch** (p. 271): arch that displaces most of its weight, or downward thrust along its curving sides, transmitting that weight to adjacent supporting uprights (door or window jambs, columns, or piers). Ogival arch: a pointed arch created by S-curves. Relieving arch: an arch built into a heavy wall just above a **post-and-lintel** structure (such as a gate, door, or window) to help support the wall above by transferring the load to the side walls. **Transverse arch** (p. 457): an arch that connects the wall **piers** on both sides of an interior space, up and over a stone vault.

Archaic smile (p. 114)   The curved lips of an ancient Greek statue, usually interpreted as a way of animating facial features.

architrave (p. 108)   The bottom element in an **entablature**, beneath the **frieze** and the **cornice**.

archivolt (p. 473)   A **molded** band framing an **arch**, or a series of stone blocks that rest directly on the **columns**.

ashlar (p. 99)   Highly finished, precisely cut block of stone. When laid in even courses, ashlar masonry creates a uniform face with fine joints. Often used as a facing on the visible exterior of a building, especially as a veneer for the **façade**. Also called **dressed stone**.

assemblage (p. 1026)   Artwork created by gathering and manipulating two- and/or three-dimensional found objects.

astragal (p. 110)   A thin convex decorative **molding**, often found on Classical **entablatures**, and usually decorated with a continuous row of beadlike circles.

atelier (p. 944)   The studio or workshop of a master artist or craftsperson, often including junior associates and apprentices.

atmospheric perspective (p. 562)   See **perspective**.

atrial cross (p. 941)   The cross placed in the **atrium** of a church. In Colonial America, used to mark a gathering and teaching place.

atrium (p. 160)   An unroofed interior courtyard or room in a Roman house, sometimes having a pool or garden, sometimes surrounded by **columns**. Also: the open courtyard in front of a Christian church; or an entrance area in modern architecture.

automatism (p. 1056)   A technique whereby the usual intellectual control of the artist over his or her brush or pencil is foregone. The artist's aim is to allow the subconscious to create the artwork without rational interference.

avant-garde (p. 971)   Term derived from the French military word meaning "before the group," or "vanguard." Avant-garde denotes those artists or concepts of a strikingly new, experimental, or radical nature for their time.

axis (p. xxxii)   An implied line around which the elements of a picture are organized.

axis-mundi (p. 297)   A concept of an "axis of the world," which marks sacred sites and denotes a link between the human and celestial realms. For example, in Buddhist art, the *axis mundi* can be marked by monumental freestanding decorative **pillars**.

bailey (p. 473)   The outermost walled courtyard of a castle.

baldachin (p. 467)   A canopy (whether suspended from the ceiling, projecting from a wall, or supported by **columns**) placed over an honorific or sacred space such as a throne or church altar.

bar tracery (p. 507)   See **tracery**.

barbarian (p. 151)   A term used by the ancient Greeks and Romans to label all foreigners outside their cultural orbit (e.g., Celts, Goths, Vikings). The word derives from an imitation of what the "barblings" of their language sounded like to those who could not understand it.

bargeboards (p. 870)   Boards covering the rafters at the gable end of a building; bargeboards are often carved or painted.

barrel vault (p. 188)   See **vault**.

base (p. 110)   Any support. Also: masonry supporting a statue or the shaft of a **column**.

basilica (p. 192)   A large rectangular building. Often built with a **clerestory**, side **aisles** separated from the center **nave** by **colonnades**, and an **apse** at one or both ends. Roman centers for administration, later adapted to Christian church use.

battered (p. 418)   An architectural design whereby walls are sloped inward toward the top to increase stability.

bay (p. 172)   A unit of space defined by architectural elements such as **columns, piers**, and walls.

beehive tomb (p. 98)   A **corbel-vaulted** tomb, conical in shape like a beehive, and covered by an earthen mound.

Benday dots (p. 1093)   In modern printing and typesetting, the individual dots that, together with many others, make up lettering and images. Often machine- or computer-generated, the dots are very small and closely spaced to give the effect of density and richness of tone.

bi (p. 333)   A jade disk with a hole in the center.

bilum (p. 863)   Netted bags made mainly by women throughout the central highlands of New Guinea. The bags can be used for everyday purposes or even to carry the bones of the recently deceased as a sign of mourning.

biomorphic (p. 1057)   A term used in the early twentieth century to denote the biologically or organically inspired shapes and forms that were routinely included in abstracted Modern art.

black-figure (p. 105) A style or technique of ancient Greek pottery in which black figures are painted on a red clay ground. See also **red-figure**.

blackware (p. 853) A **ceramic** technique that produces pottery with a primarily black surface with **matte** and glossy patterns on the surface.

blind arcade (p. 780) See **arcade**.

bodhisattva (p. 297) In Buddhism, a being who has attained enlightenment but chooses to remain in this world in order to help others advance spiritually. Also defined as a potential Buddha.

Book of Hours (p. 547) A private prayer book, containing a calendar, services for the canonical hours, and sometimes special prayers.

boss (p. 554) A decorative knoblike element that can be found in many places, such as at the intersection of a Gothic **rib vault** or in the buttonlike projections of metalwork.

bracket, bracketing (p. 335) An architectural element that projects from a wall to support a horizontal part of a building, such as beams or the eaves of a roof.

buon fresco (p. 87) See **fresco**.

burin (p. 590) A metal instrument used in **engraving** to cut lines into the metal plate. The sharp end of the burin is trimmed to give a diamond-shaped cutting point, while the other end is finished with a wooden handle that fits into the engraver's palm.

buttress, buttressing p. 172) A projecting support built against an external wall, usually to counteract the lateral **thrust** of a **vault** or **arch** within. In Gothic architecture, a **flying buttress** is an arched bridge above the **aisle** roof that extends from the upper **nave** wall, where the lateral thrust of the main vault is greatest, down to a solid **pier**.

cairn (p.17) A pile of stones or earth and stones that served both as a prehistoric burial site and as a marker of underground tombs.

calligraphy (p. 279) Handwriting as an art form.

calotype (p. 968) The first photographic process utilizing negatives and paper positives. It was invented by William Henry Fox Talbot in the late 1830s.

calyx krater (p. 118) See **krater**.

came (cames) (p. 497) A lead strip used in the making of leaded or **stained-glass windows**. Cames have an indented groove on the sides into which the separate pieces of glass are fitted to hold the composition together.

cameo (p. 178) Gemstone, clay, glass, or shell having layers of color, carved in **low relief** to create an image and ground of different colors.

camera obscura (p. 967) An early cameralike device used in the Renaissance and later for recording images of nature. Made from a dark box (or room) with a hole in one side (sometimes fitted with a lens), the camera obscura operates when bright light shines through the hole, casting an upside-down image of an object outside onto the inside wall of the box.

canon of proportions (p. 65) A set of ideal mathematical ratios in art based on measurements, as in the proportional relationships among the basic elements of the human body.

canopic jar (p. 56) Special jars used to store the major organs of a body before embalming, found in ancient Egyptian culture.

capital (p. 110) The sculpted block that tops a **column**. According to the **conventions** of the **orders**, capitals include different decorative elements. See **order**. A **historiated capital** is one displaying a figural composition of a **narrative** scene.

capriccio (p. 912) A painting or print of a fantastic, imaginary landscape, usually with architecture.

capstone (p. 99) The final, topmost stone in a **corbel arch** or **vault**, which joins the sides and completes the structure.

cartoon (p. 497) A full-scale drawing used to transfer or guide a design onto a surface (such as a wall, canvas, panel, or **tapestry**) to be painted, carved, or woven.

cartouche (p. 189) A frame for a **hieroglyphic** inscription formed by a rope design surrounding an oval space. Used to signify a sacred or honored name. Also: in architecture, a decorative device or plaque, usually with a plain center used for inscriptions or epitaphs.

caryatid (p. 107) A sculpture of a draped female figure acting as a **column** supporting an **entablature**.

cassone (cassoni) (p. 616) An Italian dowry chest often highly decorated with carvings, paintings, **inlaid** designs, and gilt embellishments.

catacomb (p. 219) A subterranean burial ground consisting of tunnels on different levels, having niches for urns and **sarcophagi** and often incorporating rooms (**cubiculae**).

cathedral (p. 222) The principal Christian church in a diocese, the bishop's administrative center and housing his throne (*cathedra*).

celadon (p. 352) A high-fired, transparent glaze of pale bluish-green hue whose principal coloring agent is an oxide of iron. In China and Korea, such glazes typically were applied over a pale gray **stoneware** body, though Chinese potters sometimes applied them over **porcelain** bodies during the Ming (1368–1644) and Qing (1644–1911) dynasties. Chinese potters invented celadon glazes and initiated the continuous production of celadon-glazed wares as early as the third century CE.

cella (p. 108) The principal interior room at the center of a Greek or Roman temple within which the cult statue was usually housed. Also called the **naos**.

celt (p. 377) A smooth, oblong stone or metal object, shaped like an axe-head.

cenotaph (p. 771) A funerary monument commemorating an individual or group buried elsewhere.

centering (p. 172) A temporary structure that supports a masonry **arch** and **vault** or **dome** during construction until the mortar is fully dried and the masonry is self-sustaining.

central-plan building (p. 228) Any structure designed with a primary central space surrounded by symmetrical areas on each side. For example, a **rotunda** or a Greek-cross plan (equal-armed cross).

ceramics (p. 22) A general term covering all types of wares made from fired clay, including **porcelain** and **terra cotta**.

chacmool (p. 390) In Mayan sculpture, a half-reclining figure probably representing an offering bearer.

chaitya (p. 302) A type of Buddhist temple found in India. Built in the form of a hall or **basilica**, a *chaitya* hall is highly decorated with sculpture and usually is carved from a cave or natural rock location. It houses a sacred shrine or **stupa** for worship.

chamfer (p. 780) The slanted surface produced when an angle is trimmed or beveled, common in building and metalwork.

chasing (p. 776) Ornamentation made on metal by **incising** or hammering the surface.

château (châteaux) (p. 691) A French country house or residential castle. A *château fort*, is a military castle incorporating defensive works such as towers and battlements.

chattri (chattris) (p. 779) A decorative pavilion with an umbrella-shaped **dome** in Indian architecture.

chevron (p. 350) A decorative or heraldic motif of repeated Vs; a zigzag pattern.

chiaroscuro (p. 634) An Italian word designating the contrast of dark and light in a painting, drawing, or print. *Chiaroscuro* creates spatial depth and volumetric forms through gradations in the intensity of light and shadow.

cista (cistae) (p. 166) **Cylindrical** containers used by wealthy women as a case for toiletry articles such as a mirror.

clerestory (p. 58) The topmost zone of a wall with windows in a **basilica** extending above the aisle roofs. Provides direct light into the central interior space (the **nave**).

cloister (p. 442) An open space within a monastery, surrounded by an **arcaded** or colonnaded walkway, often having a fountain and garden. The most important monastic buildings (e.g., dormitory, refectory) open off of it. Since members of a cloistered order do not leave the monastery or interact with outsiders, the cloister represents the center of their enclosed world.

codex (codices) (p. 243) A book, or a group of **manuscript** pages (folios), held together by stitching or other binding on one side.

coffer (p. 197) A recessed decorative panel that is used to reduce the weight of and to decorate ceilings or **vaults**. The use of coffers is called coffering.

coiling (p. 845) A technique in basketry. In coiled baskets a spiraling structure is held in place by another material.

collage (p. 1026) A composition made of cut and pasted scraps of materials, sometimes with lines or forms added by the artist.

colonnade (p. 69) A row of **columns**, supporting a straight **lintel** (as in a **porch** or **portico**) or a series of **arches** (an **arcade**).

colophon (p. 432) The data placed at the end of a book listing the book's author, publisher, **illuminator**, and other information related to its production. In East Asian **handscrolls**, the inscriptions which follow the painting are also called colophons.

column (p. 110) An architectural element used for support and/or decoration. Consists of a rounded or polygonal vertical **shaft** placed on a **base** and topped by a decorative **capital**. In Classical architecture, built in accordance with the rules of one of the architectural **orders**. Columns can be free-standing or attached to a background wall (**engaged**).

combine (p. 1085) Combinations of painting and sculpture using nontraditional art materials.

complementary color (p. 993) The primary and secondary colors across from each other on the color wheel (red and green, blue and orange, yellow and purple). When juxtaposed, the intensity of both colors increases. When mixed together, they negate each other to make a neutral gray-brown.

composite order (p. 163) See **order**.

composite pose or **image (p. 9)** Combining different viewpoints within a single representation of a subject.

composition (p. xxix) The overall arrangement, organizing design, or structure of a work of art.

conch (p. 234) A half-**dome**.

cong (p. 328) A square or octagonal jade tube with a cylindrical hole in the center. A symbol of the earth, it was used for ritual worship and astronomical observations in ancient China.

connoisseurship (p. 741) A term derived from the French word connoisseur, meaning "an expert," and signifying the study and evaluation of art based primarily on **formal**, visual, and stylistic analysis. A connoisseur studies the style and technique of an object to assess its relative quality and identify its maker through visual comparison with other works of secure authorship. See also **contextualism**; **formalism**.

contrapposto (p. 121) An Italian term meaning "set against," used to describe the pose that results from setting parts of the body in opposition to each other around a central **axis**.

convention (p. 51) A traditional way of representing forms.

corbel, corbeling (p. 16) An early roofing and arching technique in which each **course** of stone projects slightly beyond the previous layer (a corbel) until the uppermost corbels meet. Results in a high, almost pointed **arch** or **vault**.

corbeled vault (p. 99)   See **vault**.

Corinthian order (p. 108)   See **order**.

cornice (p. 110)   The uppermost section of a Classical **entablature**. More generally, a horizontally projecting element found at the top of a building wall or **pedestal**. A raking cornice is formed by the junction of two slanted cornices, most often found in **pediments**.

course (p. 99)   A horizontal layer of stone used in building.

crenellation (p. 44)   Alternating higher and lower sections along the top of a defensive wall, giving a stepped appearance and forming a permanent shield for defenders on top of a fortified building.

crocket (p. 585)   A stylized leaf used as decoration along the outer angle of spires, pinnacles, gables, and around **capitals** in Gothic architecture.

cruciform (p. 232)   A term describing anything that is cross-shaped, as in the cruciform plan of a church.

cubiculum (cubicula) (p. 224)   A small private room for burials in the **catacombs**.

cuneiform (p. 28)   An early form of writing with wedge-shaped marks impressed into wet clay with a **stylus**, primarily used by ancient Mesopotamians.

curtain wall (p. 1045)   A wall in a building that does not support any of the weight of the structure.

cyclopean construction (p. 93)   A method of building using huge blocks of rough-hewn stone. Any large-scale, monumental building project that impresses by sheer size. Named after the Cyclopes (sing. Cyclops) one-eyed giants of legendary strength in Greek myths.

cylinder seal (p. 32)   A small cylindrical stone decorated with **incised** patterns. When rolled across soft clay or wax, the resulting raised pattern or design (**relief**) served in Mesopotamian and Indus Valley cultures as an identifying signature.

dado (dadoes) (p. 163)   The lower part of a wall, differentiated in some way (by a molding or different coloring or paneling) from the upper section.

daguerreotype (p. 967)   An early photographic process that makes a positive print on a light-sensitized copperplate; invented and marketed in 1839 by Louis-Jacques-Mandé Daguerre.

demotic writing (p. 77)   The simplified form of ancient Egyptian **hieratic writing**, used primarily for administrative and private texts.

dendrochronology (p. xxxvi)   The dating of wood based on the patterns of the growth rings.

desert varnish (p. 400)   In southwestern North America, a substance that turned cliff faces into dark surfaces. Neolithic artists would draw images by scraping through the dark surface.

diptych (p. 215)   Two panels of equal size (usually decorated with paintings or **reliefs**) hinged together.

dogu (p. 356)   Small human figurines made in Japan during the Jomon period. Shaped from clay, the figures have exaggerated expressions and are in contorted poses. They were probably used in religious rituals.

dolmen (p. 17)   A prehistoric structure made up of two or more large upright stones supporting a large, flat, horizontal slab or slabs.

dome (p. 188)   A rounded **vault**, usually over a circular space. Consists of curved masonry and can vary in shape from hemispherical to bulbous to ovoidal. May use a supporting vertical wall (**drum**), from which the vault springs, and may be crowned by an open space (**oculus**) and/or an exterior **lantern**. When a dome is built over a square space, an intermediate element is required to make the transition to a circular drum. There are two systems: A dome on **pendentives** (spherical triangles) incorporates **arched**, sloping intermediate sections of wall that carry the weight and **thrust** of the dome to

heavily **buttressed** supporting **piers**. A dome on **squinches** uses an arch built into the wall (squinch) in the upper corners of the space to carry the weight of the dome across the corners of the square space below. A half-dome or **conch** may cover a semicircular space.

domino construction (p. 1045)   System of building construction introduced by the architect Le Corbusier in which reinforced concrete floor slabs are floated on six free-standing posts placed as if at the positions of the six dots on a domino playing piece.

Doric order (p. 108)   See **order**.

dressed stone (p. 85)   See **ashlar**.

drillwork (p. 190)   The technique of using a drill for the creation of certain effects in sculpture.

drum (p. 110)   The wall that supports a **dome**. Also: a segment of the circular **shaft** of a **column**.

drypoint (p. 748)   An **intaglio** printmaking process by which a metal (usually copper) plate is directly inscribed with a pointed instrument (**stylus**). The resulting design of scratched lines is inked, wiped, and printed. Also: the print made by this process.

earthenware (p. 22)   A low-fired, opaque **ceramic** ware that is fired in the range of 800 to 900 degrees Celsius. Earthenware employs humble clays that are naturally heat resistant; the finished wares remain porous after firing unless glazed. Earthenware occurs in a range of earth-toned colors, from white and tan to gray and black, with tan predominating.

earthwork (p. 1102)   Usually very large scale, outdoor artwork that is produced by altering the natural environment.

echinus (p. 110)   A cushionlike circular element found below the **abacus** of a **Doric capital**. Also: a similarly shaped molding (usually with egg-and-dart motifs) underneath the **volutes** of an **Ionic** capital.

electronic spin resonance (p. 12)   Method that uses magnetic field and microwave irradiation to date material such as tooth enamel and its surrounding soil.

elevation (p. 108)   The arrangement, proportions, and details of any vertical side or face of a building. Also: an architectural drawing showing an exterior or interior wall of a building.

emblema (emblemata) (p. 202)   In a **mosaic**, the elaborate central motif on a floor, usually a self-contained unit done in a more refined manner, with smaller **tesserae** of both marble and semiprecious stones.

embroidery (p. 484)   Stitches applied on top of an already-woven fabric ground.

encaustic (p. 79)   A painting medium using pigments mixed with hot wax.

engaged column (p. 173)   A column attached to a wall. See also **column**.

engraving (p. 590)   An **intaglio** printmaking process of inscribing an image, design, or letters onto a metal or wood surface from which a print is made. An engraving is usually drawn with a sharp implement (**burin**) directly onto the surface of the plate. Also: the print made from this process.

entablature (p. 108)   In the Classical **orders**, the horizontal elements above the **columns** and **capitals**. The entablature consists of, from bottom to top, an **architrave**, a **frieze**, and a **cornice**.

entasis (p. 108)   A slight swelling of the **shaft** of a Greek **column**. The optical illusion of entasis makes the column appear from afar to be straight.

etching (p. 748)   An **intaglio** printmaking process in which a metal plate is coated with acid-resistant resin and then inscribed with a **stylus** in a design, revealing the plate below. The plate is then immersed in acid, and the design of exposed metal is eaten away by the acid. The resin is removed, leaving the design etched permanently into the metal and the plate ready to be inked, wiped, and printed.

Eucharist (p. 222)   The central rite of the Christian Church, from the Greek word "thanksgiving." Also known as the Mass or Holy Communion, it is based on the Last Supper. According to traditional Catholic Christian belief, consecrated bread and wine become the body and blood of Christ; in Protestant belief, bread and wine symbolize the body and blood.

exedra (exedrae) (p. 199)   In architecture, a semicircular niche. On a small scale, often used as decoration, whereas larger exedrae can form interior spaces (such as an **apse**).

expressionism (p. 151)   Terms describing a work of art in which forms are created primarily to evoke subjective emotions rather than a rational response.

façade (p. 52)   The face or front wall of a building.

faience (p. 87)   Type of **ceramic** covered with colorful, opaque glazes that form a smooth, impermeable surface. First developed in ancient Egypt.

fang ding (p. 328)   A square or rectangular bronze vessel with four legs. The *fang ding* was used for ritual offerings in ancient China during the Shang dynasty.

femmage (p. 1101)   From "female" and "**collage**," the incorporation of fabric into painting.

fête galante (p. 908)   A subject in painting depicting well-dressed people at leisure in a park or country setting. It is most often associated with eighteenth-century French Rococo painting.

filigree (p. 87)   Delicate, lacelike ornamental work.

fillet (p. 110)   The flat ridge between the carved out **flutes** of a **column shaft**. See also fluting.

finial (p. 308)   A knoblike architectural decoration usually found at the top point of a spire, pinnacle, canopy, or gable. Also found on furniture; also the ornamental top of a staff.

flutes, fluted (p. 110)   In architecture, evenly spaced, rounded parallel vertical grooves incised on **shafts** of **columns** or columnar elements (such as **pilasters**).

flying buttress (p. 496)   See **buttress**.

flying gallop (p. 87)   Animals posed off the ground with legs fully extended backwards and forwards to signify that they are running.

foreshortening (p. 119)   The illusion created on a flat surface in which figures and objects appear to recede or project sharply into space. Accomplished according to the rules of perspective.

formal analysis (p. xxix)   An exploration of the visual character that artists bring to their works through the expressive use of elements such as line, form, color, and light, and through its overall structure or composition.

Formalism, formalist (p. 1073)   An approach to the understanding, appreciation, and valuation of art based almost solely on considerations of form. This approach tends to regard an artwork as independent of its time and place of making. In the 1940s, Formalism was most ardently proposed by critic Clement Greenberg. See also **connoisseurship**.

forum (p. 178)   A Roman town center; site of temples and administrative buildings and used as a market or gathering area for the citizens.

four-iwan mosque (p. 271)   See **iwan** and **mosque**.

fresco (p. 87)   A painting technique in which water-based pigments are applied to a surface of wet plaster (called **buon fresco**). The color is absorbed by the plaster, becoming a permanent part of the wall. **Fresco secco** is created by painting on dried plaster, and the color may flake off. Murals made by both these techniques are called frescoes.

fresco secco (p. 87)   See **fresco**.

frieze (p. 108)   The middle element of an **entablature**, between the **architrave** and the cornice. Usually decorated with sculpture, painting, or moldings. Also: any continuous flat band with **relief sculpture** or painted decorations.

frottage (p. 1056)   A design produced by laying a piece of paper over a textured surface and rubbing with charcoal or other soft medium.

fusuma (p. 818)   Sliding doors covered with paper, used in traditional Japanese construction. *Fusuma* are often highly decorated with paintings and colored backgrounds.

gallery (p. 236)   In church architecture, the story found above the side **aisles** of a church, usually open to and overlooking the **nave**. Also: in secular architecture, a long room, usually above the ground floor in a private house or a public building used for entertaining, exhibiting pictures, or promenading. Also: a building or hall in which art is displayed or sold. Also: *galleria*.

garbhagriha (p. 301)   From the Sanskrit word meaning "womb chamber," a small room or shrine in a Hindu temple containing a holy image.

genre painting (p. 712)   A term used to loosely categorize paintings depicting scenes of everyday life, including (among others) domestic interiors, parties, inn scenes, and street scenes.

geoglyphs (p. 392)   Earthen designs on a colossal scale, often created in a landscape as if to be seen from an aerial viewpoint.

gesso (p. 544)   A ground made from glue, gypsum, and/or chalk forming the ground of a wood panel or the priming layer of a canvas. Provides a smooth surface for painting.

gilding (p. 87)   The application of paper-thin **gold leaf** or gold pigment to an object made from another medium (for example, a sculpture or painting). Usually used as a decorative finishing detail.

giornata (giornate) (p. 537)   Adopted from the Italian term meaning "a day's work," a giornata is the section of a **fresco** plastered and painted in a single day.

gold leaf (p. 47)   Paper-thin sheets of hammered gold that are used in **gilding**. In some cases (such as Byzantine **icons**), also used as a ground for paintings.

gold foil (p. 87)   A thin sheet of gold.

gopura (p. 775)   The towering gateway to an Indian Hindu temple complex. A temple complex can have several different *gopuras*.

Grand Manner (p. 922)   An elevated style of painting popular in the eighteenth century in which the artist looked to the ancients and to the Renaissance for inspiration; for portraits as well as history painting, the artist would adopt the poses, compositions, and attitudes of Renaissance and antique models.

Grand Tour (p. 911)   Popular during the eighteenth and nineteenth centuries, an extended tour of cultural sites in France and Italy intended to finish the education of a young upper-class person primarily from Britain or North America.

granulation (p. 87)   A technique of decoration in which metal granules, or tiny metal balls, are fused onto a metal surface.

graphic arts (p. xxiv)   A term referring to those arts that are drawn or printed and that utilize paper as primary support.

grattage (p. 1056)   A pattern created by scraping off layers of paint from a canvas laid over a textured surface. See also **frottage**.

grid (p. 64)   A system of regularly spaced horizontally and vertically crossed lines that gives regularity to an architectural plan or in the composition of a work of art. Also: in painting, a grid is used to allow designs to be enlarged or transferred easily.

grisaille (p. 538)   A style of monochromatic painting in shades of gray. Also: a painting made in this style.

groin vault (p. 188)   See **vault**.

grozing (p. 497)   In **stained-glass** windows, chipping away at the edges of a piece of glass to achieve the precise shape needed for inclusion in the composition.

hall church (p. 518)   A church with a **nave** and **aisles** of the same height, giving the impression of a large, open hall.

handscroll (p. 337)   A long, narrow, horizontal painting or text (or combination thereof) common in Chinese and Japanese art and of a size intended for individual use. A handscroll is stored wrapped tightly around a wooden pin and is unrolled for viewing or reading.

hanging scroll (p. 795)   In Chinese and Japanese art, a vertical painting or text mounted within sections of silk. At the top is a semicircular rod; at the bottom is a round dowel. Hanging scrolls are kept rolled and tied except for special occasions, when they are hung for display, contemplation, or commemoration.

haniwa (p. 356)   Pottery forms, including cylinders, buildings, and human figures, that were placed on top of Japanese tombs or burial mounds.

Happening (p. 1085)   An art form developed by Allan Kaprow in the 1960s incorporating performance, theater, and visual images. A Happening was organized without a specific narrative or intent; with audience participation, the event proceeded according to chance and individual improvisation.

hemicycle (p. 508)   A semicircular interior space or structure.

henge (p. 18)   A circular area enclosed by stones or wood posts set up by Neolithic peoples. It is usually bounded by a ditch and raised embankment.

hieratic scale (p. 27)   The use of different sizes for powerful or holy figures and for ordinary people to indicate relative importance. The larger the figure, the greater the importance.

hieroglyph (p. 52)   Picture writing; words and ideas rendered in the form of pictorial symbols.

high relief (p. 304)   See **relief sculpture**.

historiated capital (p. 479)   See **capital**.

historicism (p. 963)   The strong consciousness of and attention to the institutions, themes, styles, and forms of the past, made accessible by historical research, textual study, and archaeology.

history paintings (p. 924)   Paintings based on historical, mythological, or biblical narratives. Once considered the noblest form of art, history paintings generally convey a high moral or intellectual idea and are often painted in a grand pictorial style.

horizon line   A horizontal "line" formed by the implied meeting point of earth and sky. In **linear perspective**, the **vanishing point** or points are located on this "line."

horseshoe arch (p. 268)   See **arch**.

hue (p. xxii)   Pure color. The saturation or intensity of the hue depends on the purity of the color. Its value depends on its lightness or darkness.

hydria (p. 139)   A large ancient Greek and Roman jar with three handles (horizontal ones at both sides and one vertical at the back), used for storing water.

hypostyle hall (p. 66)   A large interior room characterized by many closely spaced columns that support its roof.

icon (p. 237)   An image representing a sacred figure or event in the Byzantine, and later in the Orthodox, Church. Icons were venerated by the faithful, who believed them to have miraculous powers to transmit messages to God.

iconic image (p. 224)   A picture that expresses or embodies an intangible concept or idea.

iconoclasm (p. 245)   The banning or destruction of images, especially **icons** and religious art. Iconoclasm in eighth- and ninth-century Byzantium and sixteenth- and seventeenth-century Protestant territories arose from differing beliefs about the power, meaning, function, and purpose of imagery in religion.

iconography (p. xxxiii)   Identifying and studying the subject matter and conventional motifs or symbols in works of art.

iconology (p. xxxv)   Interpreting works of art as embodiments of cultural situation by placing them within broad social, political, religious, and intellectual contexts.

iconophile (p. 246)   From the Greek for "lovers of images." In Byzantine art, iconophiles advocated for the continued use of **iconic images** in art.

iconostasis (p. 245)   The partition screen in a Byzantine or Orthodox church between the **sanctuary** (where the Mass is performed) and the body of the church (where the congregation assembles). The iconostasis displays **icons**.

idealization (p. xxiv)   A process in art through which artists strive to make their forms and figures attain perfection, based on pervading cultural values and/or their own personal ideals.

ideograph (p. 331)   A written character or symbol representing an idea or object. Many Chinese characters are ideographs.

ignudi (p. 645)   Heroic figures of nude young men.

illumination (p. 425)   A painting on paper or parchment used as an illustration and/or decoration in **manuscripts** or **albums**. Usually richly colored, often supplemented by gold and other precious materials. The artists are referred to as illuminators. Also: the technique of decorating manuscripts with such paintings.

impasto (p. 748)   Thick applications of pigment that give a painting a palpable surface texture.

impost block (p. 600)   A block, serving to concentrate the weight above, imposed between the **capital** of a **column** and the springing of an **arch** above.

incising (p. 32)   A technique in which a design or inscription is cut into a hard surface with a sharp instrument. Such a surface is said to be incised.

ink painting (p. 810)   A monochromatic style of painting developed in China using black ink with gray washes.

inlay (p. 30)   To set pieces of a material or materials into a surface to form a design. Also: material used in or decoration formed by this technique.

installation (p. 1087)   Contemporary art created for a specific site, especially a gallery or outdoor area, that creates a complete and controlled environment.

intaglio (p. 590)   Term used for a technique in which the design is carved out of the surface of an object, such as an **engraved seal** stone. In the **graphic arts**, intaglio includes **engraving**, **etching**, and **drypoint**—all processes in which ink transfers to paper from **incised**, ink-filled lines cut into a metal plate.

intarsia (p. 617)   Decoration formed through wood **inlay**.

intuitive perspective (p. 184)   See **perspective**.

Ionic order (p. 108)   See **order**.

iwan (p. 71)   A large, **vaulted** chamber in a **mosque** with a monumental **arched** opening on one side.

jamb (p. 473)   In architecture, the vertical element found on both sides of an opening in a wall, and supporting an **arch** or **lintel**.

japonisme (p. 994)   A style in French and American nineteenth-century art that was highly influenced by Japanese art, especially prints.

jasperware (p. 917)   A fine-grained, unglazed, white **ceramic** developed by Josiah Wedgwood, often colored by metallic oxides with the raised designs remaining white.

jataka tales (p. 300)   In Buddhism, stories associated with the previous lives of Shakyamuni, the historical Buddha.

joggled voussoirs (p. 272)   Interlocking **voussoirs** in an **arch** or **lintel**, often of contrasting materials for colorful effect.

joined-block sculpture (p. 367)   A method of constructing large-scale wooden sculpture developed in

Japan. The entire work is constructed from smaller hollow blocks, each individually carved, and assembled when complete. The joined-block technique allowed the production of larger sculpture, as the multiple joints alleviate the problems of drying and cracking found with sculpture carved from a single block.

kantharos (p. 117) A type of Greek vase or goblet with two large handles and a wide mouth.

keep (p. 473) The innermost and strongest structure or central tower of a medieval castle, sometimes used as living quarters, as well as for defense. Also called a donjon.

kente (p. 892) A woven cloth made by the Ashanti peoples of Africa. Kente cloth is woven in long, narrow pieces in complex and colorful patterns, which are then sewn together.

key block (p. 826) A key block is the master block in the production of a colored **woodblock print**, which requires different blocks for each color. The key block is a flat piece of wood upon which the outlines for the entire design of the print were first drawn on its surface and then all but these outlines were carved away with a knife. These outlines serve as a guide for the accurate **registration** or alignment of the other blocks needed to add colors to specific parts of a print.

keystone (p. 172) The topmost **voussoir** at the center of an **arch**, and the last block to be placed. The pressure of this block holds the arch together. Often of a larger size and/or decorated.

kiln (p. 22) An oven designed to produce enough heat for the baking, or firing, of clay.

kiva (p. 398) A ceremonial enclosure, usually wholly or partly underground, used for ritual purposes by modern Pueblo peoples and Ancestral Puebloans. *Kivas* may be round or square, made of **adobe** or stone, and they usually feature a hearth and a small indentation in the floor behind it.

kondo (p. 360) The main hall inside a Japanese Buddhist temple where the images of Buddha are housed.

korambo (p. 863) A ceremonial or spirit house in Pacific cultures, reserved for the men of a village and used as a meeting place as well as to hide religious artifacts from the uninitiated.

kore (kourai) (p. 114) An Archaic Greek statue of a young woman.

koru (p. 870) A design depicting a curling stalk with a bulb at the end that resembles a young tree fern, and often found in Maori art.

kouros (kouroi) (p. 114) An Archaic Greek statue of a young man or boy.

kowhaiwhai (p. 870) Painted curvilinear patterns often found in Maori art.

krater (p. 99) An ancient Greek vessel for mixing wine and water, with many subtypes that each have a distinctive shape. **Calyx krater**: a bell-shaped vessel with handles near the base that resemble a flower calyx. **Volute krater**: a type of krater with handles shaped like scrolls.

Kufic (p. 272) An ornamental, angular Arabic script.

kylix (p. 124) A shallow Greek cup, used for drinking, with a wide mouth and small handles near the rim.

lacquer (p. 22) A type of hard, glossy surface varnish used on objects in East Asian cultures, made from the sap of the Asian sumac or from shellac, a resinous secretion from the lac insect. Lacquer can be layered and manipulated or combined with pigments and other materials for various decorative effects.

lakshana (p. 303) Term used to designate the thirty-two marks of the historical Buddha. The *lakshana* include, among others, the Buddha's golden body, his long arms, the wheel impressed on his palms and the soles of his feet, and his elongated earlobes.

lamassu (p. 42) Supernatural guardian-protector of ancient Near Eastern palaces and throne rooms, often represented sculpturally as a combination of the bearded

head of a man, powerful body of a lion or bull, wings of an eagle, and the horned headdress of a god, usually possessing five legs.

lancet (p. 502) A tall, narrow window crowned by a sharply pointed **arch**, typically found in Gothic architecture.

lantern (p. 458) A turretlike structure situated on a roof, **vault**, or **dome**, with windows that allow light into the space below.

leythos (lekythoi) (p. 141) A slim Greek oil vase with one handle and a narrow mouth.

linear perspective (p. 593) See **perspective**.

linga shrine (p. 310) A place of worship centered on an object or representation in the form of a phallus (the lingam), which symbolizes the power of the Hindu god Shiva.

lintel (p. 473) A horizontal element of any material carried by two or more vertical supports to form an opening.

literati (p. 337) The English word used for the Chinese *wenren* or the Japanese *bunjin*, referring to well educated artists who enjoyed literature, **calligraphy**, and painting as a pastime. Their paintings are termed **literati painting**.

literati painting (p. 791) A style of painting that reflects the taste of the educated class of East Asian intellectuals and scholars. Aspects include an appreciation for the antique, small scale, and an intimate connection between maker and audience.

lithography (p. 951) Process of making a print (lithograph) from a design drawn on a flat stone block with greasy crayon. Ink is applied to the wet stone and adheres only to the greasy areas of the design.

loggia (p. 532) Italian term for a covered open-air **gallery**. Often used as a corridor between buildings or around a courtyard, loggias usually have **arcades** or **colonnades**.

logosyllabic (p. 385) A writing system consisting of both logograms (symbols that represent words) and phonetic signs (symbols that represent sounds, in this case syllables). Cuneiform, Maya, and Japanese are examples of logosyllabic scripts.

longitudinal-plan building (p. 228) Any structure designed with a rectangular shape. If a cross-shaped building, the main arm of the building would be longer then any arms that cross it. For example, **basilicas** or Latin-cross plan churches.

lost-wax casting (p. 413) A method of casting metal, such as bronze, by a process in which a wax mold is covered with clay and plaster, then fired, melting the wax and leaving a hollow form. Molten metal is then poured into the hollow space and slowly cooled. When the hardened clay and plaster exterior shell is removed, a solid metal form remains to be smoothed and polished.

low relief (p. 39) See **relief sculpture**.

lunette (p. 223) A semicircular wall area, framed by an **arch** over a door or window. Can be either plain or decorated.

lusterware (p. 277) **Ceramic** pottery decorated with metallic glazes.

madrasa (p. 271) An Islamic institution of higher learning, where teaching is focused on theology and law.

maenad (p. 104) In ancient Greece, a female devotee of the wine god Dionysos who participated in orgiastic rituals. She is often depicted with swirling drapery to indicate wild movement or dance. (Also called a Bacchante, after Bacchus, the Roman name of Dionysos.)

majolica (p. 571) Pottery painted with a tin glaze that, when fired, gives a lustrous and colorful surface.

mandala (p. 299) An image of the cosmos represented by an arrangement of circles or concentric geometric shapes containing diagrams or images. Used for meditation and contemplation by Buddhists.

mandapa (p. 301) In a Hindu temple, an open hall dedicated to ritual worship.

mandorla (p. 474) Light encircling, or emanating from, the entire figure of a sacred person.

manuscript (p. 242) A handwritten book or document.

maqsura (p. 268) An enclosure in a Muslim **mosque**, near the **mihrab**, designated for dignitaries.

martyrium (martyria) (p. 237) In Christian architecture, a church, chapel, or shrine built over the grave of a martyr or the site of a great miracle.

mastaba (p. 53) A flat-topped, one-story structure with slanted walls over an ancient Egyptian underground tomb.

matte (p. 571) Term describing a smooth surface that is without shine or luster.

mausoleum (p. 177) A monumental building used as a tomb. Named after the tomb of Mausolos erected at Halikarnassos around 350 BCE.

medallion (p. 225) Any round ornament or decoration. Also: a large medal.

megalith (p. 17) A large stone used in prehistoric building. Megalithic architecture employs such stones.

megaron (p. 93) The main hall of a Mycenaean palace or grand house, having a columnar **porch** and a room with central fireplace surrounded by four **columns**.

memento mori (p. 907) From Latin for "remember that you must die." An object, such as a skull or extinguished candle, typically found in a **vanitas** image, symbolizing the transience of life.

memory image (p. 8) An image that relies on the generic shapes and relationships that readily spring to mind at the mention of an object.

menorah (p. 219) A Jewish lamp-stand with seven or nine branches; the nine-branched menorah is used during the celebration of Hanukkah. Representations of the seven-branched menorah, once used in the Temple of Jerusalem, became a symbol of Judaism.

metope (p. 110) The carved or painted rectangular panel between the **triglyphs** of a **Doric frieze**.

mihrab (p. 261) A recess or niche that distinguishes the wall oriented toward Mecca (**qibla**) in a **mosque**.

millefiori (p. 428) A term derived from the Italian for "a thousand flowers" that refers to a glass-making technique in which rods of differently-colored glass are fused in a long bundle that is subsequently sliced to produce disks or beads with small-scale, multicolor patterns.

minaret (p. 267) A tower on or near a **mosque**, varying extensively in form throughout the Islamic world, from which the faithful are called to prayer five times a day.

minbar (p. 261) A high platform or pulpit in a **mosque**.

miniature (p. 243) Anything small. In painting, miniatures may be illustrations within **albums** or **manuscripts** or intimate portraits.

mirador (p. 275) In Spanish and Islamic palace architecture, a very large window or room with windows, and sometimes balconies, providing views to interior courtyards or the exterior landscape.

mithuna (p. 302) The amorous male and female couples in Buddhist sculpture, usually found at the entrance to a sacred building. The *mithuna* symbolize the harmony and fertility of life.

moai (p. 859) Statues found in Polynesia, carved from tufa, a yellowish brown volcanic stone, and depicting the human form. Nearly 1,000 of these statues have been found on the island of Rapa Nui but their significance has been a matter of speculation.

mobile (p. 1059) A sculpture made with parts suspended in such a way that they move in a current of air.

modeling (p. xxix)   In painting, the process of creating the illusion of three-dimensionality on a two-dimensional surface by use of light and shade. In sculpture, the process of molding a three-dimensional form out of a malleable substance.

module (p. 341)   A segment or portion of a repeated design. Also: a basic building block.

molding (p. 315)   A shaped or sculpted strip with varying contours and patterns. Used as decoration on architecture, furniture, frames, and other objects.

mortise-and-tenon (p. 19)   A method of joining two elements. A projecting pin (tenon) on one element fits snugly into a hole designed for it (mortise) on the other. Such joints are very strong and flexible.

mosaic (p. 146)   Images formed by small colored stone or glass pieces (**tesserae**), affixed to a hard, stable surface.

mosque (p. 261)   An edifice used for communal Islamic worship.

Mozarabic (p. 433)   An eclectic style practiced in Christian medieval Spain while much of the Iberian peninsula was ruled by Muslim dynasties.

mudra (p. 304)   A symbolic hand gesture in Buddhist art that denotes certain behaviors, actions, or feelings.

mullion (p. 507)   A slender vertical element or colonnette that divides a window into subsidiary sections.

muqarna (p. 275)   Small nichelike components stacked in tiers to fill the transition between differing vertical and horizontal planes.

naos (p. 236)   The principal room in a temple or church. In ancient architecture, the **cella**. In a Byzantine church, the **nave** and **sanctuary**.

narrative image (p. 224)   A picture that recounts an event drawn from a story, either factual (e.g., biographical) or fictional.

narthex (p. 222)   The vestibule or entrance **porch** of a church.

nave (p. 192)   The central space of a **basilica**, two or three stories high and usually flanked by aisles.

necking (p. 110)   The molding at the top of the **shaft** of the **column**.

necropolis (p. 53)   A large cemetery or burial area; literally a "city of the dead."

negative space (p. 120)   Empty space, surrounded and shaped so that it acquires a sense of form or volume.

nemes headdress (p. 51)   The royal headdress of Egypt.

niello (p. 87)   A metal technique in which a black sulfur alloy is rubbed into fine lines **engraved** into metal (usually gold or silver). When heated, the **alloy** becomes fused with the surrounding metal and provides contrasting detail.

nishiki-e (p. 813)   A multicolored and ornate Japanese print.

oculus (p. 188)   In architecture, a circular opening. Oculi are usually found either as windows or at the apex of a **dome**. When at the top of a dome, an oculus is either open to the sky or covered by a decorative exterior **lantern**.

odalisque (p. 950)   Turkish word for "harem slave girl" or "concubine."

ogee (p. 551)   An S-shaped curve. See **arch**.

oinochoe (p. 128)   A Greek jug used for wine.

olpe (p. 105)   Any Greek vase or jug without a spout.

one-point perspective   See **perspective**.

orant (p. 222)   The representation of a standing figure praying with outstretched and upraised arms.

oratory (p. 232)   A small chapel.

order (p. 110)   A system of proportions in Classical architecture that includes every aspect of the building's plan, elevation, and decorative system. **Composite**: a combination of the **Ionic** and the **Corinthian** orders.

The **capital** combines **acanthus** leaves with **volute** scrolls. **Corinthian**: the most ornate of the orders, the Corinthian includes a **base**, a **fluted column shaft** with a capital elaborately decorated with acanthus leaf carvings. Its **entablature** consists of an **architrave** decorated with **moldings**, a **frieze** often containing sculptured **reliefs**, and a **cornice** with dentils. **Doric**: the column shaft of the Doric order can be fluted or smooth-surfaced and has no base. The Doric capital consists of an undecorated **echinus** and **abacus**. The Doric entablature has a plain architrave, a frieze with **metopes** and **triglyphs**, and a simple cornice. **Ionic**: the column of the Ionic order has a base, a fluted shaft, and a capital decorated with volutes. The Ionic entablature consists of an architrave of three panels and moldings, a frieze usually containing sculpted relief ornament, and a cornice with dentils. **Tuscan**: a variation of Doric characterized by a smooth-surfaced column shaft with a base, a plain architrave, and an undecorated frieze. A colossal order is any of the above built on a large scale, rising through several stories in height and often raised from the ground by a **pedestal**.

orientalism (p. 966)   The fascination with Middle Eastern cultures.

orthogonal (p. 140)   Any line running back into the represented space of a picture perpendicular to the imagined picture plane. In **linear perspective**, all orthogonals converge at a single **vanishing point** in the picture and are the basis for a **grid** that maps out the internal space of the image. An orthogonal plan is any plan for a building or city that is based exclusively on right angles, such as the grid plan of many major cities.

pagoda (p. 341)   An East Asian **reliquary** tower built with successively smaller, repeated stories. Each story is usually marked by an elaborate projecting roof.

painterly (p. xxiv)   A style of painting which emphasizes the techniques and surface effects of brushwork (also color, light, and shade).

palace complex (p. 41)   A group of buildings used for living and governing by a ruler and his or her supporters, usually fortified.

palazzo (p. 600)   Italian term for palace, used for any large urban dwelling.

palmette (p. 139)   A fan-shaped ornament with radiating leaves.

panel painting   Any painting executed on a wood support. The wood is usually planed to provide a smooth surface. A panel can consist of several boards joined together.

parapet (p. 138)   A low wall at the edge of a balcony, bridge, roof, or other place from which there is a steep drop, built for safety. A parapet walk is the passageway, usually open, immediately behind the uppermost exterior wall or battlement of a fortified building.

parchment (p. 243)   A writing surface made from treated skins of animals. Very fine parchment is known as **vellum**.

parish church (p. 239)   Church where local residents attend regular services.

parterre (p. 760)   An ornamental, highly regimented flowerbed. An element of the ornate gardens of seventeenth-century palaces and **châteaux**.

passage grave (p. 17)   A prehistoric tomb under a **cairn**, reached by a long, narrow, slab-lined access passageway or passageways.

pastel (p. 912)   Dry pigment, chalk, and gum in stick or crayon form. Also: a work of art made with pastels.

pedestal (p. 107)   A platform or **base** supporting a sculpture or other monument. Also: the block found below the base of a Classical **column** (or **colonnade**), serving to raise the entire element off the ground.

pediment (p. 108)   A triangular gable found over major architectural elements such as Classical Greek **porticoes**, windows, or doors. Formed by an **entablature** and the ends of a sloping roof or a raking **cornice**. A similar architectural element is often used decoratively

above a door or window, sometimes with a curved upper **molding**. A broken pediment is a variation on the traditional pediment, with an open space at the center of the topmost angle and/or the horizontal cornice.

pendentive (p. 236)   The concave triangular section of a **vault** that forms the transition between a square or polygonal space and the circular **base** of a **dome**.

peplos (p. 115)   A loose outer garment worn by women of ancient Greece. A cloth rectangle fastened on the shoulders and belted below the bust or at the waist.

Performance art (p. 1085)   An artwork based on a live, sometimes theatrical performance by the artist.

peristyle (p. 66)   A surrounding **colonnade** in Greek architecture. A peristyle building is surrounded on the exterior by a colonnade. Also: a peristyle court is an open colonnaded courtyard, often having a pool and garden.

perspective (p. 184)   A system for representing three-dimensional space on a two-dimensional surface. **Atmospheric perspective**: A method of rendering the effect of spatial distance by subtle variations in color and clarity of representation. **Intuitive perspective**: A method of giving the impression of recession by visual instinct, not by the use of an overall system or program. Oblique perspective: An intuitive spatial system in which a building or room is placed with one corner in the picture plane, and the other parts of the structure recede to an imaginary vanishing point on its other side. Oblique perspective is not a comprehensive, mathematical system. **One-point** and multiple-point perspective (also called **linear**, scientific or mathematical perspective): A method of creating the illusion of three-dimensional space on a two-dimensional surface by delineating a horizon line and multiple **orthogonal** lines. These recede to meet at one or more points on the horizon (called **vanishing points**), giving the appearance of spatial depth. Called scientific or mathematical because its use requires some knowledge of geometry and mathematics, as well as optics. Reverse perspective: A Byzantine perspective theory in which the orthogonals or rays of sight do not converge on a vanishing point in the picture, but are thought to originate in the viewer's eye in front of the picture. Thus, in reverse perspective the image is constructed with orthogonals that diverge, giving a slightly tipped aspect to objects.

photomontage (p. 1039)   A photographic work created from many smaller photographs arranged (and often overlapping) in a composition, which is then rephotographed.

pictograph (p. 331)   A highly stylized depiction serving as a symbol for a person or object. Also: a type of writing utilizing such symbols.

picture plane (p. 573)   The theoretical plane corresponding with the actual surface of a painting, separating the spatial world evoked in the painting from the spatial world occupied by the viewer.

picture stone (p. 436)   A medieval northern European memorial stone covered with figural decoration. See also **rune stone**.

picturesque (p. 917)   A term describing the taste for the familiar, the pleasant, and the agreeable, popular in the eighteenth and nineteenth centuries in Europe. Originally used to describe the "picture like" qualities of some landscape scenes. When contrasted with the **sublime**, the picturesque stood for the interesting but ordinary domestic landscape.

piece-mold casting (p. 328)   A casting technique in which the mold consists of several sections that are connected during the pouring of molten metal, usually bronze. After the cast form has hardened, the pieces of the mold are disassembled, leaving the completed object.

pier (p. 266)   A masonry support made up of many stones, or rubble and concrete (in contrast to a column **shaft** which is formed from a single stone or a series of **drums**), often square or rectangular in plan, and capable of carrying very heavy architectural loads.

pietà (p. 231)   A devotional subject in Christian religious art. After the Crucifixion the body of Jesus was laid across the lap of his grieving mother, Mary. When others are present the subject is called the Lamentation.

pietra dura (p. 781)   Italian for "hard stone." Semiprecious stones selected for color, variation, and cut in shapes to form ornamental designs such as flowers or fruit.

pietra serena (p. 600)   A gray Tuscan limestone used in Florence.

pilaster (p. 160)   An **engaged column**-like element that is rectangular in format and used for decoration in architecture.

pilgrimage church (p. 239)   A site that attracts visitors wishing to venerate **relics** as well as attend services.

pillar (p. 219)   In architecture, any large, free-standing vertical element. Usually functions as an important weight-bearing unit in buildings.

pilotis (p. 1045)   Free-standing posts.

pinnacle (p. 499)   In Gothic architecture, a steep pyramid decorating the top of another element such as a **buttress**. Also: the highest point.

plate tracery (p. 502)   See **tracery**.

plinth (p. 163)   The slablike base or **pedestal** of a **column**, statue, wall, building, or piece of furniture.

pluralism (p. 1106)   A social structure or goal that allows members of diverse ethnic, racial, or other groups to exist peacefully within the society while continuing to practice the customs of their own divergent cultures, thus providing to artists a variety of valid contemporary styles.

podium (p. 138)   A raised platform that acts as the foundation for a building, or as a platform for a speaker.

polychrome, polychromy (p. 521)   The multi-colored painting decoration applied to any part of a building, sculpture, or piece of furniture.

polyptych (p. 564)   An altarpiece constructed from multiple panels, sometimes with hinges to allow for movable wings.

porcelain (p. 22)   A high-fired, vitrified, translucent, white **ceramic** ware that employs two specific clays—kaolin and petuntse—and is fired in the range of 1,300 to 1,400 degrees Celsius. The relatively high proportion of silica in the body clays renders the finished porcelains translucent. Like **stonewares**, porcelains are glazed to enhance their aesthetic appeal and to aid in keeping them clean. By definition, porcelain is white, though it may be covered with a glaze of bright color or subtle hue. Chinese potters were the first in the world to produce porcelain, which they were able to make as early as the eighth century.

porch (p. 108)   The covered entrance on the exterior of a building. With a row of **columns** or **colonnade**, also called a **portico**.

portal (p. 39)   A grand entrance, door, or gate, usually to an important public building, and often decorated with sculpture.

portico (p. 62)   In architecture, a projecting roof or porch supported by **columns**, often marking an entrance. See also **porch**.

post-and-lintel (p. 16)   An architectural system of construction with two or more vertical elements (posts) supporting a horizontal element (**lintel**).

potassium-argon dating (p. 12)   Technique used to measure the decay of a radioactive potassium isotope into a stable isotope of argon, and inert gas.

potsherd (p. 22)   A broken piece of **ceramic** ware.

poupou (p. 871)   A house panel, often carved with designs and found in Pacific cultures.

Prairie Style (p. 1046)   Style developed by a group of midwestern architects who worked together using the aesthetic of the Prairie and indigenous prairie plants for landscape design to design mostly domestic homes and small public buildings mostly in the midwest.

predella (p. 548)   The base of an altarpiece, often decorated with small scenes that are related in subject to that of the main panel or panels.

primitivism (p. 1022)   The borrowing of subjects or forms usually from non-European or prehistoric sources by Western artists. Originally practiced by Western artists as an attempt to infuse their work with the naturalistic and expressive qualities attributed to other cultures, especially colonized cultures.

pronaos (p. 108)   The enclosed vestibule of a Greek or Roman temple, found in front of the **cella** and marked by a row of **columns** at the entrance.

proscenium (p. 150)   The stage of an ancient Greek or Roman theater. In modern theater, the area of the stage in front of the curtain. Also: the framing **arch** that separates a stage from the audience.

psalter (p. 253)   In Jewish and Christian scripture, a book containing the psalms, or songs, attributed to King David.

psykter (p. 127)   A Greek vessel with an extended bottom allowing it to float in a larger krater; used to chill wine.

putto (putti) (p. 229)   A plump, naked little boy, often winged. In Classical art, called a cupid; in Christian art, a cherub.

pylon (p. 66)   A massive gateway formed by a pair of tapering walls of oblong shape. Erected by ancient Egyptians to mark the entrance to a temple complex.

qibla (p. 267)   The **mosque** wall oriented toward Mecca indicated by the **mihrab**.

quatrefoil (p. 503)   A four-lobed decorative pattern common in Gothic art and architecture.

quillwork (p. 845)   A Native American decorative craft technique. The quills of porcupines and bird feathers are dyed and attached to materials in patterns.

radiometric dating (p. 12)   A method of dating prehistoric works of art made from organic materials, based on the rate of degeneration of radiocarbons in these materials. See also **relative dating**, **absolute dating**.

raigo (p. 372)   A painted image that depicts the Amida Buddha and other Buddhist deities welcoming the soul of a dying worshiper to paradise.

raku (p. 821)   A type of **ceramic** pottery made by hand, coated with a thick, dark glaze, and fired at a low heat. The resulting vessels are irregularly shaped and glazed, and are highly prized for use in the Japanese tea ceremony.

readymade (p. 1037)   An object from popular or material culture presented without further manipulation as an artwork by the artist.

red-figure (p. 118)   A style and technique of ancient Greek vase painting characterized by red clay-colored figures on a black background. (The figures are reserved against a painted ground and details are drawn, not engraved, as in **black-figure style**.)

register (p. 30)   A device used in systems of spatial definition. In painting, a register indicates the use of differing groundlines to differentiate layers of space within an image. In sculpture, the placement of self-contained bands of **reliefs** in a vertical arrangement. See **registration marks**.

registration marks (p. 826)   In Japanese **woodblock printing**, these were two marks carved on the blocks to indicate proper alignment of the paper during the printing process. In multicolor printing, which used a separate block for each color, these marks were essential for achieving the proper position or registration of the colors.

relative dating (p. 12)   See **radiometric dating**.

relic (p. 239)   A venerated object associated with a saint or martyr.

relief sculpture (p. 5)   A three-dimensional image or design whose flat background surface is carved away to a certain depth, setting off the figure. Called **high** or **low (bas) relief** depending upon the extent of projection of the image from the background. Called **sunken relief** when the image is carved below the original surface of the background, which is not cut away.

reliquary (p. 299)   A container, often made of precious materials, used as a repository to protect and display sacred **relics**.

repoussé (p. 87)   A technique of hammering metal from the back to create a protruding image. Elaborate **reliefs** are created with wooden armatures against which the metal sheets are pressed and hammered.

rhyton (p. 88)   A vessel in the shape of a figure or an animal, used for drinking or pouring liquids on special occasions.

rib vault (p. 495)   See **vault**.

ridgepole (p. 16)   A longitudinal timber at the apex of a roof that supports the upper ends of the rafters.

roof comb (p. 386)   In a Mayan building, a masonry wall along the apex of a roof that is built above the level of the roof proper. Roof combs support the highly decorated false façades that rise above the height of the building at the front.

rosettes (p. 105)   A round or oval ornament resembling a rose.

rotunda (p. 197)   Any building (or part thereof) constructed in a circular (or sometimes polygonal) shape, usually producing a large open space crowned by a **dome**.

round arch (p. 172)   See **arch**.

roundel (p. 160)   Any element with a circular format, often placed as a decoration on the exterior of architecture.

rune stone (p. 436)   A stone used in early medieval northern Europe as a commemorative monument, which is carved or inscribed with runes, a writing system used by early Germanic peoples.

rustication (p. 600)   In building, the rough, irregular, and unfinished effect deliberately given to the exterior facing of a stone edifice. Rusticated stones are often large and used for decorative emphasis around doors or windows, or across the entire lower floors of a building. Also, masonry construction with conspicuous, often beveled joints.

salon (p. 905)   A large room for entertaining guests; a periodic social or intellectual gathering, often of prominent people; a hall or **gallery** for exhibiting works of art.

sanctuary (p. 102)   A sacred or holy enclosure used for worship. In ancient Greece and Rome, consisted of one or more temples and an altar. In Christian architecture, the space around the altar in a church called the chancel or presbytery.

sarcophagus (p. 49)   A stone coffin. Often rectangular and decorated with **relief sculpture**.

scarab (p. 51)   In Egypt, a stylized dung beetle associated with the sun and the god Amun.

scarification (p. 403)   Ornamental decoration applied to the surface of the body by cutting the skin for cultural and/or aesthetic reasons.

school of artists (p. 281)   An art historical term describing a group of artists, usually working at the same time and sharing similar styles, influences, and ideals. The artists in a particular school may not necessarily be directly associated with one another, unlike those in a workshop or **atelier**.

scribe (p. 242)   A writer; a person who copies texts.

scriptorium (scriptoria) (p. 242)   A room in a monastery for writing or copying **manuscripts**.

scroll painting (p. 243)   A painting executed on a rolled support. Rollers at each end permit the horizontal scroll to be unrolled as it is studied or the vertical scroll to be hung for contemplation or decoration.

sculpture in the round (p. 5) Three-dimensional sculpture that is carved free of any background or block.

seals (p. 338) Personal emblems usually carved of stone in **intaglio** or **relief** and used to stamp a name or legend onto paper or silk. In China, they traditionally employ the archaic characters appropriately known as "seal script," of the Zhou or Qin. Cut in stone, a seal may state a formal given name, or it may state any of the numerous personal names that China's painters and writers adopted throughout their lives. A treasured work of art often bears not only the seal of its maker but also those of collectors and admirers through the centuries. In the Chinese view, these do not disfigure the work but add another layer of interest.

serdab (p. 53) In Egyptian tombs, the small room in which the *ka* statue was placed.

sfumato (p. 634) Italian term meaning "smoky," soft, and mellow. In painting, the effect of haze in an image. Resembling the color of the atmosphere at dusk, *sfumato* gives a smoky effect.

sgraffito (p. 602) Decoration made by **incising** or cutting away a surface layer of material to reveal a different color beneath.

shaft (p. 110) The main vertical section of a **column** between the **capital** and the **base**, usually circular in cross section.

shaft grave (p. 98) A deep pit used for burial.

shikhara (p. 301) In the architecture of northern India, a conical (or pyramidal) spire found atop a Hindu temple and often crowned with an **amalaka**.

shoin (p. 819) A term used to describe the various features found in the most formal room of upper-class Japanese residential architecture.

shoji (p. 819) A standing Japanese screen covered in translucent rice paper and used in interiors.

siapo (p. 874) A type of **tapa** cloth found in Samoa and still used as an important gift for ceremonial occasions.

silkscreen printing (p. 1091) A technique of printing in which paint or ink is pressed through a stencil and specially prepared cloth to produce a previously designed image. Also called serigraphy.

sinopia (sinopie) (p. 537) Italian word taken from "Sinope," the ancient city in Asia Minor that was famous for its red-brick pigment. In **fresco** paintings, a full-sized, preliminary sketch done in this color on the first rough coat of plaster or *arriccio*.

site-specific sculpture (p. 1102) A sculpture commissioned and/or designed for a particular location.

slip (p. 120) A mixture of clay and water applied to a ceramic object as a final decorative coat. Also: a solution that binds different parts of a vessel together, such as the handle and the main body.

spandrel (p. 172) The area of wall adjoining the exterior curve of an **arch** between its springing and the **keystone**, or the area between two arches, as in an **arcade**.

spolia (p. 465) Latin for "hide stripped from an animal." Term used for fragments of older architecture or sculpture reused in a secondary context.

springing (p. 172) The point at which the curve of an **arch** or **vault** meets with and rises from its support.

squinch (p. 236) An **arch** or **lintel** built across the upper corners of a square space, allowing a circular or polygonal dome to be more securely set above the walls.

stained glass (p. 464) Molten glass stained with color using metallic oxides. Stained glass is most often used in windows, for which small pieces of different colors are precisely cut and assembled into a design, held together by lead **cames**. Additional details may be added with vitreous paint.

stave church (p. 436) A Scandinavian wooden structure with four huge timbers (staves) at its core.

stele (stelae) (p. 27) A stone slab placed vertically and decorated with inscriptions or reliefs. Used as a grave marker or memorial.

stereobate (p. 110) A foundation upon which a Classical temple stands.

still life (p. xxxv) A type of painting that has as its subject inanimate objects (such as food, dishes, fruit, or flowers).

stoa (p. 107) In Greek architecture, a long roofed walk-way, usually having **columns** on one long side and a wall on the other.

stoneware (p. 22) A high-fired, vitrified, but opaque **ceramic** ware that is fired in the range of 1,100 to 1,200 degrees Celsius. At that temperature, particles of silica in the clay bodies fuse together so that the finished vessels are impervious to liquids, even without glaze. Stoneware pieces are glazed to enhance their aesthetic appeal and to aid in keeping them clean (since unglazed ceramics are easily soiled). Stoneware occurs in a range of earth-toned colors, from white and tan to gray and black, with light gray predominating. Chinese potters were the first in the world to produce stoneware, which they were able to make as early as the Shang dynasty.

stringcourse (p. 499) A continuous horizontal band, such as a **molding**, decorating the face of a wall.

studiolo (p. 617) A room for private conversation and the collection of fine books and art objects. Also known as a study.

stupa (p. 298) In Buddhist architecture, a bell-shaped or pyramidal religious monument, made of piled earth or stone, and containing sacred **relics**.

stylobate (p. 110) In Classical architecture, the stone foundation on which a temple **colonnade** stands.

stylus (p. 28) An instrument with a pointed end (used for writing and printmaking), which makes a delicate line or scratch. Also: a special writing tool for **cuneiform** writing with one pointed end and one triangular.

sublime (p. 955) djective describing a concept, thing, or state of greatness or vastness with high spiritual, moral, intellectual or emotional value; or something awe-inspiring. The sublime was a goal to which many nineteenth-century artists aspired in their artworks.

sunken relief (p. 71) See **relief sculpture**.

symposium (p. 118) An elite gathering of wealthy and powerful men in ancient Greece that focused principally on wine, music, poetry, conversation, games, and love making.

syncretism (p. 222) A process whereby artists assimilate images and ideas from other traditions or cultures and give them new meanings.

taotie (p. 328) A mask with a dragon or animal-like face common as a decorative motif in Chinese art.

tapa (p. 874) A type of cloth used for various purposes in Pacific cultures, made from tree bark stripped and beaten, and often bearing subtle designs from the mallets used to work the bark.

tapestry (p. 484) Multicolored pictorial or decorative weaving meant to be hung on a wall or placed on furniture. Pictorial or decorative motifs are woven directly into the fabric of the cloth itself.

tatami (p. 819) Mats of woven straw used in Japanese houses as a floor covering.

tempera (p. 141) A painting medium made by blending egg yolks with water, pigments, and occasionally other materials, such as glue.

tenebrism (p. 724) The use of strong **chiaroscuro** and artificially illuminated areas to create a dramatic contrast of light and dark in a painting.

terra cotta (p. 114) A medium made from clay fired over a low heat and sometimes left unglazed. Also: the orange-brown color typical of this medium.

tessera (tesserae) (p. 146) The small piece of stone, glass, or other object that is pieced together with many others to create a **mosaic**.

tetrarchy (p. 204) Four-man rule, as in the late Roman Empire, when four emperors shared power.

thatch (p. 17) Plant material such as reeds or straw tied over a framework of poles.

thermo-luminescence dating (p. 12) A technique that measures the irradiation of the crystal structure of material such as flint or pottery and the soil in which it is found, determined by luminescence produced when a sample is heated.

tholos (p. 138) A small, round building. Sometimes built underground, as in a Mycenaean tomb.

tholos tomb (p. 98) See **tholos**.

thrust (p. 172) The outward pressure caused by the weight of a **vault** and supported by **buttressing**. See **arch**.

tierceron (p. 554) In vault construction, a secondary rib that arcs from a **springing** point to the rib that runs lengthwise through the **vault**, called the ridge rib.

tondo (p. 128) A painting or **relief sculpture** of circular shape.

torana (p. 300) In Indian architecture, an ornamented gateway **arch** in a temple, usually leading to the **stupa**.

torc (p. 151) A circular neck ring worn by Celtic warriors.

toron (p. 417) In West African **mosque** architecture, the wooden beams that project from the walls. Torons are used as support for the scaffolding erected annually for the replastering of the building.

tracery (p. 502) Stonework or woodwork applied to wall surfaces or filling the open space of windows. In **plate tracery**, openings are cut through the wall. In **bar tracery**, **mullions** divide the space into vertical segments and form decorative patterns at the top of the opening or panel.

transept (p. 228) The arm of a **cruciform** church, perpendicular to the **nave**. The point where the nave and transept cross is called the crossing. Beyond the crossing lies the **sanctuary**, whether **apse**, choir, or chevet.

transverse arch (p. 457) An **arch** that connects the wall **piers** on both sides of an interior space, up and over a stone **vault**.

trefoil (p. 294) An ornamental design made up of three rounded lobes placed adjacent to one another.

triforium (p. 502) The element of the interior elevation of a church, found directly below the **clerestory** and consisting of a series of **arched** openings. The triforium can be made up of openings from a narrow wall passageway, or it can be attached directly to the wall.

triglyph (p. 110) Rectangular block between the **metopes** of a **Doric frieze**. Identified by the three carved vertical grooves, which approximate the appearance of the end of a wooden beam.

triptych (p. 564) An artwork made up of three panels. The panels may be hinged together so the side segments (wings) fold over the central area.

trompe l'oeil (p. 617) A manner of representation in which the appearance of natural space and objects are re-created with the express intention of fooling the eye of the viewer, who may be convinced that the subject actually exists as three-dimensional reality.

trumeau (p. 473) A **column**, **pier**, or post found at the center of a large **portal** or doorway, supporting the **lintel**.

tugra (p. 284) A **calligraphic** imperial monogram used in Ottoman courts.

tukutuku (p. 871) Lattice panels created by women from the Maori culture and used in architecture.

Tuscan order (p. 161) See **order**.

twining (p. 845) A basketry technique in which short rods are sewn together vertically. The panels are then joined together to form a vessel.

tympanum (p. 473)   In Classical architecture, the vertical panel of the **pediment**. In medieval and later architecture, the area over a door enclosed by an **arch** and a **lintel**, often decorated with sculpture or **mosaic**.

ukiyo-e (p. 994)   A Japanese term for a type of popular art that was favored from the sixteenth century, particularly in the form of color **woodblock prints**. *Ukiyo-e* prints often depicted the world of the common people in Japan, such as courtesans and actors, as well as landscapes and myths.

undercutting (p. 214)   A technique in sculpture by which the material is cut back under the edges so that the remaining form projects strongly forward, casting deep shadows.

underglaze (p. 799)   Color or decoration applied to a ceramic piece before glazing.

upeti (p. 874)   A carved wooden design tablet, used to create patterns in cloth by dragging the fabric across it, and found in Pacific cultures.

urna (p. 303)   In Buddhist art, the curl of hair on the forehead that is a characteristic mark of a buddha. The *urna* is a symbol of divine wisdom.

ushnisha (p. 303)   In Asian art, a round turban or tiara symbolizing royalty and, when worn by a buddha, enlightenment.

vanishing point (p. 608)   In a **perspective** system, the point on the **horizon line** at which orthogonals meet. A complex system can have multiple vanishing points.

vanitas (p. 751)   An image, especially popular in Europe during the seventeenth century, in which all the objects symbolize the transience of life. *Vanitas* paintings are usually of still lifes or genre subjects.

vault (p. 17)   An arched masonry structure that spans an interior space. **Barrel** or tunnel vault: an elongated or continuous semicircular vault, shaped like a half-cylinder.

Corbeled vault: a vault made by projecting **courses** of stone. **Groin** or cross vault: a vault created by the intersection of two barrel vaults of equal size which creates four side compartments of identical size and shape. Quadrant or half-barrel vault: as the name suggests a half-barrel vault. **Rib vault**: ribs (extra masonry) demarcate the junctions of a groin vault. Ribs may function to reinforce the groins or may be purely decorative. See also **corbeling**.

veduta (p. 913)   Italian for "vista" or "view." Paintings, drawings, or prints often of expansive city scenes or of harbors.

vellum (p. 243)   A fine animal skin prepared for writing and painting. See also **parchment**.

verism (p. 170)   style in which artists concern themselves with describing the exterior likeness of an object or person, usually by rendering its visible details in a finely executed, meticulous manner.

vihara (p. 301)   From the Sanskrit term meaning "for wanderers." A *vihara* is, in general, a Buddhist monastery in India. It also signifies monks' cells and gathering places in such a monastery.

volute (p. 110)   A spiral scroll, as seen on an **Ionic capital**.

votive figure (p. 31)   An image created as a devotional offering to a god or other deity.

voussoir (p. 172)   The oblong, wedge-shaped stone blocks used to build an arch. The topmost voussoir is called a **keystone**.

warp (p. 286)   The vertical threads in a weaver's loom. Warp threads make up a fixed framework that provides the structure for the entire piece of cloth, and are thus often thicker than weft threads. See also **weft**.

wattle and daub (p. 17)   A wall construction method combining upright branches, woven with twigs (wattles) and plastered or filled with clay or mud (daub).

weft (p. 286)   The horizontal threads in a woven piece of cloth. Weft threads are woven at right angles to and through the warp threads to make up the bulk of the decorative pattern. In carpets, the weft is often completely covered or formed by the rows of trimmed knots that form the carpet's soft surface. See also **warp**.

westwork (p. 439)   The monumental, west-facing entrance section of a Carolignian, Ottonian, or Romanesque church. The exterior consists of multiple stories between two towers; the interior includes an entrance vestibule, a chapel, and a series of **galleries** overlooking the nave.

white-ground (p. 141)   A type of ancient Greek pottery in which the background color of the object was painted with a **slip** that turns white in the firing process. Figures and details were added by painting on or **incising** into this slip. White-ground wares were popular in the Classical period as funerary objects.

woodblock print (p. 589)   A print made from one or more carved wooden blocks. In Japan, woodblock prints were made using multiple blocks carved in **relief**, usually with a block for each color in the finished print. See also **woodcut**.

woodcut (p. 590)   A type of print made by carving a design into a wooden block. The ink is applied to the block with a roller. As the ink remains only on the raised areas between the carved-away lines, these carved-away areas and lines provide the white areas of the print. Also: the process by which the woodcut is made.

yaksha, yakshi (p. 296)   The male (*yaksha*) and female (*yakshi*) nature spirits that act as agents of the Hindu gods. Their sculpted images are often found on Hindu temples and other sacred places, particularly at the entrances.

ziggurat (p. 28)   In Mesopotamia, a tall stepped tower of earthen materials, often supporting a shrine.

Susan V. Craig, updated by **Carrie L. McDade**

This bibliography is composed of books in English that are appropriate "further reading" titles. Most items on this list are available in good libraries, whether college, university, or public institutions. Recently published works have been emphasized so that the research information would be current. There are three classifications of listings: general surveys and art history reference tools, including journals and Internet directories; surveys of large periods that encompass multiple chapters (ancient art in the Western tradition, European medieval art, European Renaissance through eighteenth-century art, modern art in the West, Asian art, and African and Oceanic art, and art of the Americas); and books for individual Chapters 1 through 32.

General Art History Surveys and Reference Tools

Adams, Laurie Schneider. *Art across Time.* 4th ed. New York: McGraw-Hill, 2011.

Barnet, Sylvan. *A Short Guide to Writing about Art.* 10th ed. Upper Saddle River, NJ: Pearson/Prentice Hall, 2010.

Bony, Anne. *Design: History, Main Trends, Main Figures.* Edinburgh: Chambers, 2005.

Boström, Antonia. *Encyclopedia of Sculpture.* 3 vols. New York: Fitzroy Dearborn, 2004.

Broude, Norma, and Mary D. Garrard, eds. *Feminism and Art History: Questioning the Litany.* Icon Editions. New York: Harper & Row, 1982.

Chadwick, Whitney. *Women, Art, and Society.* 4th ed. New York: Thames & Hudson, 2007.

Chilvers, Ian, ed. *The Oxford Dictionary of Art.* 4th ed. New York: Oxford Univ. Press, 2009.

Curl, James Stevens. *A Dictionary of Architecture and Landscape Architecture.* 2nd ed. Oxford: Oxford Univ. Press, 2006.

Davies, Penelope J. E., et al. *Janson's History of Art: The Western Tradition.* 8th ed. Upper Saddle River, NJ: Prentice Hall, 2010.

The Dictionary of Art. Ed. Jane Turner. 34 vols. New York: Grove's Dictionaries, 1996.

Encyclopedia of World Art. 17 vols. New York: McGraw-Hill, 1959–84.

Frank, Patrick, Duane Preble, and Sarah Preble. *Prebles' Artforms.* 10th ed. Upper Saddle River, NJ: Pearson/Prentice Hall, 2008.

Gaze, Delia, ed. *Dictionary of Women Artists.* 2 vols. London: Fitzroy Dearborn, 1997.

Griffiths, Antony. *Prints and Printmaking: An Introduction to the History and Techniques.* 2nd ed. London: British Museum Press, 1996.

Hadden, Peggy. *The Quotable Artist.* New York: Allworth Press, 2002.

Hall, James. *Dictionary of Subjects and Symbols in Art.* 2nd ed. Boulder, CO: Westview Press, 2008.

Holt, Elizabeth Gilmore, ed. *A Documentary History of Art.* 3 vols. New Haven: Yale Univ. Press, 1986.

Honour, Hugh, and John Fleming. *The Visual Arts: A History.* 7th ed. rev. Upper Saddle River, NJ: Pearson/Prentice Hall, 2010.

Johnson, Paul. *Art: A New History.* New York: HarperCollins, 2003.

Kemp, Martin, ed. *The Oxford History of Western Art.* Oxford: Oxford Univ. Press, 2000.

Kleiner, Fred S. *Gardner's Art through the Ages.* Enhanced 13th ed. Belmont, CA: Thomson/Wadsworth, 2011.

Kostof, Spiro. *A History of Architecture: Settings and Rituals.* 2nd ed. Revised. Greg Castillo. New York: Oxford Univ. Press, 1995.

Mackenzie, Lynn. *Non-Western Art: A Brief Guide.* 2nd ed. Upper Saddle River, NJ: Pearson/Prentice Hall, 2001.

Marmor, Max, and Alex Ross, eds. *Guide to the Literature of Art History 2.* Chicago: American Library Association, 2005.

Onians, John, ed. *Atlas of World Art.* New York: Oxford Univ. Press, 2004.

Sayre, Henry M. *Writing about Art.* 6th ed. Upper Saddle River, NJ: Pearson/Prentice Hall, 2009.

Sed-Rajna, Gabrielle. *Jewish Art.* Trans. Sara Friedman and Mira Reich. New York: Abrams, 1997.

Slatkin, Wendy. *Women Artists in History: From Antiquity to the Present.* 4th ed. Upper Saddle River, NJ: Pearson/Prentice Hall, 2001.

Sutton, Ian. *Western Architecture: From Ancient Greece to the Present.* World of Art. New York: Thames & Hudson, 1999.

Trachtenberg, Marvin, and Isabelle Hyman. *Architecture, from Prehistory to Postmodernity.* 2nd ed. Upper Saddle River, NJ: Pearson/Prentice Hall, 2002.

Watkin, David. *A History of Western Architecture.* 4th ed. New York: Watson-Guptill, 2005.

Art History Journals: A Select List of Current Titles

African Arts. Quarterly. Los Angeles: Univ. of California at Los Angeles, James S. Coleman African Studies Center, 1967–.

American Art: The Journal of the Smithsonian American Art Museum. 3/year. Chicago: Univ. of Chicago Press, 1987–.

American Indian Art Magazine. Quarterly. Scottsdale, AZ: American Indian Art Inc., 1975–.

American Journal of Archaeology. Quarterly. Boston: Archaeological Institute of America, 1885–.

Antiquity: A Periodical of Archaeology. Quarterly. Cambridge: Antiquity Publications Ltd., 1927–.

Apollo: The International Magazine of the Arts. Monthly. London: Apollo Magazine Ltd., 1925–.

Architectural History. Annually. Farnham, UK: Society of Architectural Historians of Great Britain, 1958–.

Archives of American Art Journal. Quarterly. Washington, DC: Archives of American Art, Smithsonian Institution, 1960–.

Archives of Asian Art. Annually. New York: Asia Society, 1945–.

Ars Orientalis: The Arts of Asia, Southeast Asia, and Islam. Annually. Ann Arbor: Univ. of Michigan Dept. of Art History, 1954–.

Art Bulletin. Quarterly. New York: College Art Association, 1913–.

Art History: Journal of the Association of Art Historians. 5/year. Oxford: Blackwell Publishing Ltd., 1978–.

Art in America. Monthly. New York: Brant Publications Inc., 1913–.

Art Journal. Quarterly. New York: College Art Association, 1960–.

Art Nexus. Quarterly. Bogata, Colombia: Arte en Colombia Ltda, 1976–.

Art Papers Magazine. Bimonthly. Atlanta: Atlanta Art Papers Inc., 1976–.

Artforum International. 10/year. New York: Artforum International Magazine Inc., 1962–.

Artnews. 11/year. New York: Artnews LLC, 1902–.

Bulletin of the Metropolitan Museum of Art. Quarterly. New York: Metropolitan Museum of Art, 1905–.

Burlington Magazine. Monthly. London: Burlington Magazine Publications Ltd., 1903–.

Dumbarton Oaks Papers. Annually. Locust Valley, NY: J. J. Augustin Inc., 1940–.

Flash Art International. Bimonthly. Trevi, Italy: Giancarlo Politi Editore, 1980–.

Gesta. Semiannually. New York: International Center of Medieval Art, 1963–.

History of Photography. Quarterly. Abingdon, UK: Taylor & Francis Ltd., 1976–.

International Review of African American Art. Quarterly. Hampton, VA: International Review of African American Art, 1976–.

Journal of Design History. Quarterly. Oxford: Oxford Univ. Press, 1988–.

Journal of Egyptian Archaeology. Annually. London: Egypt Exploration Society, 1914–.

Journal of Hellenic Studies. Annually. London: Society for the Promotion of Hellenic Studies, 1880–.

Journal of Roman Archaeology. Annually. Portsmouth, RI: Journal of Roman Archaeology LLC, 1988–.

Journal of the Society of Architectural Historians. Quarterly. Chicago: Society of Architectural Historians, 1940–.

Journal of the Warburg and Courtauld Institutes. Annually. London: Warburg Institute, 1937–.

Leonardo: Art, Science and Technology. 6/year. Cambridge, MA: MIT Press, 1968–.

Marg. Quarterly. Mumbai, India: Scientific Publishers, 1946–.

Master Drawings. Quarterly. New York: Master Drawings Association, 1963–.

October. Cambridge, MA: MIT Press, 1976–.

Oxford Art Journal. 3/year. Oxford: Oxford Univ. Press, 1978–.

Parkett. 3/year. Zürich, Switzerland: Parkett Verlag AG, 1984–.

Print Quarterly. Quarterly. London: Print Quarterly Publications, 1984–.

Simiolus: Netherlands Quarterly for the History of Art. Quarterly. Apeldoorn, Netherlands: Stichting voor Nederlandse Kunsthistorische Publicaties, 1966–.

Woman's Art Journal. Semiannually. Philadelphia: Old City Publishing Inc., 1980–.

Internet Directories for Art History Information: A Selected List

ARCHITECTURE AND BUILDING,
http://www.library.unlv.edu/arch/rsrce/webresources/
A directory of architecture websites collected by Jeanne Brown at the Univ. of Nevada at Las Vegas. Topical lists include architecture, building and construction, design, history, housing, planning, preservation, and landscape architecture. Most entries include a brief annotation and the last date the link was accessed by the compiler.

ART HISTORY RESOURCES ON THE WEB,
http://witcombe.sbc.edu/ARTHLinks.html
Authored by Professor Christopher L. C. E. Witcombe of Sweet Briar College in Virginia, since 1995, the site includes an impressive number of links for various art historical eras as well as links to research resources, museums, and galleries. The content is frequently updated.

ART IN FLUX: A DIRECTORY OF RESOURCES FOR RESEARCH IN CONTEMPORARY ART,
http://www.boisestate.edu/art/artinflux/intro.html
Cheryl K. Shurtleff of Boise State Univ. in Idaho, has authored this directory, which includes sites selected according to their relevance to the study of national or international contemporary art and artists. The subsections include artists, museums, theory, reference, and links.

ARTCYCLOPEDIA: THE GUIDE TO GREAT ART ON THE INTERNET
http://www.artcyclopedia.com
With more than 2,100 art sites and 75,000 links, this is one of the most comprehensive web directories for artists and art topics. The primary search is by artist's name but access is also available by title of artwork, artistic movement, museums and galleries, nationality, period, and medium.

MOTHER OF ALL ART AND ART HISTORY LINKS PAGES
http://umich.edu/~motherha
Maintained by the Dept. of the History of Art at the Univ. of Michigan, this directory covers art history departments, art museums, fine arts schools and departments as well as links to research resources. Each entry includes annotations.

VOICE OF THE SHUTTLE,
http://vos.ucsb.edu
Sponsored by Univ. of California, Santa Barbara, this directory includes more than 70 pages of links to humanities and humanities-related resources on the Internet. The structured guide includes specific subsections on architecture, on art (modern and contemporary), and on art history. Links usually include a one-sentence explanation and the resource is frequently updated with new information.

ARTBABBLE
http://www.artbabble.org/
An online community created by staff at the Indianapolis Museum of Art to showcase art-based video content, including interviews with artists and curators, original documentaries, and art installation videos. Partners and contributors to the project include Art21, Los Angeles County Museum of Art, The Museum of Modern Art, The New York Public Library, San Francisco Museum of Modern Art, and Smithsonian American Art Museum.

YAHOO! ARTS>ART HISTORY,
http://dir.yahoo.com/Arts/Art_History/
Another extensive directory of art links organized into subdivisions with one of the most extensive being "Periods and

Movements." Links include the name of the site as well as a few words of explanation.

European Renaissance through Eighteenth-Century Art, General

Black, C. F., et al. *Cultural Atlas of the Renaissance*. New York: Prentice Hall, 1993.

Blunt, Anthony. *Art and Architecture in France, 1500–1700*. 5th ed. Revised. Richard Beresford. Pelican History of Art. New Haven: Yale Univ. Press, 1999.

Brown, Jonathan. *Painting in Spain: 1500–1700*. Pelican History of Art. New Haven: Yale Univ. Press, 1998.

Cole, Bruce. *Studies in the History of Italian Art, 1250–1550*. London: Pindar Press, 1996.

Graham-Dixon, Andrew. *Renaissance*. Berkeley: Univ. of California Press, 1999.

Harbison, Craig. *The Mirror of the Artist: Northern Renaissance Art in Its Historical Context*. Perspectives. New York: Abrams, 1995.

Harris, Ann Sutherland. *Seventeenth-Century Art & Architecture*. 2nd ed. Upper Saddle River, NJ: Pearson/Prentice Hall, 2008.

Harrison, Charles, Paul Wood, and Jason Gaiger. *Art in Theory 1648–1815: An Anthology of Changing Ideas*. Oxford: Blackwell, 2000.

Hartt, Frederick, and David G. Wilkins. *History of Italian Renaissance Art: Painting, Sculpture, Architecture*. 7th ed. Upper Saddle River, NJ: Pearson/Prentice Hall, 2011.

Jestaz, Bertrand. *The Art of the Renaissance*. Trans. I. Mark Paris. New York: Abrams, 1994.

Minor, Vernon Hyde. *Baroque & Rococo: Art & Culture*. New York: Abrams, 1999.

Paoletti, John T., and Gary M. Radke. *Art in Renaissance Italy*. 3rd ed. Upper Saddle River, NJ: Pearson/Prentice Hall, 2005.

Smith, Jeffrey Chipps. *The Northern Renaissance*. Art & Ideas. London and New York: Phaidon Press, 2004.

Stechow, Wolfgang. *Northern Renaissance, 1400–1600: Sources and Documents*. Upper Saddle River, NJ: Pearson/Prentice Hall, 1966.

Summerson, John. *Architecture in Britain, 1530–1830*. 9th ed. Pelican History of Art. New Haven: Yale Univ. Press, 1993.

Waterhouse, Ellis K. *Painting in Britain, 1530 to 1790*. 5th ed. Pelican History of Art. New Haven: Yale Univ. Press, 1994.

Whinney, Margaret Dickens. *Sculpture in Britain: 1530–1830*. 2nd ed. Revised. John Physick. Pelican History of Art. London: Penguin, 1988.

Modern Art in the West, General

Arnason, H. H. *History of Modern Art: Painting, Sculpture, Architecture, Photography*. 6th ed. Upper Saddle River, NJ: Pearson/Prentice Hall, 2009.

Ballantyne, Andrew, ed. *Architectures: Modernism and After*. New Interventions in Art History, 3. Malden, MA: Blackwell, 2004.

Barnitz, Jacqueline. *Twentieth-Century Art of Latin America*. Austin: Univ. of Texas Press, 2001.

Bjelajac, David. *American Art: A Cultural History*. Rev. and expanded ed. Upper Saddle River, NJ: Pearson/Prentice Hall, 2005.

Bowness, Alan. *Modern European Art*. World of Art. New York: Thames & Hudson, 1995.

Brettell, Richard R. *Modern Art, 1851–1929: Capitalism and Representation*. Oxford History of Art. Oxford: Oxford Univ. Press, 1999.

Chipp, Herschel B. *Theories of Modern Art: A Source Book by Artists and Critics*. California Studies in the History of Art, 11. Berkeley: Univ. of California Press, 1984.

Clarke, Graham. *The Photograph*. Oxford History of Art. Oxford: Oxford Univ. Press, 1997.

Craven, David. *Art and Revolution in Latin America, 1910–1990*. New Haven: Yale Univ. Press, 2002.

Craven, Wayne. *American Art: History and Culture*. 2nd ed. Boston: McGraw-Hill, 2003.

Doordan, Dennis P. *Twentieth-Century Architecture*. New York: Abrams, 2002.

Doss, Erika. *Twentieth-Century American Art*. Oxford History of Art. Oxford: Oxford Univ. Press, 2002.

Edwards, Steve, and Paul Wood, eds. *Art of the Avant-Gardes*. Art of the 20th Century. New Haven: Yale Univ. Press, 2004.

Foster, Hal, et al. Art Since 1900: *Modernism, Antimodernism, Postmodernism*. New York: Thames & Hudson, 2004.

Gaiger, Jason, ed. *Frameworks for Modern Art*. Art of the 20th Century. New Haven: Yale Univ. Press, 2003.

———, and Paul Wood, eds. *Art of the Twentieth Century: A Reader*. New Haven: Yale Univ. Press, 2003

Hamilton, George Heard. *Painting and Sculpture in Europe, 1880–1940*. 6th ed. Pelican History of Art. New Haven: Yale Univ. Press, 1993.

Hammacher, A. M. *Modern Sculpture: Tradition and Innovation*. Enl. ed. New York: Abrams, 1988.

Harris, Ann Sutherland, and Linda Nochlin. *Women Artists: 1550–1950*. Los Angeles: Los Angeles County Museum of Art, 1976.

Harrison, Charles, and Paul Wood, eds. *Art in Theory: 1900–2000: An Anthology of Changing Ideas*. 2nd ed. Malden, MA: Blackwell, 2003.

Hunter, Sam, John Jacobus, and Daniel Wheeler. *Modern Art: Painting, Sculpture, Architecture, Photography*. 3rd rev. & exp. ed. Upper Saddle River, NJ: Pearson/Prentice Hall, 2004.

Krauss, Rosalind E. *Passages in Modern Sculpture*. Cambridge, MA: MIT Press, 1977.

Mancini, JoAnne Marie. *Pre-Modernism: Art-World Change and American Culture from the Civil War to the Armory Show*. Princeton: Princeton Univ. Press, 2005.

Marien, Mary Warner. *Photography: A Cultural History*. 3rd ed. Upper Saddle River, NJ: Pearson/Prentice Hall, 2011.

Meecham, Pam, and Julie Sheldon. *Modern Art: A Critical Introduction*. 2nd ed. New York: Routledge, 2005.

Newlands, Anne. *Canadian Art: From Its Beginnings to 2000*. Willowdale, Ont.: Firefly Books, 2000.

Phaidon Atlas of Contemporary World Architecture. London: Phaidon Press, 2004.

Powell, Richard J. *Black Art: A Cultural History*. 2nd ed. World of Art. New York: Thames & Hudson, 2003.

Rosenblum, Naomi. *A World History of Photography*. 4th ed. New York: Abbeville Press, 2007.

Ruhrberg, Karl. *Art of the 20th Century*. Ed. Ingo F. Walther. 2 vols. New York: Taschen, 1998.

Scully, Vincent Joseph. *Modern Architecture and Other Essays*. Princeton: Princeton Univ. Press, 2003.

Stiles, Kristine, and Peter Selz. *Theories and Documents of Contemporary Art: A Sourcebook of Artists' Writings*. California Studies in the History of Art, 35. Berkeley: Univ. of California Press, 1996.

Tafuri, Manfredo. *Modern Architecture*. History of World Architecture. 2 vols. New York: Electa/Rizzoli, 1986.

Traba, Marta. *Art of Latin America, 1900–1980*. Washington, DC: Inter-American Development Bank, 1994.

Upton, Dell. *Architecture in the United States*. Oxford History of Art. Oxford: Oxford Univ. Press, 1998.

Wood, Paul, ed. *Varieties of Modernism*. Art of the 20th Century. New Haven: Yale Univ. Press, 2004.

Woodham, Jonathan M. *Twentieth Century Design*. Oxford History of Art. Oxford: Oxford Univ. Press, 1997.

Chapter 29 Eighteenth and Early Nineteenth Century Art in Europe and North America

Bailey, Colin B., Philip Conisbee, and Thomas W. Gaehtgens. *The Age of Watteau, Chardin, and Fragonard: Masterpieces of French Genre Painting*. New Haven: Yale Univ. Press in assoc. with the National Gallery of Canada, Ottawa, 2003.

Boime, Albert. *Art in an Age of Bonapartism, 1800– 1815*. Chicago: Univ. of Chicago Press, 1990.

———. *Art in an Age of Counterrevolution, 1815–1848*. Chicago: Univ. of Chicago Press, 2004.

———. *Art in an Age of Revolution, 1750– 1800*. Chicago: Univ. of Chicago Press, 1987.

Bowron, Edgar Peters, and Joseph J. Rishel, eds. *Art in Rome in the Eighteenth Century*. London: Merrell in association with Philadelphia Museum of Art, 2000.

Brown, David Blayney. *Romanticism*. London: Phaidon Press, 2001.

Chinn, Celestine, and Kieran McCarty. *Bac: Where the Waters Gather*. Univ. of Arizona: Mission San Xavier Del Bac, 1977.

Craske, Matthew. *Art in Europe, 1700–1830: A History of the Visual Arts in an Era of Unprecedented Urban Economic Growth*. Oxford History of Art. Oxford: Oxford Univ. Press, 1997.

Denis, Rafael Cardoso, and Colin Trodd, eds. *Art and the Academy in the Nineteenth Century*. New Brunswick, NJ: Rutgers Univ. Press, 2000.

Goodman, Elise, ed. *Art and Culture in the Eighteenth Century: New Dimensions and Multiple Perspectives*. Studies in Eighteenth-Century Art and Culture. Newark: Univ. of Delaware Press, 2001.

Hofmann, Werner. *Goya: To Every Story There Belongs Another*. New York: Thames & Hudson, 2003.

Irwin, David G. *Neoclassicism. Art & Ideas*. London: Phaidon Press, 1997.

Jarrassé, Dominique. *18th-Century French Painting*. Trans. Murray Wyllie. Paris: Terrail, 1999.

Kalnein, Wend von. *Architecture in France in the Eighteenth Century*. Trans. David Britt. Pelican History of Art. New Haven: Yale Univ. Press, 1995.

Levey, Michael. *Painting in Eighteenth-Century Venice*. 3rd ed. New Haven: Yale Univ. Press, 1994.

Lewis, Michael J. *The Gothic Revival*. World of Art. New York: Thames & Hudson, 2002.

Lovell, Margaretta M. *Art in a Season of Revolution: Painters, Artisans, and Patrons in Early America*. Early American Studies. Philadelphia: Univ. of Pennsylvania Press, 2005.

Monneret, Sophie. *David and Neo-Classicism*. Trans. Chris Miller and Peter Snowdon. Paris: Terrail, 1999.

Montgomery, Charles F., and Patrick E. Kane, eds. *American Art, 1750–1800: Towards Independence*. Boston: New York Graphic Society, 1976.

Natter, Tobias, ed. *Angelica Kauffman: A Woman of Immense Talent*. Ostfildern: Hatje Cantz, 2007.

Porterfield, Todd, and Susan L. Siegfried. *Staging Empire: Napoleon, Ingres, and David*. University Park: Pennsylvania State Univ. Press, 2006.

Poulet, Anne L. *Jean-Antoine Houdon: Sculptor of the Enlightenment*. Washington, DC: National Gallery of Art, 2003.

Summerson, John. *Architecture of the Eighteenth Century*. World of Art. New York: Thames & Hudson, 1986.

Wilton, Andrew, and Ilaria Bignamini, eds. *Grand Tour: The Lure of Italy in the Eighteenth Century*. London: Tate Gallery, 1996.

Chapter 30 Mid to Late Nineteenth Century Art in Europe and the United States

Adams, Steven. *The Barbizon School and the Origins of Impressionism*. London: Phaidon Press, 1994.

Bajac, Quentin. *The Invention of Photography*. Discoveries. New York: Abrams, 2002.

Barger, M. Susan, and William B. White. *The Daguerreotype: Nineteenth-Century Technology and Modern Science*. Washington, DC: Smithsonian Institution Press, 1991.

Benjamin, Roger. *Orientalist Aesthetics: Art, Colonialism, and French North Africa, 1880–1930*. Berkeley: Univ. of California Press, 2003.

Bergdoll, Barry. *European Architecture, 1750–1890*. Oxford History of Art. New York: Oxford Univ. Press, 2000.

Blühm, Andreas, and Louise Lippincott. *Light!: The Industrial Age 1750–1900: Art & Science, Technology & Society*. New York: Thames & Hudson, 2001.

Boime, Albert, *The Academy and French Painting in the Nineteenth Century*. 2nd ed. New Haven: Yale Univ. Press, 1986.

Butler, Ruth, and Suzanne G. Lindsay. *European Sculpture of the Nineteenth Century*. Washington, DC: National Gallery of Art, 2000.

Callen, Anthea. *The Art of Impressionism: Painting Technique & the Making of Modernity*. New Haven: Yale Univ. Press, 2000.

Chu, Petra ten-Doesschate. *Nineteenth Century European Art*. 2nd. ed. Upper Saddle River, NJ: Pearson/Prentice Hall, 2006.

Clark, T. J. *The Painting of Modern Life: Paris in the Art of Manet and His Followers*. Rev. ed. London: Thames & Hudson, 1999.

Conrads, Margaret C. *Winslow Homer and the Critics: Forging a National Art in the 1870s*. Princeton: Princeton Univ. Press in association with the Nelson-Atkins Museum of Art, 2001.

Denis, Rafael Cardoso, and Colin Trodd. *Art and the Academy in the Nineteenth Century*. New Brunswick, NJ: Rutgers Univ. Press, 2000.

Eisenman, Stephen F. *Nineteenth Century Art: A Critical History*. 3rd ed. New York: Thames & Hudson, 2007.

Eitner, Lorenz. *Nineteenth Century European Painting: David to Cezanne*. Rev. ed. Boulder, CO: Westview Press, 2002.

Frazier, Nancy. *Louis Sullivan and the Chicago School*. New York: Knickerbocker Press, 1998.

Fried, Michael. *Manet's Modernism, or, The Face of Painting in the 1860s*. Chicago: Univ. of Chicago Press, 1996.

Gerdts, William H. *American Impressionism*. 2nd ed. New York: Abbeville Press, 2001.

Greenhalgh, Paul, ed. *Art Nouveau, 1890–1914*. London: V&A Publications, 2000.

Grigsby, Darcy Grimaldo. *Extremities: Painting Empire in Post-Revolutionary France*. New Haven: Yale Univ. Press, 2002.

Groseclose, Barbara. *Nineteenth-Century American Art*. Oxford History of Art. Oxford: Oxford Univ. Press, 2000.

Harrison, Charles, Paul Wood, and Jason Gaiger. *Art in Theory 1815–1900: An Anthology of Changing Ideas*. Oxford: Blackwell, 1998.

Herrmann, Luke. *Nineteenth Century British Painting*. London: Giles de la Mare, 2000.
Hirsh, Sharon L. *Symbolism and Modern Urban Society*. New York: Cambridge Univ. Press, 2004.
Kaplan, Wendy. *The Arts & Crafts Movement in Europe & America: Design for the Modern World*. New York: Thames & Hudson in assoc. with the Los Angeles County Museum of Art, 2004.
Kendall, Richard. *Degas: Beyond Impressionism*. London: National Gallery, 1996.
Lambourne, Lionel. *Japonisme: Cultural Crossings between Japan and the West*. New York: Phaidon Press, 2005.
Lemoine, Bertrand. *Architecture in France, 1800–1900*. Trans. Alexandra Bonfante-Warren. New York: Abrams, 1998.
Lewis, Mary Tompkins, ed.. *Critical Readings in Impressionism and Post-Impressionism: An Anthology*. Berkeley: Univ. of California Press, 2007.
Lochnan, Katharine Jordan. *Turner Whistler Monet*. London: Tate Publishing in assoc. with the Art Gallery of Ontario, 2004.
Miller, Angela L., et al. *American Encounters: Art, History, and Cultural Identity*. Upper Saddle River, NJ: Pearson/Prentice Hall, 2008.
Noon, Patrick J. *Crossing the Channel: British and French Painting in the age of Romanticism*. London: Tate Publishing, 2003.
Pissarro, Joachim. *Pioneering Modern Painting: Cézanne & Pissarro 1865–1885*. New York: Museum of Modern Art, 2005.
Rodner, William S. *J. M. W. Turner: Romantic Painter of the Industrial Revolution*. Berkeley: Univ. of California Press, 1997.
Rosenblum, Robert, and H. W. Janson. *19th Century Art*. Rev. & updated ed. Upper Saddle River, NJ: Pearson Prentice Hall, 2005.
Rubin, James H. *Impressionism. Art & Ideas*. London: Phaidon Press, 1999.
Rybczynski, Witold. *A Clearing in the Distance: Frederick Law Olmsted and America in the Nineteenth Century*. New York: Scribner, 1999.
Smith, Paul. *Seurat and the Avant-Garde*. New Haven: Yale Univ. Press, 1997.
Thomson, Belinda. *Impressionism: Origins, Practice, Reception*. World of Art. New York: Thames & Hudson, 2000.
Twyman, Michael. *Breaking the Mould: The First Hundred Years of Lithography*. The Panizzi Lectures, 2000. London: British Library, 2001.
Vaughan, William, and Francoise Cachin. *Arts of the 19th Century*. 2 vols. New York: Abrams, 1998.
Werner, Marcia. *Pre-Raphaelite Painting and Nineteenth-Century Realism*. New York: Cambridge Univ. Press, 2005.
Zemel, Carol M. *Van Gogh's Progress: Utopia, Modernity, and Late-Nineteenth-Century Art*. California Studies in the History of Art, 36. Berkeley: Univ. of California Press, 1997.

Chapter 31 Modern Art in Europe and The Americas, 1900–1950

Ades, Dawn, comp. *Art and Power: Europe under the Dictators, 1930–45*. Stuttgart, Germany: Oktagon in assoc. with Hayward Gallery, 1995.
Antliff, Mark, and Patricia Leighten. *Cubism and Culture. World of Art*. London: Thames & Hudson, 2001.
Bailey, David A. *Rhapsodies in Black: Art of the Harlem Renaissance*. London: Hayward Gallery, 1997.
Balken, Debra Bricker. *Debating American Modernism: Stieglitz, Duchamp, and the New York Avant-Garde*. New York: American Federation of Arts, 2003.
Barron, Stephanie, ed. *Degenerate Art: The Fate of the Avant-Garde in Nazi Germany*. Los Angeles: Los Angeles County Museum of Art, 1991.
———, and Wolf-Dieter Dube, eds. *German Expressionism: Art and Society*. New York: Rizzoli, 1997.
Bochner, Jay. *An American Lens: Scenes from Alfred Stieglitz's New York Secession*. Cambridge, MA: MIT Press, 2005.
Bohn, Willard. *The Rise of Surrealism: Cubism, Dada, and the Pursuit of the Marvelous*. Albany: State Univ. of New York Press, 2002.
Bowlt, John E., and Evgeniia Petrova, eds. *Painting Revolution: Kandinsky, Malevich and the Russian Avant-Garde*. Bethesda, MD: Foundation for International Arts and Education, 2000.
Bown, Matthew Cullerne. *Socialist Realist Painting*. New Haven: Yale Univ. Press, 1998.
Brown, Milton W. *Story of the Armory Show*. 2nd ed. New York: Abbeville Press, 1988.
Chassey, Eric de, ed. *American Art: 1908–1947, from Winslow Homer to Jackson Pollock*. Trans. Jane McDonald. Paris: Réunion des Musées Nationaux, 2001.
Corn, Wanda M. *The Great American Thing: Modern Art and National Identity, 1915–1935*. Berkeley: Univ. of California Press, 1999.
Curtis, Penelope. *Sculpture 1900–1945: After Rodin*. Oxford History of Art. Oxford: Oxford Univ. Press, 1999.
Dachy, Marc. *Dada: The Revolt of Art*. Trans. Liz Nash. New York: Abrams, 2006.
Elger, Dietmar. *Expressionism: A Revolution in German Art*. Ed. Ingo F. Walther. Trans. Hugh Beyer. New York: Taschen, 1998.
Fer, Briony. *On Abstract Art*. New Haven: Yale Univ. Press, 1997.
Fletcher, Valerie J. *Crosscurrents of Modernism: Four Latin American Pioneers: Diego Rivera, Joaquín Torres-García, Wifredo Lam, Matta*. Washington, DC: Hirshhorn Museum and Sculpture Garden in assoc. with the Smithsonian Institution Press, 1992.
Folgarait, Leonard. *Mural Painting and Social Revolution in Mexico, 1920–1940: Art of the New Order*. New York: Cambridge Univ. Press, 1998.
Forgács, Eva. *The Bauhaus Idea and Bauhaus Politics*. Trans. John Bátki. New York: Central European Univ. Press, 1995.
Frampton, Kenneth. *Modern Architecture: A Critical History*. 4th ed. World of Art. London: Thames & Hudson, 2007.
Gooding, Mel. *Abstract Art*. Movements in Modern Art. Cambridge: Cambridge Univ. Press, 2001.
Grant, Kim. *Surrealism and the Visual Arts: Theory and Reception*. New York: Cambridge Univ. Press, 2005.
Green, Christopher. *Art in France: 1900–1940*. Pelican History of Art. New Haven: Yale Univ. Press, 2000.
Harris, Jonathan. *Federal Art and National Culture: The Politics of Identity in New Deal America*. Cambridge Studies in American Visual Culture. New York: Cambridge Univ. Press, 1995.
Harrison, Charles, Francis Frascina, and Gill Perry. *Primitivism, Cubism, Abstraction: The Early Twentieth Century*. New Haven: Yale Univ. Press, 1993.
Haskell, Barbara. *The American Century: Art & Culture, 1900–1950*. New York: Whitney Museum of American Art, 1999.
Herskovic, Marika, ed. *American Abstract Expressionism of the 1950s: An Illustrated Survey: With Artists' Statements, Artwork and Biographies*. New York: New York School Press, 2003.
Hill, Charles C. *The Group of Seven: Art for a Nation*. Ottawa: National Gallery of Canada, 1995.
James-Chakraborty, Kathleen, ed. *Bauhaus Culture: From Weimar to the Cold War*. Minneapolis: Univ. of Minnesota Press, 2006.
Karmel, Pepe. *Picasso and the Invention of Cubism*. New Haven: Yale Univ. Press, 2003.
Lista, Giovanni. *Futurism*. Trans. Susan Wise. Paris: Terrail, 2001.
Lucie-Smith, Edward. *Latin American Art of the 20th Century*. 2nd ed. World of Art. London: Thames & Hudson, 2005.
McCarter, Robert, ed. *On and by Frank Lloyd Wright: A Primer of Architectural Principles*. New York: Phaidon Press, 2005.
Moudry, Roberta, ed. *The American Skyscraper: Cultural Histories*. New York: Cambridge Univ. Press, 2005.
Rickey, George. *Constructivism: Origins and Evolution*. Rev. ed. New York: Braziller, 1995.
Taylor, Brandon. *Collage: The Making of Modern Art*. London: Thames & Hudson, 2004.
Weston, Richard. *Modernism*. London: Phaidon Press, 1996.
White, Michael. *De Stijl and Dutch Modernism*. Critical Perspectives in Art History. New York: Manchester Univ. Press, 2003.
Whitfield, Sarah. *Fauvism*. World of Art. New York: Thames & Hudson, 1996.
Whitford, Frank. *The Bauhaus: Masters and Students by Themselves*. Woodstock, NY: Overlook Press, 1993.
Zurier, Rebecca, Robert W. Snyder, and Virginia M. Mecklenburg. *Metropolitan Lives: The Ashcan Artists and Their New York*. Washington, DC: National Museum of American Art, 1995.

Chapter 32 The International Scene since 1950

Alberro, Alexander, and Blake Stimson, eds. *Conceptual Art: A Critical Anthology*. Cambridge, MA: MIT Press, 1999.
Archer, Michael. *Art Since 1960*. 2nd ed. World of Art. New York: Thames & Hudson, 2002.
Atkins. Robert. *Artspeak: A Guide to Contemporary Ideas, Movements, and Buzzwords*. 2nd ed. New York: Abbeville Press, 1997.
Ault, Julie. *Art Matters: How the Culture Wars Changed America*. Ed. Brian Wallis, Marianne Weems, and Philip Yenawine. New York: New York Univ. Press, 1999.
Battcock, Gregory. *Minimal Art: A Critical Anthology*. Berkeley: Univ. of California Press, 1995.
Beardsley, John. *Earthworks and Beyond: Contemporary Art in the Landscape*. 4th ed. ebook. New York: Abbeville Press, 2006.
Bird, Jon, and Michael Newman, eds. *Rewriting Conceptual Art*. Critical Views. London: Reaktion Books, 1999.
Bishop, Claire. *Installation Art: A Critical History*. New York: Routledge, 2005.
Blais, Joline, and Jon Ippolito. *At the Edge of Art*. London: Thames & Hudson, 2006.
Buchloh, Benjamin H. D. *Neo-Avantgarde and Culture Industry: Essays on European and American Art from 1955 to 1975*. Cambridge, MA: MIT Press, 2000.
Carlebach, Michael L. *American Photojournalism Comes of Age*. Washington, DC: Smithsonian Institution Press, 1997.
Causey, Andrew. *Sculpture since 1945*. Oxford History of Art. Oxford: Oxford Univ. Press, 1998.
Corris, Michael, ed. *Conceptual Art: Theory, Myth, and Practice*. New York: Cambridge Univ. Press, 2004.
De Oliveira, Nicolas, Nicola Oxley, and Michael Petry. *Installation Art in the New Millennium: The Empire of the Senses*. New York: Thames & Hudson, 2003.
De Salvo, Donna, ed. *Open Systems: Rethinking Art c. 1970*. London: Tate Gallery, 2005.
Fabozzi, Paul F. *Artists, Critics, Context: Readings In and Around American Art Since 1945*. Upper Saddle River, NJ: Pearson/Prentice Hall, 2002.
Fineberg, Jonathan. *Art Since 1940: Strategies of Being*. 2nd ed. New York: Abrams, 2000.
Flood, Richard, and Frances Morris. *Zero to Infinity: Arte Povera, 1962–1972*. Minneapolis, MN: Walker Art Center, 2001.
Goldberg, RoseLee. *Performance Art: From Futurism to the Present*. Rev. and exp. ed. World of Art. London: Thames & Hudson, 2001.
Goldstein, Ann. *A Minimal Future? Art as Object 1958–1968*. Los Angeles: Museum of Contemporary Art, 2004.
Grande, John K. *Art Nature Dialogues: Interviews with Environmental Artists*. Albany: State Univ. of New York Press, 2004.
Grosenick, Uta, ed. *Women Artists in the 20th and 21st Century*. New York: Taschen, 2001.
———, and Burkhard Riemschneider, eds. *Art at the Turn of the Millennium*. New York: Taschen, 1999.
Grunenberg, Christoph, ed. *Summer of Love: Art of the Psychedelic Era*. London: Tate Gallery, 2005.
Hitchcock, Henry Russell, and Philip Johnson. *The International Style*. New York: Norton, 1995.
Hopkins, David. *After Modern Art: 1945–2000*. Oxford History of Art. Oxford: Oxford Univ. Press, 2000.
Jencks, Charles. *The New Paradigm in Architecture: The Language of Post-Modernism*. New Haven: Yale Univ. Press, 2002.
Jodidio, Philip. *New Forms: Architecture in the 1990s*. Taschen's World Architecture. New York: Taschen, 2001.
Johnson, Deborah, and Wendy Oliver, eds. *Women Making Art: Women in the Visual, Literary, and Performing Arts Since 1960*. Eruptions, vol. 7. New York: Peter Lang, 2001.
Jones, Caroline A. *Machine in the Studio: Constructing the Postwar American Artist*. Chicago: Univ. of Chicago Press, 1996.
Joselit, David. *American Art Since 1945*. World of Art. London: Thames & Hudson, 2003.
Legault, Réjean, and Sarah Williams Goldhagen, eds. *Anxious Modernisms: Experimentation in PostwarArchitectural Culture*. Montréal: Canadian Centre for Architecture, 2000.
Lucie-Smith, Edward. *Movements in Art since 1945*. New ed. World of Art. London: Thames & Hudson, 2001.
Madoff, Steven Henry, ed. *Pop Art: A Critical History*. The Documents of Twentieth Century Art. Berkeley: Univ. of California Press, 1997.
Moos, David, ed. *The Shape of Colour: Excursions in Colour Field Art, 1950–2005*. Toronto: Art Gallery of Ontario, 2005.
Paul, Christiane. *Digital Art*. 2nd ed. World of Art. London: Thames & Hudson, 2008.
Phillips, Lisa. *The American Century: Art and Culture, 1950–2000*. New York: Whitney Museum of American Art, 1999.
Pop Art: Contemporary Perspectives. Princeton: Princeton Univ. Art Museum, 2007.
Ratcliff, Carter. *The Fate of a Gesture: Jackson Pollock and Postwar American Art*. New York: Farrar, Straus, Giroux, 1996.
Reckitt, Helena, ed. *Art and Feminism*. Themes and Movements. London: Phaidon Press, 2001.
Robertson, Jean, and Craig McDaniel. *Themes of Contemporary Art: Visual Art after 1980*. 2nd ed. New York: Oxford Univ. Press, 2009.

Robinson, Hilary, ed. *Feminism-Art-Theory: An Anthology, 1968–2000*. Malden, MA: Blackwell, 2001.

Rorimer, Anne. *New Art in the 60s and 70s: Redefining Reality*. New York: Thames & Hudson, 2001.

Rush, Michael. *New Media in Late 20th-Century Art*. 2nd ed. World of Art. London: Thames & Hudson, 2005.

———. *Video Art*. 2nd ed. London: Thames & Hudson, 2007.

Sandler, Irving. *Art of the Postmodern Era: From the Late 1960s to the Early 1990s*. New York: Icon Editions, 1996.

Shohat, Ella. *Talking Visions: Multicultural Feminism in a Transnational Age*. Documentary Sources in Contemporary Art, vol. 5. New York: New Museum of Contemporary Art, 1998.

Stiles, Kristine, and Peter Selz. *Theories and Documents of Contemporary Art: A Sourcebook of Artists' Writings*. California Studies in the History of Art, 35. Berkeley: Univ. of California, 1996.

Sylvester, David. *About Modern Art*. 2nd ed. New Haven: Yale Univ. Press, 2001.

Varnedoe, Kirk, Paola Antonelli, and Joshua Siegel, eds. *Modern Contemporary: Art Since 1980 at MoMA*. Rev. ed. New York: Museum of Modern Art, 2004.

Waldman, Diane. *Collage, Assemblage, and the Found Object*. New York: Abrams, 1992.

Weintraub, Linda, Arthur Danto, and Thomas McEvilley. *Art on the Edge and Over: Searching for Art's Meaning in Contemporary Society, 1970s–1990s*. Litchfield, CT: Art Insights, 1996.

CREDITS

Chapter 29

29.1 © 2007 Photo The Philadelphia Museum of Art/Art Resource/Scala, Florence; 29.2 AKG-Images/Hervé Champollion; 29.3 Erich Lessing/Art Resource, NY; 29.4 Gerard Blott/Réunion des Musées Nationaux/Art Resource, NY; 29.5 Rheinisches Bildarchiv Köln; 29.6 By kind permisison of the Trustees of The Wallace Collection; 29.7 Photograh © 1990 The Metropolitan Musuem of Art/Art Resource, NY; 29.9 Picture Press Bild - und Textagentur GmbH, Munich, Germany; 29.10 John Hammond/The National Trust Photo Library; 29.11 © 2010 The National Gallery, London/Scala, Florence; 29.12 © 2008 Photo Scala, Florence/BPK, Bildagentur fuer Kunst, Kultur and Geschichte, Berlin; 29.13 Ikona; 29.14 © 1999 Photo Scala, Florence, courtesy of the Ministero Beni e Att. Culturali; 29.15 © Achim Bednorz, Koln; 29.17 Nick Meers/The National Trust Photo Library; 29.18, 29.19 Image by courtesy of the Wedgwood Museum Trustees, Barlaston, Staffordshire, England; 29.20 © Crown copyright. NMR; Object Speaks National Museum of Women in the Arts, Washington, DC; 29.21 AKG-Images/A.F. Kersting; 29.22, 29.24 © 2009 The National Gallery, London/Scala, Florence; 29.23 Photograph © 2007, The Art Institute of Chicago. All Rights Reserved; 29.25 © National Gallery, London/Scala, Florence; 29.26 Photo: Katherine Wetzel. Virginia Museum of Fine Arts, Richmond; Art and its Contexts The Royal Collection © 2010 Her Majesty Queen Elizabeth II; 29.27 National Gallery of Canada, Ottawa; 29.28 The Detroit Institute of Arts; 29.29 © Tate, London 2010; 29.30 Photograph © 2006 Board of Trustees, National Gallery of Art, Washington, D.C.; 29.31 The Library of Virginia; 29.33 National Gallery of Canada; 29.34 © RMN/ Gérard Blot; 29.35 Caisse Nationale des Monuments Historiques et des Sites, Paris, France; 29.36 Art Resource/Réunion des Musées Nationaux; 29.37 Cussac/Musées Royaux des Beaux-Arts de Belgique; 29.38, 29.47, 29.48 Art Resource/Musée du Louvre; 29.39 Photograph © 1980 The Metropolitan Museum of Art; 29.41 The Hispanic Society of America; 29.42 Erich Lessing/Art Resource, NY; 29.43 Oronoz-Nieto/Museo Nacional del Prado; 29.44 Enrique Franco Torrijos; 29.45 Denver Art Museum; 29.46 Robert Frerck/Odyssey Productions, Inc.; Object Speaks a, b, c Art Resource/Réunion des Musées Nationaux; Object Speaks d Musee Fabre; 29.49, 29.50, 29.51 © RMN; 29.52 The Cleveland Museum of Art, Ohio. Purchase from the J. H. Wade Fund (1927.437); Technique © RMN (Musée d'Orsay)/Michèle Bellot; 29.53 Bibliothèque Nationale de France; 29.54 © National Gallery, London/Scala, Florence; 29.55 Photograph © Museum of Fine Arts, Boston; 29.56 Philadelphia Museum of Art/Scala, Florence/Art Resource, NY; 29.59 English Heritage/National Monuments Record; 29.57 Photograph © 1995 The Metropolitan Museum of Art/Art Resource, NY; 29.58 © 2005 Photo Scala, Florence/BPK, Bildagentur fuer Kunst, Kultur und Geschichte, Berlin; 29.62 Art Resource, NY; 29.60 Leo Sorel Photography; 29.61 Art Resource/The New York Public Library Photographic Services; 29.63 Courtesy of Philip Pocock

Chapter 30

30.1 Bridgeman-Giraudon / Art Resource, NY; 30.2 Roger-Viollet Agence Photographique; 30.3 Art Resource, NY/Giraudon; 30.4 Dahesh Museum of Art. © 2006 Dahesh Museum of Art, New York. All Rights Reserved.; 30.5 Erich Lessing/Art Resource; Art and its Contexts Sterling and Francine Clark Institute, Williamstown, Massachusetts. Photo by Michael Agee; 30.6 Société Française de Photographie; 30.7, 30.10 Library of Congress; 30.8 Science Museum; 30.9 Fine Arts Museum of San Francisco, Gift of Drs. Joseph and Elaine Monsen, 1986.3.62; Technique Library of Congress; 30.11 Science & Society Picture Library; 30.12 © Staatliche Kunstsammlungen Dresden/The Bridgeman Art Library; 30.13, 30.18 Hervé Lewandowski./Art Resource/Musée du Louvre; 30.14 Jean Schormans/Art Resource/Musée d'Orsay; Art and its Contexts © 2007 Image copyright The Metropolitan Museum of Art/Art Resource,NY/ Scala, Florence; 30.15 The Carnegie Museum of Art, Pittsburgh; 30.16, 30.19 © 2007 Image copyright The Metropolitan Museum of Art/Art Resource,NY/ Scala, Florence; 30.17 © Art Resource, NY/Musée d'Orsay, Paris/RMN; Closer Look John Webb/Courtauld Institute of Art; 30.20 The State Russian Museum/Corbis. All Rights Reserved; 30.21 Jefferson Medical College of Thomas Jefferson University, Philadelphia; 30.22 Art Resource/Philadelphia Museum of Art; 30.23 Gregory R. Staley Photography; 30.24 Hampton University Museum, Hampton, Virginia; 30.25 Photography © The Art Institute of Chicago; 30.26 Musée Marmottan, Paris/Bridgeman Art Library; 30.27 The Nelson-Atkins Museum of Art, Kansas City, Missouri. Photograph by Mel McLean; 30.28 Musee d'Orsay, Paris. RMN Réunion des Musées Nationaux/Art Resource, NY; 30.29 Witchita Art Museum, Kansas; 30.31 Image copyright © The Metropolitan Museum of Art / Art Resource, NY; 30.30 © National Gallery, London/Scala, Florence; 30.32 © 2002 Photo National Portrait Gallery, Smithsonian/Art Resource, NY/Scala, Florence; 30.32, 30.34 Photograph © 2006 The Art Institute of Chicago. All Rights Reserved.; Object Speaks a Brooklyn Museum of Art/ Central Photo Archive; Object Speaks b Van Gogh Museum, Amsterdam (Vincent van Gogh Foundation) (s0115V/1962); 30.35 The Museum of Modern Art/Licensed by Scala-Art Resource, NY. Photograph © 2000 The Museum of Modern Art, New York; 30.36 Albright-Knox Art Gallery, Buffalo, New York; 30.37 Spencer Museum of Art, The University of Kansas, Lawrence. 30.38 The William Morris Gallery, London, E17, England; 30.39 Detroit Institute of Arts. The Bridgeman Art Library Inc.; 30.40 Musee du Louvre/RMN Réunion des Musées Nationaux, France. J. G. Berizzi/Art Resource, NY; 30.41 Nasjonalgalleriet, Oslo. Photo: J. Lathion © Nasjonalgalleriet 02. © Munch Museum/ Munch - Ellingsen Group, BONO, Oslo/DACS, London 2010; 30.42 Koninklijk Museum voor Schone Kunsten, Antwerp. Image courtesy of Reproductiefonds Vlaamse Musea NV © DACS 2010; 30.43 Hirshhorn Museum and Sculpture Garden, Smithsonian Institution. Gift of Joseph H. Hirshhorn, 1966.; 30.44 Bayerische Staatsgemaldesammlungen, Neue Pinakothek, Munich © ADAGP, Paris and DACS, London 2010; 30.45 Art Resource/ The Museum of Modern Art/SOFAM, Brussels. Photo by Ch. Bastin & J. Evrard; 30.46 Vincent Abbey Photography; 30.47 Digital Image © The Museum of Modern Art/Licensed by SCALA/Art Resource, NY; 30.48 San Diego Museum of Art; 30.49 The Samuel Courtauld Trust, Courtauld Institute of Art Gallery, London; 30.50 The W. P. Wilstach Collection. Philadelphia Museum of Art/Art Resource, NY; 30.51 V&A Picture Library; 30.52 © Paul Almasy/Corbis; 30.53 © Corbis; 30.54 Courtesy of the Library of Congress; 30.55 © Art on file/Louis H. Sullivan/ Corbis; Elements of Architecture Frederick Law Olmsted & Calvert Vaux/City of New York, Department of Parks

Chapter 31

31.1 The Museum of Modern Art, New York/Scala, Florence/Art Resource, NY. © Succession Picasso/DACS 2010; 31.2 Photograph © Board of Trustees, National Gallery of Art, Washington, D.C. © ADAGP, Paris and DACS, London 2010; 31.3 San Francisco Museum of Modern Art. © Succession H Matisse/DACS 2010; 31.4 © 1995 The Barnes Foundation. © Succession H Matisse/DACS 2010; 31.5 Photograph © Board of Trustees, National Gallery of Art, Washington, D.C. © Succession Picasso/DACS 2010; 31.6 The Museum of Modern Art/Licensed by Scala-Art Resource, NY. © Succession Picasso/DACS 2010; 31.7 Solomon Guggenheim Museum. 54.1412. Georges Braque © ADAGP, Paris and DACS, London 2010; 31.8 Photography © The Art Institute of Chicago. Photo: Robert Hashimoto. © Succession Picasso/DACS 2010; 31.9 Mildred Lane Kemper Art Museum, Washington University in St. Louis. © Succession Picasso/DACS 2010; 31.10 © Succession Picasso/DACS 2010; 31.11 Staatliche Museen zu Berlin, Preussischer Kulturbesitz, Nationalgalerie. Art Resource, NY. © DACS 2010; 31.12 The Nelson-Atkins Museum of Art, Kansas City, Missouri. Photo: Jamison Miller; 31.13 Digital Image © The Museum of Modern Art/Licensed by Scala-Art Resource, NY.; 31.14 Photo: Joerg P. Anders. Location: Kupferstichkabinett, Staatliche Museen zu Berlin, Berlin, Germany © DACS 2010; 31.15 Kunstmuseum Basel. Photo: Martin Buhler/Kunstmuseum; 31.16 The Metropolitan Museum of Art, New York. Photograph © 2007 The Metropolitan Museum of Art, New York; 31.17 Walker Art Center, Minneapolis; 31.18 The Solomon R. Guggenheim Museum, New York. © ADAGP, Paris and DACS, London 2010; 31.19 Emanuel Hoffman Foundation. Kunstsammlung Basel, Switzerland. © L & M Services, B.V. The Hague 20100105; 31.20 © L&M Services, B.V. The Hague 20100105; 31.21 The Museum of Modern Art/Licensed by Scala-Art Resource, NY © ADAGP, Paris and DACS, London 2010; 31.22 The Museum of Modern Art, New York, NY, U.S.A. Digital Image © The Museum of Modern Art/Licensed by Scala/Art Resource. © ADAGP, Paris and DACS, London 2010; 31.23 Digital Image © The Museum of Modern Art/Licensed by SCALA/Art Resource, NY.; 31.24 Musée National d'Art Moderne. Centre National d'Art et de Culture. Georges Pompidou. Réunion des Musées Nationaux/Art Resource, NY; 31.25 Stedelijk Museum Amsterdam; 31.26 © Estate of Vladimir Tatlin/RAO Moscow/Licensed by VAGA, New York, NY; 31.27 Hirshhorn Museum and Sculpture Garden, Smithsonian Institution © ADAGP, Paris and DACS, London 2010; 31.28 © Philadelphia Museum of Art/ Scala, Florence, Art Resource, NY. © ADAGP, Paris and DACS, London 2010; 31.29 Kunsthaus Zurich Dada-Archive. © 2005 Kunsthaus Zurich. All rights reserved.; 31.30 © Philadelphia Museum of Art/Scala, Florence, Art Resource, NY. © Succession Marcel Duchamp/ADAGP, Paris and DACS, London 2010; 31.31 Philadelphia Museum of Art © Succession Marcel Duchamp/ADAGP, Paris and DACS, London 2010; 31.32 Solomon R. Guggenheim Museum, New York. © DACS 2010; 31.33 © 2005 Photo Scala, Florence/BPK, Bildagentur fuer Kunst, Kultur und Geschichte, Berlin. © DACS 2010; 31.34 Colby College Museum of Art. Photo: Peter Siegel; 31.35 Photograph © 2000 The Metropolitan Museum of Art/Art Resource. © The Saul Steinberg Foundation/ARS, NY and DACS, London 2010; 31.36 Photograph © 2006, The Art Institute of Chicago. All Rights Reserved; 31.37 The Minneapolis Institute of Arts. © Georgia O'Keeffe Museum/DACS, 2010; 31.38 © Digital Image, The Museum of Modern Art, New York/Scala, Florence; Closer Look Photograph © The Metropolitan Museum of Art; Photograph © 1986 The Metropolitan Museum of Art/Art Resource, NY; 31.39 Gerald Zugmann Fotographie KEG; 31.40 Anthony Scibilia/Art Resource, NY. © FLC/ADAGP, Paris and DACS, London 2010; 31.41 Heidrich Blessing/Chicago Historical Museum. © ARS, NY and DACS, London 2010; 31.42 David R. Phillips/Chicago Architecture Foundation. © ARS, NY and DACS, London 2010; 31.43 Thomas A Heinz, AIA, Photographer © Copyright Western Pennsylvania Conservancy 2007 © ARS, NY and DACS, London 2010; 31.44 Photo Grand Canyon National Park Museum Collection; 31.45 Collection of The New-York Historical Society, Neg #46309. Photo: Cass Gilbert; 31.46 © Rodchenko & Stepanova Archive, DACS 2010; 31.47 Van Abbemuseum. © DACS 2010; 31.48 © DACS 2010; 31.49 The Menil Collection, Houston. © 2010 Mondrian/Holtzman Trust c/o HCR International, Virginia 20186 USA; 31.50 Florian Monheim/Artur Architekturbilder Agentur GmbH, Cologne, Germany. © DACS 2010; 31.51 Photo: Jannes Linders Photography. © DACS 2010; 31.52 The Museum of Modern Art/Licensed by Scala-Art Resource, NY. © DACS 2010; 31.53 Bauhausarchiv-Museum fur Gestaltung, Berlin, Germany. © DACS 2010; Art and its Context Adk, Berlin, George Grosz-Archiv/Akademie der Kunste/Archiv Bildende Kunst © Estate of George Grosz/Licensed by VAGA, New York, NY; 31.54 Busch-Reisinger Museum. Harvard University. Photo Michael Nedzweski/© President and Fellows of Harvard College, Massachusetts. © The Josef and Anni Albers Foundation/VG Bild-Kunst, Bonn and DACS, London 2010; 31.55 Stedelijk Museum, Amsterdam. © 2010 DACS, London; 31.56 The Solomon R. Guggenheim Foundation, New York. © Salvador Dali, Gala-Salvador Dali Foundation, DACS, London 2010; 31.57 The Museum of Modern Art/Licensed by Scala-Art Resource, NY. © DACS 2010; 31.58 Wadsworth Athenaeum, Hartford Connecticut.© Succession Miro/ADAGP, Paris and DACS, London 2010; 31.59 The Museum of Modern Art/Licensed by Scala-Art Resource. © Calder Foundation, New York/DACS London 2010; 31.60 © Tate, London 2010/Henry Moore Foundation. Bowness/Hepworth Estate; 31.61 Henry Moore Foundation Archive. Reproduced by permission of the Henry Moore Foundation; 31.62 © Donna VanDerZee. All Rights Reserved; Object Speaks Art Resource/The New York Public Library Photographic Services © Succession Picasso/DACS 2010 © Calder Foundation, New York/DACS London 2010; 31.63 Schomburg Center for Research in Black Culture, New York Public Library Photographic Services/Art Resource, NY; 31.64 Howard University Libraries/American Art from the Howard University Collection; 31.65 The Phillips Collection, Washington, DC. © ARS, NY and DACS, London 2010; Art and its Contexts Courtesy of the Library of Congress; 31.66 The Art Institute of Chicago © Estate of Grant Wood/DACS, London/VAGA, NY 2010; 31.67 National Gallery of Canada; 31.68 Photo by Trevor Mills, Vancouver Art Gallery; 31.69 Schalkwijk/Art Resource, NY. © 2010 Banco de México Diego Rivera Frida Kahlo Museums Trust, Mexico, D.F./DACS; 31.70 © 2010 Banco de México Diego Rivera Frida Kahlo Museums Trust, Mexico, D.F./DACS; 31.71 Courtesy Guilherme Augusto do Amaral/Malba-Coleccion Costanini, Buenos Aires; 31.72 Collection Art Museum of the Americas OAS, Gift of IBM; 31.73 Photograph © 2006, The Art Institute of Chicago. All Rights Reserved. © The Estate of Francis Bacon. All rights reserved. DACS 2010; 31.74 The Museum of Modern Art, New York, NY, U.S.A. Digital Image © The Museum of Modern Art/Licensed; 31.75 Solomon R. Guggenheim Museum, New York. © ADAGP, Paris and DACS, London 2010; 31.76 Albright-Knox Art Gallery, Buffalo, New York; 31.77 The Museum of Modern Art, New York/Art Resource, NY © ADAGP, Paris and DACS, London 2010; 31.78 The Metropolitan Museum of Art. Photograph © 1998 The Metropolitan Museum of Art, New York/ Art Resource, NY. © The Pollock-Krasner Foundation ARS, NY and DACS, London 2010; 31.79 Hans Namuth Ltd. © The Pollock-Krasner Foundation ARS, NY and DACS, London 2010; 31.80 Photo: Geoffrey Clements © ARS, NY and DACS, London 2010; 31.81 © 2010 Digital Image, The Museum of Modern Art, New York/Scala, Florence. © The Willem de Kooning Foundation, New York/ARS, NY and DACS, London 2010; 31.82 National Gallery of Canada. © SODRAC, Montreal and DACS, London 2010; 31.83 Collection of the artist on extended loan to the National Gallery of Art, Washington, DC. Photograph © Board of Trustees, National Gallery of Art, Washington, D.C. © ARS, NY and DACS, London 2010; 31.84 Hirshhorn Museum and Sculpture Garden, Smithsonian Institution. Photography by Lee Stalsworth © 1998 Kate Rothko Prizel & Christopher Rothko ARS, NY and DACS, London; 31.85 The Museum of Modern Art. © 2009 Digital Image, The Museum of Modern Art, New York/Scala, Florence ©

Page numbers in *italics* refer to illustrations and maps

Napoleon III, king of France, 963, 974, 976, 977
Napoleon in the Plague House at Jaffa (Gros), 944–945, *945*
Nash, Paul, 1060
National Endowment for the Arts (NEA), 1120
Native Americans
   influence on art, 1068, 1076
   Northwest Coast cultures, 1068
   Spanish influences, 941, *941*
Nature Symbolized No. 2 (Dove), 1042, *1042*
Nauman, Bruce, 1096–1097
   Self-Portrait as a Fountain, *1096*, 1097
Navajos, 1076
Nazis, 1018, 1054, 1055
Neoclassicism
   architecture (American), *958*, 958–959, *959*
   architecture (English), *916*, 916–917, *917*
   architecture (French), 930–932, *931*
   architecture (German), 958, *958*
   defined, 911
   in England, 915–917, 919
   in France, 930–938, 944, 950
   in Italy, 911–915
   in nineteenth century, 943, 944, 950, 956, 958–959
   painting (American), *902*, 903, 929–930, *930*
   painting (English), 920–927, *921–925*, *927*
   painting (French), 932–937, *932–937*
   painting (Italian), 911–913, *912*, *913*, 914, *914*
   painting (Spanish), 938–940, *939*
   pottery (English), 917, *918*, 919
   in Rome, 913–915
   sculpture (French), 937–938, *938*
   sculpture (Italian), 914–915, *915*
Neo-Expressionism, 1106–1108, *1107*
Neo-Impressionism, 993
Neo-Palladianism, 916
Neshat, Shirin
   Rebellious Silence from "Women of Allah" series, 1121, *1121*
   "Women of Allah" series, 1121
Netherlands
   See also Dutch art
   De Stijl, 1052, 1057
   Rationalism, 1052–1053
Neumann, Johann Balthasar: Vierzehnheiligen church, Bavaria, Germany, 910, *911*
The Newborn (Brancusi), 1036, *1036*
New Image of the World (Schoenmaeker), 1052
Newman, Barnett, 1081
   Vir Heroicus Sublimis, *1080*, 1081
New Negro movement, 1061
New Realism, 1088
Newton (Blake), 929, *929*
Newton, Isaac, 904
New York City, *957*
   AT&T Corporation Headquarters (Sony Building) (Johnson), 1106, *1106*
   Central Park (Olmsted and Vaux), 1014, *1014*
   Empire State Building, 1050, *1050*
   The Gates, Central Park (Christo and Jeanne-Claude), 1103, *1103*
   Guggenheim Museum (Frank Lloyd Wright), 1104–1105, *1105*
   New York School, 1079, 1081, 1083
   Seagram Building (Mies van der Rohe and Johnson), 1104, *1104*
   skyscrapers, 1048, *1049*, 1050
   Trans World Airlines (TWA) Terminal, John F. Kennedy Airport (Saarinen), 1104, *1104*

Trinity Church (Upjohn), 957
   Woolworth Building (Gilbert), 1048, *1049*
New York School, 1079, 1081, 1083
Nietzche, Friedrich, 1026
The Nightmare (Fuseli), 928, *928*
Nochlin, Linda, 1099
Nocturne in Black and Gold, the Falling Rocket (Whistler), 999, *1000*, 1000–1001
Nolde, Emil, 1027, 1055
   Masks, 1027, *1027*
North America. *See* America
Northwest Coast cultures, 1068
Nude Descending a Staircase (Duchamp), 1037

O

Oath of the Horatii (David), *934*, 934–935
Object (Luncheon in Fur) (Oppenheim), 1058, *1058*
Odalisques, 950
Ofili, Chris, 1115
   The Holy Virgin Mary, *1116*, 1117, 1120
Oh, Jeff … I Love You Too … But … (Lichtenstein), 1093, *1093*
Oil painting, 985
O'Keeffe, Georgia, 1041, 1042–1043, 1100
   City Night, 1043, *1043*
   An Orchid, 1043, *1043*
Oldenburg, Claes, 1093, 1128
   Lipstick (Ascending) on Caterpillar Tracks, 1093, *1093*
Olmsted, Frederick Law
   Central Park, New York City, 1014, *1014*
   World's Columbian Exposition, Chicago (1893), 1012
Olympia (Manet), 977–978, *978*
One and Three Chairs (Kosuth), 1096, *1096*
133 People Paid to Have Their Hair Dyed Blonde (Sierra), 1133, *1133*
On the Bank of the Seine, Bennecourt (Monet), *984*, 985
The Open Door (Talbot), 968, *968*
Opéra, Paris (Garnier), 963–964, *964*
Oppenheim, Meret, 1058
   Object (Luncheon in Fur), 1058, *1058*
An Orchid (O'Keeffe), *1043*
Orientalism, 963, 966, *966*
Orphism, 1032, *1032*, 1033
Ospina, Nadín: *Colombia Land*, *1131*, 1131–1132
O'Sullivan, Timothy, 968
   The Home of the Rebel Sharpshooter, 968–969, *969*
Oursler, Tony, 1128
   Multiplexed, 1128, *1129*
The Outbreak (Kollwitz), 1028, *1028*
Owens, Craig, 1109
The Oxbow (Cole), *955*, 955–956
Ozenfant, Amédée, 1033

P

Paik, Nam June, 1125
   Electronic Superhighway: Continental U.S., *1125*, 1125–1126
Painting
   See also Figure painting; History painting; Landscape painting; Portraits
   Abstract Expressionism, 1073–1079, *1074–1080*, 1081, 1083
   academies, 924, 926, 932, 937, 944, 962–963
   Action painting (gestural), 1074, 1075–1077,

1075–1078, 1087, 1088
   Art Nouveau (French), *1006*, 1006–1007
   Arts and Crafts (English), *998*, 999
   Ashcan School, 1040, *1041*
   Der Blaue Reiter (The Blue Rider), 1029–1031, *1030*
   Die Brücke (The Bridge), 1026–1028, *1027–1028*
   Color Field painting, 1074, 1079, *1079*, *1080*, 1081
   Cubism (French), *1016*, 1017, 1021, *1024*, 1024–1025, *1025*, *1031*, 1031–1033, *1032*
   Cubism (Italian), 1033, *1033*
   Cubism (Russian), 1033, *1034*, *1035*
   Dadaism, 1039, *1039*, 1040
   De Stijl, 1052, *1052*
   Expressionism, *1028*, 1028–1029, *1029*
   Fauvism, 1019–1021, *1020*, *1021*
   Futurism, 1033, *1033*, 1034, *1034*, *1035*
   genre paintings, 932
   Harlem Renaissance, 1064, *1064*, 1065, *1065*
   Impressionism, 978, 984–991, *984–991*
   in Mesoamerica (Spanish influence), 941, *942*
   Neoclassical (American), *902*, 903, 929–930, *930*
   Neoclassical (English), 920–927, *921–925*, *927*
   Neoclassical (French), 932–937, *932–937*
   Neoclassical (Italian), 911–913, *912*, *913*, 914, *914*
   Neoclassical (Spanish), 938–940, *939*
   Neo-Expressionism, 1106–1108, *1107*
   nineteenth century (English), 997–1001, *998*, *1000*
   nineteenth century (French), 964, *965*
   oil painting, 985
   pastels, 912
   Post-Impressionism, 992, 992–993, 995–997, 996–997, *1007*, 1007–1009, *1008*
   Postmodern, 1106–1109, *1107*, *1108*
   postwar (English), 1071, *1071*
   Pre-Raphaelites (English), *998*, 998–999
   primitivism, 1022–1024, *1023*, 1026–1028, *1027–1028*
   Realism (American), 979, 981, 981–982, *982*, 983, *983*
   Realism (French), 971–973, 971–979, 975–979, *980*, 989
   Realism (Russian), 979, *981*
   Regionalism, 1065, 1067, *1067*
   Rococo (French), *906*, 906–910, *907*, *908*, *909*, 932
   Romantic (English), 927–929, *928*, *929*, 953, 953–955, *954*
   Romantic (French), 944–948, 944–949, 950–952, *950–952*
   Romantic (Spanish), *940*, 940–941
   sand painting, 1076
   scientific subjects, 922, *923*, 924–925
   surrealism, 1056–1058, *1057*, *1058*
   Symbolism, *1001*, 1001–1003, *1002*
Painting (Wols), 1072, *1072*
Palladio, Andrea (Andrea di Pietro della Gondola), 916
Panthéon, Paris (Church of Sainte-Geneviève) (Soufflot), 930–932, *931*
Paris
   Arc de Triomphe, *949*, 949–950
   Bibliothèque Nationale (Labrouste), *1010*, 1010–1011
   École des Beaux-Arts, 944, 962, 965, 979, 989,

NOTES

NOTES

NOTES